# A Moment in Hist

## The Life and Times of
## Felix Mendelssohn Bartholdy,
## 1809-1847

By: Abigail R. Smith

# Featured Credits

(Full list of credits in back of book)

The Letters of Felix Mendelssohn
The letters of Felix to Ignaz and Charlotte Moscheles
Various accounts from Felix Moscheles
The letters of Fanny Mendelssohn
The letters of Ferdinand Hiller
Watercolours and sketches by Felix Mendelssohn
Paintings and Sketches by Wilhelm Hensel

# Editors and Consultants

Cathy Miller
Kate Urchoticky
Gerald Smith
Andreas Smith
Audrey Krukow
Honorata Nowak

# Table of Contents

Each chapter has a selected number of pieces to accompany the reading. The numbers in brackets are the spots to start the music. The suggested tempo of reading is moderato, or about the pace of out-loud reading.

# Introduction

The Violin. The instrument that I happen to choose. Though considered one of the most difficult, I fell in love with it since I had begun learning it in my youth. I did not know where it would take me, but never did I expect to end up where I did. Starting as an amateur at thirteen, by my twenty-fifth year, I, Ferdinand David, became concertmaster of The GewandHaus (Ge-Vaunt-Haus) orchestra in the city of Leipzig.

The orchestra at that time was under the direction of Felix Mendelssohn, who obtained the position the same year I was appointed concertmaster in 1835. I thought my life had now been set. After having occupations with my violin here and there, my concentration could now focus on doing the work of concertmaster. An honorable station for a violinist. Yet it became more complicated than I anticipated. The job began to double as our conductor's busy career caused his absence more often than not. His work of organizing concerts and conducting rehearsals were left to me. Almost more often than him.

Yet, you most likely have not heard of me much in the history of music. I'm mentioned on the subject of the Violin Concerto in E minor by Mendelssohn. He wrote the concerto after I suggested he write one. It took him six years to complete, but it became one of the greatest concertos in violin repertoire.

Anyways, this book is not about me, It's about Mendelssohn. To keep you, the reader, interested in this biography, it will be in the form of a story rather than a boring old report. Most of this story will be factual, based on the letters of Mendelssohn. Some details and subtle plots are to add elements to the story.

Now, without further ado, I shall tell the story of the life and music of:

Felix Mendelssohn Bartholdy.

# Chapter I: Reflecting

Music to accompany chapter:
Bach, Prelude and Fugue No. 1 in C [1]
Fanny Mendelssohn, Notturno in g minor [2]

Year of 1815

[1]

In the earliest of memories that could carry one such through the times; from the woes and sorrows of life; from the feelings of dismay as well as heartfelt emotions; was that of the sweet vibrations of Bach preludes echoing from a well tempered clavier. The melodies, clear as day upon pondering over them. No other enjoyment could replace the fond memories of Bach's music tapped at the pianoforte. Taken aback with every note by the one who played them ever so to perfection.

Many would be in disbelief that the touch of the ivories was that of a girl at the tender age of ten. She is not the main figure of this story, but has the most important influence. This young and talented girl goes by the name of Fanny. The eldest child of the Mendelssohn family. Her gift at the piano made her to be the musician of the family as her father, Abraham, felt quite sure of. Her mother, Lea, had musical skills and had begun teaching Fanny in her sixth year. Within a matter of four years, her abilities showed.

The touch at the ivories were soft then rose as the melody reached its climax. Sitting underneath the instrument, taking in every note, sat Felix. Six years of age and not yet had one lesson. Something though, about the music fascinated him. With his mother and sisters' talents, music already became a large part of him.

Shelves, containing manuscripts of music, consumed this room of the house. The home in which the Mendelssohns' resided settled in the city of Berlin, then of Prussia. As a family of the upper middle class, they had a decent standard of living. Abraham had a prosperous occupation as a banker.

As the Bach prelude continued, Fanny neared to the final cadence-

"Felix!" A bewildered voice called. The piano's music halted as Lea entered the room in search. Felix came from under the piano.

"Felix!" Fanny wined as she flipped the page in her music book, "You made me ruin the piece!"

"Oh now Fanny, it's not his fault, I startled you when I came in. Don't blame your Bruder on such things."

"You were looking for him..." Fanny mumbled under her breath. Felix went to his mother. She held a French lesson book, "You shouldn't go hiding when you know it's time for your language studies. You worried me."

"Sorry Mutter..." Felix shuffled his shoes against the wood floor.

"On you go, as I must give Fanny her piano lesson. Be sure that Paul and Rebecka are doing something productive." She instructed while handing him the book. Felix went off as Lea began Fanny's piano lesson.

Felix sighed as he set the book down at the dining table next to his younger brother Paul. Rebecka's book laid open at the table, but her seat rendered empty. Felix huffed and checked the parlor next door. She was speaking with their father there. Felix turned back to the dining room and flipped to a chapter in the book he was studying.

Abraham and Lea made sure that their children had the best education they could get. Even as they were quite young. Rebecka had turned four and Paul was two. Abraham was in charge of teaching the children arithmetic and French. Lea taught them German, literacy and fine arts.

As Fanny being the eldest, Lea had begun teaching her the fine things of being a lady. Along with music she learned art and poetry. As well as common house work, intellectual subjects and everything between. Felix knew within the next few years, Abraham would teach him the ways of business. His father's wishes were for him to carry on the bank in the family's name.

The children had many opportunities and privileges in their upbringing, but it was far from easy. To make sure they got the most out of their days, they were to be up every morning at the fifth hour for their studies. Paul was an exception since he was young yet. Only on Sunday were the older ones allowed to sleep in. Until the sixth hour that is.

Sunday was a rather special day. Abraham would invite members of society over as a social gathering, called salons. He invited many aspiring guests such as musicians, scientists, poets, authors and artists. Lea made sure the best food and tea were served on the occasion. It was quite exciting each week.

As Felix worked on his secular education with his siblings, he began to lose his focus. The door to the music room where Lea was giving Fanny lessons remained open. He couldn't help but listen. Fanny was learning a new piece. It sounded more challenging than anything she had played before and she had a hash with it. Mistakes were prevalent. Felix had never heard her have such a difficult time.

She had recently been taking up lessons with a local instructor. Her skill improved to the extent that Lea thought it best to find a professional. An accomplished pianist by the name of Ludwig Berger took up the position.

He even composed some. Clementi, a composer known for works at the keyboard, had taken Berger as a student years ago. Felix was familiar with Clementi's music since Lea had taught Fanny to play some of his pieces. Lea still gave Fanny lessons by helping her with the music given. Lessons with Herr Berger were once a week.

Lea's side of the family had a deep love of music. Sarah Levy, her aunt, had been a professional keyboardist in the 18th century. She happened to be a pupil of Wilhelm F. Bach and supported the music of C.P.E. Bach. Both some of the many children of Johann Sebastian.

"Felix...Felix...Felix!" Abraham scorned, "What is it that distracts you?"

"Oh...it's nothing." Felix shook out of the doze and turned back to his French studies. After their studies, Felix tip-toed back to the music room where Fanny still sat practicing. He brushed the door open, not to disturb her. She worked through a passage as he crept up behind to get a look at the music.

As he peeked over her shoulder, she vigorously struck the keys in frustration. With a huff, she got up and stormed out of the room, shoving past him. She left the music at the piano. Felix sat at the piano to inspect this music. It was a book. He turned to the cover and it read as so:

### J. S. BACH
### Two and Three Part Inventions. Works for Keyboard.

It was the same composer that wrote those preludes that his sister played so perfectly. It seemed out of place for her to become frustrated. He turned to the first page. Invention No. 1 in C.

Felix had watched Fanny play dozens of times and tried to follow the sheet music. It bewildered him as to how she could read two lines at once.

The melody lines looked even more complicated as things overlapped. He looked at the first bar. It consisted of a single strand of notes.

He placed his fingers on what he thought were the notes and pressed the keys. Pausing, he veered to the lower line. It had a similar strand of notes as the first line continued on. He picked through it. The playing didn't sound at all correct. A Mozart this age would be laughing at such skills. Fanny had played segments of the piece with struggle, yet the melody rendered distinguishable for her.

As he continued in the slow, rather clumsy manner, someone walked up behind him. He glanced back and froze. His father appeared intrigued while reading the music over his son's shoulder with his spectacles. Felix chuckled in nervousness. Abraham then commented, "I'll have your Mutter help you with that."

~~~~

That is when music began for Felix. At least the part about his mother teaching him piano at six. I wouldn't know every detail as during those days, I had not known him yet. At the time, I resided with my family, born in the city of Hamburg in 1810. The Mendelssohn family had lived in Hamburg before journeying to Berlin in 1811. It happened to be that my family took up residency in the Mendelssohns' previous home.

Rumors went around soon after the Mendelssohns' leave of Hamburg. They had left in haste, leaving little behind. The reasoning alluded to their family's business, The Mendelssohn Bank. Abraham worked alongside his older brother Joseph, who established the bank in Berlin.

(*The Hamburg Home*)

10

When the family lived in Hamburg, much unrest from France gave concern to the bank. It was later found that the bank had an involvement in swindling Napoleon Bonaparte of his attempt to take over Prussia. When the French Emperor's 'Reign of Terror,' invaded the city of Hamburg, Abraham in a trance, took his wife and children in the dead of night to flee. They went straight to Berlin where Joseph occupied a house that also served as the bank's main office.

We won't be discussing too much on the subjects of politics and war. There's other books for that. Yet, before we continue with Felix's story, I'll give background on their family history.

The Mendelssohn name had become well known in the midst of the eighteenth century. Abraham's father, Moses Mendelssohn was a person of influence in his day concerning religion and philosophy. The family's heritage was Jewish. Felix and his siblings never met their grandfather since his death happened in 1786. Abraham wasn't fond of his father's beliefs. He wanted what was best for his children so they could get 'ahead in life'. As to blend in with the common beliefs in Berlin, he professed his family to be Christian, having his children baptized. Lea and Abraham got baptized six years after their children.

(Abraham Mendelssohn-Bartholdy)

(Lea Mendelssohn Bartholdy)

*(Jakob Salomon Bartholdy)*

Some still were not fond of the family's past beliefs, such as Abraham and Lea themselves. Lea's side of the family was Jewish as well. She came from the Iztig family. They had impacts on cultural, religious and musical history here and there. In wanting to separate from their family ties, both Lea and Abraham adopted the surname Bartholdy. It was a suggestion from Lea's brother, Jakob Salomon Bartholdy. He had adopted the Bartholdy name from a property he happened to inherit in Luisenstadt.

The name however didn't always appeal to the Mendelssohn children as will be mentioned later on. Now, back to the story...

~~~~

The year drew by after that day Abraham happened upon Felix attempting to play Bach at the piano. His mother was now teaching him the techniques of what became his new favorite outlet.

Before becoming a pupil of Ludwig Berger just as his sister, the family temporarily traveled abroad to Paris in 1816. Abraham had to go on a business trip and decided to bring the family with. Once arriving and obtaining a place to reside, Abraham had to tend to his work straight away. Lea and the children were left to find something to do in the meantime. Their stay would last at least a few weeks.

Lea happened to know of a lady who had an accomplished reputation for teaching and composing at the piano. She was currently taking residence in Paris. Her name was Marie Bigot. Lea thought it a perfect idea to have her give the children lessons.

It would keep Fanny and Felix's practice up to par during their lengthy trip. Plus having a different teacher in a foreign country would give them all the more experience.

Marie's music was praised throughout European musical circles. She had lived in Vienna with her husband for five years. There she had met Joseph Haydn, who adored her compositions and Antonio Salieri.

Her husband happened to be the librarian of Count Razumovsky. Razumovsky was the brother-in-law of Prince Lobkowitz. Both were patrons of music in Vienna, particularly to Ludwig Van Beethoven. Lobkowitz famously had the composer's third symphony performed at his palace on June 9th, 1804. It was a turning point in music from that day on. Razumovsky played the violin and commissioned Beethoven to write three string quartets. The relationships between these people led Marie to have a friendship with Beethoven. He was impressed with her playing. He had her be the first to play through his newly composed piano sonata, the 'Appassionata'.

Marie and her husband later moved back to France. She composed and introduced much of Beethoven's music to Parisian society. Sadly, her husband was then taken prisoner in 1812 to Russia due to Napoleon's campaign. It left Marie to support her children by giving piano lessons.

When Lea arranged to meet, Marie quickly became acquainted. She had much excitement upon meeting Felix and Fanny. They learned much from her as she had many stories and experiences to tell. Fanny enjoyed Marie's input as a composer as she so aspired to become.

~~~~

Upon returning home to Berlin in 1817, their grand aunt, Sarah Levy, arrived by a planned arrangement. She had been inclined to come after learning of the children's musical progress. Almost as soon as she came, she herded them to the music room.

Fanny performed some of the Bach Inventions for her. She had become fluent with every two part invention over the last year. Felix practiced a few short Mozart pieces.

Sarah recommended that Abraham and Lea introduce them to Carl Zelter. He was a conductor, teacher and composer. He led the Sing-Akademie zu Berlin, a music society that hosted concerts. Originally it consisted of only a choir. An orchestra was added after Zelter took the leading position. Abraham and Lea both knew of him and the Sing-Akademie as they were members of the choir.

(*Carl Freidrich Zelter*)

Within the week before Sarah's leave, Abraham invited Zelter to the house. Zelter accepted and arrived one evening during the week. The first impression of Zelter made Felix believe him to be an old, stern man. Zelter wandered the parlor as the family had tea and visited. He stopped by the windows, holding his tea, to observe the outside. His thoughts seemed elsewhere as he sipped his cup.

After tea, they all strolled to the music room. Felix happened to be standing next to Zelter as they gathered by the piano. Fanny sat down to play. Once she started Zelter became deeply enthralled. She played the Bach pieces as she had for Sarah. When she finished, the old man turned to Felix, "I'm told that you play also?"

Felix nodded and made his way to the Klavier after Fanny stood. He played some various minuets of Bach and Clementi for Herr Zelter. Upon finishing the final chord, Zelter smiled, "Excellent! A decent young musician." He patted Felix on the back. He then turned to the children's father, "Abraham, I would be inclined to accept Fanny as my pupil and have her join the Sing-Akademie. I would be very willing to teach her theory and composition.

She may stay a student under her regular piano instructor if you wish, but I'd be willing to give instruction at the keyboard as well."

"I'd be happy. She does aspire to compose, especially after learning from Marie Bigot." Abraham inclined. Fanny couldn't wipe the smile from her face. Zelter then asked her, "Pray, tell me, what is your age?"

"Eleven." Fanny curtsied.

"Well, I shall plan to start teaching you next week. As for the young boy, I'd be willing to give a few lessons for a start, I'd like to see him join the Akademie within the next couple years." He looked towards Felix. Abraham nodded in agreement. Zelter smiled, "Dankeschön und Auf Wiedersehen, Herr Mendelssohn." He shook Abraham's hand. After he made his leave, both Felix and Fanny raved with excitement.

Their parents for the rest of the evening felt a sense of pride. Their children were doing great artistically and intellectually. It made them feel satisfied with the work they put into their education.

~~~~

Felix continued his piano studies with his new teacher in the year of 1818. He had progressed at his instrument enough that at age nine, he made his first public performance at one of the salons his parents hosted. A virtuoso horn player, Joseph Gugel, provided the music. He needed a piano accompanist for a chamber piece. He offered Felix the position. It was a horn duet by Joseph Wölfl.

The performance turned out as a decent success. Much applause was given. Abraham and Zelter were impressed but weren't enthusiastic on too much applause as it sometimes led to overpraise.

From the first lesson with Zelter, he learned more techniques. He was also taught the beginning concepts of theory and counterpoint. Felix quickly came to realize that his instructor had a strict way of teaching.

Zelter preferred him to work on the mathematical sequences of Bach as well as the balance of Mozart's piano sonatas.

One day, while Felix sat at the piano at home, he felt inclined to read through a Beethoven sonata. He had become fascinated by the composer. Many musicians of the younger generation yearned to play the strong emotions that Beethoven conveyed at the keys. His music was revolutionary and had a feeling of power when one was able to play it. Felix heard various performances of Beethoven by attending local concerts and salons. The chords in his music were strong and inspiring. Beethoven was in his forties, still composing new and exciting works. By then it was known that the composer's hearing was in slow decline. From his early thirties, his ears began losing their abilities.

Felix thought that the first sonata of Beethoven seemed good to start with. He happened to find a copy among some of Lea's piano music. She had played it some before and Marie Bigot played it when she taught Felix and Fanny. He set it on the piano stand and began to practice.

By his next session with Zelter, he could fluently read the first movement. The lesson went on as normal with his usual exercises and assignments. After the hour of instruction, Felix mentioned with enthusiasm, "I've been learning something new over the past week."

"Oh, it is hopefully not distracting you from what I assign?" Zelter had a half joking tone. Felix shook his head, "Nein, it's not a bother, it's quite fun." He dug through his sheets of music, but couldn't find the sonata. He had left it at home. Felix sighed in disappointment, "I forgot to bring it."

"Can you play some of it at least so I know what it is?"

"Ja, I have most of it memorized."

"Let me hear it." Zelter encouraged. Felix turned back to the keyboard in excitement. He began playing the opening notes that created the motif of the sonata. Before he hardly finished the motif, his fingers stopped abruptly upon a hard flick against his wrist. He refrained from the keyboard and looked at Zelter in confusion. The expression on his master's face made him conclude that he had done something wrong. Zelter then scolded, "I do not need my student to be playing such chaotic music as that."

"But I didn't get far into it? What's wrong-"

"The music of Beethoven is too loud and rough. My students play music that helps with their technique. Not scribbled up rubbish." Zelter gave his pupil an expression of disapproval. From then on Felix thought it best to keep this music to himself.

~~~

## [2]

In 1819, Rebecka and Paul became piano students of Herr Berger. Rebecka showed some promising talent but her interests veered towards singing. She began practicing much with her voice and it developed decently for her age. Paul seemed to enjoy the piano lessons, but he soon became intrigued by the sound of the cello. He was young and small for such an instrument, but many cellists that visited the home taught him some things. Paul would watch with every bit of attention.

Fanny was quite consumed with the instruction of Zelter and attending the Sing-Akademie. Her regular practice consisted of the works of Bach and counterpoint. She now, aged fourteen, could play 'The Well Tempered Clavier' book I and II by memory. It impressed Abraham very much as he had requested she learn them. She now used most of her time composing music of her own. Felix became intrigued upon hearing her way of expressing music. He listened closely to the style.

It sounded dramatic but not in exaggeration. It had a mature sense to it. Felix knew all in all, this was Fanny.

It excited him that his own sister could write such music. He began playing her compositions for his practice as well as to test them out. She liked having a second opinion. Felix commented while practicing her work, "Soon you'll be just like Marie Bigot! I bet in a few years every pianist will want a copy of Fanny Mendelssohn's music."

"That would be quite the dream. Perform in public just as aunt Sarah." She gave a sigh as she pondered all that she would do. Felix continued playing. Their practice session made the afternoon hours that day some of the happiest.

That evening, Felix sat in his room, doing miscellaneous things such as sketching and reading. He could hear that a conversation was being held in the parlor between Abraham and Fanny. It was too muffled to hear from his room though. He didn't think much of it, until their voices started raising into an argument. Felix set his crafts aside and went to see what it was about. As he neared the parlor door, he heard Abraham snap, "It is not a proper profession for a lady!"

Soon after the remark, Fanny burst out of the room in tears. She rushed straight to her room. Felix coward a bit as he saw the furious look on his father's face as he paced about in the parlor. Felix quickly turned back for his room to not be noticed lurking by the door. When he returned to his room, he thought about what they could have been arguing about. He had only one guess. It made him sigh with sadness. His sister's dreams had been torn to pieces all in one day. Abraham did not want his daughter to have a public career.

Felix didn't think it fair for his sister. At the same time it made him worry about his own desires, but for different reasons. For Fanny, Abraham wanted her to marry someday in adulthood and concentrate on that.

Felix's worries lied with the fact that he was Abraham's eldest son and would want him to put his interests in the family business. He knew within the next few years he would have to choose what he wanted. A career in music or a career in The Mendelssohn Bank. One choice would be more challenging to convince his father, but he was willing to stand his ground if need be.

The thing that was a bit ironic with his father was that Abraham had such an enthusiasm for music. He collected various manuscripts, sang in the Akademie's choir, wanted his children to have music in their lives, but became the near opposite when a career choice was involved. Felix felt quite confused at times with his father's opinion and demands. The thoughts and commotion of the moment tired him. The day had been well and happy, but turned sour at the end. He decided to retire early for the night.

~~~~

Felix joined the Sing-Akademie soon after turning ten years of age. Most of his time he spent at the Akademie as it served as an educational place in many aspects. It had many events and rehearsals through the seasons. He sang in the choir among the altos. The music of Bach, Handel and lesser known composers were sung frequently. He became aware of the structural patterns of compositions such as fugues and voice leading.

Felix also took up the violin and viola. The lessons were from a violinist by the name of Eduard Rietz. Rietz played in the orchestra at the Akademie, but had recently joined the Berlin court orchestra. He was bright, instructive and open. Felix looked up to him not only as a teacher, but as a trusted friend. He was only eight years Felix's senior. Eduard was so passionate about the instrument he mastered and it reflected. One of the many things Felix liked about him was his nice handwriting. When writing a few pointers in the music, the neatness of the pencil made it impossible to ignore. Eduard Rietz was a good and pure musician.

When Felix turned eleven, he became interested in composition. Fanny had used up all her manuscript paper at the time. Abraham was in Paris on business again, so Felix resorted to writing to his father. He made a request for paper, but his letter was rendered rather unspecific. Abraham penned back, educating Felix:

My dear Felix,

You must specify what music paper you wish to have. Ruled? Not ruled? How is it you want it ruled? When I went to the paper shop, I did not know what to buy. Read over your letter before you send it off and ascertain whether, if addressed to yourself, you could execute the commission contained in it .

—Abraham

Felix eventually obtained paper and began composing, with the help of Zelter. The first work was a piano piece that seemed decent enough. Soon after, it was followed by nineteen other piano works, a violin sonata he could practice for himself, a wedding cantata and two comic operas. His pieces were performed at salons by ensembles of musicians. The little composer conducted by standing on a chair. Though he seemed to be quite busy with these first compositions, this would only be the beginning.

# Chapter II: The Poet

Music to accompany chapter:
Carl Maria Von Weber, Der Freischütz Overture [1]
Mozart, piano concerto no. 1 in F [2]

[1]

The year 1821 proved well. Felix was in his twelfth year and he completed a piano quartet. This major work of the youth impressed Abraham so much that he sent it to a local publisher to get it in print. Though it was an accomplishment, Felix felt slightly out of place as Abraham had never sent any of Fanny's music. She didn't mention anything about it, at least not to Felix.

As time went on, Felix completed some string symphonies. The musicians at the family's Sunday afternoon salons performed them. Fanny played her compositions as well. Felix assumed Abraham allowed her to play her music only for private gatherings.

In the city of Berlin, public concerts were a common event and the family went to many of them. Opera was one of the most popular for theatrical performance.

During the month of June, a new opera was premiering in Berlin at the Konzerthaus. The composer was Carl Maria Von Weber. Felix knew of him as he had much music that circulated about. Carl had a decent career and he was only in his mid-thirties. He played piano in high regards and was also skilled at the guitar. He conducted his operas and compositions when he wasn't at the keyboard. Originally he came from Eutin, Germany, born in 1786.

He happened to be a cousin of Constanze Weber, the wife of the late Mozart. It was what sparked the idea for Carl's father to teach him music at an early age, hoping he would be a child prodigy as his nephew-in-law had been.

The result was that Carl became a decent young singer and pianist with a good career ahead of him. He had a few instructors here and there as his family frequently moved.

*(Carl Maria Von Weber)*

In a stop in Munich, he happened to study the art of lithography, a form of printing from a flat surface treated with oil and water, from the inventor of the process himself, Aloys Senefelder.

His family later moved on to Salzburg. One of his instructors there was Michael Haydn, the younger brother of Joseph Haydn. Yet, life in Salzburg took a bad turn as Carl's mother and young sister succumbed to tuberculosis in 1798. Weber traveled to Vienna later the same year in an attempt to get lessons from Joseph Haydn, but to no avail. All in all, he had a well rounded musical education.

The opera that was to premiere was 'Der Freischütz'. Based on a tale by Johann Apel with the same title. The premise of the story was of a hunter who obtained a number of magic bullets to hit whatever he wished (Sound safe, Right?). The purpose was to win a shooting contest to get the woman he loved and fight off evil.

Weber did the opera justice by the music he composed for it. It was so new and fresh. The beginning of the overture captivated the audience.

The rising chords made by the strings gave the feeling of a cold chill through a dark, forested landscape.

As the music built, it was as if the instruments were setting the scene in the minds of the listeners, giving light into the next motifs of the overture. The curtain rose as the overture neared its end, so the story could begin.

With the music of Weber, the intensity forced the listener to keep their attention. If the hearer dozed for a moment, the jump of the next chord could wake the deepest sleeper. It had such high energy like that of a person's heart ramping. His music had an intense, heroic sense.

When most think of a composer writing heroic music, Beethoven usually comes to mind. He was known to write with broad and grand chords of the victor riding from the success of a battle in a proud stride. Flares of quick passages were added now and again when in context. A prime example was his third symphony, called 'Eroica Symphony.'

In Weber's heroic touch, the hero is rather on his horse in the midst of battle, racing to victory. The exciting loud blares of hunting horns cheered the hero on.

The layer that gave Weber's music a noticeable tone, was the brass. The sounds of them were more crisp and colorful than any other work before. Adding to that were the woodwinds that correlated with the brass. Every instrument that used breath in his compositions became as crisp as biting into an apple.

The premier was a great success for him. 'The Hunting Chorus,' was a favorite among the audience. After the end of the dramatic and exciting work, everyone applauded. Weber turned around after conducting and gave a smile along with a sigh of relief. As the audience quieted down to disperse for the evening, Weber shook hands with the members of the orchestra, thanking them.

Felix watched him shake hands with his violin teacher, Rietz, who had been playing violin in the pit. As Rietz started talking to Weber, he happened to notice the Mendelssohn family among the crowd.

"Felix!" He gestured to the boy. Felix instantly went to his teacher. The other members of the orchestra were packing up. Rietz turned to Weber, "You have to meet one of my students. He's been practicing violin and viola for a few years with me. His main teacher is Herr Zelter with his regular instrument, piano."

"Hello," Carl shook Felix's hand. Felix noticed how well dressed Weber was. He had very refined attire, and very modest. His voice had a bit of a rasp as if it were slightly strained. He continued to say, "I've met Zelter before, when I went to Weimar to meet the poet Goethe. Zelter is quite acquainted with the poet."

"You've met Goethe!?" Felix replied in amazement. Weber chuckled slightly, "Ja...he didn't care for me much I dare say, but I got along with Zelter fine." His talk turned to a positive smile. Rietz told Felix, "Oh, you must not know. Zelter has been talking to your father. He would like to take you to meet Goethe in Weimar."

"I wasn't told anything yet." Felix jumped in happiness. Johann Wolfgang Von Goethe (Ger-ta) was one of the most known people in German society. He had become a successful author early on in his twenties during the eighteenth century. Beethoven used the poetry of Goethe in many lieds and Schubert did so as well. Goethe was in his old age now, but had a high influence. Weber assured Felix's excitement, "I'm sure you'll fare better with the old poet. He's a picky man, but your energy will impress him."

Felix then asked Weber, "What was it that helped you write such an opera? I've tried my hand at writing a few very short ones in my free time."

"Well, a lot goes into a full-scale theatrical performance. What helps is having a basis such as the folk tale this opera was based on. Then a librettist will create a basis for the stage play, then the composer will write the music. Sometimes the story itself inspires the music, but other times, if I'm having a hash with finding inspiration, I study other composer's music if it corresponds with what I'm doing. You can learn a lot by studying scores and things.

Sometimes one composer's small idea can grow into something big for another. Some ideas for this opera were influenced by an unperformed opera. I happened to study a score when I was in Dresden. The King of Saxony showed me a score he obtained from Poland. I'm not fluent in the polish language but the score had intriguing musical aspects. I believe Karol Kurpinski was the name of the composer. He had a very decent way of structuring a piece. Things such as structure and style can help. Don't ever be shy of taking inspiration from others. You'll still have your own voice and you'll learn better music that way." Weber took a bit of a breather after that spiel. Felix took in every bit of information.

"Do you by chance have any engagement after this?" Rietz changed the subject. Weber shook his head, "I don't believe so."

"I say, we should have dinner at my place. I've not eaten since early lunch."

"I'd be obliged." Weber nodded. Rietz turned to Felix, "You are invited as well of course."

"I'll ask my parents." Felix raced back to his family, who had been waiting ever so patiently in the lobby. As Felix left to ask, Rietz and Weber continued to chat. Standing nearby, overhearing their talk, stood one of the orchestra directors, Gaspare Spontini. He was an Italian composer of opera and worked as a conductor at the 'Königliche Opernhaus' in Berlin. Rietz worked with him a lot. Weber was happy upon meeting him. Gaspare gladly greeted him, but didn't greet Rietz with the same enthusiasm.

Spontini and Rietz didn't get along in the best regards. Yet, Gaspare had the audacity to incline to Rietz, "Eduard, I overheard you are hosting dinner with Herr Weber."

"Yes, my student Felix may be joining as well."

"Ah, that child. I wondered if I may be invited as well? I'd like to visit with Herr Weber on the subjects of opera, since we both compose." He turned to Carl. Weber shrugged, "I don't see why he can't join. I am familiar with your operas signore Spontini. It would be intriguing to talk."

"I suppose…" Rietz said, trying to hide any irritation in his voice. A little bit later, Felix came back to the auditorium.

As he walked towards them, Gaspare whispered to Rietz, "Can you tell him that we'd rather keep dinner for us adults. I don't feel like having some young brat at dinner."

"Felix is no brat. Plus it's at my house, you have no say!" Rietz spat back in a whisper. Gaspare backed away in a huff as Felix came back to the group. He told Rietz, "My parents said it was fine for me to come since you were hosting. They want me back home before ten."

"That gives a few hours. Plenty of time," Rietz answered. Felix heard Spontini give a rather loud sigh. Rietz glared at him. Felix and Weber both shrugged not understanding the quarrel between them.

The group packed up their things to leave the Konzerthaus. As Weber walked towards the door, Felix noticed he limped slightly. Rietz didn't say anything of it, so Felix didn't either. He worried about him though. Spontini spoke up and asked Weber upon exiting the front doors, "Are you alright? You seem like your leg is bothering you."

"Oh, I'm fine. It's my hip. I've had trouble with it since birth. It prevented me from walking in my first four years.

No matter though, I kept busy. I was singing and playing the piano before I could walk." He chuckled, making the conversation chipper. Felix liked the fact that Weber was positive and expressed it with such ease.

The group stopped a carriage passing by and rode it to Rietz's house. When they got to the humble little flat, Rietz mentioned in embarrassment, "I forgot that I let my servant go home for the evening, not expecting guests. I regret that dinner will be quite informal. No worry though, I shall cook dinner. How does pasta and parmesan cheese sound? I'll bake some potatoes on the side as well."

"Are you sure you're a good cook?" Spontini questioned, "If we would have gone to my place, we would have some fresh and formal Italian pasta."

"I think macaroni and cheese sounds good!" Felix chimed as he sat at the table. Weber shrugged, "It sounds fine with me. I could eat anything, I'm starving." He joined Felix. Rietz brightened up, "Pasta and cheese it is then. If you want a little fun fact since we all are musicians, Pasta and Parmesan is a favorite dish of Beethoven."

"See, perfect after a full day of music." Weber commented. Rietz went to the stove to kindle a fire. Spontini sat by Weber to start conversation, but every once in a while he checked on Rietz's cooking skills, making sure he was properly cooking the pasta. Meanwhile, Weber was becoming more intrigued by Felix as they spoke. Felix had so much to talk about and Weber's interest boosted his self confidence. Weber asked him, "How old are you? With all you know, you must be at least thirteen or fourteen, but you look younger."

"I'm twelve. Next February I shall be thirteen, but that's months away." Felix fidgeted with some of the cutlery as he waited for food. Spontini moved the fork away that Felix kept moving about as it got annoying. He scolded, "Table manners child."

"Sorry…" Felix blushed in embarrassment. Rietz finished boiling the pasta a while later. He then mixed in the cheese. After some potatoes finished cooking, he served it. The meal turned out great. Felix enjoyed how casual it was. It felt even more relaxed than dinner with his own family. Spontini was a bit stern but eased up as the evening went on.

At around the ninth hour, they finished eating. Rietz offered Felix, "If you don't mind, I bet Gaspare will accompany you home as his home is on the way. I think Weber's place of stay is the opposite way."

"I don't mind." Felix said. Spontini sighed quietly. Weber spoke up, "I can take Felix home. I don't mind one bit. Besides I may not get to visit with him again in a long while as I must depart Berlin in a few days."

"All the better." Rietz smiled. After that, everyone helped clean up. Spontini, Weber and Felix departed Rietz's home. Weber and Felix walked down the street to find a carriage. There weren't many about at the late hour, but as they walked a few blocks, one came around. They chatted while the coachman drove to Felix's address. When it stopped in front of the house, Weber told Felix, "You are a charming little child, I hope to hear of you in future. I'm sure we will meet again."

"I hope so as well. Danke." Felix headed into his house. Abraham made sure he got back safely. Felix told him all about dinner before heading to bed. The day had been one of the best.

~~~~

## [2]

A few months later, Zelter began informing Abraham when he planned to take Felix to Weimar to meet Goethe. Abraham agreed to let Felix go as it would be a very important engagement. Zelter had written to Goethe a few years back upon taking Fanny as a student, exclaiming her talent. As Felix had become skilled over the years, he thought the boy's visit would indulge the old author.

Goethe had admiration for the arts and sciences. He studied nature and color theory. In his own youth, he had attended a concert of Mozart in the composer's days as a child prodigy.

Soon, Zelter and Felix were on a coach headed to Weimar. The trip would take at least a full day. As they sat in the coach, Felix read through many letters that his parents and Fanny gave him, reminding him to be well mannered and to tell them all about the experience upon his return.

Fanny was especially enthralled about her brother's future visit to Goethe's home. Felix felt a bit nervous about her opinions since Zelter didn't offer her to go. He opened her note:

*Dearest Brother,*

*When you are with Goethe, I advise you to open your eyes and ears wide; and after you return, if you can't repeat every word that fell from his mouth, I will have nothing more to do with you. It's better for us to lose you for a little, that during that time you may lay up the most precious recollections for your future life. Also, don't forget to sketch his house and describe the instrument there. Rietz sends his best regards. Don't drink too much beer,*

*Adieu, my little Hamlet,*

*~Fanny*

Zelter and Felix arrived at a humble home at dusk. It was a long rectangular building with many windows and a quaint garden behind it. The decoration of statues and carved art in and outside the house reflected the aesthetic of Ancient Greece. In short, it was beautiful.

A servant escorted them into a music parlor full of guests. The oldest man in the room seemed to draw most of the attention. It was the poet. Once Zelter and Felix entered, he turned to them. His worried expression turned to relief, "I began to think you decided to forgo my invitation."

"The coach happened to be slow." Zelter explained to the kindly voiced man. Goethe nodded in understanding then welcomed them warmly to his home. He had other visitors as he did often. The aged man was hesitant to include new people in his social circle as Weber had told Felix. Yet, contrary to Weber's experience, the poet eyed Felix with intrigue.

No longer did Felix arrive, he had been made to sit at the piano. Everyone circled around. Goethe inclined to Zelter, "Carl, please give your student a tune to improvise."

Zelter nodded and hummed an unfamiliar Lied. Goethe brighten up upon recalling it. Felix looked up nervously at his teacher, "I'm not quite familiar with that one."

"Here..." Zelter leaned over the piano. Felix watched closely as he stiffly played the melody of triplets. After he finished, Felix recited the tune, then began improvising an allegro. The growth of the melody and sound flourished in the creativity of the moment. After giving a grand finish, everyone clapped in enthrallment. One of the guests commented, "That poured out like liquid fire."

"What sort of dreams are driving you to go on in such a rambunctious fashion!?" Zelter questioned in a tone of surprise. Felix shrugged. Goethe kindly encouraged, "You will have to play much more before I am convinced of you."

*(12 year old Felix playing piano for Goethe)*

The young musician went on with some fugues of Bach, then a minuet upon Goethe's request. Felix begged to play the one from Don Juan. Goethe complied to it, but after finishing the poet mused, "That was beautiful but what about the Overture?"

"It can't be played," Felix retorted, "It's too beautiful to alter and make it playable at the piano. Instead I shall play the Overture to Figaro." He began to move about the keys, playing each part to satisfaction.

After that little sprawl, Goethe commented, "So far, you've played me what you know. How about something you've not seen before?" He went to a desk and took out an organized pile of manuscripts. He chose one that had Mozart's signature. The writing was rather small, but readable. Felix went ahead and sight read it the best he could.

Goethe seemed impressed but festered, "That's nothing though, anyone can read that. Here is more of a challenge."

He pulled another manuscript from his collection and put it at the piano. This one appeared quite a mess. Felix laughed as he studied it, "How could anyone read this? Such handwriting!"

"Do you know who wrote it?" Goethe implied. Zelter looked over the boy's shoulder and answered, "Why that's Beethoven. It's recognizable by a mile away as it looks like he used a broomstick then wiped his sleeve over the ink. I have a few of his manuscripts myself."

Felix glanced at Zelter in astonishment at his claim of owning sheet music of Beethoven. It excited him though, knowing that this manuscript was Beethoven's. The poet urged on, "Show us what you can do."

Felix began, playing it slightly roughly, giggling and searching for the right notes out of the scratched out ones. The melody seemed distinguished so his wrong fingerings shifted quickly to the right ones. After finishing the tune he told them, "Now I shall play it for you." This time he knew where every note needed to be. After playing it fluently he then remarked, "That is Beethoven."

"Indeed it is. My poem 'Wonne der Wehmut' is what he set it to." Goethe smiled then inquired, "You compose I imagine?"

Felix nodded. Zelter dug out the sheets of the piano quartet from his bag. He handed it to the poet. After inspecting it a bit, in haste Goethe pleaded, "Stay in Weimar for a few days. I shall invite some musicians to play this with you. There are guest rooms here for you."

Zelter and Felix agreed to stay. Felix couldn't believe he was staying in such a landmark of a house. They had dinner together with a few other select guests. Felix was in complete awe the entire time, until the hour of bed. Goethe, all in all, had deemed young Felix a decent well mannered boy.

~~~~

The next afternoon after enjoying a calm beautiful morning, with a walk in the gardens and breakfast, Goethe had some musicians invited over. A violinist, violist and cellist had agreed to come. Though the composer was unfamiliar, they were unable to pass on an invitation from the great poet.

They all sat in the music room, holding their instruments, waiting to play the music set before them. They spoke among themselves about being in company with Goethe, but not much about the music. They didn't take note of Felix until he sat at the piano. They appeared baffled by his young character. Their subtle whispers made him feel a bit shy. Once Goethe entered the parlor, they were silent. When he gestured to them to play, they held up their instruments and didn't question anything. Everyone played the work as intended.

Once the closing chord ended the piece, everyone nodded in satisfaction. Goethe and the string players gave their complements. The poet then turned to Felix, "Please, go cool down in the garden, you're perspiring."

Felix instantly jumped from the seat and raced out the door in excitement, but halted before exiting through the main door. In silence, he stood close to the doorway of the music room to eavesdrop.

The smiling poet turned to Zelter and the string players, "Musical prodigies are probably no longer so rare; but what this little man can do in playing at sight borders the miraculous, and I could not have believed it possible at so early an age."

"And you heard Mozart in his seventh year at Frankfurt, when you were twelve?" Asked Zelter.

"Yes, but what your pupil already accomplishes, bears the same relation to the Mozart of that time that the cultivated talk of a grown up bears to a prattle of a child."

Zelter added, "True, many begin as Mozart but no one ever reached him."

Felix's thoughts dazed over their references. He then continued his way toward the garden with his sketchbook as to not forget Fanny's request. All he could think upon though was the fact that they thought him as good as Mozart.

~~~~

Back in the city of Hamburg, I had only by now heard slight details of the boy near my age at the time that had the 'Mozart' status.

Ever since Wolfgang Amadeus Mozart's father, Leopold, made his son's talent a success back in the 1770s, many parents wanted the same for their children. Some went so far as to push their child's limits to the extreme.

Such a thing happened to Beethoven. He did become a talented child as he had passion for the piano early on. His grandfather had been a decent court musician, but his father, not so much. His father instead took advantage of his son's talents by keeping him up late into the night to impress friends with music as they drank into drunkenness. If young Ludwig's skills happened to be dissatisfying, his father resorted to beating him. It is supposed that is what led to his gradual deafness later on.

With all of the pressures of his father, he still failed to meet the standards in musical society at the time to be considered a 'Mozart', which only infuriated his father all the more. Ludwig was still in high regard with talent. He found work as an organist to support his younger brothers, when his father failed to make a living.

He had traveled to Vienna in his adolescence to branch out in his performing skills, but it was hindered upon urgent letters from his father concerning his mother, who was ill of consumption (tuberculosis).

Upon his return home to Bonn, his mother died. A few years later, Beethoven found his real success in returning to Vienna and studying with Haydn.

Another that fared harshly due to the pressure from his parents was the Italian violinist Niccolo Paganini. In his childhood, he was taught the mandolin by his father as a pastime. However, when he was old enough and became interested in the violin, he was to practice full time everyday. If he did not meet his father's standards in hours of practice, he wouldn't get super. Yet, for Niccolo, the practice paid off and made a very successful career.

The style in which Paganini played always caught my interests. In the year 1821 I had not yet taken up violin, but music did interest me. My family still resided in Hamburg and later encouraged my musical path once I became serious. I had a rather normal family that still fed me and treated me with kindness.

Felix happened to be one of a few youths achieving such status of a 'Mozart'. He was lucky though to have kind parents in the matter. They were encouraging but the biggest difference was that his parents didn't want his talents overly known. They were more reserved in the matter as Abraham at the time allowed music in his youth. In his traditional ideals, music was an adornment for a wife to do in free time. Not a career. Yet Felix would be challenging his ideals.

~~~~

In the following year of 1822, the family traveled to Switzerland. The beautiful landscapes prompted Felix to sketch it all. Nature fed his muse for composition. He wrote more string symphonies, also a violin and piano concerto as well. Fanny continued to compose excellent music. All the children gained inspiration from the journey as everything was so beautiful.

Once the family returned home, Felix and Fanny's compositions were rehearsed and performed on Sunday afternoons. The salons were an intricate event each week, but full of endless memories.

*(Felix Mendelssohn)*          *(Fanny Mendelssohn)*

# Chapter III: A Gift

Music to accompany chapter:
Moscheles, Piano concerto no. 3, (until next piece) [1]
Mendelssohn, Symphony no. 1 in c minor [2]


Year of 1824

[1]


"Get up." The familiar voice of a maid called. It was the early fifth
hour. Felix continued snoring, trying to catch up on much needed slumber.
The maid called again, this time sternly, "Wake up, you'll
be late."

In a sudden burst of energy, he scrambled out of bed. An opened
book setting on his chest fell to the floor as he got up. He picked it up in
haste, skimming the pages to find his place. The book was the Shakespeare
play 'Romeo and Juliet'.

"You fell asleep late reading again, didn't you?" The maid scowled.
She walked to the nightstand that had a fully melted candle. The entire
thing had been covered in hardened wax. She began to council, "You do
realise that candles cost money? This is the third time this week you've
wasted them. Your father wasn't happy last week when he had to
order extra."

"I'm sorry, but I couldn't help it. I've almost finished the book."

"I know very well that both you and Fanny have read that book
many times." She referred to their shared love of Shakespeare, "From
now on, I'll be sure that you aren't staying up late. Your mother was
frustrated after I told her how hard it is to wake you up. For goodness
sake, you are fifteen now. Learn some responsibility."

Felix sighed and went to pick an outfit for the day. Today deemed important, so he chose his most modest linen and wool garments. An important figure in music had taken up residence in Berlin during a tour. A composer and performer by the name of Ignaz Moshceles. Lea sent him an invitation to have dinner with them that day. It was Felix's hope that Ignaz would give him some music lessons upon his short stay.

Felix was ready for the day by six. He grabbed his general books of study and trudged to the dining table. His siblings were already into their books. Lea warned upon his entrance, "Today is very important as you know. It's a must to be on time on such days," referring to his tardiness. Felix silently opened his book of grammar studies.

The afternoon consisted of music and theory studies. Zelter had given him some counterpoint studies and wanted him to incorporate them into a composition. It kept Felix busy for an hour or so. Fanny joined him after finishing some needlework with Lea. After they composed some, they read some books. No letters from Mr. Moscheles arrived. Felix felt a wave of disappointment as the hour of dinner came.

The family sat together at the table with a nice meal consisting of roasted lamb and duck. It had been made nicer than usual since they had been expecting a guest. The family felt disappointed at Ignaz's absence. Abraham tried to brighten the mood, "Well, it's nice to have a fancier family dinner every now and again."

Lea and the children nodded. The food was quite savory and satisfying. After dinner was eaten and cleaned up, Lea decided to write to Ignaz again. She went to the stationary desk in the drawing room and penned:

*Berlin, November 18th, 1824*

*We much regretted not seeing you at dinner today; pray, let us have the pleasure of your company, if not earlier, at least next Sunday. Have you kindly thought over our request concerning lessons? You would sincerely oblige us by consenting, if you could do so without interfering with arrangements you have made for your stay in this place. Please do not set down these repeated requests to indiscretion, but attribute them solely to the wish that our children should be enabled to profit by the presence of the 'prince des pianistes'*

*(Prince of pianists)*

*With sincere regards, yours,*

*Lea Mendelssohn Bartholdy*

**She folded up the letter and straight away had it sent. Hopefully the letters were actually getting to him. On the other hand, he probably had a lot to do on his limited stay in the city before moving to the next.**

**It was a few days later when a letter of reply came. Ignaz agreed to meet Felix but gave sparse meeting arrangements. Felix felt inclined to go to Ignaz's house right away. Lea prevented him in the moment of his excitement and went to the writing desk:**

*Berlin, November 23rd, 1824*

*Being uncertain whether my son will find you at home, I write this line to ask if you feel inclined to visit the Sing-Akademie.*

*Felix at any rate will call for you, as his way lies in that direction. If you are disengaged, will you join our family dinner at three O'clock, or, should that be impossible, will you accompany Felix after the "Akademie" (It lasts from five to seven O'clock), and be one of our small circle at tea?*

*If I may be allowed to renew my request that you will give lessons to my two eldest children, be good enough to let me know your terms. I should like them to begin at once, that they may profit as much as possible during the time of your stay here.*

*With sincere regards and esteem, yours,*

*Lea Mendelssohn Bartholdy*

She handed the letter to the servant and instructed, "This is to arrive at Mr. Moscheles. He must get it as it is important. Now go, Schnell!" The servant left in a hurry. Lea turned to Felix, "I'll have you go over to his residence in an hour. The letter will have reached him by then. I asked that he accompany you to the Akademie if he can't be at dinner, then here for tea. Hopefully he offers lessons. Be sure to hold that conversation when brought up."

Felix nodded. In the meantime he decided to go to the music room with Fanny to show her a piece he'd begun to write. It was a sonata that had made much progress over the week since he had started it. He always felt inclined to ask Fanny for approval of his work. She had more experience in composition. Felix listened closely to her opinions.

After correcting and adding notes and phases, the hour went by. Felix packed up his compositions and Klavier music. He grabbed the letter of Ignaz that contained his address. Lea headed out the door with him and stopped a carriage driving by. She told Felix, "Remember to persuade him to give Fanny lessons as well."

"I will." Felix climbed in the chaise.

The carriage drove on across the city to the address written on a note he handed the coachman. At precisely noon, he arrived outside the complex in which Moscheles was staying. A servant from the complex came and escorted him in by the request of Ignaz. When Felix entered the flat, he was welcomed by Ignaz who was at the piano in the main room. His piano took up most of the space due to the small size of the flat.

Ignaz Moscheles was originally from Bohemia, born in Prague in 1794. His father played guitar and had determination for one of his children to become a musician. His sister seemed to be eager but ended up quitting piano lessons, leaving them to Ignaz. Soon after his father's death, he moved to Vienna, where he gained much musical influence. His instructors included Johann Albrechtsberger for theory and Antonio Salieri for composition.

Ignaz, now in his thirties, had a successful career as composer and pianist. His current home base was in London England where he had a wife by the name of Charlotte.

He gestured to Felix to sit at the piano with him. He had a piece of music already out. A duet. He asked, "Can you read this with me?"

*(Ignaz Moscheles)*

"Ja." Felix placed his fingers on the keys of the lower voice of the duet. Ignaz smiled and placed his at the upper melody. They began playing after counting in. The piece was quite beautiful, one Felix had not heard before.

After playing it, Ignaz said in an impressed tone, "That was perfect on the spot. You read as well as any professional."

"Danke, but may I ask, who is the composer of this? I've never heard it before."

"It's an obscure piano work by a composer by the name of Schubert. I do not know much about him. I picked up this piece from a supposed friend of his on my travels through Vienna. It was a painter I liked and bought a painting. He then begged me to play and keep this duet written by a friend of his. It is quite beautiful. It Is strange how some of the most beautiful things render their creator unknown."

"Maybe someday we'll hear of him." Felix mentioned.

"Right. Anyways, what did you bring along with you?" He pointed at the small stack of music. Felix showed him his favorite pieces. He brought a Beethoven piece to see if Ignaz would enjoy it. To his surprise, he let Felix play an entire sonata. Ignaz asked, "You like Beethoven?"

"Ja, his music has so much to it. I don't get to play it often as my teacher doesn't care for the intensity."

"I had teachers like that. When I was ten, I had a chance to hear Beethoven's eighth sonata. I wanted so badly to play it. At the time I couldn't afford sheet music, but I happened upon the pages at a library and copied it for myself. My teacher rebuked the playing of such music. When I became serious in my career and studied at the conservatory in Prague, my instructor mostly wanted me to play Mozart, Bach and Clementi. I enjoyed my time at the conservatory still, but everything was made up for it when I got to work with Beethoven in Vienna."

Felix's eyes widened, "You worked for Beethoven!?"

"Yes, he commissioned me to prepare the piano score for his opera. It was tough work but we were in good company. He's not as chaotic as many make him out to be. He is a little, but not terrible." Ignaz smiled. Felix looked at him in astonishment. He couldn't believe that Ignaz not only met Beethoven, but worked for him. Ignaz then changed the subject and grabbed a manuscript from Felix's pile of music. It was a composition. Felix played it for him as well as some others. Ignaz asked Felix quite a few questions on how he composed. Felix gladly explained and asked Ignaz questions as well.

After visiting and playing piano for a few hours, Ignaz mentioned, "I do believe the time is nearing four already. We've missed your family's dinner and aren't you to be at the 'Akademie' by five?"

"Yes, my mother wishes you to escort me and come to tea at my house afterwards."

"Tea? That sounds quite English. I'm very fond of England. I chose to reside there with my wife Charlotte. Have you been to Britain?"

"No, but I'd love to someday...but I must inquire, if you would be in favor of giving my sister and I lessons. Our mother and father insist."

"Does your sister play as well as you?" Ignaz questioned. Felix gave a firm reply, "She is a better keyboardist than I. She composes as well."

Ignaz nodded in intrigument. He then said, "I shall teach with what time I have. Now, let's get to the Akademie."

*(Sing-Akademie zu Berlin)*

They rode a carriage to the Akademie. It was a bit early, but Zelter was there as usual. Ignaz was glad upon meeting him. They happen to speak much on the subject of Bach. Felix had some interest in the conversation, but it wasn't anything new to him. Zelter always spoke much about Bach's music. Ignaz found much interest as he had only come across pieces of Bach through his time at the conservatory. Zelter smiled upon hearing this, "I have a large collection of Bach's manuscripts in my office. Would you like to see?"

"I'd be obliged." Ignaz answered. Felix lifted his head from boredom. Zelter never offered to show someone the collection. Felix had only heard of it but never got to see it. He went to follow, but Zelter turned to him, "Felix, can you go and make sure the auditorium is ready for rehearsals?"

"I'd like to stay in company with Ignaz." Felix knew his teacher did not want him to go with. Zelter pressured, "Everyone will be showing up for rehearsals soon, I want everything set." He tried to sound nice in front of Ignaz.

Felix gave him a dead stare, knowing he wasn't meaning to be kind. Ignaz suggested, "I think Felix should stay in company. I think his mother wanted him to stay with me as my visit here is limited."

"Alright. My office is this way." Zelter headed down a corridor. They stopped at a room. Zelter unlocked it and they went in. He went straight to the large oak cabinet that lined the back wall of the large office. It had many openings to store things on the shelves. Each one was crammed full of books of scores and papers.

Zelter gladly let Ignaz get a glimpse of the many Bach manuscripts. Felix had not known he kept so many. Abraham had collected a good amount of Bach's manuscripts at an auction before fleeing Hamburg. Zelter made sure some of his father's collection resided with the Akademie. Now that Felix saw the hundreds of sheets crowded in one large cabinet, he felt that Zelter was rather hoarding them than collecting them.

As Zelter allowed Ignaz to skim through the music, Felix glanced at his instructor in confusion. He never let anyone near his precious Bach collection. As Ignaz held some to study, Felix tried to get a glimpse. Zelter grabbed them before Felix could hold them. He even went as far as shewing him away if he leaned too close. He didn't want Felix near them.

Ignaz was far too awestruck to notice the silent quarrel between Felix and Zelter. After Ignaz looked at many of them, there was one he especially was fond of. Zelter looked at it and exclaimed, "That's a very good keyboard work. This happens to be a copy and I have a few copies of this one, plus the original. You can have this one."

"Danke, I'll certainly play it much." Ignaz smiled. Felix's mouth nearly dropped. This was nothing like Zelter. He must have really liked Ignaz. Zelter then told Felix, "You must go to the auditorium. Rehearsals start in fifteen minutes." He gently nudged him out of his office. Felix huffed and listened.

Rehearsals with the choir went on fairly normal. Ignaz watched from one of the seats. The orchestra wasn't with them today, so Felix couldn't tell Rietz about Zelter letting Ignaz keep a copy of a Bach manuscript.

Sitting beside Felix were his two friends. The one on his left was named Eduard Devrient. He was an excellent singer. The other on his right was Karl Klingemann, who was also a great singer and a poet.

As Zelter had the women practice their section, Felix began whispering to them. Both Eduard and Karl were surprised at Zelter. They murmured and giggled a bit upon the subject. Felix suddenly felt a light slap to his shoulder. He turned around and one of the older gentlemen in the choir gestured to him to shut up. Felix turned back and kept quiet for the rest of the rehearsal.

When the choir rehearsal ended after two hours, Ignaz accompanied Felix back to his home where they were to join for tea. Ignaz liked it very much as it reminded him of his residence in England. Felix noticed he had a particular way of having tea by his manners. It made him very much refined. Lea loved it as well as she tried her best to make tea in the way the English did.

After tea, Ignaz left for the evening. Upon arriving home, he pondered on Felix's skill at the piano. His instructor had taught him much. Ignaz sat at his piano. He continued on with his work, but his thoughts distracted him. It affected his concentration on the music. He decided to set the piano aside for a while and write in his diary instead to get his thoughts off his mind. He penned a bit about his day and the lesson with Felix. Already thinking of inviting him over again before his leave. He then wrote, concerning the lesson with him, 'I am aware I am sitting next to a master; not a pupil.'

~~~~

The next week after Ignaz's leave, Felix was in the music room, writing much on a manuscript he had been penning the past week. It was his hand at a first attempt of a full scale symphony. He worked intensely on it. Much of his inspiration sprouted from Weber's music. He wanted something energetic and grand. Abraham walked in and asked, "Son, you have a bit?"

"Wait a minute." He continued writing for a while. Abraham ordered, "Put the music down."

"Just a minute-"

"Now." Abraham demanded. Felix immediately set it down. His father explained, "I'm taking you to visit my brother Joseph and to show you around the offices at the bank. He is excited to teach you some things. You'll be staying at the bank's residence for a few days."

"A few days!? What about my practice?" Felix felt bewildered.

"Joseph has a decent piano, but you won't be doing a lot of music while you're there. It will be a little break to introduce you into your future profession." Abraham went to his son and patted his shoulder in pride. Felix looked at his father with wide eyes. He was in fear for his future. Abraham told him, "We shall leave within the hour, so get packed for a few nights."

"Alright…" Felix got up from the piano, taking his score. Abraham warned, "Leave the music. It will still be here upon your return."

Felix left the music room and went upstairs to go pack. He wasn't happy with any of it. After he got his things together, he rushed back to the music room. He put his score in progress in his book satchel. Right as he closed his bag, Abraham called, "Felix, time to go!"

Felix rushed to the entryway. Before he went out the door with his father, Abraham stopped him. Right away he opened Felix's bag and grabbed the score. Felix gave a huff. Abraham scolded, "You are not going to be working on music while you're there."

"But Vater!? I can't let it set around for days!"

"Put it back now."

"Maybe I don't want to visit Uncle Joseph." Felix mumbled. His comment was met with a smack. Abraham became heated with frustration, "You are going to put that score back in your room and you are going to Joseph's house."

Felix put the score back straight away. His face stung from his father's hand. After setting it at his desk, he and his father finally headed out. The carriage ride was silent all the way to the bank house.

When they arrived at the quaint building that served as a home and business, Joseph welcomed them in. He most eagerly greeted Felix. Abraham warned Joseph discreetly, "He's being a bit ignorant. Don't mind being stern with him."

Joseph's smile at Felix faded some. Abraham and Joseph both showed Felix around the house. It was a well suited home with intricate decor to show professionalism. The offices for the bank were on the first floor. A building towards the city center served as the vault, but the main offices were in this home. Abraham worked here often.

*(The Bank Haus, Jägerstraße 51)*

After Felix settled his things in a guest room, Abraham and Joseph showed him to the main office. It was large and well kept with two large work desks. Abraham explained, "I shall leave you here now for Joseph to teach you. I'll be back in three days. Listen to your uncle and be a good apprentice. No composing."

"Apprenticeship?" Felix echoed. He didn't like the idea of being called Joseph's apprentice when he didn't want to be in this profession. Abraham patted Felix on the shoulder then left. Joseph gestured Felix to sit at one of the desks. He hesitantly obeyed. His uncle assured him, "I can already tell you are not fond to learn from me, but you must." He grabbed some papers from the desk's built-in cabinet.

Felix listened as Joseph explained each aspect of keeping track of money and to do it with accuracy. Felix sensed his uncle had a deep passion for teaching his nephew the profession.

"This folder has all of the calculations for this month and what should be in the bank. I'll show you how to make sure that what has been calculated here is correct." He opened a folder. Another folder he dug out had all of the expenses.

Joseph handed Felix a quill and had him start adding up totals and checking the numbers. It felt like good hearted work and something he was capable of. Joseph told him he was already quite good and would be excellent once he trained more often.

Felix did not feel satisfied. There was something missing. This was work to make money, keep busy, move on. It did not fill the desire to create something heartfelt then later enjoy the result upon completion. It made Felix sigh.

Joseph noticed his nephew's absence of enthusiasm. It only made him keep encouraging, "You are doing well. You'll love this work once you realize how much it has to offer. It may not seem like it now but you won't regret taking it up. I know in time you'll like it."

After a few hours of basically doing what Felix found out was Abraham's job, Joseph let him off for the day. As soon as he was off, he found the decent piano in the sitting room. He practiced and played. The maids in the house paused their cleaning in the kitchen to clean in the sitting room to hear Felix. They were quite happy. Joseph was still at his desk. Upon hearing the beautiful melodies echo through the house, he gave a sigh. In honesty he hoped his brother wouldn't pressure Felix into doing something he didn't want to do.

~~~~

[2]

When the three days at Joseph's house passed, Abraham took Felix home. He asked his son, "Did you learn a lot?"

"Ja." Felix sighed. He wanted to tell his father how much he didn't care for it, but he knew it would only hurt his feelings.

50

Abraham told him, "In a few weeks, I'll have you go back to train with him more. I expect that after you complete some university studies later on, you'll then find your new settlement at the bank house." He went on and on about Felix's future.

"Why can't music be my career?" Felix finally pleaded. Abraham eyed him in disappointment, "Music is a pastime. You'll have a good wife and she will have good taste in music just as Fanny. As well as cook and take care of the house. Your job is to provide for her and your future family by having a steady career. Doesn't that sound nice to you?"

"What about a music teacher? Zelter has a good career."

"Having that sort of career isn't always practical. You know that Beethoven had not the best reputation and Mozart was a debtor in real life, not having a good station that we are fortunate enough to have! The bank will keep your family afloat."

"Can I do anything creative!?"

"Listen to me. Art, music and poetry are pastimes for a wife to please their husbands, not sustainable careers! I am letting you enjoy these things in your youth so you can remember a good childhood."

"Can I still compose?" Felix asked in a somber tone.

"Only if you agree to continue learning from Joseph and I." Abraham bargained. Felix huffed, knowing he had no choice. He couldn't bear the conversation any longer. He didn't answer to any more demands. Once they arrived home, Felix raced to his room. Straight away he continued with his symphony that was in progress.

~~~~

During the long winter month of January, Lea's mother, Bella Salomon came to the home to attend one of the Sunday concerts. Though she lived in the same city, her visits were special. She had excitement upon visiting her grandchildren.

Bella quite loved Fanny's talents and admired her as a fine young lady. Fanny was now eighteen going on nineteen in November. Her newest compositions consisted of works for piano and Lieder for Rebecka to sing.

Rebecka had become quite a singer within the last few years of music lessons. The twelve year old's inclination to sing impressed many guests.

She also had quite a gift for language and literature. Fluently she could read the works of Homer in Greek.

*(Rebecka Mendelssohn)*

Paul's interests were devoted to learning the cello. He had grown enough to be able to handle one. The nine year old fell completely in love with the instrument. Lea encouraged him to prepare music for their home concert. He practiced some short pieces to his heart's content. In other aspects, Paul had grown and matured into a well mannered young boy.

Bella became very much intrigued as Felix showed her the finished manuscript of his first full symphony. Since an entire orchestra couldn't come to their home, an ensemble of musicians had been invited to play the work.

The children enjoyed bonding the day with their grandmother as she had come early in the day. They had tea and lunch together. When evening came, musicians and guests arrived.

Cheese and wine were served as they visited in the parlor. Within the hour they then headed to the music room. Once everyone settled, Fanny went to the piano along with Rebecka beside it.

Though Rebecka was a decent singer, she soaked up the attention. She always had to perform at least three or four Lieder. Once she finished and took her bow, she went to an open seat by her mother. Fanny then continued the performance with her newest compositions.

All of the guests watched her in awe. She had such grace at the keys that it mesmerized her audience. Felix wished her talent could fare as aunt Sarah, but it would remain only within the walls of their home. Abraham listened with the utmost intent. Felix hoped his father would change his mind concerning Fanny.

With a grand finish, the music ended. The clapping echoed through the entire house. She bowed humbly and took her seat. Next, little Paul grabbed his cello. It wasn't a full size cello, but it was still a burden for him to drag around. Abraham helped him. Once Paul got set, he began playing some Bach and Clementi minuets that Fanny arranged for him to play. It sounded so pure and innocent.

After his finishing applause, the ensemble of musicians got set for Felix's composition. Felix handed out the music for them. The musicians sat and tuned. This miniature orchestra consisted of a string quintet, a horn and a few winds. Felix stood up on a makeshift conducting pedestal and held up his hands ready to conduct. The musicians raised their instruments, ready to play.

As soon as the rosin on the bows and breath activated the instruments, the music came to life. The room echoed with melody and excitement.

Felix felt the same energy as he had when attending Weber's concert. He had learned much from Weber's way of composition and captivating the listeners.

For the next half hour or so, no one would be distracting their ears. The strings jittering through quick passages gave indication to a distinct style. This was Felix's sound.

~~~~

The last movement of the symphony ended with energy. Everyone applauded the work. Felix turned and bowed and courteously moved aside for the musicians to give their bows. After it was all over, the guests began to disassemble for the evening. Bella stayed of course. She was so enthralled by the concert. She felt proud to have such talented grandchildren.

Later that evening, as Felix wandered the house, Bella called him to the parlor where she sat in her lonesome. Most of the guests had made their leave. The remaining ones were back in the music room as Fanny and the rest of the family played some casual music for the evening.

Bella gestured to Felix to sit in the chair beside her. Once he sat, she grabbed a bag beside her and took something out. It looked like a book of papers bound together. Felix's eyes brightened as he noticed that it was a score. Bella told him, "I mean to give you this. Your aunt Sarah, my sister, wanted you to have it as well. It's a copyist score of an old orchestral piece."

She handed it to Felix. He looked at the front. Right away his excitement flared. It was an orchestra piece of Johann Sebastian Bach. He looked at the title. St. Matthew Passion. Felix guessed that it was an old church piece. Most professional music in Bach's time was church music. Since the time of Mozart and Beethoven, music started to become freelance. Bella explained, "This piece has not been performed since the time of Bach."

"Really?" Felix stared at it in awe. Bach had died in 1750, so this piece had not been performed in almost a hundred years. Felix began to recall upon examining the music that Zelter had this piece in the Sing-Akademie's collection. He attempted to get it performed. Sadly it didn't turn out due to the complexity.

Bella then told him, "It took a while to convince Zelter to lend the manuscript to get it copied. Eduard, your violin teacher and his younger brother Julius did the work of copying it."

"Dankeschön." Felix couldn't wipe the smile from his face. He headed to his room with his gift. Sitting at his desk, he examined it front and back, analyzing each section. He began to wonder:

*Is it possible to make a more playable arrangement?*
~~~~

That next year in 1825, Abraham set out on another business trip to Paris. This time taking only Felix. Felix received a letter of invitation to the conservatory in the city from one of the most highly rated musicians in Europe. His name was Luigi Cherubini, a composer of opera. Upon learning about the young Berliner, he wanted to meet the boy.

Since Abraham had work, it was practical for them to journey there. Abraham hoped to teach Felix about foreign business between his musical engagements. Felix consented to accompany his father in some.

As soon as they arrived in Paris, Abraham dropped Felix off at the conservatory. It was quite nerve racking. Abraham had to go out on business. Felix had Cherubini's letter with him, so he made his way to the front doors. As he roamed the main entry, he noticed many students and instructors about. Some holding instrument cases, others with canvases and art supplies as well as many of the ballet department. Some looked his way as he was quite young to be in such a place.

He headed towards the music department. Upon roaming the halls, he felt some relief as he gazed upon another near his age.

Felix assumed he was a pianist as his fingers were quite long and well suited for the instrument. Felix stopped him and asked, "Can you tell me where I can find Signor Cherubini?"

"Cherubini? What is it you want with him?" His accent was not French, rather Germanic. Felix showed the boy his letter. The fair blond nodded, "Go straight down this hall. You'll hear him before entering the room."

"Merci." Felix said in politeness. The boy then asked, "So that letter…your name is Felix? Are you quite a musician as Cherubini must think?"

"I play and compose. I came from Berlin. My father happened to have business in Paris. About you though? You don't seem to be from around."

"My name is Franz Liszt. My family came from Hungary. I play the piano. Currently I am in residence here." He held out his hand. Felix shook it, "Well, I guess I should be going, Danke for the greeting."

Felix continued down the corridor. He walked until he heard the faint sound of arguing. It grew louder upon nearing a room. When he reached the door, he opened it slightly. A man stood by the piano, singing an operatic piece for tenor. His voice had the most mature sound that Felix had ever heard. An accompanist played the piano. As the man sang the climax of the piece, a loud voice from another standing a few paces away shouted, "STOP! STOP!"

The singer and accompanist both sighed in despair. Felix peeked in more and saw the one that yelled. He seemed angered and frustrated. His appearance accompanied his stress. That was Cherubini.

He stormed towards the singer, "You must control your falsetto. You are trying to impress me. I don't want to hear your power, this is a love song. Not a victory piece! Start again!" He clapped his hands together.

The determined tenor took his stance again and sang with infatuation. Felix thought the singer changed to the music's mood. After completing the piece, Cherubini told him, "Better. Next time I want it flawless. Now go practice." He pointed to the door. Upon looking towards the door, Cherubini noticed Felix. Felix felt his nerves jump being intimidated. Yet, the maestro's stern demeanor softened. After the singer and accompanist left, he gestured to Felix, "Please, come here young one. I see you accepted my invitation."

Felix came in and Luigi told him, "Carl Weber told me of you when he passed through here. He gave me the information to contact Spontini. I've heard much of you. I'm taking word from Weber. Spontini rather spoke bluntly."

"Oh…" Felix didn't know what to say. Cherubini guided him to the piano. He opened an orchestral score and told Felix, "Play this for me."

Felix examined the score as a whole, checking the key and other obvious things. It was a work that rather made sense and phrased well. Most likely it was an opera overture to one of Cherubini's. Felix then put his hands on the keys and read the score, playing it as a piano arrangement. After that Luigi had him play other various things as well as Felix's own compositions.

When Felix was done, Cherubini nodded, "Very well done young man. Have you had the chance to meet Franz Liszt? He's a very well brought up pianist. I believe he is only a bit younger than you. I suggest you go to one of his performances. He has one tomorrow evening."

"I saw him in the halls. I'd like to." Felix felt intrigued. Cherubini told him the details. After Felix left Cherubini, Abraham waited for him outside the conservatory. They took a chaise back to their place of stay. Felix mentioned, "Tomorrow Cherubini would like me to accompany him to see a good pianist perform at the conservatory."

"Oh, good. You may go as long as you accompany me on some business beforehand."

"Alright..." Felix sighed. They returned to their lodgings, which was a nice hotel. As it was the evening, Felix and Abraham both retired to bed to get much needed rest.

The next morning, they awoke early and got breakfast as the hotel offered it. The food was some of the best. Abraham ate a croissant and pastries with his coffee. Felix wanted something less plain and got blueberry crepes with a latte. Everything, even the bland foods were savory.

After breakfast, Abraham took Felix to tend to some work. From that point on, Felix's inclination for the city began to decline. He knew his father's work would be boring. It consisted of filling out paperwork at an office building which was an extension to the family bank. When that was done, Abraham took Felix back to the conservatory.

Felix found Cherubini this time in the same room as before, but instructing a group of singers. They were acting out a section of an opera. He raged at them for not being accurate. Much was blamed on the accompanist. The man was breaking a sweat in nervousness. It was only making his playing worse. Finally Cherubini yelled at him to make his leave. Felix felt bad for the pianist, but his heart thudded as Cherubini demanded, "Felix! Come here!"

Felix entered the room without question. Luigi's attitude was quite different with him than yesterday.

Cherubini pointed to the Klavier, "Accompany." His voice felt like sharp thorns. The only way of escaping these thorns was to do as he wanted. Felix sat at the piano and looked at the music before him. This opera score was far more complicated than the one yesterday.

The group of singers stared at Cherubini in disapproval for snapping so harshly at a kid. Cherubini announced, "We are starting at measure 37!" He counted them in. Felix had no clue what the opera was. He just played what he could make of the score. He wasn't used to pressure of this sort. Especially when mentally arranging a rather large, messy score on the spot. He had to pick and choose the main parts to play. At times Cherubini didn't agree with his arranging and scolded him. The rough session ended eventually to Felix's relief.

Many of the singers commended Felix before leaving their rehearsal. They seemed embarrassed upon Cherubini's rage. The tenor that Felix saw the day before explained in a whisper that Luigi had attitude problems. After the singers left, Cherubini told him, "Franz plays within the hour."

"Fine." Felix spoke bluntly. He refused to say much as his respect for this man was lost. Cherubini sensed it but rather ignored the boy's attitude. He guided him to where Liszt would be playing. It was in a large, elegant room in which piano recitals were held at the conservatory. They took their seats among the already gathered crowd.

The young blonde that Felix had met yesterday came and walked to the piano. He noticed Felix and gave a rather cocky nod. Felix smiled back, yet he began to sense that Franz acknowledged him as to show him up. He wasn't fond of the competitive spirit that was festering in the air.

Felix watched as young Franz sat at the piano with complete etiquette. He then gazed upon the keys of the piano, then the audience. With his arms raised over the keys, his hands barreled to the first chord of his piece.

~~~~

*April 1825*

*Dear Mr. Moscheles,*

*I am writing to give you my experience in my current time in Paris. I'm with my father. The city still has its beauty and good food as I remember coming in years past. Yet this trip has not fared as pleasurable. I must tell of the concert I attended a few evenings ago concerning a pianist a few years younger than I. His name is Franz Liszt. You wouldn't believe his ability unless you were there, yet at the same time, it was rather a hash. I wasn't as impressed as Cherubini said I should be. Liszt had much energy and skills that any other boy his age wouldn't. Yet I wasn't fond of his flashy style. It was to show off to his listeners. In short, he has more fingers than brains. His improvisation skills were completely wretched. At the same time Franz is a true artist that you can't help liking even if you disagree. His compositions I favored not. I guess the only thing he really lacks is originality. I hope to meet you again in the coming time. My father gives his regards and I to you and Mrs. Moscheles.*

*Your friend,*

*Felix M.*

Felix set down his quill and folded up the letter. He set it aside then looked at another unopened one that had come to him. It was from Fanny. Felix and Fanny had been writing back and forth through the weeks in their separation. It was rather bantering between their experiences. Felix had written to her upon his growing disappointment in the city. He attended a few other concerts and events that fared bland. Fanny wrote back in response to Felix's negative feelings on Paris:

*25th, April, 1825*

Alas! You both travel to Paris and hear no decent music, or very little, and we stay calm at home and are forced to stretch our ears. In one week we've had Jessonda, Aceste, Samson and the Pastoral Symphony, and the last two will be at Sanpupi's (Spontini's) concert on Good Friday the day after tomorrow. What do you think? This much seems clear: Your talent for fickleness develops brilliantly in Paris. My son, your letters consist nothing but criticism –

Oh, the beautiful paintings you've seen, why no word of them? Nothing on public gardens, the city, the buildings? I feel that the tiresome salon music has killed every ounce of enjoyment for you –

**She then wrote of her joys in the flowers and gardens back at home:**

We all crouched around the ground to look for violets, including Klingemann, yet he made fun of us. We claimed that he dug up violets. He put on his glasses then sat on a chopped tree trunk to arrange the flowers and things he had gathered in his handkerchief. Can you picture this grandiose figure? Our garden is already splendid. How beautiful it will be in May when the lilacs are in bloom. Yet you don't even acknowledge the green trees.

Have I not mentioned that Klingemann has already taken 3 violin lessons from Rietz? One has to admire his zeal. We think he should become a main pillar in Rietz's symphony society. Rietz has received 3 students including our neighbor, little talented Eda Benda. –

Her mention of the symphony society referred to what Rietz had been putting together. He had left his position in the Berlin court orchestra due to quarrels and disagreements with Spontini. Rietz decided to make his own Philharmonic Society. Fanny ends her letter, addressing Abraham as so:

Dear father, I greet you a thousand times over, Farewell. If only we could meet up in Potsdam.

-Fanny

The letter rather irritated Felix. He didn't like how she implied so much on his negative outlook on the trip. In the meantime he set the letter aside as he had things to tend to. A few days later he penned in strong reply:

9th, May, 1825

I was rather angry over your previous letter and decided to send a scolding your way...You write of me preconceptions of the land where milk and honey flow, as you call this Paris? Are you in Paris or am I? That I must know better than you!

-Felix

The grumblings of Paris did not stop until his return home.

# Chapter IV: Shakespeare

Mendelssohn, String Octet in E-flat, movement I [1]
Mendelssohn, Overture to A Midsummer Night's Dream [2]
Mendelssohn, Die Hochzeit des Camacho Overture [3]

## [1]

Abraham felt a wave of success as he shook hands on an engagement he had acquired. The family would be moving to a new house, still in Berlin. Not just any kind of house. An estate. It was settled in a quiet neighborhood. The purchase also included not only the main house, but also some guest houses. The structures surrounded a large park containing many gardens.

Once the deal was set the family moved in. When the children entered the house, they were amazed. A large staircase showed the wealth of the home. The grand halls contained tall intricately engraved pillars. It reminded Felix of the marble works of art from the renaissance.

Once the children looked about in circles, Rebecka blurted, "I'm choosing my room first!" She raced up the stairs. Felix followed close behind, then Fanny, then young Paul. Rebecka reached a room and went in without even looking at the others. Felix glanced at the rooms then found one that had a window facing the beautiful gardens. He went to go in, but was pulled back by the collar of his coat.

"I'm getting the garden view." Fanny pushed in front of him. She shut the door after entering. Felix snorted in irritation at his sister. Paul had taken one of the other rooms already, leaving two rooms. One was the large master bedroom. Obviously his parents would be taking that one. The other was a quaint bedroom with a window facing the streets. Felix went in and looked about. It seemed a decent place to reside.

The vast neighborhood and lake nearby gave more options for recreation and sport. The children now had the outlet of swimming in the summer and ice skating through the winter.

Soon after settling, Felix acquired a horse from his father. The gardens were large enough for riding and the estate contained the necessary accommodations for keeping one. Felix fell in love with taking it for long leisurely gallops. He also became athletic in other activities such as tennis and fencing.

*(Mendelssohn estate, Leipziger Straße No 3, Berlin)*

Though the large house seemed to bring a promising new life, the days only grew busier for Felix as he, now sixteen, had more education. The thought of more overwhelmed him, but the tutor his father hired was good and kind. His name was Herr Heyse. Felix felt more at ease as his tutor taught him many of the things he enjoyed. His instruction consisted of classical literature, art, languages and philosophy.

Felix kept occupied with music through the busy schedule. Though his father was encouraging him to pursue the bank, Abraham still sent Felix's finished compositions to the publishers.

The constant early days left all the children tiresome, but more so with Felix. He adopted the habit of napping whenever he had the chance. More often than not he would be snoozing on the sofa during the gatherings hosted by his parents. Despite the chatter of guests and clanking of silverware, Abraham resorted to waking him for dinner or to entertain.

Some of the salons rendered too important to sleep through. Highly regarded guests came at times. One guest that Felix found interest in was the scientist Alexander Humboldt. He had traveled to many lands and told much of his experience. Abraham tried to keep Felix in Humboldt's company since the scientist had founded the college in Berlin. He hoped his son would have a better chance of entering later if he were in good favor with the founder.

With Abraham and Lea hosting more salons, the children's musical talents were the highlight of the gatherings. Both Fanny and Felix's compositions were in high preference. All of Berlin society came to their home to hear the work of mere teenagers.

~~~~

In the days with the chill of the autumn weather, Fanny and Felix spent much of their spare hours in the large music room. The room had much elegance from the regency style decor. Felix opened the patterned blue and white curtains to let in what light was outside. The sky was bright but grey. He kept the window shut as it would chill the room. Though the fireplace had some embers, the air still felt bitter through the nose.

Keeping a large house warm was challenging. The music room happened to lack the circulation of the fireplace. Fanny wore a heavy wool cloak over her dress. She kept her hands in her pockets when not playing the piano to keep her hands from stiffening. Felix stood near the fireplace while playing his violin.

They were practicing Mozart's violin sonata in e minor. Felix's violin resonated through the house. Fanny's accompaniment at the piano added fullness. Nothing could have sounded more beautiful. As the violin's tone soothed Felix's ears upon bowing the strings, Fanny paused after a cadence, ending the phrase. Felix held the violin down in confusion, "Is something on your mind?"

"I've recently been thinking about something..." Fanny paused a second, "It's been on my mind for a long time," She sounded hesitant to speak, "I want to take my own compositions more seriously. I plan to ask father if I can publish. He may not let me perform in public, but I hope to publish."

"You should. I don't know why he's not sent anything of yours before." Felix encouraged. Fanny smiled with determination, "Let's go talk to him now."

~~~~

Fanny's idea turned to turmoil. Abraham would not have it. Felix stood in the middle of the argument.

"Music is not a profession for a lady. It's a pastime." Abraham stated. Fanny begged, "Please, what is wrong with my music? I'll fix it."

"Nothing is the matter with your music. It is written to perfection. You are my daughter, a finely brought up lady. Your music is to please your future husband. I will not argue further on this subject." Abraham turned back to his newspaper as he sat by the fireplace.

"What about aunt Sarah? What of Marie Bigot!?" Fanny continued.

"Marie Bigot died of consumption due to constantly trying to provide for her children! She overworked in her career! I shall not see the same in my daughter!" Abraham near yelled. Fanny backed away and looked to Felix. She wanted him to say something.

With his father's strong opinion and his own back and fourths, he remained silent. Fanny looked at her brother in confusion. When she realized that he wouldn't help, she stormed out of the room. Abraham muttered, "She should know better."

Felix began to feel bad. He stayed near the fireplace. He finally confessed, "Aunt Sarah had a decent reputation."

"But she is not my daughter. My daughter is going to play music for her future husband and be a fit wife." He hissed. He then muttered to himself, "One child attempting to make music as a profession is enough."

His comment hurt. Felix began to feel as if his aspirations were what made his father reluctant to let Fanny achieve her own. Before Felix could leave, Abraham told him, "You had better not be encouraging your sister in these ideas. I am sticking to my opinion."

Felix left the room to find Fanny outside. Glaring at him. Felix couldn't bring any words to mind. Without any sound, she retired upstairs to her room. He wished to do something to apologize.

Felix went upstairs as well to his room. Upon entering, he rummaged through his bookshelf. After skimming it over, he grabbed one. It was Shakespeare's Hamlet. A favorite of his, and Fanny. He took the book and headed to Fanny's room. He knocked on the door. No answer. He called softly, "Please can I talk to you?"

Still no answer. He tried again, begging, "Please Fanny. I want to talk. Please...please...please..." Felix pleaded until she opened the door and snapped, "Get out of here you annoying little-" She paused as he handed her the Shakespeare book. Her expression turned to confusion. He explained, "I want you to have it."

Upon him giving her one of his favorite books, she sighed and let him in. Once he came in, he told her, "I'm sorry about earlier. I tried to convince Vater after you left."

"There wasn't anything that would change our Vater's opinion." Fanny sighed. Felix then mentioned, "I thought of an idea for you to publish."

"Felix, I don't think anything will convince Vater."

"But I know a way. You could publish under my name. I'll give the music to Vater. The only thing is, he would have to think it's mine."

"Surely Vater would know it's not your work. He knows our music."

"I'll say I'm getting some different influences. You'll give me the music and I'll copy it in my hand. Be sure to write other music so he thinks you're still writing in your own time."

"I will think about it..." She left the conversation at that.
~~~

The next day, Herr Heyse came at his usual time in the morning to instruct Felix. Today they worked on studies of language and classical literature. Heyse had brought a copy of the play Andria, an ancient Roman comedy adapted by Terence from two Greek plays. Felix had been studying the Greek language.

As Felix recited a section of the play to Heyse, making sure of correct pronunciation, Felix paused then asked, "Are there any copies of the play in German?"

"Not that I know of, but you are learning Greek, you don't need a German copy." Heyse commented. Felix shrugged and continued on.

The lesson lasted a few hours. Heyse told Felix before leaving, "Tomorrow we will go over some English studies and more of the play. I want you to work on your pronunciations, especially your English. Your lisp is quite noticeable when you speak it."

"I will." Felix nodded, grabbing his English book. Heyse then left. Felix practiced phrases, trying to say things correctly. He then moved back to his Greek lesson. As he worked, he began to get an idea to help him study better. He grabbed a quill and a stack of paper. On the first sheet he wrote:

*Mädchen Von Andros*
*Terence*

He then began translating the play to German. The work would help him understand the play better as well as the language. As the next hour became consumed with the work, Fanny joined him at the table. She had a piece of newly composed music. Felix slid it into his stack of papers as she handed it to him. She wanted to publish.

~~~~

The weeks went by with study, music and everyday activities. Through the commotion, Felix felt inclined to compose something for his violin teacher. He wanted to give Rietz something special he could play with friends. After learning much of the fundamentals of bowed instruments over the years, he felt more confident in composing for them. He decided to write an octet.

Upon finishing a lesson with Rietz that day, he went home, sat at his desk and grabbed some manuscript paper. The ideas were already flourishing. In the first movement, the melody grew humbly in strides. As the section continued, he used the melody throughout the voices. Each layer contributed to the intricately woven phrases.

Over the next few days, it became a challenge to balance time for composing, practice and education. On top of that, his sister gave him more compositions to copy. Abraham hadn't caught on to Felix's copying skills and had sent Fanny's work in the mix of his own. His father did notice his son in a rather stressful state as he tried to continue his training in banking.

Concerning his usual attendance and lessons at the Sing-Akademie, Zelter concluded that Felix had progressed enough to become an assistant. Before then, he had been in apprenticeship as many of the well trained students were. A position as an assistant gave him more responsibilities.

More and more the taxing days exhausted Felix. The early morning wake up calls of the maid resorted to almost dragging him out of bed. To get all that he wanted done, he resorted to working late into the night in secret. The maid usually made sure he was in bed at decent timing. Yet, as soon as she left, he quietly got up, lit a candle and continued working at his desk. He was careful not to waste candles. The octet for strings and Fanny's commissions to copy were making rapid progress.

He had flourishing excitement as he neared the end of penning the first movement of the octet. The enthusiasm sparked him to write a part where the entire ensemble plays a transition of parallels in four octaves at once. His hearing mind envisioned the sheer power of it, breaking the rules of counterpoint, returning to the main melody to rise again.

~ ~ ~ ~

After working a while to his full abilities in all of his subjects, he managed to finish the translation of Andria. At his lesson with his tutor, Felix grabbed the stack of papers and set it in front of Heyse. It was a full German translation of the play. Heyse was confused at first, "Where did you find this? Did you use it to cheat on your Greek work?"

"No, it's my writing. I've translated it from the original Greek. I've learned a lot by doing so. I want you to have it."

Heyse looked astonished and impressed. The lesson that day felt good as it consisted of art. He practiced watercoloring. His painting skills were elevated in natural scenery and architecture. Felix showed Heyse some pencil sketches he made a few years back when his family traveled to Switzerland.

Heyse enjoyed the scenes of the mountains and quaint villages. He noticed one sketch contained people walking about in a city center. The buildings were drawn well, but the people were sketched rather sparingly. Their outlines made them only noticeable. He asked Felix, "Why didn't you finish drawing in the people?"

"I had to erase many times as I found it hard to get their silhouettes right. I just left it. I still find it hard to sketch people." Felix said in disappointment. Heyse gave him a few pointers. He learned much from his teacher. Heyse frequently gave him homework though.

~~~~

The month of October began to sweep by. The octet was near completion. Yet the late nights were catching up to Felix. One afternoon, he groggily came down the stairs after completing homework from Heyse. As he neared the dining room, he heard Abraham exclaim, "Why have our candle purchases gone up? We aren't using that many!"

Felix entered the dining room to see Abraham and the maid speaking. The maid looked to Felix straight away. She knew who was using them up. Felix concluded that he needed to finish the string octet that night. After spending time downstairs and eating dinner, he decided to head early for bed. The maid thought it suspicious.

After an hour of his retirement, the maid went upstairs to check on him. She slowly opened the bedroom door. The candles were out and he was snoring. Before she left, she noticed a fresh candle on the nightstand. She silently went in and took it.

The second she left, Felix huffed in frustration. He got out of bed and fumbled around the room. His eyes got used to the dark by a little. He then went to the window and opened the curtains. To his luck, the moon was full and gave some light. A spark of happiness motivated him. He went to his desk and continued the last bit of the string octet.

~~~~

"What on earth are you doing there!?" The frustrated maid stormed into the room. Her thistled tone made Felix jump awake. He was still sitting at his desk. His head rested on the pile of manuscript paper. His hand ached with an ink covered quill still in his grasp. He sat up. His tired state confused him, but then his thoughts gathered upon looking at the music in front of him. He quickly wrote on the last bar, but the quill was dry. Frantically he dipped it in the inkwell then wrote. The maid went to him and demanded, "Is this what you've been doing through the night!? Have you been staying up late in secret!?"

"I guess it doesn't matter now, I've finished what I wanted." Felix gathered up the pile in an orderly fashion. The maid snapped, "Such a mess! Your sleeve and hand are stained with ink! I am sick of your antics. Your siblings are less trouble. You need to think about how much sleep you're getting. My job is to do common house work and to be sure everyone is up at the time wanted, not dragging a sixteen year old out of bed."

"Then wake me up at a later time. Heyse doesn't come until seven." Felix put the papers in a safe spot then flopped into bed. The maid snapped, "Your parents want you up early so you can study beforehand."

"I've already studied." Felix instantly snored upon hitting the pillow. The maid now had enough, "I am going to be speaking to your Vater." She left in a trance. Felix sighed, knowing he had pushed boundaries, but he needed a morning to rest. He did just that, at least until his father barged in, "Get up now."

The maid complained, "I found him sleeping at his desk, working at this music! I was sure he had been to bed at decent timing but has been disobeying." She grabbed the pile of manuscripts. Abraham took the papers and looked at them. He seemed quite intrigued, but went back to Felix, "Get up, you can not be staying up late anymore. You have time during the day for composing."

"I hardly do!" Felix sat up in annoyance, "Every day, all day is study and practice. Why can't I have a break!?"

"Don't use that tone with me. You will not regret that you did work and study early each morning. Now it's already six thirty, Heyse will be here in half an hour, so get dressed for the day." Abraham demanded. Felix got up and listened to his father.

After the morning chaos, Herr Heyse came and began the lesson for the day. It consisted of secular studies in allude with his training in banking, upon his father's request. When the long, boring lesson ended, Felix got ready to head to Rietz's house for his violin lesson. He took the manuscript for the octet with him.

Rietz was enthralled upon looking at the freshly composed music before him. Felix told him, "I finished it early this morning."

"More like through the night? You're tired in appearance." Rietz half teased. Felix smiled in mischief.

"We must play some of the parts together before your lesson's end. I hope you plan to have it performed at the next salon your parents host."

"I'll be sure of it." Felix said in determination. They lifted their instruments again to try the piece. Ritz played violin while Felix played viola. They enjoyed it immensely. Rietz knew upon reading through it, this piece was a great work of art waiting to be performed at full capacity.

~~~~

As spring turned to summer in the next year of 1826, the days grew sunnier. The string octet became a favorite work among ensembles and music attendees. Yet, some not so sunny news had reached Felix.

Abraham one morning read the paper, then handed it to Felix somberly, "You may want to read this."

Felix took the paper and skimmed it while eating breakfast. There were many articles as usual, then one struck him. He felt as if bricks had fallen on his shoulders. It was a fragment from the London paper. Carl Maria Von Weber had died. The news saddened Felix as he wished to have had another chance to meet him. Alas, it wasn't now possible.

Weber had traveled to London for some concerts a few months prior. He began struggling with tuberculosis (Then called consumption). As his health was in decline, he inquired to go back home. He was forced to stay in London as he wasn't fit for travel. A friend and musician, Sir George Smart, thankfully let him stay at his home until his health improved. Yet, Weber didn't make any progress and went to bed one night, never waking. He was thirty-nine.

~~~~

Paul and Rebecka went outside after their studies to play in the Garden. Felix was with Heyse in a lesson still. It was a rather long one. Before the lesson finished, Heyse mentioned, "I took your translation of Andria to be published. It was accepted. One of the instructors at the university happened to see it and was impressed. So much so that he wants you enrolled for the next semester."

"Really?" Felix asked, holding excitement. Heyse nodded, "I believe you are ready to study at university. You're seventeen, so you'll be an excellent scholar by the time you're twenty."

Felix smiled. The lesson ended, so he joined Paul and Rebecka after being cooped up inside. He took some paper and sketched the flowers. After drawing a while, he picked up the book he had been reading recently. It was 'A Midnight Summer's Dream' by Shakespeare. The story became his favorite since Heyse had given him the book. Fanny had read it as well.

[2]

As he read, the wind blew, rustling some leaves nearby. The sound lingered in his mind. The single note of the wind began to echo into a chord, then two, then three, then four. Subtle from the light breath of flutes. He penned the music on his sketch paper.

After spending time in the garden, reading and sketching, he went to his room to compose. All that was on his mind were the plots of the Shakespeare play, filled with fairies and weddings. The play would serve as his muse for this composition. He began depicting the sprites through light flurries of the high strings after the flutes' windful chords.

The low strings were then plucked in a pitter patter like way, as if a maiden were running through an enchanted forest. Her white dress flowing in her trance. The sprites follow her, encouraging her to run faster. The maiden obeys in her need.

Yet, the flutes give the indication as she halts to see a young fawn grazing the sweet succulents. She continues on in a hurry, hoping to not be late. Anticipation flourished among the lilies and wildflowers. In her need to catch breath, the flutes indicate her slowing pace once more.

When running a bit further through the whimsical woods, she enters a wedding scene; the grand chords burst from the orchestra upon the bride's arrival. It was her day taking place in the mystical woods among the sprites and forest creatures.

Though the setting was outdoors, the shape of the music moved down in a grand trance as if one of royalty were stepping down a beautiful marble staircase. The orchestra's sound moved back up in boldness.
Then refrained back down.

It was as the orchestra moved higher and higher into a cloud of sound, underneath this cloud, the crisp sound of a certain brass instrument moved down, distinguishing itself from the other instruments in a perfect sense. Felix jotted the notes: A, G#, C#. The Ophicleide. It was a low brass instrument. The feeling of the instrument gave the reminisces of the brass in Weber's exciting music.

On the side, he decided to make a rough outline to get the full picture of the piece. He wanted to know where the music would be going to tell the story with sound itself. The outline came to be suitable for Sonata Form, which was a standard form used in a lot of music. It helped organize which keys to transition to and what to repeat. The emphasis on repeating the main motifs would help the listener familiarize the work and remember it. Zelter of course encouraged that form as it was deemed one of the most practical. Once he had somewhat of an outline, it gave a nice basis for his next move in the work.

As he continued the days with the piece and read the play for more insight, he decided to consult a friend. His name was Adolf Bernhard Marx. He was a musicologist working as a music critic. Felix had become acquainted with him as he had much intrigue on Marx's way of characterizing music through words.

Upon showing Marx the Overture in progress, Marx gave much suggestion on the poetic tone aspects of the work. The art of mimicking things with the instruments. Felix had already done some of that already but Marx furthered it with in depth advice.

One idea came with the strings. Felix grabbed a separate sheet of paper and sketched some tonal shapes moving from high to low in dramatic exaggeration. It was the Hee-Haws of a burrow in which the play famously contained.

~~~~

By the time the month of August came that year, he had finished the Overture to 'A Midsummer Night's Dream.'

(Adolf Bernhard Marx)

Upon completing it, he arranged it as a piano duet. Once it was played through by him and Fanny, she approved of the work.

A few weeks after finishing the composition, Felix's studies moved to the University of Berlin. There, his lectures and instructors expanded. He excelled in his studies. His status as an assistant at the Sing-Akademie allowed him to conduct some concerts and organize a few things. He hoped in his future to take over after Zelter retired, but Abraham hoped his son's interests would lie elsewhere.

In November, Felix's dear friend Ignaz Moscheles was touring through Berlin again. He was invited over to the Mendelssohn home, as by now he was well acquainted. When he came, Felix and Fanny both went to the piano and played the arrangement of Felix's new Overture. Ignaz was astounded and wished to hear an orchestra play the score.

Ignaz played some of his own compositions as well. He gave Felix the music of a series of studies he wrote.

Upon Ignaz's leave of Berlin, Felix then began to write to him to stay in touch with his friend. He grabbed an E major Sonata to enclose. He then penned:

*November 28th, 1826*

*You kindly expressed a wish, dear Mr. Moscheles, to have my sonata, and I therefore shall present it to you. Should you come across it, let it remind you of one who will always respect you.*

*Once more a thousand heartfelt thanks for the happy hours I owe to your "Studies;" they will long find an echo in my mind. I am sure they are the most valuable of your works. That is, until you write another.*

*My best wishes accompany you on what I trust will be a happy and pleasant journey. Please remember me kindly to Mrs. Moscheles, and believe me Ever Yours,*

*Felix Mendelssohn Bartholdy*

~ ~ ~ ~

In February of 1827, when Felix turned 18, he was packing up a horse drawn sled that would be taking him to the city of Stettin for a concert. He had received a letter from the composer and conductor Carl Loewe requesting to have the Overture to 'A Midsummer Night's Dream' premiered. Loewe came across the work through Marx. They had been fellow students of composition together.

When Loewe began planning for a concert, Marx eagerly told him of Felix's new overture and had a copy sent. Loewe agreed to have it performed. He also wanted Felix to play with the orchestra in some other selected works.

The journey would be long and cold since the month of February still had phases of snow. Stettin was eighty miles away. His father seemed hesitant about it but helped him pack. He spoke to Felix beforehand on how to deal with travel and weather. It would take a full day and a half to get there and traveling in any sort of drastic weather has its risks.

The morning when the sleigh was packed, the calm sun and grey sky indicated only a chill. The sled would hopefully ride smooth against the snowy terrain. Regular carriages weren't as common during the winter season.

Felix wore his warmest wool coat, lined with leather. He had proper footwear, wool scarf, winter cap and other necessary garments to protect himself from exposure. Abraham was sure to hire an experienced coachman in case anything were to happen. Lea made sure enough food was packed by gathering a basket full of essentials. It consisted of dried meats and fruit.

Once everything was ready, Felix grabbed the remaining things such as his music and violin. He then climbed into the sled and waved to his family, "Auf Wiedersehen!" As his parents and siblings waved back, the journey carried on.

The sled gilded against the finely packed snow along the city streets. The city soon became a sparse landscape of a few houses and farmland. Then it turned to a snowy wilderness with scattered forest. The heavy snow banks began to force the two horses to trudge, slowing the ride every now and again. A few hours into the trip, the coachman began to visit with Felix. Many times Felix sat next to him at the driver's seat.

"So how long has this been your line of work?" Asked Felix.

"Oh, about fifteen years. I enjoy going places and having good conversations. You wouldn't believe some of the passengers I've had to listen to too." The middle aged man chuckled.

"What is your name?"

"Johnathan." His voice resonated with jubal, "Now what is bringing you all alone to Stettin?"

"A concert." Felix grabbed a manuscript from his satchel, "The orchestra there is premiering my work."

"I don't believe it, one as young as you." He stated.

"I'm also going to be playing piano and violin in the orchestra. You should watch. They are doing Beethoven's 9th symphony."

"I may. Then I'll believe you." He half teased. Felix then commented, "I am 18, an adult, so I'm not as young as you think."

"Well you are a young adult." His smile soon began to fade as he looked to the sky. He turned to Felix, "Go back in the sled and get as much sleep as you can." His tone seemed worrisome. Felix tilted his head, "It's late morning, I'm not tired."

"You must. I sense a storm coming. You'll need to save as much energy as you can. When it starts, put that wool blanket over you." Johnathan grabbed a blanket for himself. Felix listened and grabbed a blanket. He then laid in the back seat of the sled the best he could. There wasn't any good position to have a comfortable sleep, but he managed to nap.

After an hour or so, he felt a few snowflakes land on his face. Felix sat up from his rest.

Some flurries were blowing about but nothing to dread over. Within another hour, the snow fell consistently, adding beauty to the landscape. Felix opened his mouth, catching the cold crystals. Johnathan glanced back to check on him, "I would get under the blanket, the snow is going to pick up from now as well as the cold."

Felix obeyed him, but before retiring to nap again, he grabbed a book and some dried fruit to eat. It was still light enough even under the blanket to read. As another hour drug by, the sled suddenly thudded into harsh terrain. The deep thick snow almost stopped the sled. Felix peeked out from the blanket. His heart skipped in shock. The snow was coming down hard. It confused his sense of direction. Johnathan seemed to somehow know where they were. He had most of his face covered by his long hat.

A strong winter wind blew. Felix gasped as the cold air hit against his face. He felt as if he were breathing in sharp fractals of ice. Johnathan noticed him and ordered through the howling wind, "Stay under the blanket!"

Felix huddled back under it. The air had winded him. He did his best to warm back up. The hard wood floor of the sled hit against the cold snow, which made it more of a challenge. After a while though, he finally felt warmer. Every ounce of energy he had left him. The snow collected against the blanket weighing it down on him, which helped conserve heat. The weighted blanket and his tired state caused him to drift into a heavy sleep.

Felix awoke to calmer weather. He sat up, but night had fallen. There wasn't much to see. The air had become drastically colder. He wrapped his scarf over his face. Jonathan suggested he sleep more, but he felt too bored out of his mind to do so.

Johnathan had a lamp for light so Felix lit one as well, which helped him keep warm a little. He then grabbed a quill and paper to write back to his family of his experience thus far. As he began to write, the ink began to freeze soon after he opened the inkwell.

Then the quill snapped as it had become brittle with frost. He wouldn't be writing. The rest of the night dragged with the constant need to keep warm.

~~~~

The next morning, the sun gave a slight change to the temperature. The sled gilded easier across the newly formed blankets of snow. Johnathan stopped only once in the night to rest a bit, but he didn't rest long. He mentioned, "We shall arrive in Stettin by noon. I know of a decent inn we may stay at. I believe it happens to be close to the concert hall."

The horses managed to continue through the snow. The lonely trail turned to countryside then town, then into city. Stettin was a decently big city.

Johnathan stopped the sled at a street side near a long brick building. The white snow against the walls and roof complemented the red bricks. A young stable boy came up and grabbed the horses' reins. Johnathan gave him a tip. Felix grabbed a few bills and handed it to Johnathan, "I could have done that."

"Oh, it's fine, I can spare you a few expenses. Your father was quite generous. Plus I'll be seeing you play some music."

They both went inside and got a room. It felt relieving to be near a fireplace. The second they entered the room, Felix got a blanket and laid in front of it. Johnathan hung his socks and coat by it so they could dry. Yet Felix couldn't stay beside the fire long. He had to go rehearse with the orchestra. The concert was tomorrow night. He grabbed his music and violin.

Felix still felt tired and chilled from the journey. Thankfully the concert hall was within walking distance. It was a large artistic structure, showing that it was a place of theater and music. When Felix entered the building, a man was standing in the lobby looking a bit stressed.

He paced back and forth. Upon hearing Felix enter, the aged man lifted his head, "You must be Felix."

"You must be Loewe." Felix held his letter, "The snow storm caused me to arrive later than anticipated."

"I'm glad you've arrived in one piece. That storm was terrible here. We've run through your Shakespeare piece already and the Beethoven. We were waiting for you to run your double concerto and Weber's Konzertstück."

"Alright, I'm ready to rehearse." He stretched his fingers. They both headed to the auditorium where a full orchestra sat, waiting.

There were two pianos as the double concerto he wrote involved two pianists. Loewe would be playing the piece with Felix. For the Weber piece, Felix was to be the soloist. He had been practicing the violin parts for the Beethoven symphony, so he wasn't worried about it.

As Felix sat at the piano, the members of the orchestra whispered among each other. Carl hushed them and rehearsals continued. There were only a few things to fix. Felix was enthralled to finally hear a full orchestra play his music.

Once everything was ready the next evening, The concert hall became packed. At the nineteenth hour, Loewe and the orchestra got set up. Felix stood off to the side of the stage to hear his Shakespeare overture. After Carl introduced the piece, he turned to count the orchestra in. The flutes whispered their chords that mimicked the breeze.

Felix couldn't believe how it sounded. It was better than he imagined it in his head. The flavor and pattern of the music had become real. He could clearly envision the story he had read those months ago.

After the end, the audience roared with applause. Carl then introduced Felix to the stage and they both went to the pianos to play the double concerto. After the cheers of that, the Weber piece was played. As Felix played the piano, it saddened his spirits. It made him miss the bright composer of this work all the more.

With the ending of the Weber piece, Felix then joined the first violins to play Beethoven's ninth. His public debut was a success. From then on he knew, this was the official start of his music career.

~~~~

## [3]

With success...doesn't always come with more success. In Felix's return from his great debut in Stetten, he began ambitious work on his next project. In the years passed, he had penned the music for an opera. It was complete, but needed further editing if it were to set foot in the opera house.

The opera was titled, 'The Wedding of Camacho.' The libretto was based on a story of 'Don Quixote'. Karl Klingemann had written up the text for Felix to compose the music around.

He eagerly worked at editing the opera. As it came together, Eduard Diverant hung out with Felix after rehearsals at the Akademie. He became interested in the opera, wanting a part if it got performed. Felix entitled him to the character of Camascho.

Among editing the opera, the month of March became dreary for the history of music. News from the city of Vienna was posted in the papers. March 26, 1827. The composer Beethoven had died. Felix felt pangs of sadness upon hearing of the death of one of his favorite composers.

84

The news was all over and reports from the funeral said that it was the largest for any composer in history. Felix noticed that mentioned in the list of torch bearers of the funeral, was Schubert. Felix remembered playing a Schubert piece with Ignaz. With the tragic news, Felix continued editing his opera.

*(Beethoven's Funeral 1827)*

After deeming his opera done, he and Eduard presented the score to Spontini as he was Berlin's opera director. Felix's spirits were rendered crushed as he and Eduard watched Spontini skim the score. He muttered much criticism. Before he directly spoke, he looked up at Felix from the score. He gestured to the ambitious young man to walk with him. Felix followed and they went to a window where the tall buildings surrounding OpernHaus towered over. One building had a large intricate dome. Spontini pointed out the window telling Felix, "You should have bigger ideas, as big as that dome."

Spontini did not care for this work. He expected much more from Felix. He wouldn't have it in the opera house. Yet, Eduard and Felix managed to convince him to let rehearsals begin at the Schauspielhaus, a smaller theater in Berlin.

They found singers for the parts. A baritone by the name of Heinrich Blume took the role of Don Quixote. The rehearsals were rather a struggle as they went on. Felix stood in the auditorium with Klingemann, listening to Blume sing. Blume's voice slowly developed a rasp. Felix noticed and whispered to Klingemann, "He better get his voice back in order."

"He wasn't feeling well before rehearsals started," Klingemann whispered back, "He looks rather yellow in the face. I think it's jaundice."

Felix facepalmed. Blume would need to be excused until he was better. They continued practicing the parts that did not involve the main role, but Blume would need to get caught up, causing delay. At times Felix wanted to suspend the work. Yet, he stopped himself from doing so as his mother Lea encouraged the opera. She very much wanted her son to become a composer of opera. To please her dreams, Felix pushed the rehearsals forward.

Eventually, it came together enough for a premier in late April. A well wishing crowd filled the Schauspielhaus. Felix sat among the audience to see his work at the stage. It gave him hope as the overture began. The libretto gave the audience their entertainment, but the music rather as only adornment to the theatrical aspect. Felix sensed that the crowd clapped to not offend the singers and musicians. The music wasn't necessarily bad. Everyone sang and played well. The composition itself was deemed too innocent for the experienced attendees of opera. They wanted more mature aspects in sound. It was obvious a youth had written the work, trying to imitate the sounds of Rossini and common opera.

Felix had spent much time studying the operas of Mozart and Weber to gain some influence. It must not have rendered enough to give the success he had wished for. Felix became anxious and overly conscious as the opera neared the end of the first act. As soon as the orchestra went into an interlude, Felix got up from his seat and headed for the exit.

In his early return home, he had to tell his mother the fact of the matter concerning his opera skills. She was distraught, but Felix knew she would get over it. The real matter came up when within the week, reviews of the performance showed up in the papers. Abraham was the first to notice them. He was enraged. The reviews were not kind concerning the music. The part that made Abraham the most unhappy were the robust comments towards the young composer's family name. Felix determined:

He would not set foot in the world of opera again.

# Chapter V: Bach

Mozart, Symphony no. 40 [1]
Bach, St. Matthew Passion oratorio [2]

Year of 1828

## [1]

Felix in his nineteenth year had grown much as a young adult. His stature was much more refined and his appearance suited him. Since attending classes at The Humboldt Universität zu Berlin in 1826, he had traded his long brown curls for a nice trim. He also made sure to dress in good taste as it showed he took his studies in all seriousness.

Life as a student at the Universität zu Berlin was quite an accomplished one. The family's financial backing enabled Felix to have such an education. He took in depth lessons from instructors. Some of whom were renowned in their subjects.

While his talents flourished all the more, music seemed destined to become Felix's future prospect. His close friends and now colleagues, Eduard Devrient and Karl Klingemann, both distinguished themselves as writers. Eduard wrote in the dramatic arts, becoming a talented actor. He sang wonderfully and Felix always went to him if he needed a singer for a new Lied.

Karl traveled to England in much of his time. He became a member of the Hanover embassy. It was the German embassy in Britain. Felix hence then didn't get to see him as often, but they kept in touch through writing. Karl later began composing his own poetry, giving it to Felix to base the Lieder on.

Felix was still acquainted with Ignaz, who's current home was still London. Ignaz traveled constantly through Europe. He stopped in Berlin every now and again of course to catch up with Felix's budding career. As Ignaz spoke of his tours, Felix began to express interest. His questions became more in depth on the subjects of going abroad. His travels to Paris were always with his father and Stettin was within the same jurisdiction as Berlin. He knew a real trip abroad on his own accord would render much different.

After speaking with Ignaz, he began researching maps in the university's library. In his journal he penciled notes of places he wanted to go. His interests were after the fine arts of Europe. Many of his colleagues made plans on what they called 'The Grand Tour,' where newly graduated scholars traveled abroad to get a sense of the world before marrying and settling.

If he were to start his journeys straight after completing his studies, he'd have to plan quickly. The winter semester was in session and ended in the spring. He wanted things done accordingly. There was another person where he could get advice. Felix left the library to go home to his father.

~~~~

"Well, I agree that you should travel and see the world. Beyond the Swiss alps and France. You say you spoke with Ignaz?" Abraham asked as he flipped through the journal of notes that Felix wrote on various aspects of travel. They were subtle ideas at the moment, but Abraham was intrigued.

"Ja. He has a lot of experience." Felix felt a wave of enthusiasm. Abraham became stern as he set the journal down, "Are you thinking that in traveling you're going to find success as a musician?"

"If it offers the opportunity," Felix implied, "My main concern is to learn about the world and see fine art from Italy to England."

"In that case, I shall write to Ignaz as I believe he would be a good chaperone to stick to." Abraham affirmed, "When are you planning to start these travels?"

"Late March to early April soon after I complete my studies." Felix stated. Abraham nodded, becoming serious again, "Now, since you plan to leave soon after university, I imagine when you arrive back, you will be willing to begin your career at the Bank?" His father implored. Felix looked at him bluntly, "Ignaz makes a decent living. He has many connections and I believe he can help give my career it's start."

"I have one condition in which you may travel. You are to be sure you can make your future living as a musician. I suppose if your attempt fails, you have a business to come back to. I hope you know you are now pushing the business into your younger brother's hands."

Felix felt a slight guilt. His father always seemed to demand a part of him. It was his happiness or his sense of sureness. If he pursued the bank, his happiness would befall him. With music, he did not know where his career would go. Felix spoke up despite his feelings, "I am sure of what I want to do."

Abraham nodded. His father had come to terms. Felix gave a sigh of relief and left the house for his studies. As soon as he left, Abraham laid his head on his desk and ran his fingers through his hair in utter anxiety. He couldn't fathom the way the conversation went. He pondered whether Felix even felt any sort of remorse on declining the family's business. Felix put the responsibility on Paul rather painlessly.

Abraham stood from his desk and went for a much needed walk in the gardens. There, he happened to find Paul riding Felix's horse. It trotted across the thin layer of snow, blanketing the park. Paul appeared happy and carefree. Abraham decided to leave conversation with him alone for the time being. Paul did not need the stresses of being told his future then and there.

After a calming stroll, observing the sleeping trees, Abraham returned inside to the warm heat of the fireplace. He went to his office. At his desk he sat, grabbing paper and a quill:

Berlin Dec. 12, 1828

My dear Sir and Esteemed Friend,

My son, in whom you take to kind an interest, is about to leave his home in a few months, and to go forth into the world. He is a musician and a musician he means to remain; and in furtherance in his musical education, he proposes to make some stay in Italy, France, England and Germany, with a view of becoming acquainted with the great works of art. The predominant artists and art institutions of these countries, and for seeing himself what music aspires to, and to what it has achieved.

What a comfort it is to know that in the vast metropolis, so strange and so new to my son, he is to be welcomed by such true and warm friends as yourself and Karl Klingemann.

To him, please remember me most kindly when you see him, and do not fail to present my kindest regards to Mrs. Moscheles.
Your most truly,

Abraham Mendelssohn Bartholdy

Abraham set the quill down with a sigh. Upon doing so, he heard someone enter in the main doors. He grabbed his letter and headed downstairs to see who was home. It was Felix. A servant was taking his coat. Abraham handed his letter to the servant to send. Felix asked, "Is that the letter for Mr. Moscheles?"

"Yes, I am in hopes he will be willing to accompany you. Anyways, how were your lessons today?"

"Very well, Devrient intends to stop over today. I want him to sing through something. I've been arranging that Bach score grandmother gave me a few years back. I hope to have it performed at the Akademie before I leave."

"Oh, the Passion?" Abraham commented, "Zelter might be against it as he tried to have that performed. It was quite the hash. Are you sure that's a wise decision?"

"Upon studying the work, I think I can get it arranged for the Akademie musicians. I can't help but try. I feel that it must be heard. Zelter can not keep Bach's music locked up forever. Eduard and I will organise everything if we must, with Zelter's help or not." Felix then headed for the stairs. Abraham grabbed his arm to stop him once more, "May I speak of something. In the parlor." His tone sounded subtle but Felix knew the matter had to be somewhat serious if it were a sit down conversation.

Once they settled in the parlor, with some tea, Abraham began, "Now, I know you want to go out and make your way musically with your travels, but I must warn you of success. Success in anything I mean. Ignaz is a known musician as are other acquaintances of yours. People know their names well. I think it's time I'd ask of you to consent in dropping the Mendelssohn name and stick to Felix Bartholdy. I suggest it highly for you since your occupation will give you a reputation."

"Vater...I feel I can not straight up change the name I was born with. I am a Mendelssohn. Yet, I am very much intending to keep the Bartholdy name in accompaniment with it. Uncle Bartholdy wasn't even born with that name. I want to keep my name." Felix sipped his tea to veer his eyes from his father's frustration.

"But think of how it would look in Society. Do you want those disgraceful reviews to show up again in the papers as with your opera attempt? People will not think of you in the highest regards. They will only think of your grandfather. In my youth I was always known as the son of my father. I wasn't my own person. I've been doing what I can to be my own man. I'm trying to make it the same for you. People will only think of you as the grandson of Moses Mendelssohn."

"But I will make my own way. With my own real name." Felix set the tea cup down, "I must get to my room. Eduard will be here soon. I must finish some arrangements so we can run some parts." Felix got up and continued to his room. Abraham gave a sigh. His wishes for his child would be harder to pursue than he thought.

~~~~

The next day at the Universität, as Herr Ritter's geography class was in session, Felix had much on his mind. The conversation with Abraham was rather towards the back of his priorities. He thought more about his practice session with Eduard. It had gone exceedingly well, making him feel more determined than ever to organize the Bach oratorio for the Akademie. He had not spoken to Zelter about it yet, but he planned to after his studies that day.

The other half of Felix's mind wandered to his geography textbook. It was open to a map different from the one being studied. As the class was lectured on the great savannas of Africa, Felix's eyes gazed at maps of Europe and England. He lightly penciled lines from Rome to Vienna to London and so forth.

As Felix pretended to listen to Ritter's teaching, a classmate beside him whispered, "Planning your Grande Tour?"

Felix smiled, nodding. Herr Ritter's concentration instantly moved towards Felix, "Is something funny?"

His old raspy tone startled the day dreamer.

"Nein." Felix quickly stated. Herr Ritter eyed him in discernment. His voice carried on, announcing to the class, "Remember that this lesson will be a main subject of the final test." He walked to Felix and flipped his book to the right page, "I would be sure to pay attention and hold off all of your Grand Tour dreams until after class." Ritter returned to the front of the room. The geography lesson continued in dullness.

History class was better, but still dull. Eduard Gans was the instructor for that class. He was much more calm than Ritter. The lesson happened to be about Ancient Rome. It was the only thing keeping Felix awake as it was something other than recent war and political unrest. Plus he planned to journey to Italy.

The next class of his was rather more exciting. It was science, instructed by Alexander Humboldt. Felix was well acquainted with him in his visits to the family's hosted salons. He made the studies of science all the more interesting as he had traveled on my excursions to make discoveries. Felix felt that he learned more on geography from Humboldt rather than Ritter. Both were known as great advocates of geography, but Alexander had more information on the nature of different areas. He mentioned that after the winter was over, he would be going to Russia.

Humboldt was rather different than most people in the aspects of travel. Usually after young men took their grand tours abroad, they married and settled somewhere for the rest of their lives. He on the other hand had never married. He chose to keep traveling throughout his life. Ignaz had married but his spouse did not mind his travels. Felix found it quite fascinating that these people kept going places.

After the lecture, Felix stayed behind to talk with his instructor. Humboldt was working at his desk as the other students streamed out.

Felix slowly packed up his books debating whether Alexander was too busy or not. Humboldt noticed Felix looked inclined to speak, "Is there something on your mind?"

"What makes you want to keep traveling through the years?" Felix walked to his desk. Alexander set his reading spectacles down on his papers,"Well, it is my nature to learn more of the world. I feel I can not settle. It is part of my work but also feeds my interest."

"Do you ever think about settling?"

"I sometimes imagine myself if I had done so in my youth after my initial tours and expositions. I think about where I'd be right now if that was the case, but when I recollect, I find I am glad I chose what I did. I've had many irreplaceable experiences that I wouldn't trade for anything. I have had love in my life, but nothing to the extent of marriage. As for you, you may find yourself in your future tour, planning to never end your journeys, but someone could unexpectedly capture your heart in the snap of the fingers. Especially you. Young, talented, fresh out of studies, well rounded gentleman. Love is a much more difficult science, but we all know of it at least once in a life."

"It's that unexpected?" Felix was intrigued. Humboldt then asked in suspicion, "Shouldn't you be in your philosophy lecture right now? Herr Hegel will wonder where you went."

"He may, he may not. Depending if the debates of the class turn into chaos or not." Felix grabbed his books and headed out the door. As he got closer to Hegel's room, he could hear the arguing from the end of the hall.

Felix snuck into the class as two students were leading some sort of debate on a theory of their teacher's. He settled in the nearest open seat. Upon looking up, Hegel stared at him. He had watched Felix enter late, but didn't disrupt anything.

Just as Alexander Humboldt, Hegel was well acquainted with the Mendelssohn family from visiting the Sunday music gatherings on occasion.

*(Hegel's lectures in Berlin 1828)*

Once the class was over, the argument left into the university's halls. Felix trailed behind, not wanting to get too caught up in the debating. Before exiting the classroom though, Hegel stopped him, "I know you came in late today. It's the second time this week. It's not like you. Is everything alright?"

"Ja, I had been talking to Herr Humboldt about some work." Felix excused. Hegel raised an eyebrow, "Well, I overheard Herr Ritter complaining of you not in the right of mind in his lesson earlier. I take being on time a personal virtue of a man in society. Do you not respect my time of instruction? You are almost finished with your studies here and I wish you to not fail the final exams. I know you are busy with music, the Akademie and future travel. Don't let these things cause your education to dissolve."

"Don't worry, I'll be sure to respect your valuable time." Felix then headed off. He was in rather a rush now to get to the Sing-Akademie. He wanted to speak with Zelter before their usual chorale meet.

The horse carriage stopped at the Akademie and Felix jumped out. He rushed to the door, nearly slipping on the light dusting of snow. He found Zelter straight away as he was entering the building.

"Zelter!" Felix heaved from his quick jog.

"Felix? What is bringing you here so early?" He asked as they both walked in. Felix continued, "I've decided what to do for the performance I want to put together in March."

"Oh! Do tell me what it is you decided." Zelter was curious. Felix grabbed a large book of manuscripts which made up the tremendous score. He opened it and Zelter glimpsed over his shoulder. There were quite a few marks in pencil. Some instruments were altered. The recorder had been switched to clarinet and an extra bass section had been added. The old instrumentation indicated it to be of baroque origin. Some of the cantatas were marked in disregard. It was obviously being arranged into a simpler performance.

Modern dynamic markings had been penned in. The original lack of such markings gave a hint to Zelter straight away of the composer. He began to gaze upon the score in bewilderment as it looked familiar. Then it hit him. That Bach piece that Bella Salomon had ever so much begged to have a copy of. He couldn't believe he had parted with his personal copy for a short time to let Eduard and Julius Rietz copy it. Then given to, at the time, the fifteen year old boy, who was now standing in his nineteenth year.

Zelter put a hand on Felix's shoulder. Felix smiled, still studying his arranging skills. He then glanced at Zelter, excited to hear his opinion. Yet, Felix froze upon becoming face to face with a death defying glare.

He froze as his instructor's grip on his shoulder became rather rigid. Zelter snapped, trying to keep composure,"I very much disagree that this could possibly work. I have tried it as you very well know. It will not work. There are too many things that hinder the performance. Look at how much you marked and condensed."

"I very well know what I've marked. I made it more agreeable to the Berlin audience. I'm keeping the important aspects of the music. It will help Bach's music to be heard among the orchestra and choir as it has not happened in almost a hundred years. You are always wanting to save his music. What is the use in keeping precious manuscripts when they are left to not be played. We must make an effort in at least arranging it."

"I will not have it. Choose another piece." Zelter demanded. He took a hold of the book as if to take it. Felix instantly shut it and caressed it safely at his side. Zelter gave him another glare before releasing him. Felix couldn't believe his teacher's attitude. As Zelter turned away, Felix sneered, "Just because you tried it doesn't mean it can't happen!"

"My dear pupil," Zelter turned back in a flash, "This conversation is over." He stormed away to tend to other work. Felix sighed in remorse. He sat in the lobby whilst waiting for choir rehearsals to start.

Slight drops of water fell from his eyes as he stared at the score he had spent nearly five years editing. The music played in his head upon looking at it. The beginning, with the dark growing interlude of the orchestra made the feelings rise. Later the voices bled into the scene that the orchestra created. Berlin needed to hear this music.

As the hour drew closer, the first to enter for rehearsals happened to be Eduard Rietz. The orchestra would be with the choir today. Felix kept his head buried in the large book. It did not fool Rietz. He noticed the young man's somber state straight away. He calmly sat next to Felix, "Is something the matter?" Felix didn't answer. He didn't want to be seen in any sort of distraught state.

Rietz noticed the score, "Oh, that piece! I remember making that copy for you. I see you've been making your own edits to it. Are you choosing that one for the concert in March?"

"I was…" Felix sighed, "Then Zelter rebuked it to shreds."

"Oh…he is particular about Bach's music…." Rietz glanced at the score. He smiled upon the intricate edits made. He patted Feix on the back, "I think we can work something out."

~~~~

In the next month, the new year of 1829, Felix began to write to Mr. Moscheles concerning travel. Felix wrote a proper introduction then went to business:

*Berlin, January 10, 1829*

*I intend to start at the beginning of this year and devote three years to traveling: my chief object being to make a long stay in Italy and France. It is desirable that I return to Berlin for a few days in the middle of December before leaving for Rome. I intend to devote eight and a half months of the present year, during which I can absent myself, to visiting first those cities of Germany I am not acquainted with such as Vienna and Munich and then if possible, extend my journey to London…"*

He thought through his trip in the moment, thinking of what his father suggested as to how long it takes to get from one place to another. He continued:

*Now the question I want you to decide is this: Whether it would be better to begin or end with London.*

In the once case I should be in Vienna in early April, remaining there until about middle of July and then go to Munich via the Tyrol and then down to Rhine to London, where I could stay until December then return by way of Hamburg to Berlin.

In the other case, I should be to London in April then remain there until July, go to Rhine, through the Tyrol to Vienna then back to Berlin. Evidently the former of these tours would be more agreeable and as such I would willingly select it; but in following the latter, should I not have a better chance to see the two capitals to the fullest advantage?

The season in Vienna is coming to an end, as I am given to understand, in May. Whereas London extends all through June and beyond?"

**Felix had many questions for his friend and wrote everything that he had doubts on. He took a quick break from such a lengthy letter and got some coffee that had been freshly brewed at the hour. Once coming back, he noticed the book of 'studies' Ignaz had given him. It reminded him to thank him. He wished much to do so in person, but wrote in his letter:**

I have yet to thank you for your second book of your splendid 'Studies.' They are the finest pieces of music I have become acquainted with in a long time. Instructive and useful to the player as they are gratifying to the hearer. Might you feel disposed to write a third book? You know what service you'd be rendering all lovers of music. With best regards to Mrs. Moscheles, I have the honor to remain,
Yours most respectfully and truly,

Felix Mendelssohn Bartholdy

~~~~

That next week at the Akademie, the usual rehearsals were happening for the orchestra. They were running through Mozart's symphony No. 40. Felix and Rietz were next to each other among the first violins. They kept making eye contact with one another in communication for timing. Rietz was the concertmaster so it was his job to help the musicians count by means of gesture. Zelter was conducting the rehearsal of course and he wasn't in the best of moods.

Felix and Rietz also had a plan between the two of them. They both had folders beneath their chairs containing the orchestra parts of the Bach oratorio. Their plan was to hand out the music discreetly during break time. Eduard Devrient was to be sure that the choir received their parts.

They knew Zelter would throw a fit if they passed out precious copies of Bach. He would make some sort of excuse to take it all and put it in the Akademie's vault, where it would sit and rot.

All week during rehearsals, Zelter had been impossible to please. Felix felt a sense of guilt for Zelter's mood as it was because of their argument. The day prior was proof of it. During his one on one lecture, Zelter had grabbed a large stack of Bach's Klavier music and didn't let Felix leave the piano until each one was played through to his satisfaction. He was purposely picky.

The stack was so large that Zelter eventually left to tend to some other work. His office was next door. As soon as he heard no piano from Felix, he made sure he was still playing. Felix honestly didn't mind his slightly ridiculous task.

This orchestra rehearsal though felt far worse. Zelter stopped the entire orchestra due to a supposed distracted violinist. It was slightly true as Felix kept glancing at Rietz. Zelter finally announced, "I think it's time for a break."

Sighs of relief echoed through the musicians. Felix set his violin down and whispered to Rietz of the plan. As they spoke, Zelter called to Felix, "Come here, we need to take a walk."

Felix glanced at him then turned back to Rietz, "I'll give you my folder. Hand them out while I talk to him. I'll-" He was interrupted as Zelter pulled him away. Rietz took the folders to take care of business. Felix became agitated as Zelter hurried him to his office.

Once they got there, Felix was nudged in and Zelter near slammed the door shut. Felix knew he was in steep trouble. Zelter straight away snapped, "I have been in extreme frustration with you in the past week. This is the last straw. If you can not get your act together, I don't want you at rehearsals."

"I haven't done anything." Felix retorted.

"You were distracting! You kept looking to Rietz rather than the music! Your bowing was off! Do I need to tell your Vater of your behavior? You're an adult now! I shouldn't be having such a conversation." Zelter sat at his desk in disappointment. Felix kept silent. He didn't feel the need to argue with his teacher more. Zelter calmed down a bit and explained, "I've given thought about the concert you wanted to arrange. I am willing to be flexible."

"You are?" Felix brightened in an instant. Zelter searched a drawer for something. He grabbed a copy of Beethoven's 5th piano concerto. Setting it on his desk, he said, "I am willing to let you play a Beethoven concerto. You may conduct from the piano."

Felix loved that piece and it was a rarity for him to allow Beethoven's music at the Akademie. Yet, he knew his teacher's intentions. Zelter would rather have Beethoven's music performed rather than Bach's oratorio. If Felix found success in the Bach piece, Zelter feared for his own skill.

102

Felix smiled from the kind suggestion, but begged, "Bitte, I do not want to argue anymore. This piece is tempting, but I am set on what I want to do. I've already put in the work. I am organizing the oratorio. All I need is your permission to have rehearsal time with the orchestra and choir," He then became stern, "I will not let that score sit in silence."

Zelter got up from his chair and stood face to face with Felix. His tone felt like blaring trumpets, "As your teacher you will not speak to me in such disrespect. I do not give you permission. It's the Beethoven piece or none at all."

"It's the Bach piece or none at all." Felix tested. Zelter had enough. He wasn't going to take any more mouthing from his pupil. In his most sharp voice, he demanded, "Give me that score. I know you have it in your bag."

"Nein!" Felix held his ears at his tone. Zelter instantly grabbed hold of Felix's bag. Felix clung to his bag and snapped, "You have your own copy. You will not take mine."

"You are to give it to me or I shall take it myself." He ordered already rummaging through his things. Felix shewed him away, "Alright...I will get it, just calm down." He slowly searched his book bag. Zelter crossed his arms, knowing Felix was purposely taking his time. Before grabbing the score, Felix unexpectedly dashed towards the desk. He grabbed the Beethoven score then sprinted out of the office.

~~~~

The month of February arrived and much happened. The members of the Akademie had been practicing Felix's arrangement of Bach's oratorio, The St. Matthew Passion, for over a month in small groups outside of the Akademie's rehearsals. The progress was growing, but they needed time at the Akademie as March was getting closer. Eduard Devrient and Felix were set to convince Zelter to have them happen.

After choir practice that day, Felix and Eduard waited around until they knew Zelter would be at his office. They strolled there and found the door closed. Eduard knocked.

"Come." Zelter called, sounding busy. Eduard entered first. Zelter smiled upon his entry. Then Felix trailed behind causing Zelter's smile to fade. Straight away he stated, "If this is to convince me of your ideas, it will not work. You do not have the means to do it."

Eduard budded in, "I've sung through Felix's arrangement and I find that it does work. The rest of the choir thinks so as well. It is possible."

"Please, we just need some real rehearsal-" Felix began but Zelter hissed, "I've told you time and time again! It will not happen, it's too complicated and you are far too young in your career for such a task!"

"I am soon to be twenty on the third, only two days away, I am almost finished with my studies. I'm not your little student anymore. I'm an adult." Felix stated. Zelter crossed his arms whilst giving him a look of disapproval. The room fell silent for a few minutes. Zelter then huffed, "Fine. Have your rehearsals. Have the concert you foolish children. Don't complain to me when the performance flops." He pointed them both to the door.

~~~~

In the coming day, official rehearsals for Bach's oratorio began. Zelter stayed out of the way to let Felix deal with the work. The first rehearsal was with the choir. He had them positioned on stage. There were 158 singers to organize, so he decided to divide them into two choirs. He positioned the piano in the middle.

As he sat at the Klavier between the two choirs, some gave way to complaints, "Who's to conduct if you're playing the piano?" "How will the orchestra see you?" "Who will conduct them?"

"Don't worry, Rietz will watch me as he will be able to see me. He will help the orchestra count in. I will conduct and use this to make the conducting more noticeable." He grabbed something sitting on the piano stand. It was a conducting baton. Something that was relatively new. Some of the choir members laughed. One commented, "You'll look ridiculous at the piano and holding that all at once."

"Well, if it helps the performance then I don't mind looking ridiculous." Felix glanced back at Zelter. His teacher facepalmed. Felix turned back to the score and gave a breath of determination. The choir agreed to start singing.

Felix raised the baton and it started roughly. Some of the stubborn singers fell away from trying. Felix assured them, "I know you all can sing this. You were successful in small groups. We just need to put it together. Please keep trying. We will get this."

They tried some more, this time fixing a few of the dynamics and the flow of the sound. Towards the end of the session it formed into a decent choral. The singers gave sighs of relief once the rehearsal ended for the day. As everyone dispersed, most had a positive outlook. Some weren't as enthusiastic. A few singers afterwards bantered with Zelter. Felix ignored their negativity.

The weeks went by and each rehearsal with the choir improved. The orchestra had been working in small groups, but once they rehearsed together, it wasn't too terrible to prepare them. Some of course in the orchestra weren't in favor of Felix's arrangement. In honesty, most thought the concert would be a fail. The set date for the performance was to be the 11th of March.

~~~

In the midst of the university work and rehearsals, Felix woke up one morning at his usual time. This day he decided to use it to catch up on homework and organize himself.

Once he dressed, he headed downstairs. It was still dark as the maid had not lit the morning candles yet. Since it was too early for breakfast, he took a walk in the gardens. It happened to be a nice morning as the sun broke in the skyline. It was a bit cold but the fresh air felt nice.

When he returned to the main house, he happened upon his father in the parlor having coffee and reading the papers. Abraham set the papers down upon hearing Felix enter, "They've announced the concert in the paper. It should be a good turnout. Your Mutter and I have spoken to many friends."

"Oh good." Felix grabbed the paper and glanced at the advertising in awe. Abraham then commented, "I see that they put Felix Mendelssohn Bartholdy as conductor. I would have rather preferred Felix Bartholdy."

"Vater, I am not dropping my name." Felix wasn't in the mood to discuss such a topic this early before the big concert. Abraham sighed, "I am in a turmoil that you do not heed my advice. This concert may have your name but the next one I want to see it changed. This concert I believe will stay in the local eye, but when you travel, I want it changed." Abraham gave his son a stern expression. Felix left the parlor, finished with his father's suggestions.

Later that day, Felix found Fanny in the drawing room with Lea and someone else. Felix knew who it was right away as he had a pencil and sketchbook at hand, drawing Fanny. This was Wilhelm Hensel. He was well acquainted, but mostly to Fanny. It was in the obvious he loved her. Lea did not permit anything more than friendship upon their first meeting. She was making Wilhelm wait five years before anything serious. That five years was soon to be up.

When Felix entered the room, Wilhelm turned around. He appeared excited at Felix's entry. Fanny smiled, "Oh! brother, Felix. I regret not reminding you as you've been busy the past weeks. Wilhelm decided to visit for a sketching date."

(Fanny Mendelssohn 1829)

(Wilhelm Hensel 1829)

Wilhelm smiled, "I hear there's to be a concert soon. I'd like to join." He continued sketching a rather beautiful portrait of Fanny. Wilhelm was a master at art, but had no ear whatsoever for music. He still loved Felix and Fanny's skills. Wilhelm was a kind man and Felix shared art with him. He wouldn't mind it one bit if he soon became his brother-in-law.

After visiting a bit, Felix left the room. He returned to his own room to study for his classes as the final exams were drawing near. They would be no easy task with everything else he was doing in preparation for the concert.

~~~

All of Felix's efforts began to become worth the while. The month of February neared its end and rehearsals were going well.

As the week of the performance came, Zelter began to assist the choir as he noticed the progress. It quite surprised Felix.

In other aspects, his Universität studies were in their final days and his instructors demanded his utmost attention. Herr Ritter could have cared less if Felix were conducting a large concert. As long as he paid attention to his teachings then he got along with him.

Gans was rather indifferent. He wasn't as strict as other teachers. Felix had much respect for Humboldt's class, so he did his best. Hegel was happy as long as Felix showed up on time. He was rather excited upon this concert of Felix's and aspired to show up.

By the time March came, everything seemed to come together. Felix completed his Universität studies with ease and the concert that was to be at the Akademie deemed prepared. Zelter sat down with his student in his office. He began, "Well...I guess your Bach dreams are coming true. But will the audience like it?"

"I think it will go over decently if anything. I'll be sure it is announced well among the city." Felix answered, "I'd be satisfied if at least a small crowd comes in."

"We shall see." Zelter anticipated.

~~~~

March 11th, 1829

[2]

In the auditorium of the Sing-Akademie, all of Berlin society filled every seat. The dark, growing interlude from the orchestra before them consumed their attention.

There, seated at the piano between the two choirs, bâton in hand was the twenty year old Felix Mendelssohn, conducting this sacred sound that had not been heard by the public in almost a hundred years. The St. Matthäus Passion oratorio by Johann Sebastian Bach. What Felix had envisioned for this great work after five years of arranging the score was now presented around him.

Felix watched carefully the score at the piano as to play and conduct with utmost accuracy. This concert would be giving way to a new concept at the concerhall. The revival of forgotten works.

After this concert, which would be marked as the greatest revival of Bach's music, the music of Johann Sebastian Bach would be deemed the greatest works in the history of music. His near forgotten music would be revived and become the standard basis of every instruction in theory and composition.

Reitz was using gestures with his violin bowings to guide the musicians in the orchestra. Devrient took head of the chorus, giving a breath in gesture to the singers to bleed into the tones of the orchestra.

The voices echoed acoustically in accord to the harmonies that had been composed strategically to work together, producing a music that could fill any attendee with awe. The natural earthy tones could warm and sooth any ear.

Felix couldn't help but smile as it all was going as he had wished. Zelter sat off to the side among the audience. He glanced at their faces, each one with a mesmerized expression. This music that he had locked up for so long was now free from it's imprisonment. A sense of gladness came over him upon the outcome of the concert.

~~~

The crowd roared with excitement after the closing cadence. Much commentary was made as they dispersed the Akademie. Felix and the musicians were scattered about backstage. Zelter found Felix and gave him a handkerchief as he was sweating, "I guess Bach's music isn't meant to be locked away. All of Berlin must have showed up. It was extravagant."

"Danke. My family is hosting dinner tonight, you are certainly welcome to join. Hegel and many others will be there."

"I think I may. It's hard to pass the company of Hegel." Zelter then walked off. Felix headed for his home but it took a while as many greeted him and congratulated the performance.

When he arrived home, guests were already having drinks in the dining room. Before the servant took his hat and coat, Lea came to him with a hug, "The concert went over so well. Everyone is talking about it and are growing impatient for you to join the gathering."

"May I go to my room a while though. I'm exhausted." He got his coat off. Abraham was walking in and overheard. He assured, "You'll get to rest when it's time for bed. There are guests waiting. I will not have them wait longer."

Felix obeyed and went to the dining room. Many of the guests were his parent's friends. He noticed Hegel sitting at the table so he headed that way. As he neared the spot beside him, a lady took it. Felix sighed and took the next nearest spot, which was by the lady.

Once the rest of the guests arrived, everyone sat at the table and dinner was served. It was a good variety of meats and fruit. Everyone was pleased. As they ate, Hegel began conversing with the lady sitting between him and Felix. She was rather uninterested in his speech and turned to Felix. She whispered, "Who is that idiot beside me?"

Felix smiled with humor, "That is the philosopher Hegel. Quite a smart man." She was rendered speechless. The rest of the evening went on, but Felix became so exhausted that he retired to bed once dinner finished. He was excused after giving goodbyes to every guest.

Once he made it to his room, he flopped into bed without bothering to change from his concert outfit. The day fared far too exhausting. He still could not believe the success of the concert. He wondered if by next morning he'd be waking up from a dream. Yet, this was far from some mere dream.

# Chapter VI: London Society

Paganini, caprice no. 24 [1]
Beethoven, Violin Sonata No. 9, Kreutzer [2]

## [1]

The violin bow ricoshade across the four strings. The resin gave way to the sound. The striking of the chords; the shrill scales played with ease; pizzicato played with such skill that it deemed inhuman. All from one man and one violin. No orchestra, no accompanist. This man, this creature, could fill an entire concert hall with the flick of the wrist.

Felix and Fanny sat amongst the audience gathered in this recital hall. The hall was decently large. It was owned by an acquaintance, hence their invitation to this concert. Every seat had been filled and it was worth every daring second.

Felix stared in awe as the man with long locks of black hair conquered the wooden instrument in his hands. His long, thin structure helped his fingers stretch incomprehensibly far across the fingerboard. The violinist swayed aggressively with the bow's movements. At the end of the piece, he hammered the last chord, lifting his bow in the air. The concert's end. The panting musician moved to a relaxed position.

This was Niccolo Paganini.

The audience in attendance burst with applause. Felix and Fanny glanced at each other, exchanging their impressed expression. Niccolo bowed and walked away from the small stage. Everyone scattered about afterwards. Felix wanted to meet Niccolo, but the crowd was rendered too thick. He was lucky to have seen the virtuoso play up close.

~~~~

Back in Felix's musical aspirations, he would be making his leave abroad in a few weeks. In the midst of the busy month, a letter from Ignaz was received in response to his concerns on travel. Ignaz suggested that Felix begin his journey with London. Felix needed to start preparing. He turned to his father to inquire about the best way to get there. Abraham had some connection in Hamburg and got information on the ships that sail to England.

Felix wrote a response to Ignaz of the progress of his plans:

*Berlin March 26, 1829*

*According to your advice, I have made inquiries about the boats between Hamburg and London. The first sails on the 4th of April and after, one every week. It will be impossible for me to leave by the first or second, as I have hitherto not been able to make any preparations."*

He goes on to write the success of Bach's oratorio in Berlin. Marx, the musicologist, helped further by having Felix's arrangement published for wider audiences. It was still March and there was to be a second performance at the Akademie. Berlin audiences requested for a third, but Felix knew it wouldn't be possible. He agreed to conduct the second, but Zelter would have to take over. He sighed and wrote:

*The whole thing has so interfered with the completion of my own compositions and other business that I shall require at least a fortnight to prepare for my departure; then I want to stay a few days in Hamburg, so I shall leave only by the third steamer on the 18th of April, due in London on the 20th."*

Paganini is in Berlin; he gives his last concert on Saturday, and then goes directly to London, where I believe he will meet with immense success, for his never-erring execution is beyond conception. You ask too much if you ask of a description of his playing. It would take up the whole letter; for he is so original, so unique, that it would inquire an exhaustive analysis to convey an impression of his style.

Concerning London, Can you really take rooms for me as you suggested in your letter? Anything would be welcome however small, if in your neighborhood. If so please let Klingemann know; he would have time to send the address to Berlin. Secondly, I want your advice as to whether I should really bring the scores to some of my compositions, if so, what would be best to select? I was thinking of my Overture to a 'Midnight Summer's dream;' Do you think that is suitable? And if I pack manuscripts in my portmanteau, shall I be able to pass the custom-house without difficulty? In that case I should bring several compositions and submit them to your judgment previous to making a selection.

Please give my best regards to Mrs. Moscheles, and believe me,

Your most sincerely,

Felix Mendelssohn Bartholdy

~~~~

As the plans of travel were nearing with each day, Felix walked about in the gardens in thought. The early spring brought a few flower buds. He picked a few blushing pink sprouts and arranged them into a miniature corsage. As he knew he'd be away from home for many months, he needed to be sure he gave his farewells to everyone he wanted. One person was on his mind at the moment.

Felix exited the garden, carrying his little bundle of budding flowers. He then went down a few blocks from his home, stopping at a tall three story, dark brick house. It was the home of the Pistor family. They were one of the neighbors.

One of the singers of the Akademie was the Pistor daughter, Betty. She was good friends with Fanny and Rebecka. Felix met her many times with the Pistors' visits to the Sunday salons and the choir rehearsals at the Akademie. Both she and Felix were in a small singing group that sang on Fridays. Felix was the accompanist. They spoke at times and he liked her company. He thought it important to see her before his leave.

Felix knocked at the door. It was a few minutes before a maid answered. She let him into the entryway. As he entered, Mr. Pistor, Carl, rushed down the staircase, "Who is it calling?"

Upon seeing Felix, he brightened his demeanor, "Ah, Felix. What brings you here?"

"I have to give some farewells as I am to leave Berlin on a lengthy trip in a few days time."

"Oh that is quite a surprise. I am happy for you, it is nice of you to stop here." He smiled. Mr. Pistor was a man of science. His main skill was constructing instruments for the use of scientific research. Much of what he learned, he picked up from Felix's uncle, Nathan Mendelssohn. Mr. Pistor was also a lover of music. Like Abraham, he had a collection of Bach's manuscripts. Felix had helped him organize them.

"Is by chance Betty around?" Felix inquired. Mr. Pistor's expression changed, on a negative standpoint. Felix knew the question would cause such. It was obvious that Felix had admiration for his daughter. For Mr. Pistor, it would not be favorable in the eyes of his extended family; they had their own opinions of the Mendelssohns.

Mr. Pistor himself had nothing against the youth's heart for his daughter, but if anything exceeded a mere friendship, it could ruin his family's view of his branch of the line.

"Felix...Betty has gone out of the house to accompany some friends today. I'm sorry but she won't be back until later." Mr. Pistor sighed. Felix nodded, "Alright, but at least bid her farewell for me."

"You have my word." Mr. Pistor promised. Felix exited the house. Mr. Pistor watched him through the window as he ventured down the sidewalk. He gave a sigh of relief then continued on some projects in his office upstairs.

Felix walked a ways down the pavement. He paused a few minutes then turned around. On coming back towards the house, he inspected the windows. No one was looking out. He then went to the small gate wedged between the Pistor home and the next. It was unlocked, so he discreetly opened it and went along the path between the houses. The little alley led to a good sized flower garden behind the Pistor home.

In his hopes, at the tree, sitting at the swing, book at hand, was beautiful Betty. Her long blond locks were draped over her book. She read in all peacefulness until the swing was gently pulled back and pushed. Dropping her book from the unexpectedness, she snapped, "Bruder! Must you always disrupt my book!" She turned to see Felix, "Felix? Sorry, I thought you were my brother. Usually he interrupts my reading. Anyway, why didn't you just call at the door? I would have come."

"I did. Your Vater told me you were in the company of friends."

"Oh. He's pulling that today. You shouldn't have snuck here though, Vater is in his office. The window is right there." She pointed to it. Felix shrugged, "I have no fear. It is important I found you as I intended to give my farewells."

116

**"Farewells!?"** Betty sounded stunned.

"I am going abroad in a few days. This is our last visit before I am gone for many months." He sighed as he continued to push the swing. Betty stopped it and stood to face him. She gazed at him as to savor their visit. He then gave her the corsage of flower buds. She smiled but then told him, "You must leave in haste though. I can't let my father catch you. He'll never let you back. You must know that our togetherness can only be but a mere friendship. You know how the other sides of my family are. Please don't give them an excuse to ruin our acquaintance."

"I promise to return and if it comes to anything, I promise to make things work out. I love you." He lightly pecked her cheek. She blushed. As he looked up from the light kiss, Mr. Pistor glared at him from the upstairs window. Betty didn't notice, so Felix wrapped up their conversation and left the garden in haste. In the following days, not a word or note was heard from Mr. Pistor, nor Betty. Instead he received Ignaz's response to his previous letter:

*London, 1829*

*My dear friend, I have noted your questions and hope to answer them all to prepare you for the journey. I have secured rooms at said address: No. 203 Portland Street, Oxford Street. Keep this letter in case you forget said address. I also wish you very much to bring some of your compositions. Please of all I inquire you bring your Overture to 'A Midsummer Night's Dream,' as well as that cantata of 16 parts, 'Hora es.' You shall not have any trouble getting through the customs-house. Safe travels and give your father greetings,*
*Your sincere friend,*

*Ignaz Moscheles*

~ ~ ~ ~

When the day had come of Felix's leave to London, he stood in his room, packing up his portmanteau. A few select outfits and manuscripts were sprawled about the bed. Klingemann and Ignaz mentioned that in London, people dressed in good taste. He took his best outfits and the accessories to go with.

His outfit of choice for the trip itself was well suited for the journey and showed a decent appearance. He wore a linen shirt with a navy blue wool waistcoat over it. His black coat was sturdy and had good form. It would give protection if the weather rendered cold or rainy. He grabbed a standard top hat to wear. It would help keep his head warm, with fashion. He would have to keep this outfit clean the best he could. It would get dirty after a few days worth of travel, but he wanted to enter London in style.

As Felix finished tying his black silk cravat, he glanced out the window. The coach to Hamburg was waiting outside the house. It gave him a surge of excitement. He finished packing and brought it all downstairs. His parents and siblings were gathered in the entryway to give their farewells. Wilhelm Hensel was visiting to say goodbye as well.

Felix inquired to them all, "I should be home in the autumn in time for the anniversary. I will write." He alluded to his parent's 25th anniversary within the year. They wanted him to put together something special musically to entertain the guests. He would have plenty of time to compose during the long stretches of travel.

Felix embraced his father tightly. His mother slathered him in kisses. Felix felt embarrassed as his siblings and Wilhelm giggled.

"Alright Mutter, please." Felix rubbed some of the kisses from his face. Lea teared up, "I won't see my child for months! You're growing up too fast." She dabbed her eyes with a handkerchief.

After his siblings gave their hugs, Felix announced, "Auf Wiedersehen. I'll be back before you know it." He grabbed his bags and stepped outside with the utmost confidence. As he headed out the door, Fanny followed him. She stopped him outside, "I have a request as well for you to compose. It is possible I may need some music for a wedding that may take place in the autumn. I will write to you once I find out."

"Is it Wilhelm?"

"Ja. Dearest brother I believe with my heart he is soon to ask. I felt you must be the first to hear of my belief."

"I shall prepare something."

With that, Felix continued to the carriage. Once he settled, the horses trotted through the city. The coach happened to pass by the Akademie. Felix asked the coachman to stop a minute. The coachman allowed it and Felix jumped out. He ran to the Akademie's doors. To his hopes, both Zelter and Rietz were there. He gave his well wishes for the upcoming performances of the Bach oratorio. In return, the two of them gave their heartfelt regards to the young traveler soon to embark. When Felix returned to the coach, it officially set off from Berlin to Hamburg.

~~~~

By mid-afternoon the next day, Felix arrived in Hamburg. The boat to London wasn't leaving until early tomorrow, so he found himself a room at an inn. Once he settled his belongings for the time being, he decided to go out for some lunch. The inn had a pub but didn't serve anything hearty to satisfy his hungry state. The innkeeper suggested a restaurant down the street.

As he went to find this restaurant, the streets were busy with passersby. Among the chatter and clopping of horse hooves, he heard a melody playing from a violin. A Beethoven sonata. Felix turned about to find the busker, but no one had an instrument at hand.

It sounded close by. He then looked at the building he stood near. It was a tall home on a street corner. A window was open, letting the music sing into the air.

Staring up at the house, Felix froze from the reminisces of dejavoo. The faint burning memory of his father pulling him out of bed in the dead of night; the rush of packing a carriage and leaving in haste to Berlin. He was only three upon the event. This house was the first home he ever knew.

~~~~

## [2]

In the upstairs room of the Hamburg home, I practiced my violin, playing Beethoven's Kreutzer Sonata. The air outside felt fresh as it breezed in through the window. I was then in my nineteenth year, visiting my family home.

My own career already had much success. In the previous years, I had obtained a position in Berlin, living there. I did become more familiar with Felix Mendelssohn, but we met on subtle occasions. Our separate musical engagements crossed paths only a handful of times.

While he was busy at the Sing-Akademie, I played among the first violins at the Königsstädtisches Theater. I heard much of the successful performances of Bach, but invitations for positions abroad distracted my focus.

As I was soon to leave for Estonia, I decided to pay a visit to my Hamburg home. It felt nice to be with my parents and they were happy to see me after I had lived in Berlin in the past few years.

After playing through the first movement of the strong sonata, I took a break. I set my violin down and went to the window to look out. The usual horse carriages and citizens were tending to their business. Before I turned back, I looked down and saw a man staring up.

He must have stumbled upon my playing. As I looked at him, I realized it was Felix. He didn't break his stare. A slight array of horror filled his eyes. I waved and he shook himself out of his daze. He called from the street, "Excellent rendition!"

"Danke!" I called back as he hurried off.

~~~~

The next day upon boarding the boat to London, Felix's enthusiasm took an unexpected blow. Ten minutes of the boat floating on the water, not yet departing, he felt a rush of nausea come over him. He stood on the top deck, rocking with the boat in hopes to become accustomed to it.

As the steamer took off, the rise and fall against the current made his stomach turn. He went from feeling slightly nauseous to horribly ill. It didn't fathom in his train of thought that he was prone to getting seasick. The sickness began to make him homesick as well. He wished his father to be with him. In his moment of regret, he took it out on the steward of the ship.

"Turn the boat around! I can't take this anymore! I want to go home!" Felix clung to the railing. The steward rolled his eyes, "We've left the dock already. It's three days to London. Get cozy." He patted his shoulder. Felix threw up over the side of the boat, "I'm dying!"

"You are not dying. You'll get your sea legs after a while." The steward helped him stand straight. As he tried to help him sway with the boat, a large wave caused the boat to dip unexpectedly. A feeling of dizziness hit Felix with such force, he fell flat on the deck, fainted. What a start to London…

Felix woke in a small cabin of the ship. The bed was a hammock so it could sway with the boat. It didn't make things easier. Each wave that managed to lurch the boat, lurched his stomach, making him hurl. It frustrated him horribly as his nice outfit suffered in the process.

He tried to sleep, but the effort rendered useless. Instead the sickening sea let him sleep by means of making him faint.

On the 21st of the month, the boat thankfully docked in London by mid-morning. In the entire time at sea, Felix never gained his sea legs. Before leaving the boat, he managed to find a bucket of clean water and a rag. He cleaned off his coat the best he could, hoping to not look like a sick drunk walking the streets. The rocking of the boat would mess up his balance once he got back on land.

After cleaning up a bit, in re-determination he walked onto the docks, luggage at hand. A moment of bewilderment beseeched him when entering the London streets. He needed to find the custom-house. There was a note he received of it's address, but he needed something more specific. He grabbed a map he saved from his geography book.

After studying it, he found that the custom-house was only a few streets away. He looked up from the map. There was another problem. A thick fog sulked through every road and alley of the city. It was impossible to see from one side of the street to the other. Felix hoped it would clear soon.

The streets began to look similar in the smoky air. Felix resorted to his map rather than surroundings. After turning a few corners, closely following it, he found himself standing in the middle of an alley. He huffed in frustration. His huff turned to shock as he noticed the state of the neighborhood. The streets were muddy and the horse manure reeked. The alley led to a dust yard. A few workers in their tattered clothes sorted through baskets of old rags and garbage. Among the ones working were children, quite young.

Felix had not seen such dirty living conditions. Berlin had certain neighborhoods that weren't the best, but the dark side of London fared far worse for the poor of the city.

There were two, stocky grown men taking a break from their work. Their faces expressed tiredness and irritation. They eyed the young man in well kept attire, lost in his way.

Felix felt their stares and kindling thoughts. He forced himself to turn around. He didn't want to get tangled up in a brawl.

Back on the main streets, he became more confused in the fog. Many people ran into him as he toiled in the walkway. One finely dressed English gentleman bumped into him and hissed, "Watch where the bloody hell you're going!"

Felix opened his mouth to apologize but the man continued on. A voice then called in Felix's direction, "Oi, you, young lad."

Felix turned to see a man nearby leaning against a chaise. He continued to say, "I know you're lost. You've been walking the same street for the past twenty minutes. You could've stopped a cab."

"I wouldn't be lost if only this fog would clear up."

"You mean the smog. It never clears."

"Smog?" Felix glanced at the sky. The man laughed, "I notice you are a foreigner. First time abroad?"

"I've traveled in my childhood. It's my first time in London though. Say, you must be a cab."

"That I am. Where is it you need to be?" He asked.

"I must find the custom-house." Felix gave him the address. The coachman nodded and they climbed in the chaise. He took him straight to the right place. The coachman assured, "This building is the custom-house."

"Oh, danke!" Felix said in excitement. The coachman gave him a confused glance. Felix corrected, "-Thanks."

After Felix paid the coachman, he grabbed his luggage and headed inside. He gave a sigh of relief as he set his things down on a bench. There were many people waiting to have their papers checked, so Felix grabbed a book to read in the meantime.

As soon as opening the book, a familiar voice chanted with jubilation, "You've made it!"

"Karl!" Felix looked up instantly to see Klingemann racing towards him. They shook hands in greeting, having not seen one another in a few weeks. Klingemann asked as he noticed his friend's weary state, "How was the trip? You look a bit of a mess."

"It was...an experience." He answered. Klingemann assured, "Well, you are lucky that I work around here. I'll get you checked in." Klingemann gestured to Felix to follow. They went to one of the offices and Klingemann sorted through Felix's legal papers. Felix then asked, "What about the rooms Ignaz said he found for me?"

*(Karl Klingemann)*

"About that...the rooms are still currently being occupied, but that's no matter. You can stay with me, I have extra space that is suitable for a few days. Your official place of stay will be open on the 25th." He stamped a few papers then put them back in Felix's folder, "Let's get you to my place. I imagine you're hungry and tired."

"Ja, I could fall asleep right now." Felix grabbed his things and followed Klingemann out of the custom-house. Klingemann stopped a carriage and they rode it a ways into the city. It stopped at a tall complex. Klingemann guided him in and helped Felix get his luggage up the stairs. When they got to the third floor, they walked down a hall until Klingemann stopped at a door. He unlocked it, "It is a bit small, but it's a humble abode. I do have a guest room, but it's very small. It will be good for a few days but you'll get claustrophobic after a few nights." He showed him in. The flat was decent. The 'guest room' was a single bed taking up a closet like space.

Klingemann told him, "I'm sorry but I do have work to tend back at the custom-house. I'll let you rest here and I must mention, the Moscheles' home is only a few blocks down. After you rest up, you'll want to call on them. I have an extra key for this flat." He handed it to Felix.

"Danke." Felix went to the guest room and slid his luggage under the bed. As soon as Klingemann left for business, Felix flopped onto the bed. As soon as his face hit the pillow, he slept hard. The traveling thus far had worn him out completely.

Felix woke up after a long three hour nap. The fourteenth hour had struck. He still relaxed in bed, catching a few more snoozes. Once he felt rested enough, he went to his luggage and gathered some music. He then fixed his outfit up a bit and walked a few buildings down to Ignaz's home. He had the address and found it much more conveniently.

Upon entering the complex, he went up some stairs. He did not know the specific flat where Ignaz lived. As he roamed the second floor, he heard the faint sound of a piano. It was Ignaz's playing. He followed it to the right door.

After knocking, a kindly faced woman answered. She smiled, "Oh, you've come, my husband is practicing at the moment, but do come in."

The woman was Charlotte Moscheles. She had not the chance to meet Felix until now but heard much of him over the years. She knew him by Ignaz's words and description. She showed him in, "You must have had such a hard trip, you look so tired."

"I have rested some from the harsh journey. I've learned that the sea doesn't agree with me."

"Oh you poor thing. I know how that can get. The first time my husband came home from a tour, he was ill for a week. He's gathered his sea legs over the years though." Charlotte went to the dinning table where a tray of tea sat. She grabbed two of the cups with the saucers, "Tea came at the hour. It's fresh." She handed Felix a cuppa.

She then led him to the room next door where the music played. When they entered, Ignaz looked up from the piano and jumped with excitement. Felix nearly threw his tea in the air. Charlotte took it from him as Ignaz greeted Felix. Felix asked after the handshakes, "May I know what piece you were just playing?"

"It's a Fantasia for piano and orchestra. Something I'm dedicating to the writer, Sir Walter Scott. I have a concert on the 7th of next month. Did you bring your Shakespeare overture?"

"Of course," Felix grabbed the score from his folder. Ignaz looked at it as a precious piece of art, "There is to be another concert at the end of May and one in June. I'd like to see this performed in June. It's a charity concert to raise money to help victims of those dreadful floods happening in Silesia. Sir Goerge Smart is organising it. He suggested Beethoven's 5th piano concerto as well. I told him that you could do it. For the concert in May, could you possibly conduct your symphony in C."

"My music played in London!?" Felix questioned. Ignaz nodded. They both became filled with enthrallment.

126

Charlotte budded in on their enthusiasm, "Felix. Before you have your music performed in London, you first need to learn the ways of the city and society. You don't want to embarrass yourself upon gatherings. Things are a bit different here than in Berlin."

"I know you'll teach me well." Felix smiled on the fact that he'd be learning how to be a proper Londoner. Charlotte went back to the other room to get more tea. Ignaz suggested, "Today we can call upon some of my acquaintances to introduce you to for a start," He then called Charlotte, "Darling, was it Mr. Chappell who wrote, inviting us to a late tea this afternoon?"

"Yes, he also invited Mr. Cramer, Mr. Taylor and Mr. Collard." She answered. Ignaz told Felix, "You probably know the proper ways of tea as your mother hosts gatherings as such. The one I went to seemed quite casual, but I imagine she's hosted formal ones."

"Ja, sometimes on special occasions there are sandwiches and pastries to go along with the tea."

"Ah, so you should know the proper way of eating." Ignaz stated. Felix nodded but in slight confusion as to what he meant. He thought it was no big deal as he knew table manners. Tea at his home had it's formalities. His mother got inspiration from 'British tea'.

At around three o'clock, they took a carriage to a quaint townhouse. It was a large well kept structure made up of a few homes. Mr. Chappell lived in one of the center houses. When they called at the home, they were shown in and led to the dining table where Mr. Cramer, Mr. Taylor and Mr. Collard sat. Another lady sat next to Mr. Taylor. Mr. Chappell took his seat at the far end.

It was different than Felix had expected. Straight away he could tell the manners were far more intricate. He wished Ignaz hadn't assumed that 'formal' tea at his home was exactly 'British tea'.

In the situation, he felt nervous to even grab a chair as everyone seemed to sit in a certain order. He waited and took the last open spot between Charlotte and Mr. Taylor.

Felix greeted Mr. Taylor and began conversation with him. His first name was John. He worked in Wales as a mining engineer. Sitting next to him was his sister, Mrs. Austin. Charlotte addressed her, "It's such an unexpected pleasure to see you Mrs. Austin. How was your visit to Bonn?"

"Very well, I came back only a day hence. It feels good to return to England." She looked curiously at Felix. Charlotte introduced him, "This is Mr. Mendelssohn. He's from Berlin."

"A Mendelssohn? I met one while in Bonn. He was a professor at the university there."

"That would be my cousin." Felix said in surprise. Mrs. Austin smiled and looked at Mr. Taylor. John suggested to Felix, "You should come meet my family, I have three daughters who would be thrilled to meet you. Two of my sons still live with me as the others are in Wales tending to work while I'm not there."

"I'd love to." Felix accepted. Mrs. Austin assured, "We should all take a walk through the park tomorrow, the weather has been faring well this week."

After everyone agreed on the idea, a maid brought the tea and began pouring it into the elegant cups. The set was fine china, with beautiful purple lilacs painted on the white porcelain. The tea tray had already been set full of scones, sandwiches and cakes. Felix was famished as he hadn't eaten all day. He waited though to see what was next.

Once the tea was served, they began picking up their cups and taking small sips. Felix carefully held his cup along with the saucer underneath in case he spilled. It felt logical. Mr. Chappell gave a disturbed glance.

Felix set it down knowing he'd done something improper already. He didn't know what exactly as no one spoke of it.

The conversing continued. Mr. Chappell asked Felix, "How long have you studied the English language? You speak quite well."

"Since my youth I've studied a handful of useful and educational speeches." He answered. Mr. Chappell then encouraged, "You look hungry. Please, have some food, I see you eyeing it."

No one had taken any of the food yet, so Felix hesitantly reached for a sweet raspberry scone. Everyone seemed to disapprove. Felix began to wonder if he should have taken the plain one instead. He tried to ignore the stares by grabbing the cream. It only made it worse as he poured a dab in the peppermint tea.

As he stirred it in, the spoon clanked against the cup. He stirred slower as Mr. Chappell cleared his throat. Charlotte spoke up, "Mr. Chappell, if you do not mind, I wish to excuse myself and Felix for a moment." She stood from the table. Felix followed her out of the room.

Once they got out, Charlotte asked him in concern yet with care, "I know you told Ignaz that your mother hosted tea, but have you ever had formal tea outside of home?"

"No. Please excuse me but I do not know why they keep staring."

"Here, let's take a moment and talk a bit about tea etiquette." She went to a small table in a neighboring room. There happened to be a decorative teacup and saucer on it. She sat down. Felix pulled up a chair. She began,"There are a lot of rules for proper manners. It's more than just knowing not to slurp the tea." She grabbed the tea cup and saucer. She set it in front of Felix, "Pick it up as if you were to take a sip."

Felix grabbed the handle of the cup, which he did now correctly from watching everyone earlier, but he picked up the saucer. Charlotte made him set it back down, "The saucer always stays at the table. Remember not to blow on the tea, even if it's too hot."

Felix listened but rather didn't understand these picky rules. Charlotte handed him a teaspoon, "Show me how you stir."

Felix stirred it as he would, but Charlotte corrected, "Stir it up and down, not in circles or it will make too much noise. The first kind of tea served was peppermint. Milk and sugar are only for black tea. Now with the food, the tea sandwiches are eaten first, then the scones and deserts. Be sure to break the scone apart, but do not dunk a scone in the tea. All of the food should be eaten with your fingers..."

Felix nodded. Charlotte added, "And put the napkin on the left side when it is over."

They stood from the table and re-entered the room. Everyone greeted them back. Mr. Chappell asked in speculation, "Did Charlotte teach you some things? You were absent for a bit."

"I believe so." Felix grabbed a tea sandwich. His scone was still on the plate, but he left it to eat later. Mr. Chappell smiled, "Very well, there's some fresh earl grey tea as the other grew cold from your leaving."

"Thank you." Felix put some milk and sugar in it and stirred it properly.

When tea finished after more conversation, everyone set their napkins down properly and got up. Felix felt more confident as he learned better tea manners.

On the ride back to Ignaz's home, Ignaz suggested to Felix, "I think it may be best if Charlotte teaches you the details of London society.

You do have good manners, but you need some help. The social aspects here are different from what you are accustomed to."

Charlotte mentioned, "You seem to learn quickly, so I think you'll be fine. Since tomorrow we are going to spend time in the park. You'll want to get a proper hat and jacket."

"Proper Hat? I do have one but didn't wear it since it's not cold out." Felix noticed many gentlemen walking outside with fine top hats, though there wasn't a chill. Ignaz had a rather nice hat as well. Charlotte and many ladies around wore a bonnet. She explained, "A fine gentleman in public wears a nice hat as an accessory. Plus you don't want too much sun."

"Alright, I do have some extra money from the concerts I conducted before I came so I should be able to get a decent one…"

"A new suit will help you blend in with the city. The hat and jacket you have are fashioned after styles in Berlin. I can take you to a good tailor tomorrow morning." She offered. Felix felt a slight burden of having to buy a new outfit. Ignaz added, "I do believe Herr Klingemann shall be joining us tomorrow as well. Mr. Chappell wanted to invite him."

"Oh good." Felix chimed. The carriage then stopped by Klingemann's home. Felix disembarked and told Charlotte, "See you tomorrow. I'll call at your door at ten." With that he went back to the flat.

Felix gave a sigh of relief upon returning to the little guest room. It enclosed him, giving him a much needed break from this new outside world. He gathered some of his manuscripts and looked through them while sitting in bed. He brought a makeshift keyboard to practice on without upsetting any neighbors. He was glad though that Ignaz had a real piano.

After writing and organizing some things, the hour got late, so he cleaned up everything and retired for the night.

~~~~

The next day, Felix was in a carriage with Charlotte on their way to a tailor. They rode through a beautiful neighborhood of large houses. Neatly paved brick streets and miniature flower gardens embellished the street sides and yards. It was quite a sight to see. The smog wasn't as dense as they were far from the factories that produced smoke.

At the end of the road, shops and restaurants lined the street. They appeared fancy and expensive. Though it all looked high priced, Felix assumed the tailor would be reasonable as Charlotte was a reasonable woman. She wanted the best for Felix. Appearance wise and cost wise. Over the course of only a day, he'd begun to look up to her as a mother.

When they arrived at the tailor's shop, they found the tailor himself at work. Straight away the bright eyed craftsman greeted Charlotte. She was well acquainted with him. He couldn't have been more than five years older than Felix.

"Who is this you have brought?" The tailor noticed Felix standing a pace or so behind Charlotte.

"This is Felix. He needs a new outfit." Charlotte nudged Felix forward. The tailor held out his hand, "My name is Zachary. Where are you from?"

"Berlin." Felix shook his hand. Zachary examined his current outfit, "I imagine you want something a bit more...British?"

"I think so." Felix felt in offense as Zachary looked at the label of his coat in disgust. He assured, "I'll find you something that will suit you. Come with me." He walked towards a door. As Felix followed Zachary, Charlotte went to look at the women's accessories.

Felix looked around in awe as they entered a room stocked of every sort of garment. From fine linens to shoes, there were many choices. Zach shuffled through some linen shirts and silk waistcoats.

"You'll want more than one coat and a few different waistcoats depending on the occasion." He grabbed waistcoats of various colours. The standard coats that went over them were either black or a dark grey. The pants tended to match the coats.

There were many options on the style of coat such as morning, dress and frock. Some had elegant pleated shoulders while others looked broad and slim. The various lengths changed the look as well. Felix skimmed some racks and happened upon something unique. A deep blue dress coat with a refined shape. He couldn't help but take it from the rack. Nearby he found a pair of long white pants. Zach noticed him piecing a suit together, so he handed him a brown silk waistcoat, "This will go well with that."

After finding a linen undershirt and shoes, Felix eagerly headed for the fitting room. Zach stopped him, "There's something you need yet to get the correct silhouette." He skimmed some shelves.

Felix had noticed many gentlemen with a silhouette of broader shoulders and slimmed waist. He figured it was the style of coat, until Zach unexpectedly handed him a corset. He took it in confusion and told him dumbfoundedly, "I'm not wearing a corset!"

"I assure this is styled for a gentleman. It has become a standard undergarment among the refined. Charlotte mentioned that you are to make public appearances in the concert halls and London society. Your figure must be favorable." He nudged Felix to the fitting room. Felix thought it rather ridiculous.

After the corset had been tightened, he felt stiff and constricted whilst fitting the other layers of the outfit over it.

After buttoning up his coat, he asked Zachary with a worrisome tone, "Are you sure it's not too tight? It feels like it's crushing my ribs."

"It's only crushing a few of the lower ones." He bluntly stated as if it were a normal fact. Felix paused in unsettlement by his words. He wasn't joking.

When he turned about near the mirror, the suit looked sharp, but the sleeves and pant legs were too long. Zachary grabbed some sewing tape to calculate the correct measurements. It took a while as Felix chose three other outfits.

After the painstaking process of patiently getting measured, Zachary finally said, "These outfits will work. I'll get them hemmed. It will take an hour or so. How about you go look at the hats and cravats in the meantime."

*(Example of 1820s mens' fashion)*

Felix changed back to his regular outfit. After feeling that he could breathe again, he went to the front room to find Charlotte. She looked at the accessories with him. He tried on some top hats as Charlotte gave insight. Some hats were far too tall in his preference. The smaller ones were styled for a lady's riding outfit. He then found a few standard gentlemanly hats that favored him.

After finding a nice sturdy black wool top hat and some cravats, Felix and Charlotte waited for the suits. Once they were ready, Felix tried them on once more to be sure they fit.

Though he hated the feeling of restraint, his favorite outfit was the one with the blue coat. The hat and a black cravat completed it to the full. He felt like a proper Londoner from then. He chose that outfit to wear out.

Felix then paid at the front desk. The price wasn't as fun as choosing the outfits. Charlotte handed him some money to help. After it was paid for, they took a carriage, heading back to Klingemann's home so Felix could put the other outfits with his luggage.

After that, everyone met at the park for the afternoon walk. The weather was well suited with the sun out. The 'smog' wasn't as bad as yesterday. Cramer, Chappell, Ignaz, Klingemann and an unfamiliar man were already at the park. Felix and Charlotte caught up to them.

The new person was a friend of Klingemann. Mr. Rosen was his name. He was a professor of Sanskrit at the University of London and worked in the Hanover Embassy with Klingemann. Mr. Rosen was quite intrigued upon meeting Felix. The Berliner's attitude and attire made him appear as one of the most proper gentlemen walking about. Felix was busy talking to Karl, not noticing the passerby giving glances.

Soon Mrs. Austin joined the walk with Mrs. Taylor and the Taylor daughters. John and his sons had to be elsewhere. The eldest daughter was named Anne. She was nearest to Felix's age and right away appeared stuck with awe at his appearance. The youngest was Honora. She was very playful and imaginative. Susan was the middle sister. Felix deemed her the prettiest.

As their group walked on, Mr. Rosen trailed to the back where Felix was speaking with Klingemann. He joined their conversation. They were speaking of common things. Felix told Karl of his experience at tea with his improper manners. Karl laughed, "Oh, you'll learn after a while. It is quite picky but in all it is relaxing."

"I hope I get these English manners down." Felix said. Mr. Rosen budded in, "I bet in a few days you'll be the politest young man in Britain."

"I don't know if I'd go that far." Felix chuckled. Rosen went on to say, "I fancy that I'd like the two of you at my house for dinner. I am able to have guests on the 25th."

"I will be moving to my official place of stay that day." Felix said.

"Where are you staying? You could come over after moving in."

"It's on Portland Street."

"Please, I inquire, I'm only a street away from there."

"Alright. I can make time." Felix bartered. Karl added, "I will be there as well. You have wonderful food."

The group continued walking and talking of other common things. After they walked the entire park, they dispersed back to their homes.

The next two days Felix kept company at Ignaz's home. They shared music and improvised at the piano together. When they improvised, it was almost like a game as they tried to trick each other with unexpected melodies. They changed keys on the spot and added more voicings as they carried on.

Before Felix left, after many hours of practice and fun, he offered to help Ignaz copy the orchestra parts for the upcoming concert. The work would take some time, but he wanted to help his friend. Ignaz was glad to have anything done to lighten his load.

~~~~

When the 25th came, Felix gathered his belongings and headed to his new abide. The place was roomy and included many furnishings.

136

There was a large room containing the living area in one half and a kitchenette with a dining table in the other. Another room contained the bedroom.

It was mid-afternoon when he finished getting settled. He wanted to work on things for Ignaz, but Mr. Rosen sent a note, reminding him of his dinner proposal. Felix wished he could cancel but he knew Rosen wouldn't forgive him. He was looking (rather overly) forward to his coming.

When the hour came, Felix found Rosen's home with the given address. He entered with Klingemann who happened to arrive at the same time. The dinner looked very well made. Mr. Rosen greeted them, "Pleasant for you to come. I've got roasted peking duck." He guided them to their seats. His wife and children were at the table as well. They spoke upon many subjects while eating. Felix was rather in distraction though, penning a letter to Ignaz. He hoped to have time to help make the copies of music.

"Felix?" Mr. Rosen questioned, "Did you not hear what I asked?"

Felix looked up in bewilderment. Klingemann elbowed him, whispering, "Don't write during dinner."

"I'm sorry, what is it you have asked?"

"I want you to improvise something on the piano there. I'd so much like to hear it. I've heard much of your skill at improvising." He pointed to the upright piano against the wall. Felix got up from his dinner and went to the old instrument. He began on a melody of a sonata, then blended the notes into some common English tunes he had heard while riding through London. Everyone enjoyed it as they recalled the folk tunes. Felix didn't necessarily know them but they weren't too complicated to incorporate.

After playing some more and finishing dinner, Mrs. Rosen and the children headed to the parlor for the evening. Felix stood to make his leave, but Mr. Rosen questioned Felix, "Where are you going?"

"Back to my flat." He answered. Mr. Rosen inquired, "You must not know, it is custom that after dinner the men stay for a smoke and visit more so."

"Oh." Felix sat back down. Klingemann straight up lit a cigar, as did Mr. Rosen. Karl handed Felix one and lit it for him. It was a common thing for men to smoke, but he had not become accustomed to it. He tried it and instantly thought he'd hack up a lung. Mr. Rosen chuckled. Klingemann suggested, "Just keep breathing, you'll get used to it."

Felix took his advice, but after many minutes of coughing, he gave it up. After much conversing, the evening came to a close. Felix and Klingemann retired from Mr. Rosen's home. When Felix got back to his official home in London, he did not go to bed. Instead he kept the candles lit and began working on Ignaz's project. The concert was in a few weeks so he needed to be sure to have it done.

~~~

Many things progressed as the concert got closer. Felix had found his time to make the orchestra copies. Ignaz was so happy to see it done. The rehearsals for his concert were going smoothly.

With each day, Felix's English manners improved with the help of Charlotte. Together they attended other local theatrical events, such as the plays of Shakespeare. He made many new acquaintances and received many invitations to social gatherings.

His talents not only at the piano impressed the Londoners, but it was his way of speech as he spoke with elegance. He could read the works of classical literature in their original language, intriguing any scholar.

His ability to draw and paint the scenes of the land were above that of an amateur. Along with those things, his taste in attire rendered him one of the most fashionable gentlemen.

Many, new to meeting the young man, thought him to be a fellow Englishman, until his accent gave him away as a foreigner. At times Charlotte helped him when his manners weren't up to par. Occasionally he made a drastic mistake at tea or dinner, but his apologies were far too sincere for anyone to not put into account.

After Ignaz's concert successfully came and went, the next planned concert came up. It was in the latter part of May. Felix conducted some of his own works such as his first symphony and an orchestrated version of the Scherzo from his string octet. He played Weber's Konzertstück at the piano. The music was a hit in London.

Yet, it wasn't until the benefit concert in June that would establish Felix in London Society. There he planned to conduct the Overture for 'A Midsummer Night's Dream'. Sir George Smart was the man organizing the concert to be hosted at the Argyll rooms in London.

The rehearsals went well, but many curious people attended the sessions to listen. Sometimes crowding about amongst the orchestra. (Mostly ladies curious about Felix) They didn't bother the musicians, so Felix just went with it.

When the day of the official concert came, Felix arrived early to the concert house. He went through the lobby, but found the auditorium locked. No one was around, so he wandered the open halls. There was a small room containing an upright piano, so he decided to improvise in the meantime.

Back in the lobby, someone unlocked the auditorium as the orchestra arrived. They got set up, but wondered where Felix was. Much of the audience flooded in early. (Mostly ladies)

Many heard a piano faintly coming from a distant room, but didn't think much of it. One of the violinists searching for their conductor heard an improvised version of the Beethoven concerto. He found Felix in a rush, "The concert is to start soon! What are you doing!?"

"Oh!" Felix got up and ran. Yet he turned the opposite way. The violinist called out, "Where are you going!?"

"I must get dressed!" Felix rushed to a room to change into his favorite outfit. It was the one with the blue coat and white pants. After changing, he dashed about backstage, but halted himself to walk casually onstage. A full crowd was already assembled and the orchestra was set. He began the concert without any waiting.

After the London audience heard the overture to their beloved play of Shakespeare, they were enthralled to the full. Felix then played at the piano with the orchestra in Beethoven's 5th piano concerto. To the audience's surprise, he played it from memory. Felix preferred having sheet music as it was a formality, but his rendition in the moment favored to his satisfaction.

Felix became the talk of the town after that concert. The success of it led to other musical engagements and gatherings. It all attracted the attention of journalists and music critics. They asked many questions to later write their reviews in the papers. One of the last questions each asked was: 'What would you like to go by in the papers?' In which Felix answered confidently without any hesitation:

"Felix Mendelssohn."

# Chapter VII: From the Caves to the Lochs

**Mendelssohn, Scherzo (III) from String Octet [1]**
**Mendelssohn, Symphony No. 3, Scottish, Movement I [2]**
**Mendelssohn, Hebrides overture (Fingal's cave) [3]**

## [1]

When the summer season came, Ignaz left London for a concert tour in Denmark, leaving Felix to stay in London. He had much to do and many to keep company with. Reviews and recaps of the successful concert resided in newspapers for over a week. Copies of the English papers even reached back home in Berlin.

In the midst of the mid-summer, he received many letters from his family. There was one that came a bit later than some others. It was from Fanny, but it wasn't the most cheerful one:

*July 8th, 1829*

*I have finished my contribution to the large family letters to you, dear Felix, and must now add this small private dispatch, whose contents are as follows: It's come to father's attention that your name was mentioned merely as Felix Mendelssohn in many English newspapers. He thinks he detects an ulterior motive in this fact and wants to write to you today about it, as Mother, who tried to dissuade him from doing so told us yesterday. I do not know if he will still carry it out, but last night, Hensel and I decided to write you this letter in any case.*
*If it's unnecessary then it won't hurt you, possibly it could be of value; and if it's unpleasant then you'll forgive me—*

*I know and approve of your intention to lay aside someday this name we all dislike, but you can't do it yet because you are a minor, and it's not necessary to make you aware of the unpleasant consequences it could have for you. Suffice to say that you distress father by your actions. If questioned, you could easily make it look like a mistake, and carry out your plan at a later, more appropriate time.*

*~Fanny*

~ ~ ~

**Before the summer's end, Felix had the desire to visit Scotland. The idea came to him as he had heard much of the scenery and the inspiration that it could yield. He began planning straight away, writing to Klingemann of the subject:**

*July, 1829*

*My friend of England,*
*I write to you to tell you: Next August I am going to Scotland, with a rake for folk lieder, an ear for the lovely, fragrant countryside, and the heart for the bare legs of natives. Klingemann, you must join me and soar to Scotland.*

*~Felix*

~ ~ ~

**By the near end of July, Felix packed for a two week trip into the highlands. He had a desire to see the meadows and hills; castles of old. He planned to meet the writer Sir Walter Scott at his home of Abbotsford. It would be an adventure filling experience. Klingemann agreed to accompany Felix. He hoped to get much inspiration for his poetry and writing.**

142

After packing as well, he met Felix at one of the streets where they hoped to catch a coach leaving the city. They found one on its way to York. Klingemann knew of a decent inn there.

The trip to York was nice as the carriage they happened upon had no other passengers, making it roomy. The weather fared decent in the two days of travel. The inn there was welcoming and offered a good meal. They spend a day and a half in York.

Their next departure was set in the afternoon. This time they went by mail coach, which wasn't the most comfortable. They traveled all through the day before making another stop at an inn settled in a country village. It was calm and restful. Felix and Klingemann preyed on a good night's sleep. The mail coach would be taking them to Scotland, leaving early the next day.

~~~

The morning sun rose, casting light on the dew of the grass and thrushes. They glimmered in such light. The coach was going a more steady pace when Felix and Klingemann awoke from snoozing. The air was calm with a slight chill. They were still tired from departing at the early hour before dawn. The coach was headed for the city of Durham in which they would arrive that evening. The landscape was now Scotland.

The coach made a stop as there was a body of water to give the horses a drink. The passengers dispersed the area to take in the sights. Felix grabbed his sketchbook, a gift from Wilhelm, and began penciling the old cathedral. He then took the water colours he brought along and painted the drawing. He added texture to the lush leaves and flowing river.

*(Mendelssohn Watercolour of Durham 1829)*

Later that evening upon entering the edge of the city, it was anything but calming. It had begun to rain and the roads became mud. The coach's wheels rolled over every dent and rock in the road. Felix and Klingemann found seats inside the coach as they were the only passengers left. The others had dispersed elsewhere.

Suddenly, the horses halted in the middle of a street and the coachman pounded on the cab's top, indicating the two travelers to get out. The streets were empty due to the hard rain. Klingemann yelled to the coachman, "Would you be kind to take us to stay somewhere?"

"That's not my problem, now get out before I charge you both extra. I've other places to be." He hissed. Felix and Karl grabbed their things and were left to fend for themselves in the cold rain. They searched for the nearest inn, which was a challenge as the lamps glowed dim in the wet weather. After walking a few paces down, some lightning flashed, enabling them to see one.

Without hesitation, they entered the inn. The front room was a small sitting room. Old candles gave some light. The building had a cabin-like feel. Yet water still fell on them as the rain leaked through the ceiling. It smelled musty as well. Felix asked Karl between chattering teeth, "Should we find a better place?"

"I believe we stay here or risk catching hypothermia. Besides this is only an entryway. We've not even been inside the actual inn yet." Klingemann tried to lift his spirits.

They both walked in. The true distasteful scents of the inn hit their faces like a brick wall. A few people were scattered about in the tavern. They looked from the rough side of town. Every eye veered to the nicely dressed gentlemen. Karl whispered to Felix, "I think we came in at the wrong end of the city."

Before Felix could answer, a lady walked from behind the bar of the tavern. Her kitchen dress was dark green with a puke yellow apron, stained with wine and brandy. Her dirty gold locks looked tangled and sticky. She appeared to be thirty or forty. Her stance became stern upon noticing Felix and Klingemann. She was the innkeeper.

"What is it you two would want from here?" She walked rather close to them. Felix stepped back at a pace. This woman had not bathed in a long time; if not ever. He nearly retched at her smell. Karl managed to maintain his stance to answer, "A room for the night. Two beds. If that doesn't work, one of us can sleep on a chair or something. We just need to crash."

"I have two single rooms open." She gestured to them to go up the stairs. Klingemann went first. Before Felix followed, the innkeeper forcefully took his luggage, "I can help you with that dear sir." Her tone changed to deceiving kindness. Felix didn't want to argue and continued on up the stairs with Karl, who still carried his own luggage. Felix helped him of course.

The stairs creaked and felt unstable. When they got up the stairs, the innkeeper handed Karl a key and pointed him to his door. Karl told Felix, "I am retiring for the night. See you in the morning." He left. Felix then turned to the lady, "I shall take my key as well. Just point to the room and I'll get my stuff."

"I'll help you get everything in the room." She walked towards a door.

"That is not necessary. I can manage." He noticed she rummaged the outer pockets of his bags. He only kept a few things in them, but nothing of value. His money he kept close to him in his coat.

The innkeeper ignored his request and unlocked the door herself. She carried his luggage in. He followed to be sure she didn't open anything. Upon sitting the bags down, she wistfully turned to him. Her demeanor was deemed unfavorable in Felix's eyes. Her intentions in the obvious were ill mannered. He wanted the keys and for her to leave, "Give me the keys now."

She handed him the keys in slowness. Felix snatched them from her hand. After taking the keys, she inquired, whilst stepping close, "I can take your coat for you. It's still drenched from the rain. I can get it dry."

"Please go, I shall manage my own things. Leave me to rest." He covered his nose with a handkerchief to avoid her horrid stench. She took the gesture in offense, eyeing him in disappointment. She made her leave. Felix made sure to shut and lock the door behind her. He then turned back to the room.

The first glance deemed it not the nicest. Rather dirty. Disgusting. It was better than catching hypothermia, but after being in the room a while, he began to debate what would be worse.

The wooden floorboards creaked terribly as they were worn and chipped. As he observed the floor closer, he noticed a few roaches scouting for food. A mouse rushed from under the bed as he sat on it. He took his coat off and laid on top of that, not daring to lift the blankets. He wanted to be as far from the mattress as possible as who knew what was crawling about in it. Felix was hesitant to blow out the candle, but he needed to try to sleep.

As soon as the room was completely darkened, it became full of the unsettling sounds of the scratching and chewing of rodents. After a bit he ignored all second thoughts and fell asleep.

~~~~

Felix stirred awake as the sun had risen above the skyline, letting light stream into the room. Upon opening his eyes and seeing everything in natural light, he wanted to barf. The wood wall panels had water damage and mildew. The ceiling fared the same.

He sat up a bit, but froze. A mouse was sitting on him, chewing at his silk waistcoat. He brushed it off and looked at the silk in frustration. It wasn't torn, but it had been frayed. He put on his overcoat which hid the tattered silk.

After grabbing his luggage, he exited the room eagerly. There he met with Klingemann, who was closing the door to his room. He didn't appear at all happy as he incessantly scratched at his head. Karl looked to Felix, "That innkeeper is not getting a cent. We need to find some clean water or a lake. I need a bath. I think the bed gave me lice."

"A mouse tried to eat me." Felix showed him the chewed silk. They both headed down the stairs.

The tavern was empty, so Felix and Karl snuck towards the door. As Karl reached for the handle, someone stopped them both by yanking the back of their coats. They turned around to see the innkeeper standing in anger. She hissed, "Were you two about to walk out? Without paying?"

"Ja." Karl bluntly admitted, "This disgusting place gave me head lice!"

"A mouse ruined my clothes!" Felix snapped. The lady rolled her eyes. She sternly said, "Either you pay, or you both will be staying here a week to work here."

"You can't make us stay." Karl hissed, opening the door to leave otherwise. Felix followed, but the innkeeper pulled him back, "One of you at least will be staying."

Karl instantly turned back and pried Felix from her grip. Once she let go, the two of them dashed out of the inn. They felt much relief after jogging a few blocks away. A man driving a chaise rode by and Karl called to it. The coachman stopped to let them on. Karl asked him, "Do you know of any place to find clean water?"

"There's a nice brook on the outskirts of town. The water is crystal clear."

Karl and Felix climbed onto the chaise. The coachman drove on. Once they got to the brook, they felt happy to find clean water. Once they cleaned up, the day fared much better.

They then found another carriage headed to Edinburgh, the main city of Scotland. The scenery on the way had the beauty they hoped for. Riding through the gorgeous mountain views of Arthur's seat. Felix of course sketched much of the land.

Upon arriving in Edinburgh early in the day, they were not slow to start sightseeing. The city had charm and a calmness.

Soon after finding a decent inn, clean and well maintained, they headed to the Palace of HolyRoodhouse.

The palace was a sight to see with it's beautiful castle structure giving homage to the past monarchy of the land. It gave much essence of the Tudor days. The gardens were well planted and blossomed with many sorts of flowers. The air smelled divine and would please any king or queen that opened their window.

A servant escorted Felix and Klingemann inside to give them a tour. The decor gave much insight of the palace's history. Some rooms were fashioned in the Tudor style as such in the days of the Palace's most known monarch, Queen Mary. The dining hall had more of a modern touch, but it still gave the impression that the table was suited only for kings, queens, dukes and duchesses.

As they went through the large structure, they stopped near a winding staircase, leading to a room. The servant explained a darker side of the Palace's history, "Up there is where David Rizzio was found with Queen Mary. He was a court musician but later became a private secretary of the Queen. He was murdered out of jealousy as he had influence on Mary. Three rooms down over there was where he was stabbed 57 times." He pointed to it.

Felix went up the winding steps and opened the door. The little room it led to gave a chilling sense. If the room could speak it would have much to say from what happened all those years ago. Felix then went to check out the other room the servant spoke of. It was a few paces away from the staircase. He opened the door to a dim room. A far corner rendered dark and full of mystery. Felix dazed at the room so full of history. His uneasy thoughts became interrupted as someone grabbed at his shoulders, "Baa!"

"Karl!" Felix jumped in pure fright. He turned around to face Klingemann, who stood behind him, giggling.

Karl noticed Felix didn't enjoy such a scare and tried to cheer him, "Oh, I'm just having a bit of fun. You were in such deep thought, I couldn't help myself."

"Well you shouldn't joke around here, this was somebody's place of murder." Felix pointed out the obvious. Karl nodded, taking his advice. After observing the room a bit longer, they headed back to the main entrance of the Palace.

They next took a hike through the yards to go see the old chapel where the queen of Scotts had been crowned all so long ago. Felix envisioned a beautiful Gothic cathedral with high walls, an elegant throne and crafted tapestries.

Upon arriving, Felix's imagination rotted. There was a plot of land containing tall grass and some trees. As they walked further, they found a tall crumbled up structure of brick and iron fencing. A large slab of rock that appeared to be a chair sat worn and eroded. Ivy crept up the crumbling brick wall of a once beautiful Chapel.

*(The Chapel Ruins)*

## [2]

Upon standing in the middle of the open structure, Felix gazed up at the large exposed window holding only a few bits of the iron frame showing it's design. The sky gave a sudden gloom, saddening the chapel's state.

The scene sparked his hearing mind. A sound of longing and reminiscing captured the structure and the fields of green flowing grass surrounding it. The chords were heartfelt with beauty, but the inner depths of the sound were an empty void, begging the question, 'Why? Why has such a beautiful thing been resorted to rubble?'

They stayed at the ruins a while before heading back to the main palace. While on their way back, Felix grabbed some writing paper and penned a letter for home:

*My dear family,*

*In the twilight we went to the palace where queen Mary lived and loved. A little room is shown there with a winding staircase leading up to the door. Up this way they came and found Rizzio in that little room, pulled him out and three rooms off there is a dark corner, where they murdered him. The chapel close to it is now roofless, grass and ivy grow there and at that broken alter, Mary was crowned Queen of Scotland. Everything around is broken and mouldering and the bright sky shines in. I believe in that old chapel, the beginning of my Scotch symphony.*

*-Felix*

~~~~

To the south of Edinburgh with a days worth of more beautiful scenes, was the home of the writer Sir Walter Scott.

Both Felix and Karl had high hopes to meet the well acclaimed poet. Felix's reasoning alluded to the fact that lots of Scott's work was used in Lieds of various composers.

Klingemann as a poet himself, couldn't wait to get some insight from a well off writer. There was no guarantee that they would meet Sir Scott as it was possible that he wouldn't be home.

They arrived at Abbotsford house, having left Edinburgh at the sixth hour. It took six tiring hours to get there. Like so many grandiose structures in Scotland, the large home was a castle, standing as if it were watching over a kingdom of its own. The carriage strolled closer to the house on the long driveway. The well trimmed acres of yard growing green in the sun gave such openness.

When they disembarked the carriage, a servant watching for guests stepped out to greet them. They were allowed to enter and take a tour as was a standard custom with manor houses. The main living quarters where Sir Scott resided was a private section of the house.

Felix and Karl were the only visitors at the moment and it happened to be that Sir Scott was home. Karl asked their guide kindly, "May it be possible to greet Sir Scott? We are both writers of sorts."

"I shall see if he's in any mood for a greeting. It is a rare thing for him to be unless he knows you." The servant headed for a staircase. Felix and Karl waited and continued looking at the house. The fireplaces gave much needed comfort from the windy weather outside. Books were neatly placed on shelves as well as stacks of books piled on desks and tables not as neat. Small statues and decor scattered on other surfaces and above the fireplaces.

The servant came back to them with a negative shake of the head at their request. Scott wasn't in the mood for visitors.

Felix and Karl sighed in disappointment. They had driven so far. Felix tried to convince the servant, "We traveled all the way here to meet him. Is he still sleeping? It's noon!"

Just as he stated the fact, Sir Scott walked into the main room. Felix and Karl turned to him, staring at him like fools. Walter was in the act of gathering his hat and frock coat to leave Abbotsford. Yet upon seeing the expression on the young gentlemen visiting, he subtlety paused and spoke sparingly to them. It lasted a mere half hour of unconventional conversation. Not much of poetry or insight. With that Walter bid his farewells and left the home.

Felix and Karl continued through the manor house, observing some poems and books on display. All in disappointment of the waste in traveling eighty miles. Karl wrote of it but in a sarcastic way of it being a success:

July 31 1829

Most astonished friends! O most amazed readers! Under us the great man is snoring, his dogs are asleep and his armoured knights awake: It is twelve o'clock...I lay quiet on the sofa when someone rushed into the room. Thinking of only Felix, I made some scurrilous remark.

That moment I discerned an elderly man, 'Oh, Sir Walter!' cried I, jumping up, with apologizing blushes. Walter replied, ' I have much pleasure in meeting you, your friend has already beautifully told me what and how much you will write and may have already written.' Meanwhile, hands were shaken and we all proceeded in happy ecstasy to Abbotsford.

P.S. by Felix: This is all Klingemann's invention. We found Sir Walter Scott in the act of leaving Abbotsford, stared at him like fools, drove eighty miles and lost a day for the sake of at best one half-hour of superficial conversation.

*Melrose compensated us but little: we were out of humor with great men, with ourselves, with the world, with everything. It was a bad day.*

~~~~

The following day, they continued their Scottish tour by taking a boat from Edinburgh to the highlands. Felix wasn't too thrilled about facing the sea, but Karl assured him that it was the quickest route. The water fared calm so the voyage wasn't as bad as Felix anticipated. His little bit of nausea he managed to distract by opening his sketchbook.

After being in the boat a deal of the day and docking, they found stay in the city of Perth. It was beautiful sitting beside the bank of the river. They found a well maintained inn. The streets and buildings were decent and clean through the city.

There was a fairly new art gallery. It was built only five years prior. Felix had much excitement to go see it. He liked any sort of master works of various artists. All day in Perth he spent roaming the halls and rooms containing fine art. The oils on canvas, pencil sketches and sculptures captured beauty. Klingemann strolled with Felix a while, but wanted to see the other parts of the city, so he left to do his own thing for a few hours.

When Felix finally left the art gallery for the evening, he met Karl back at the inn. There was a fine restaurant next to their place of stay. Karl suggested, "Why don't we get something a bit fancy tonight? I'm a bit tired of tavern food."

"Ja, we haven't splurged our money on food. I guess this is the city to do it in." Felix answered.

They walked over to the restaurant and got a table near a window, looking out into the river. It was pretty as the evening sun sparkled over it. Felix began speaking to Karl much about some music he planned to write. That ruined chapel had struck his muse so much.

154

As they spoke, a man walked up to their table. He was carrying a large satchel holding canvases and painting supplies. The man asked Felix, "My good sir, I couldn't help but overhear you speak of music. Your character made me wonder, are you that Mr. Mendelssohn by chance?"

"Why ja." Felix smiled. The man introduced himself, "My name is James or Mr. Childe. I've heard much of you from the London papers. I'm a painter and do portraits. I've done a few prolific authors and actors, I would like to make a painting of you. I've got some water colours with me."

"That would be nice to have a portrait done in Scotland." Felix thought about it. James turned to Klingemann, "I don't want to leave you out on an offer as well."

"Na, I'm not keen on my looks much. I've had a sketch done recently." Karl declined. Felix assured him, "You don't look bad. Wilhelm's sketch did you justice in goodness. Anyways, I'll sit in for a portrait, but only if you join my friend and I in the tavern at the inn for some good Scottish Beer."

"Of course!" James happily replied, "There is a bright room with windows right over there. The light is perfect for a portrait." He pointed to it. Felix and Karl paid their dinner bill then followed James to the beautiful open room. It was a place to stand about and drink champagne.

James set up his canvas and water colours. He began sketching Felix as he stood near a wall holding his hat. Felix made sure to pose in style.

*(Felix Mendelssohn 1829 by James Warren Childe)*

After finishing the painting he gave it to Felix to inspect. He approved of it. The three of them then walked back to the inn for some beer. As they drank and chatted, Felix suggested, "Why don't we play chess or something?"

"I'm game." James said. Karl stood up, "I'll go get my chess set!" Karl jumped up the staircase in excitement to get to his room. The other people in the tavern looked at him as if he were mad. Felix and James laughed.

After a few rounds of drinks and chess, the hour struck late, indicating time for sleep. Felix and Karl were leaving for their next destination in the morning, so any rest in a good inn was needed. The city of Perth though was one of the best stops.

~~~~

The next day as the open carriage reached the outskirts of a city, the countryside was beautiful. Felix began drawing incessantly. They arrived at Dunkeld, which occupied much of his art. The flowing rivers rushing across the rocks were refreshing upon visiting Rumbling bridge and Hermitage. It was all a sight to the eyes. Such things were what they had come to the highlands for. The weather fared well upon hiking and riding through the lands. They had to walk a great deal to see certain things they wanted, but it was worth the while.

The next place of stay they came to was quite of interest. A tall white castle; estate like, sat in the midst of the mint green grass which flowed with the breeze. Purple thistles scattered about here and there. The sky was a pasty bright grey, ready for a sprinkle. The carriage carried on towards the estate. The dark, dirt path had old grey stone lining the sides of it.

The building was Blair Atholl. It was the ancestral home of Clan Murray. Felix and Klingemann were excited to be staying in such a place. As they came to the front of the home, a few people were scattered about. Some of the men, who were local, wore traditional clan uniforms, complete with kilts specific to Clan Murray. The ladies wore typical dresses, having the plaid pattern of the Clan.

Felix was excited upon seeing a man holding a bagpipe. He had not heard one yet in his time there. The man with the instrument began playing.

At first, Felix and Klingemann were intrigued to hear the traditional calls of Scotland. After a few minutes, Felix began to hold his ears in annoyance. The man kept playing and playing. Klingemann didn't seem too bothered. Yet.

Felix inclined Karl to head inside. Still upon entering the grand main room, the bagpipes blared with full force. Felix asked a lady that seemed to reside here, "How long does that man play?"

"About half an hour, thrice a day. The eighth hour, noon, and the eighteenth hour. If it's raining outside, he plays here in the main hall. He keeps track of the hours." She then walked away. Felix looked to Karl, "We'll stay here a night. I don't think I'll be able to stand two."

"Oh Felix, it's not that bad. It is beautiful, traditional music. Maybe you'll grow accustomed in a day." Klingemann tried to cheer him up. They were then shown to their rooms. The guests' rooms were quite large and elegant. Felix set his luggage in his room which had a window facing the clear open grassland. Bagpipes were still blaring, so Felix decided to visit Karl's room.

His room was more quiet and he was relaxing from the carriage ride. Felix sat in a chair across the room and they spoke. Karl felt at home in Blair Atholl. He enjoyed the history and its traditions.

As Felix listened to his friend's enthusiasm, he opened his sketchbook and began drawing the room. He drew Klingemann as well and titled the drawing, 'The Fair Maid of Perth.'

*('The Fair Maid of Perth' Sketch of Karl Klingemann by Felix)*

After finishing the comical drawing he showed it to Klingemann. He burst into some laughter. Felix smiled then finished up some details. The sound of the bagpipes thankfully halted as time for dinner came. The food of Scotland was filling and hearty.

The next day was only cloudy, so they decided to visit the falls of Bruar and of Moness. They were both beautiful bodies of falling water surrounded by forests. The paths gave much means for hiking and admiring the landscapes.

As Felix drew the land often, Klingemann inclined, "You have been sketching so much and I have not contributed to any sort of art yet on our journey. What if every time you stop to sketch, I make a poem for every place you begin to draw."

"That will be quite fun." Felix grabbed his pencil already, drawing the trees as they rode past some.

There was something about trees that felt so natural to pen. The winding trunks were like an automatic starting point on the paper.

When lush leaves appeared on the page, Klingemann took in his surroundings and began writing up some rhymes depicting the fine air of Scotland. They both created much through the day, enjoying every bit of it. It carried on at many nature sites as Felix couldn't hold back from his book. Felix assured Klingemann that he'd use his poetry for future Lieder. The adventure took up the day until dinner and bed.

~~~~

The next morning, Felix woke to the ear piercing pipes. It forced him out of bed. Usually he was up earlier, but he was tired. The music sounded louder than yesterday. The man playing was obviously in the main hall, which meant it was raining out. Felix looked out the window to see a developing downpour.

He gave a sigh, knowing Karl and he would be staying at least another night if the rain kept up. At least the castle had much to look at in its charm. As Felix still relaxed in bed, he grabbed some letter paper and wrote to home:

*August 3rd, 1829*

*This is a most dismal, melancholy, rainy day. But we make shift the best we can, which is indeed not saying much. Earth and sky are wet though, and whole regiments of clouds are marching up. Yesterday was a lovely day, we passed from rock to rock, many waterfalls, beautiful valleys and rivers, dark woods and heath with red heather in blossom. In the morning we drove an open carriage and walked twenty-one (English) miles. I sketched a great deal, and Klingemann hit upon the divine idea, which I am sure will give you great pleasure, of writing some rhymes at every spot of which I make a sketch.*

*Yesterday and today we have been carrying out the plan, which answers charmingly:*
*He has already composed very pretty things.*

*—Felix*

~~~

There was a break in the rain by early afternoon, so Karl and Felix made their leave of Blair Atholl. Yet the fun continued in a light horse drawn cart, riding through mud and the misty air. Another storm was nearing, forcing them to stay the night at Tummel Bridge.

They found an inn near the bridge in the nick of time as the wind and rain rushed over them. It was humble, made of wood. After they occupied a guest room, the storm outside strengthened. Karl and Felix sat in some chairs near the fireplace in their room. It was large with two nice beds, decorated with crimson curtains. Yet the room was rather empty other than the beds to sleep.

Karl and Felix sat quietly in the dark evening, keeping dry as a wall collected droplets of water. Felix poked at the fire every so often to flare it up. The wind howled and whistled. Doors banged and the window-shutters burst open in the affair. The sound of water echoed from the nearby stream and the pouring sky.

The floor of the room was made up of thin boards of wood in which a conversation penetrated through from the servants' room below. They were singing drunken songs and laughing. Somewhere in the house dogs were barking.

Instead of some soft English slippers to keep their feet warm, they were given Scottish shoes made of leather and wood to wear through the house. As not a servant offered any food in the midst of their drinking, Felix went down the wooden, winding staircase to head for the kitchen.

A servant girl leaned at the bottom of the stair post, holding a bottle of whiskey. She tried to offer Felix a glass, but he was rather too hungry.

Many were at the inn, wandering. The young boys wore kilts, running about in play as older ones stood, speaking to one another in the native Gaelic. Though Felix was linguistically inclined, he couldn't make out their speech. Though the house had much commotion, he felt a bit lonely as the culture was so far different that he didn't know what to make of it.

Felix found the door to the kitchen. As he was about to go in, a waiter was coming out and asked him, "Is there something you need?"

"My friend and I would like some tea and something to eat."

"There's freshly brewed chamomile with honey and potato cakes have been made as well, I'll get a tray for you to take." The waiter turned around and was gone for a bit. He came back with a full platter of tea and cakes for two. Felix thanked him then took it upstairs. The bit of food filled them for the night.

The weather finally seemed to calm for the next day. They gathered their belongings outside the inn next to the horse cart. Once they got the horse fastened to pull the cart, they drove through the wide country. The vast land was filled with dark green foliage and deep blue bodies of water. The depth of the colour gave a lonely mood.

The cart took them to Fort Williams, which flourished with history. It was a busy town as it was a popular destination for those looking for historical sites. Much of the history came from the 18th century during the Jacobite uprisings. Felix and Karl stayed in the town a night before taking a steamer down Loch Linnhe, headed to Oban. Oban was a town by the sea.

After arriving in the late afternoon, Felix felt inclined to venture up a hill at the north part of town.

There he saw the Dunollie Castle. Behind that, the island of Mull and peninsula of Movern were visible. He sketched the charming scenery.

*(Sketch of Dunollie Castle, Mendelssohn)*

"Felix!" Karl called from afar, "The ferry for Tobermory leaves soon!"

"Alright! Just a minute!" Felix smudged the tree's detail, creating depth to his drawing. He cast a shadow on the high rocks with his pencil, adding shade. After getting the important aspects of the scene, he walked back down the hill.

The ferry to Tobermory wasn't terrible and when the steamer anchored at the harbor, it was bustling with young people of the town. The Atlantic Ocean rendered quite a sight with much water. Klingemann was intrigued by it's vastness. They found a respectable private house to take room. Everything was well so far in their time journeying the Hebrides.

Though Felix's feelings of the sea were a negative means of travel, something about the ferry that took them from Oban to Tombermory struck his hearing mind. When they settled in the nice home to stay, he went to the writing desk and began penning what fueled his muse.

It was a beginning sketch of a distinctive motif that moved down. It repeatedly played over and over in his head. Each time he heard it, something more added to the motif. One part that stuck out was a single note from flutes starting simple. They then rose, giving the illusion of anticipation.

After completing a few bars, he decided to write back home as he had not written much to his family in his time in the highlands. He neatly noted:

*August 7th 1829*

*In order to make understandable how extraordinary the Hebrides affected me, the following occurred to me:*

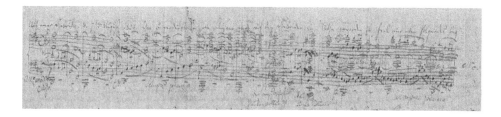

*–Felix*

~~~~

Karl and Felix made plans for what they wanted to do the next day. They had heard much about the islands of Staffa and Iona. There was an ancient cave called Fingal that was a must see sight. Yet to get there, they would have to leave early the next morning on a ferry and the sea tended to be rough in that area.

They were warned that the weather wouldn't be the most calm. Karl told Felix upon the information, "We don't have to go to the islands and cave if you don't want to. I don't want all of this sea sickness ruining the trip for you."

"I really do want to see the cave, I have much anticipation to go. I can manage." Felix felt determined as the previous few times at sea finally seemed to not bother him 'as much'. He rather wasn't thinking of the fact that the past two boat rides rode on near still water.

~~~

The next morning at the fifth hour, Felix and Karl were at the harbor, waiting for the ferry. It was dark out, but the lamps lit the area. The waves rumbled about in the darkened ocean. Felix stared at it, not knowing if he could bear boarding a boat. It was rather late to change their plans as their passes were purchased and the ferry was docking.

The sailors struggled a bit to dock the boat, but managed. A group of passengers eagerly boarded. Felix felt queasy looking at the unstable ferry. He silently refused to step on, holding up the line until Karl nudged him from behind.

~~~~

## [3]

*10th August 1829*

*For that the Atlantic did, it stretched its thousand feelers more and more roughly, twirling us about like anything. The ship-household kept its breakfast almost for itself, few people on board being able to manage their cups and saucers, ladies as a rule fell down like flies and one or the other gentlemen followed their example; I only wish my fellow-sufferer had not been among them, but he is on better terms with the sea as a musician than as an individual or a stomach...*

Klingemann was sitting at the mess of the scene in which was the deck of the ferry, writing of such experience. Felix sat violently ill of the rising sea. Having thrown up every bit of food he'd eaten, it rendered him to pointlessly gagging. Karl was not the sort to be bothered by water, but even this ride was unsettling. He still managed to keep his breakfast down.

Two daughters and a mother sat on the deck as well. The mother was not suited for the sea and the arrogant girls could have cared less. They sat quietly in annoyance at the cold air and disgust by the sickened passengers. At the same time, a man entertained himself and a few others by playing a tambourine whilst whistling the familiar 'Huntsman Chorus' from Weber's opera.

Next to Karl, an old woman sat, nudging and irritating him. She wanted to be sure to see the Island of Staffa and pushed Karl to be sure to get a clear view of it. Karl was rather trapped between the nagging old lady, taking her bothersome shoves and Felix, who consistently leaned onto him during fits of fainting out of illness.

Thankfully they neared Staffa. There was no means of the ferry to dock, so it anchored a ways out. The passengers wanting to visit the Island boarded some smaller boats to reach the basalt pillars of the land. Every moment of this trip for Felix was a torcher as the boat floated with the swelling body of water.

Once they got onto some land, which was the stumps of the pillar rocks, they ventured towards Fingal's Cave. In Karl's eyes, the shapely walls of the cavern looked like endless pipes of an immense organ, black and resounding, and absolutely without purpose and quite alone with the wide grey sea within and without.

*(Fingal's Cave)*

As the sea water crashed against the rocks, the old woman who had been a bother to Karl, pushed her way through the group to see the cave of Staffa. She wanted to see it as her age was advanced, numbering her experiences of extraordinary sights.

Felix gazed upon the swelling abyss of waves. He began to hear the crescendo of the winds and strings from the piece he noted the night before. The movement of the waves consumed his daze as he unconsciously leaned closer to look down. Something had struck his curiosity about the deepness. He stepped onto one of the pillar rocks, at the edge.

Yet his tolerance for turbulent seas got the best of him. Karl noticed his dizzy state and pulled him away from standing so close to it. Felix snapped out of his doze, feeling a rush of adrenaline. Karl suggested to his friend, "Why don't you sketch the cave? It might lift your spirits."

"I'm not much in a mood to sketch such ill fated water." Felix groaned. Karl sighed, wishing for his friend to have a better time at this unique destination. The cave was admired a while longer before exiting back to the little boats.

When they boarded them, Karl noticed something on the high cliffs. There were cute little birds nested on the side. They looked like adorable little penguins. He pointed them out, "Hey look! Puffins!"

"They're so cute!" Felix instantly admired them. It was something unexpected to see and quite extraordinary. The birds ended up being the only brightening thing to lift his mood. It lasted only a short while.

The boat left the Island and the unpleasant smell of the steamer filled everyone's noses upon arriving back to it. The water rocked everything more so this time. No one boarded without at least slightly feeling unwell. Klingemann watched the two arrogant daughter's delicate faces run pale. The old woman trembled as the boat moved up and down. She boarded the steamer with some difficulty. No one spoke as the ferry moved on through the Atlantic.

The man that had tapped at the tambourine and whistled remained somewhere below deck. The scent of stale ham lingered in the air as the cook decided to fire such. Many complaints were aimed at the captain. In return, the captain agreed to take a shortcut back to Oban by way of stopping in Iona.

The stop at that Island was well worth the rest and beauty. There were ruins of an old cathedral, remains of a convent and graves of ancient Scottish Kings. A sense of loneliness flowed throughout Iona.

The illness of the sea seemed to disappear all at once after Iona. Even Felix felt well fared. Yet as everything could not be perfect, irritability replaced sea sickness. A light rain drizzled. Felix sighed, managing to look out into the sea, "I wish the rain would stop."

"It's more of a mist." Klingemann corrected.

"It's raining." Felix corrected back. They bickered about the simple act of the weather.

168

There they knew they needed a break from each other after spending so much time crammed in a boat or a carriage in the past week or so.

As they expected to be back in Oban by the seventh hour, they had only reached Tobermory. As everyone was tired and worn, the captain anchored the ferry off to the side a few paces from the harbor. Few had the wakefulness (the arrogant travelers) to take a boat to the shore.

Felix and Karl were too exhausted and to follow that idea. The ferry had a cabin, but no beds. Everyone in the tired state resorted to sleeping on the floor. There were few blankets and pillows given, but many used their frocks to keep warm and boots to rest their heads.

*(The steamers and boats by Mendelssohn)*

Felix and Karl found a corner, close to the steamer's engine. Some warmth from the steam heated the wall there. Felix laid his coat down and huddled, trying to get every bit of warmth. Karl sat beside him, leaning against the wall to get some shut eye.

They were content at first, until others in the crowding room sought it as a good resting place as well. It became quite claustrophobic around them. Unconventionally, the travelers that stayed on the boat were dusty, smelly sailors and highlanders. Karl later wrote of it:

*August 1829*

*At times, when half asleep, I tried to drive away flies from my face, and then found they were the grizzly locks of an old Scotsman.*

~~~~

After making it back to Oban and leaving the town, they went to the city of Glasgow. There, they visited a cotton mill, which was a relatively new and flourishing business. The noise of the mill sounded like that of the falls of Moness. The manner of it all made time in the highlands move at an alarming pace. Felix felt he needed to write back to home, but so much had happened. He still had the paper of his musical sketch of the Hebrides. He added to the letter:

*How much lies betwixt my last letter and this! The most fearful sickness, Staffa, scenery, travels, people— Klingemann has described it all, and you will excuse a short note, the more so as what I can best tell you is contained in the above music.*

~~~

After Glasgow, they traveled a ways north to see some of the famous Lochs such as Ben Lomond, Loch Katrine and Loch Lomond. Felix once again continued his sketching that had been halted from his previous ill feelings at Staffa.

He drew a landscape of the reeds and greenery. Karl watched him draw and sighed, "Would it not be a dream to live in such a scene?"

"I would very much like a splendid cottage over there. If I ever fell in love someday, my wife would be outside reading away and I would be composing and drawing the scene from afar." Felix began doodling in a garden-like cottage with a figure of a girl in a fine dress and bonnet. A servant held some refreshments. The imagery reminded Felix of the poem, 'The Lady of the Lake', by that disappointing Sir Scott....

170

*(Loch Lomond by Felix)*

They took a rowboat to cross the Loch as there appeared to be a light from a real house there. As they were in the middle of the Loch, they had to row harder as a sudden wind swept through. The boat see-sawed fearfully. Their stuff was thrown about, making a mess. Klingemann became anxious as everything went topsy-turvy. Felix braced himself, ready to jump out and swim if needed. It was strange as he was such a fantastic swimmer in the water, but couldn't handle movement whilst floating on it. Thankfully they made it to the safety of the other shore.

There they found a small house where other travelers were taking a rest. It consisted of a larger main room with some chairs and two guest rooms. The owner was a man that lived on the basics and welcomed anyone to stay.

Felix and Karl got their luggage reorganized in the main room. An irritable young Englishman sat cursing to himself of his companions.

He did not care for such wilderness. Outside the house, a group was cooking dinner a few paces away amongst the forest. Felix and Karl wanted to check it out and gladly the food was shared with them. It was quite a little experience.

The next day though, rain poured again. Their highland adventure was nearing the end in the way of the weather and bleakness. They returned to Glasgow to take room. There, they penned letters and diary entries of their trip through Scotland.

Klingemann penned, poetically reminiscing:

*August 15 1829*

*Ever-memorable country! The Highland smell will be remembered by us, a certain smokey atmosphere which every highlander has about him. I once, while going along, closed my eyes and then correctly stated that five Highlanders had passed by for my nose had seen them...At last we issued from the highlands longing for the warm sun, which we had not seen for days...and we might have become Highland-sick and wished ourselves back had we not known the reality within the mountain land was grey and cold and majestic. It was a sweet farewell to the heights which we at once abuse and love.*

*~Karl Klingemann*

Felix's letter had a different way of recalling his experience in the country. He nearly forgot that the hustle and bustle of London was contained in this entire area called Britain. He wrote:

This, then, is the end of our Highland journey and the last of our joint letters. We've been happy together Roaming the country as gaily as if storms and rain had not existed. But they did exist....To describe the wretchedness and the comfortless, inhospitable solitude of the country time and space do not allow....Whiskey is the only drink. There are no churches, no streets or gardens. Many huts have no roof and crumbling walls, and many houses have been destroyed by fire...It's no wonder the highlands have been called melancholy. But we two have been happy enough, laughing, rhyming, sketching, growling at each other and at the world...eating everything eatable and sleeping for twelve hours every night. We won't forget it as long as we live.

—Felix Mendelssohn

# Chapter VIII: Coed Du Hall

Mendelssohn, Scottish Symphony 2nd movement [1]
Mendelssohn, Three Fantasies Op. 16  [2]
Mendelssohn, Symphony 5, movement IV  [3]

## [1]

Felix and Karl boarded a mail coach leaving Glasgow, headed for Liverpool. The coach was going the impressive speed of ten miles an hour. It was a fast trip out of Scotland. Felix deep inside knew that trip would be the last time of truly feeling the freedom of wandering and sketching for the fun of such things. It was now time to head back to the hustle of English society. At least for Klingemann.

Karl had business back in London, so he bid Felix farewell at Liverpool. Felix was saddened, but had made his decision to venture through the Lake District, see Wales and make it to Ireland.

After a day's worth of traveling, Felix arrived at an inn in the Welsh city of Llangollen. Upon entering the tavern and taking a seat, the atmosphere didn't suit him well. Whether it was Karl's absence or the musicians playing their harps, his impressions on Wales was hindered. He penned to his family:

*August, 1829*

*Ten thousand devils take all national music! Here I am in Wales and heaven help! A harper sits in the hall of every reputable tavern incessantly playing so-called Folk melodies. That is to say, dreadful, vulgar, out of tune trash with a hurdy-gurdy going on at the same time! It has given me a toothache already.*

*Anyone, who like myself, can't stand Beethoven's national songs ought to come to Wales and hear them bellowed by rough nasal voices to the crudest accompaniment and then try to keep his temper. As I write, a fellow in the hall is playing this:*

He scribbled the god-forsaken melody on the paper then wrote in exclaim:

*It's making me so angry, I can't go on!*

Felix wrapped the letter to send. He stayed seated a while at the tavern to try the Welsh beer. It tasted decent enough. A satisfying drink with a meal of rarebit and bara lawr. It lifted his mood some. He especially enjoyed the bara lawr that was served on toast. He wasn't sure what the green sauce-like spread was made of but he found it appetizing. He saw the name of it on the menu. It tasted fishy. As the innkeeper came by, he asked, "What is the bara lawr made of? It's quite good."

"That's laverbread. Made of seaweed." The innkeeper answered, "A very common dish to forge here in Wales, especially by the sea."

Felix looked back at the dark green food. He wasn't expecting it to be seaweed, not knowing such a thing was edible. Seaweed was tasty. Since the music of Wales didn't favor Felix, the food made up for it.

After eating a square meal, Felix looked at some maps of Britain. He knew not much about the way to Ireland, so he asked the innkeeper as he came by again, "Sir, might I heed some advice from you? I am wondering a way to Ireland, do you know the best route?"

"Ireland is a good beauty to see, but I must say in regret that a trip there may be more of a hash than it's worth. The season is yielding quite ill fated weather. A voyage over the crossing would not be a pleasurable one. Getting there will be a challenge as the rain is to be falling most of the week."

"Alright. Thank you -Diolch yn fawr." He tried his best to speak the local language. The innkeeper smiled at his politeness. Felix scratched his Ireland idea. He had enough seasickness in the past few weeks, he was done with it.

Now he needed to decide what to do next. He wanted to leave Llangollen before the rain. A carriage would be bound to get stuck in a muddy mess. He then remembered the Taylor family he had met in London. They had a home in Wales. It was in the country near the village of Rhydymwyn. The village wasn't far from Llangollen.

As the weather remained fine at the moment, he took a carriage. The ride was decently beautiful. Within a few hours, the carriage turned at a driveway. It led into a most charming landscape of hills and green. At the end of the finely graveled road was Coed Du Hall. A large home the Taylor family rented.

*(Coed Du Hall)*

As the carriage neared the home, passing the well groomed yard, Felix saw two of the Taylor daughters in the gardens. Closer to the house, in a nearby meadow, their mother was there, riding a donkey as it grazed peacefully among the wild roses.

Felix had the coachman stop and he jumped out to greet Mrs. Taylor. She dismantled from the burrow and shook his hand upon meeting, "Oh such a surprise from London, dear Mendelssohn. What has brought you here?"

"I've just come from a tour of Scotland. My companion, Herr Klingemann had to return to the city, but I decided to keep furthering through Britain. I had hoped to make it to Ireland, but alas, the weather will soon be in the season of rain and rough voyages I am to hear." Felix looked at the donkey. He grabbed an apple he happened to have in his bag and fed it to the burrow. Mrs. Taylor mentioned, "I wouldn't be going anywhere too far in the next few days or so. The mud is terrible."

"That is why I am wondering if I may stay a week at Coed Du Hall? If I may ask John."

"John and his eldest son are away for the next day, so the decision must lie with me." She smiled as the donkey began to nip at Felix's bag, wanting another tidbit. Mrs. Taylor then giggled, "I suppose you should stay, the donkey insists. In the meantime for a room to be prepared, there is a nice inn at Rhydymwyn to stay at. But please, before you leave for the day, take a walk with the girls, they soulfully will be very much obliged."

"I saw Anne and Honora in the gardens, but pray tell me where is Susan?"

"She is out in the woods riding somewhere. May you also, if you would be so kind as to stay for tea?"

"Of course." Felix replied with a smile. He left Mrs. Taylor then went to where he had seen Anne and Honora.

Though he enjoyed their company much, it was really Susan he wanted to see. In London when meeting he couldn't help but take note of her beauty.

When the girls noticed Felix coming, they cheered in excitement upon the visitor, running to him. Anne couldn't contain her joy, "Oh it's so well to see you here! I did not know you'd be coming!"

"Ja, I've been making my way around. I am to stay for a walk and tea."

"Any amount of your stay is a privilege." Anne gracefully smelled the daisies she had picked. Felix went on to explain, "I'm to stay in the village nearby for a night or two so a guest room may be prepared. I'll be staying here a week."

"Really!?" Both girls exchanged glances. As they continued to chat in the garden, one of the Taylor sons rushed to the group. He was the youngest son, in his mid-adolescence. Anne seemed a bit annoyed at his intrusion on the conversation. She asked him, "Peter, why are you running about so frantically? Have the woods caught fire?"

"No. I heard from mother that Mr. Mendelssohn came to visit and you were going for a walk. Please may I join?" He begged.

"I suppose..." Anne sighed. Her tone caused Peter to look to Felix, "If you don't mind sir?"

"Of course you can. I didn't get to speak with you much in London." Felix inquired. He figured Anne and Peter were just having a normal brother-sister quarrel. He understood as he had older and younger siblings. Honora didn't mind any of it.

Anne quickly took Felix's arm as to escort him the way to the walking paths in the woods. Peter and Honora followed beside. Felix sensed that Anne had wanted the walk to only be he and her.

Though he did care about Anne and loved her company, he didn't think it well to give her the wrong impression.

The group walked through the calmness of the trees and every now and again, a stag would be seen grazing the mulberry bushes. When they neared a heap of stone, Felix went towards it in wonder. It looked like it used to be a structure of some sort. He stepped onto one of the stones, "What is this?"

"It's part of an old mine. Hence why the stones are dusted with bits of coal." Anne explained, "Do be careful, the entrance of the mine is on the other side a few of those stones, it would be a horrid fall." Her tone expressed worry as Felix climbed another large rock to look over it. Felix assured her, "I am just going to glance at it. I've not seen a real coal mine before, I'm curious."

"When my father returns he will show you a real one that is functioning and safe," Anne then commented, "As you should know, curiosity killed the cat."

"Alright." Felix sighed, coming back down. As they walked along some more, they heard horse hooves clamping against the dirt path. Then a little ways down, Felix felt a slight wave of breath taken aback. A beautiful grey horse came their way. It's rider wore the most beautiful blue outfit for a leisurely trot about. Her happiness in doing so shone as gold. It was Susan.

Felix looked at her in complete awe. Anne noticed and took his arm as to escort him again. Susan rode up to them and looked enthralled to see Felix. She dismantled from her horse to greet him. She held out her hand and Felix took it and casually kissed it as to greet an elegant lady. Anne glanced at Felix as he had not welcomed her in the same fashion.

"Such a pleasure to see a familiar face of London." Susan smiled, blushing. Anne glared at her younger sister.

Felix began blushing as well, but did his best to hide the fact of youthful admiration. He stated, "I am happy to know such a family is taking a home here in this side of Britain."

Susan and Felix met gazes for a few moments in silence. Peter and Honora were chasing frogs and toads jumping about. Anne couldn't handle such awkwardness anymore and nudged Felix, "Let us all go back to the house, tis near time for tea."

Susan and Felix shook out of their moment and everyone headed the way back to Coed Du. Susan rode her horse as Felix walked beside it, holding the reins to guide it in their pace.

When they returned to Coed Du Hall, Susan took her horse back to the stables. The others went inside. Felix turned about the main hall. It was like a breath of fresh air, open and clean. Anne mentioned, "My cousins are staying here a few days yet. They are from Ireland."

"How nice." Felix commented. Everyone went to the parlor where a casual tea had been set. Sitting on a couch were two girls in their early adolescence. They glanced up from whispering upon seeing a new guest. Anne introduced Felix. The two girls greeted him then went back to their murmurs and whispers, laughing and eyeing Felix as if he had done something funny.

The hour of tea made for some of the calmest moments. Susan sat next to Felix on an elegant parlor couch. Anne of course sat on the other side of him, striking up conversation whenever Susan did. Felix enjoyed both their company. Mrs. Taylor listened to them talk in awe. She began to have hope in Felix's stay that the enthusiastic young man would become even more acquainted with her daughters.

After the teapots were emptied, Felix made his leave to the suggested inn at the village. It was a two story brick building, very pleasant. Everything there was spotless.

180

After getting a room, he unpacked some luggage to get reorganized. The rooms were very peaceful as the evening came about. Once he blew out the candle to sleep, the atmosphere gave some of the most relaxed rest.

~~~~

The next day, Felix ate breakfast at the inn's tavern. He tried some of the other traditional Welsh dishes he hadn't yet. They were good, but he of course got a serving of the bara lawr to get his fill of it. It tasted even fresher as the village was closer to the sea than Llangollen.

He spent his time inside as the rain fell lightly outside. A harpist decided to sing a morning tune in hopes to cheer the weather, to Felix's dismay. Felix went back to his room and sat at the little stationery desk. He sorted through some manuscripts of music and began on some compositions. He made an outline of a short operetta for the upcoming silver wedding anniversary of his parents. At the same time, he sketched an organ work in case Fanny would be having a wedding.

He made use of the day, writing, then going down to the tavern for lunch and dinner. It felt good to catch up on work as well as rest from sickening travel. Though Wales would not be as adventurous as Scotland, it was a perfect way of winding down from the rough journey in the Highlands.

~~~~

## [2]

When the 27th of August came, Felix returned to Coed Du Hall. His guest room was prepared and so very nice. He fell in love with the bright calm decor and fresh air flowing through the windows. The cousins from Ireland had left, leaving a room for him.

After unpacking some, he headed to the main hall to look around the quaint home. He was welcomed by John as he had returned home from traveling. His son that had gone with him returned to his own country home.

The eldest sons had families of their own and worked with John in the mining company.

"I had not realised you were staying with us." John was surprised upon seeing Felix. Felix felt like an intruder and explained, "I came by a day or so ago and spoke with Mrs. Taylor. I figured that she would write to you?"

"No matter," John assured, "I'm perfectly happy that you are here, it was just unexpected. Why don't you come and have demitasse with me?"

"Sure." Felix followed him to the sitting room. A maid brought in a tray of small coffee cups. A few sandwiches had been made as well. John and Felix were the only ones enjoying the small coffee. The rest of the family were outside, tending to their gardens. John spoke of many varying subjects as to learn more about Felix. They had met in London at Mr. Chappell's home, but this was much more casual. It gave Felix a sense of home.

As the hour of demitasse neared its end, John noticed Felix eyeing the piano in the windowed area of the room. John encouraged him, "You must be itching to play the piano. I imagine in traveling it's hard to find a decent instrument. Please, go play some."

Straight away Felix went to the beautiful grand. He touched a few keys and upon hearing it in tune, he sat on the bench. A fantisful improvisation echoed. John set his cup down and walked towards the windows that surrounded the piano. He gazed outside into the gardens as the tune carried. Felix smiled as he thought of the green leaves and all the different flowers blooming. Each kind sparked his hearing mind. Upon finishing the little tune, John commented, "I had no idea how delicate the piano could sound. It fits so well with the nature and scenes."

"Nature happens to inspire much of my music. Something about it gives way to song." Felix turned to him.

John then changed the subject, "I do assure that in two days time, my family and friends will be heading to one of the mines a few miles out. We are hosting a dinner. Something festive for the workers. You are welcome to join."

"I'd love to." Felix became excited at such.

"I heard that you have an adventurous spirit. I'll let you see inside of a working coal mine when we go." John added. Felix stood from the piano in all joy.

From the first day of Wales to the present, his thoughts of the land were becoming more favorable.

~~~~

The rest of the day, Felix wandered the home, had dinner with the family and composed in his room. The night was calm with the sounds of crickets. He peacefully penned up his operetta by candlelight. He titled it, 'Son and Stranger'. For the organ piece, he wrote in another section. There was no say yet from Fanny about the wedding.

Hours went by into the cool moonlight. At midnight Felix set down his quill and blew out the candle. The bed was soft and one of the coziest. Through the open shutters, the songs of toads and crickets put Felix to sleep. Everything felt perfect. He couldn't imagine leaving such a home.

The next morning at the table, a hearty breakfast of Welsh cakes were presented. Tea and coffee were served as well. John read a newspaper as Mrs. Taylor and the girls spoke about their gardens. John's son, Peter, watched Felix pen some music.

After breakfast, everyone went to do their own things. Felix went to the piano to improvise and test out his operetta. Klingemann had written verses and story lines to base the music.

Though Felix still had a negative outlook on opera, he decided to keep this work within the family gatherings.

After using up some ideas, he looked up from the music and gazed out the windows. The three Taylor daughters were in view, running through the wildflowers and grasses. Each one had their own distinct way thither through lush grass and admiring each blossom. He placed his hands on the keys and played his feelings. The daughters' personalities began to influence his improvisation. So much so he began to sketch three unique caprices based on each of them.

For Anne, her favorite flowers, red roses and carnations were captured in sound by an Allegro vivace in A major. The softness gave the feelings of their wafting scent. Honora loved the vines with the trumpet shaped flowers so he thought up something to mimic the blossoms, which was no easy task. In an e minor scherzo, he put a crisp fanfare-like phrase at the beginning. For Susan, her caprice was especially pretty. It depicted a meandering rivulet, flowing free in the woods. Felix figured he could finish the pieces then give it to them upon his leave.

That evening, dinner consisted of lamb chops and roasted carrots, tossed in a specially homemade maple bourbon glaze. Honey roasted chopped almonds and scallions were used as the spice to top it off. The aroma filled the house. The sight of this meal could make anyone's mouth water.

The family took their seating at the large table. Honora and Peter sat together and Mr. and Mrs. Taylor took the end seats. Felix was squeezed between Anne and Susan. Everyone got a plateful of the delicious meal. It's taste was the most divine.

As Felix bit a mouthful of roasted carrots, Susan begged to him, "After dinner, may you teach me some piano? Father heard you play and said it was beautiful. I've heard many good musicians."

"I've been learning piano as well, may I join." Anne budded in. Felix was still chewing, holding his answer. He didn't want to rush as to not waste the flavor of such food. The sisters were rather looking to him with overcrowding eagerness. He finally swallowed, "Of course."

Instantly their eyes brightened up. Susan then spoke of the pieces she enjoyed. Felix was enthusiastic as she mentioned Mozart and Haydn. Mrs. Taylor smiled as the two spoke in all youthful manners. Anne budded in when she could and looked towards Susan with a daring glance. Susan began to catch onto her sister's intentions. Felix turned to Anne as he began to feel her stares as well. Anne smiled at him in all kindness.

Desert was then served. It was blackberry Monmouth pudding, which was another traditional Welsh dish. It was a creamy whipped pie of pudding, blackberries and fluffy cream on top. When it was sliced, the layers of it were a beautiful purple and white. Upon tasting it, Felix couldn't help but ask, "Is there a recipe I can take home with me? As well as that bourbon glaze? My family back in Berlin must try this."

"Oh! I can certainly get it written down." Mrs. Taylor had an excited tone. The maid left to go write a copy of it. She came back with some note cards and handed them to Felix. He glanced over them and pocket them.

After the pudding was devoured, Felix headed for the piano with Anne and Susan. The girls stood around the instrument as he sat at the bench. They listened to him play. There was no music on the stand but he recalled a folk melody and did his own version of it. Susan couldn't believe their own piano could have such etiquette. When Felix finished with a few flutters of notes, he asked, "Do you have any sheet music?"

"Yes," Anne went to a cabinet and picked out a piece. Felix looked at it, "It's a duet. Schubert in fact. Fantasie in f minor." He smiled, playing some of the upper melody. Anne sat next to him, "I know how to play this one." She placed her hands on the keys. Felix nodded and he played the lower voicing.

Though the music sounded superb, Felix noticed the piece she chose had a lot of phrases where their hands were close together. At one point in the piece, their hands crossed. Anne at times made a 'mistake' and her hand bumped into his.

Susan found a Mozart duet. When the Schubert piece finished, she discreetly shewed Anne away to sit. Felix looked at the Mozart piece and they began playing. Susan had more skill at the keys, yet she needed to hold her fingers better. After finishing the piece, Felix suggested, "Be sure to place your fingers correctly and don't let them slouch on the keys. You'll want to keep the strength of them up and keep your joints loose for a smoother attack." He showed her his stance. She watched and then copied his manner.

In an instant her playing improved. She turned to him,"Your playing is by far the prettiest. I'll have to call you the chief piano player."

"I believe it's all about how you go about playing. You are lucky to have such a fine English piano." Felix fluttered some notes. They continued on with much music and lessons.

~~~~

[3]

The next day, the family packed up a large lunch for some festivities. They were going to be having a picnic outside one of the mines with the workers. Everyone took part in preparing it. Felix helped carry some baskets as the family and him hiked to a mine a few miles away. The weather was thankfully sunny and calm. The beauty of the land was breathtaking.

When they arrived at the picnic site, a group of locals were already gathered in the grasses, drinking wine and brandy. A big wood paneled shed with a few surrounding wood structures stood in the middle of the grassy yard. Inside the building was where the deep coal mine was contained.

Excitement stirred all the more amongst the gatherers when the Taylor family and Felix brought food. The occasion gave the utmost joy. Straight away the meal was served and drinks were drank. Felix enjoyed every bit of it. He loved being involved in the true state of the local culture. As in London, the people began to think of him as one of their own, only his speech giving him up.

After eating and drinking a while, John told Felix, "You must come and see inside the mine. Though we dig for coal, there are beautiful rocks and things."

"Sure!" Felix slightly slurred as he finished a shot of brandy. Most everyone was having their fair share of drink. John led Felix to the entrance of the large wood building. The inside looked even bigger than out. It contained a mechanism which was a pulley system to lower a lift into the deep opening in the earth.

John lit a lantern and gave it to Felix. He then used the pulley system to get the lift to the surface. The platform was only suited for one person to stand on. John gestured Felix to get on it. Felix was unsure of it as the lift wobbled a little while stepping on it. John assured him, "It's safe, I assure you."

Felix took his word for it and clung to one of the ropes. John then lowered it down. As the lift reached a few body lengths down, if Felix hadn't had the lamp, it would have been pitch black except for the small bit of light from the entrance.

The lift continued on, lower and lower. A few interesting rock formations were here and there. The naturalness of the earth's crust began to inspire Felix's hearing mind as it was a new experience. The sound of a grand orchestra came whilst seeing the vastness and depth of such a structure.

At 500 feet below ground, the lift stopped. Felix paused in the moment. His surroundings were dead silence and near darkness. He looked up. The entrance was barely visible. It was a mere dot of light in the deep hole. Heart wrenching minutes passed as the lift still stayed put. He tugged at the ropes and called out to John, "Pull me back out!" He hoped his voice carried up. It echoed through the shaft. It still didn't move. The lamp on low fuel dimmed more and more. Soon his surroundings were pure darkness.

As he thought he'd been abandoned, the lift was pulled back towards the surface. The second it reached the normal ground, Felix stepped off the lift and sat on the ground, trying to calm his nerves. John went to him in worry, "Felix, are you alright? It was just a mine."

"It was so dark! You left me there until the lamp burnt out." His eyes were still adjusting from being in such darkness to natural light. John snickered a bit, "Well, I had to make sure you got the full experience of it."

Felix stood back up and shook himself out of his nervous state. He and John then rejoined the party outside. They were still drinking and speeches were being given in toast. Felix met many miners, learning about their lives and interests. Yet the evening went on with mostly drink. Felix resorted much to the company of Anne and Susan, flirting and speaking poetically in his best English. Anne of course loved every word of admiration, though his talk was intended for Susan.

The picnic went on until late evening.

~~~~

The morning sun shone through the window, feeling like a slap in the face. Felix groggily opened his eyes to see a maid opening the curtain in his guest room. He had somehow returned to bed last night. As he was in a sleepy state of confusion, the maid walked to the desk, studying the manuscript of composition sitting out. After noticing Felix awake, she left to tend to other work.

A sharp headache came over him. He didn't think he had drank that much. He snoozed in bed a while then made himself get up. It was late morning, but there was still enough time for breakfast. He dressed into something decent and headed for the dining room. Mrs. Taylor was in the sitting room and saw Felix pass by. She called for him. He turned around and entered, keeping composure.

"Sit please," said she. He listened and took a spot on the couch across from her. They both sat in silence as she watched Felix closely as if studying him. He sat naturally trying to ignore his throbbing head. She finally spoke up, "You appear in a bit of a disorderly state."

"Just a small headache." He mentioned. She then joked, "I would be surprised if you didn't. You got into quite a bit of the brandy last night."

"A bit of a bad headache actually," He rubbed his forehead. Mrs. Taylor stood and gestured to Felix, "Here, come to the kitchen with me. I've something that may help."

Felix eagerly followed. Once they got to the kitchen, Mrs. Taylor opened a cabinet and grabbed a glass jar of some chocolate milk. She poured some into a drinking glass and handed it to Felix, "Chocolate milk is quite a useful remedy in the case of a hangover."

Felix drank it and within a few minutes the sugar from it helped ease his symptoms. The milk calmed his nausea. He then asked Mrs. Taylor as she gave him more, "How did I get back to my room? I don't remember coming back..."

"John and Peter walked you back as you started sleeping at the picnic table. You didn't cause a ruckus or anything. You just got sleepy."

"Oh good, I was worried. I assure you I truly am no lush." He sipped some more chocolate. Mrs. Taylor assured, "It's easy to get caught up with those miner's way of fun. I would stick with chocolate for today.

In fact, chocolate is becoming the popular drink in London. Anyways, the girls went to go sketching this morning and wanted you to join, but you were still sleeping. I imagine they are still out drawing if you want to catch up with them."

"I would like to." He finished some more milk then went back to the guest room to grab some sketch paper.

Outside he found the girls in the garden closest to the woods, drawing and laughing. When Felix came to them, they excitedly shared their art. Felix began his own sketches of some roses and the trees. The girls were surprised that he had such skill. Susan teased, "Aren't you just talented in every aspect. Look how perfect that flower is. It's a spitting image."

"I assure this is not top grade art. I'm only an amateur." Felix erased half of it to retry. Anne tried to stop all of his erasing, "You're ruining it by doing that. It was so good the first time."

"Hey quick, draw that girl walking way over there." Honora pointed at a girl holding a basket. She was collecting raspberries in the neighboring grassland. Felix sketched and began bursting into laughter. Anne tried to get a peek of it, but Felix kept it hidden. Susan leaned in to see, but he wouldn't let anyone get a glimpse as it was in progress.

He became so winded with laughter that he fell back in the grass and dropped the sketch paper. Anne grabbed it and laughed hard at it's appearance. The others looked in curiosity. Anne commented, "Alright, you aren't skilled at everything. What is this? It's hardly a person! Her face looks like that of a camel!"

"I can't sketch people right. It's my weakest aspect in drawing." Felix still laid in the grass in laughter. Susan teased, "We should probably hide this sketch in case that girl comes over here." She folded it and pocketed it. Once they calmed from their antics, they continued drawing the hills and forests.

As the day went on, they spent it all outside. They ate lunch, sitting in Mrs. Taylor's garden. Two of the Taylor sons joined them. One was Peter, the other was a year or so older than him. His name was Anthony.

After they finished lunch, they decided to go out into the woods in the early evening. They wanted to build a fort. Each of them helped by gathering branches and fallen logs. Felix helped with much zeal, dragging the largest tree scraps he could find. There were many fir trees in these woods.

The air was hot on the summer day, tiring the group, but they were determined to make a good structure. They started putting together their findings in an open area in Susan's garden. By the time the sun began to set, their little house of branches was finished. Anne then said, "All we need now is a fire."

The boys gathered more wood and built one in the thicket of the trees. When it was lit, they all sat around, telling stories and laughing. Susan began to sigh, "If only we had some music on this perfect evening."

"Could anyone get something to play on?" Felix asked.

"We are near the gardener's cottage, he has a fiddle." Anthony recollected. Honora encouraged, "You must go get it." The other girls agreed. Peter and Anthony ran off to seek out this fiddle. When they came back, Felix looked at the instrument in amusement. The strings were broken but one. Felix took it and tuned the string the best he could.

Upon moving the bow across it, he gave way to fits of laughter. It had the most wretched screech. His laughs spread to everyone else. Then a wave of seriousness bestowed him and he managed to gently glide the bow over the one string, forming a single voiced melody in all decency. The soft, ruddy phrasing went on until the dark of night forced them to return to the house.

The next few days at Coed Du Hall were filled with more happy memories. Even if the rain trapped them inside, the house would echo with music from the piano. The true and heartfelt expressed feelings of Felix's nature in the day were known by the way he improvised and played.

Eventually the day came when Felix had to return to London. On his day of leave, when it was still morning, the girls gathered around the piano, listening to him play one last time. It was new music to them. After finishing three pieces, he grabbed the sheet music from his folder and handed them the pieces that he made for each of them. They were baffled and enthralled.

It was the best farewell gift they could wish for.

~ ~ ~ ~

After the long, saddening ride of leaving Wales behind, Felix returned to his flat in London. The city was as busy as ever. He felt ever so heart warmed to find a pile of letters from home. The first one he opened was a wedding invitation. It was for Fanny and Wilhelm. A note was folded with it. Felix rushed to read it.

*My Dearest Brother,*

*I suggest you leave London as soon as possible. Do not forget the music I asked of you. Father is currently in the Netherlands. You could meet him there and we shall welcome both of you home. I can not wait to hear what it is you have composed for my wedding day. I miss you ever so and wait with all eagerness for your return,*

*Sincerely,*

*Fanny*

Felix frantically gathered the letter pile and put them with his other luggage. He decided to read the rest on the way back home. After a quick reorganization, he took his things and raced out the door. The next ship out of London was bound to leave soon.

He returned the keys to his landlord then hurried to the nearest parked gig. He loaded his luggage and hopped on, ordering the coachman, "I must get to the harbor as quickly as possible. The next ship shall leave soon. I can not miss it."

The coachman nodded and made his horse carry on at a fast pace. The horse suddenly became agitated, quickening on it's own, into a gallop. The coachman tried to slow it, but the horse wouldn't let up.

A large coach of four horses was trudging up the street coming their way. Felix in fright snatched the reins from the coachman in an attempt to make their horse turn. It only made the animal lose control, causing the gig to lean towards one side. The whole thing wobbled and tipped after the wheel snapped under the weight. Both the coachman and Felix were thrown from their seats. A bloodcurdling scream echoed through the streets.

*(Learning to drive a Dennett by Henry Thomas Alken)*

# Chapter IX: Home sweet Home

Beethoven, Symphony No. 5 movement I [1]
Mendelssohn, Son and Stranger Overture  [2]

## [1]

Everything in one moment had become a blur. It took only a single turn of the chaise to halt every plan. All of the horses were spooked, causing them to rear and whinny, kicking dust. A man nearby who knew how to handle horses managed to calm the startled creatures.

A few paces from the toppled chaise, the coachman managed to stand. His legs and elbows ached from the impact. His injuries were a few scrapes and some road burns. He stretched his arms to be sure he hadn't broken anything. All was moving well.

On the other side of the chaise, Felix was laying next to the gig. The splintered up wheel was in shambles beside him. He was in a daze after he had smacked his side against the cobblestone. As he managed to turn himself onto his back, he knew something wasn't right. A horrid pain started in his foot and eased it's way to his knee. He yelled as it escalated. The yell was more in anger at himself in the fact that he had gotten hurt on his first trip abroad, all because he was in a rush.

*What of the wedding!? What would Fanny think!? What would Vater think!?*

If the injury proved to be bad enough, he would have to stay in London longer. He would be missing Fanny's wedding. The only hope of his music reaching her was by way of the post.

The coachman rushed to Felix upon noticing his state. He looked at his leg and sighed, "I don't think you'll be leaving London today. You need a bed and a doctor. Can you possibly get your rooms back for longer?"

"I don't know," Felix cried as he tried to bend his knee. As he shifted his leg, it felt like bricks falling down on it all the way to his foot. He sat up in a fit of frustration. The coachman made him lay back, "You shouldn't be moving. I don't want you to risk worsening the injury."

"I can't stay in London longer! My sister is to be married! I must be there for her! I must get back home at any cost." Felix argued. The coachman gestured to a man nearby, "Help me take him back to his place of stay."

Between the two of them, they picked Felix up. They found another carriage to transport him back to his place of stay. The ride was slower. The entire ordeal agitated Felix. He complained and became irritable.

Upon finding the landlord, the coachman explained the situation. The rooms were thankfully still available. The landlord helped further by calling for a doctor.

When Felix was brought back to his room, he was put straight to bed. The coachman stayed and waited for the doctor. In the meantime Felix attempted to shift his leg. The coachman warned, "You're only making things worse by moving it. From experience I know."

"I can't be in London longer. I need to be there for my sister." Felix huffed with tears as he felt hopeless.

A few minutes later a doctor arrived. The coachman let him in and informed him of his concerns. The doctor upon hearing of the injury assured, "I will look at it. It sounds like a bad sprain." He headed to the bedroom.

The second the doctor entered, Felix explained in urgency, "I can't be stuck in London! I must head back to Berlin."

"I'll decide if you're fit for travel." The doctor gave a stern answer as he set his bag down on the bed. As he took his vitals, Felix continued to explain, "My sister is to be married soon. I must meet with my father in the Netherlands. The boat will be leaving- AUSCH! DAS TUT WEH!" He yelled in the middle of his speech as the doctor moved his leg. It sent a jolting pain through his nerves.

The doctor stepped back in thought. Felix begged after the pain calmed, "Please, I need to get back home, it's not that bad is it?" His heart pounded for his answer.

"I'm sorry, but you must stay in bed. You landed wrong on your leg upon falling. Your leg isn't broken, but your foot and knee are not in a good state. You risk permanent damage if you put weight on them. You're going to be here a few months before you're fit to travel. Even then it could be risky and won't feel the best. Definitely after getting home, you'll have to keep off it for a few more weeks."

"Nein! Bitte! Please!" Felix tried to plead. The doctor convinced his bed rest by gently lifting his leg. The second he touched it, Felix near screamed. The doctor assured, "You aren't going anywhere. I inquire that you stay six weeks in bed. You shall still be confined here in your rooms after that as you mustn't walk too much. If you want to get home, you must let your leg rest. It needs a lot of time."

"I want to go home now!" Felix became irrational. The doctor ignored his unrealistic nature and tended to a few minor bruises and scrapes from the impact of his fall. After checking his pulse, he declared, "You are still in shock from the accident, your pulse is hard and ramping. You need to calm down. Sleep will help."

"How can I sleep!?" Felix retorted. The doctor had enough of his irritability and told him, "I'll give you something to help you sleep." He searched his bag and gathered some medicines.

After mixing some sort of tincture together, the smell of lavender filled the room. He put the mix in a vial and handed it to Felix.

The lavender aroma was strong upon drinking it. Another strong taste made him drowsy. In a few heavy blinks of the eyes, Felix had no more complaints. Only soft snores and sweet dreams of Scotland.

The doctor checked his pulse once more and he was much more calm. He turned to the coachman before leaving, "Be sure someone watches him frequently." With that, he left.

The coachman sighed, debating what to do. He needed to get back to his work, but couldn't leave Felix in case he woke in a panic. He had no choice but to stay around. Thankfully though, there was a knock at the front door. The coachman answered. It was Klingemann. He came in with much worry, "How is he? Is it bad? I came as soon as I heard of the accident."

"He is fair. His leg is injured quite terribly, but it could have ended much worse." The coachman showed him to the bedroom. As Klingemann walked up to the bed, Felix nodded awake as if he sensed his friend's presence. Klingemann assured him, "I shall write to your father and family so you don't have to worry about it. You need rest."

"I must at least finish the last bit of the organ music for Fanny." Felix sat up. Klingemann made him lay back, "You do not need to compose, you need sleep." Karl then went to the writing desk. The coachman left now knowing there was someone to keep an eye on Felix.

Klingemann stayed the rest of the day. He penned a letter, informing Abraham of the accident. Felix tried to encourage Klingemann to lessen the situation with his writing skills, but Karl did not want to lie to Abraham. He wrote everything the coachman told him as well as the doctor's orders. It was sent out as soon as it was folded up.

Karl kept Felix company as he was bored laying about. They spoke of their memories from Scotland and the highlands. Felix told Karl all about his experience in Wales, staying at Coed Du Hall. He wished to be there once more.

When the sixth hour came, Karl called for a maid to make something for super. She put together a hearty shepherd's pie. The English dish was bland but filling. Karl then made his leave for the evening, instructing the maid to keep an eye on Felix.

As soon as Karl left, Felix asked the maid, "Hand me that folder over there." He pointed to his music folder. The maid listened. As he sat up in bed, she questioned, "Shouldn't you be sleeping? Resting?"

"I've been resting all day, I'm bored out of my mind." He snatched the folder from her and grabbed a pencil sitting on the nightstand. The maid left him alone and tended to cleaning the main room.

Felix frantically worked at the organ music for Fanny. Yet his rushed inner pressure only frustrated the progress of it. He erased notes in anger, scribbled harmonies to fill the page and got nowhere with it. After an hour or so, the maid came back and forced him to give it up.

He in pure stress gave an agitated yell into his pillow, muffling it. The music would not make it to Fanny. He felt that he had disappointed his sister before she even knew it. In the midst of his aggravation, he shut his eyes to sleep.

~~~

Fanny paced around her room at home in Berlin. She wore a most elegant white silk gown. Lea and a seamstress were with her, adjusting her wedding dress, making sure it fit. Her pacing was of worry. The wedding was in two days time and Felix had not arrived home with their father.

198

In a moment of hope, the main door downstairs opened. Fanny raced down the steps to see a servant taking Abraham's coat. She gave a sigh of relief, but then asked, "Where is Felix?"

Abraham handed her a letter. It was from Klingemann. She looked at the opened paper. As she skimmed it, she became full of mixed emotions. Sorrow came over her on the fact that Felix got hurt in the accident, but then disappointment entered her eyes.

"Did Felix not even enclose the music I requested? Why did he not send that at least? Why must this happen? I need wedding music! I guess I'm going to write it myself!" The dressed up bride raged to the music room, grabbed a quill and manuscript then began composing an interlude appropriate for her vows to Wilhelm Hensel.

In her writing, she discarded her thoughts about Felix's failure to contribute to her day and only thought of her future life as Fanny Hensel. Abraham was happy that she had much excitement on changing from a Mendelssohn to a Hensel

One child taken care of in ridding the name.
~~~

Weeks later, back in London, Felix still was confined in his flat. He was now allowed out of bed every now and again, but not for a long amount of time. The doctor visited once a week to make sure his leg was healing right. Klingemann came often as well as Mr. Rosen. Ignaz was still out on a tour and Charlotte had not heard of the accident. Karl and Felix thought it best not to get them worried about it.

Many letters arrived after Fanny and Wilhelm had wedded. It made Felix feel so left out as the family described their day of uniting. The guilt was heart weighing. Fanny sent a sketch of her composition for the occasion. Felix wrote back trying to lighten her mood by telling her how much talent she had in doing so.

Wilhelm was ever so happy to have Felix as a brother-in-law. It made Felix smile as he admired a few of the drawings he sent of various members of the family.

Abraham sent a rather discerning letter, discreetly mentioning that Fanny no longer had the Mendelssohn name. He strongly referred to her as Fanny Hensel. Felix had now mixed feelings on returning home. He needed to be with family, but he knew that when he was to be stuck in bed longer after travel, his father would trap him in conversation about the London papers excluding the Bartholdy name.

Abraham knew the name in concern to his daughters would be much easier to hide as all they had to do was fall in love. It wasn't so easy for Felix. Paul had agreed to pursue the bank, which wasn't an overly public job, so Abraham had less concern for him. Felix sighed at all such letters. He had to set it aside.

In his time still in London, he finished the small operetta for his parent's anniversary. He also began penning a string quartet with a certain someone on his mind. Betty Pistor. He was looking forward to seeing her again, if circumstance allowed. For the first two notes of the quartet he used B and E.

~ ~ ~

After being stuck in London for three and a half months, the doctor gave him permission to travel home. Felix now managed to walk on his leg in short amounts of time. After too long, it ached. The doctor gave strict orders of bed rest upon his return home.

Felix packed everything up and went out the door to make his second attempt at leaving London. Karl accompanied him this time. They took a sturdy carriage to the harbor. The streets were more calming. The London fog had lifted a little.

When the carriage arrived at the docks, Felix felt some anxiety. The ride at sea would be horrid. Karl assured Felix while helping him get his luggage aboard, "Try to sleep in the cabin. I happened to talk to the doctor before accompanying you and told him of your sea sickness. He gave me something to give to you. Hopefully it helps." Karl handed Felix a small vial of medicine, "It should settle your stomach for a night at least. I would only drink it when the waves are at their worst."

"Danke." Felix pocketed it. Karl then left him. The ship was the same one he arrived in London on. The familiar steward rolled his eyes as Felix boarded. The boat's sway at the dock made Felix lean on his leg every once in a while unexpectedly. He found a cabin straight away to lay down as his leg ached. Once the boat sailed, he knew it was going to be the longest three days of his life.

~~~

Hamburg, a few days later:

In a break from much traveling of my own, I was once again visiting my home in Hamburg, spending time with my parents and practicing violin of course.

After a long session, I decided to go out for a walk. The weather was grey, but decent for a stroll. As I wandered the street, seeing the usual locals, giving a wave, I bumped into someone. They nearly fell and snapped in frustration, "Please watch where you are going."

I turned to see a well dressed man in London styled attire. It was Felix. He seemed rather in desperation, holding some letters of address. I asked, "Is everything alright?"

"I'm trying to find a place of stay," his tone became kinder upon recalling my face, "I've been to three different inns and they're all full. They keep referring me to another. I injured my leg in a carriage accident a few weeks ago and I must rest it."

"There is room at my place of stay. I am currently visiting my parents' home but I shall ask them to be sure it's alright." I gestured to him to follow. Felix asked as he trailed behind, "What is your name again? I know we have met in Berlin."

"Ferdinand," said I, "I remember that you are Felix." I stopped at my house. Felix looked at it with a strange pang of shock. I noticed, "Is it suitable for you? I assure you it's a humble home."

"Oh, it's alright." He followed me in the house. Oddly he looked all around studying the walls and halls. I told him, "I shall be right back." I left to go find my parents. Felix stood in the main entrance taking in every sense and remnant that the house gave him. The faint memory of the structure and style sparked his deepest, oldest memories.

I found my father reading in the study. He looked up as I entered. I explained, "An acquaintance of mine by the name of Felix is looking for a place to stay for the night. May he stay with us?"

"We have room. Of course." My father answered, getting up from his seat. We both walked back to the entryway to find Felix in a state of reflection. He snapped out of it upon seeing us. My father gladly greeted Felix as a guest, "You are certainly welcome to stay Herr..."

"Bartholdy." Felix answered. I tilted my head at Felix not knowing the choice of name. Felix didn't explain, but then it made sense to me. I remembered his family used to live in this home, which explained his wandering eyes. My father would be asking loads of questions if he knew Felix was a Mendelssohn.

"I don't think I know a family by the name of Bartholdy around. Nice to meet you." My father already seemed skeptical as Felix continued to gaze about the house.

202

Felix smiled kindly and thanked us both so very much for the accommodation. My father then asked after initial greetings, "Where is it you are from?"

"Berlin. I've had a hash trying to get home. Between being stuck in London and finding places to stay, it's been a trip." He gave a sigh of relief.

"Why don't I show you to the guest room." I suggested. Felix followed me up the stairs. When we came to the small guest room, he smiled upon entering. It was a warming smile. I told him, "Settle here. Then, if you'd like, we will have some dinner in about a half hour."

"Dankeschön." Felix nodded and shut the door behind him. Upon being alone in the room, he gave a breath of nostalgia. This little room had been his. The feeling rather made him want to get to Berlin even more. He missed his parents and siblings.

As I tuned my violin in my room, I noticed Felix by the door. I gestured to him to come in. He noticed my violin had a good tone. I told him, "It's from 1742."

"Oh nice." He commented, "You definitely deserve such a fine instrument as you have such skill."

"Danke. I know you have much skill at a bit of everything musically. The orchestra I was in played your Midsummer Night's Dream Overture. I know you've written other things. Have you got anything new? I ask as I am trying my hand at composition."

"Ja, I'll get something I've been penning." Felix went to his room then brought back the string quartet he had started. I looked at it and started playing the violin part. Felix smiled then said, "I don't want to tell too many people but I've dedicated it to someone back in Berlin."

"Is it a girl?" I asked the obvious as love was the usual reason for dedicating a work. Felix blushed a little then explained, "The first two notes are the first two letters of her name."

"It is a well thought idea." I said. We both spoke much, officially getting to know one another. Felix mentioned, "After I leave, I definitely want to keep in touch. I will write to you."

"Most definitely. You must tell me how this Betty will like the string quartet." I chuckled. After friendly chatter, we went downstairs to have dinner. He sat next to me at the table and met the rest of the family. Much was discussed. I asked Felix, "What took you to London? I've heard it's quite foggy and the air is bad."

"I have some friends there and Scotland intrigued me." He answered. My father budded in, "Since you were in London, you must have heard of the concert halls performing some new music of a young man. I think his name happened to be Felix."

"Oh really..." Felix nodded, "I did hear new works of many composers. I like Moscheles' music."

"This chap had been mentioned in the newspapers a few times though. Mendelssohn was the last name. He's been quite the talk of London in the music scene. I am wondering if he's from the family that used to live here. The father worked for the Mendelssohn Bank I believe. Years ago they fled this city without a trace. I just wondered what became of them." He eyed Felix in wonder.

"Well," Felix sipped some wine, "I would not know," he then veered the conversation, "So Ferdinand, I'd like to hear some more violin from you before the evening draws to a close."

"Of course." I said, "I'll go get it now while you all get seated in the parlor." I set my napkin down and went upstairs in excitement.

Everyone else sat in the parlor with some drinks. I joined them with my violin and stood in the front of the room near the crackling fireplace. My father suggested I play some sonatas of Haydn. I chose some of the adagios for a calm evening. Felix watched with much attention. The ruddy, earthy sound of the violin gave emotion through the calmness of the room.

After a few movements of select sonatas, my father turned to Felix, "Surely you play? My son said you have an ear for music."

"I do take violin lessons. I'm no virtuoso, but I manage." Felix mentioned. I eagerly handed him my instrument. He stayed seated and held it to his chin. He bowed the melody to a Mozart sonata. Upon the humble end, my father stated, "Surely you play in an orchestra in the least. You play as any professional."

"Every now and again." Felix didn't want to give away too much. My father implied to Felix, "Well if you put your skills to much use, surely we will be hearing of Felix Bartholdy in the papers."

Felix shrugged then handed back my violin. It was late by the time we were done with music, so everyone retired to bed.

The next morning Felix packed straight away to leave. He did stay for breakfast and was ever so thankful for the nice stay. He gave farewells to each of us. My father, he thanked lastly. Upon doing so, he whispered to Felix, "Auf Wiedersehen Herr Mendelssohn."

Felix gave a shy smile then left.

~ ~ ~

Felix found a carriage and continued on the last stretch home. He felt a sense of cured homesickness while passing through familiar areas. In no time, the carriage halted on Leipziger Straße.

Felix disembarked the carriage with his luggage. Lea came out of the house first to help and gave him urgent hugs and kisses. He blushed in embarrassment as passerby smiled upon the heartwarming welcome home. Felix begged, "Please Mutter can we go inside."

"I'm sorry, I have not seen your face in months! I've been worried sick! The news of the accident gave me a near heart attack!" She hugged him protectively, "Klingemann wrote to us of the doctor's instructions. You are to be straight to bed, I do not want you to take any risks."

"My leg is much better than it was a few weeks ago. I should be fine walking around a bit." He headed into the house with Lea.
The next to greet him were Paul and Rebecka. Felix was fazed at how much they had grown within the time he was gone. Rebecka was eighteen and Paul was sixteen. It all seemed to dawn on him how old they were.

He nearly jumped at the sight of Fanny, standing near the doorway. Her arms were crossed. As were Abraham's as he stood beside her. They obviously weren't the happiest. Felix couldn't believe his twenty four year old sister was married. She was a Hensel now, living with Wilhelm in one of the guest houses at the estate.

Felix went to greet her. She gave a hesitant hug, which was light at first then grew tighter upon realizing she had truly missed him. Felix sniffled, "I'm so sorry I couldn't be there for you at your wedding. I almost had the music done, but Karl wanted me to rest rather than compose."

"I made the music myself when I knew yours wouldn't make it."

"That's my sister." Felix chimed feeling a bit more chipper about it. He then turned to his father, who still had his arms crossed. He bluntly stated, "Let's get you to bed and get you off that leg. We also need to talk." He grabbed a copy of an English newspaper. Felix knew what the conversation was going to be already. He went to his room and sorted his luggage then laid in bed. Abraham let him get some much needed rest.

After an hour or so, Abraham knocked at Felix's door. He walked in as he still heard him deeply snoring. Felix was out like a candle. Abraham tapped on him. Felix jolted awake from the deep slumber. He gave a sigh as Abraham pulled up a chair beside the bed to talk. The London papers were in his hands. Felix stayed silent. He couldn't walk away or make an excuse now.

Abraham began, "How is it the carriage crashed? Did you tell the coachman to drive fast? I know how you are in a rush on such matters. You can not rush travel. You're lucky that you didn't get more hurt."

"It's not entirely my fault." Felix confessed. Abraham held a letter, "Klingemann talked to the coachman and he said you grabbed the reins from him."

"A large coach was about to run into us." Felix sat up. Abraham then opened a newspaper, "You also completely ignored my request on your name. You didn't even bother to add Bartholdy!"

"Please I have only been home an hour. Why can't you just be happy to see me home and alive. You haven't even hugged me." Felix gave his father a sad glance. A bit dramatic. Abraham gave his son a stern glance. Felix knew his talk wouldn't ease his father's frustration. Abraham sighed, "What am I to do with you. I gave you the means to have a successful trip, but you've already gotten hurt. You haven't even gone to Italy yet where Ignaz nor Klingemann will be able to watch over you."

"Well I think I'm learning my ways about. I'll be more careful."
Felix implied.

"You're not continuing your trip until winter ceases." Abraham bluntly stated as he got up and left, shutting the door. Felix grunted in disappointment.
~~~

## [2]

Within the next coming months, as the wedding anniversary neared, Felix started assigning parts for the little operetta he planned out. His siblings and a few other friends such as Eduard Devierent had parts. He also wanted to include the newest member of the family, Wilhelm.

As Felix took his horse for a wintry ride in the gardens, he found Wilhelm outside he and Fanny's home. Upon seeing Felix riding the horse, Wilhelm went to him in question, "Does Abraham approve of you riding? I don't think you should be risking getting your leg hurt again."

"I'm not standing on it, besides in a few weeks it will be fully healed."

"My point exactly." Wilhelm put his hands on his hips in sternness. Felix dismantled from his horse. He then told Wilhelm, "I'm assigning parts for the operetta. I want you to have a role."

"Are you sure you want me? I'm quite tone deaf."

"Oh please, everyone has some singing ability. Besides, the Mayor is only one note. All you have to sing is one long note." Felix encouraged.

"I am speaking in honesty."

"Just one note." Felix held the sheet music, still trying to encourage. Wilhelm took the copy, "Alright..." He looked at the sheet music, not having a clue what the writing meant. His wife would need to help him with this.

~~~

When late December arrived, preparations for the party were in place. Felix left Fanny in charge of the operetta rehearsals.

208

On the day of, she warned Felix, "Do not laugh when my husband sings. He is trying. I know you."

"I won't, I know he's trying. It's one note, how bad can it be?" Felix questioned. Fanny gave him a stern face. Felix still shrugged knowing Wilhelm could sing a note.

There was much fun with food and drink when guests arrived. Abraham and Lea had invited basically everyone. Zelter showed up. He appeared very aged from the last time Felix saw him. He spoke to Felix of the Bach performances as they were still popular. He mentioned some alterations he made to the arrangement. Felix didn't care in the moment and continued greeting other guests.

Reitz wasn't anywhere to be seen, but the Pistor family came. Felix tried to make his way towards Betty, but Mr. Pistor came in front of him, speaking of every subject he could think of, trying to keep Felix away from her. Betty noticed Felix as he waved. She glanced at him, but nothing more.

When it came time to perform the operetta, Felix sat at a chair to conduct as to rest his foot. Everyone took seats to have a listen. It began smoothly and pleased his parents. Felix flipped through pages, using a baton to direct. Then Wilhelm sang his note…

The held note that was to carry through for a long while sounded so shaky. His voice swayed back and forth trying to find the right note. Felix couldn't contain himself as it tickled his ears. He covered his mouth with the hand he wasn't conducting with, trying anything to hold his giggles.

The audience behind him noticed he was acting strange. Fanny eyed him, discreetly shaking her head. Whinnies left Felix's mouth. A few of the listeners gave way to snickers. Wilhelm finished his note, looking down in embarrassment. The operetta soon ended with claps. Everyone still enjoyed the music. The party was a success.

~~~~

A few days after the big wedding anniversary, the year reached 1830. In the midst of everything going on, he realized he had not kept in touch with Charlotte or Ignaz. He wrote to Charlotte explaining everything that had happened in the past few months:

*January 6th, 1830*

*Dear Madam,*

*I hardly know how to ask for your pardon for my sins, for I have a load of them on my conscience; yet were I to trouble you with a string of excuses, you might think that a new sin....These last few days have been the only quiet ones since we parted. First, there was our Highland tour in anything but favorable weather, bad roads, worse conveyances, still worse inns and landlords, and the richest and most picturesque scenery....Then I returned to London with the misfortune of being thrown from a gig, and was obliged to be six weeks in bed and two months in my room. At last I was able to travel home; but my injured foot, which was still very weak, made the journey both painful and dangerous...when I did reach home, I was condemned to another imprisonment of several weeks...the happiest and most disagreeable days of my life are following each other in rapid succession. Of course I feel rather upset by all this. Witness this careless and confused letter; yet I would not put off writing lest I should add to my sins. Please give my regards to Ignaz and wish him well.*
*Yours truly,*

*F. M. B.*

~~~~

Later that day, Felix paid a visit to the Sing Akademie to catch up on the latest things there. Rietz had missed Felix very much. He surprised Rietz by sneaking up behind him during his time of violin practice.

After Rietz struck a final chord, Felix clapped, causing his violin teacher to jump around, "You're back!" They instantly went into conversation to catch up.

Felix then found Zelter heading for his office. Upon seeing Felix, he invited him in to show him his own edits to the Bach oratorio. Felix was skeptical of the matter, knowing his teacher had to find some way to 'correct' Felix's work. After skimming a freshly copied score, the adjustments Zelter penciled rather made Felix's arrangement more of a hash. They quarreled a bit over it, but in the end, Felix was done, he decided that it was time to move onto better things.

The early spring brought a dusting of snow, soon to melt in the upcoming weeks. Felix had now turned twenty-one. The growth in age made him feel more inclined to plan his next trip abroad for the spring, after the weather deemed favorable.

~~~

Once again to Wilhelm's disapproval, Felix was out riding his horse in the gardens. Felix felt confident as a horseman and gave Wilhelm the excuse that the horse needed exercise.

After trotting about, Felix returned the horse to the stable then headed back in the house. He went to his room to grab something. A pile of manuscripts were laid neatly at his desk. It was the string quartet for Betty. He carefully rolled the pile up and wrapped a fine red ribbon around it, tying a bow.

Felix then took off his riding coat and put on a black London frock coat. Refined, but not too fancy. He wore his top hat as well. The outfit looked fashionable for cold weather. He then took the nicely ribboned music and headed out to the Pistor home.

Upon arriving, he knocked at the front door. No answer. He tried again. Nothing. Felix went to the gate.

There was a lock on it. As he was bracing himself to climb it, the front door opened. It was the maid. Felix went to her and she blocked him, "Mr. Pistor does not want you here."

"Please, I need to talk to Betty." He walked closer. The maid glared, not budging. Felix saw Betty walking by in the entryway. He called to her and forced his way past the maid. The maid grabbed his coat, trying to prevent his entry, but he called to Betty, "I need to speak with you."

Betty turned to him in confusion. She gestured to the maid to release him. Felix then walked up to her with the music. He noticed the sound of much chatter in the parlor a few rooms into the house. Betty appeared occupied, but Felix handed her the wrapped music. She took it, not saying a word. Felix then explained, "It's a string quartet I've dedicated to you. It shall be played at one of the salons. I wrote your initials B. P. on the cover. I missed you, so much has happened in the past few months." He quickly pecked her cheek.

The maid gave the most baffled expression. Betty gave an expression of horror as well. Felix asked in a worried tone, "What is the matter-" he jumped as someone caught him by the shoulders from behind. The person spoke in a half joking, half serious tone, "It seemed you shall have to make that little quartet dedicated to B.R. instead." The man who spoke forced Felix around to face him. It was a man he did not know, but he went on speaking, "You must be that Felix I hear much about. Mr. Pistor warned me of you."

"Warned? I don't understand." Felix looked towards Betty. She held up her hand. Placed in elegance on her finger was an engagement ring. The little white diamonds sparkled. Felix stared at it in shock. Betty explained, "I am soon to be Mrs. Rudorff."

Felix looked back to Herr Rudorff, who was clenching the arms of Felix's coat. He stated, "I am sorry that we couldn't meet on a proper occasion. Betty's side family is visiting to celebrate my proposal.

They speak some about you. I don't think they will enjoy knowing that you came and gave Betty a kiss."

"First of all, I did not know she was engaged," Felix defended himself, "Secondly, it was a light kiss." As Felix tried to lessen his mistake, Herr Rudorff told the maid, "Please go get Mr. Pistor."

The maid hurried off. Rudorff, after instructing the maid, coughed. It sounded like an ill cough. He informed Felix, "I'm not sick, I just got over a bad illness."

"Well you still hacked all over me!" Felix hoped whatever he had didn't spread to him. Suddenly Mr. Pistor rushed to them. He was infuriated, "Felix! What on earth are you doing here!?"

"I am sorry, I came to visit but it was all a mistake." Felix tried to step away from Rudorff, but he wouldn't unhand him. Betty finally told Ruldorff, "Let him go. I don't think he will be stopping by here after this." She pried one of his clenched fists from Felix's coat. Rudorff eyed Felix once more before releasing him.

Felix turned for the door, but Mr. Pistor now stopped him. He grabbed the string quartet from Betty and shoved it back in Felix's hands. Felix held it in sadness. Mr. Pistor sighed at his somber expression, but pushed him out the door, slamming it behind him.

Upon returning home, Felix went straight to his room and flopped into bed. He threw the string quartet at his desk and sobbed. The day wasted away with tears.

~~~

The next week, Felix sat at the breakfast table, still in a depressed state. As Lea, Abraham, Rebecka and Paul gladly ate, Lea noticed Felix taking a few small bites. She looked at him closer, "Are you alright? You seem a bit sick."

Felix shrugged, not noticing anything but his sorrow. Abraham looked at him, "I know it's hard when someone you like is to be married, but you must look to other things. Remember the doctor said your leg is completely healed."

"Soon I shall be leaving for Italy." Felix felt slightly more optimistic. Lea still seemed worried. It was her motherly instincts, "I still think something is wrong."

"I feel fine." Felix stated. He left the breakfast table. Most of his food still remained on the plate. He went to his room and began looking at maps of Austria and Italy. He penciled some routes he wanted to take to visit Salzburg and Vienna. In Italy he was looking forward to Venice and Rome. As he did some planning, he felt a mild headache. He thought it to be the reminiscences from his sadness over Betty.

When dinner came, the family ate together again. This time Lea knew Felix wasn't in a healthy state. His face appeared tired and pale as his eyes watered. Every now and again he covered a dry cough. Abraham spoke up to him, "I think your Mutter is right in saying something isn't right. You need to go rest in bed. I think the early spring is causing a cold."

Felix listened and left the table, still leaving the food at the plate. Though it was early evening, he laid in bed to huddle from sudden cold chills. His body begged for sleep. Upon shutting his eyes, he instantly fell into a deep slumber.

When waking in an extremely groggy state, he shivered as the blanket was moved away from him. He could hardly lift his tired eyes as he felt a hand against his forehead. In the moment he noticed he was in a cold sweat and felt terribly ill.

He opened his eyes the best he could to see a doctor standing at his bedside. It was the same one that had come to check on his leg.

Just last week he determined his leg healed, but now he was back under different circumstances. Lea peeked into the room, staying by the door, "How is he?"

"He is catching a fever. I noticed a rash on his arms. It's starting to develop on his neck and body. I fear that he's caught measles," the doctor stated while inspecting him, "It's very contagious. Be sure to keep your distance."

Lea left to inform the family not to come in the room. Felix felt a wave of disappointment. He was too tired to express it. His Italy plans would be pushed back. Just when things were looking positive…

Felix spoke with exhaustion, "How long will this last?"

"You could be sick a week or so. It's only the beginning of it," the doctor explained, "The fever might worsen and the rash will become more apparent. You'll be very tired." He grabbed a handkerchief to wipe the sweat from his face.

After tending to him the best he could, he tucked the blanket over him to help his chilled state. Felix gave up on his worried thoughts on everything and went to sleep.

~~~

A week Later in Dorpat Estonia:

In mid-April I returned to my current flat in Dorpat after a long day of rehearsals. I was tired after such a day, but came to my rooms to find a letter waiting for me. It was from Felix. I was eager to read it and opened it:

Berlin, 13th April 1830


Ferdinand David!

I begin this letter to tell that I am not writing, but am forced to go by way of dictation. My terrible luck has continued as I have been stuck by measles. I am currently recovering after a dreadful week, but am not allowed to read nor write in my time of rest. Yet I have much been wanting to write to you. I've found much around Berlin a bit different in the few months I've returned. Everyone, family and those at the Akademie have missed me so. My violin teacher, Reitz, especially so. Though as I have been gone, I feel so less attached to the engagements of Berlin. Zelter made many alterations to the Bach oratorio in my absence. The popularity of the work is still well. Yet the winter brings quietness in the concert halls. I wish you well in your time in Dorpat.
Your friend,


Felix Mendelssohn Bartholdy.


Postscription

With the letter, I am sending you that string quartet. In all of my horror in returning home, I came to find Betty in engagement. Though it saddened my state, I am happy for her. I still mean to dedicate the quartet to her, but wanted to send it to you as I know you'll get some performances. After my illness is gone, I plan to travel to Italy as I am craving for another adventure.


-F. M. B.

# Chapter X: Abroad Again

Mendelssohn symphony 5, 1st movement  [1]
Beethoven Sonata no. 8, 2nd movement [2]
Beethoven Symphony no. 3, 3rd movement, Scherzo [3]

## [1]

In the full spring morning, Felix woke, feeling in complete freshness. His fever and illness had lifted. He sat up in bed, enjoying the feeling of good health after such a horrendous week. A tray of eggs, bacon and orange juice sat on top of the nightstand. He took it and had a well made breakfast in bed. It made him feel like royalty.

Also on the tray were some letters and notes. He looked through them to catch up on what he missed in the past couple of weeks. Most of them were from friends, wishing him to get well.

One of the folded letters had a more official appearance. It was from the University of Berlin. Felix opened it and read it through carefully as it was quite lengthy. It gave him mixed thoughts. They were offering him a position as head of the music department. It sounded like a good deal to have such a career, knowing it a rare opportunity for a twenty-one year old. Yet there was still so much he wanted to see before settling into a job. Italy consumed his plans.

Felix threw the job offer aside and penned a decline. He then finished breakfast and encouraged himself out of bed. His legs felt stiff from such a long bed rest, so he stretched a while then dressed for the day. It felt nice to look decent after being so far under the weather.

He then went downstairs to have his job decline sent. As Felix handed it off to the servant, Abraham walked in and questioned, "Who is that for?"

"The Universität." Felix answered as he gestured to the servant to go.

"What did they want?"

"They offered me a position as head of the music department."

"Oh! What a surprise. That's quite an accomplishment. I now have much hope for your welfare." Abraham stood proud.

"I declined." Felix didn't dare look at him. Abraham lifted his son's head by the chin, "What in the hell is wrong with you?"

"I am to leave for Weimar in a short while. Then I'll be to Vienna, Italy, France then back to London. Why get an official position now? Plus I am near to finishing a symphony. I'm inclined to have it performed for a festival in Augsburg." Felix was referring to the event the 300 the anniversary of the Augsburg Confession. The directors organizing the festival were seeking out music.

"Are you sure that they will take it? With your name? For that festival? You know how people view us in concern of such subjects. I've told you time and time again, I advise you to get rid of the Mendelssohn name."

"I am in assurance that they'll use it. I based the last movement on some Hymns that would be appropriate for the occasion." Felix tried to justify. Abraham shook his head in disapproval, "They won't care about the Hymns when they see your signature."

"Why are you so obsessed with covering up the name!?" Felix began to rage, "I know our family has a history, but I view it as my own name and nothing more! Everyone has a name. I don't want to be under a fraud name!"

Abraham quickly met his talk with a smack. He clutched the collar of his coat with both hands, nearly lifting him, "You do not understand what your Mutter and I have dealt with in order for you and your siblings to have a good upbringing. Your disrespect for that name will be your downfall if you don't learn to accept it."

Felix stared at him, frozen in shock. Abraham's furious eyes penetrated into his soul. They were both silent for at least a minute. Some servants peeked from around the corner of the hall at the commotion. Paul happened to be eavesdropping by the stairs. Abraham took no note of any of them. Felix glanced up at Paul peering from the staircase's balcony.

Felix's veering attention prompted Abraham to demand, "Look at me!" He jerked his coat, "from now on, before you make any more foolish moves, you will completely adopt the Bartholdy name."

"No!" Felix blurted loudly in English. Abraham ordered back, "Wir sprechen Deutsch in diesem Haus!"

"I am going to speak what language I want. You're the one that taught me!" Felix continued in posh English. Abraham was done. He released him, "You're going to bed. Obviously that sickness prevented you from getting good rest." He straightened Felix's coat. Felix froze again. Abraham pointed towards the stairs, "Go now! Get out of my sight!"

Felix obeyed him in that matter. The argument made him feel quite tired, so he laid in bed. Unexpectedly he slept through many hours as his emotions needed to catch up on rest. Still, he was determined to keep the Mendelssohn name.

~~~

After penning the last bit of the symphony Felix intended for the festival in Augsburg, he made arrangements to meet with the directors. He sent out some notes.

Before putting them in the post, Abraham forced him to sign the letters as 'Felix Bartholdy', to ensure that the directors would at least agree to meet.

Within the week, a letter arrived, instructing Felix to meet at the Konzerthaus. In eagerness he took his symphony score, which he signed as 'Felix Mendelssohn-Bartholdy'.

Upon arriving at the Konzerthaus lobby, he was greeted in all politeness by a group of four directors. Yet it felt rather shallow as they got a good look at him. Two of the directors were middle aged and two were a bit older than Felix. The last one was in old age. He seemed to be the one with the most say.

Their speech began to indicate that they were only tolerating the meeting. One of the middle aged ones looked at Felix in disgust, sneering something in a whisper to the director beside him. He was obviously trying to offend Felix. The young composer did not let it faze him though. He was sure the score would convince them.

Felix handed the music to the oldest director. The others circled around to get a glimpse. Each one nodded and whispered as it was flipped through. Their expressions lightened slightly while examining the fourth movement, which included the well known hymns that corresponded with the festival. Much also was inspired by his stay at Coed Du Hall, in the depths of the Welsh mine.

After inspecting the score, they fell silent. A rather awkward silence. Felix waited for a response. Finally the oldest came forward, "I am distraught to say that we find the music..." the director searched for his words,
"Too dry."

"Please, I'll fix the music," Felix began to feel the sting of rejection. One of the younger directors further explained, "We don't think the attendees want music from someone of your... background." He bluntly pointed to his signature of Mendelssohn.

Felix felt his confidence leave him as they shoved the score back in his hands and walked away. He had been rejected. Whether the music was truly 'dry' or not, his father was right all along.

~~~~

Felix trudged through the front door of the house. He didn't bother letting the servant take his coat. Abraham was in the parlor, reading. He saw Felix storm in the hall. Abraham sighed, setting the book on his lap, "Felix! Parlor. Now."

Felix paused at the stairs, gave a sigh, then turned around. He entered the parlor in silence. Abraham adjusted his spectacles, "May I need to ask how it went?"

"They thought the music was 'too dry'." Felix muttered.

"And?"

"And because of my 'background'." Felix mumbled in irritation.

"Did I not warn of such an outcome?"

"But it wasn't fair! They were judging me on things that I can not control. I can't change who my family is!" He retorted.

"That's why you need to use the Bartholdy name!" Abraham nearly threw his book at Felix. Felix stood without a word for a minute then finally huffed, "That's it. I leave for Weimar tomorrow. Early morning. If you need me, I'll be packing."

Abraham shook himself in agitation, turning back to his reading. He did not like his son's consistent relentlessness. Maybe it was a good thing to get him out of the house and far away.

Felix packed up in haste as the morning could not come soon enough. He couldn't take the sight of Berlin anymore. The music folder he put together contained much of his work, but he left the freshly composed symphony out. Instead, he shoved it in a drawer where it would be forgotten; never to be performed. At least not in his lifetime.

~~~

Felix headed to Weimar the next day. He felt refreshed upon leaving. The longing pull of adventure tugged at his determination. He planned to pay a much wanted visit to Goethe's home, which he had not seen since 1821.

It was Sunday morning. The early hour rendered grey and cloudy, but later the sun burst forth, giving light to the day. In the outskirts surrounding Weimar, there were a few villages. Many were dressed in their best attire as they were coming out of the Sunday church services. The fresh smell of tulips filled the air.

As the open droshky drove on from a quick break, Felix found himself a bundle of flowers to enjoy as if on a pleasure ride through the country.

The air was fine so he set his hat and cloak with his luggage. The beautiful light blue pattern of his waistcoat looked ravishing as he held some lilies-of-the-valley. He felt confident, traveling completely solo. Many passersby and the coachman conveyed a sense of envy at such a free spirited youth. (At least in Felix's mind.)

The whole day he enjoyed without composing a single bar of music. A rarity. He did though pen about the day, describing it as;

*A delicious day, one soon not to forget.*

When arriving in Weimar, the city was more charming than he remembered. He spent some time riding an open carriage through the park as well as walking around the city.

Everything was lively with carriages in the streets and people strolling the park. A few young couples were enjoying lovely picnics under trees and in the sunshine.

After using up the day, wandering about, he took a cab to Goethe's. The house was as he remembered from his twelfth year. Still elegant and inspiring. A servant escorted him inside, leading him to the dining area. There, a table of four guests sat. There were two ladies and two children. Felix took an open chair next to a lady who gave him a glance of curiosity.

She set down her glass of white wine to say something, but before she could speak, Goethe entered the room. His entrance gave Felix a sense of anticipation. The appearance of the old man had not changed much, but his eyes and expression showed his tiredness.

Goethe silently took the chair at the end of the table, close to Felix. Everyone gave their host a questionable glance. He continued to not talk and began eating. Everyone shrugged and ate, talking amongst themselves. Felix noticed the poet eyeing him closely. He didn't understand his reasoning for such a mood, but concluded that he was testing his demeanor.

Dinner looked well with schnitzel and potatoes. The lady sitting beside Felix finally got to talk, "My name is Ottilie, I am Herr Goethe's daughter-in-law. You are Felix?"

"Ja." He looked across the table as Ottilie introduced the older lady, "That is my mother, Ulrike and those two boys are Walther and Wolfgang. They are my sons, Goethe's grandchildren."

"Pleasure to meet you." Felix smiled. Ottilie then fell into a whisper, "Goethe speaks so much of you. He waited every second for your arrival."

"Oh, I'm glad I could make it. I plan to stay a day or two." Felix inquired. Upon hearing that, Goethe turned to Felix.

He finally broke his silence, "I insist that you should stay longer. There is much to catch up on my friend. You have grown so much in maturity and refinement. I would like time for a painter I know to come and make your portrait. I'm trying to get up to date portraits of my acquaintances. I invited the artist to come in a fortnight. Please, stay."

Goethe's tired, aged eyes suddenly became that of youthful expression. Having now watched the happy and bright young gentlemen, it paused his aging in a mental sense. Goethe wanted him to stay much longer than Felix intended.

Everyone at the table noticed how much Felix's presence lifted Goethe's mood, which wasn't a normal thing. Hardly anyone gave him such joy as he expressed in the moment. Felix felt more at ease after he spoke and answered his question, "I shall have to see what my weeks bring."

Ulrike then suggested, "You should accompany Ottilie and I to Tiefurt and Berka tomorrow before dinner. I would very much like you to do so. We are going to stroll the gardens."

"Of course." Felix answered. Goethe enticed Felix, "Yet before you walk with them, I know you will be playing some piano after breakfast for me?"

"Ja." Felix noticed his day becoming booked already. Since that was the case, he told everyone, "I think I shall sleep so I can be well rested for the busy day ahead." He stood and a maid showed him to his guest room.

~~~

The next day, the early morning was calm. Felix sat alone at the dining table. A tired maid came in and set a plate of eggs and hot cakes in front of him. She was not used to such an early riser. The strong oolong tea she poured for him woke her senses a bit. Felix thanked her much.

An hour later, around six, Goethe walked in to find Felix finishing up his last bit of eggs and tea.

He joined him at the table, "You're quite a morning dove."

"Got to make the most of the day." Felix sipped his second cup of oolong. Goethe asked as the maid brought his plate and coffee, "Does not coffee suit the morning better?"

"My time in London has acquired my taste for strong tea to wake me. Coffee is good on occasion though. I enjoy demitasse." Felix mentioned.

As Goethe ate, they spoke of many subjects. After he finished his plate, the poet encouraged, "Let's go to the music room. I want to hear a few new compositions of yours. There's much music I've not been able to enjoy in your time away. I am in assurance that you've improved over the years. I'm desiring to hear it all."

"I shall." Felix set his napkin down. They both went to the piano in the room next door. Felix grabbed some sheet music from his folder. He brought the three Welsh pieces he had composed for the Taylor daughters. Upon listening, Goethe couldn't help but smile as he sat in a chair near the singing instrument.

After playing the pieces, Felix spoke about his trip in the highlands and Wales with much eagerness. In listening, Goethe commented, "You have been to so many places and you have much on your mind to speak. It amazes me as you are not yet thirty, let alone even halfway into your twenties."

Felix shrugged and blushed in the matter, trying to keep his polite composure. He tended to carry about in subjects of interests. Goethe checked the time, "It is nearing noon. The girls should be coming to take you to Tiefurt. We will have to continue the music later. I told them you are not to go to Berka."

"Why not?" Felix tilted his head. Goethe chuckled and straightened the young one's coat, "There is a very pretty girl there. I don't want you plunging into misery."

Felix shrugged, but went with the old man's opinions. He stood from the piano and headed towards the entryway where he found Ottilie and Ulrike. Ulrike had a basket of lunch. They took a carriage to Tiefurt, a large manor house with beautiful gardens. They enjoyed the good spring weather. Most of the afternoon hours were spent observing the birds and flowers.

After a small picnic they returned to Goethe's home. Goethe had invited a few others for dinner and music afterwards. Felix of course was musical entertainment. He played pieces of Weber, his own music from the British Isles and others. The night was full of dance and song.

Goethe returned to his room at nine o'clock for the night. The rest of the party then began the real frolics and went on until the midnight hour.

~~~~

The next afternoon, Goethe enticed Felix to the piano again, begging to hear music he had not been able to listen to in so long. Felix was obliged and decided to do something a little special. He told him, "Since you aspire to hear the classics, I must play them in chronological order and give you the history of such subjects, beginning with Bach."

Felix went straight into a fugue then a few chorales. Goethe smiled at the sounds of a musical mathematician filling the air; each note lining up in perfect harmony. Bach knew the ways of making music. After Felix finished another fugue, he gave Goethe an earful of history, "Bach had twenty children, he also wrote over a thousand works. Much of it is still being discovered."

"I guess he was busy." Goethe replied.

"I do enjoy Bach's arrangements of Vivaldi's music, but I know not much of Vivaldi. He's quite obscure." Felix pecked at a few notes of a fugal subject, originally of Vivaldi.

Next he played a few sonatas of Haydn and Mozart. He spoke between each piece, informing Goethe of it all. Goethe was quite overwhelmed as it was a lot of information along with the complexity of the music.
Felix enjoyed every bit of it.

*(Felix playing to Goethe)*

Felix's admiration for the history of his art made his music differ from the modern composers of the time. Most were keen on moving forward in the age of Romanticism. The past was to be left and music was to move on. Yet such ideals began to change after Felix revived Bach's orchestra music.

Though Felix wrote in the Romantic style, he was a renaissance man at heart. He wanted his compositions to stay true to melody with well maintained harmony. Influence of the classical era gave balance to his work.

Sometimes his interest in history took the best of him in the eyes of fellow composers. Some thought his music did not express his innermost feelings. Felix did convey his emotions, but it was in part of his upbringing in high society that caused him to be more reserved. The rage such as Beethoven wrote wasn't a factor in Mendelssohn's way of composing. Though Felix gladly played and conducted the music of Beethoven, his own music conveyed otherwise. At least through most of his happy life.

"Now I will play a symphony of Beethoven." Felix put his hands happily at the keys. Goethe groaned a bit, "May we skip Beethoven for today? I am not in such a mood. I think you've covered everything otherwise."

"But we can't skip Beethoven if you want me to play you a full history of music. Beethoven is a must on such subjects."

"Alright. One movement though." Goethe accepted. Felix gladly continued and chose the first movement of the well known fifth symphony. When striking the motif, the old man jolted at the fearful emotions the shapely music conveyed. He had not heard such a piece before. The symphony by then was nearly twenty years old, so Felix assumed that Goethe had to know it. Goethe didn't always keep up with the times.

After finishing the piano arrangement, Felix turned to Goethe with a smile. The poet commented, "This music causes not emotion, only astonishment.

It is grandiose. It gives the feeling that the house might collapse. Imagine a group of men playing that."

Felix snickered a bit at the old man's shock of the classic piece. The poet stood and stated, "You speak so much of music, the history, the fundamentals and you play with etiquette. Why don't you use some of your energy to research other things such as science or mathematics?"

"Those things are fascinating, but they don't give way to my interests enough to make time for them. I have art and literature to widen my skills." Felix lightly played a c minor scale at the keys. Goethe became silent in an angered mood. Felix knew he caused upset as the grumpy man exited the room. It was his way of scolding Felix.

After a bit of silence, the piano continued with improvisation. The sweet sounding adagio echoed as if the piano itself were reminiscing its own regret. The apologetic music gradually drew Goethe back into the room, where he saw Felix playing, eyes closed whilst conveying his emotions at the keys.

Goethe walked up beside the piano, unable to be angry at such an innocent and aspiring young musician. The aged man needed to remember that he was once young and had different determinations as a writer.

When Felix made a closing perfect authentic cadence, he gave a sigh. He opened his eyes and jumped, not expecting Goethe to have come back. The poet commented, "You have enough. Hold on to what you have."

~~~

A full week passed and Felix had not left Goethe's company. The portrait artist wasn't to come until the next, giving reason for Goethe to keep Felix in his company. Each time Felix spoke to Ottilie of leaving, she requested a walk up and down the gardens, persuading him to stay longer. Goethe told her to do so. Felix had much determination to move on with his journey, but after the sincere requests, he felt he needed to stay a bit longer.

The days were filled with music and talk on every artistic and academic subject. It was a rarity in recent times for Goethe to invite guests to dinner and parties, but since Felix's arrival, the home was filled with acquaintances both young and old.

Goethe invited several well standing young ladies to introduce Felix to. Felix, though preferred to keep company with the poet, finding his wise words more interesting than the ladies eyeing him in frustration as he didn't induce conversation.

Eventually Goethe noticed his reluctance and told him in encouragement, "My young friend, you must join the ladies and make yourself agreeable to them."

"I'm much content speaking to you." Felix excused. Goethe's sigh to himself was apparent. The ladies held their glasses of wine, gazing at Felix with dreamy eyes, yet still with frustration. Felix didn't want to be thrown into their love speeches and flirts as their glances showed their desire.

Goethe was trying to help his friend find love and enjoyment with the company of other young persons, but Felix did not want to find love. He still had much to see and had not yet been to Italy.

Goethe grumbled about the young man's stubbornness to Ottilie, but she informed her father-in-law otherwise.

~~~~

The next week, the artist Goethe called finally arrived. He was very talkative and too much so. When he entered, he shook hands with Goethe, already plunging into conversation. Felix tried to speak up, but was outspoken. He did not catch the artist's name. The painter finally turned to Felix, "You must be the one Herr Goethe wants a portrait of. The light in this room is very feasible, let's get you a chair." He left to go find one.

When he returned, he set the chair in the lightest area and Felix sat down. The artist then grabbed his canvas and pastels, setting up a few paces in front of his subject. He then went to Felix and turned his head to face in a good position. Felix still didn't get a chance to speak as the artist's mouth rambled about getting the right pose for a perfect characterization.

After finally deciding what angle he wanted Felix to face, the artist went to his canvas. Felix patiently sat, trying not to move too much. Though the portrait felt like it was taking forever, Felix thought it good to get a current picture done.

The artist's running conversations didn't make the time any more pleasant. Goethe observed the art forming into a picture of much likeness. It came together and finished after what felt like another forever.

Goethe picked it up and smiled at the professional piece of art. Felix stood up and stretched from sitting in one position so long. He then checked out the portrait. To him the art was top notch, but in critique of his own appearance, he thought he appeared rather sulky in the expression.

After the artist was paid and on his way, Goethe strongly advised Felix to stay for dinner as he knew the young musician would be trying to make his leave. Felix agreed to stay one more night, but it had now been a fortnight since arriving. He needed to move on.

At dinner, it was quiet as it was only Goethe, Felix and Ottilie. No guests. Ulrike and the grandchildren were elsewhere for the evening. Felix savored the time as it was most likely to be the last with the poet. He knew that Goethe's age was up there and didn't expect a chance to be back anytime soon. It did give him much sadness, but he kept his outward appearance in all joy as not to fright his hosts. Yet Goethe knew Felix and could read him like a book, though he only had sparing company with him through his old years.

In many discreet attempts, Goethe begged Felix, "Why must you leave tomorrow? What more would you be losing by staying more? Bitte, stay longer."

"I have stayed far longer than my intention. By many days, weeks in fact." Felix ate the well made pasta. It was purposely made savory in an attempt to incline him not to leave. Ottilie made comments, supporting Goethe's wants, but not as strongly.

Goethe then stood and went to a cabinet nearby. He opened it and grabbed a book. It was a thick book. He came back to the table and handed it to Felix, "This is something for you."

Felix took it and read the cover. It was a copy of 'Faust', one of Goethe's best works. It would give him much to read on his travels. Felix opened the front cover and inside were some letters of introduction, if he needed any, and written on the inside cover was a special note:

*To my dear young friend F. M. B., mighty, yet delicate master of the piano. To remember the happy May days in your visit in 1830.*

*-J. W. Von Goethe.*

"Aww, Dankeschön." Felix smiled with all enthusiasm. Goethe smiled at seeing his friend so happy. He hoped the gift would entice him to stay longer, but after the well tasting food was consumed, Felix stood from his seat, "I must retire for the night. I need to rest well for tomorrow."

"Please," Goethe stood, "Play more music before you go to bed. I must hear some as I now will be suffering without such sounds." He nudged Felix towards the piano room. Felix told him in reluctance, "I do not want to be guilted into hours of improvising, I need sleep. I've played every night for you."

"Not just one tune?" Goethe's aged eyes swelled with water. Felix's heart ached at such a look. He gave a sigh, "One more, then no more."

The three of them sat in the music room and Felix brushed a slow Ab Major scale across the keys. He then looked to Goethe and Ottilie in the evening candlelight, catching his last happy moments with them. He gave way to a tiny sigh, turning to the instrument he had become well acquainted with in his lifetime.

[2]

The music was calm and warm. Bittersweet in a sense. The choice of Beethoven was not Goethe's first, but this piece did not have the harshness or raging, nor even the heroism. It was a different side of Beethoven. This was the feeling of the unforgivable and indescribable. Bitter longing. The hurt. Questioning the big picture of what could be or could have been.

The calmness in the light of the candles gave the sweet incense of fond memories. The days of childish innocence, before the changes of life. A remembrance that there once was happiness. After storms cease, the loss of love and reason begs the wisher to return to the peaceful days without a care. To take away all of the inhumane occurrences. Yet now knowing all that would be gone through, woe and sorrow, why bother with the thought of returning.

Though Felix's feelings differ much from Beethoven's reason for composing it. Beethoven was in his twenty-seventh year when he penned the sonata. Already by then he had much happen in his life with loss and heartbreak. On top of that, his hearing had begun to decline at that age, hindering his ever so promising success as a performer at the piano.

Though his career could have ended; and almost did at that. Instead, he took what he still had which was the will to compose. He scratched his prospects of piano virtuosity and put his energy into composition.

Despite all that happened, if things had gone the other way, Beethoven's music would have sounded a lot different.

Felix, on the other hand, was only twenty-one and had not gone through the trials that Beethoven had at that age. He still had a happy home to go back to, he still had his parents, his siblings were in good standing and he had many opportunities. Pure innocent happiness depicting nature flowed in Felix's music.

The calm second movement of the sonata though was a perfect choice for a perfect night. The natural and old keyboard's dry, earthy tone pleased the ears. As he went along the piece, he treated Goethe by lengthening various sections with graceful impromptu passages to savor the moment a bit longer. Yet the last notes could only be sustained for so long.

His stay in Weimar was near the end. He refused more persuasion.

~~~

Felix took a carriage headed to Salzburg, Austria. The leaving of Weimar was hard, especially for Goethe who tried ever so strongly to encourage a longer stay. Felix, in behavior contrary to himself, was stern.

Salzburg, The birthplace of Wolfgang Mozart, was on the way to Vienna. Felix thought it best to stop there, yet some troublesome travels beseeched his journey through the Bavarian mountains.

Felix sat alone in the enclosed coach, trying to sketch the landscape. His mood took the best of him. In part, Klingemann wasn't with him to share poetry, contributing to loneliness. The drawings of the Austrian landscape dissatisfied Felix and he tore them from his book, throwing them out the window.

The coachman caught the antics and snapped from the driver's seat, "Don't be littering about!"

The response was silence, so the coachman suggested, "Why don't we stop soon. Capuchin Hill is nearby, I think you need to take a hike. You've been riding for days." He halted the carriage as they arrived at the tall hill that sat at the fringes of Salzburg. Felix got out of the carriage and began to walk about. Some structures of the city could be seen nearby. The hill was filled with trees and shrubs.

The coachman's real reason for stopping was then conveyed. He told Felix, "There is a place of stay just around the hill. I shall leave you here."

"Wait…" Felix followed the coachman as he grabbed his luggage. Before Felix could testify, the coachman spilled his luggage all over the ground. As Felix went to gather it back up, the driver mounted his coach and hurried off, leaving Felix abandoned.

Felix groaned loudly in the matter. His luggage wasn't too heavy so he carried it and began hiking the forested hill. As he went in his way, the trees began looking similar. He had circled somehow. It frustrated him all the more in his hither and thither. He finally got some of his brains together and headed for the summit to go from there.

Upon reaching the top of the hill, he could see the city and where he needed to be. As he observed the land, the grey clouds vigorously gave way to rain. Felix in a mood grabbed his umbrella, trying to keep dry. The cold rain caused a muddy mess and puddles formed here and there, wetting his shoes.

In a race down the hill, hands full of luggage and covering from the weather, he spotted a monastery at the foot of the hill. He reached it and rang the bell, shivering as his feet were chilled. In his hope for an answer, a monk came to the door. He seemed in hesitation. Felix asked, "Do you have any room, so I may stay for a night?"

"One moment." The monk shut the door.

As Felix waited, he dug in his pockets and luggage for money to pay. In his astonishment, he only had a bit of money left on him. Not enough for the monk to let him stay. He abandoned the monastery before the monk's return.

In the meantime, he decided to take temporary shelter at the post office. It wasn't far away. He had a stack of letters that needed sending. He now needed to pen request to his father for more funds.

When entering, he rested a minute and recollected himself. He became determined that his frustrations were over and everything would be well. He then wrote his request to Abraham and put it in the stack of letters.

As he walked up to the front desk, a lady looked at him in bewilderment. He set the stack of letters on the desk, "I must have these sent through Leipzig to reach Berlin. I have enough to pay for their sending."

"No you are not." The snarky woman pushed the letters away. He was wrong about his mood changing for the better. His tone showed it, "Why!? I need to get funds from home! How am I to go anywhere or stay anywhere if I don't have money!?"

"That's not my problem. You do not have the permission to send through here."

"Why not?" Felix became ever so agitated. Before the lady said anymore, a man, who appeared to manage the post, asked, "What is the matter here?"

"This man wants to send his letters off." She scoffed. The manager eyed Felix, noticing his muddied shoes and pants. His mess of papers were sticking out of his luggage. He then explained, "You need to get your papers examined at the customs-house. Otherwise, off to the streets with you."

236

"Fine." Felix turned and raced out the door to find the customs-house. It was a challenge in such weather. His clothes were becoming wet despite the shelter of the umbrella.

Once he found the customs-house, a man at the main desk pointed to a chair in the empty waiting area, "Sit please."

Felix sat, waiting….waiting…waiting. He skimmed some books sitting nearby. The main office had the door opened slightly. Two men were laughing in jokes. Not another soul that wanted papers checked entered or was waiting. The man at the front desk continued on a project of his own.

After a full hour, the two men in the main office noticed Felix waiting. One exited the room and went to a secondary office as he worked there. Felix near slammed his book down, but forced himself to keep some composure.

The man in the main office called him to enter. Felix felt some relief but not much. He sat down and the customs officer took his papers to examine. It wasn't as fast as when Klingemann helped him into London.
This officer took his time, in laziness he glanced at Felix every now and again, being sure the paper's descriptions matched him. He spoke none.

Felix started his requests, "I need to get some letters sent out to Berlin, but the post is being unwilling. They told me to come here. I also want to request a carriage and some horses to take me out of Salzburg to Ischl once I'm sent the sufficient funds."

"You mean to say you don't have sufficient funds right now?" He spoke saucily.

"That is why I need to send the letters!" Felix began to feel like he was drowning helplessly. The customs officer nodded and gave a face of carelessness. He dug around for some papers, scribbled a signature and handed it to Felix, "Give the post that. If you want horses you must get permission from the police."

"The Police!?" Felix hit the desk in utter rage. The customs officer warned whilst standing, "If you keep up your little mood, I'll send you there myself."

"You mean arrest me?"

"I can make a reason if need be. You look a complete mess and not in good standing. You look like a rift raft."

"I've been traveling for days and my carriage driver abandoned me! I'm no bum!" Felix stood in offense. The customs officer pushed him towards the door, "Leave now, good day."

Felix stomped his foot after the officer shut the door. The man at the main desk watched him make his leave. They were not much help, but at least his letters could be sent.

The police station was on the way back to the post, so he entered, trying to calm himself down so as to not give the police any trouble. He walked to an officer at the front desk. He was reading a paper and drinking coffee. Felix stood and waited. The officer finally looked up, "Can I help you?"

"I came from the customs-house. I need a carriage and horses to Ischl. They told me I needed to get permission from the police."

"Have you a passport?"

"Nein."

"No permission can be granted until you have a passport."

Felix face palmed and left the conversation all together. He went back to the post where he could at least get something accomplished. In the meantime after sending out his letters and requests, he was stuck in Salzburg.

As he had little to no money left, he had to figure something out as to find a bed and meal. In all of the commotion the day had brought, he realized he hadn't eaten. His stomach growled consistently.

As the weather cleared, he wandered the streets with his luggage. He did have fresh clothes with him, but he was still walking the muddy streets. He faced the fact that he would have to look dusty for the time being.

Felix found a small inn. Before entering he counted all of the cash that remained after going to the post. It was surely enough for a bed in the least. He went in and a man came to him in an instant, "We don't accept beggars."

"I assure, I'm not from the streets. I'm traveling and need a bed." He handed the innkeeper the money. The innkeeper nodded and handed him a key, "Third door to the right up the stairs."

"Danke," Felix nodded. He took his luggage and headed up the stairs. When finding the room, he reorganized and changed into a clean outfit. He needed to explain to the innkeeper his situation, but had to dress decently to appear well maintained. He had not a cent left for food, so he hoped to convince the innkeeper that he would repay him.

When coming back down the stairs and to the tavern, the innkeeper noticed his better attire and good standing. He kindly asked Felix, "Is there something I can get you to eat? You look famished."

"About that, I must confess. I'm completely out of funds. The mail coach left today with my requests to acquire more. It won't be back for a few days."

The innkeeper gave Felix a disapproving glance. He asked, "How old are you? You seem too young to be going places far away all alone. Your accent is of Berlin."

"Twenty and one." Felix began to feel tired from hunger. The innkeeper seemed reluctant to give him food, but after watching him eye the plates set before a few guests he felt that he should do something. He told him, "I'll get you a hearty meal and a bed and you pay as soon as that mail coach gets back. If you do not, I will be sure to take you to the police."

"Alright..." Felix felt some relief, but hoped the mail coach would arrive back with his funds soon. He sat at a table and was given a warm super of beef and potato stew. Such food never tasted so good after craving anything to eat. The innkeeper was surprised as he had finished the well filled plate rather quickly.

Felix thanked him then went back to his room to get a good rest after such a harsh, frustrating day. The bed wasn't the coziest as the mattress was thin, but he did not care. He was lucky to have gotten a bed.

~~~

Four days later, as it was mid-morning, Felix began to worry about the mail coach's arrival. The innkeeper was in suspicion as he gave Felix breakfast. When he set the plate in front of him, he sat beside him. Felix looked to him before touching the eggs and bacon. The innkeeper didn't speak a minute, making Felix wonder if he was doing something wrong.

Finally the innkeeper spoke, "I am confused by you. You cleaned up well from when you walked in. You sit each time at the table with much manners as if you have been brought up in well efficiency. Yet you still lack the payment you owe. I am beginning to believe you've been taking advantage of my inn."

"I assure I am not. The mail coach should be here any moment. I am not a thief."

"It's been four days." The innkeeper stated. He then told him in bluntness, "Eat your breakfast then you shall be going to the station." He pointed to an officer standing near the door. Felix turned back to the innkeeper, "Please Sir, the funds will be here soon–"

"Eat or you'll be going now." He sternly spoke. Felix turned to his food and ate slowly, hoping the mail would arrive in the next few moments. The innkeeper caught on to his slow eating. He gestured to the officer to take him. Felix then begged as the officer grabbed his arm, "Please, the money will come!"

"It would have been here by now." The innkeeper snapped. The officer forced Felix from his seat. Felix huffed in the matter. Nothing in his time in Salzburg was going right.

As the officer took him towards the door, a mail man entered, asking out loud, "Is there a Herr Mendelssohn staying here?"

"Ja! Ja!" Felix tried to free himself from the officer. The officer thought he was making an excuse and pulled him towards the door. The mail man stopped them and handed Felix a handful of letters, "These were in the lock pouch and I almost forgot about them."

"Danke!" Felix thanked him. The officer let him go so he could open them. The innkeeper stood nearby to see if he would get his pay. A letter from Abraham contained all of the withdrawn funds he needed to pay the fees and continue his journey.

After that ordeal, Felix packed up and his luck turned. A carriage with travelers exiting sat outside the inn. He asked the coachman, "Where is this carriage headed?"

"Vienna." He answered. Felix loaded his luggage and boarded the coach. It was a city he had planned to get to. Nothing could have been more perfect. The coach stayed at the curb side a while to get the horses some food and water before carrying on.

Felix organised himself and read the other letters he got. Most of it was from home. Fanny was ill with a cough, so Felix penned a short piece for her to play once she recovered.

When he looked up from his music, another carriage had pulled up beside the one Felix was in. He looked over with intrigue. Inside, there was an old woman, but she was dressed in the most extravagant, richly garments. She had to be of nobility of sorts. Felix felt compelled to say something to her as she glanced at him. She gave a snooty expression and told her coachman, "Drive on."

After her carriage was gone, Felix asked his coachman, "Who was that? She had to be of some importance from the looks of her."

"That is a Baroness from Vienna. She and her family take leisure rides to Ischl."

"Oh." Felix couldn't believe he saw a real Baroness from Vienna. The coachman climbed back onto the driver's seat when the horses were rested and energized. It felt so pleasing as the carriage drove out of dreadful Salzburg.

~~~

[3]

The beautiful blue Danube sparkled in the sunlight. The artistically architectured palaces and cathedrals were the gems of the city. Music was everywhere, whether it was that of a well trained busker or whistling passerby going about their business, it was a pleasure to the ears. Felix had arrived in the capital of music. Vienna.

This day though, the streets were particularly busy. The carriage slowed as crowds of people halted the traffic. Felix wondered what all of the commotion was about. The coachman suggested to Felix, "You may want to go on by foot from here as you won't get anywhere otherwise. There are many festivities happening. The King of Hungary is to be crowned."

"That's quite exciting." Felix exited the carriage, taking his luggage. He maneuvered around the crowded roads, looking for a place to stay. The events of the day rendered most inns and rooms full. He had to walk quite a ways from the city center until he found a humble looking hotel. There was one room left.

After he set his luggage in the simple yet finely decorated room, Felix treated himself by setting some manuscript paper and an ink well at the desk by the window. He sat, gazing out into the city holding the most charm he'd ever known. While savoring the moment, he grabbed a quill and penned any music he could bring from the scene. He didn't care what music, he just wanted to complete the goal of composing while in a room in Vienna.

After his little happy moment of composition, he put the music away and went out to go explore this city, rich with history. He frolicked the streets and looked up at the many houses and complexes. All he could ponder over was the fact the Beethoven had lived in various rooms throughout the city. Vienna was practically a must for any aspiring composer.

Felix came across Mozart's abide as well. He heard that Wolfgang's children were still alive. One had an awe for composition. He hoped to meet them in future to learn what it was like living in such a household.

As he took in the sights Vienna had to offer, he happened to get caught up in a crowd watching a parade of guards and horses go by. It was the procession for the new king of Hungary. Felix watched it a while and wrote to his brother Paul of the scene.

He then left the crowds to stop in a cafe to get coffee and savory chocolate cake in which Vienna was popular in regards to food.

Once the platelet of a handsome slice of dark cake, coated in liquid chocolate and dusted in cocoa powder was set before him, he knew his means of diet in this city would be rather an unhealthy one. Yet it was the tastiest thing he had ever come across. He decided the much walking about at the many sights and palaces would make up for any weight gain.

The rest of the day consisted of more exploring such as strolling the gardens of large palaces, art galleries; finding the concert halls and opera houses. He had no plans to have his music performed at them as he was merely passing through Vienna for a few days. He did make some acquaintances in the short time and played some piano for private and casual get togethers. He planned to definitely come back.

As the beautiful evening sunset came, Felix decided to eat at a lovely restaurant. The schnitzel in Vienna was the finest. Though the beer was good, Felix favored the fine wines as it gave him anticipation for the sweet wine of the neighboring country of Italy.

# Chapter XI: Italy part I

Mendelssohn, Italian symphony movement I   [1]
Mendelssohn, Italian symphony movement II   [2]

[1]

## Italy at Last.

Felix wrote home after the carriage crossed the border. He felt he had accomplished much by making it to the country he had ever so desired to see. Now knowing this was Italy, the land felt as if it were bursting with flutes.

Felix intended to reach the city of Venice. The way there would be a bit of a trip yet. The vetturino agreed to get him as far as he could. There were a few stops between then. Already Felix had seen a few towns and cities, stopping in fine art galleries. Each one was full of precocious master works.

There then was a long stretch of travel and the vetturino drove at a snail's pace. Felix gave a sigh as he sat next to the coachman in the driver's bench. The only thing holding his complaints were the fresh air and the achievement of reaching the country. The two horses' hooves padded against the dirt road, snorting and carrying on.

As evening neared, the distance covered didn't impress Felix. The vetturino parked the carriage in a safe grassy area in the woods. Felix asked,
"Surely we aren't resting now?"

"The horses are hungry. I'm tired. There's an extra pillow and blanket in the back." He dismantled from the driver's seat. Felix huffed, but hopped down from the carriage to walk around.

He went to the horses and petted the tired creatures. The coachman
unhooked them from the cab and let them graze.

"What have you for supper?" Felix questioned. The coachman shrugged,
"I'm more tired than hungry. Unless you brought food, I'm not planning on
finding a tavern until morning." The coachman went in the carriage
to sleep.

Felix turned to his luggage, not wanting to speak to the lazy man anymore.
He found a jar of sauerkraut and pickled eggs to munch on. He sat near the
grazing horses, making a small picnic for himself as to join them in dinner.
A bottle of old savory wine completed the meal.

After getting a fill, he packed everything up. By then it was growing dark.
The horses were resting together in the grass as if they knew tomorrow
would be another long day. Felix made sure they were settled. The
vetturino rather carelessly had gone to bed, not checking if they were still
fit after pulling for hours.

Felix then took the blanket and pillow given to him and went to the cab.
When opening it, he found the coachman taking up all of the room. His
snores were loud. Felix shut the door, feeling annoyed. The night
thankfully was beautiful and the stars were sparking. It was chilly but not
terrible. He decided to sleep under the stars.

Felix took a spot beside one of the horses and leaned the pillow against its
side. He found an extra blanket to set on the ground. After making a place
to sleep, he laid down. He stared up at the sky as it looked quite beautiful.
The wistful breeze then put him to sleep.

~~~

Felix awoke to one of the horses nudging him with its nose. It whinnied a
bit until the coachman called to him, trying to wake him. Felix opened his
eyes. It felt far too soon to do as such. It was still dark.

The vetturino had hooked the horses to the carriage already. He stated as Felix sat up, "We're continuing on."

"What time is it?" Felix picked up the pillow and blankets. The coachman crawled onto the driver's seat, "Four in the morning. You complained of not getting far, so we shall start earlier. You can sleep in the cab."

Felix gathered some lastly things and made a bed in the carriage, falling asleep once more. The horses carried on through the country at a slow pace. By mid-morning, little distance was covered. Felix stepped outside of the slow moving cab and crawled onto the driver's bench. The coachman handed Felix the reins, "I need to stretch my legs." He hopped down from the cab and walked alongside the horses. Felix debated speeding up the horses, but figured it not a good idea in case they became agitated.

Hours later they drove into Resciutta. There, in the town was a bridge to cross. The vetturino mentioned, "I hope you are fluent in your Italian. No one speaks an ounce of German on the other side of the bridge."

"Oh." Felix felt a bit nervous. He knew fragments of Italian and could communicate but not as well as French or English.

Upon crossing the bridge, the style of houses became that of tiles, flat roofs and deep windows. Many small chapels were scattered through the land with monks and nuns close by. Every now and again a beggar or two would follow beside the carriage, trying to get a coin or food. The coachman hurried the horses during such occasions but always returned to the slow pace. They drove on many roads winding through orchards. Vineyards were visible in any open plain. By evening they found an inn settled in Udine.

After purchasing a room, Felix ventured down the street and found a humble looking restaurant. It was small and lonely, so Felix sat at a table. A waiter, happy to have a customer, gave him a menu. Felix skimmed it over. The waiter had no one else to tend to so he eagerly set bread and fine wine at the table.

"Cosa vorresti mangiare?"

"Um...I would like- I mean-" Felix's tongue skated and stumbled from English. The waiter knew not a word. Felix corrected his speech to Italian, "Vorrei gli spaghetti." He pointed to what he wanted. The waiter nodded and went off to have it made.

Once the food was set, the pasta couldn't have tasted better. With the wine and a desert of gelato it was well...until the waiter gave the bill. It was more than what was said on the menu. Felix, slipping in his language stated, "Signor...è giusto?"

"No, no, è giusto. Ti sei perso alcuni calcoli." The waiter sounded affirmative. Felix didn't catch all of his words and tried to speak more, but after a bit he gave up in the process. The waiter smiled kindly, taking the money. Felix sighed when returning to the inn as he knew the waiter ripped him off.

~~~

The next day of Sunday, Felix and the coachman continued on to Venice. The way there brought many sights of flowers, happy people and festivities through the villas. After covering many more dragging miles, the vetturino let Felix off at a harbor to reach Venice by boat.

The rowing of the crossing to the city was calm. Unlike the seas around Britain. Soon the dim lights of the city appeared. The boatman quietly rowed into the city, passing under bridges and interesting lines of houses along the canal. The further into Venice they went, the more commotion of the local people there were.

He found stay in a hotel, beside the canal. The window looked over the gondolas passing by with their singing gondoliers. The beautiful city gave Felix the sense of the art he wished to see.

He became acquainted with various local painters, as well as admiring old masterpieces. In his excitement, he could not believe he really made it to Venice.

At the desk in the room styled of the renaissance, he penned to Zelter, telling him of his trip thus far. He eagerly wrote about the music he had come up with in his stay in Vienna before arriving to Italy:

*To professor Zelter*

*I finished two pieces of sacred music in Vienna- a choral in three movements for chorus and orchestra and an Ave Maria for a choir of eight voices, a capella. The people I associated with there were so dissipated and frivolous, that I became quite spiritually-minded, and conducted myself like a divine among them. Moreover, not one of the best pianoforte players there, male or female, ever played a note of Beethoven, and when I hinted that he and Mozart were not to be despised, they said, 'So you are an admirer of classical music?' - 'yes,' said I.*

*Tomorrow I intend to go to Bologna to have a glance at the St. Cecilia, and then proceed by Florence to Rome, where I hope to arrive eight or ten days hence. I will then write to you more satisfactorily. I only wish to make a beginning to-day, and to beg you not to forget me, and kindly accept my heartfelt wishes for your health and happiness.*

*Your faithful,*

*Felix*

After penning to his old teacher, he turned to some family letters, reading them with enjoyment. It was hard to communicate as it took weeks to receive letters at such a distance apart. Concerning Fanny, she was a mother.

The baby was now six months old, but Felix still could not believe he was an Uncle. She had much to do now, but wished more time for her music, yet at the same time felt too busy. Felix wrote to her:

*November 1830*

*...If you had the inclination, you certainly have sufficient genius to compose, and if you have no desire to do so, why grumble so much? If I had a baby to nurse, I certainly should not write any scores, and as I have to compose Non Nobis, I cannot unluckily carry my nephew about in my arms. But speak seriously, your child is scarcely six months old yet, and you can think of anything but Sebastian? (Not Bach!?) Be thankful that you have him. Music only retreats when there is no longer a place for her, and I am not surprised that you are not an unnatural mother...*

*—Felix*

Another speck of trouble beseech him as well. It was another go around with the post, trying to send letters to friends and family. He noticed upon taking a letter for his friend Devrient, the postman took it with much suspicion. Felix had sent a few letters here and there containing music and well wishes to his family, so he didn't understand why the postman was acting so strange towards him.

The postman still took the letter, so Felix headed back to his place of stay. He couldn't help to feel that as he walked back, that he was being watched. No one was standing about in the obvious, but he knew something wasn't right.

After entering his hotel room, he sat at the desk with manuscripts, a quill and ink. He continued some music as the evening moved by, working by candlelight. In a sense, he felt a bit like Vivaldi, who was a composer in Venice back in the early 1700s.

The water of the canal flowing gave a calm ambiance. Some gondolas quietly rowed by with their lamps. The gondoliers saved their song for daylight.

His wakeful dreams were suddenly halted by a knock at the door. He set his quill down and went to answer it. In a moment he paused, wondering who it could possibly be. A strong voice then demanded with a hard pound, "Open up now!"

Felix opened the door and an officer pushed his way in. A few others were behind him. Felix felt a wave of confusion as the first officer grabbed him and moved him out of the doorway. The others began searching the room and his luggage. They shuffled through the music and letters. The officer that had a hold of him questioned in broken English, "What is your business?"

"I...I'm just visiting." Felix glanced as the officers began taking various manuscripts. He attempted to rush to them, but was held back. The officer stated, "You have been enclosing music in letters. It is suspected that you are sending secret ciphers in them. Who is your correspondence?"

"I have none!" Felix was utterly confused. He hoped they wouldn't take the large musical scores in progress. They seemed to be taking the short pieces he noted. It was a frustration all the more. The officer told him sternly, "We shall be taking the music to the customs-house. If we find anything in your letters, we shall find you. You seem nothing but young and naive, but I know such ones are used in such a manner." He let him go and they all left, taking what they wanted.

After the door shut, Felix sat where he was, not believing that they really thought him to be a messenger. He had nothing to hide, but he hoped they wouldn't suspect something that they believed a secret of some sort. Ending up in prison would be a horrid thing to happen while abroad.

~~~~

After his shady stay in Venice, he left and ventured through Bologna to Florence. The vetturino he received for this track was much faster. He spoke much of nature as well as politics, which became quite annoying. The troubling thing of this man though was he stopped at terrible little inns, offering little to no food. If there was any, it was bad. It reminded Felix much of the horrid inn that Karl and he stumbled upon in Scotland. Yet this was multiple stops and days. The coachman seemed to get by fine.

After tolerating a few nights of starving and little sleep, Felix finally confessed to the vetturino as they trudged through the countryside, "I need something to eat. Real food."

The coachman looked at him, noticing his state, "There is an inn coming up in the next few miles." He then grabbed a jar of pickled eggs to share. Felix wondered how much food the coachman had been hiding. The food in Felix's luggage had been eaten through in the days of getting no super. As Felix took a few eggs, the vetturino put the jar away, "That's enough, I need food too." He honestly did not want to share.

After a few more hours of a hard day of travel through the Apennines, they made it to a small inn. It was cold and the wind blew leaves and soot in. Felix wished for any decent meal. The innkeeper gladly took Felix's offer of money and led him to the kitchen. There, a fire was burning, making it the only warm room. Others were standing about. They appeared to be peasants.

The innkeeper threw a watery soup together. Adding hardly any meat or vegetables to it as if being overly frugal. As it heated, Felix sat in a chair close to the fire, trying to get warm. He was expecting a hearty, filling soup as his stomach ever so begged for such.

The innkeeper finally handed him a bowl of the soup. It looked like flavored water. He wanted to complain, but he needed something to get energy. Felix drank the flavorless broth. It had nothing of nutritional value. The innkeeper had cheated him with his money and expectation.

It only added up as the bed was poor for a good sleep. From the moment of laying down, Felix was determined to be strict on offers.

~~~

## [2]

The next morning already brought another stride of hunger. The coachman woke him early in the fourth hour, pestering to continue on. Felix dressed and gathered his things. He then headed to the tavern. No breakfast was served. The coachman hurried Felix outside to the carriage, "I want to get us to Rome fast. I've business to attend to and I imagine you do as well."

"I am not in a hurry. Rather I wanted a pleasure ride there, not tired and starved as you make the trip out to be."

"Well your pleasure of food and sleep awaits you in Rome." He climbed onto the driver's seat. Felix entered the carriage, instantly sitting down and falling asleep. When the sun came up, Felix distracted himself with Goethe's books and poems as well as music. He worked much at the Hebrides overture and the Scottish symphony. Lately yet, something new came to mind. The fast staccato of strings and flutes inspired him again.

After many more miles of the horses pulling the carriage through the Italian country, the landscape turned into a grand ancient city. There were some fresh structures as well as ruins of old. They had arrived in Rome.

Felix had a few letters of introduction to ensure he found good rooms. The coachman dropped him off at said address. It was an apartment complex. The three story building was fashioned in Italian culture with tiled roofing and vines creeping up the side.

Felix unloaded his luggage. The vetturino wished a lofty sum, but Felix kept determined to be strict, paying only what was deserved. The coachman took what Felix offered then went on his way.

Felix then walked across the cobblestone path to the main door of the apartments. Upon entering into the lobby, the landlord met him. Felix gave his letters of introduction.

The landlord smiled upon looking at them and led Felix to a perfectly sound apartment on the first floor. It was beautiful with the surprise of a grand Viennese piano in the main room. A nearby window gave a landscape of architecture and sunshine. The floors were of stone and the walls were a burnt orange in tiles, giving a sense of cultural design. The bedroom was a luxurious affair. Felix flopped onto the soft elegant bed upon seeing it. The landlord couldn't help but smile at the young man's awe for the place. He asked in broken English, "Does this suit you?"

"Es ist so Schön!" Felix could help but speak in his mother tongue. The landlord then assured, "I'll be sure you get some lunch. You look quite hungered. Traveling here can be rough." He left. Felix still laid in bed, recollecting the fact that yesteryear ago, he was in London, stuck in bed because of the carriage crash. Now he was in complete bliss at last.

He enjoyed a few minutes, sprawled upon the comforting bed, breathing in the air of Rome. A light knock on the door made him sit up. It was a servant with a tray of pita bread, grapes and sausages as well as wine to wash it all down.

It felt ever so relieving to eat and drink real food. After digging into the bread and spiced sausages, he gulped down a fair serving of fine Italian wine. The servant was a bit shocked at how much the food excited him, but it was obvious how hungry Felix was. He finished it so fast the servant took it back almost as soon as setting the table. Felix still had some grapes and wine. As he snacked on the grapes and held the wine bottle, he gazed out the window.

It was a nice part of the city in which he resided. The letters of introduction were what helped much. Many locals were walking about, going on with their normal routine.

Felix spent the remainder of the day resting and checking out the well built piano. He played to his content. A few servants every now and again peeked in the apartment to see who was playing such a beautiful melody.

~~~

The next morning, breakfast was sat at the table. It was ever so comforting to begin the day with breakfast. He sipped the frothy cappuccino and ate the warmed cornetti. The sun was bright and shining into the room.

After breakfast it was all playing, singing and composing. Many ideas came to mind as well as old ones. He continued to work on the Hebrides Overture that he began over a year ago. It was nearing it's finish. Originally he had it named, 'The Lonely Island,' but changed it to the 'Hebrides'.

The Scottish symphony still needed much work. Another symphony idea crossed his mind, distracting the progress of other works. His collection of Goethe's poems were sparking music to his ears as well.

A surprise came to him as he worked at the keys. The landlord came in, handing him a letter. Felix paused the music and took it, hoping it to be from home. Instead it was something unexpected and good. Someone he knew had arrived in Rome. His name was Charles Bunsen. He and his wife had a large home in the city in which they visited every so often. Abraham most likely informed them of Felix's stay.

Charles had invited Felix to dine with them in the evening. Felix of course wrote an accepting note. He then put his music away for the day and made plans to go sightseeing before dinner.

There were grand things to see within Rome. Like in Venice, it felt surreal that he was in such a city. He remembered penning lines in his geography book back in his days at the university. That now felt like ages ago, yet at the same time the memory was as vivid as yesterday.

Upon going out to sight see, he took a carriage to the ancient coliseum. It was large and quite extraordinary. Felix had seen many sketches of the famous structure, but it was very much different in real life. A drawing can only depict so much.

That afternoon, he visited the Vatican as that was its own city within Rome. He learned much of culture and how the people viewed their government and religion. He sent letters of his observations to home for his siblings to read.

As he continued on, he heard some news that the pope was ill and it was likely he wasn't going to live much longer. It was possible he was already dead. A new one would be elected in February. Felix was curious of how it would go as the season of festivities and carnival were to take place. The locals seemed to carry on with their preparations.

After wandering vast ancient structures and large cathedrals, it was nearing dinner, so Felix took a cab to Herr Bunsen's abode. It was a large vast home, full of true renaissance decor and art. Felix took much interest in the small details carved in stone and marble. The Bunsens were a well off family as Charles had a sufficient occupation as a diplomat and was quite a scholar. He was younger than Abraham but quite older than Felix.

Upon entering, Mrs. Bunsen greeted Felix with much kindness. She had a fine dark green silk dress with black embroidery. She wasn't thin nor too fat, but it was noticeable that she had a well to do lifestyle. Charles followed soon after her. He was so very happy and told Felix in excitement, "Now we shall have more music. Another musician is here as well."

"How nice." Felix shook Herr Bunsen's hand. They then went to the dining room where an array of guests sat. All very rich looking. Felix had a nice outfit but it didn't overdo his status.

As he sat, the other guests smiled at him. Most were older and their expression showed that they thought of him as a young, innocent child. There were two ladies near his age, eyeing him as the most refined of the guests.

Felix sat quietly as food was served and everyone spoke. Right away he noticed a man that spoke in a German tone. Felix didn't catch his name and didn't wish to as he heard his speech to the lady beside him. The naive girl laughed as the man spoke in musical terms, deeming himself a 'musician.'

Felix avoided his attention until he was pointed out by Charles. The 'musician' asked Felix, "So you are a musical one as well?"

"I play and write." Felix sipped some wine.

"Ah, you are German as well." His tone was quite posh. Felix in the moment wished he were a Frenchman or anything else. This man's demeanor felt like an embarrassment. The 'musician' continued on, trying to impress the ladies, "The art of melody is such a delicate thing. Music must be handled every day." He nodded at his own words. Everyone else agreed.

"Why?" Felix questioned the man. The 'musician' paused in his self agreement and seemed a bit embarrassed at Felix's comment. He searched some words then coined, "Earnest purpose is a must. I have heard your name and heard your Tu es Petrus. That has some gleams of earnest purpose."

"Oh..." Felix felt rather fed up with this 'musician.' He then asked him, "So, what grand music is it you must be composing with such earnest purpose?"

"Well...I have a lot of business with a property in Frascati. I'm about to lay down the profession of music." He confessed.

Felix almost sneered at such a remark. He penned to Fanny after dinner of such a man giving up music and exclaimed in writing:

*We have not got so far as that yet!*

After noting some things to Fanny, Charles and others begged Felix to the music room to play some piano. They all wanted to hear Bach's music. Felix willingly played a number of fugues and Chorals. He then began talking about the various oratorios by Bach. They enjoyed learning about the one Felix conducted the year prior and what work went into it. Charles then dug something out from his music cabinet. It was a piano arrangement of another oratorio of Bach. This was the St. John Passion. Charles mentioned, "I've shown this to the Papal singers and they deem it impossible for human voices."

"I think the contrary. People thought it impossible with the St. Matthew Passion. Also I've heard there is to be a score of this one published."

"Interesting." Charles nodded. The rest of the evening was filled with music.

~~~

Felix's days in Rome were happy and healthy. Each day started with a good breakfast, then he played piano and sang new Lieder to his content. He was leading a joyful little life in his room in Rome. Most of the time.

Letters from Abraham had been abundant upon arriving. Since Felix had found a place of stay in Rome, his father's letters had become irritable in the sense that he feared for Felix's welfare for finding a future living. He was young and carefree, but Abraham wanted his son to be serious and prepared.

Felix wrote simple replies back, consenting to instructions and sometimes carrying them through. Felix cared for his father's opinions, but at the same time, home was two weeks away.

258

He tried sending music for his father, but knew with his mood, his father probably wouldn't read the notes. If the music would even reach him.

After more demanding notes from Abraham, Felix wrote to his siblings of the matter, to help ease their father's worries and frustrations:

Rome, November 22nd, 1830,


My dear Brother and Sisters,

You know how much I dislike, at a distance of two hundred miles, and a fortnight's journey from you, to offer good advice. I mean to do so, however, for once. Let me tell you therefore a mistake in your conduct, and in truth the same I once made myself. I do assure that never in my life have I known my father write in so irritable a strain as since I came to Rome, and so I wish to ask you if you cannot devise some sort of domestic recipe to cheer him a little? I mean by...yielding to his wishes by allowing my father's views of any subject to predominate over your own; then, not to speak at all on any topics that irritate him; and instead of saying shameful, say unpleasant; or instead of superb, very fair. This method has often a wonderfully good effect...For, with the exception of the great events in the world, ill-humour often seems to me to proceed from the same cause that my father's did when I chose to pursue my own path in my musical studies. He was then in a constant state of irritation, incessantly abusing Beethoven and all visionaries; and this often vexes me much, and made me sometimes very unamiable. At that very time something new came out, which put my father out of sorts, and made him I believe not a little uneasy. So long therefore as I persisted in extolling and exalting my Beethoven, the evil became daily worse; and one day, if I remember rightly, I was even sent out of the room. At last, however, it occurred to me that I might speak a great deal of truth, and yet avoid the particular truth obnoxious to my father; so the aspect of affairs speedily began to improve, and all soon went well.

...My father considers himself both much older and more irritable than, thank God, he really is; but it is our duty always to submit our opinion to his, even if the truth be as much on our side, as it often is on his, when opposed to us. Strive, then, to praise what he likes, and do not attack what is implanted in his heart, more especially ancient established ideas....In short, try to smooth and equalize things; and remember that I, who am now an experienced man of the world, never yet knew any family, taking into due consideration all defects and failings, who have hitherto lived so happily together as ours.

Do not send me an answer to this, for you will not receive it for a month, and by that time no doubt, some fresh topic will have arisen; besides if I have spoken nonsense, I do not wish to be scolded by you; and if I have spoken properly, I hope you will follow my good advice.
Your brother most truly,

~Felix

~ ~ ~

Felix continued his days in Rome, spending much time at the piano, alone in his apartment. He had multiple projects he worked on and revised. Other times, he was at the homes of friends, playing for various social gatherings and music get-togethers.

There were many artists wanting background music as they worked at their crafts. Many had a piano in their studio. Felix enjoyed offering his talents as he liked watching the paintings and pottery form into works of art.

One one occasion at a small gathering of a few men, in a beautiful apartment decorated in lush green indoor plants and which contained an open balcony of fine carved stone, Felix improvised various segments of operas on a fine piano. The music's sound echoed as it bounced off the marble paneled flooring. Shades of brick red and orange, lined with a tan hue colored the room. The rooms were owned by a man named, Horace Vernet. He was hosting the gathering of music and sweet wine.

Horace was the most intrigued by Felix's impromptu skills. He suggested many opera themes for Felix to use. Felix knew every one and made his own versions of them based on the theme. The music went on for a full hour or so.

After finishing the final phrase of notes, the guests clapped and gave their commends. When they dispersed from the piano, Horace went to Felix and whispered as not to let the others hear, "You must come with me to make an exchange for I am also an improvisatore."

"What do you mean?" Felix was curious. Horace smiled, "A secret. Come."

Felix followed him to a room next door. It was a drawing room. No one else occupied it. The room had bottle green wallpaper on the upper half and fine glossed wood paneling on the bottom. A heavy wood table sat in the middle. A large open corner had a nice chair.

Horace gestured to Felix to sit in the chair. Felix complied, but was still curious as Horace wouldn't give a say as to why he took him aside. Yet like a child, he couldn't conceal his reasoning long.

"Have you some time to spare?" He asked, setting up a canvas. He wanted to paint Felix.

"Of course," Felix consented. He then in humor made a funny face as Horace looked at him to start drawing. Horace laughed then asked, "May you pose casually with a happy expression? I'd like a cheery picture."

Felix crossed his legs, posing with elegance and gave a slight smile, yet not too much. Smiling too much for a picture wasn't considered a decent look as it was considered too silly. Horace though encouraged, "Smile a hair more."

Felix slightly moved his mouth, but didn't want his gritty teeth showing. Horace then went to a cabinet and grabbed a cloth, a canister of water and a jar of powder. He dampened the cloth, put some of the powder on it then handed it to Felix, "If you're shy of your teeth, this will clean them."

Felix took it and cleaned his teeth with the salty dental powder, feeling much better. He hadn't paid much attention to his teeth since traveling. The most common way of brushing was finding a birch twig and fraying the end to use that, but without any salt or cleaner, they became quite unpleasant.

Horace seemed to be the sort that took more care of his teeth than most. He noticed some of Felix's teeth were causing him an ache, so he suggested, "You know, you could go to the barber, they might have something to help."

"If I remember to clean them it will be fine. I've been traveling so much and don't get good means of cleaning them. A barber will just find some to pull out and I am not going for that. My sister had a tooth pulled and sent me a letter telling me of the ache." He scrubbed his teeth more. After getting decently clean teeth, Felix smiled more for the painting.

"Perfect!" Horace sketched an outline. It took an hour or so to get the pleasing picture that Horace wanted. They chatted in the meantime as Horace carefully gave the canvas brush strokes of color. When the painting was finished, Horace stepped back, "Tell me what you think."

Felix went to the canvas and saw a picture of much likeness. He told Horace, "Surely you aren't an improviser, you are a professional!"

*(Mendelssohn by Horace Vernet)*

"You think?" He picked up the portrait, noticing his own mistakes. Felix saw no flaws, but asked, "Didn't you want to paint a smile?"

"I wanted it to look refined but just wanted to see you smile." Horace chuckled as he unpinned the canvas, rolling up the painting. He handed to Felix, "It shall be yours. For playing so good at the piano."

"Thanks." Felix took the handheld sized roll. The both of them then joined the other guests until the gathering ended in the evening.

~~~

When Felix returned to his apartment, he progressed on his craft of composing. He deemed the Hebrides Overture finished. Now his energies could go to the symphonies in progress such as the Scotch and the Italian one, both in which were haunting his brain.

263

In the midst of the joy of composing in Rome, bad weather gave way to reality. The room became cold and the stone floors felt like ice. It was winter, but instead of a cold blanketed snow, it was a bitter, frosty breeze. The wind blew the shutters open, blowing dust and leaves in. When rain hit, it made a sopping mess all around the window. Felix remained in the bedroom, in bed on such days to keep warm. The last thing he wanted was to catch a chill.

While hiding in the bedroom from the weather, Felix took the time to sort through letters. Some were being halted or arriving late due to the occurrence that happened in Venice. All of the letters containing music had been sent back to him in Rome. The one he had sent to Devrient had gone through, but it had been delayed, causing a delayed reply. Some letters were lost in the matter. Felix figured it would all resolve on its own with time.

Abraham sent a letter of information that gave worry to Felix. Goethe was not in good health and it was likely his time to die in the coming year or so. The thought crushed Felix, but he knew from his leaving Goethe's home in Weimar, it was to be the last. Yet the old poet's time was not yet, so he didn't let the somberness depress him.

~~~

Felix continued sightseeing with some English friends he happened upon. Since Rome was large, people from all over came to the city. Unlike the Italian countryside and villages where no one knew a word of German or English, he was able to find many friends to speak fluently to. He felt though at many times, his tongue was confused in languages and mixed about in his head.

One of the interesting places Felix happened upon gave too much interest. A large home came into view while riding in the carriage. An English lady in a fine dress mentioned to Felix, "That place contains a large collection of fresco paintings. It used to be owned by a man by the name of Bartholdy."

"You are speaking of my late Uncle. Jacob Bartholdy. I was told of his home in Rome but didn't think it was this grand!" Felix couldn't wait to see the inside of it.

Jacob had been a leading patron of the fresco technique of painting. Various artists had done up an entire room in the home. Since Jacob's death, two English ladies had purchased the home. Felix found things that had been either redecorated or resorted. The wall of frescoes was left alone, but the room itself had been made into boarding quarters. All in all, it was done up nice.

Felix got to see his uncle's portrait as well. It was all striking to him as it was the only time he'd visited the Bartholdy residence. It surprised him. The art made him feel an inclination to start painting and sketching again.

# Chapter XII: Italy Part II

Mendelssohn, Italian Symphony Movement III (to next piece) [1]
Berlioz, March to the Scaffold from Symphonie Fantastique [2]
Mendelssohn, Italian symphony movement IV [3]

## [1]

In February of 1831, Felix turned two and twenty. The month was busy with festivities commencing in the city. Everywhere, guards were parading and the drums were beating. The new pope had been elected.

Felix walked in the commotion as crowds of people gathered in the streets, spectating the parades. It was loud with cheer. Felix found himself caught up in confetti throwing, causing him to turn about and bump into someone.

"Aie!" They exclaimed as they tripped. Felix helped the man up, switching his language to French, "Je suis vraiment désolé."

"How do you know I speak French?" The man fixed his wispy strides of ash brown hair.

"Your coat appears to be of French tailoring and your accent."

"Oh…" The ditzy man recollected. Felix concluded that the man was older than him by a few years. His choice in fashion made him appear younger in mindset. His clothes were nice, but his cravat was a messy knot. He looked as if he'd been out with friends all night. The man held out his hand, "My name is Hector Berlioz."

"I'm Felix Mendelssohn," They shook hands. Berlioz nodded, "Ah, I have heard of you. You see, I studied music at the conservatory in Paris. I'm working on a career in composition. I'm getting along well with it."

"I hope to hear your work," Felix smiled as they found a quiet path to converse. He continued, "You play piano I imagine?"

*(Hector Berlioz)*

"Well, not like most composers. I've had a few lessons here and there. I'm more fluent with guitar and other instruments. I didn't get much of a chance growing up to find my musical abilities. I loved it, but you see, my father sent me to university to study medicine."

"That sounds tough. I've heard medical school is quite hard, that is if you can stomach it." Felix felt queasy just thinking about it. Hector nodded, "That was my problem. I handled the schooling for a few years, but one day when I was to visit the morgue with a classmate, I jumped out the window and ran away. I then finally got a chance to pursue music when I was accepted to be a student at the conservatory."

"If you have the desire to make music, it's never too late," Felix commented. He then added, "I'd take music school over medical school any day. You must be quite smart if you made it fine in other aspects of learning medicine."

Berlioz shrugged, "You can do a lot just to please your father....and the schooling did have it's benefits..." His tone turned rather suspicious. Felix didn't think much of his oddness.

They continued towards the main area of the city. There, with the election of the pope, many events were happening, mostly concerning religion. Felix found the long occasions quite tiresome. The culture of Italy was different to him, but he spectated the various events. He did have personal interest in religion, complying to what his parents had brought he and his siblings up in. When traveling, his idea of the two most important items to obtain were a Bible and a piano.

Hector perceived the occasions boring and uninteresting. He was indifferent when it came to religion. In the moment of standing in an open area, listening to speeches, he spotted a pastry shop nearby selling cannoli, so he decided to head that way. Felix followed as he wanted something sweet to eat.

The shop smelled divine upon entering. There were a few small round tables for seating and the decor made the shop quaint and clean. At the main counter, the pastries on display included gelato, chocolate and sparkling drinks. Both Hector and Felix were set on getting cannoli and coffee.

After purchasing a few rolls of the creamy treat, they sat down to visit. Hector had many questions for Felix concerning composition. Most of what he learned had been from textbooks, but he knew it was important to consult other fellow musicians. Felix in his usual way spoke much about Bach, Haydn, Mozart and Beethoven.

Hector nodded at all of the information, but after Felix spoke his heart out, Hector questioned, "I see you do like the old composers, but what about anything current? New? Music needs to be pushed forward."

"Well Ja, but I think for new music to sound good, it needs influencing, not completely from scratch. Some rules must be set."

"I think you study the music of dead composers too closely."

"But I love it." Felix took a bite of cannoli. He flinched upon doing so. Hector noticed, "I think you need to go to the barber. An aching tooth might mean it's infected."

"Nein, it's fine. I just washed them. I've been making sure to."

"But if it's already infected, you must get it out. Let me see it." Hector demanded. Felix opened his mouth and pointed out the one that ached. Hector scolded, "If you don't go to a barber now, I will pull it out."

"You aren't a barber. I'm not getting it pulled."

"Trust me. I went to medical school. I may not have finished, but I know an infected tooth when I see one."

"Well I'm not getting it pulled right now. I have too much that I want to see today." Felix crossed his arms. Hector gave a hard response, "If you put it off, you won't be around to sightsee anything. Besides, there's a barber just down the street."

[2]

"Oh how convenient..." Felix felt anxious as he couldn't argue. The two finished their pastries then headed out the door. When entering the sidewalk, Felix began walking the opposite way to the barber. Hector turned him around, "It's this way."

"Oh..." Felix followed him in reluctance. He felt as if he were walking to a scaffold as he knew getting a tooth pulled wasn't at all pleasant. They came to a small brick building with the blue, red and white ribboned pole indicating the barber shop. Barbers mostly shaved and cut hair, but some were also 'skilled' dentists.

"Are you sure a barber would really know what they are doing? Can't we find a doctor or someone who specializes in teeth?" Felix stopped before opening the door. Hector laughed, "Who else is there besides a barber? That would be quite silly for someone to go to school just for teeth." He nudged Felix to go in.

Upon entering the small shop, the barber was busy giving a man a haircut. When he saw more customers come in, he pointed to two chairs in the waiting area. Felix nervously sat and Hector took the other chair, picking up a newspaper. Felix watched as the barber worked, making sure he acted nice. The man seemed kind as he chatted with the current customer he was cutting hair for.

Hector noticed Felix gawking about in a fright, so suggested, "You should read something to calm down. It's a quick tooth pull that shan't hurt... for long."

Felix took his advice and happened upon a Bible to comfort him. He began reading it with deep interest. Hector noticed his choice of book, "You don't *really* read that, do you?"

"I find it the utmost importance of reading." Felix told him, his voice shaking.

"It's an outdated silly old book, full of stories. Why bother with it?" Berlioz stated, crossing his arms. Felix's voice became blunt and serious, "Hector. Please, don't make fun of it. It is a truthful book. It has practical advice even if you disagree."

"Advice as what?"

"There's much to read upon being practical, decent and kind. How to have happiness in life, managing work and money responsibly.

There's so much, you should read it." Felix encouraged in brightness. Berlioz shrugged and rolled his eyes.

"Alright, who's next?" The barber called. Felix's enlightenment faded. He stood nervously, declaring to the barber, "My tooth is aching."

"Sit here and I'll take a look." He patted the seat. Felix sat in the rather uncomfortable barber's chair. It felt sturdy and stiff. The barber organized a few utensils to clean his teeth such as floss and dental powder. He set a candle on a stand for extra light. It still rendered the room a tinge dim.

The barber gently tilted his head back to examine his teeth. Felix reclined the best he could, but the chair was completely unsuitable for dentistry. He still had his doubts as to how qualified this man was to be prodding at his teeth.

"An upper molar in the back is pretty bad," the barber informed, "I'll get it out." He rummaged a drawer nearby. The contents of the drawer had nothing but sharp and unpleasant things. It made Felix's stomach churn. He tried to dissuade the barber, "Are you sure that's the only solution? Can't I just get a filling. I'd be pleased with that."

"I'm sorry, but a filling won't fix the problem." He set a tooth key on the stand beside the chair. Felix near jumped at the sight of it. He questioned in a tremble, "It will be painless right?"

The barber grabbed a bottle of brandy from a cabinet, not answering the question, "Drink a few gulps of this. Be sure to wash it in your mouth."

"Alright." Felix felt a bit more at ease with the refreshments offered. He drank a fare share. The barber then grabbed a cloth and soaked it in some dental powder, "Right now I'm going to clean your teeth."

"Okay." Felix opened his mouth, but in unsureness. The barber carefully began scrubbing his teeth, trying to ease his nerves.

Felix felt calmer, but had a feeling that the barber was distracting him from something else. Each time he wanted to sit normally, the barber instructed while keeping his head tilted back, "Don't move, I'm still cleaning your teeth."

Felix cooperated as the salty cleaner soothed his aching tooth. It felt nice to get a thorough cleaning. The barber then sighed while grabbing the tooth key, "This is the hardest part of my job."

"Wait!" Felix refrained as the barber held the wretched thing towards his mouth. In a nervous smother, he went to stand, but realized he couldn't. His arms had been strapped against the armrests, trapping him in the chair. The barber had done it in the time of distracting him. In a frantic panic, Felix tugged at the restraints, "This is inhuman! You shouldn't treat your patients like this!"

"I'm sorry, but you don't seem the sort to keep still and this must get done." The barber tightened him to the chair further by strapping his body. Felix struggled, "This is too tight! You're hurting me!"

"Calm down, you're alright." The barber continued tightening him to be sure he couldn't move.

"Nein! Nein! Nein!" Felix yelped as the barber forcefully shoved the tooth key in his mouth. When the metal bashed against the aching tooth, tears streamed down Felix's face. The barber sighed, "This will take one try...or two." He began prying at the infected tooth.

"Ausch! Ausch!" Felix snapped at the barber, trying to bite him. The barber in frustration gripped his jaw tighter to keep him still. Felix grimaced as the rather rusty old thing was forced towards the back of his mouth.

The barber tried to assure, "Just keep still."

"Please nein-" Felix was interrupted as the barber began forcefully prying. In the midst of screaming and wailing, the barber struggled to get a good hold on the tooth. Felix wasn't helping as he, in another nervous smother, managed to bite his finger, causing the barber to back away in a yell, "Ouch! I can't do this, you are far too difficult." The barber, now overly frustrated, threw the tooth key down on the stand. Hector set down the newspaper, "I'll do it."

Before Felix could make any complaints, Hector in a flash grabbed the tooth key. He pried at the tooth as if he had been trained in such a field. It didn't make the procedure any less painful. Felix couldn't discern if this was a helpful gesture or torture. He deemed it the latter.

After many heart wrenching moments, Felix didn't think he could bear the pain any longer. A split second after a flick of the wrist, the tooth toppled to the floor.

~~~~

"It wasn't that hard." Hector stood by Felix outside the barber's shop. Felix held a handkerchief in his mouth while sitting on a bench, looking like the most miserable man in the country. His mouth and jaw ached horridly. Hector mentioned, "I've seen a few tooth extractions in my schooling years and it's quite the hash. You only screamed a little."

"I preferred the toothache over this pain." Felix stated with watering eyes. Hector sighed, "Well it had to get done. If you would have left it, over time, the infection would have killed you. Maybe you'll now remember to keep your teeth in check when traveling."

"I will." Felix chewed at the handkerchief, trying to sooth his mouth. They both then carried on down the pavement to see what else was happening in town. Hector mentioned, "I wonder if the Carnival festivities will still commence tomorrow as there is much happening religious wise."

"I don't know. I guess we shall find out tomorrow."

"I'll be walking around the Colosseum if you'd like to join." Hector offered. Felix debated, "I don't know. I've not been around you a day and already I've had a tooth pulled."

"I promise you won't be going to the barber again." He said. Felix nodded, "Alright. I shall join you. I should be in better shape tomorrow. I'm very tired right now."

Hector stopped a carriage passing by and paid the cab to take Felix to his apartment. Felix thanked Berlioz and they went their separate ways for the day.

~ ~ ~ ~

The next day, there was a dusting of snow on the ground. Felix felt the need to treat himself after enduring the day before. He wore his favorite outfit with the blue coat when going out. His mouth ached still, so he kept a handkerchief at hand to chew at.

The chill didn't seem to stop any locals from their daily walks and business. Felix took a carriage headed for the Colosseum to meet with Hector again. The festivities of Carnival seemed rather quiet. Yet as the carriage turned a corner to a center street, the confetti flew. It went everywhere and people wore their decorative masks as well.

In the midst of the confetti, people and other carriages, Felix was pelted in an array of sugar comfits. The powdered sugar covered his coat. He looked up to see some young ladies throwing them at him from a balcony. Felix had seen their faces before at gatherings and balls.

As the carriage drove on, another familiar lady threw powered candy as well. Felix grabbed a handful of confetti and threw back. The second he started throwing, many acquaintances noticed him. Confetti and bonbons were tossed like snowballs.

Felix's coat became as white as that of a miller. Before the carriage exited the busy road, a masked woman threw Felix a bundle of flowers.

The carriage carried on through the bustling street and stopped at the Colosseum. Felix spotted Hector. Hector turned to him and asked in confusion, "What happened to you?"

"The carnival is pretty wild down the street." Felix brushed the powdered sugar from his coat. He and Hector then began walking about. Hector asked Felix, "So in your travels, are you going to stop in Paris by chance?"

"Ja, my plan after Italy is to take a pedestrian excursion through Switzerland then I must get to Munich to have my music performed there, then I'll be in Paris."

"I was thinking, when you get to Paris, we could meet again. I'll be back there by the time you come as I am leaving tomorrow morning. Some of my music will be performed and I would like you to come."

"I definitely will." Felix accepted. Hector thought his new friend's opinion would be ever so important. Felix then mentioned, "I'm going to be leaving Rome soon and head to Naples as my journey must continue, so I guess we won't meet again until I get to Paris." Felix shook Berlioz's hand. They went their separate ways after strolling a few hours.

Back at Felix's apartment, he still had his bouquet of flowers the masked woman had given him. He worked on drying the flowers so he could keep them and show them to his siblings. His rooms were calm and away from the commotion near the city center. He spent the remainder of the day at the piano, working on the Italian symphony and music for Goethe's poem, 'Walpurgis Night.'

Felix was going to miss composing at the fine piano, in the stylish apartment, but he needed to move on. There were still so many places to go and sights to see.

~~~~

In April of 1831, Felix caught up on letter writing in his new abide in Naples. It was much calmer than the hustle and festivities of Rome. Yet, the weather was much more dreary. Even so, the peaceful surroundings inclined Felix to write letters, sketch and compose in detail.

He got to take a side excursion to the ruins of Pompeii, but found the ruins a melancholy affair. It appeared completely burnt and deserted. As he recollected on the ancient tragedy, many English and French ladies frolicked about, sketching and painting the old city.

Some sights were a challenge to enjoy. As Felix strolled along a seashore, gazing at the distant islands, someone tapped his shoulder. Felix turned to see an old white haired man. He looked crippled and hungry. Feeling pity, Felix gave the beggar a few scudi to send him on his way. Yet as soon as the man went off, Felix was surrounded by a group of beggars. It ruined his stroll as he was forced to finish his sight seeing of the ocean. Each one tugged at his coat and followed him. Some of them were children, rattling their jaws and crying, 'Muoio di fame.'

Felix felt terrible, but he couldn't pander to each of their needs as there were so many. At the same time, he knew only a few were actually in need. A carriage happened to be nearby, so Felix took it back to his rooms.

The days in Naples began to tire him. He was living healthier as he went to bed at nine to wake at five. Yet at the same time he was lazier, taking a siesta during the day on top of the hearty amount of sleep. The laying about sent him into thoughts of the friends and family he ever so missed. The sound of a full orchestra begged to be listened to as he had not heard one in such a long time. There were orchestras in Italy, but not well rounded ones.

The choirs fared the same. He wrote to Zelter of such. The voices were never together and they seemed to battle each other in song.

The holy music was sung in complete dullness with bad tone. Felix was not impressed with the Italian choirs. He missed his London friends ever so as they could play and test out his freshly composed music with ease.

Felix debated leaving Naples for Sicily, but Abraham sent letters, discouraging that choice. Felix complied to his father's wishes, but with much reluctance. Instead he decided to return to Rome. He couldn't help but get a taste of the city once more before leaving Italy.

On his way there, he happened upon some friends heading to Ischia. It was a place near Rome full of beautiful scenery. Felix wanted to join and paid the coachman to take his luggage back to his rooms in Rome. He only grabbed a small knapsack of three shirts and some poems of Goethe for the side excursion. His friends on the trip were Ed. Bendemann, Theodore Hildenbrant and Carl Sohn.

Felix joined their carriage. The whole way to Ischia was nothing but beggars. When there weren't any, the carriage parked and the group hiked around the lake and hills. The landscape inclined Felix to draw. He also read Goethe's poems as to take in the meaning whilst wandering the forests. In their stay at Ischia, they breakfasted on fruit and in the evenings dined on fish. The trip lasted a few days before heading back to civilization.

Upon returning to his apartment in Rome from the little side excursion, Felix received more family letters. Paul had sent a letter. It intrigued Felix as his young brother was becoming dignified. He was making arrangements to travel to London. Felix felt such pride as Paul was getting out on his own. At the same time, it made Felix miss that smokey nest called London. He missed his friends of Britain. The concert goers of England had not yet forgotten Felix's name as some newspapers noted. Felix couldn't wait to hear a good Philharmonie again.

After spending a few days and getting his last taste of the grand Italian city, Felix made the decision to fully end his stay in Rome. He needed to move on with his journey. The next city on the way out was Florence.

The route out of Rome was beautiful, but the horrid vetturino once again stopped at horrid inns that starved him. Felix had enough of it as they made it half a day's journey from Florence. As the horses steadily walked along the dirt path, nearing the next village, Felix yelled at the coachman, "Stop the carriage now!"

As soon as the carriage halted, Felix jumped out and grabbed his luggage in an angered mood. The vetturino rolled his eyes at Felix, thinking him to be acting as such a child. Yet Felix was tired and hungry, rendering him to be moody. After grabbing his luggage, Felix hissed at the insolent vetturino, "Drive to the devil!"

The man hurried off gladly. Felix went on by foot to the village ahead. It was called Incisa. The summer day was hot, so Felix was sweating and thirsty by the time he reached town. A carriage house stood as one of the first buildings to see when walking into the village. He went straight there as he intended to get a better ride to Florence.

Upon entering, a landlady was tending to some sweeping. Some stable boys were at work as well. Felix in tiredness set his luggage down. The hard at work, middle aged landlady turned when hearing him enter. She fetched him some water and acted with kindness.

"Grazie," Felix gulped down the fresh water. He then spoke his business, "I need a carriage to Florence, I must be there by evening."

"I can get you a decent carriage." The landlady spoke decent English. Felix offered his price, but she requested four times as much. Felix refused such an offer as it was cheating. The landlady then said, now speaking fast Italian, "You'll have to find a carriage elsewhere."

Felix caught her words as his Italian had been improving, but knew she was trying to confuse him. Felix huffed and walked out to find other means of a carriage. He went to a few inns but only found offers on post-horses.

Not suitable for luggage. It forced him to return to the carriage house. This time he demanded the landlady, "I want horses at a fair price."

"You take my offer or leave." She swept the floor more harshly. Felix crossed his arms, "I want to see the regulations." He knew in such matters they were supposed to have them.

"I don't have time to show you them." She snorted and raised the broomstick at him, "Leave or I shall make you!"

Felix stepped towards the door as the stable boys eyed the commotion. The landlady turned her back on him, continuing her sweeping near a door that led to another room. Felix in a sudden fit of rage stormed towards the woman and seized her. She in an instant bashed him in the gut with the broom's handle. Felix gasped as it winded him, but he managed to push her in the room nearby. The woman yelled but Felix shut the door on her. He felt regret as he knew his anger caused him to be harsh, but she was on such disagreeable terms.

When turning away from the door, a group of stable boys gathered together, forming a mob. Each one had their fists clenched. As Felix froze, the landlady opened the door, clenching her broom in pure fire. She ordered the stable boys, "Get him!"

[3]

Felix sprinted off, carrying his luggage as the boys were at his heels. They yelled and cursed at him. Felix glanced at each house, trying to find the Podestà. Yet in reality, no such a person was in town. They lived four miles off.

Felix was fit athletically as a runner, but he was slowed. Though he had hurt his leg in the carriage crash a year prior, it was weak when strained. He knew he should have worked more on strengthening it, but had been busy and didn't think much of it after it was deemed healed.

One of the stable boys noticed Felix slowed with each step. It made the boy only sprint faster, knowing he could catch him.

In the moment of running in the middle of a street, Felix could only go so far. He didn't know where to turn. As he frantically turned about, one of the adolescents managed to pull him backwards. Felix dropped down with his luggage, making a mess of it. The other boys caught up and surrounded him. Their fists were raised. Felix shut his eyes tightly and braced himself for their throttles.

After a few moments of nothing, he opened them again. A well dressed gentleman that had walked into the scene distracted the boys' attention and their respect. The man instructed the adolescents, "Leave him be. I am sure whatever it is he has done can be made up in better ways."

The boys listened to the man. Felix felt much relief after such an affair. He picked up his luggage and stood by the respected man. The boys warned the gentleman, "That man is mad! He's not right! He's crazy!"

The man ignored their warnings and turned to Felix, "What happened?" He was genuine with concern. Felix explained everything involving the landlady and the prices. The man nodded, "Come with me." He led Felix to a vine-dresser. There, he had a little carriage for hire and at a fair price.

The stable boys followed Felix as if to find a chance to take him back, but their respect for the kind gentleman rendered them to only continue their warnings. They pressed into the building. Felix kept beside the respected man who understood his situation. In the whole matter, the carriage came and Felix was on his way to Florence.

The sun was quite bright, so Felix opened an umbrella to get some shade. This carriage ride was deemed far better than the one before. The coachman drove quickly, but still mild enough so Felix could enjoy the scenery. When the carriage entered the streets of Florence, Felix felt such relief to see the large cathedral with the famous domed roof.

He expected to gain much insight at the museums and galleries, seeing the sculptures by Michael Angelo and the paintings by Leonardo da Vinci.

*(Mendelssohn Watercolour of Florence)*

After finding rooms, he seeked out somewhere to eat as the hassle of the day took up the lunch hour. As he walked, there were grand sculptures outside museums to see in the dim sunset, giving a sense of beauty of its own.

Felix treated himself to a fine dinner in a beautiful restaurant. The building was old, but still beautiful with Renaissance art and carved wood decorating the door frames. He dined on real Italian pizza and for once was not cheated by the waiter on price. He picked up better Italian speech within his stay. After eating, he went home and got good rest.

The entirety of the next day was spent roaming the art galleries. Felix, being an admirer of art, found it almost surreal to see the famous paintings and statues depicted in his study books. It gave him much inspiration and the strive to draw and paint. It influenced his musical ear as well as the beauty of it burst with song.

The journey through Italy was nearing the end with each day. The final city Felix found stay in was Milan. Much happened there though. The carriage ride was entertaining as he read an episode of 'Armida', surrounded by a group of Italian actors singing Rossini's, 'Ma trema, trema'.

Upon arriving in Milan, all he could ponder over musically was Beethoven's A major sonata in which was dedicated to Madame Dorethea von Ertmann. She lived in Milan as her husband was an Austrian general stationed there. She could have been the one Beethoven intended in his love letter in which he titled the recipient his, 'Immortal Beloved'. Felix strived to find her as anything involving Beethoven took his interests.

After asking a few locals, he found the grand home of General Ertmann. Before walking up to it, he penned a few pretty speeches as to address Madam Ertmann in a good manner. He wore a nice black coat over his well chosen outfit, completing a proper greeting. When walking up to the gate, what appeared to be a watchman stood nearby. Felix asked him, "Is by chance General Ertmann around? I wish to speak to him."

"You are speaking to him." The old man confessed. Felix felt some surprise but conducted himself, "I am a musician and heard that Madam Ertmann played Beethoven's music well. I wish to hear some."

"You like Beethoven? She is inside. You seem a nice gentleman. It is so hard to find one who loves the music of Beethoven around here. My wife would love to have you come in. She doesn't play piano much anymore though I'm afraid." He gestured to Felix to follow him. They entered the gate. The yard and flower gardens felt so regal and open. The sound of the piano could already be heard upon nearing the front doors. General Ertmann showed surprise with a few tears as he had not heard his wife play music in a long time. A room down the hall near the doors, sat a fine lady playing the keys of a Mozart sonata. She halted as she heard footsteps walk in the music room.

"Darling. I've happened upon a gentleman. He enjoys Beethoven's music."
General Ertmann inquired. Madam Ertmann turned around in her seat and
smiled kindly. Felix smiled back, holding his music folder. The kindly faced
old woman gestured to him to set the music at the piano. He did and she
then patted a spot beside her on the piano bench. Felix sat, feeling quite
shy as they welcomed him easier than anticipated. They were of quite high
a station in society, so he didn't know what to expect. He felt more at ease
as they shuffled through some music, speaking of the well crafted music
Beethoven composed. Felix spoke his proper speeches as well to assure her
that he was an educated man.

After playing through various works for an hour or so, Madam Ertmann
couldn't help but find much intrigue in Felix as he was young to know
Beethoven's music so well. She shared her stories of meeting Beethoven
and his reasoning on dedicating a sonata to her. One story was quite
touching as she seldomly explained that years back when her young son
died, Beethoven invited her over and improvised at the piano for an hour to
comfort her, saying they would be 'Speaking to each other in tones'.

Felix enjoyed her piano skills as she knew the techniques of a good rounded
sound. Some passages she played too quickly though, but it gave character.
She enjoyed Felix's music as the creativity of the composer gave her the
reminisces of taking lessons from Beethoven those years ago. Of course
Felix was different from Beethoven, but they were both creative and
played piano with complete passion and talent. Madame Ertmann had
longed for such delicate improvising at the keys as Felix accomplished. The
Ertmanns invited him to come back.

Felix spent the next few days paying visits to their home. Though the
company was well in Milan, Felix had trouble keeping himself groomed
during his stay. He managed, but it was a challenge. The trouble lied with
the lodgings. It was settled in a desolate part of town. He had been stuck
with it as the other lodgings were taken. The walls were thin. He could
scarcely sleep as stormy weather woke him in the night.

It rendered him looking tired. The other trouble was that fleas were prevalent on the bed and around the rooms. They kept him awake as they had a nasty bite.

Felix carried on his days in Milan as he became acquainted with another person of utmost importance to him. Madam Ertmann sent him an invitation to dinner and an evening of music. Felix of course was obliged and came accordingly. Other guests had been invited as well. One caught Felix's attention. He had dark hair, but his face had a slight familiarity. At the same time he knew he'd never met this man. He was older than Felix by some years, around Ignaz's age.

As everyone entered the dining room, Madam Ertmann encouraged Felix, "Why don't you sit by Karl, I bet you'd like to be in his company." She gestured to the man that puzzled Felix's mind. His mind was not puzzled anymore as everything clicked by hearing his name. This man was Karl Mozart, the eldest of Wolfgang's two sons. Felix became overly excited, but only on the inside as he needed to keep composure. Karl noticed his spark of enthusiasm though. He held out his hand kindly for Felix to shake. After such a greeting, they gladly sat by each other.

Felix learned much by conversation with Herr Mozart. Karl told him of his residence and occupation in Milan, which gave Felix relief that he had stopped in this city. He noticed how much Karl looked like his father as he had seen paintings of Wolfgang. His way of speech was so much like Wolfgang's manner in letter writing and such. He also had a well trained ear for composition. His manner of talking about music showed he was very much a true Mozart. He confessed in humbleness, "I do some music when my regular job gives the time, but my younger brother, Franz Xaver is the one who got the aspiration to compose."

"You surely have some of your father's gifts. I can tell from your speech and passion for music." Felix assured. Karl smiled at his kindness.

284

After dinner, the guests went to hear music. A few had talent at the keys and filled the room with the well tuned instrument. To Felix's surprise, no one played any Mozart. Beethoven was the main choice. He figured Karl didn't want to be in the shadow of his father. Yet a baroness whispered to Felix, "You better play something of Mozart's or his son would be quite mortified."

Felix went to the piano and at first felt shy of playing a Mozart piece in front of Karl. Yet he carried on with the overture of Don Juan. After it, Karl came up to the piano. His expression looked breathless. Felix wondered if he made a mistake in choosing the piece. Yet Karl suddenly burst into enthusiasm, "Please play the overture to Flauto Magico of my Vatter"

Felix complied with relief and played it through. Karl nearly hopped with happiness in hearing his father's music. It was as if he were back home in the apartment in Vienna, hearing Wolfgang play in his usual cheeriness of laughs. Felix couldn't help but smile at Karl.

~~~

The next day Karl invited Felix to accompany him to visit a group of friends at a home near the Lake of Como. On the way, Karl told Felix many stories of his childhood. One fun story was of how he and his brother would irritate their father by sitting at his piano, playing incomplete scales as Wolfgang was busy in the other room. The sound of the incompleteness prompted their father to rush into the room and finish the lines. Felix laughed at such an interesting fact.

They soon arrived at a humble abide that had a decent view of the lake. When they entered the home, Felix found that the company were locals from the city.

There was a Doctor, the Apothecary, the Judge and others as such. They all stayed a few days, spending time visiting about art and plays. There was a lively discussion of the French writer George Sand.

They admired the 'man's' books. The plays of Shakespeare were then talked of. Felix enjoyed how they loved the works, but then the Doctor stated,"Some of Shakespeare's plays are rather a childish affair."

"Really?" Felix asked, "What ever ones do you mean?"

"A prime example that is a waste of a read I say to you is 'A Midnight Summer's Dream.' So childish with the fairies and things."

"Oh..." Felix trailed off his speech. He wanted so badly to say it was a wonderful play and he wrote music for it, but didn't want to be laughed at, so he stayed silent. He regretted doing so. The rest of the stay at the house consisted of sketching, bathing in the lake and taking a rowboat around. Yet the plan of rowing was shortened as a dark canopy of clouds hovered over.

After returning to Milan days later, Eduard Devrient wrote to Felix, wishing him to write an opera. Thinking it foolish he hadn't written more. Felix wrote back that he had a libretto in his hands soon to be done and planned to accomplish one. It was rather an excuse though as he told him of all the other things he was writing. In truth, he was indecisive of the opera libretto. After writing, he packed up and took a coach headed for Switzerland. The leave of Italy saddened him but at least it helped him think up good music.

# Chapter XIII: The Alps

Beethoven, Symphony No. 6 in F, 'The Pastoral' Movement I [1]
Beethoven, Symphony 6 movement IV-V, 'Storm and Shepherd's song [2]

## [1]

The golden rays of the rising sun crept over the lavender grey mountains and shone over the green hills surrounding the city of Lucerne of Switzerland as the carriage arrived. Felix intended to stay a few nights in the city to get his taste of the grand Swiss Alps.

On his way to the Alps, his journey was a bit amusing as he observed other travelers. A couple from England showed utter boredom at the sight that the snow capped mountains had to offer. They wished to be elsewhere. Felix, when seeing the Alps, was breathless as he recollected the landscape from his childhood when his family took a trip through the mountains. The views were as he remembered. Blue sky, grey mountains in the distance and green grass in valleys.

Another man, who was from Germany, had awe for the scenery. He looked as if he wanted to make his purchase of the wilderness of Switzerland. Felix giggled a bit as the man shook his head, determining it too expensive.

At Felix's lodgings in Lucerne, he continued to try and find some muse for Devrient's wish for an opera. His thoughts were all over in the matter, discouraging his means of starting. The past attempt at opera didn't help either. He came across Schiller's 'William Tell,' and found intrigue in it. He wrote to his siblings many of the amusing plots. Yet alas, Rossini already made use of such an idea.

Days later, pushing further through Switzerland, Felix found himself in the town of Charmey, seated by a lake.

He stayed in a nice clean wood room at a humble cabin. The air of Switzerland was crisp and healthy. In the early hour, Felix ventured on a pedestrian tour around the bright blue lake. He took with him for the hike only a knapsack to carry over his shoulder. It contained the simplest of things. An extra shirt, a brush, comb and sketchbook. He was quite alone on the humble footpath but loved the lush green grass and the calmness of the hours.

After spending the early morning moments to himself, he decided to head back to his rooms as his stomach growled for breakfast. The excursion was well; almost as energizing as food itself, but he still needed a serving of milk and seasoned sausages.

When he returned to the cozy room, he wrote to his siblings as he waited for the milk to be warmed. He loved the room so much as the fireplace crackled. It was a real treat to get a place as good as so, but such things were costly. Especially in Switzerland. He needed to peruse on.

After breakfast, he packed his things to prepare for a walk across the Dent. When paying the landlady and telling her his plans, she explained, "You'll have no guide, all of the men are at work."

"I can carry on myself if needed, it's not a problem." Felix was accustomed to doing things himself in this country as the price for guides and inns were outrageous. The landlady thought he needed help and suggested, "There is a girl who can help." She headed out to fetch her. Felix still thought he could manage and continued packing. Before he picked up his luggage to go, a girl (a pretty one) came, loading his things in a wicker basket. The strawberry haired girl then held out her hand, "I'm Pauline."

"Felix." He shook her hand, thanking her. They both set off on foot through the country. The land had so much to offer in view. Castles, villas and tall walnut trees were scattered here and there. Pauline was a healthy and happy girl, who enjoyed everything about where her village was settled.

288

It took much activeness to get about on foot as there were many rocks, holes in the paths and intense heat. The rough yet beautiful terrain could wear out the strongest pair of boots. Felix had been walking much already so he would be getting a new pair in the next stop.

There were many pastures of cattle and farmers out in the sun, collecting milk. It was a useful thing to come by a drink of fresh milk. It was utmost refreshing after a hard hike every few miles. Pauline was used to such a walk as she hardly broke a sweat. Rather, she joyfully frolicked the roads and climbed to her content. Felix was fine as he loved the exercise, but was sweating and drinking near a gallon of milk at each stop.

Another treat of the Alps were the distant tunes of yodeling, echoing in the air as if the mountains were speaking to one another. The call of the Alp horn gave its sound as well. Everything on this bright journey was a pleasure.

Pauline spoke much of life around her village. She pointed out a broken hedge along the way, "Many of the young people come around here for an afternoon dance then have a late night of a fire and coffee. The men have wrestling and running matches by morning. Tomorrow there is to be a dance across the lake. Musicians bring their instruments. Yet my mother is not letting me go as she fears that I may fall in the wide lake. Many of my friends are told not to as well..."

"Better to be safe than sorry." Felix stated. They were both silent a moment, but Pauline spoke up upon coming across a neat cottage in the meadow, "Oh, I must bid a good-day to my cousin if you don't mind."

"Not at all." Felix watched her run for the house as two girls came out the front door together. Pauline joined them on a bench and they all chattered. Felix noticed the adults of the cottage out herding cattle in the vast distant hills. It was a sight to see.

Felix and Pauline continued after the rest and Felix told her much about his time in Italy. She thought it quite interesting and nerve racking all at once. She couldn't imagine being in such a metropolis.

At noon they came to the village of Allière, resting a time there after the full morning of walking. Pauline gave Felix his things from the wicker basket as she had to return to her home. Felix still had further to go. They shook hands, feeling a somberness of their short growing relationship.

After Pauline left, Felix felt he could manage his things. The help was nice, but he was fine either way. At times he preferred to carry his own things. A man who noticed Felix's guide leave took advantage of the moment. Felix was getting some shut eye on a bench. When opening his eyes, he saw the old, rather fat man coming up to him. His demeanor was provoking. He suggested in a robust tone, "I see you are left without a guide, I can accompany you on your way of where it is you are going."

"I'm fine thank you. I can manage." Felix clung to his things as the man reached for his bags. The old man felt some offense and tried to convince Felix to hire him. Felix from then got up and went on his way by himself.

Along a path, he happened upon a cherry orchard. The people were gathering the fruit as well as enjoying the sweet red bulbs. Felix joined a group sitting under a tree, who welcomed him. He laid in a grassy area, relaxing as he got a filling of cherries.

Later he reached Latine and wandered the main street that had a few markets. Felix skimmed a meat market as a hearty meal sounded tasty. A man, not terribly older than Felix, purchased some lamb to roast. He noticed Felix was foreign and greeted him kindly, "Hello, are you having a fine day?"

"Ja." Felix couldn't help but smile at the man's tone. The man suggested, "Why don't you come with me, I have spare lodging at my place.

I'm sure you will be looking for lodging. The inns here are outrageous, please, I insist as you will in turn give me company."

"Dankeschön!" Felix felt relief to find such a kind man. As they walked down a few roads, the man introduced himself, "My name is Michael. I noticed you were not from around. My main means of living is being a guide so I know a traveler when I see one."

"I'm happy to have come across you then, my name is Felix." They walked to a clean wooden house. When entering, Felix was intrigued at the furnishings. Much of the chairs, tables and door frames were hand carved with beautiful designs. Michael admitted, "My other work consists of carpentry. The house and all of my furniture is made by me."

"It's beautiful." Felix turned about. Michael was quite proud of his woodworking skills. He told Felix, "I hope you like lamb. I'm roasting that for dinner."

"That sounds divine." Felix accepted but admitted, "I must say that I am to be at Château d'Oex tonight so I will be going after super."

"That's fine. I can help you get there." Michael prepared the lamb meat to roast. They continued speaking as it cooked. When it was done and served, it gave the pure essence of a nice home meal.

By late evening, Felix made it to Château d'Oex with Michael's help. Michael made sure the innkeeper gave Felix a well maintained room. After settling in a good and quiet room, Michael departed from Felix's company. Felix hoped to meet him again someday. The day rendered Felix exhausted, but he still made time to write to his family. By candlelight he penned his experience in Switzerland thus far, comparing it from Italy:

*It feels nice to know there is still honesty in the world: Happy faces, total absence of beggars and no saucy officials.*

~~~

As Felix by now should have known, contentment in travel did not last. In a stay at Boltigen, it rendered uncomfortable. The main inn was full, so he observed the surrounding buildings to find another place of stay.

Across the street stood a house open for lodging. The outside appeared old and worn down. Some people, rather homeless looking, walked in. Felix went ahead and decided to go as it was the only place open for the night.

Inside the home, it was more a fright in the night. When Felix walked into the entryway, lit by dim candles, he was met with a swarm of ragged people who were from the streets. They all dispersed around the house to find a place to rest. Felix went into the living room. An old scraggly man slept in a chair. The sofa was open, but Felix was unsettled by the creaking of an old grandfather clock as it struck with a hoarsely tone. The home wasn't necessarily disgusting, but it was dusty.

Felix roamed the halls, looking for an open bedroom. Each one was taken, so he resorted back to the living room, where the dry toned clock ticked. He set his knapsack down and laid on the tattered sofa. The old man in the chair peacefully snored. Felix wished he could do the same.

The wall panels of the room were thin as a baby could be heard in complete clearness in the next room. It screeched the whole night. Felix tossed and turned on the couch, unable to ignore the fact that the baby cried in every possible key, expressive of every possible emotion; first angry, then furious, then whining, and when it could screech no longer, it grunted in a deep bass. The infant's shrills gave Felix to thought of why people wished so much to return to childhood as children are so 'happy'. Children still flew into a rage just as adults and had sleepless nights as well as passions and so fourth.

~~~

The next morning after managing a few hours worth of rest, Felix set out for another day. In his walk to find a place for breakfast, he happened upon a 'Constitutional' to read. There were articles of politics and such, but one article was about the cholera disease that was supposedly spreading about. Many denied it. One man in Dantzic caught it, but recovered. In the midst of reading, it began to rain, so he put away the paper.

In the next coming days, the rain worsened. It poured all day and into the evening. Felix took shelter in a home in Wyler. A kind man and his wife hosted him. They lived a rather primitive lifestyle, but Felix was happy to find such a humble home. They let his coat, shoes and stockings dry by the fireplace. He was quite cold and huddled by the fire with a wool blanket. The lady gave him a cup of coffee to warm him inside.

As soon as the clothes dried he put them back on. He struggled with his shoes as the leather had shrunk from being sopping wet to warmed. The landlady noticed and offered, "Do you need a shoe-horn?"

"Ja." Felix answered. She came back with a tablespoon instead but it did the trick. He felt better once getting the freshly toasted shoes on his feet. The last thing he wanted was to catch a chill when he still had much backpacking to do in the coming days. The raging rain was putting his plans to a halt. He hoped it to end by morning, but the landlady gazed outside, "I've not seen it rain so much in a long time."

Felix gave a quiet sigh, turning back to his coffee. The lady then mentioned, "I'll be making beef and potato stew for supper. It might be simple, but you look like you need some fattening up."

"I'll eat anything." Felix stared at the fireplace. As the lady went to cook, the landlord came from the bedroom and sat at his chair by the fire. He grabbed a pipe for an evening smoke.

With the wet weather, the stew cooking, the fire and the pipe smoke, the home had an array of scents throughout.

It gave the sense of average home life. The feeling was what Felix had hoped for in his experience in the Switzerland country.

When the stew was finished, the three sat at the small, round wooden table and ate the hearty meal. There was fresh apple juice to drink. It's taste gave the impression of how crisp the apples used to make it were. The landlord and lady visited much with Felix. The lady ever so wanted to hear Felix play piano, but they didn't own one. Instead after dinner, he treated them by reading poems and stories he had brought along. It made a good close to the day.

~~~

## [2]

The next morning Felix awoke in bed to the sound of dripping rain. He snoozed hoping it would stop. He planned to make his leave that morning. The water still trickled against the roof. He gave a sigh and made an effort to get out of bed. The wind whistled coldly outside. The weather was to be disagreeable, whether he chose to continue on or not, so he decided to pack and hope for it to clear. The landlady had already set some bacon and orange juice at the nightstand, so Felix ate while getting dressed.

As he was packing up, the shutters suddenly burst open with the force of a strong wind. Rain and leaves blew in, making a mess. Outside it looked like a hurricane sweeping through. Trees were near to flat and the grass was being torn from the dirt. Felix had to shut the shutters with much strength then locked it. He gave a breath of relief. The small old house creaked against the turbulent storm.

Felix unpacked his things as he wouldn't be leaving. Instead, he grabbed a blanket, joining the landlord and lady in the living room. He sat on the rug by the fireside. They seemed quite scared of such a storm with the wicked lightning, making Felix feel unnerved. He jumped at the thunderclaps.

294

As the morning turned to noon, the storm's anger seemed to become furious. The landlord and lady seemed to not know what to make of any of it. The house was strong but creaked much. Felix was ever so thankful that he had a roof over his head and a warm fire beside him.

The landlady distracted her fears by tending to her needlework whilst sitting on the sofa. The landlord sat in his chair and smoked while staring at the fire in deep thought. Felix was laying on the floor with the soft rug under him, sticking close to the fire. He set a newspaper in front of him to keep him entertained, reading while wrapped in the heavy wool blanket.

There were many articles in the paper but they only gave more unrest. There were many reports across Europe of war and conflict. Another article had more about the cholera spreading. All things to hinder his travels across the lands. He set the paper aside, not wanting to hear of such. He grabbed a book instead. The storm perused on with wind and downpour.

The landlady smiled at the sight of Felix reading in such coziness by the fire. It seemed to remind her of years passed when her own children were still at home. She couldn't help but glance at him silently reading after every stitch in her needlework.

As noon passed, the storm finally cooled. Everyone gave sighs of relief. The landlady set her thread down, "What a storm that was. I hope nothing was destroyed."

A knock on the door then disrupted the calm. The landlord answered and a young boy in a panic explained, "All of the bridges have been washed away! Every path is blocked!"

"Oh no." The landlord grabbed his coat to go out and inspect. Felix was curious of the damage, but the landlady told him as he was about to get up, "I wouldn't bother going, you'll get soaked and chilled again."

Felix listened and continued reading his book. The landlady wanted more time to enjoy Felix's company. The landlord was gone an hour or so. When he came back, his pants were covered in mud as well as his coat. He was quick to set his shoes aside as to not get the floors too messy. He then informed, "It is true that the paths are blocked and bridges swept away. There was a terrible landslip at the Lake of Brienz."

"Oh dear." The landlady set down her needlework. Felix gave a sigh as he was stuck for the time being. The landlord assured him, "You'll probably be able to get on your way still tomorrow morning if all is completely calm. I'm sure a few passage ways will be cleared somewhat and passable if you're going by foot."

"Alright." Felix nodded. The landlady seemed in sadness as he stood from his cozy reading. In honesty, she wished him to stay. Felix didn't notice the aged woman's melancholy state and returned to his room.

~~~

The next morning the weather was wet, but calm. Felix packed straight away and headed off in the early hour. The landlady gave him some biscuits to eat along the way for breakfast. He thanked his hosts' kindness with well immense and paid them of course.

The next phase of the hike did not fare well. The paths Felix walked along were sadly cut up, muddying his boots and pants. He felt in disgust as the sloppy mess got in his shoes. His stockings would be ruined.

At about the eighth hour, the rain sprinkled. It created a mist among the landscape. By the ninth hour, the weather began it's violence again. This time Felix was in the middle of it. His hair, face and outfit dripped with water. He had chosen not the best color of pants to wear on his foot travel. His white pants were covered in mud to the knees, making him appear to be wearing long boots. His blue Paletôt was soaked as well.

He searched through the thicket of the raindrops, looking for any sort of shelter. A few meters away, he spotted a half built hut, so he ran there and crept in. No one else was there so he took his shelter. Inside there was a mass of dry fodder, so he nestled comfortably among the fragrant hay. He needed to be sure that he got a fresh dry outfit at his next stop, or he risked catching hypothermia.

As the rain raged on, another man came into the hut to take cover of the weather. He was a soldier. Felix peered at him as the man in uniform kicked his boots off and stockings. He grabbed a fresh pair from his bag. The soldier noticed Felix, "You should get a fresh pair of stockings and shoes," he pointed at Felix's muddy ones then asked,"Have you anymore?"

"Nein, I'll get some at my next stop."

"I wouldn't wait that long. Here," the soldier gave him an extra pair of his, "You don't want to risk getting immersed foot."

"Danke," Felix felt thankful to have a dry pair of stockings. As he changed, the soldier went off, unable to wait for the rain to halt. Felix made the same choice as well, continuing on a separate path.

The dry stockings didn't last long. Water seeped into everything. It even began to soak through his bag. He quickly took his sketchbook from it and shielded the precocious drawings by buttoning his waistcoats over it. It only kept it dry a little.

After walking a good hour, Felix came to the town of Interlaken. The sight of ruined streets and trees were everywhere as the storm had pushed through there. He was happy to find his next stop, but was ill received at the inn. He entered and asked for a room. The landlord sneered, "We are full."

"But I saw a couple leave on my way in!" Felix raged. The innkeeper shrugged and walked away. Felix checked other inns but they fared the same. He was forced to walk to Untersee where he found a comfortable lodging.

The next day he was able to acquire a carriage to Nuss-Baum Platz. There he got to do something a little less taxing than hiking. He toured a famous glass gallery, then found a stay at a tidy, rustic inn. The scenery out the window provided muse so he practiced drawing, sending some sketches home to his family.

In a musical finding, he happened upon a monastery in Engelberg. The monks were looking for an organist in the moment. Felix was obliged to play for them. He stayed a few days as they gave him a few duties as organist. The bit of pay was nice as well. Other musicians played through some works with him.

In a performance at the suitable instrument, Felix improvised a Fantasia. He ever so wished to write it down but no paper was available in the moment. The general idea of it was notable enough to remember when paper was found.

After having much to play on the organ, he journeyed on. It so happened that at many places he stopped, an organ could be found. He was able to practice and stretch his fingers. His feet, playing at the foot pedals, were making good progress. The organ was such a vast instrument for one person. Yet some of the keyboards were limited, being short notes or pedals in ranges. He couldn't play Bach's principal works on every organ, but still practiced sections of Bach's 'Well tempered Clavier' the best he could. He assumed there would be a perfect organ to play in Munich. Rietz sent a letter telling him of a friend that played an excellent bass section of the D major fugue, so Felix had to try it.

One of the organs he came across had trouble as he played it. It was noticed that the deep C sharp buzzed softly without ceasing.

Felix and a few other musicians tried to fix it. They pressed, shook and thumped the keys but it kept humming. The fault laid in the bellows. Felix resorted to going up to where the pipes were. He took stairs leading to the floor above. Taking his handkerchief, he stuffed it in the affected pipe. The hum stopped. He returned to the keyboard, but the C sharp could not play. He shrugged and continued his practice.

~~~

In the near end of Felix's pedestrian tour of the Swiss alps, he walked along a path in his lonesome as he could not find a guide this far. He headed for Tourgen. The feeling of being independent determined his spirits while passing through the woods. He felt that he had truly learned the Swiss way of yodeling, so he frolicked about the forest, yodeling his heart out several airs at the pitch of his voice. He was in high spirits.

His spirits were crushed as he arrived at the inn of Tourgen. Every person was rude and saucy, so he gave a spit of fire to them, "You will all be hanged! I shall go on!" He took out a map and the village of St. Gall was near. No guide wanted to go with him, so he carried his own luggage there.

On his way down the street, he happened upon a fine old peasant who wanted to help for a cost. He asked only two Batzen for a two hour hike to his home where he would help find Felix a carriage to Munich. Felix gladly paid and followed. They came to a newly built wooden house. Inside, the man's family sat at a round table. The mother read a thick book, a son shuffled cards and a pretty daughter sewed. It was charming.

The old man tried to find means of transportation out of Switzerland for Felix, but no coachman in the neighborhood wanted to drive that far. He resorted to sending his son with Felix to walk out until they found one headed for Munich. When they set out, the weather was a mix as it wasn't sure what it wanted to do. The sun peeked out from small rain clouds. Eventually after hiking a few miles, a carriage came by and Felix was on his way out of Switzerland.

# Chapter XIV: Munich

Mendelssohn, Piano concerto no. 1 in g minor  [1]

[1]

In Munich, Felix was determined to work hard at his music. He began penning a piano concerto as the carriage crossed the border out of Switzerland as he wanted to have a grand concerto of his own. It was set in g minor. He wanted a strong sound from the piano so he made much use of melodies in octaves.

Whilst making notes, he glanced at some letters from home. Mostly from his mother. Lea worried about her son's health. Felix assured her in writing that he was eating and sleeping well. The guide driving the coach knew his way around. He and Felix got along and ate together. Sometimes Felix disrupted the guide as he hummed trumpet and oboe tones in his sleep. In turn, the guide would wake him from his morning snoozes.

Felix arrived in Munich in early October. Perfect timing for the Oktober Festival. He could not wait for the full week of Bier, dancing as well as music with his friends. Skipping about to polka in a Bier Hall was definitely on the checklist.

As the carriage drove into the bustling city streets, he felt a happiness to be in civilization again. He gave a letter of address to the guide of a place that was prepared for him to stay.

Felix felt a bit confused when the carriage parked at a busy street lined with stores. The said address was on the street level and had the look of a shop with its glass door. He asked the guide, "Are you positive this is right?"

"It's what the note says."

"I guess I'll find out." Felix hopped off the carriage and unloaded his luggage. He entered the place and felt sure it was right. A piano, bed and other necessities were placed in the small makeshift apartment. The glass door had a thick, decorative curtain for privacy. Beside the door was a window with shutters. At the moment the shutters were open. It was only a step into the street with passersby. Some already were peeking in, giving a friendly wave and a 'Guten Morgen'. A few seemed to be snooping in the apartment. Felix shut the shutters soon after getting his things organized.

Within the day ahead, he got to learn of his neighbors. In the apartment above, the landlord and his daughter lived. They were kind and the daughter was of course pretty. Next door there was a Greek man lodging. He was learning piano. The progressing music could be heard when the shutters were open. It was enjoyable as The traditional tunes of Greece could be heard. Sometimes the tunes inclined Felix to practice dancing, yet he quickly learned the man to be odious.

When Felix began his own regular practice, he opened the shutters, letting in the fine crisp air. As he played a lush, sweet melody, the neighbor man happened to be coming from the market. He stopped and peeked through the window, "Show off!"

Felix jumped to a wrong chord as the comment startled him. He looked up from the keys, explaining, "I must practice. You should be doing the same."

The man had nothing back to say so he carried on. His bitterness was made up as the landlord's sweet daughter walked by every now and again, wearing her round silver cap. Felix thought her slender and ever so pretty. His heart fluttered when she happened to notice him. In turn it caused his fingers to flutter a trill at the keys in his romantic improvisation.

Concert plans arranged for Felix's music were pushed back due to the hectic week of Oktoberfest.

Each evening had a concert, ball or party already booking out every venue. Felix's hands were full enough in other means. Friends constantly interrupted his composing as they begged him to join in their activities. When his friends left him alone, the lovely weather tempted him to go for a walk. At the same time, copyists made him stay home as they gave him much work. Felix enjoyed every bit as it felt good to be back in society.

When rehearsals for the future concert were soon to commence, Felix prepared the set list. The first half would start with the symphony in C, then 'The Midsummer Night's Dream', finishing with his new piano concerto in g minor. For the second half, after selected works of others, he was instructed by directors to improvise at the keys. Many had heard of his skill at improvising and wanted to hear for themselves. Felix felt nervous at such a request. It was one thing to improvise alone or in a casual setting, but it didn't seem proper in a large concert hall. In London he had done so, but it was on a more organized basis. He wasn't sure if he really wanted to fulfill the request.

Felix set his debates aside to turn his focus to his daily schedule. It had become reoccurring. From morning he composed, corrected and scored until one o'clock. He then went to Scheidel's coffee-house in the Kaufinger Gasse. Since going the same time each day, he learned every face in the same place. Two played chess, three in day dreams, five at the newspapers, six eating dinner and Felix himself, sitting with a nice set of coffee and dinner. After eating, a friend by the name of Herr Bärmann went to fetch him for a walk to discuss the coming concert. After a walk, they ate cheese and drank beer together. Felix then would return home to work.

Felix wasn't the only young aspiring pianist in Munich. In the paper, there was a new name. A polish pianist by the name of Frederick Chopin was to play in the Konzerthaus. There were many good reviews of his technique. The man helping Chopin make a name for himself was Freidrich Kalkbrenner.

Kalkbrenner was from Paris with a well known name as he was a composer and piano manufacturer. Felix ever so wanted to hear Chopin, but he had too much on his hands at the moment.

Felix's friends often came to his apartment for musical picnics in the evenings. They would invite other friends as well. Word of the gatherings at Felix's room spread among musicians and music lovers. Felix at times tried to keep the gatherings small as his place of stay couldn't hold a lot of people. Kalkbrenner heard of the gatherings and Felix's skill. He felt inclined to pay a visit.

When a formal, well written letter of request reached Felix's hands, he was in hopes that Chopin would come with Friedrich, but Kalkbrenner didn't say anything of the pianist. Instead, Friedrich requested a time for only he and Felix. Felix couldn't deny the request as he deemed it an important engagement. He sent an accepting note for him to come that afternoon as no gatherings had been planned.

When the sixteenth hour struck, there was a knock at the door. Felix stood from the piano and was quick to answer. There at the door was a dark haired man, dressed as finely as a gentleman possible. He seemed rather to be dressed to impress.

*(Freidrich Kalkbrenner)*

Felix welcomed him into his Munich home. Kalkbrenner glanced about and commented, "This is quite a small place for the gatherings I hear of."

"I try to regulate who's invited. Yet one of these days my friends are going to go all out and invite everyone they know." Felix chuckled. Kalkbrenner gestured to him at the piano, "Please. Play some."

Felix sat down and began improvising a floral tune. Kalkbrenner leaned against the instrument, arms crossed in deep thought. He seemed a mix of opinion. Felix hoped he sounded as good as Kalkbrenner was expecting. The tune lasted a few minutes, then closed. Kalkbrenner turned to Felix, "That was improvised?"

"Ja, but it is in part based on one of the Welsh tunes I wrote a few years back. There's so many options for one tune." His voice resonated with passion. Friedrich nodded and mentioned, "Chopin can improvise anything you give him. He has such a unique sound. My help has furthered his technique as I am the last of the great classicists in musical society."

"Oh..." Felix wanted to laugh at his comment of being the last classicist, but he held it in. The statement gave Felix insight to Friedrich's personality. He was a conceited and self centered man. Such musicians tired Felix to the full.

Kaulkbrenner wasn't what he claimed to be. Beethoven was considered to have transitioned music from the classical to the romantic style. Rather, it would be better to call composers such as Beethoven, Schubert, Rossini, Weber and some others that lived in between the 18th into the early 19th century, composers of the regency era. Of course Beethoven's early years were definitely based on the classical forms, but throughout his life, the music's basis relied more on feelings rather than balance, and powdered wigs became last season. The true heart of classicism died with Mozart. Of course Kalkbreener could compose in the classical style, but that didn't make him the last great classical composer.

"Have you heard him?" Kalkbrenner continued. Felix shook out of passing ideas, "Oh. Chopin? Nein. I want to, but I'm so busy here.

I will be in Paris after this and heard that you and he were to be there soon. I bet I can catch a concert then."

"He shall be playing many concerts there. I believe he'll be the best pianist in Paris." Kalkbrenner stated. Felix nodded, not taking the man's confidence in Chopin personally. He knew his own abilities and didn't want to make any negative assumptions of Chopin before hearing him, or meeting him. Kalkbrenner then asked Felix, "May I improvise something for you?"

"Of course." Felix stood from the piano. Kalkbrenner took his spot in all prosperity, then began a Fantasie and played with perfection. It felt almost too precise for an improvisation. Felix listened closely, catching on to something. This was not improvised. It was a written piece. Friedrich continued on, trying to appease. When he finished, he turned to Felix, "That is improvising. You see my young fellow, you have much to learn."

"Sounded good." Felix gave a kind smile. Friedrich did have skill, but he was trying to play up his talents. Felix preferred the man to be himself. Kalkbrenner then asked Felix, "What sheet music do you have? I'd like to see."

"I have some of yours," Felix chimed, digging through the stack of music. He grabbed one titled 'Effusio Musica'. He then slyly stated while setting it at the piano, "I was going to ask you to play it, but it appears you've already fulfilled my wishes!"

"Oh…" Friedrich stared at the note for note notation of the 'Improvised Fantasie'. He then turned to Felix, his tone turning as if he swallowed a sour apple, "I believe the hour is drawing where I must go. Paris shall be when we meet again." He was quick to get up and make his leave. From then, Felix knew Kalkbrenner didn't like him, but didn't want to show it. He hoped not to get in any entanglements with the man.

In other means concerning true friends, they requested to host the large musical soirée in Felix's room. Felix was unsure as they made a list of thirty guests. He didn't want to disappoint his friends, so he agreed to host. In preparation, he made sure the home was clean and ordered plenty of wine, cheese and sausage. His friends gave in to help the expenses to make it a good gathering.

Upon the evening of the event, the small apartment filled with more and more people. They ranged from friends, friends of friends, musicians, one's of dignified society and of course, party crashers. There were definitely more than thirty people. Some sat on his bed, others on the dining table and counters. Musicians were scattered about, playing at their turn. There were singers, violinists and woodwindists. Felix, being the host of the party, was made to play the most at the piano. His poetic friends created some verses for Lieder.

When others sat at the piano to play, Felix stood among the spectators to listen. He felt overcrowded as some tried to move closer to the piano. A few others (ladies) wanted to stand beside Felix. After wonderful violin, piano and flute music, everyone enticed Felix back to the keys, wanting him to improvise. He tried to decline as he was tired, but the guests refused no for an answer.

Felix complied and improvised on some themes. All he really had on his mind were wine-glasses, benches, cold roast meat, and ham. Everyone though loved his piano etiquette. The music resonated through the complex. People were in the halls, visiting the landlord's home, standing in the street and everywhere else to get a listen of Felix's music.

The room became hot from the crowdedness and the noise was deafening as the piano played over people speaking in cheer, drink, chatter and song. Felix finished to a cadence after a few more variations then stood from the piano. Everyone clapped and rooted. Felix gave a bow. The party continued with dance as a guitarist and accordionist began polka tunes. Food and more wine were passed around for dinner.

There was no means for the meal to be sit down, but the formal guests didn't seem to mind. They were reserved but content. The other guests sat anywhere and everywhere, having the time of their lives. Felix was in between formal and partyful. He liked to have his dinner at the table, having refined conversation with dignified guests. He also spent time drinking with his casual friends but didn't get to the point of falling over in a childish affair as some young men foolishly did. No matter what station the guests had, each one had someone to talk to and had a happy time. The party lasted until half past one in the morning.

~~~~

Felix woke up the next morning in bed, rather not remembering laying down. He was still in the same outfit from the gathering. An empty wine glass sat beside him in bed. Wine glasses and dishes were rather everywhere, making a mess of things about. It looked like a pack of wild animals had trampled through his room. He found Herr Bärmann asleep in a dining chair and another man passed out on the floor. Felix didn't think the party was hardcore, but it had been something.

In his need to get organized, a postman came with a very fancy letter. Felix took it. As he read it, he felt another array of disorganization. He was to play for the royal court in Munich! In front of the Queen! The dukes and duchesses! That evening!

Felix couldn't decline as it was a demand. He needed to be presentable. Straight away he dug out his best attire. Herr Bärmann woke with a snore. Felix was tying a fine black silk cravat over the collar of his formal white shirt. Bärmann asked him, "What are you getting done up for?"

"The Royal Court." Felix put on his best black coat. Bärmann yawned as he was too hungover to care. Felix woke the passed out man and made him leave. He then turned to Bärmann, "I must get all of this cleaned up, can you help?"

"I suppose…" Bärmann stood from the chair and picked up discarded wine glasses. Felix finished straightening his coat then picked up dishes and rags scattered about. Once the room was spiffy, Bärmann left as he had his own business to tend to. Felix went to the piano to figure out what he should play that evening. It was a hard choice as a Queen would be hearing the music.

By the time he got his choices made and his regular work done, it was time to head to the palace. A special note he gave the postman agreeing to come. Soon a special carriage pulled up the street. It wasn't a big fancy coach, but everyone looked at Felix curiously as the carriage was marked as royal transport.

When the carriage turned a path, a large palace of Bavarian architecture came into view. The beauty stunned Felix as the yard was open trimmed grass with decorative hedge trees along the wide main road up to the structure. To top off the look, there was a sparkling body of water with a grand fountain.

When escorted into the palace, the inside was all the more grand with lush red carpets making a path over the slippery marble floors. The walls were an array of hand painted scenes, gold lined frames and elegantly draped windows.

Felix felt nervous to step on the carpet as the servant led him down a corridor. He had nice shoes, but didn't want to mess anything up. When he entered the main hall full of high society, he did his best to keep his posture up to par. The court of dukes and duchesses were gathered at both sides of the room. The Queen, in her royal garb, was seated at her throne. Next to her an empty one sat, the King's, but he was elsewhere.

In the center of it all stood a well kept grand piano. As the servant guided Felix to the instrument, the court glanced at him, whispering amongst themselves. The Queen sat quietly in all grace.

Felix stood next to the piano bench as the servant announced to her, "Your majesty, Herr Felix Mendelssohn."

After bowing politely, the servant walked away. Felix kept his stance, unsure what to do next. The Queen kindly gestured, "Please. Sit." She had a warm smile. Felix obeyed but felt uncomfortable as those of the court stepped closer to the instrument. A few ladies held fans, feverishly waving it at themselves in anticipation. The gentlemen observed the musician in deep thought before he even pressed a key yet. Felix glanced at the Queen, waiting for instruction. She spoke, "Play something."

Felix turned to the keys and began with some pieces of his own. The whole court seemed to recall the music. Felix gave sighs of relief constantly to himself as the Queen appeared pleased. She especially liked his improvising skills.

After moving to a final cadence on the current impromptu, he thought he was finished, so he turned to the Queen. She seemed in a daydream while looking at him. Felix froze in the moment, but she snapped out of her doze and commanded, "Improvise on some Royal Themes. You aren't done yet."

Felix nodded and recited a few themes then burst them into a presto, making it an exciting affair. Later he made a sweet, resonating adagio. After painting his ideas in music, he ended with grand chords. The Queen shook from another doze and commented, "It is strange the power you possess for carrying away an audience."

"Oh I do apologize for carrying away her majesty."

"Don't apologize, you play so wonderfully." She then gestured to him to join the other guests. Felix got a glass of champagne and stood among the crowded court. It was a world of difference from the evening before. Everyone was highly polite and polished. Felix was the roturier among them, but he was good of heart and managed pretty well.

At times he bumped into an excellency, but his proper apologies were accepted. They had adored his music too much to think lowly of him.

Being among royalty was an honor but Felix felt a lot more relaxed upon returning to his apartment after the formal evening.

~~~~

In the coming days with work and routine, Felix found spare time each day at noon to give lessons to a little Mademoiselle who wished to learn from him. She was bright and very good at the piano. Her name was Lia. She was small, pretty and a pale girl in her late adolescence, full of genius and a gift of composing songs. Felix loved the sound of her voice as it was unique. It was soft and tender and she had grace at the keys. Felix couldn't help but like her. He gave her instruction in two part counterpoint and composition. Originally she had been trained by the books, but it rendered her confused. Felix knew the proper way of explaining counterpoint and it made much more sense to her. Sometimes the books made it more complicated than necessary.

In other regards, rehearsals for the coming concert began. There were thirty-two violins, six double basses and two sets of woodwinds. Felix was happy to have such an orchestra to work with. Herr Bärmann helped as he was the one who organized the musicians together.

In the first rehearsal, Felix stood in front of them with his baton, ready to hear his symphony in C. He counted them in and thought his ears were bleeding from the first measure. They blared the fortes rather than punching them with a crisp tone. Every instrument section had their own tempos. Felix clicked his bâton against the stand calling to them, "Start over, bitte. Clean sound, bitte."

They started again. It still sounded horrible. When Felix stopped them in frustration, Herr Bärmann suggested, "Why don't I work with them. I'll let you go cool down. There's a piano in the room over there."

310

Felix went away to a private room with a suitable piano. For two hours he practiced conducting by himself while Bärmann tried to get the musicians' act together. Felix returned and suggested to Bärmann, "Why don't we try the concerto?"

"That may suit better for now." Bärmann gestured Felix to the piano. He sat feeling anxious as the newly composed concerto had not been played by an orchestra before. Bärmann counted them in. From the get go, each musician rushed in which in turn made Felix start out of tempo. He tried to fit his playing to the orchestra's speed, but they were falling apart. Felix in frustration stood from the keys in the midst of it and yelled over their playing in angered German, "Halt! Halt! es ist nicht zusammen! Lass uns die Ouvertüre versuchen. Das Konzert ist in zwei Tagen!"

The musicians flipped their music to the Overture to a 'Midsummer Night's Dream.' They gave sighs and seemed unsure. Felix grabbed his bâton again and took Bärmann's place. When counting them in, the flutes' windful chords echoed in the concert hall. It was the most dry and off tune thing he heard. When the violins mimicked the sprites, it was so rushed that they fell apart in tempo. Felix face palmed, "I may as well take this piece off the bill."

"Please, I assure you next time they will be better. Just let them rest today. I think you need time away too. It's just one of those days," Bärmann encouraged, "There is a ball tomorrow. You should go and get your mind off this. Rehearsals will be better next time, I am sure."

"Alright." Felix left for the day. He hoped the concert would be prepared accordingly. There were only two days until then.

~~~~

The Sunday ball lifted Felix's spirits. There was dancing, cheese and crackers with a fine 'punch' to drink. It all helped ease the worry of the coming concert. The ladies whispered to one another behind their decorative fans, telling each other of how pleasing of a dancer Felix was.

The other gentlemen observed Felix, trying to learn good dancing skills to impress their dates.

"He knows every step and pattern of the minutes." A lady commented, waving her fan in a flutter while watching Felix gracefully turn about in the company ôf a pretty girl. Another young lady stated in response, "If only I could catch a dance with him."

After the pleasant evening, Monday morning came. It was the day of the planned concert. Felix made sure rehearsals started early in the day as he feared a lot would need to be fixed. Thankfully, the orchestra gathered and seemed more organized. He had them start with the Overture. Felix counted them in and they ran through it. Again. And again. They played it until Felix was pleased. He did the same for the other pieces. It took a lot of time to perfect everything.

After finally getting the right sound in order, everyone went home to rest before the concert. When it came time to return to the Konzerthaus, the rattling of the carriages excited Felix. To his surprise, the royal court, King, Queen and all arrived for this concert. It was requested that Felix make a speech before the performance. That was the most trying part of the evening. He prepared a talk that would be pleasing, but he felt it was an awkward ordeal.

When everyone seated, Felix stationed himself in the prompter's box. He tried to speak over the murmuring crowd, "Meine Damen und Herren...."

No response. He spoke louder, "Meine Damen und Herren, bitte..." The audience quieted and moved their stares up to Felix. He paused a second as the King and Queen looked at him. After a moment of silence, he began his speech, addressing the musicians and the benefit of the concert. It went smoothly. After the speech, he headed for the stage to conduct. He held his nice English bâton, ready to count the musicians into his symphony in C.

312

The orchestra sounded phenomenal. Felix didn't know what had changed with them as it sounded better than the rehearsal earlier in the day. They crashed the fortes and played the scherzo delicately. The King applauded first, then the rest of the crowd. Next was the overture to the Shakespeare play. It was very pleasing and most everyone by now was familiar with it. The execution sounded whimsical. After the humble end, Felix set his bâton down and sat at the piano to play his new concerto. Upon playing it, it instantly became a favorite. The third movement, with the ear tickling melody, captivated every listener. It received a long applause.

Felix was sweating as he bowed. He left the stage as Herr Bärmann took over to play various works for the second half. Felix went to the anteroom to cool down. As he laid on a sofa, napping, someone tapped on him, "Herr Mendelssohn?"

Felix woke from his rest to see the King in his ever so formal uniform. In an instant Felix sat up, but the King assured, "Oh please, you don't need to stand in the moment. I just came back here to ask you something. I feared you'd be busy after the concert, so I came now."

"Of course, anything." Felix nodded. The King then gave his question, "Are you by chance related to the Bartholdy that had an abide in Rome? With the fresco paintings? I noticed your name was Mendelssohn-Bartholdy."

"Ja, my uncle Jakob on my Mutter's side."

"Really? I visit there whenever I am in Rome. I find it to be a cradle of modern art." He then chimed, "My wife tells me you improvise well at the piano. I may have to entice you to do so before the end of the concert."

"Oh…" Felix felt a bit nervous. He hoped the request to improvise would have been forgotten. Felix questioned the King, "Are you sure you want me to improvise here? Would you rather hear it at another time?"

"Are you declining my demand?" He sounded displeased. Felix in an instant replied, "Nein your majesty. I shall improvise."

"Good. Otherwise your neck would be at stake." His displeasure turned to a tease. Felix laughed slightly, wondering if he really meant such. The King then left. Felix began organizing his thoughts to set his mind to improvising. It was all interrupted as an attendant told Felix, "The King has summoned you back to the stage."

"I'll be right there." He rushed out. As he entered the stage, the musicians sat quietly as the audience watched him as if they were waiting for him to do something. The King then called out explaining, "Please. Improvise for us at the piano."

Felix obeyed and got seated once more at the instrument. He was still sweating from the concerto (and nerves), so he wiped his face with a handkerchief. It felt rather in distaste to be improvising at the keys during an orchestral concert. He thumbed some notes, thinking of a theme. The King then suggested, "Please do a royal theme."

Felix began and played a set of variations on the spot. It sounded smooth and structured. He knew what he was doing. The audience applauded loudly after the grand finale. Felix felt far from satisfied with himself. He heard his mistakes through his nervousness. No one else may have noticed, but to him it was a hash. He felt so foolish as it was in front of royalty.

Afterwards, the Queen went to Felix to give her good regards. Felix apologized all so much as he still felt annoyed at his playing. The Queen sweetly assured, "Dear one, all is courteous. You made no mistake."

Though the Queen gave assurance that it was well, Felix discerned that he would not improvise in public again. Even if the King demanded it. Felix thought it to be;

*Both abuse and absurdity.*

314

# Chapter XV: Lieder Ohne Worte

Mendelssohn, Songs Without Words no. 1 [1]
Chopin, Op. 10 Etude No. 3 'Tristesse' [2]
Chopin, Romance from Piano concerto no. 1 [3]

## [1]

The winter chill blew into the cab riding across the dusting of snow, headed for Paris. Felix gave a warm breath to his cold hands. He was in the middle of penning some piano works that had been on his mind. They were styled as a Lied, but solo piano. It was as if a voice should come and sing with the keys, but no words could express what the music gave. They were songs without words.

When entering Paris, a layer of snow beautifully covered the elegant buildings. It was a cold December. Felix debated what he was to achieve in such a city. In Italy he had been lazy, sleeping and eating about. In Switzerland; a wild student, walking the country, taking what he could for a bed and meal. In Munich; a consumer of cheese and Bier. In Paris he decided to speak more of people, politics and music. The city had changed since the last time he had been there. It was a plethora of culture and music as well as unrest, uproar and disease.

Felix penned to his father, discussing a libretto idea for an opera. He was in a tangle of the subject. Abraham suggested that Felix find a French poet, but Felix debated using Shakespeare's 'The Tempest.' In all honesty, Felix wasn't up to doing an opera.

The coach stopped at an address Felix obtained from a friend. It was a small complex of two stories. Felix couldn't wait to get a nice, warm room with a cozy bed. The landlord met him outside and led him to a door on the ground floor. Inside contained a dark small room, cold as ice.

"Is there by chance a warmer place available?" Felix chatted through his teeth.

"Not until the new year. You get this room or go somewhere else." The landlord took his pay. Felix set his things on the hard steel framed bed. The mattress was poorly packed with feathers. The blanket was tattered, making it a useless item. A window looked over a small damp garden. In the room above, a man could be heard singing political tunes while strumming a guitar.

Felix found the means to light a candle to brighten the depressing room. The fireplace had some hot coals, but nothing that could warm the place. Felix's feet were as ice. The cold state made him in no mood to compose and he missed the weather in Italy. Even in the winter season, Rome was better.

As his rooms were deemed too bitter, he became outgoing. His main friend in Paris was Ferdinand Hiller. He was a musician, younger at twenty years of age and had been a childhood friend. Felix soon received an invitation to dine at Herr Hiller's home.

When finding the humble apartment, Felix knocked at the door. Surprisingly it was not Hiller that answered. It was an older man, strangely familiar. Felix apologized, "I'm sorry Monsieur, I thought this to be the home of Herr Hiller."

"Ah, but it is. You are Felix are you not? Come in, the table is set. Hiller had to take care of some business, so I answered." The man let Felix in the home. He noticed on the sofa in the sitting room was a violin case. This man was Monsieur Baillot, one of the most skilled violinists.

As Felix hung his coat, Baillot explained, "I know you from years ago when you came to the conservatory to meet Cherubini. He showed me some of your compositions and I do say I was impressed. Now you are so grown and I imagine your music has done the same."

"I'm always trying to improve."

Herr Hiller walked in from another room, meeting his guests standing about, "Felix! How much you've grown. I see you've met Baillot. How is your sister Fanny?"

"Getting on well. Married and with child. She still composes." Felix handed him a manuscript of her work. He brought it knowing Hiller admired her music to the full. He examined it with deep interest, "Her way of writing is so neat and flawless. I remember hearing her play at the Sunday salons."

"I've been away from home for over a year and miss it too." Felix felt a slight homesickness. Hiller handed back the music and in turn grabbed something of his own that he composed, "I think you may like this."

Felix took it and skimmed it. It was an enthralling piano work. When something pleased Felix to the utmost full it showed in the obvious. A surge of excitement came over him. It caused him to drop on the floor and rolled about, channeling his built up energy. Baillot laughed, "It's a good thing this floor is carpeted."

Felix stood back up exclaiming, "This music is written so well! I can't wait to hear it played." His slightly overgrown hair was a bit of a mess now. Hiller teased, "With that hair, you look so much as Meyerbeer!" He was referring to Guacimo Meyerbeer, a composer of opera.

Felix's enthusiasm instantly faded. Meyerbeer happened to be a distant cousin of his. He wasn't fond of him. The comment made him feel self conscious. Hiller knew Felix to be sensitive, so he encouraged, "Come, let us not waste time in the parlor and have dinner." They all headed to the dining room. There, their chatter continued, catching up on life.

~~~~

The next day, Hiller and Baillot spent the afternoon at a café. Felix soon arrived to join in coffee. Hiller gave way to chuckles upon his appearance. He had freshly trimmed hair. Baillot implied, "Felix, your hair looks well cut. Was there a reason you got a trim?"

"Hey, they have chess here!" Felix distracted their amusement, "Let us play a match." He sat at one of the chessboard tables. Baillot joined him and Hiller sat close by to watch.

Felix being an avid chess player rendered hard to beat. Baillot tried a few times, but always a hair off. After the afternoon hours passed, the old man assured, "Next time I will beat you."

Felix shook his hand in sportsmanship. The three of them then left the café to go their separate ways for the evening.

As Felix walked towards a carriage, he thought over his plans music wise in Paris. Unlike Munich or London society, it was a struggle. He contacted the directors of the Paris Conservatoire to host a concert, but there was much quarreling. There were much larger names in Paris at the moment. Meyerbeer had his operas, Paganini was packing the concert halls, Berlioz found opportunity, Franz Liszt was making a career and Chopin had arrived.

Felix consulted Baillot on the matter as he had influence in Paris. He suggested finding Cherubini, but not to guarantee anything as the aged man's grumbling mood only grew. For the younger generation of directors, what they wanted musically was that of The Romantic school.

Felix thought the Romantic School had infected all of Paris society. The music depicted nothing but darkened themes of murder, misery, the plague, the gallows, etc. A prime example was Berlioz. Felix loved him as a dear friend, but couldn't come to adore his music. Berlioz invited him to a concert that included his orchestral work, Symphonie Fantastique. The style had received good success in Paris. Berlioz happened to not be conducting, so he sat with Felix in one of the boxes above the floor level.

As soon as the music started, Felix began to feel sick to his stomach. To his ears, it was a frightful muddle, an incongruous mess. He felt the need to wash his hands if he ever had to handle such a score. The music kept going in all morbidity, sending shivers up his spine.

Berlioz noticed Felix in an ill state as he refrained in his seat. He discreetly grabbed something from his pocket and handed it to Felix. It was a vial of some sort of medicine. Berlioz instructed, "Drink it. It will help your nerves. Drink it quick though."

"What is it?" Felix took a swig of the liquid. Berlioz whispered, "Opium."

"What!?" Felix spat it out, "You mean to drug me!?" He whispered aggressively. Berlioz huffed, "You just wasted half of it."

"You shouldn't even have this. I can't believe though in the whole time of getting my tooth pulled you had this…" He poured the rest of the vial on the floor. Berlioz's attitude changed in a mere second. He snapped at Felix, taking him by the coat, "What are you doing!? How am I to find my composition inspiration now?"

Felix stared at him in fright as his expression looked like that of a mad man. They were the only ones sitting in the box, so no one noticed them. Hector obviously had taken some advantages of his days in medical school. Felix asked him, "Are you alright mentally?"

"I'm fine." Hector let him go, realizing how his behavior had become. Felix felt uneasy the rest of the concert as Hector didn't speak anymore.

Later Felix was asked to write a review of the concert. He wrote one deeming the music sickening. Even though Felix's opinions were negative, Berlioz still kept company with him. He sat in at a musical gathering at Hiller's home where he heard Felix play Beethoven at the piano. Berlioz determined that Felix understood Beethoven, but didn't understand Berlioz.

~~~~

In the meantime of no concert opportunities, Felix became a bit lazy; eating out with friends, sleeping, not composing and blaming the cold air. His letters conveyed tiredness and his mother sensed it. She worried about her son as he had been traveling hard for nearly two years. Felix assured that he was getting on well. In catching up on things in Berlin, nothing much had changed. The only sad news was the passing of his old philosophy professor, Hegel.

Soon a concert of interest finally came up and Felix was determined to go. Chopin would be playing in a recital at the Pleyel rooms, along with other well acclaimed pianists. The papers spoke grandly of Chopin. Felix sensed that Kalkbrenner had a strong influence on the papers' claims.

On the day of, he went to the Pleyel rooms and found a chair in the fancy recital hall. Everyone was dressed quite elegantly. Felix of course had a nice suit. He sat next to a gentleman, facing the other way. He had rather long hair; longer even for a gentleman that preferred long hair. When the man turned around, Felix felt a wave of shock. This was no man. It was a lady holding a top hat and wearing trousers!

"Who are you?" Felix had to ask. The woman near laughed at his disapproval, "Aurora, but most know me by my pen name. Sand."

"You're George Sand!?" Felix could not believe all of those books he read were by a woman under a pen name, who wore trousers. The other gentlemen didn't seem to take note of her dressing and greeted her as any other lady. Obviously people knew her.

Felix's disapproving thoughts were interrupted as Kalkbrenner sat next to him. He greeted him in all kindness, "Ah, a familiar face from Munich. It's nice of you to be here. I heard that you got to play music for the royal court of Munich. The King approved much of it. May I ask how you got to be in such a company?"

"The Queen first invited me to improvise at a gathering of the court."

"Oh. You must have been such a commoner among them." Kalkbrenner glanced at Felix's appearance as if he were unsuitable to be in the presence of aristocratic society. Felix stated, "They were all kind and good hearted to me. They loved my music." Their conversation ended as everyone took a seat, indicating the beginning of the recital.

The first to play was a familiar man who went to the elegant dark wood piano. He had medium length blonde locks. His smile showed pure white, clean teeth. A lady in the audience waved her fan as she blushed at him.

Felix's self confidence went down the drain as the man noticed him and gave a cocky nod.

He sat at the keys and glanced at the audience, then raised his hands over the keys. His fingers were incredibly long. Felix glanced at Kalkbrenner, who seemed to have a worried expression. The man at the keys then played a plethora of thirds and octaves. Chords as big as his finger span. This was Franz Liszt.

After a few impressive tunes, he played variations on a theme of Paganini. It was obvious Lizst adored his music. Felix, having seen Franz play when they were adolescents, felt his music had improved. It was still a bit much, but it was exciting. Everyone clapped and ladies swooned after the performance. Felix was curious of how this Chopin played if he was supposed to be the best pianist in Paris as Kalkbrenner claimed.

After Franz made his leave, the recital hall became filled with murmuring as the next pianist had not entered. Kalkbrenner seemed in a nervous rage. After a few more minutes, he stood and went to the door that was near the piano's platform. He was gone a while.

Finally the door opened again and a young man appeared. He stood in the doorway, trembling. His completion looked a bit worrisome as his face was on the pale side and his stature, rather thin. His brownish dark blonde hair was nicely styled and his outfit well maintained. Upon seeing the audience, his eyes seemed to widen all the more. Everyone looked at him, waiting.

Kalkbrenner came up behind him and strongly nudged him out of the doorway. He told him in a whisper before heading back to his seat, "You better play your damn best."

Felix, sitting in the front, heard Kalkbrenner's comment and thought it awful. It was obvious the pianist was near scared to death. The nervous mess of the man went to the keys. He wiped his face and hands with a handkerchief. This man had much smaller hands than Liszt and drowned in anxiety rather than haughtiness.

The ladies that had swooned over Liszt now seemed unimpressed, except for one woman. George Sand. She looked at the musician with awe.

Felix glanced at the program as he was unsure if this was really Chopin. The paper didn't seem to be mistaken. Before he looked back up, the man finally began to play.

## [2]

Felix could not believe the fragrant sound that blossomed from the keys. All anxiety seemed to be lifted as soon as the wistful notes resonated. Chopin's music was like a poet describing love. Fanciful, free and romantic. Felix shut his eyes and dreamed in the moment. When opening them, he observed Chopin's technique. His fingerings seemed different, not always correct, but it gave the same result in sound, if not better.

Chopin continued with ballads, waltzes and polonaises. Clenching his eyes shut at times out of fright as the audience stared at him. Felix glanced at Kalkbrenner, who glared at Chopin as if he did not approve entirely of the rendering of the music.

After Frederick finished the final cadence of an etude, he gracefully lifted his hands from the keys and appeared much more calm. The recital hall was silent for a moment.

*(Fredrick Chopin)*

Felix in a rush applauded aggressively. The rest of the audience then followed. Chopin turned to Felix and seemed struck with awe as if he knew him. Felix didn't find Chopin familiar, but was determined to become acquainted.

After giving his bow, Frederick made his exit. The next pianist took his place. Felix didn't pay any sort of attention to whoever it was, his mind was far too distracted by Chopin's music. He day dreamed through the rest of the performances, no matter how big the musician's name.

When the recital ended, Kalkbrenner straight away asked Felix, "Have you any engagements tonight? I'd be pleased if you would join Chopin and I to dinner. I'm much intrigued to know more of your concert for the King and Queen."

"Sure." Felix gave a kind tone. He only accepted on the basis that Chopin was coming along. George Sand overheard and begged, "Is it too much to ask if I may come Monsieur?"

"No." Kalkbrenner turned away to engage conversation with another. George rolled her eyes, storming away. Felix felt bad, but couldn't do anything. When it was time to leave, Kalkbrenner gathered Felix and Chopin so they could find a carriage to a restaurant.

Upon meeting, Chopin told Felix in a soft voice, "I've seen you before." His polish accent was thick as he tried to pronounce his French. Felix understood him fine. He could relate as he had a strong German accent, "You have?"

"When I was eighteen, I happened to be in Berlin. I heard you play at a recital, but I felt too nervous to meet you. Your music gave me much insight."

"Danke." Felix blushed. Already Felix and Frederick had become friends.

Kalkbrenner seemed cheered at first, but that soon faded as they rode in a carriage. The two young pianists spoke nonstop. They liked each other's techniques and way of composition. Each time the subject of technique came up regarding Chopin, Kalkbrenner tried to veer the conversation. Frederick sensed it and became nervous as Felix continued on.

At the restaurant, Kalkbrenner took over the conversing. He made sure of it. Chopin's manners became very reserved at entering. Kalkbrenner went to a waiter telling him, "I want the finest table. This is Chopin, the best pianist in Paris. We must have the best seats."

Chopin appeared in much embarrassment at Kalkbrenner's claim. Felix thought it awful that Kalkbrenner used him as a way to look good in public. The waiter explained, "I will seat you at the table we have left." He pointed at seating near the kitchen door. Kalkbrenner for some reason didn't think it favorable and hissed out loud, "Listen. I am in company with Chopin. That there is also Mendelssohn. You had better get us a better table."

Felix couldn't tolerate Kalkbrenner's comment and instantly told the waiter, "The table is perfectly fine, we shall sit." He and Chopin sat down and became busy in conversation. Frederick seemed to have much relief to talk to a decent and kind musician.

Kalkbrenner still stood by the waiter, arms crossed in a posh stature. Felix glanced at Freidrich, who eyed Felix with much contempt. Yet when he finally sat down next to him, he became full of kindness towards him. He interrupted his conversation with Chopin, asking more about how he became in royal company. It was all he seemed to care about. Thankfully he soon had to go use the restroom, so he left the table.

Felix turned to Frederick eagerly, "So, have you anything going on tomorrow?"

"No- wait- I forgot. I'm to be at the conservatory with Kalkbrenner. He has been making me attend some of his own music classes on piano technique as he believes mine needs much work. I know I do some things different as I am majorly self taught. My mother started my piano education but my first real instructor was a violinist. He had good pointers but he was no pianist."

"You do not have bad technique. Skip it and we shall spend the day with much more favorable musicians."

"I don't want to displease Kalkbrenner. He has helped me much."

"I think he's helped enough. You have proven yourself well, you should be in control of your own career...in fact, let's go find my friends now." Felix stood. Chopin seemed quite unsure, "I don't think we should abandon Freidrich. He is in charge of me. I have a performance next week and he's helping me organize it. We are still looking for musicians."

"You are old enough to be in charge of yourself. Besides, I'm a musician and my friends are. There's plenty to go around for what you need."

"Alright." Chopin got up with confidence. They both left the restaurant, abandoning Kalkbrenner. In the streets of the evening light, Felix spotted Hiller and Baillot going for a stroll. All was well when introducing Chopin.

~~~~

That next week, Felix and his friends helped Chopin organize his coming performance. The concert involved other composers as well. The pieces Chopin chose for his part involved six performers. Piano and strings. Felix volunteered to play viola. Baillot of course took up violin. The rest of the spots weren't hard to fill. There was no shortage of musicians.

Frederick seemed relieved in happiness in the company of his new friends. The rehearsals were well and positive. Yet the day before the concert, Kalkbrenner came to catch up on the progress of the performance.

He didn't speak to Chopin at all. Instead he gave much kindness to Felix at each break or chance he got. Felix thought it strange, even after he proved Freidrich a fake at improvising and abandoned him at the restaurant.

In other means, the concert happened in the early afternoon the next day. Chopin found much success in his segment of the concert. It even gave opportunity to the other musicians including Felix. He was surprised to find a dinner invitation upon returning to his rooms. It was from the Comtesse de P.

Felix wrote an accepting reply then noticed another dinner invitation. This one from Kalkbrenner. He wanted Felix to his home, as his main abide was in Paris. Felix tossed it away as he had a better engagement.

He left his rooms in the evening to the large home of Comtesse de P. Her dinner was quite formal. The long table fit a party of people. Felix sat next to the Comtesse. Among one of the guests was Franz Lizst. He sat towards the other end of the table, surrounded by ladies that had attended a concert of his a few hours prior.

Though Liszt had much company, everyone became intrigued by Felix. His speech that evening rendered especially witty. He had brought drawings with him, making everyone astounded at how well the landscapes were penciled. The Comtesse handed him her favorite books of poetry to read out loud. Some poems were in Greek and Latin. Liszt was interested in learning that Felix also played violin and viola.

After dessert was served and eaten, the Comtesse begged Felix, "Please may you play at the piano your latest Song without Words? They are such nice tunes, or anything you find appropriate."

"Of course Madame." Felix went to the grand piano within the large dining hall. He gave Liszt a glance, as a way of a comeback for all the times he nodded before playing.

Franz didn't seem to like being on the other side of the fence. Felix then sat at the keys and raised his hands in the air just as Liszt. He then plunged into Liszt's Hungarian Rhapsody No. 4.

Bursts of laughter came from the ladies sitting next to the composer of the piece. It began to cripple Felix's playing. Through the taunting laughs, Felix managed to make it to the end with struggle. He stood to see every guest holding their giggles. The Comtesse held a laugh as well.

Franz stood up and went to Felix. He gently took hold of his hands, "Your fingers are far too delicate and nimble. Since you butchered my music, I shall play yours with much ease. Have you some music I could read?"

Felix handed him his g minor concerto without a word. Franz took it then sat. Instead of raising his arms over the keys in his usual attack, he decided to imitate Felix's stance; pretty and delicate. At sight he read the work. Felix could not believe the accuracy and emotion put in. It was the best performance that piece ever had.

After Franz finished the marvelous rendition, Felix looked at his hands. They were quite big and his fingers were incredibly long. The webbing between them was much less than the average person. Felix joked, "I would have asked to do a boxing match instead but I don't think I'd fare well in that option either." He laughed a bit. Franz brightened him, "We both have our own skills. Let's leave it at that."

The rest of the evening went on in cheer. Felix played some of his Songs without Words to please the Comtesse. He also began to have a better acquaintance with Franz as they spoke more at the table. What could have ended up an unpleasant evening, turned out to be one of the best.

~~~

At the strike of noon, Felix sat in a dining hall, next to Hiller. It was in a grandiose home, showing its price by far. The table, fine mahogany. The chairs, maple with intricate carvings.

The walls, gold leafed embroidery. The floors, checkered marble. Even the food looked like royalty. A grand piano, produced by Kalkbrenner's company, stood in the room as well. Felix and Hiller had accepted a lunch invitation from Friedrich.

Hiller was amazed at it all; for now. He was not yet acquainted much with the man. Felix knew every bit of decor was for show. Kalkbrenner wanted to impress at his best.

While waiting, Felix in excitement told Hiller, "The other evening I had dinner at the Comtesse de P's. Liszt was there and you will not believe what happened. He played my g minor concerto at sight!"

"Of course he did. If he would have done it a second time, he would have something to add to it–"

Their conversation ended as their elaborate host entered the room in his finest attire. He gracefully took a seat across from Felix. Hiller already felt quite out of place. The atmosphere to Felix reminded him of his time at the royal palace in Munich among the court, where he was a commoner. A few servants served a large platter of a finely roasted ham.

The food looked picturesque as the meat had a mouthwatering smoked skin and rested on a decorative bed of lettuce. Roasted carrots and soup accompanied the main course. A servant cut the meat and served it.

Hiller dug into his food straight away, thinking this to be the best lunch invitation he happened upon. Felix admired his plate before enjoying it. Friedrich properly laid his napkin on his lap, situated the silverware and made sure the plate was placed correctly.

They each ate in silence for the first bites as the food had extravagant taste. Friedrich then swallowed and spoke up, "So Felix, how does a musician find commissions from royalty?"

"The Queen asked for me. She heard about my improvisation skills at piano." Felix sipped some French onion soup. Friedrich nodded, then asked, "Have you any concerts coming up here in Paris?"

"Not yet, I have to get the conservatory to accept my music. I'm not their first choice at the moment."

"I bet you would have a grandiose concert, playing on a Kalkbrenner piano of course. Why don't you try my piano over there? It's the finest Kalkbrenner piano in existence."

"Not today." Felix bluntly declined. He didn't want to feed into the narcissistic musician. As Felix looked towards the piano, Friedrich glared at him. Hiller noticed and didn't like the haughty musician's expression. When Felix turned back, Kalkbrenner was all smiles and kindness.

~~~

In the coming week, while the conservatory still fussed over doing a concert, Felix decided to get some music published. There was quite a bit he wanted in print. A quintet, octet (the latter also arranged as a duet), 'Midsummer Night's Dream', seven songs without words, six songs with words, six pieces of sacred music and the symphony in d minor.

Some publishers interested in his music requested a few alterations. So Felix gathered together the music that needed revising. He deemed the Hebrides Overture needed to be put in that pile. The modulations in the middle savored more counterpoint than the train of oil, seagulls and salt fish. He liked the work too much to be performed in an imperfect state. The Italian symphony was a mess in editing as he couldn't decide on themes. When consulting Fanny by letter, she thought the original was best. It left Felix feeling torn, so he set it aside.

In other engagements, he received notes every day inviting him to parties, music gatherings and balls.

It excited him to go to each one, but it distracted his composition work. To make time, he set aside the early hours of the day.

As Felix played at various small gatherings among musical society, his talents were quickly recognized. Word finally convinced the conservatory and they selected his music for two concerts. The pieces that interested the music directors were his piano concerto and the overture to 'A Midsummer Night's Dream'.

Rehearsals then consumed Felix's time to the full. The conservatory's orchestra was one of the finest he had ever worked with, minus the fact that the second Oboe was missing for the Overture. In one run through of the piece, it was noticed that the drummer had left, so Felix took the timpani sticks and played a fine closing drum roll.

For the performance, Felix took seating in a box next to some young armature musicians. Someone else was conducting, so he came as a concertgoer. The two musicians beside him whispered and giggled amongst themselves before the concert. When the orchestra got settled on stage they quieted. Felix had much confidence when his Overture sang throughout the concert hall. Yet by the time the strings started mimicking a burrow, the music scholars chattered in negative tones. They got up and left without knowing they were right by the composer.

~~~

After the concerts at the conservatory came and went, life in Paris became political turmoil. Talk and opinions of current affairs became frequent among the citizens. Felix's friends spoke of politics nonstop. He on the other hand wasn't keen on political speech and tried to avoid talk of anything risky. Only his letters to home contained a few subtle opinions, stating that his way of being a doctrinaire was by reading his newspaper each morning, forming his own opinions of peace and war then only among friends confess he knows nothing of the matter. To him, his friends appeared quite foolish with their gripes of temporary subjects.

It was true that there was much chaos as street raids often commenced, but Felix distracted himself from the frightful fights by composing or reading. Currently there were some fantastic novels in the bookstores. Victor Hugo had become a popular name in the world of literature. Just within the year, Hugo published, 'The Hunchback of Notre Dame'. It made the old cathedral noticeable as a destination, in which pushed the people of Paris to have the rather neglected structure restored.

Felix took his copy of the book with him on a stroll to see Notre Dame. The gothic structure was breathtakingly tall and intricate. At a bench nearby he sat to read. The essence of the story felt more so conveyed while at the real setting.

"Enjoying some of Victor's stories are we?" A familiar voice came up to Felix. He set the book down to see Franz Liszt. Felix nodded, "His writing definitely makes one feel within the story." He glanced at the cathedral behind him. Franz smiled and gestured to Felix to follow him, "I do wish you to come with me to where I am going. I think you'll find it quite of interest."

"Alright." Felix followed Franz as he walked down the street. They went a few blocks before stopping at a decent neighborhood. Franz went up to a door in a line of crowded city houses. After knocking, a servant answered and let them in. It was a nicely decorated home. The rugs were soft and the flooring was polished. In the main room, a refined man sat on a sofa by the fireplace, reading the paper. He looked up to see Franz, "Oh, bonjour. I'm so glad you have come and you've brought a friend. Is he musically inclined as well?"

"Monsieur Hugo, This is Herr Mendelssohn. Oui, he is musical." Franz introduced. Felix still held the book in his hands, disbelieving that Franz had been headed to the author's home all along.

Victor smiled and gestured to them to sit on the other couch. Once they settled, the servant brought some coffee and croissants. Victor explained to Felix, "I've been acquainted with Franz for a while. He's been teaching me piano. I can now play my favorite composer at the keys."

"Who?" Felix enthused.

"Weber."

"He has such good music. I met him in my youth once." Felix recollected a bit. Franz added about Victor's playing, "You've progressed to being able to play a melody with one finger."

Hugo laughed as he knew he wasn't really much of a musician, "I have progressed at least."

"The important thing is that you have good taste in music. That makes a world of difference." Felix commented. After speaking of music, the conversation rotated to current affairs of social society. The talk made Felix feel a bit disappointed. Part of it was the fact that he wasn't a permanent resident of Paris. Franz and Victor were, so it concerned them. Things were arising in the city and whispers went around that it's citizens would soon one day rebel, barricading the streets. Hugo had interest in social misery and wanted to incorporate it into a future project.

After spending the afternoon with Victor Hugo, Felix and Franz left his home to go elsewhere. Franz suggested, "I think Chopin and your friend Hiller are at the Café downtown. We should go join them."

"Sure." Felix continued following him about. They found Chopin and Hiller at a table outside the café, eating croissants and sipping cappuccinos. There were two open seats, so Felix and Franz gladly took them. The conversation was much more chipper than politics. Hiller was speaking to Chopin about the lunch he and Felix attended at Kalkbrenner's home, "Friedrich seems rather desperate to be in Felix's company."

"I don't doubt it," Chopin stated, "He has an obsession with being in company with anyone who has associated with royalty. He aspires to be an aristocrat."

"That explains why he keeps asking how I got to play piano for the court in Munich." Felix sipped some creamy cappuccino. Hiller then looked towards the street then whispered, "Speak if the devil."

The group looked over to see Kalkbrenner in his finest suit, strolling on the other side of the street. He paused by a lamp post, spying on them from afar. Felix continued drinking, feeling Friedrich's eyes on him. Hiller warned Felix, "I wouldn't accept any more invitations to dine with that man again. He seems too determined for high social status."

After they finished their cappuccinos, they left the café to go their separate ways. As soon as Felix was a few paces from the others, Kalkbrenner rushed up to him. He blocked the sidewalk, "Would you be so kind as to accompany me on a walk?"

"I'm sorry, I have work to tend to." Felix turned around. Friedrich walked beside him, "Is not your place of stay the other way? You were headed there, were you not?"

"How do you know where I'm staying?" Felix felt intruded. Kalkbrenner continued his questioning, "Have you really any business? I would very much like to invite you to dinner." He kept up with Felix's walking pace. His mannerism was so determined. It was no wonder Chopin felt a nervous wreck at the piano with him hovering and micromanaging.

As Felix was about to speak again, Hiller, Chopin and Liszt walked up to them. Each of them acting overbearingly friendly. Hiller asked Kalkbrenner, "We were just going to dinner, want to join?"

"Not today." Kalkbrenner huffed, only wanting Felix's company. He left the conversation all together. Hiller escorted Felix home as Franz and Chopin went their own ways.

~~~

## [3]

On the third of February, Felix turned 23 years of age. He could seldom believe the time gone by. The rooms he first acquired in Paris, he traded for a warmer apartment. One closer to Hiller's home. The neighborhood had much more charm as it was near the city center.

That evening, he was invited to a music gathering at Baillot's residence. It was a calm gathering. Some piano was played as well as soft cello music. Baillot then took his violin towards the end of the evening. He played one of the most beautiful melodies in the moment, giving more peace to the night.

The instrument resonated throughout the room as the guests stood or sat where they could ponder. Felix sat at a table, daydreaming as Baillot gently bowed his feelings into his instrument. It was a soothing adagio. Felix felt memories bursting in his train of thought. Only one other could play as this. He turned to Hiller in a whisper, "I only know one man who could match this skill. My violin teacher back in Berlin."

"Oh..." Hiller trailed off a bit. He put his hand in his pocket, holding a note. It had been given to him and he was instructed to give it to Felix. The postman allowed Hiller to read it beforehand. Yet in the moment, Hiller thought it best to leave it for the morning. A few hours would not change the effect of it.

Felix continued reminiscing as he wished to see Reitz again. His violin teacher had not written in a long while. Felix sensed something as Hiller throughout the evening seemed to be trying hard to stay joyful for Felix's sake. He would not confess anything. Felix shrugged off the feeling and kept happy company until the hour of returning to his apartment.

Hiller told him before he got a carriage, "I believe I've left something at your place, may I come with you?"

"Of course." Felix called up a carriage. When they arrived at the complex and entered the flat, Felix in tiredness tended to his bed, fluffing the pillow and such. Hiller took his chance and slid the note under Felix's shaving kit that sat by a mirror. He wouldn't notice it until morning. Hiller then headed for the door, "I found what I was looking for. I'll be back tomorrow to visit." Hiller made his leave.

Felix blew out the candles then flopped in bed, falling asleep from a good evening and not a care in the world.

~~~~

*Paris, February 4th, 1832*

*You will, I am sure, excuse my writing you only a few words today as I heard of my irreparable loss. Many hopes, and a pleasant bright period of my life have departed with him, and I never again can feel so happy. I must now set about forming new plans, and building fresh castles in the air; the former ones are irrevocably gone, for he was interwoven with them all. I shall never be able to think of my boyish days, nor of the ensuing ones, without connecting him with them; I shall never hear music or write it, without thinking of him; all this makes the rending asunder of such a tie doubly distressing. The former epoch has wholly passed away, but not only do I lose that, but also the man I so sincerely loved. If I never had any special reason for loving him, or if I no longer had such reasons, I must have loved him all the same, even without a reason.*

*He loved me too, and the knowledge that there was such a man in the world–*

*one whom you could repose, and who lived to love you, and who's wishes and aims were identical with your own— this is all over: it is the most severe blow I have ever received, and never can I forget him,*

*Your,*


*—Felix*


Hiller knocked at Felix's door in the mid-morning. There was no answer. He asked the landlord if he had gone out but the landlord shook his head. Hiller knocked again. Nothing. He then slowly opened the door. His friend was sitting at the dining table, head buried in his arms.

Hiller's heart lurched at hearing Felix's quiet whimpers. He walked to him and hugged him, which in turn made Felix weep more. A letter Felix penned sat at the table. Copies of the string octet sat, sprawled out. The nice handwriting gave indication as to who had made the copies of the composition. There was as well, the tear soaked note of the announcement of Eduard Reitz's death. He died of consumption. Reitz was only twenty nine. It was the first major loss in Felix's circle of friends and family.

~~~


On the other side of things, Abraham wrote, wondering of his son's plans as Felix had now traveled Europe. Felix felt confident that he had an idea of what he wanted to do for his future. He still had yet to travel to London once more (if the cholera pandemic wasn't out of control), but he would be residing in Germany when ready to settle in a permanent home. He did not know which city, but the perfect one would come due in time. If he failed to sustain himself in Germany, he had a backup plan to live in some foreign country.

In the midst of heartbreaking news and future decisions Felix was summoned back to the conservatory for another concert. He was to play Beethoven's G major concerto.

The whole royal court was to be present as Felix's good reviews from the Munich court reached Paris. Since playing for royalty was a serious matter, Felix had some nervousness.

The request of the royal concert also reached the ears of Kalkbrenner. His desperation turned to envy in a flash, trying anything to dissuade the conservatory from choosing Felix for the concerto. The directors brushed off his complaints as the concert was already decided upon. The Queen requested Felix. No one else.

Kalkbrenner feverishly began sending Felix requests to dine with him, but Felix knew better. His friends warned him as well, so he discarded every invite. He wrote to home of the matter:

*March 15th, 1832*

*I told you that I am to play Beethoven's Concerto in G major two days hence, in the Conservatoire, and the whole court is to be present for the first time at the concert. K— is ready to poison me from envy; he at first tried by a thousand intrigues to prevent my playing altogether, and when he heard that the Queen was actually coming, he did everything in his power to get me out of the way.... He is the only musician here who acts unkindly and hypocritically towards me; and though I never placed much confidence in him, still it is always a very painful sensation to know that you are in the society of a person who hates you, but is careful not to show it.*

*—Felix*

Felix decided to avoid the man altogether. Yet, the sour musician knew where Felix enjoyed being in company. Every afternoon he played his chess matches against his friends at the café.

On the day of the big concert, Kalkbrenner entered the café as Felix was engaging in a game of chess. He got a coffee and sat a few paces away, watching as Baillot and Felix concentrated on their match. Felix was losing this one. Others circled about to see Baillot finally defeat Felix's winning stride. It was an intense scene as Baillot made his next move,

"Checkmate."

"You win." Felix smiled, leaning back from such thinking. Everyone cheered for Baillot. Felix stood from his chair, ready to leave the café after much fun. It was time to head to the conservatory for rehearsals. As he walked down the pavement, he was abruptly pushed forward. His hands caught his fall, but he landed hard on one of his wrists.

"Oh, I do apologize, I assure I tripped," Kalkbrenner pulled Felix back up and brushed the dust from his coat, "Is your wrist alright?" He grabbed it. Felix pulled his wrist away, "Do not come near me again."

"It was an accident." Kalkbrenner blocked the path. Felix shoved passed him, clutching his wrist. He called for a carriage to be sure he wasn't followed. Once sitting down, he looked at his wrist. It turned out to be fine after moving it a bit. It could have been worse. Felix knew Kalkbrenner was desperate as there were only hours before the concert.

~~~

That evening, the royal court arrived for the concert. The rehearsals beforehand had gone well, ending early, so Felix spent the extra time preparing in the dressing room. He decided on his favorite outfit, the one with the blue coat. It was almost complete as he tied the formal black cravat. As he situated it correctly, he stood in front of the mirror. He looked quite well. When admiring his attire, a voice behind him warned, "Don't look into the pond too long, you'll fall in."

Felix jumped and in an instant turned to face Friedrich, "How did you get in here!?" He backed up a pace.

Friedrich assured him, "I only came to give good luck at this grand concert....It would be a shame if you suddenly couldn't get to the stage. The Queen would ask any capable musician to play the concerto. Luckily, I'll be by the stage."

Felix was quick realize he had intentions, so he made a sprint for the door. Friedrich pulled him back and shoved him out of the way, causing him to fall against the mirror. It cracked as his back hit it. Felix managed to pick himself back up, but by that time Friedrich had left the room, locking the door. While pounding at the door made no use, Felix resorted to yelling. It was a few agonizing minutes before Hiller found him in a panic, not taking note of the situation, "The King and Queen are getting impatient. You're late!"

"We must hurry, Kalkbrenner is trying to take my place." Felix dashed past Hiller. They both rushed to the stage. The closer they got to the auditorium, the louder the ranting of an impatient audience became. Hiller brushed past Felix as he spotted Kalkbrenner backstage, about to go on. As he pulled Friedrich back, Felix entered the stage, calming the crowd. He sat at the keys and the concert went on as normal.

Afterwards, the whole court gave their positive remarks. The Queen especially loved Felix's skill and sent him many complements. Kalkbrenner watched from afar the company Felix received, causing him to leave the conservatory in a huff.

~~~~

Felix's time in Paris was coming to an end. There were still nights of music and last minute opportunities. A rather odd request came from a church as they inquired to use his string octet for a funeral mass in commemoration of Beethoven. Felix thought it the strangest idea to have that piece chosen for a funeral mass, yet he couldn't refuse. He laughed at the thought of a priest at an altar with the scherzo of his octet in the background.

Felix attended the event and every part of his idea of the scene happened. The feeling of the composition seemed a bit of a chipper choice for a melancholic occasion, but the people considered it fine sacred music.

The last performance Felix took part in was Baillot's concert. He played a Mozart piano concerto. It went very well. All of the musicians afterwards threw a dinner party at a nearby restaurant. Felix decided to join, but not too long as he wanted to pack that night to leave Paris by morning. He sat by Hiller and Chopin through the evening. Hiller mentioned to Felix, "I hope you'll be safe getting to London. I hear the cholera is terrible."

"It's probably not as bad as here." Chopin pointed to some newspapers on the table. Felix shrugged, "I'm not worried about it. I'll be careful not to get too close to anyone. After London, I think I've decided on residing in Germany."

"That sounds nice," Chopin commented, "I think my official home is here in Paris."

"This place suits you well." Felix sipped a mug of water. He grimaced after tasting it. Hiller questioned, "Something wrong?"

"Water tastes bad."

"It's not poisoned is it?" Chopin teased, "Us composers must be careful after Mozart's demise."

"Oh that's such folklore." Felix rolled his eyes. Hiller and Chopin chuckled. After a few teases, Felix stood to make his leave for the night. All of his friends bid him farewell. It saddened him, but he needed to be back with his London friends.

He eagerly packed up his luggage to make for an easy leave in the morning.

Yet as he folded up his clothes and gathered his music, a slight stomach ache became a bother. He figured it to be the food at the restaurant, but Chopin's comment lingered in the back of his mind. Reconvening himself the thought to be foolery, he went to bed.

~~~~

The next morning, London was going to have to wait. Felix couldn't will himself out of bed as he had awoken to a mild fever and terrible stomach ache. The landlord came to his door as he knew Felix intended to leave by morning, but it was now noon. When he saw Felix ill in bed, he instantly called for a doctor.

When a doctor came, he diagnosed him, "I believe you have caught cholera. You're showing a few of the same symptoms I've been seeing all too often lately. Your case is quite mild."

"Let me guess, I'm stuck in Paris a while." Felix replied.

"You'll have to stay at least a fortnight in quarantine. There is not enough known about this disease. I can't risk you spreading it." The doctor left it at that.

Felix read and wrote letters to friends and family in his time stuck in his rooms. As he thought that would cheer him, his father sent a note with a blow to his heart. Goethe had died. It put Felix in a gloom all over again as it reminded him of Reitz. He concentrated on his composition instead. The newspaper came every morning giving Felix some more to read. It was full of articles on cholera and such. It wasn't determined how it spread, so many were refraining from attending events and occasions in case it was from person to person.

After the extra two weeks in Paris, a cold winter and the loss of friends, the spring gave bloom to the lilacs and lilies. Felix left Paris to return to his favorite city: London.

# Chapter XVI: Like Father, Like Son

Haydn, Trumpet Concerto in Eb Movement III [1]
Handel, Happy We [2]
Mendelssohn, Bei der Wiege [3] *

## [1]

The swords clanked against each other. Their steel sound echoed in the large room. The skill of attack and defence was the object of this sport. Both opponents circled each other, wearing proper fencing gear. The swords hit until one of the fencers poked the tip of his sword against the padded shirt of the other. Straight away the winner took his helmet off, "Ha! I have finally beat you!" Klingemann cheered, still holding the sword against his opponent.

"Oh no!" Felix took his fencing helmet off, dramatically going to the ground as if death were succumbing him. Klingemann laughed then in sportsmanship helped Felix back up, "I'm so glad you have come back to London."

"As am I. I felt as if I'd not seen Ignaz and Charlotte in so long." Felix felt much happier being among his London friends. The season this time fared much better as the smog had lifted, making the city more visible within. The rooms where Felix resided were the same he had before, giving all the more feeling of comfort. Though he made friends, old and new in Paris, he felt more at home in London. Klingemann told him, "We shall have to go to the concert hall. The orchestra is doing a rehearsal of Beethoven's pastoral symphony. I believe they miss you quite so." He began putting away his fencing gear. Felix followed and they both left the gym.

* A guitar and vocal arrangement can be found at the Tea and Guitars YouTube channel

As they entered the lobby of the concert hall, the fragrant sounds of the countryside echoed down the hall, reminding Felix of Switzerland. Klingemann headed for the auditorium as Felix went up a staircase to sit in a box. It was nice to see the orchestra rehearsing from above. He spotted many friends among the musicians. After the piece reached it's finale, Felix headed to the ground floor of the auditorium. When hardly making it down the aisle towards the stage, a member of the orchestra shouted, "There is Mendelssohn!"

"Welcome to him!" The other members gave their excited uproars. Felix went to greet them, feeling happy that the musicians loved and missed him. Music wise, Felix and Moscheles had various concerts underway. For Felix, his newest compositions were met with great success. The 'Hebrides Overture' and the g minor piano concerto became ragingly popular.

Among aspiring keyboardists, Felix's concerto became common for ones making their debuts. Felix attended a concert to hear a seventeen year old by the name of William Sterndale Bennett play the work. The young man played with such ease at even the most challenging of passages. Felix was so impressed with Mr. Bennett's skill, he inquired to contact him. He found Bennett after the concert and the young man was enthusiastic. Felix told him, "I hope we keep in touch. If you are willing, I'd like to take you on as my pupil."

"Yes. I would very much like that."

"I shall give you my information before I leave London."

"Thank you so!" Bennett jumped in joy. Felix left him at that and continued with his own business. He still had much to do with concerts and composing. The Scottish symphony was not yet complete and he still could not make a firm decision on the Italian symphony. He revised it much. Fanny sent her suggestions as he often begged for her opinion.

Felix's time in London was going smooth and ever better than the woes and struggles in Paris, but a letter from his father changed that. Abraham informed Felix that Professor Zelter had become dangerously ill. Felix gave way to much worry over the information. Zelter was old and past his prime. In all hopes, Zelter would recover and Felix would greet him upon his return to Berlin. Yet the recent death of Goethe did not lift Felix's spirits.

Felix worried about the Sing-Akademie as well. Without Zelter, there would be no one to watch over the precious collection of Bach's music. The collection, if Zelter couldn't return to the Akademie, would be dispersed. Felix wrote to Abraham, telling him to do what he could to prevent anything from getting tossed away. He wanted to see the collection before any such thing was decided upon. Felix also pleaded to his father that he help Zelter in any way by means of watching over the Akademie.

It was obvious that Zelter should be retiring and Felix intended to speak with him on the matter. He wanted to take over his position. Zelter at the moment may not have been thinking of handing his job on, but Felix had good standing with the Akademie to acquire it.

Over the course of a few days, Abraham's letters described the decline in Zelter's health. Felix decided he needed to leave London if he wanted a chance to talk to his old professor. There was still business in London so he deemed that in a fortnight he'd make his return to Berlin.

Abraham was not enthused with Felix's intention to obtain the Akademie position. It seemed better for someone in advanced years, not a young aspiring man. It was also the fact that the salary was small. By any means, Abraham wanted his son home as Felix had been abroad for over two years now. He wanted to discuss in person a better decision on his future.

In his last few days in London, Felix calmed his anxiety by spending time with friends, rehearsing for concerts and composing. On days off, he walked through the gardens near his residence to smell the lilacs.

To keep his mother worry free of his health, he often performed gymnastics to keep his strength up. There was much space in the gardens to stretch and roll about.

~~~

The steamer departed the London dock in the night. Felix laid in the cabin's hammock with an aching stomach. This time it was not sea sickness; nor illness. It was the fear of returning to a changed home. Berlin would be a different place and he did not know what to make of it. It was only days prior that he received the news of the death of his beloved professor Zelter. The information gave a sickness of its own.

In other aspects, Felix would get to meet new members of the family such as his nephew Sebastian and Rebecka's husband. She had recently wedded to the mathematician Peter Gustave Lejeune Dirichlet. It was unknown what mood Abraham would be in over the fact that his younger sibling married before he.

After passing through Hamburg and trudging the next thirty six hours by carriage, Felix arrived on Leipziger Straße in Berlin. A calm feeling was felt in the darkened evening. The estate looked the same. Candles were glowing through a window or so. His family was waiting for him.

When opening the front door, the entryway was dark and quiet. He hung his coat and hat on the rack then proceeded to the parlor where the fireplace was providing a dim spark. To his relief, Abraham was in his chair, reading his book and Lea was peacefully knitting on the couch.

Felix stood in the doorway a while, watching them in their peaceful state. He took in that small yet precious moment. Lea finally looked up to see her son who she had not seen in two years time. Her gazing expression caused Abraham to look up from his book.

As Felix walked in, Lea set her needlework down as if she did not know what to make of the sight before her.

Finally her senses came to and she dashed to him. She gave the tightest hug he'd ever had. His heart filled with the utmost content, but after a bit admitted, "You're crushing me."

She let go and replaced the hug with motherly kisses. Abraham came, giving an embrace. He seemed happy to have Felix home, unlike last time. Paul came down the stairs and cheered at the sight of Felix. Felix's eyes gave to shock at how much Paul had grown. He was now eighteen, going to college and making a career in banking with Abraham. Lea informed Felix, "Fanny and Rebecka are coming tomorrow with their families."

"Good. I miss them ever so." Felix gave a sigh of relief. It felt so strange that the only other child left in the main house besides Felix was Paul. Abraham had much on his mind concerning Felix as Rebecka, being younger had already found settlement. Paul was deemed in good standing. Felix didn't take note of such things. He wanted to enjoy being back with his family.

~~~~

The next day, Felix strolled around the gardens with Fanny to catch up. She brought along her son, Sebastian, for Felix to finally meet. The little boy was able to walk and speak a few words. Felix held him as they admired the blooming flowers. Fanny had joy at heart at seeing Sebastian with his uncle.

Felix told Fanny all about his adventures abroad and the memories he gained. Fanny was intrigued by each story, but Felix began to feel as if he were talking of a distant dream. He knew the past events took place but it seemed to have gone by in the snap of the fingers.

In turn, Fanny spoke of her life. Music still took up her time as she organized the Sunday salons and composed new pieces each week. Her ideas were flourishing. She seemed eager to ask Felix something, but held back as if she were unsure of the subject. Felix listened patiently in hopes to hear her question.

As she finally felt willed to ask, she began, "Felix, I know this may be an old subject and you may agree or disagree. I'm not sure your feelings of it since you've traveled and seen so much...I was wondering-"

"Felix!" Wilhelm interrupted as they happened to be near the guest house. Felix set Sebastian down and ran to greet him. As they spoke, Fanny caught up beside her husband, holding Sebastian. Felix watched as the family stood together, looking ever so happy. It gave an inner sense of joy to see his sister's family.

Later that day, Felix went to the stable to see his horse. The equine expressed excitement at seeing him. It whinnied and nestled at him. Felix smiled, "Did you miss me? I missed you." He gave the horse a few apples then saddled it up. Paul had made sure the horse got regular exercise, but it seemed quite restless as Felix sat on it. It pranced out of the stall then bucked slightly with energy when entering the gardens.

"Whoa." Felix used the reins to control the horse as it frolicked and jumped. At times it bolted about. Felix muttered to the horse, "You do know a person is riding?" The horse grumbled a bit and continued skipping about.

A few paces away, Felix spotted Rebecka and her husband, Peter, walking the gardens. Peter was quite intrigued as Felix trotted the horse towards them and hopped off with much grace. Rebecka introduced her husband and Felix gave a shake of the hand. He couldn't help but notice how happy the couple seemed together.

~~~

Inside the estate, in his office, Abraham sat in his chair, gazing out the window. He watched Felix speaking with Rebecka and Peter. The scene sent him into deep thought on a subject. Marriage.

Felix's carefree spirit often remained in his own little world of music, travel and art. Too often for Abraham's ideals.

In his mind, Felix needed to find love towards a decent young woman to make a well maintained family. The trouble lay in the fact that Felix seemed uninterested in serious love.

It was true he had affection for Betty Pistor, but that attachment rendered severed with Betty marrying off. Since then, the young love tyrant had a stubbornness to find a woman. If Felix wasn't going to find a lady for himself, Abraham had plans of his own...

"Honey?" Lea called by the doorway. Abraham jumped from his doze, "Ja?"

"I just was checking on you. You seem so lost in thought."

"Oh, I'm admiring the garden outside." He excused. Lea glanced out the window and noticed her children outside. She knew what was on her husband's mind and assured, "Felix will find a wife someday. Give him time."

"But he's nearing four and twenty and has been abroad. He should be settling. I know he won't be given the position at the Akademie as he wishes. I've heard rumors that the committee choosing have their prejudices."

"There are plenty of other positions out there. With his skill, he should end up fine.

*(Felix at age 23)*

349

Don't worry so much. If you push him into something too quickly he could fare unhappy in the long run." Lea embraced Abraham. Abraham gave a sigh whilst still gazing out the window at Felix.

~~~~

Days soon turned into weeks since Felix's arrival home. Life in Berlin was slow and calm. Felix made sure to be among the first to send applications for the Sing-Akademie position. It was now nothing but a waiting game. There were quite a few fighting for the job. He decided to still enroll though he did not yet know the terms. If the attempt failed, there was much to do with publishing proposals for his compositions.

When visiting the Akademie for rehearsals, Felix felt pangs of sadness when entering. There was a sickening emptiness. Reitz nor Zelter were there. He felt the dreadful gaps of those who had made the Akademie so bright. A director filling in Zelter's place didn't lift Felix's spirits any bit. His friend Devrient still attended, helping him cope enough to make rehearsal bearable.

Later that evening, the entire Mendelssohn family dine together at the main house. A nice meal of pheasant was prepared. It felt refreshing to eat with much conversation commencing. Felix found it entertaining to watch Fanny scold her child for not eating the vegetables. Sebastian only wanted desert. Wilhelm sketched on a small leaf of paper. Paul sat next to Abraham and they were discussing banking. Lea spoke with Rebecka and Peter.

Felix had a manuscript penning some music. As he wrote and ate dinner, he unconsciously began chewing at the table napkin. His mouth still felt the reminiscing need to be soothed. Abraham glanced at Felix as the cloth frayed, "Stop chewing on that. It's disgusting. You're ruining the napkin."

"Sorry..." Felix set it aside, feeling embarrassment as everyone had confusion over this odd habit. Lea continued a different conversation by asking Wilhelm, "Hensel? Would you be willing to sketch Paul?"

"Ja." Wilhelm grabbed his sketchbook. Lea instructed, "Be sure it's a side profile. It suits him better."

"Mutter!" Paul felt embarrassed at her comment. Wilhelm was sitting on his side of the table so began a side sketch. It turned out quite flattering.

*(Paul Mendelssohn by Wilhelm Hensel)*

Abraham then informed Felix, "I forgot to mention that your friend Herr Marx is applying for the position of music at the Universität."

"Good for him. I shall send a letter recommending him. I'd like to see him get the job." Felix grabbed some letter paper.

As dessert was served, which was lemon curd and biscuits, Fanny mentioned, "This Sunday should be quite a big salon since we skipped out on the last few. Vater, I did invite all that you suggested."

"Good. I figured there were many who had not heard Felix in a while would want to come. Felix? Have you much new material to play?" Abraham asked. Felix looked up from his letter, "Ja papa."

"Wunderbar! Be sure to dress your best."

"I will." Felix nodded.

For the remainder of the week, Felix organized a list for Sunday. He had plenty of new material such as his concerto and 'Lieder ohne Worte.' There were always the old classics as well such as Bach, Beethoven and Mozart.

In other means, Felix became rather lazy in concern with searching for a job. He kept waiting on the Akademie position but no word came of anything. To compensate, Felix continued composing and sending things to the publishers, so Abraham wouldn't think him a complete oaf.

When Sunday came, Felix felt his heart ache as he dressed for the afternoon's occasion. The salons wouldn't be the same without Reitz or Zelter attending. It felt near pointless to participate as it would only bring somberness.

A light knock on the door caused him to finish tying his fine black silk English cravat. Lea peeked in, then smiled while walking in, "My child, you look so mature."

"Danke Mutter…" Felix gave a rather fake smile. It didn't fool Lea one bit. She gave a motherly hug, "What ever is the matter?"

"I miss Reitz…and Zelter." Sniffles escaped Felix's nose. Lea comforted him a while then suggested, "We should be getting downstairs, there are quite a few guests already here. They are excited to see you."

"Alright." Felix followed Lea out of the room. As they reached the stairs, the chatter of guests echoed through the halls.

Once they entered the music room, many people greeted them. Felix turned about, surrounded by unfamiliar faces. He spotted a few close friends here and there, but most rendered unrecognized. One thing was for certain. Many young ladies had been invited in company with their parents.

When the hour struck, everyone took their seats as Fanny went to the piano. She spoke a short speech then went right into playing. Felix felt his breath taken as he had not heard his sister at the keys in so long. Her sound had matured more than ever. Wilhelm sat off to the side, sketching whilst listening to his wife. The music gave him much muse.

Paul then took a cello and set up to play. He had still been taking lessons in spare time. It was a joy to watch him brush the bow across the strings, showing such passion for the instrument. Bach's cello preludes hummed into everyone's ears.

After Paul finished, Fanny returned to the keys to accompany Rebecka's voice in some freshly composed Lieder. Rebecka sang like the blossoming roses, but her tone indicated that she still loathed in the attention.

Last but not least, it was Felix's turn. When standing, the young ladies among the spectators gave way to excited whispers, waving their fans in a blush. Felix hoped their attendance wasn't his father's doing, but deep inside, he knew the truth.

In ignoring his inner conclusions, Felix sat down at the piano, giving the audience a glance. They stared at him intently. He was not one to have stage fright, but for some reason their gazes effected his conscience. It made him understand how Chopin felt when giving a concert.
He opened his mouth to speak, but no words came. Abraham gave his son a stern nod. Felix turned to the keys and began playing his 'Lieder ohne Worte'.

The room filled with the soothing sounds of written music along with improvisations here and there to give a unique performance.

Felix closed his eyes, pretending to be in Paris at the Pleyel Rooms. His added impromptu phrases had taken inspiration from Chopin which intrigued the audience all the more.

After many select songs without words, he completed his part in the salon with a piano rendition of his concerto. The last movement made for quite a workout. By the time he stood from the keys, he was sweating.

Everyone clapped then dispersed their seats. Felix headed for the door as he wanted to get some rest, but Abraham called, "Felix, come here."

Felix obeyed with a sigh. His father was speaking with the parents of a lady. By discreetly grabbing the back of his arm, Abraham pulled his son into conversation. Knowing the intentions, Felix hastened in speech, doing nothing more than speak politely to each girl and parent.

~~~~

Days after the salon, Felix made no social progress with any particular lady, so Abraham decided to further matters himself. He picked up a letter he had received. It contained a few requests. Taking a quill, he began writing a reply.

At the fourteenth hour that afternoon, Abraham summoned Felix to the parlor for a chat. The maid set a tray of tea before them. A serious conversation. Felix settled with a cuppa, while Abraham opened a letter of invitation, "Herr and Frau Sommer invited you to their home to stay the night. They enjoyed your music last Sunday and wish you over for dinner tonight."

"How nice." Felix thought of it. The Sommers had a large estate; larger than the Mendelssohn home. It sounded like an undeclinable invite, but Felix knew the underlying plot. They had a daughter named Lorian. Her family had a lot of money and high status, giving many young men interest, until they met her.

354

Felix heard from friends that she was the most overbearing girl they had met. He didn't think he could handle a stay, giving his honest opinion to his father, "I don't want to go."

"You are. It would be rude to decline from the Sommers. You need to branch out. Your younger sister is already married. Paul with his good standing should be wedded in ease. It's time you've found someone."

"I'm not interested in looking for love." Felix stated. Abraham strengthened his stern tone, "You are going and I'm not letting you out of it. Now go pack. I've already written an accepting reply."

"Vater!" Felix groaned as he nearly threw the teacup down.

"Get up stairs and pack for one night. Now!" His father's sharp tone forced Felix from his seat. He silently went upstairs. As soon as reaching his room, he slammed the door and flopped onto his bed, burying his face in his pillow.

After a bit, he got back up. A letter from Mr. Moscheles sat at his desk. Felix opened it to learn that Ignaz was in Hamburg visiting Charlotte's relatives. In wanting him to come to Berlin, Felix wrote a begging reply:

*Berlin, Aug. 10 1832*

*Dear Moscheles,*
*....Now look here, since I have your letter from Hamburg I am doubly convinced that come you must, were it but to spend a few days with us here...no where else shall you be permitted to take up your quarters than in Green-score Hotel, Leipziger Straße, No. 3 - That is to say, in my room. It faces the street, but is very quiet and pleasant and as large as your whole house on Norton street; and the bedroom next to it is of the same size.*

*I should move a story higher, where another room could be cleared for servants or anyone you choose to bring; a piano awaits you; the stove acts well; in short you see, I am cut out for a house-agent. I really do not exaggerate, you should be comfortable in quarter, and all would be well...Much obliged, but I am not composing at all, and am living much as an asparagus does; I am very comfortable doing nothing. When you come I shall feel quite ashamed at not having anything new to show you...*

*Yours,*

*Felix*

**A servant entered his room with a small note. Felix folded his letter and traded it for the note. He looked at it:**

*Felix! Time to go!*

*~ Abraham*

**Felix rolled his eyes. It was common to send short notes even if in the same household as to not shout through the home. Felix threw a suitcase together and went down stairs. His outfit was casual, nothing formal. Abraham noticed and took Felix back upstairs to choose a better outfit. Felix sighed as his father gave him a better black coat. Upon putting it on, it gave him a more shapely figure. Abraham completed the outfit by straightening a nice maroon cravat to make a more pleasing appearance. He then sent him off by carriage to the Sommer's estate. Felix wasn't happy as he didn't want to attract the likes of Lorian.**

When arriving at the large mansion, Herr and Frau Sommer greeted him in all joy. Felix had expected other guests to show up, but it was only he and the family. They seemed overly polished and polite as many young gentlemen had walked through their doors for dinner, only to leave in haste. Yet the Sommers changed their tactics by inviting Felix to spend the night so it would be rude if he left early.

Upon hearing the chatter in the main hall, a young, excited girl with pinned up blond hair and brown eyes rushed in. Her facial complexion wasn't unkept or anything, just not all that attractive. Her overbearing attitude matched her figure. Robust and tall. In an instant she stood beside Felix and took his arm, "I shall escort you to dinner."

Felix already felt a reluctance to go through with his stay, but there was no possible way out. Lorian sat Felix next to her at the table. His chair was situated rather close. She gave him no chance to give the gentlemanly gesture of helping her get seated. It made him feel a lack of etiquette.

As a decent dinner of roasted chicken was served and eaten, Lorian did most of the talking. Her parents were happy as Felix forced himself to listen and answer her questions. In honesty, they had nothing in common. When dinner neared done, Herr Sommer suggested, "Why don't you two go for a stroll in the atrium? I have many flowers there."

"Good idea," Lorian took Felix by the arm. Felix was still chewing chicken as she pulled him down the hall towards the indoor garden.

Once they came into a hall of budding flowers, green leaves and ivy crawling up the walls, Lorian gave way to relief, "At last we are alone." She guided Felix to a bench made of stone, carved in the style of Greek art. As she held his hands, Felix hoped the evening would end as soon as possible. He didn't make conversation, causing Lorian to sigh, "You are so quiet. Have you anything to bring up? I feel I have been talking to myself all evening."

"Nein. I've nothing new in my life." Felix kept reserved. Lorian knew he wasn't fond of her, but she didn't want another man to slip away. Her demeanor changed as she commented in a light tone, "How smart it was of you to choose a maroon cravat. Maroon is my favorite color."

"Oh nice..." Felix knew Abraham purposely chose that color. Lorian then gazed upon his coat, "The coat goes so nicely with it."

"Please nein." Felix retorted as her hands fell to his waist. To his dismay she leaned her face towards his. Felix leaned back to avoid her incoming kiss. So much so that he fell backwards off the bench. In an instant he stood back up, "It is late. I shall retire to my guest room."

"I'm sorry!" Lorian stayed seated as tears of regret fell from her eyes. Felix left in embarrassment. There was no possible way he could be in love with that woman. He went to his guest room, being sure to lock the door.

The next morning at breakfast, Felix nor Lorian spoke. Felix ate his blueberry sauced toast in silence. Lorian took small bites of strawberries, whilst glaring at him. Herr and Frau Sommer could sense the two found no likeness in each other.

When Felix returned home, he threw his coat off in a huff. The servant took his hat in the least. Abraham walked by, noticing Felix's mood. He asked in suspicion, "How was it?"

"Do you really want to know?" Felix snorted in irritability. Abraham gave a stern glare, "You did not ruin the visit did you?"

"It wasn't me who soured it. I can not love a woman who has not a thing in common with me. She didn't truly care about me. All she noticed was my figure."

"I'm sure if you had put effort in she would have noticed more."

358

Felix attested, "So it's normal that a lady should try to force a kiss on the first meeting? I found it quite offensive. I can not love her."

Abraham gave a sigh and let his son leave. He did feel disappointment that Lorian had the audacity to rush at Felix. At least Abraham now knew that when his son found someone, she would be true and beautiful.

~~~

A few days later, Mr. Moscheles came to the home after complying to Felix's request. Felix had done up his room to make it suitable for Ignaz as he wanted the best for Mr. Moscheles. For himself, he moved to a temporary room on the third floor.

Once Ignaz settled his things, he and Felix went to the music room. They shared in improvising and catching up. Ignaz had news and could not contain his excitement, "Charlotte and I are to have another child due next year. We are going to move to a new home to support our growing family."

"Wunderbar! What names are you deciding?"

"I'll write it to you when the child is born. Right now it's a secret. Yet we don't know if it's a boy or girl, so that is part of it as well." Ignaz gave Felix some suspense. Felix then asked, "So where is this new home going to be?"

"It's called Chester Place, still in London of course."

"I can't wait to see it. Hopefully next time I'll meet the new little Moscheles." Felix expressed his excitement by playing a flurry of notes at the keys. Ignaz asked, "Have you anything new and exciting? I know you wrote saying you've composed nothing new, but you should have something to speak of."

"Well...I have been trying to get Zelter's position at the Akademie. It isn't decided who is to take it. There is much gossip over the ordeal as the directors are deciding between Carl Rungenhagen or I. I thought I had a good chance but Carl is older and already deputy director. If I had made it back in time before Zelter's death I'm sure he would have helped me get the job." Felix sighed.

"Don't fuss too much if you don't get it. When something doesn't work out, something twice as good comes around." Ignaz assured. Felix smiled at his positivity. They then continued their impromptu duet.

After a week-long stay, Moscheles left Berlin. Once he was gone, the upcoming months of winter were cold and dreary. Felix scarcely went out of the house. He took the horse for a snowy trot on occasion but not much else. No word from the Akademie was affirmed. It made Felix feel a sense of nothingness. He didn't bother composing, but rather revised a thing or two or played piano. In most of his time he lazed about, sleeping and eating. Life seemed to be at a halt for the winter season.

~~~~

## [2]

*Berlin, February 27th, 1833*

*Dear Moscheles,*

*Here they are, wind instruments and fiddles, for the son and heir must not be kept waiting until I come, he must have a cradle song with drums and trumpets and janissary music; fiddles alone are not nearly lively enough.*

*May every happiness and joy and blessing attend the little stranger....*

**(Little Moscheles)**

*So he is to be called Felix, is he? How nice and kind of you to make him my godchild in formâ! The first present his godfather makes him is the above entire orchestra; it is to accompany him throughout his life....*

*Dear me! But I am ever so happy when I think of your happiness, and of the time when I shall have my full share of it. By the end of April, at the latest, I intend to be in London, and then we will duly name the boy, and introduce him to the world at large. It will be grand!*

*Ever yours,*

*Felix Mendelssohn Bartholdy*

**Felix finished up the doodle he felt inclined to sketch upon being informed of the birth of Ignaz and Charlotte's new baby, Felix Moscheles. It moved Felix with happiness that they had named the child after him.**

The honor made him feel the responsibility to get to know and help the child in any way he could.

Abraham walked into the drawing room to find Felix at the writing desk. He looked over his son's shoulder, "That's quite the silly little sketch."

"It's for little Felix Moscheles, I'm going to put together an album of sketches for him. It will be his first present from me. I also intend to pen a little cradle song for him. I'll work it out as Klingmann will give me some poetry when I see him in London."

"When do you intend to be in London?"

"April." Felix gave a quick answer. Abraham stood beside Felix, quiet for a minute then informed, "I was thinking that I may join you. I'd much like to see this smokey nest you ever so love."

"Oh…" Felix didn't know how he felt about his father's idea. It could easily turn into a disaster if Abraham pressured him or quarreled. Many scenarios ran through his mind, but contrary to his thoughts, Felix casually smiled and nodded.

~~~

As the month of March leaped by, the board of council of the Sing-Akademie made their choice of director. It was Herr Rungenhagen. The outcome gave way to gossip among society. Once again, Felix was sick of Berlin. The longer he lingered in the city, the more it made him miss Reitz and Zelter. He was now four and twenty and it was hard to fathom that Reitz had been gone a year.

One temporary escape from the city was a music festival in Düsseldorf. The committee organizing it wanted Felix to conduct. It was deemed to be an important engagement as the city happened to be looking for a music director.

Conducting the festival would give a good chance of obtaining the job. Abraham felt happy in seeing his son willing to travel to find a position.

When Felix arrived by carriage to Düsseldorf, he found the place intriguing. The Konzerthaus seemed decent enough. Members of the festival committee gladly welcomed him and rehearsals commenced.

Though the committee deemed kind, Felix couldn't help but notice a few members of the orchestra glaring at him. Their irritation worsened as Felix stepped before them with his baton. These musicians were not used to modern conducting methods. Felix continued on and the given music was played capitally. The program contained an assortment of compositions; new, old, and sacred works.

When everything was performed as intended, everyone nodded in satisfaction. The committee meanwhile, whispered amongst themselves of this talented young man. One of them put together a contract of terms to discuss after the evening's festival. They were determined to hire Felix in the soon future.

An hour before the concert, the orchestra took a rest. Felix decided to take a stroll around the Konzerthaus to get fresh air. He exited through a back door that led to a quiet alley. The wind gave a chill, but it cooled him down. He walked in his lonesome, thinking to himself. His thoughts halted as he neared the front of the building. There, he noticed an eager audience streaming in the doors early. It made him happy that there was to be a good turnout.

Yet in a sudden moment, a cluster of people stormed towards the Konzerthaus in the most disruptive manner. A few officers on guard blocked them as their demeanor appeared rather violent. Felix stood where he was, still close to the alley, watching such a commotion.

A moment later, a hand fell on his shoulder. Felix turned to see a member of the committee. He seemed worried as he guided Felix towards the back of the building, "The concert is to start soon. I don't want you to be late."

"What are those people so angry over?" Felix questioned, trying to catch a glimpse. As they were still an earshot from the quarrel, a man among the group snapped, "Get a different conductor or I shall go in and remove him myself!"

Felix instantly tried to turn back as the quarrel concerned him. The committee member stopped him by clenching his arm. He warned, "You do not want near that quarrel. I'm making sure you get back inside safe and sound. There is much prejudice in this city."

"Oh." Felix gave a sigh.

When they returned, the orchestra was settled onstage already. Felix grabbed his baton and joined them. The audience clapped to welcome him despite the commotion that happened outside. It helped Felix calm down from any worries. He turned to the orchestra and counted into the first piece. Everything went smoothly.

After a grand finish of a symphony, the concert completed successfully. Felix and the orchestra took their bows then dispersed. The sound of soothing chatter echoed through the auditorium of a content audience. Felix packed his music, smiling at the results. Once he went backstage, he found the committee members standing together. One handed him a contract explaining, "Take this, read it over and give us your answer by the autumn season."

"Danke." Felix's smile only grew. The paper contained their terms of agreement for the position of director. He carefully put the contract in his portfolio. Though there was time to think about it, he knew what his answer would be.

~~~

364

April couldn't have arrived soon enough. Felix packed his luggage and headed downstairs where Abraham had his luggage packed as well. The rest of the family gathered to give their goodbyes.

After hugs and kisses were given, father and son set off, London bound. Once they were on their way, Felix felt a sense of contentment to have his father along. It helped ease any homesickness.

The first stop after a long carriage ride was Hamburg. Abraham shuddered a bit when entering the city he had run away from all those years ago. Felix noticed him stare at the old family home that still sat on the corner. The carriage stopped at an inn, brushing away Abraham's thoughts.

After they purchased a room for the evening, Abraham suggested to Felix, "We should eat in the tavern, have a few drinks and play cards. I brought my deck."

"Alright." Felix felt surprised at his father's sudden inclination to play games. They went downstairs and ate a decent meal. Abraham then ordered he and Felix a few glasses of Bier. Felix shuffled the card deck and set up a game. They had a good couple of bonding hours.

~~~

The next day, Felix and Abraham boarded the early morning steamer for London. Abraham had no trouble with seasickness but was astonished at how ill Felix became. It confused him as he had taken Felix and Rebecka on a sea voyage in their childhood, rendering fine then. It struck him odd that Felix developed such violent seasickness.

When the days on the water passed, the two travelers arrived at the London scene. Abraham stuck close to Felix as he knew nothing of this vast world of smog. Felix held Ignaz's letter of address, "We must find Chester Place. I believe if we find a cab on that street there we shall find it."

"I'm just following you." Abraham looked all around him, distracted at all of the commotion in London. Felix called to a stationed carriage with the driver waiting for a customer. He showed the coachman the address.

As they hopped on the coach, a voice called their way, "Hello Herr Mendelssohn!" Klingemann jumped onto the carriage, joining them. Felix quickly explained to Karl, "We must write a Lied! I must have a cradle song for little Moscheles." Felix grabbed some manuscript paper.

"You pen the music first then I'll make some verses." Klingemann watched Felix jot down notes. The music had been in his head for quite some time. When he finished a two page piece, Klingemann wrote his verses then signed the corner of the page.

*(Chester Place)*

The carriage stopped at a street of complexes as soon as the Lied was complete. Felix put it with the book of sketches. Before walking to Chester Place, Felix stopped across the street from the building, "You two go ahead, I must make one more sketch to present to little Felix."

"Alright. Don't be too long." Klingemann gestured to Abraham to follow him. Felix dug out the sketchbook once more and began drawing Chester Place. It looked like a humble and happy home.

*(Bei der Weige manuscript)*

As he finished the final touches of the sketch, Ignaz came to the balcony of his flat and called, "I'm waiting for you dear Felix!"

"Coming!" Felix raced towards the home. Ignaz greeted him at the stairwell. He guided Felix inside the flat where Charlotte sat in the parlor, holding the new child. Felix's eyes gleamed at seeing the cute face of the baby. Their eldest child Emily, who was six years of age, sat next to Charlotte, admiring her little brother.

Felix grabbed the sketchbook and handed it to Emily, "This is for little Felix. There are sketches and autographs for you all to enjoy. There's blank pages if Felix takes up sketching later."

"Thank you!" She skimmed the already made sketches. Felix took the page of the cradle song and handed it to Ignaz, "Klingemann and I composed this together. Be sure to play it."

"I will." Ignaz took it. Klingemann then told Ignaz, "Go get Felix the thing you got him."

"Oh yeah," Ignaz raced to the room nearby and was heard rummaging a drawer. He came back with something unique. It appeared to be a thick ribbon. Ignaz explained, "It's a new fashion of cravat. Very English."

"Danke!" Felix took it. Abraham looked at it and noticed Klingemann wearing one of the same fashion. It looked nice. Felix folded the fine fabric to try it later. Charlotte then gestured to Felix to sit beside her. As soon as he sat, she handed him the baby, "Thank you. My arms are tired today." She got up to do some things.

"Isn't he the dearest little thing?" Felix smiled as little Moscheles opened his eyes. After looking around a while, the baby closed his eyes again and a slight smile grew on his little face. He was content. Abraham sat beside Felix to see the baby as Ignaz took a chair nearby. He told Felix, "I have some concerts arranged for us in your time here."

"Excellent." Felix nodded, rocking the baby. Charlotte came back to the parlor and took the child back. Felix let her sit in his spot. Young Emily went to the piano and begged her father, "Can you play the piece Felix composed? Karl should sing it."

"Alright, we can try it. You're always so eager to hear new music." Ignaz sat at the piano bench next to his daughter. He then paused as an idea came to him. Turning to Felix, he suggested in excitement, "May I try this accompaniment on guitar? It seems to suit. I have my father's instrument."

"Of course." Felix assured in deep interest. Ignaz left the room, coming back with a nice mahogany guitar. He sat in a chair with a footrest nearby. Once he was situated, Karl stood next to the music stand to catch a glimpse at the sheet music. Felix felt excited as the baby would get to hear his present.

[3]

Ignaz began the on the spot guitar arrangement with the bright and clear chords. They rang out like the chipper chiming of a glockenspiel. Klingemann gave a breath while reading the music, making a humble entry with his tenor voice. He sang his lyrics of slumber and dreaming. The pitch of his voice had a rustic feel, making the melody as a calming lullaby.

Charlotte smiled while rocking her baby along with the rhythm. Little Felix Moscheles appeared to be dreaming along to the music composed just for him. Felix senior gazed at the child then at Ignaz, ever so happy that the piece worked out. Karl's words in song told the child to dream of joy and sorrow, the people he would come to love; however many came and went. To be patient as there were always new friends to follow. Each verse had an air to be said by the cradle of an infant who had yet to experience the world.

Klingemann then joyfully sang a section containing a sweet and succulent melody that could bloom any flower. He let his words flow letting the feelings give the ease to do it.

The guitar then led the voice into the words of being patient in almost an ear tickling giggle. The repetition of telling their new little friend to be patient would in hopes remind him to be as so.

After the first line of verses, Klingemann looked to Ignaz, who gave a nod. Karl paused the next line as Ignaz improvised a solo. It galloped gracefully like a harp. It then melodied it's way to a cadence where Karl entered with the next set of verses, his voice smooth as butter. Though the music went on in pleasure, near the end, little Moscheles began to cry. It was a hard cry of an upset child. Klingemann and Ignaz finished up the best they could. Karl then teased Felix, "Good job, your music makes babies cry."

"I tried to make it cheerful." Felix personally felt bad. Charlotte assured, "The music is fine. I think little Felix is just hungry." She got up and took her child to the nursery. The others continued playing music, switching to the piano. Abraham had much pleasure in listening to Felix and Ignaz play the music of Bach together. They could do anything they wished at the keys; improvising based on written music or from their own imaginations.

The sight of Abraham sitting on the sofa, leaning against the armrest with the expression of pure content burned into Felix's memory. He couldn't help but feel joy in the fact that his father seemed so happy in the moment. It was a feeling not felt from him in a great while.

~~~

The next day, Felix got dressed but took longer than usual. He stood in front of the mirror with every article of clothing except his cravat. The ribbon was tangled in his hands as he could not figure out how to tie it. Each time he tried, it looked crooked or not right. He felt too embarrassed in the moment to ask.

After practicing a few times in the mirror he gave it up for the time being. It was a beautiful piece of clothing, but decided not to stress too much over figuring it out.

The day would be spent mostly at Chester Place, so he tied the cravat he usually wore. Klingmann had work to tend to and Ignaz had students of piano around town to teach. Abraham was tired from traveling so spent the day napping. Felix decided to use his day by helping Charlotte around the house with the children. She seemed in a busy state with the new child, so Felix entertained Emily by giving her piano lessons and sketching.

When Charlotte needed a rest from holding little Moscheles, Felix held him to let Charlotte retire for a nap. The baby slept most of the time. Felix enjoyed humming to him as it seemed to keep the child calm. The day made Felix give way to some thoughts if this was what it would be like if he had a family and children of his own.

Abraham quietly peeked out of his guest room and watched how well Felix was around the children. He noticed the sense of happiness his son had. It gave him hope that this experience would drive his son to make a family. Abraham entered the room to Felix smiling at the infant. He commented, "Having fun?"

"Oh," Felix looked up, "Ja."

Abraham smiled then headed out to roam the city. He wanted to develop his own taste for London society. Having been to Paris and Switzerland multiple times, he was no beginner at being on his own for a while.

~~~

In the month, Felix and Ignaz's concert engagements commenced. Though Felix thought his Italian Symphony still needed revising, he prepared a rendition to be performed. He continued consulting Fanny over the matter by letter, but she assured the first draft to be the best. In any means, London went crazy over it.

Abraham decided to attend these concerts. It felt interesting as in the past when Felix traveled with him, it was banking business. This time Abraham was going along with Felix to musical business. When he watched his son play and conduct, he felt a sense of pride. The London audiences greeted him with whole hearts.

Felix and Abraham's relationship grew over the course of their London trip together. They had become the best of adult travel partners as the summer season went on. Abraham seemed less anxious of Felix's outlook after seeing the successes of London. Felix in turn began understanding his father better. Yet happy times too good to be true had interruptions eventually.

As they took a carriage for a visit to Portsmouth Dockyard, they admired the large ships coming in. When the carriage parked, Felix hopped off. Abraham stood to step off. As he did, the horse buckled, jolting the carriage. Abraham tripped as he lost balance. He landed hard on the cobblestone. Upon the fall, Abraham's shout echoed across the harbor, "DAMIT!" As well as a handful of other words that Felix did not ever think was in his father's vocabulary.

"I think I broke my leg...or my arm!" Abraham cried. Felix and the coachman managed to help him stand. He was able to put weight on his leg. It wasn't broken. As Felix took his arm to help him back in the carriage, Abraham yelled some but managed to sit back in. Felix told him, "I think you might have hurt your arm more than your leg. If your leg were broken you wouldn't have been able to get up."

"How would you know!?" Abraham was in a mood. He clutched his upper arm as if his shoulder were hurting him. Felix stated, "Let's go back to Ignaz's home. He has a nice room where you can rest and get a doctor. When I fell out of a carriage it took months as you know," Felix then teased, "Yet it may take longer for you since you're old."

372

"I'm 57! I'm not old! Since when did you go to medical school?" Abraham sneered in his frustration. The carriage headed out of the docks and back to Chester Place. Ignaz came out of the complex as he happened to notice Felix and the coachman helping Abraham out of the carriage. He had a wave or worry and asked, "What happened?"

"He tripped. His ankle is only sprained I think, but his shoulder is what I'm worried about." Felix stated.

"I'll go call for a doctor." Ignaz sprinted off.

Once they got up the stairs and in the house, Abraham felt much disappointment as he limped to bed. Charlotte gave way to worry upon seeing him. Little Moscheles was crying in all the commotion. Felix went to Charlotte and assured, "Everything will be alright, my Vater got in an accident. Sorry for the sudden hassle, I shall repay you for any extra stay we may need."

"You are fine dear Felix. Things happen, as you know." She alluded to Felix's past incident. She then added, "Plus you help me much with the children."

Felix gave sighs of relief as the baby quieted when things calmed down. He went to the guest room to find Abraham resting. Ignaz soon came back with a doctor following close behind. Straight away the doctor tended to Abraham then informed, "Your leg has a few bruises, but nothing terrible. On the other hand I'm afraid you broke your collarbone. I shall wrap your arm in a splint but it will take much time to heal."

"When would I be able to travel?"

"I'd give at least a week and a half before going anywhere. Be very careful when you do go. I do believe you'll heal best after getting home, but right now you need to stay." The doctor wrapped his arm and shoulder then went on his way.

The next days at Chester Place were spent in a rather calm sense. Charlotte tended to her needlework while little Moscheles was next to her in the crib. Emily played with some wooden farm animals.

Felix and Ignaz had moved a Klavier in the guest room so they could practice and play music to entertain Abraham as he was in bed rest. He enjoyed it much as Felix studied a collection of Bach's Fugues and arranged some of Moschele's music. Ignaz did much composing. It was interesting to hear his creativity in its purest form.

The visit to London was deemed to a close after another week passed. Abraham was fit to travel home. When giving the Moscheles family their farewells on the 29th of August, Felix grabbed a score from his satchel and handed it to Ignaz, "This is the score to my 'Hebrides Overture'. I want it kept in safe hands. Take it please."

"Felix are you sure?" Ignaz was astounded. Felix nodded and Ignaz accepted it. They then parted outside of Chester Place. A carriage waited across the street and took Felix and Abraham to the docks. Felix worked on editing the Italian symphony while in the cab. Abraham had an ache in his collarbone so Felix set the music down and adjusted the cloth splint for him.

"I think I will miss London." Abraham commented.

"We should definitely come back together. Hopefully none of us will be falling out of carriages next time." Felix gazed out the window to catch the last glimpse of the smoky streets. When the carriage arrived and parked near the docks, Felix and Abraham stepped out carefully. They then boarded the nearest boat due to Hamburg. It departed within minutes.

An old gentleman walking the London docks went to the carriage Felix and Abraham had exited. He gave the coachman a note of address and climbed in the cab.

374

Upon doing so, he found a bound stack of manuscripts on the seat. He mumbled to himself, "What is this garbage?" He looked at it in confusion, unable to make out the massive and complex scoring of music. Before wasting another minute he threw it out and the cab continued on.

As the carriage drove off, there on the dirty grounds of London laid the scoring of Mendelssohn's Italian Symphony.

# Chapter XVII: Düsseldorf

Mendelssohn, Spinning Song [1]
Mendelssohn, Overture 'The Fair Melusine'  [2]
Mozart, Overture 'Don Giovanni' [3]
Haydn, Symphony No. 94, second movement 'surprise' [4]

## [1]

In the autumn of 1833, Felix signed a contract with immense satisfaction. He folded it carefully into a letter for a servant to send. It was off to Düsseldorf. Felix accepted the terms of a three year engagement, a salary of six-hundred thalers per annum and three months leave of absence.

Abraham deemed it a decent move and wasn't long before Felix made his official residence in Düsseldorf. It felt like a fresh breath of air when the carriage parked at a street side where an old spacious home sat. It was owned by a friend who was renting out rooms.

"Herr Schadow!" Felix called to a man coming towards the home.

*(Friedrich Wilhelm Schadow)*

"Felix! You've made it." Herr Schadow waved. He was the landlord and a patron concerning fine arts. As a painter himself, Schadow helped revive the academy of Düsseldorf.

Felix followed him into the colonial house. The inside had a most regency feel in decor. Herr Schadow explained, "I have rooms on the ground floor for you. I hope you found my terms favorable."

"I did." Felix assured, handing him the down payment. Schadow pocketed the money and suggested, "How about later you sit in for a sketch. It would be nice to chat as I practice drawing."

"Sure." Felix headed into his new abide. Schadow left him to settle.

As Felix roamed the main living area, the first thing noticed was a nice grand piano set up for him. He tapped a few of the freshly tuned keys. Also in the main room was a sofa, coffee table and fireplace. A separate section near the living area contained a stove and a round dining table. Lastly, a bedroom was tucked away further into the abide. In the moment he felt hope with this new life.

His thoughts were interrupted as the sound of an old rusty upright piano vibrated through an interior wall. He had a neighbor. Felix observed the music. They were playing Rossini's airs desperately slow.

After a day or so, he found that his neighbor was a lady. He memorized her piano routine. Two hours at the keys, playing the same pieces along with the same mistakes. Upon hearing the first chord, Felix knew each piece by heart. Yet the lady was more likely tormented as Felix played piano at all hours.

Schadow soon knocked at the door, bringing in his sketching supplies and a stack of papers. Felix turned around while at the piano as he entered. Schadow set the stack of papers on the piano's lid explaining, "There is some work for you before your first meeting with the orchestra. There is a score that has not yet been copied and a few other scores that need deciding if deemed ready for a performance."

(Felix by Schadow 1834)

"Alright." Felix shuffled through the seemingly endless pile of manuscripts. Schadow took his pencil and sketchbook, "First though, I must make a good sketch of you."

"Of course." Felix posed while sitting at the keys. Schadow began the outlines of a portrait. They had a good chat, but Felix's mind pondered over the large amount of work before him. He felt relieved when the portrait finished.

~ ~ ~ ~

The next Monday brought the first day of Felix's new position. After a good night's rest and a refined outfit to wear, Felix headed to the academy with Schadow in all freshness. Contrary to the good start, the day was soon to turn into a typical Monday. The orchestra trudged in, tired from the occasional weekends off.

When the musicians seated in the large rehearsal room, Schadow announced, "I have good news today. You have a new director." He gestured to Felix to step foreword. Slight grumbles passed around. It was the same trouble as during the festival last spring. Felix hoped such things wouldn't interfere with his duties.

Despite the muttering, Felix stepped before the orchestra at the conducting desk, "As you all know, my name is Felix. I shall do my best to bring out your best in the music that shall be presented to the public." He glanced at the musicians as they sat in silence, holding their instruments. Most listened commonly, but a few gave a dirty glance at their new director.

378

After initial greetings, Felix gestured them to the music. They lifted their instruments in obedience. When he counted them in, the sound was dry and rusty. Felix determined they had potential and could get them decent in the upcoming weeks.

After running some short pieces, rehearsals ended. Schadow informed Felix as he packed up, "I have received notice that the crown prince Frederick is in Düsseldorf. He wants you and I to dinner."

"I'll be ready to go in a second." Felix put the scores in his satchel. The both of them took a carriage back to Schadow's home so they could dress properly for the occasion.

At the hour of dinner, they arrived at the Prince's grand accommodation. They were welcomed to the large dinning hall where a plethora of guests were seated. A servant showed Schadow to a seat. The last open chair stood nearest to the foot of the table, beside the host. Prince Frederick gestured Felix to come. Felix obeyed, sitting beside the Prince and another acquaintance, the poet Herr Immermann. He worked with the theater society of Düsseldorf.

After being welcomed, Prince Frederick spoke straight away, "My dear Mendelssohn, I'm so glad you've found settlement here in Germany. I was so upset as you were everywhere but here in the last few years. I've not caught a concert in a while. How is your time here so far?"

"It's well. I think the orchestra will be decent in due time." Felix eyed the rather large platter at the table center holding a ridiculous amount of Cornish hens.

"You mean they are not decent right now?" Schadow questioned. Felix stated as the servants served each guest a miniature hen, "They are a bit rusty but will be sufficient after a few rehearsals."

"I inquire," Immermann budded in, "That you should join the theater society. I'd like some operas conducted. Older ones. I know you like reviving classical works."

"I would be delighted." Felix set a napkin on his lap as a nicely roasted hen was placed before him. Immermann's idea correlated with Felix's intentions; to bring back the works of Mozart, Beethoven and obscure composers. It was questionable how the public would react. With that, everyone began eating and speaking in all casualness.

~~~

A few weeks into the position of director, Felix became near to drowning in work. The complex schedule limited his time for leisure and composition. If he didn't have a pen in his hand, he was either conducting or in a meeting with various committees. There were many groups such as the theater society, choral society, orchestra and church.

The theater society with Immermann took a large chunk of time. They held meetings concerning the improvement of the stage. It was decided to join the theater and orchestra together to prepare classical operas that hadn't seen the public eye in years. It was a different concept as audiences were always craving something new, not old. Though Felix wasn't successful at composing opera, he could contribute to the stage by organizing them. Felix began feeling comfortable working with the orchestra...when the musicians cooperated.

Besides the plans of opera, much sacred music had been commissioned by the church. The rehearsals of sacred music gave way to the most struggle in the attitudes of the musicians. Some decided it better to murmur about Felix conducting rather than concentrate on the music. They couldn't get past their opinions of Felix's family background.

As the muttering became apparent over the music, Felix glared at the ones speaking while conducting.

He wasn't going to stop the music for such insolence, but then the whole orchestra messed up a section of triples...again. Felix hit his bâton against the stand, this time angry, "Every time! Every time you play the triplets wrong! For the millionth time, a triplet is not a quaver and two semi quavers! It's a strict eins-zwei-drei, eins-zwei-drei." He patted the rhythm on his leg, "Not eins...zwei-drei. Eins...zwei-drei!"

Felix's face turned a slight red. Before trying again, an older hornist chuckled, "Don't get too much of a temper tantrum over it."

"Shut up!" Felix hissed as others snickered along. The older men viewed him as a child and Felix couldn't stand such. He scolded them, "I have been respectful to you so you should respect my directing. I am your director, not a child."

"Since you're our director, when are you organizing our pay?" A younger violinist questioned.

"I'll get to that soon. First let's finish this rehearsal." Felix flipped a few pages in his score. The musicians listened for the last few minutes. It was the only calm moment in the entire day. After correcting some things he stated, "I will get contracts organized this week for your pay. Otherwise we are done today."

Eagerly, the musicians began packing up their instruments...somewhat. Another horrifying thing about this group was the care of their instruments. The violinists merely carried their fiddles about, only covering them with their coats when a rain fell. It affected sound quality. The only careful ones were the trombonists and percussionists, the rest were ignorant and rather abominable in sound. Felix gathered his scores, not wanting to deal with their antics in the moment.

Outside the music academy, Immermann caught up with Felix. The sight of the poet tired Felix. With all of the trouble dealing with the philharmonic, Immermann wanted him to do more for the theater.

"Are you free tomorrow? There is a rehearsal with a few singers for Don Juan. I'd be pleased if you conducted rehearsals."

"You know I have my duties with the orchestra for sacred music right now."

"This will be after orchestra rehearsals."

"I have other obligations. Tomorrow I must organize contracts to pay the musicians."

"You do know you agreed to be part of the theater society right? Act like it." Immermann stormed off in irritation. Felix called out to him, explaining, "I need rest and time of my own. Besides, when things get put together with everyone, I'll be conducting those rehearsals."

"And those rehearsals shall be twice as long." Immermann pressured from afar. Felix gave a small sigh and walked to a carriage to get back home.

Upon arriving back to Schadow's comfortable home, Felix felt little relief. Before he got to his rooms, Schadow stood in the main hall, gazing out the window in his usual way, "Rehearsals went well?" He asked as if he had eyes in the back of his head.

"It wasn't the greatest. We ran the church's commissions. Tomorrow I give the musicians their contracts." Felix in honesty was nervous concerning the payment terms. There were two contracts for each musician on their salary, in which they would have to agree. Schadow kindly reminded, "Remember that the committee has a Prix fixe and you must be sure you're making enough for my rent. Be careful how kind you are to them. I tell you as you are young and may give way to their begs. Be stern."

"I've calculated the wages. It's figured out." Felix ended the conversation in haste by walking to his rooms.

As soon as shutting the door, setting his bag down and flopping into bed, he vented to his overwhelmed state with tears. The anxiety of the day's events got to him. The mutterings of the musicians, the long frustrating rehearsal, the demands of Immermann and organizing payments; it all made his feelings pour.

Holding in his inner anxiousness caused a great deal of headache. He began to wonder if he were biting off more than he could chew. The job he thought to be a dream come true was faring differently. Yet to his dismay, it was only going to get harder...

~~~~

The next day, the contracts were ready for the musicians. Felix sorted them in the early hours. By the afternoon he brought the stack of papers to his conducting desk. All of the orchestra members crowded around to take their copies. In eagerness they grabbed them...until they looked at the fine print.

"What sort of trick is this!?" A middle aged violist hissed at Felix. A trombonist exclaimed at his paper, "Such robbery! I have a family to feed!"

Felix stood at his desk in a sigh in the midst of groans and complaints festering all around him. Begging and bartering came next, snapping over a dollar more or less. The negotiating reminded Felix of his father's little proverb, 'Asking and bidding make the sale'.

Felix complied with suggestions using common sense until everyone came to an agreement...somewhat. Most still thought the pay was insufficient, but signed their papers otherwise. Everyone then dispersed for the day as Felix planned a long rehearsal for the next.

While walking outside the academy, Immermann caught sight of Felix entering a carriage.

He felt offended that Felix cut orchestra rehearsals short to go home when he could be helping the theater. Immermann rushed inside the academy to find the nearest place to pen a letter.

Meanwhile, Felix felt ever so happy to be home early. He used his time to compose...in relaxation. Sprawled out on the sofa in comfortable lounging attire with the fireplace crackling. To top it off, he poured himself a healthy glass of red wine. A small plate of sliced clementines and dark chocolate accompanied.

With a score and pen at hand, he sketched his latest idea. An oratorio for orchestra and voices struck his muse. Oratorios were typically based on religious texts or themes. Examples include Bach's St. Matthew Passion and Handel's Messiah. Felix decided to title his St. Paul and base the music on the chosen texts. Though it was common to consult a church head to help organize the text, Felix preferred doing his own research. He consulted a pastor when he felt it necessary. In hopes, the oratorio would be done by the time another music festival came around.

Schadow lightly knocked at the door and came in to find Felix in his most comfortable leisure time. He handed Felix a letter, "It's from Herr Immermann."

"Oh..." Felix opened it. He tossed it aside after skimming it. It was a long paragraph ranting at Felix for not coming to the theater. Schadow glanced at the note, "Are you not going to reply?"

"Not right now. I am devoting the rest of today to self care," he set his music aside and stretched out on the couch, "Right now, I nap. After that I shall have a warm bubble bath whilst dining on fresh cherries. Then for super I shall have more wine and hearty pasta."

"Well la-ti-da-da." Schadow stole some chocolate as Felix shut his eyes. He left to let Felix enjoy his pampering day.

As Schadow continued work of his own, Felix's plans began to influence Schadow. He decided to make a nice dinner for himself and taste a bit of whiskey.

~~~

## [2]

The next morning, Felix stood at his conducting desk, refreshed and ready for a long rehearsal. There was one small problem. Every orchestra chair stood empty upon the hour. Felix practiced conducting in his lonesome for a bit, but then put his arm down in disappointment. A sigh escaped his mouth.

Suddenly, a middle aged woman came into the auditorium and met Felix at the stage. She wore a refined dark green dress. A feathered navy blue hat covered her pinned black hair. The choice of dark clothing and her rich demeanor gave a rather scary essence.

"Herr Mendelssohn?" The woman asked poshly. Her tone indicated he was to be scolded. Felix turned to her, "Ja?"

"Excuse me, but I must speak with you, as you are the director of the orchestra in which my talented nephew is part of. He is the flautist that sits there usually." She pointed to the center front chair. Felix grumbled within himself. The man that sat there was one of the most wretched of performers. This aunt of his deemed just as wretched. She continued on, "My nephew's talents are worth a good pay. A good pay I tell you. I believe you have miss calculated his monthly worth."

"I am sorry Madame. I've stated my terms and the papers are signed." Felix grabbed the stack of contracts. The lady sneered, putting her hands on her hips, "Do you have any compassion? My nephew deserves more!"

"I have to live too!" Felix shielded himself with the stack of papers as the woman stormed towards him.

She unexpectedly snatched his conducting bâton from the music stand. Felix in an instant dropped the contracts and covered his head as she started hitting him. When he managed to pry it from her hands, she hissed, "I'll be back if you don't change your terms!" She wistfully turned away.

Felix cleaned up the mess of contracts scattered about. While picking up the last few papers, someone walked up beside him, kindly taping his shoulder. Felix jumped, thinking it to be the aunt, but looked up to see much more of a gentlewoman. Her tone was soft, "Felix? I'm sorry to have startled you, but I must speak with you."

"Go head." Felix inquired, standing up. The reserved woman burst into tears while holding him at the shoulders. She begged in utter dramatic sorrow, "Please! Please! My husband needs to provide for our family! I have a child that needs food! Please give him the pay to help us! Please!" She sobbed into his chest, hugging him. It caused Felix to drop all of his contracts again. He looked up to the ceiling with a sigh as the woman wouldn't let go of him

"I am sorry. The pay I gave is sufficient. The contracts are signed." Felix then  noticed a few orchestra members peeking into the auditorium at the side of the stage. There were three of them. Felix sighed, "I know you have something to say, so just tell me now."

"We are hungry!" "Our children need food!" "I have high rent!" They each pleaded, so utterly beneath contempt. Felix face palmed. The woman still cried on his shoulder. He gently stepped away to pick up the contracts once more, this time setting them down on the music desk. The musicians waited for an answer. Felix stated, "You signed already. You have sufficient means for a living. Stop trying to get more. This conversation is done." Felix turned to his desk. The three musicians went away humbly, but showing a miserable expression. The wife wept in her hands when walking away.

Over the course of an hour, many others came to bargain and haggle. Out of thirty people, only a trombonist stated, "I am satisfied." The whole ordeal took four days to convince the orchestra back into their usual routine.

Felix wasn't the only director struggling with the musicians of Düsseldorf. It so happened that Julius Reitz, the younger brother of Eduard Reitz, directed the choral society. Felix knew him well as Julius had a part in copying the Bach oratorio for him those years ago.

The chorus of Düsseldorf consisted of 120 singers, yet it was more like 120 drunks...in one rehearsal room. They sang, but came to rehearsals after drinking and antics. Their energy was at the maximum when the sessions were to begin. Julius wasn't an authoritative man and did his best to get them singing, but they often shouted at him.

At times Julius requested Felix to rehearsals. The chorus never looked forward to such days, especially when his music was to be sung. Felix had an authoritative attitude when necessary and took his music, especially sacred works in all seriousness.

When he arrived at the hour, only Julius occupied the rehearsal room. The chorus was late. Felix took a chair and spoke to Julius as they waited. Soon, outside the door voices echoed in song, "Fünf Flaschen Bier an der Wand, fünf Flaschen Bier!"

"Oh dear..." Julius sighed. Felix stood from the chair, "This ought to be fun as it seems they have already gone through 95 bottles." He stood sternly as the singers entered in cheer. Their joy halted when noticing Felix with his arms crossed, glaring at each of them. They silently took their seats in shame.

Once everyone settled, Felix took his seat behind Julius who was set to conduct. Everything surprisingly started out great.

The singers obeyed and sang as they were supposed to. Yet when one found some sort of fault in the music and refused to go on, things went downhill.

"I refuse to sing that high!" A tenor shouted at Julius in the midst of the music. Felix looked up in pure anger, looking to see who made such a comment. As the others sang on, a soprano hissed, "This part is stupid!"

Felix darted up from his seat and stormed closer to the choir, glaring at the ones causing trouble. Julius kept conducting as some still sang. An insolent young man in the front, who had much to drink, grabbed a bottle of champagne hidden in his coat. He popped it open as Felix walked by. The cork flung in the air and the fizz sprayed all over Felix's pants. In an uproar, everyone laughed drunkenly. The young man snickered at Felix, "I believe you've wet yourself."

"Shut up! Give me that champagne now!" Felix snatched the bottle and threw it against the wall, breaking it. The laughter ceased and the room filled with a shouting match. Felix scolded them in all fury like boots at an inn.

"Now you had better listen!" Felix scorned, "There is to be a concert in a few days! I want no more drinking or screwing around! You are all adults!"

"We can do what we want since we are adults!" A tenor snapped back. Others yelled, giving their opinions. The shouts gave a new anxiety. Felix never had such a hash with performers. Finally, when the arguments ceased, they managed to sing through Cherubini's requiem.

"Alright, now we must get through Handel's oratorio." Julius flipped open a score. A soprano spoke up, "I am to sing the solo."

"Nein, it's me!" Another lady festered. An alto fought, "My voice is changing, I'm suited for it!"

As the quarrel began turning into a fist fight, Felix stepped between the ladies to break it up. That only worsened the problem as they tangled him in the pushing and shoving. Felix finally stepped away and told Julius, "Just leave rehearsals at that for the day."

~~~~

As time pressed on, Felix was wearing himself out physically and mentally. He began escaping music by reading. He preferred books based on fairy tales so he could feel far away from the reality of life.

Lately he had picked up a story by Hans Christian Anderson. It was called 'The Fair Melusine.' It took his imagination into a world of mermaids and love. Though he was trying to take a break from music, the story began to inspire sound. He sketched an outline of an overture.

On days at work, the muse of the story consumed his mind. During rehearsal breaks, at the conducting desk, in a carriage or walking about, he found time to write any sort of melody or harmony fragment. He tried to carry pen and paper at all times.

He wrote to his father about his composition. Abraham rather thought it all foolish daydreaming; another overture full of pixies. He wished him to 'hang up on a nail' these dreams on elfin and fairy stories and work on something graver.

The orchestra and theater soon joined together for the classical operas. It only made it harder for Felix to accomplish his creative outlet, but he was excited to move forward with the operas. Being prepared were Der Freischütz, Entführung, wasserträger, die Zauberflöte and Don Juan. There were various plays as well.

As a whole, the rehearsals became a torturous affair with the grumbling members of the orchestra and the drunkards of the chorus. Added to it were actors and set crew working around everyone. Each day there were two rehearsals, ten hours each.

After a few hard days, Felix began to show signs of overwork. The twenty hours of rehearsals were killing him. The time spared for sleep rendered useless as something always kept him awake. His emotions, pressure or his aching stiff arm from conducting.

Herr Immermann noticed Felix walk into rehearsals more and more in a fog. It made him worry, not for Felix, but for the sake of the performances. Immermann called to Felix as he saw him trudging to the conducting desk, "Felix, we must talk."

"What do you want?" Felix's tone was rather grouchy. Immermann then channeled his worries, "I have not been able to work as much with the plays so I need you to take control in regulating the other aspects of the opera such as the acting and scenery."

"You mean you ask me to do your job?"

"If I'm out working with the plays there will be no one else. It will all go wrong otherwise. I'm off now. I'll check on the progress later. Danke." He left to go work with the actors doing the stage plays. Felix gave a sigh as the orchestra and singers were set up before him, waiting for instruction. It was going to be a long rehearsal.

~~~~

One fine morning in the eighth hour, a carriage pulled up beside Schadow's home. Karl Klingemann stepped out and breathed in the fair air of Düsseldorf. He was there to see how Felix's first official job was going.

After Schadow welcomed him in, Karl went to Felix's door and knocked.

"Come in." Felix called. Karl eagerly opened the door, but before taking his coat off, he was horrified at the state of the place. Papers were everywhere. Piled, sprawled or stuffed in folders. Some stained with tea or coffee. It consisted of music, bills and contracts.

Karl turned about, trying not to step on anything. When he came to the dining area, he found Felix at the table, composing as he chewed vigorously at a handkerchief. A cup of coffee sat beside him. He looked as if he'd not slept in days.

"Felix?" Karl asked in worry. Felix turned and smiled at seeing his friend. He set his music aside to greet him. Karl was in a state of shock as this was nothing like his friend. Felix told him, "I'm so happy you've come to visit. I was just about to head to rehearsals. You can accompany me."

"Alright. Are you fit to go?"

"I'll be alright. I must or Immermann will be upset." He dropped his quill on the table and stood. His outfit was fine but his hair was a mess. He had some scruff on his chin and his sideburns were growing out. Klingemann lent him a comb. Felix quickly brushed his hair then headed out the door with Karl following behind.

When they arrived at the Konzerthaus for rehearsals, Klingemann watched from a seat a few rows back. He was baffled at the state of his friend as he conducted. His arm could hardly move high enough for the musicians to see. He looked as if he'd fall over at a given moment. Though the orchestra and singers were coming together well, Felix was falling apart.

Immermann walked in during the first act of Der Freischütz and sat next to Karl. Karl had a deep respect for Immermann as he was a great poet, but he could not get past the fact that he was essentially hurting his friend. Immermann whispered to Karl, "It's all coming together well is it not?"

"I'd say hardly." Karl muttered back. Immermann took offense, "Why? What is wrong?"

"Are you blind? Look at the conductor. The opera is coming together but he is in shambles. If you do not give him a few days break, I shall find a way to stop the operas' production." Karl spoke in the utmost threatening tone. Immermann huffed, "Alright. Three days he gets. I shall cut rehearsals short today."

Immermann stood and headed towards the front. He tapped on Felix. Karl felt much happiness at seeing the relief on his friend's face as Immermann spoke to him.

~~~~

[3]

By December, after rest, spending time with Karl, continuing rehearsals and finding success in performing these classical operas, the final opera of the season was Don Juan. Immermann, in a rather foolish sense, raised ticket prices since the other operas were popular. The public thought it an arrogant move. The whole ordeal caused three days of scandalous gossip. Members of the company that had doubts ran away, including two members of the orchestra. Despite the price complaints, the auditorium sold out.

When the hour of the performance struck, the members of the orchestra were set and waiting. Backstage behind the curtain, a few actors scurried about to their places. Once they settled, Immermann instructed Felix, "Time to go."

Felix nodded and entered the orchestra pit. The audience continued muttering and whispering, which wasn't common. The musicians were ready, so Felix counted them into the overture. It was a bit awkward as some spectators decided to raise their voices in conversation.

After the completion of the overture, the auditorium echoed with a humble applause as the curtain rose.

The singers entered for the first duet, but they had a hard time perusing as the restless audience gave way howling and whistling. Felix tapped his baton against the conducting desk to control the veering heads of the orchestra.

When the disturbances grew louder than the music, Immermann came to the side of the stage and gestured for the curtain to be lowered. The opera was on hold until things quieted. When they did calm down, the curtain rose again. Shouts started up soon after, drowning out the first act.

In the next interlude, a young man in the crowd spotted Immermann standing to the side and threw a newspaper at him. It caused Immermann to go off in a huff. The curtain lowered again.

Felix wanted to put his bâton down right then and there. It felt embarrassing as the audience behind him complained. The musicians gave sweats of nervousness. Felix held his baton up again, "Alright men. We shall have to trudge on."

As Felix gave the next counts, a loud bang echoed through the concert hall. Felix jumped, tossing his bâton. He caught it and quickly counted in. The musicians followed, but jolted as another bang echoed. This time a bright spark ignited next to Felix. He nearly fell off the conducting pedestal in fright. Glancing behind him, the insolent young man causing most of the antics waved. He then lit a firecracker and chucked it at the orchestra pit. It landed at Felix's feet, but it was a dud.

Immermann came back to the side of the stage as Felix set his bâton down, deeming it unsafe to perform. The voices became hoarse in shouting. Immermann could not afford to let this concert go, so he snapped at Felix in a whisper, "Keep going!"

Felix sighed as he took the bâton once more. The orchestra and singers were especially nervous, but Felix called to them with encouragement.

As they pursued on, yells continued and firecrackers were tossed, smoking up the auditorium. Thankfully no one got hurt.

At the end, the performance received some claps from loyal audience members. When the curtain gave the final drop, Immermann and Felix called for every performer backstage to speak with them. No one listened. Instead the actors and musicians shouted at them like a fiery rain.

"What are we to do?" Immermann consorted with Felix. Felix crossed his arms, "I am not conducting again until the theater committee gives an apology. Why didn't you stop the performance? I could have gotten hurt if that man were firing a gun!"

"The show must go on! I've sold the tickets for tomorrow evening. You will be conducting!" Immermann hissed. Felix turned away, "I refuse!"

"You are. The orchestra will refuse to play if you don't conduct. They've grown fond of you as they sound better than before. Now go home, get rest and be back." Immermann snubbed. Felix headed for the halls to leave, but turned back as crowds of the audience lingered about. He exited through an alley door instead.

It was a quiet night as a soft snow fell. Carriages were stationed at the nearby street, so Felix headed that way. As he walked, someone came beside him. They put their arm around his shoulder, speaking in utmost cheer, "My dear sir, I thank you!" It was the young man who had caused the riot, "My name shall be in every paper!" He sprinted off before Felix could confront the tyrant.

~~~~

The next day, Felix awoke, got dressed and made a decent breakfast for himself. He didn't want to think about what was to come for the evening's performance. Schadow knocked at Felix's door, coming in with the morning paper. He informed, "You may want to read this."

Felix took the paper and the headlines said it all. It was full of gossip from the night before. Everyone who took part in the tumult was scolded. The instigator of the riot justified himself, declaring that in spite of it all, he had great enjoyment, being especially grateful to Felix for a fun concert. The Association for the Promotion of Music issued a manifesto, denouncing the ordeal so the next concert could go on, but the Theatrical Committee warned that if the slightest disturbance occurred it was done.

"Immermann sent a note this morning," Schadow handed it to Felix, "he has come down with a fever and won't make it tonight."

"Oh...how convenient." Felix grumbled. Schadow suggested, "Why don't you go into the market this morning. There is a fair today. Get yourself a treat, there will be many baked goods. Take a break and do something for yourself."

"Alright." Felix grabbed his satchel and headed out. The closer he walked to the market, the more people there were, drinking and dancing about; getting tipsy in the street, as if not the case every day. The smell of fresh baked goods filled the air. Nearby, a group of people crowded around a newsstand, catching the opera drama whilst eating cakes. Felix laid low and bought a cherry tart for himself.

~~~~

When evening came, the preparation of the opera rendered a mess as a few other council members had decided they were ill along with Immermann. Felix was left to organize both the orchestra and actors himself. He felt a sense of dread when the hour of showtime came. Thankfully, everyone cooperated.

Felix took his place at the music desk before the orchestra. The audience received him with good applause. A flourish from the trumpets blared to boost his confidence. Felix counted into the overture with the audience, admit a row, quiet as mice. This time, the opera went perfectly.

Everyone played and sang with confidence. At the final, the last chord echoed through the auditorium, followed by an unforgettable silence.

The crowd burst into applause and cheer. Felix turned and bowed, then let the orchestra stand. The feeling of the concert left everyone joyful. Immermann was missing out. Some singers eagerly came to Felix as he packed up his score. A tenor warmly shook his hand, "Felix, we want to admit to you; before tonight, we honestly didn't like you, nor these classical performances."

"Oh." Felix didn't know how to answer that statement. An alto then finished the speech, "After this grand concert, we are impatient for another and we would go to the death for you!" They all hugged him. Felix gave a sigh of relief as the day had been worth the while.

After the crowd made their leave, the musicians gathered in a nearby tavern to celebrate. Champagne and expensive cheeses were served. Felix ordered chocolate for himself as he didn't feel like drinking the night away. He felt calm for once in Düsseldorf.

~~~

Though the successful opera season ended, the stress of the next work week did not cease. Irritability strung up among the musicians as Felix decided the orchestra should perform the classic works of Beethoven.

As they worked at Beethoven's 'Egmont', the orchestra began to belabour to one another as Felix conducted in 6/8 time. The murmuring distracted Felix's attention. He glared at the ignorant tyrants. During the air, 'Glücklich allein ist die Seele die liebt', voices spoke over the music. Felix in a fit of rage grabbed his score and tore it in two. As soon as he did, the orchestra's playing magically became more expressive. The rest of the rehearsal went more pleasing.

Outside of his directing duties, the months after the opera season gave him time to work on his own compositions. He completed the overture to 'The Fair Melusine'. Ignaz adored the work when Felix sent a copy.

Abraham still wished his son to work on more serious things rather than tales of mermaids. His ideals leaned towards the completion of the St. Paul oratorio. Felix continued working at it, writing to his father that it would be complete in due time.

In other aspects, Felix found much more time for secular activities such as late parties and balls. His love of dance made it impossible to resist going to at least a few. Other days of leisure were spent with friends, many of which were painters. They were devoid of the slightest arrogance or envy and lived together in true friendship. The circle included Hildenbrant, Bendemann and tall quiet Lessing. They helped him get back into practicing watercolors. Another local artist hosted lessons on Sundays so Felix joined to brush up.

Another project Felix happened upon was giving piano lessons to a young girl who begged him to teach her. Felix made time. He only taught a few selective people as he was busy otherwise. The girl was the daughter of a manufacturer and had a prettiness to her. Yet in a matter of a few weeks, the girl's family was to move away. On her departure, Felix gave her copies of Mozart and Beethoven.

The day after, Felix was surprised to receive a package from the postman. He opened it to find a parcel of fine black cloth to make an entire suite. It was from the girl's father.

On a stroll along the grasslands with his friend Lessing, who was riding a horse, Felix showed him the cloth he had received. Lessing hopped down from his horse and looked at the cloth, "You'll have an excellent outfit with such fabric, such luck."

"I'm quite excited. It was unexpected but I'm grateful as I needed a new suit." Felix jumped a bit. He then said, "Your new horse has a good temper. That's luck of its own."

"Ja, he is a good companion," Lessing patted the horse, "I do strongly suggest you get one. It's a useful purchase. The countryside is a must to ride out to. So peaceful."

"I shall pen to my Vater. I'd like to consult him on the idea." Felix stated as Lessing climbed back onto his horse and carried on in the utmost leisure.

Within the week, Felix had the black fabric made into a most fashionable suite. He also figured out how to tie the cravat Ignaz had given him. It saved much time. After consulting and receiving consent from Abraham, Felix bought a nice bay horse; a good tempered steed. It became his most favorite aquatint.

On a good day, adorned in his new outfit, he rode along the countryside. Passerby asked if his cravat was English in which he gave a happy reply that it was. Often, Felix took his horse to a lovely spot where the apples grew and flocks of sheep could be visible in the distant hills. Other days he headed to Ruhr as it was a common spot for swimming and bathing. Close to the shore with the tall grass and stones, the clean water was chin deep and a little steam flowed. It gave all the more calmness.

Felix learned that his horse had a shyness of new terrain so it had to be encouraged much. On one trot, a storm happened to form. Every flash and sound made the horse start violently. Felix managed to keep control and guide it home, but he felt quite sorry for the creature.

In his laziness with heavy storms, he found no inspiration for composition. He worked at his oratorio some, but in truth, not much progress was being made. It vexed him that he was in a state of relaxation, but he enjoyed every bit of it.

~~~~

Felix's world of work slowly began creeping up on him again as Herr Immermann requested he attend more of the theater's meetings.
Felix was tired of complying to Immermann's wishes and only wanted to be a friend of the theater, not a main vessel. There was much more important business as Felix joined alongside Julius in preparing the orchestra and choir for a performance of Handel's oratorio, 'Deborah'.

As Felix sat in one of the boxes of the Konzerthaus during a rehearsal, some men entered, taking seats beside him. He didn't take note of them until one spoke up, "I love the way Handel composes."

Felix turned his head straight away to see Ferdinand Hiller and Frederick Chopin next to him. He burst with joy, "Hiller! Chopin!"

"Felix!" Herr Hiller hugged him in greeting. Chopin gave the same greet as well. Felix's voice carried across the auditorium as he spoke, "I missed you both ever so! We shall lunch together, shall we not?"

"Of course," Hiller kept his voice low, trying to calm Felix's tone. Felix instantly quieted, noticing a few singers looking up from the stage in annoyance. The three then went off for lunch. Felix felt ever so joyous to catch up with his friends of Paris. They ate at the best restaurant in Düsseldorf.

That evening they returned to the Konzerthaus as the performance of the oratorio happened to be then. Julius was to conduct so Felix joined his friends in renting a private box. It yielded much fun as they drank champagne, whispered and watched.

~~~~

Felix woke at decent timing in the dawn. He had a few early hours to himself until the ninth hour, when there was a knock at his door. He answered and it of course was Hiller and Chopin.

They didn't want to waste any time on their visit. Felix eagerly showed them around. Chopin commented as he looked about, "You have such a fine taste in decor."

"Danke, I desire to make any house I live in a home." Felix straightened a hanging painting. It was one of his watercolors. Chopin stood in deep thought, studying such art. Hiller ventured to the fine piano and began playing new material. Felix joined beside it to listen. Ferdinand spoke of his upcoming projects as he continued a tune. The grand ideas gave Felix much anticipation. Hiller then called to Chopin, "You must show Felix your new works."

"Well...they are still in progress..." Chopin shied away some. Felix encouraged, "Even if it's nothing complete, I'd still like to hear it."

"Alright." Chopin sat down. He thumbed a soft floral piece to warm up, then gradually went into a newly composed work. Felix stood astonished at the technique of his playing. It was a new piece, with new techniques. He produced effects at the keys much in the same aspect Paganini did with the violin. At the end of the piece, Felix clapped and jumped. Hiller had to take him by the shoulders to keep his feet on the ground. Chopin blushed at the enthusiasm.

Felix listened more as both Chopin and Hiller shared all of their ideas. It was all impressive, but some ideas seemed overly influenced by the music scene of Paris; rather losing sight of sobriety and true music. Felix came to the conclusion that maybe he did too little in finding something new. He shook off his complicated thoughts, determining all in all that the three of them learned and improved each other.

~~~

The next day, Felix felt a terrible sense of irritation. He was to conduct a rescheduled festival which would take up two days of his time. It was out of town so he would be parted from his friends.

As he grabbed his luggage to leave, Hiller assured, "Chopin and I plan to stay awhile. We will still be here when you return."

"Oh good. I hope this to be a quick engagement." Felix waved in farewell to Chopin and Hiller as the carriage departed for an eleven hour trip. Only a few hours in, Felix became impatient and cross. It lasted all the way to Aix-la-Chapelle. As soon as arriving, he went straight into the orchestra pit.

The festival went decently but Felix couldn't wait to get back to Düsseldorf. Eleven more tiring hours in a carriage required much patience. Felix had none, making it a torture to the coachman.

When returning to Düsseldorf, the carriage pulled up to Schadow's home in the sunny afternoon. Schadow happened to be exiting the front door with Chopin and Hiller. When seeing Felix hop out of the carriage, Schadow mentioned, "Ah, Felix, we were going for a stroll if you want to join."

"Of course, I'll get my bags inside first." He took his luggage from the coach. After settling it in his room, he came back to the group. They walked down the road towards the gardens.

Chopin and Hiller enjoyed Schadow's company as the older man was dignified, easy mannered and had a teacher-like sense to him. He had many words of wisdom to the three young musicians. Hiller then mentioned, "Chopin and I decided to go to Cologne tomorrow. We shall take a steamer, ride out on some post horses then head back to Paris by carriage."

"You're leaving so soon?" Felix questioned somberly, "I must at least accompany you to Cologne."

Schadow looked to Felix with sternness, "What of your oratorio that needs finishing? Your Vater wishes it done."

"It will be ready in good time." Felix replied quietly, but with firmness. Their walk ended with coffee and a game at bowls.

The evening was spent at Schadow's home, joined with the artists Hildenbrant, Lessing and Bendemann. It was all fun in good manner. They drank and played cards in the main hall. Chopin was reserved the entire time. He spoke in all softness, only sticking to Hiller and Felix as he was shy of the others. The painters took little notice of him.

Hiller sat next to Chopin on the sofa as the others started a chess game. He asked Frederick quietly, "Why don't you speak more? You'd have a much better time."

Chopin nodded humbly but didn't answer. Hiller encouraged further, "Frederick? Have you anything to talk about?"

"Um...not really." He didn't like the group suddenly staring at him. Felix broke the awkward silence by inviting, "Please play us some piano."

"Oh, I don't know..."

"Please," Felix took his arm, pulling him from the sofa. He guided Chopin to the piano. Everyone circled around to Frederick's dismay. After much convincing, Felix finally stated, "Just close your eyes and play."

Frederick shut his eyes tight and played whatever came to his heart. After a solid interlude of music, he opened his eyes to see every face smiling at him. The painters made many comments, adoring his music. Schadow especially found much interest. Chopin finally felt at home with the group and expressed his true self in happy speech. He ended up talking the most by the evening's end.

~~~~

The next morning, Felix, Hiller and Chopin were on a steamer headed for Cologne. The ride was smooth all the way there as they laughed and spoke.

The moment was one wished to never end, but the boat soon docked and they took post horses towards Cologne. Felix couldn't stay long with them as Schadow strongly suggested he work on the oratorio, but he planned to ride to the city with them.

In the outskirts, they reached a church and bridge. Hiller parked his horse and dismantled to look at the sparkling water. The day was warm and perfect. He made a remark to himself in extravagance, "Such a lovely, unforgettable scene."

"Hiller getting sentimental; heaven help us!" Felix called, turning his horse around, "Adieu Farewell!" With that he departed the company of Chopin and Hiller. Felix journeyed home in his lonesome.

When returning to his rooms, there was a note sitting on the dining table. Felix picked it up. The light and pretty handwriting appeared to be that of a woman's. It contained poetry alluding to the fact that he should find a wife. Felix chuckled a bit. He then went to the piano and put together a little tune, deeming it a Bachelor's song.

As Felix had no means of repaying the orchestra for testing out his Overture to 'The Fair Melusine,' which wasn't popular among them, he decided to host a dinner at the academy of roster veal with bread and butter. Wine as well to let them get tipsy. Felix didn't take pleasure in doing so, but they needed fun sometimes.

At the dinner, Felix gave speeches and the musicians had a grand time. Some trumpeters and trombonists brought their instruments, giving a flourishing fanfare. Felix played his Bachelor's song at the piano, but no one knew the meaning.

~~~

Felix's time in Düsseldorf from then on became taxing with annoyance. After setting the dining table with coffee, a pen and music, he began serious work on the oratorio to have it complete in due time.

## [4]

When finishing a bar, the bell rang. He got up to answer, finding a choirboy grumbling about his music. Felix took care of the matter then went back to composing. He penned another bar. The bell rang. He got up. Singers and seedy musicians were at his door, needing lessons on their parts. Felix took care of their matters, snubbing them in the process. Once matters were solved, Felix sat back down. He penned another bar. The bell rang.
He got up.

Felix opened his door in utter provoke, making a postman jump in a spook. Felix calmed as the postman handed him a letter. He opened it to find a note from Immermann demanding him to the theater. Felix straight away grabbed his coat to go out. There was reasoning behind his willingness.

When Felix arrived at the Spielhaus, Immermann greeted him in surprise, "It's nice that you are finally willing to come to theater rehearsals. For a while I almost forgot that you were a member of the theater society."

"I came to give my resignation." Felix handed Immermann a contract, "As much as I care about the theater, I quit." Felix kept his speech in all politeness. Immermann pressed his lips together viciously in anger as if he fained to eat him.

When Felix finished speaking, there was a silence. Immermann glared a while, then managed to say, "I guess you may resign but I will only let you go, under one condition that you promise to occasionally conduct. I cannot fully let you go."

"Alright I promise." Felix spoke with ease. Immermann then went away in irritation. Felix felt like a fish thrown back into the water. He nearly skipped all the way home as he was proud of standing up for himself.

When he returned to his rooms, he sat at the table with the oratorio score and managed to get much done, not disturbed once. It seemed as if the clouds had lifted. The freeness of the day also gave him time to read and catch up on letters.

One letter had much importance. It was an offer from an acquaintance by the name of Herr Schleinitz. He wanted Felix to come to the city of Leipzig as there was bound to be an open position with the orchestra. It was the new year of 1835 and Felix's contract with Düsseldorf was to expire the next fall. The idea of staying in Düsseldorf grew grim as his favors veered towards Leipzig. Publishers there were interested in his music. Breitkopf and Härtel wanted to publish anything he had to offer.

The first step in escaping Düsseldorf was complete by resigning from the theater. Abraham learned of Felix's actions. Straight away he wrote a scorning letter to his son. It reached Felix's hands days later. It read:

*My son,*

*I must once more resume the subject of the dramatic career, as I feel very anxious about it on your account. You have not, according to my judgement, either in a productive or administrative point of view, had sufficient experience to decide with certainty that your disinclination towards it proceeds from anything innate in your talents or character. I know no dramatic composer, except Beethoven...in which you have made only one public effort, which was partly frustrated by the text and was neither very successful nor the reverse...*

*With regards to the administrative career, it gives rise to another series of reflections which I wish to impress on you. Those who have the opportunity to become more acquainted to you and those who you desire to express more fully cannot fail to love and respect you.*

*But this is far from sufficient to enable a man to enter life with active efficacy...when you advance in years, both others and yourself are much more likely to lead to isolation and misanthropy...*

The letter went on and on. In short, Abraham approved of Felix's resignation, but not the manner in which he did.

As the month of January pushed on, more letters came upon the subject of Leipzig. Herr Schleinitz wrote up the terms. A good salary, better than his current one was offered. There was also a plan to host a benefit concert to ensure a decent bonus. Felix felt such a thing improper and unnecessary. He had much suspicion on the six months of vacation time. A lot can come together for an orchestra in such time. Being away six months could suffer any progress.

On the other side of things, Felix received another letter from Abraham. He and his father began frequently writing back and forth. Though at times they bickered, their relationship had grown strong since visiting London together. A conversation in writing went as so:

*Berlin March 10th 1835*

*My dear son,*

*This is the third letter I have written to you this week, and if this goes on, reading my letters will become a standing article in the distribution of the budget of your time; but you must blame yourself for this, as you spoil me by your praise. I at once pass to the musical portion of your last letter.*

*Your aphorism, that every room in which Sebastian Bach is sung is transformed into a church, I consider peculiarly appropriate; and when I once heard the last movement of the piece in question, it made a similar impression on myself;*

but I own I cannot overcome my dislike to figured Chorales in general, because I cannot understand the fundamental idealen which they are based, especially where the contending parts are maintained in an equal balance of power...

At Fanny's last morning music, the motet of Bach, "Gottes Zeit ist die allerbeste Zeit, and your 'Ave Maria', were sung by selected voices. A long passage in the middle of the latter, as well as the end also, appeared to me too learned and intricate to accord with the simple piety...

It is undoubted a fact that without Zelter, your own musical tendencies would have been of a totally different nature...

–Abraham

~~~~

Düsseldorf, March 23rd, 1835

Dear father,

I have still to thank you for your last letter and my 'Ave.' I often cannot understand how it is possible to have so acute a judgment with regard to music, without being yourself technically musical...I thank you a thousand times for this, and also your opinion of Bach...it pleases me to see your definite sense of music....

**A knock at the door interrupted Felix. He set the pen down with a sigh, wondering what needy musician wanted him now.**

**When answering the door, he was toppled by an unexpected hug. Lea had come in surprise to visit her son. Felix cheered and hugged back.**

His mother released her hug but held him at the shoulders, telling him in all joy, "My boy is living on his own! Oh I am so proud!"

"Love you Mutter." Felix felt a cured homesickness. He let Lea into his home. After she observed her first impressions, they went to the living area where Felix set a tray of tea.

While sipping some fresh green tea, they caught up. Felix informed her of his current situation, "I am quite inclined to quit my position with the Düsseldorf orchestra. My contract ends in October. I am wanted in Leipzig as they offered terms better than what I have now."

"I think that would be a good move. They must want you there badly." Lea seemed intrigued. Felix explained further, "Some terms seem too good. I'm going to write to persuade them not to hold a benefit concert for my sake. I hope they are not trying to replace or hurt the job of someone by hiring me," Felix then changed the subject, "Would you like something to eat? You've probably been on the road for hours on end."

"I'm starving. The tea is well but I do need food." She reclined on the couch to take a nap. Felix went to the kitchen and kindled the stove. There was a Cornish hen hanging in the food pantry. He bought it from the local market recently so it was fresh.

Since the hen was small, he chose to cook some various vegetables such as carrots, radishes and acorn squash to make it a more shareable meal. Also in the pantry there were many spices to add flavour. He grabbed rosemary and a nutmeg. There was no butter as he despised it.

While the stove heated, he put the hen in a cast iron cooking vessel, along with the vegetables. He then set a bundle of fresh rosemary beside the meat. Lastly, he graded much nutmeg over it to get the desired taste. Cooking was usually done by a servant, but Felix wanted to do something special for his mother. He deemed himself capable as he was a man of many skills.

After getting the vessel in the oven to roast, Lea couldn't help but sit at the dining table. The air filled with the scent of savory chicken. Felix gave Lea and himself a plate. As he placed the silverware, he mentioned, "For desert I have lemon curd and biscuits on hand."

"So sweet of you." Lea smiled while her son fetched the finished chicken. He came back with a platter of a picturesque meal. They both admired the food before digging in. The waiting didn't last long as their appetites were greater than their patience. It was a most lovely evening spent together.

~~~

The next morning, Felix awoke feeling rather out of sorts. He got out of bed to get dressed for the day, hoping a fresh outfit would help. As he buttoned his waistcoat, he paced about the room, feeling ill in the gut. In debating whether he was going to puke or not, the ache seemed to settle in the moment.

Yet in the room next door, he heard his mother violently barfing. The sound of it then made him hurl. He felt better, but in haste went to check on Lea. She was in a state of horrid sickness, almost feverish. Felix told her as he helped her back to bed, "I'm calling for a doctor. I think something is wrong with the both of us." He hurried off.

Outside the rooms, Schadow found Felix in the halls in a panic. He stopped the anxious man asking, "Is everything alright?"

"My Mutter came down ill this morning. I'm going to get a doctor for her."

"Nein, I'll do it. You look sick yourself." Schadow headed out. Felix went back to stay with Lea. Her state put him in a terrible worry. The minute he heard the front door open, he rushed to the doctor that had come. He showed him to the bedroom where Lea stayed.

After the doctor tended to her, he informed Felix, "She has a horrible case of food sickness. Her ill state may last a while.

When she is able, I suggest accompanying her back home where she can get comfortable rest and good food," he then handed him a bottle of medicine, "Give her some of this once a day."

"I will." Felix's voice weakened a bit as he felt his own wave of ache in his gut. The doctor looked at him, "What did you both eat recently."

"I made chicken yesterday, but it was fresh." Felix felt confused.

"Where did you get it?"

"Just in the market down the street." Felix stated. The doctor grabbed more medicine and handed it to him, "Don't go there anymore. Their meat is bad. I've had many calls under the same circumstance." The doctor took his pay then left. Felix went back to Lea's room to find her sleeping. Though it wasn't his fault, he felt terrible that he had cooked the hen.

In the days to come, Felix decided to use the three months worth of vacation to take care of himself and Lea. He made arrangements to return to Berlin after their illness lifted some. Felix wasn't worried so much of himself as he seemed better by the next day. Lea however, recovered slowly. When she was able, they left Düsseldorf the following week.

The ride home was long and fearful. Felix had much anxiety for his mother as the traveling did not help her state. Nothing would be calm until they got to the safety of home with Abraham. Felix had packed all of his belongings, intending not to return.

In the carriage, as Lea slept in the seat across from him, he penned his resignation as Music Director of Düsseldorf. He had better engagements in Leipzig.

# Chapter XVIII: The Gewandhaus

Bach, Brandenburg Concerto no. 5 movement I [1]
Robert Schumann, von Fremden Ländern und Menschen [2]
Clara Schumann, Piano Concerto 1, movement 1 [3]
Beethoven, movement II of Piano Concerto 5 [4]

## [1]

Felix straightened his framed watercolour paintings in his new roomy abode. He had already unpacked so he touched up the place. The city overwhelmed him with joy as it was where Bach once lived. Felix had accepted the position offered as the Music Director of the Gewandhaus in Leipzig.

*(Felix age 26)*

His duties were to start later in the week, allowing him time to settle. As he finished decorating, the doorbell rang. Felix answered to see his dear sister Fanny and brother-in-law Wilhelm.

"Fanny! Wilhelm!" Felix threw his arms in the air from excitement. Fanny gave her brother hugs. Wilhelm gave a tight shake of the hand; the other held a sketchbook. Felix let them in, inviting them around the coffee table in the living space, next to a kindling fireplace. Some tea had been made at the hour, so Felix served a tray for them.

Their conversation started with Lea's welfare. Felix had much worry as Lea had not fully recovered upon his leave of Berlin. Abraham had assured that she would be fine and insisted Felix pursue the offered position in Leipzig. Fanny calmed his anxiety, "Mutter was walking the gardens before we left, her health is getting stronger."

"Oh good!" Felix gave a breath of relief.

"How are you though? Your new home?" Fanny gazed about. Felix smiled, "I love it. It is a good abide. My official position at the Gewandhaus will begin later this week."

Wilhelm opened the sketchbook in his hands, "I've been making a lot of drawings lately. I wanted to show them to you. I see you have been working at watercolour."

"Ja, I took regular lessons in Düsseldorf." Felix studied Wilhelm's sketches. It consisted of portraits of friends and family. The sight of them made Felix a tinge homesick.

After discussing various subjects into the late evening, Wilhelm became tired and decided to retire to the guest room for the night. Fanny and Felix stayed up, spending time as siblings. Felix set out wine for deep talk. The conversation veered towards Fanny's inclinations.

412

She told Felix, "Bruder, I've been meaning to get an opinion from you. It's about my music. As you know, I've been composing some serious works."

"All of your music is serious and well written." Felix sounded confused at her statement. She continued, "Even though our Vater does not approve, I am ready to try my hand at publishing. Whether he likes it or not, I am my own woman and not under his roof."

"Are you truly sure that's a good idea?" Felix sipped some wine. Fanny looked up to her brother in question, "Are you not on my side of things?"

"You have a family to take care of. Your children. Your house. Your husband. Publishing will add to that list as it is an utmost serious obligation. Once you are an author, an author you remain for the rest of your life. Do you understand?"

"I think you were around Vater too long when you went to England together. Are you hearing yourself? You're turning out just as him!" Fanny sneered in disappointment. Felix set his wine glass down, "I am not like Vater! I have my own opinion!"

"Wilhelm agrees with my idea. I have my husband's consent, so don't be angry if in a few years time, the music of Fanny Hensel is on every music stand in Europe." She sipped her wine. Felix stared at his sister leaving a void in the room. The ticking clock felt like the beats of a heart. Fanny broke the silence, "I'm going to bed for the night. We leave tomorrow." She left to join Wilhelm. Felix wanted to punch something, but instead headed for bed himself.

~~~~

The next morning at the breakfast hour, Fanny and Wilhelm sat at the table. Felix set a nice meal of hotcakes with sweet maple syrup. Butter was set out for Fanny and Wilhelm. Felix assured whilst topping each plate with a serving of bacon, "The meat is well done, I've made sure to cook them to perfection."

Once Felix joined with his plate, they ate in silence. Wilhelm glanced at the watercolour paintings hanging about. Fanny kept her eyes at her plate, still unhappy about the conversation the night before. Felix ate, trying to keep an uplifting expression. He opened his mouth between bites to speak, but the bell rang, so he set his napkin down to go answer. He opened the door to see Chopin standing alone in the corridor.

"Bitte, come in." Felix gestured to him, "Some family and I are eating breakfast. I can set an extra plate, if you want."

"Sure." Frederick entered. Felix led him to the dining table. Fanny was curious as the unfamiliar man sat quietly in the chair across from her. Felix introduced them, "This is my friend, Frederick Chopin. He's a pianist and plays ever so beautifully. He has come unexpectedly."

"Nice to meet you." Fanny forced herself to sound polite. Chopin sensed the tension, "Should I have come at a better time?"

"Nein," Felix assured, "this is my sister, Fanny, and her husband Wilhelm. Fanny plays wonderfully as well."

"I sure hope to hear you." Chopin was intrigued. Fanny nodded, finishing up her food. She then went to the piano in the other room to play her 'serious' music as Fredrick and Felix ate. Wilhelm sketched in his book.

After all the plates were finished, Felix cleaned up and everyone joined Fanny at the keys. She played with all her heart and it impressed Frederick to the full. When she finished, she turned to Chopin, "Now you must play. I am eager to hear you."

Chopin traded spots with her and pressed some keys. He then began a waltz in shyness. Felix noticed he was quite nervous as Fanny watched. She nodded some but didn't show enthusiasm.

414

As the hour drew near, Fanny and Wilhelm got ready to leave. Frederick stayed at the piano, playing soft tunes as Felix escorted them to the door. Felix assured Fanny in a whisper, "Chopin does play very well, he's shy, I assure. I know you are unamused."

"I'll take your word. Anyways, Adieu my hamlet." She waved and exited with Wilhelm.

As soon as they left, Chopin dashed into some grandiose etudes. His playing had suddenly become lively. Felix watched in awe. He wished Frederick would have had the courage earlier. Many locals knocked at the door upon hearing piano as they knew Chopin to be in the city. Felix let some Leipzigers in but didn't let his house get too crowded.

After Chopin calmed down, he told Felix, "I am able to stay a day if that's alright. Tomorrow I must leave though."

"Ja, do stay. I could listen to your playing any time."

"Have you anything new?" Chopin asked, scooting over on the piano bench. Felix sat and played some lines of his St. Paul oratorio in progress, singing as well. It was soon to be finished. Chopin smiled whilst listening. In turn, Frederick showed Felix a new concerto, which sounded divine.

Felix was more especially enthralled at a notturno. He watched and listened closely. After Chopin played it, Felix recited a considerable amount by ear as he wanted to play it for his younger brother Paul when he saw him again.

The fun continued that day as the postman brought a carefully wrapped package for Felix. Chopin was curious as Felix unwrapped a large stack of thirty two great folios bound in thick green leather. On the back with gold letters in nice English fashion were the titles of Handel's music.

Inside upon opening it had the following words, 'To Director F. M. B., from the committee of the Cologne Music Festival, 1835.' These pieces were to be prepared for the Cologne music festival. There was much to be discovered with the volumes as other publications weren't as complete.

The rest of the day, Chopin and Felix looked through the folios, playing the music. Chopin sight read sections of an oratorio while Felix sang to get a sense of it. He had a sufficient choral voice. By evening they supped on sausage and vegetables.

The next morning Chopin packed to make his leave. He assured Felix, "I promise to return next winter. I am so happy to have such a friend as you."

"I promise to have a new symphony by then and to have it performed in honor of your coming back." Felix smiled. Chopin jumped a bit in flatter then grabbed his luggage, making his leave.

After Chopin's going, Felix was by no means alone. Ignaz arrived in Leipzig a day later to meet his mother who was traveling from Prague. Felix feverishly wrote, begging him to visit. Ignaz settled at a nearby hotel then accepted the invitation to Felix's abide.

When Ignaz walked in, Felix found him all the same as usual, only slightly older. It was most likely the effect of fatherhood which matured any man. Ignaz always thought Felix to be growing.

Straight away Ignaz went to the piano to look through Felix's second book of 'Lieder ohne Worte' that he had recently completed. They were delightful and charming masterpieces. After sharing music, Ignaz asked Felix, "Would you want to accompany me tomorrow to meet my maminka? She is bringing homemade cake, it is divine."

"I'd love to but I start my duties at the Gewandhaus. I'm already receiving commissions of concerts to prepare.

Yet, this weekend I've been invited to be introduced to a young pianist that would like a concerto performed. It is a young girl by the name of Clara Wieck. Her Vater wants me to hear her. Would you like to join?"

"I'd love to. I could bring the spare slices of cake from my maminka."

"Excellent!" Felix chimed.

~~~

Felix awoke early the next day to prepare for his first day at the Gewandhaus. He wore an outfit of refinement and professionalism. The thought of working with a new orchestra excited him but also made him nervous. It was questionable if it would fare better or worse than Düsseldorf.

When the carriage parked at the streetside of the place, Felix observed it from the outside. It was an old structure that appeared on the dull side. The building had obviously been transformed into a concert hall. He disembarked the carriage to observe it closer. The doorway contained a plaque of the orchestra's motto engraved in Latin: Res severa est verum gaudium. Felix nodded at it and continued in.

Standing in the lobby was Herr Schleinitz, a fellow director who helped hire him. He greeted Felix, "Welcome Herr Mendelssohn. I thought I'd show you around before meeting the musicians. They should come within the hour."

"Oh good." Felix turned about in the well maintained interior. It was a world of difference compared to the outer structure. Schleinitz led him to the auditorium in which caught Felix's interests. It was tall and elegant with chandeliers. The ceiling was adorned in decorative art. Felix asked Schleinitz, "How is it those chandeliers stay lit? I don't see any candles in them."

"We have gas lighting. Here I'll show you." Schleinitz went to a wall where a small knob stood. He gestured to Felix to turn it.

417

Felix did and the lights turned off in capital speed. He turned it again and everything came back on in the same fashion. He began turning it back and forth in confusion until Schleinitz grabbed his arm, "Ja, it is real. No candles."

"This is crazy!" Felix stared at the lights. Schleinitz turned Felix's attention by guiding him towards the stage at the head of the room. The seating in the hall was different as the benches didn't face the stage. There were two groups of chairs at each side of the auditorium, turned towards each other.

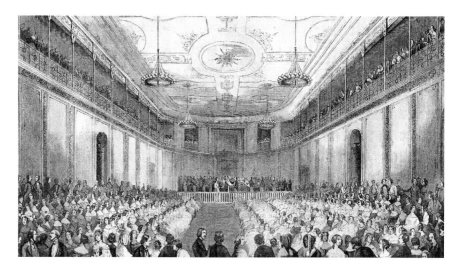

*(Inside the Gewandhaus)*

Schleinitz then explained, "There is to be a concert in only a day hence. You won't get to rehearse much with the orchestra beforehand; it was something they had been preparing with the previous director. Nothing should be too troublesome."

"As long as they've been practicing, it should be fine." Felix turned as some musicians entered. When the orchestra assembled they seemed quite pleased to have Felix at the conductor's desk. Yet the concertmaster's seat remained empty. Felix asked Schleinitz, "Who is Konzertmeister?"

"We don't have one at the moment. The old one moved away." Schleinitz explained. Felix nodded then spoke his thoughts, "I know a man for the job. I'll make arrangements later." He then turned to the scores on the music stand. One caught his eye so he announced, "Let us start with the Beethoven symphony."

As the musicians opened their music, Felix grabbed his English bâton to conduct. Straight away a violinist grumbled, "Oh, one of those conductors."

"What is wrong with a bâton?" Felix questioned. Schleinitz went to Felix, "I am sorry to inform but they've not had a director that used a bâton before. They aren't used to such."

"Well, I assure it is now a standard. It is not terribly modern. Spontini uses a large bâton and Weber used to roll up a piece of paper. I try to make it look refined." Felix raised his bâton, which had the thickness and style of a magician's wand.

When counting the musicians into their music, they obeyed accordingly. The splendid tone was like a breath of fresh air compared to the Düsseldorf orchestra. There were still things to be improved, but a course of six months would make this orchestra shine like no other. Felix felt happy at this new beginning. It would be regular official business.

That next evening Felix conducted the concert. It was a bit nerve racking as time only allowed for the one rehearsal. The concert hall, with the audience, had a profound silence when the music rested. The musicians played adagio in the most masterfully manner that even the most delicate notes could be heard. The allegro sections weren't as together, dragging as they were accustomed to slower tempos. Felix tended to use a faster speed. He liked to express his inner energy.

In 4/4 time they went capitally. The violins attacked with a degree of vehemence that startled Felix at times but delighted the public. A few other works weren't up to standard.

One rehearsal beforehand wasn't sufficient enough, but the Beethoven B flat Symphony went splendid. The Leipzigers clapped and shouted after each movement. Each person listened like popinjays as Zelter would have described it. After the concert the orchestra received many congratulations.

~~~~

## [2]

The weekend soon came after the initial first days at the Gewandhaus. The work had fared satisfying. Felix rejoined with Ignaz and together they headed to the Wiecks' household to meet Clara and her father.

Their home was settled in a well to do neighborhood. Herr Wieck made a decent living teaching piano as well as obtaining the income from Clara's concerts. Clara was in high regard as a young pianist. Felix had interest in meeting the girl, but the fact that her father encouraged her performing and publishing was so very different from his upbringing. It made him question Abraham's ideals.

When knocking at the door, there was the faint sound of a decent melody playing from a piano. Felix knocked again and they waited more. Ignaz held a wrapped package of the cake slices his mother baked.

A maid answered the knocks. She whispered as she let the two guests in, "Herr Wieck is teaching a student, he shall be with you shortly."

Ignaz and Felix sat on a decorative bench in the entryway. The piano in the other room continued softly, playing a sweet melody; rather good for a student. Felix shut his eyes, relaxing in the tones. Suddenly a loud voice barreled over the music, "Falsch!"

The piano's soft notes jumped to a jumbled chord as the player had been startled.

It caused both Felix and Ignaz to lift their heads towards the room. The stern voice exclaimed, "Measure fifteen is supposed to be softer! How many times do I have to tell you!?"

"Es tut mir leid!" A man's voice apologized hoarsely, "I fear my hand will never regain its strength."

"Keep working on stretching it. You need to gain flexibility. Here..."

"AUSCH!" The student's voice echoed through the house. Felix became curious about the commotion, so he headed towards the door. Ignaz stopped him, "I don't think we should go in yet."

"I want to see what's happening." Felix grabbed the doorknob. He creaked the door open to get a peek. Inside was a music room with a Klavier stationed in the middle. Standing at the side of the piano was a young girl, observing the scene. Felix assumed it to be Clara.

At the keys was a man, close to Felix's age. He had dark blond locks. Instead of playing, he clutched his hand as if it were in pain. Standing beside him, in a stance of frustration was a middle aged man. It was Clara's father, Freidrich Wieck. He calmed his voice and sighed to the man at the piano, "Robert, you may have to keep your concentration towards other things, such as your journalism and critiquing. I believe we are beating a dead horse in strengthening that hand."

[3]

"I don't understand why it's not healing enough." Robert stood in utter somberness. Clara went to him, "You still have skill and yield beautiful melodies. Bitte, take my word for it. Don't give up piano."

"I'll take your word." Robert smiled at the sixteen year old. She gazed back, blushing at the twenty-five year old, who was dashing in her eyes.

Friedrich crossed his arms, noticing such looks. He intervened by telling Robert, "I've got guests coming. Herr Mendelssohn is to be here."

"Really?" Robert brightened. Herr Wieck came towards the door. Right away he noticed Felix standing and snooping in. Friedrich felt some embarrassment in not noticing him before. He called Felix, "Come in."

Felix entered with Ignaz close behind. Herr Wieck gave an expression of surprise. Felix quickly explained, "I hope you don't mind that Mr. Moscheles decided to join me in coming."

"Oh not at all, it is all the better!" Herr Wieck exclaimed. Robert stood in complete awe at the sight of Ignaz. He could hardly speak when Moscheles asked his name. Robert finally formed his words, "Schumann. Robert Schumann. Mr. Moscheles, you must know, I attended a concert of yours and it is what helped sparked my love of music. Your compositions are superb."

"Thank you. I heard you playing well earlier."

"Danke." Robert felt flattered. Felix asked, "Do you compose? I think I have seen your name in regards to journal reviews."

"Ja, I compose when I can. I am very busy with the literature aspects of music such as reviews and essays. I had much intent to pursue piano, but I've been afflicted with a hand injury." Schumann sighed.

"You still play suitably from what I heard. I don't want to leave without hearing you again and some of your own works." Felix stated. Robert then questioned Felix, "Do you write? Literary speaking?"

"I write letters frequently and subtle things as so. I wouldn't keep a diary or anything of that sort if that's what you mean."

422

"I see." Schumann nodded. Ignaz set the wrapped slices of cake at a nearby table. Clara pranced towards him to get a slice. Ignaz unwrapped one, revealing a fine chocolate cake with a snowflake pattern in confectioners sugar on top. He let Clara take it, "My maminka from Prague made it. It's her famous recipe."

Clara tried a bite, "It's fantastic!" She then devoured the entire piece. Felix was distracted in talking with Robert so Ignaz handed him a piece. He ate subconsciously but paused his speech as he noticed how tasty it was. Turning to Ignaz he instructed, "Bitte, tell your Mutter this was the best cake I've ever had."

"I will." Ignaz felt proud that his mother was such a good baker. Herr Wieck then encouraged Clara, "Show Felix your concerto."

"Ja Vater." Clara obeyed, seating herself at the keys. Felix stood beside, leaning against the instrument to listen close. Friedrich grabbed the score and set it before Clara. Straight away she started playing. Felix pricked his ears at such impressive strides.

As the music went on, Herr Wieck went to Felix in a whisper, "I want you to host a concert at the Gewandhaus for her. She shall play as soloist. You conduct."

"I can work something out. This piece seems sufficient for the orchestra." Felix nodded. Herr Weick smiled. Ignaz listened but his attention veered between Clara and Robert. They seemed to meet in eye contact through most of the concerto. The deeper their glances, the deeper Clara drove emotion into the instrument. Yet her concentration was forced fully to her music for the last movement.

After the finish, Clara gracefully lifted her hands from the keys in all etiquette. Everyone clapped and Felix commended, "You are full of the utmost grace. That was beautiful."

"Danke," Clara bowed her head in a polite manner, "I'd like to play something else for you. Something I thoroughly enjoy." She went to the music shelf and pulled out a piano book. It was the first volume of Felix's 'Lieder ohne Worte'.

As soon as she started playing her favorite selections, Felix felt his ears in a soothed state. Clara played his work so fluidly. She enjoyed the composition immensely. When she was tired and in need of a break, she begged Schumann, "Robert, bitte, you play. Felix wants to hear you again. Be sure to play Felix's work, 'The Calm Sea and Prosperous Voyage', as your interpretation is ever so lovely."

Robert sat after she stood. He played as she wished and did so in capital fashion. His playing had a high level of capacity when he didn't push the limitations of his hands. The pieces of his own were worth taking note of. Yet after a few more pieces, his troubled hand got the best of him, ending his playing for the day.

Both Felix and Ignaz were impressed by Clara and Robert. Felix had much intent to become well acquainted with Herr Schumann and felt a strong will to help him in the prospects of composition.

Upon their leave, the weather had become fickle with rain. Felix thankfully had brought along a frock coat. Ignaz however only had a light coat. He didn't say anything and planned to get to his hotel in haste. Robert stopped him and confronted, "Mr. Moscheles, I have a cloak I can lend you. You shall not go out in the rain in improper attire."

"Thank you." Ignaz felt a slight embarrassment of the favor. Robert handed him a warm cloak. With that, Felix headed home and Ignaz, his hotel.

~~~~

The next week, Felix returned to normal duties at the concert hall. On Monday morning, Felix joined a discussion with Herr Schleinitz and another musician, Herr Hauser, on the subject of the coming concert season.

Many artist, new and old wanted their work performed. Herr Schleinitz and Hauser suggested artists left and right. Felix found a lot of new music colorless, but listened to his fellow directors' opinions.

"How about that second symphony by Ignacy Feliks Dobrzyński? He received second prize for that composition in Vienna." Schleinitz gave his idea. Felix nodded, "I'd be willing to conduct that. I must say, the young girl Clara Wieck has a new concerto. Her performing skills are superb. Mr. Moscheles is in the city as well."

"Those would make good concerts. Along with those, the orchestra could play various works of Beethoven as those always seem to go over well." Hauser suggested. The three then thought in silence, not having any other ideas. Hauser broke the thinking with a tease, "I did receive a letter from Kaulkbrenner. He'd love to have you conduct a concert for him."

"How about nein. I'm not conducting for a little fish patty." Felix retorted. Hauser corrected, "He's more like an indigestible sausage. I'd not let him play a note here."

Their conversation ended as the orchestra began gathering in the auditorium. Felix tended to his work when they were set to play. The instruments looked ravishing and healthy, producing a pleasing sound. These musicians took care of their instruments by putting them in their cases. Felix could tell a world of difference in sound compared to the Düsseldorf orchestra. Each musician was ready when counted in, making the day prosperous.

In the evening, everyone packed up to go home. Felix headed to the hotel in which Mr. Moscheles was staying. Each evening Felix joined him for tea and music. Ignaz already had a tray of fragrant jasmine brewing.

Felix sat in one of the two chairs angled towards each other beside the coffee table. He grabbed a tea cup to take in the soothing comfort of hot herbs.

"How was work?" Ignaz asked, pouring himself a cuppa.

"All is well. I spoke with Herr Schleinitz and Hauser on the subjects of concerts. They agree to host one for you and for Clara's concerto."

"Excellent. I'd like you to play at my concert. There is a piece for two pianos. I also may want your ever so popular 'Hebrides Overture' to creep in as well."

"That would be splendid." Felix agreed then set his cup down in all seriousness, "I do sense that after these concerts, we may depart for some time. You'll be off to London I imagine and I am going to pay a visit to Berlin."

"We shall make the most of the soon coming November with concerts together. I'm certain we won't be separated too long." Ignaz stood from his seat. Felix got up as well but apologized, "I do say I am sorry, but I can't stay for piano tonight. Early tomorrow my pupil, Bennett is coming to my home for instruction. He is composing well. I must retire for the night."

"That is good. Invite him to accompany you here sometime, I'd like to hear him." Ignaz encouraged. Felix smiled then bid farewell.

~~~~

It was the morning of early November, with the sky a cloudy grey, when the horses eagerly clopped towards the sight of civilization. My carriage arrived in Leipzig. I grasped the letter of introduction in my pocket to be sure it was safe. It contained the note of recommendation from Herr Mendelssohn. This is where I came to take my position as concertmaster of the Gewandhaus.

426

With my violin case beside me, I felt relief to be in my home country of Germany. My previous place of stay was Moscow, Russia, where I had many musical engagements. Yet, when I received notice from Felix of the open position in Leipzig, I felt a strong need to leave the cold country. The trip was excruciatingly long. I felt discouragement as the carriage pulled up a quiet street to park beside an old cloth hall.

(Watercolour of the Gewandhaus by Felix)

*(Ferdinand David)*

"Surely," I asked the coachman, "This is not really the concert hall?"

"It is the Gewand-haus." The coachman pressed the obvious. I gathered my things and stepped out, not wanting to argue. He was in a mood from long travel, yet as was I. My spirits lifted as I noticed a man walking up the street carrying a flute case. I went ahead and entered the front doors.

When I came to the lobby of the highly renovated interior, which gave me much surprise, a man greeted me, "Hallo, you must be the new Konzertmeister, are you not?"

"Ja," I handed my letter of introduction, "My name is Ferdinand, or Herr David. I've come upon the request of Herr Mendelssohn."

"I am Herr Hauser, now let me look at these papers quick..." Hauser skimmed them over, recognizing Felix's handwriting. After deeming the papers legit, Hauser encouraged, "Come, I shall show you around."

While exploring my new place of work, I felt a sense of much needed happiness. The other musicians were nice and greeted me with enthusiasm. They seemed ever so grateful to receive a concertmaster. Yet when everyone took their seats, there was something missing. Something quite important. I turned to Hauser, "Where is Felix?"

Hauser gave a sigh,"Sorry if he did not give word. He took a short leave of absence to visit his parents in Berlin. He should be back by next week. In the meantime, I believe you will be making sure things are well around here. Your real duties will be determined when Felix returns. I imagine you have much experience so I'll leave you to it."

"Alright." I gave way to slight confusion as Hauser ventured off. I stood at the music desk with my violin case at hand. The musicians of the orchestra stared at me, waiting for my instruction. This wasn't what I had expected on the first coming.

With forced confidence, I unpacked my violin and tuned it. I then flipped through the first score I saw at the conducting desk and instructed everyone to begin with said piece. In thankfulness everyone cooperated even though they hardly knew me.

~~~~

In the warm, homely estate on Leipziger Straße no. 3 in Berlin, Felix felt much comfort being with his family. He sat on the sofa in the parlor, sipping tea near the fireplace. Lea sat at a drawing table, silently working at her knitting. Fanny's child, Sebastian and Rebecka's child, Walter, were on the floor nearby, playing with toys. Felix looked towards Abraham, who was sitting in his usual chair close to the fire, reading a book. It was a most calming hour.

The children bantered a bit over their toys. Sebastian took a wooden horse from Walter, "I want that." In turn, little Walter cried. Felix set his teacup down and went to the children. He informed Sebastian, "Your cousin had that first, now give it back to him. Share."

Sebastian listened to his uncle but in hesitation. There were other wooden animals to play with, so Felix spent time with his nephews, joining in their little game, using imagination. Lea couldn't help but smile at the sight of the three. Felix got into it quite intently. Abraham rolled his eyes, but the children loved it. Fanny then walked into the room, "Bruder? Playing with children's toys?" She teased. Sebastian and Walter giggled. Felix stood up, "Just keeping my nephews in good company."

"I'm kidding, that looked quite adorable. You'd be an excellent Vater," Fanny hinted.

"If only he'd find a wife, all would be well." Abraham commented, not veering his eyes from reading. Felix shrugged and the room went in silence. Abraham suddenly felt a strain in his eyes. He set his book aside thinking he had read too long. Lea asked as he rubbed his head, "Are you alright honey?"

"I'm fine, only a headache." He stated, closing his eyes for a bit. Lea continued tending to her yarn. Her senses for the health of her husband were in worry. Felix meanwhile headed out of the parlor towards the stairs to his room. When taking the first step, a ring at the door turned him around.

The servant went to answer, but Felix had a strange inclination to get it. He raced ahead of the servant. When opening the door, he expressed excitement, "Ignaz!" Felix threw his hands in the air, "You must have followed me home!"

"I was passing through before returning to London. It was on the way and figured you'd be obliged to let me take a rest here. Plus my passport is on hold so I can't do much right now." Ignaz explained. Felix smiled, "Oh bitte, do come in. You may take my room, I do not mind at all."

"Thank you." Ignaz entered. Felix helped him carry his luggage. When passing by the parlor, Felix mentioned to his parents, "Ignaz is staying here a while. His passport is on hold. Do not fret, I've offered my room."

"Okay sweetie." Lea called back.

"Be sure it's clean!" Abraham stated in the midst of his nap. Felix turned to Ignaz, "Don't worry, my room is spotless."

"I have no worry knowing you. Always organized in housekeeping." He followed Felix up the stairs.

When entering, Felix straight away picked up a few manuscripts laying here and there. He assured, concerning the bed, "The servants put out clean bedding today so all is well. I shall sleep in the room upstairs. My sister's old rooms are taken up by my nephews as they like to stay often."

After Ignaz settled and Felix took what he needed to stay upstairs, they went to the music room. Fanny joined, standing by the instrument as Felix and Ignaz played. They improvised and dueted on the works of Bach. In between pieces Fanny asked Ignaz, "How long are you staying?"

"I plan to be here until tomorrow unless the police don't get my passport by then."

"I hoped you'd stay until Sunday. You would have been pleasing to hear at the next salon." Fanny gave a breath of disappointment. Felix teased, "Let us hope the police take their time."

"Charlotte might be a bit upset if I'm gone any longer. I miss my children." Ignaz sighed thinking about his lovely family. Fanny looked to Felix, "As for you, you shall play next Sunday. I'd like to hear your final decision of the Italian symphony at the keys. I liked the original interpretations you sent me."

"Let me get the score. It should still be with the other scores I gathered upon returning from London with Vater a little over yesteryear ago." Felix rushed from the piano and up the stairs. In his room he searched every cabinet and shelf as the music wasn't where he thought it to be. It became quite distressing to have an entire symphony lost.

When returning to the music room with no score, Fanny raised a thick eyebrow. Felix confessed in frustration, "I can't find it."

"I hope you remember what you wrote," Fanny scorned,"I was looking ever so forward to hearing it."

"I don't know where it could have gone." Felix sat at the piano bench with Ignaz. As the tension between brother and sister were sensed, Ignaz assured Felix, "If you can't find it, I can obtain copies from the musicians that premiered it in London."

"Danke…" Felix felt a pang of guilt, hoping not to put Ignaz through such trouble. To cheer up, he continued at the keys with a Bach fugue.

~~~

There was no sign of a passport the following day. When the postman came with no such papers, Ignaz ran his fingers through his hair, "Oh dear, Charlotte will be upset! My Emily will not forgive a longer absence." He paced about the main hall. Felix assured Ignaz, "Do not worry, I shall write to Charlotte to calm your woes. I am positive she will understand."

"Thank you. You are a true friend. A letter from myself most likely would sound like an excuse." Ignaz felt relief. Felix went off to the writing desk. He grabbed a leaf of paper to pen a convincing letter:

*Dear Charlotte*

Before finishing the address, Lea entered the room in a state of worry. Felix turned to her while dipping the pen in ink, "Is something the matter?"

"I am worried about your Vater. He decided to stay in bed this morning as his eyes are still a bother. He seems so out of sorts, should we call for a doctor?"

"I say if he is still unwell tomorrow call for one. It could be a bad headache as he sometimes gets." Felix advised. Lea suggested, "I shall be sure to make him herbal tea. Hopefully that will help."

"Be sure there is some calming chamomile in it." Felix continued penning the letter to Charlotte. Lea left to fetch the tea. Felix felt a sense of uneasiness. It was nothing like Abraham to sleep in, even in an ill state.

After folding the letter with care, Felix handed it to the servant to send. He then headed to the music room as the sound of the piano echoed. Ignaz was in his own world, pouring his worries into the keys. Felix stood quietly behind him. It was rare to see Mr. Moscheles with such emotion in his lonesome.

Abraham unexpectedly came into the room and sat in a chair by the door. He seemed to be feeling his way about as his sight beseeched him. Felix looked at his father closely. He had the look of a tired man, listening to the music whilst staring at nothingness.

~~~

With another day passing, Ignaz was still stuck in Berlin. He was determined to stop worrying so much and savor the company at the Mendelssohn home. Felix took enjoyment in his extended stay as every moment with Ignaz was one to be remembered.

On that day, a doctor rang the bell. Lea had sent for one as Abraham's eyes had not improved. He remained in bed all morning and afternoon. Felix kept close to his parent's room where the doctor tended to his father. Lea was beside Abraham, listening closely to what the doctor had to say.

Felix didn't want to overcrowd the room, so he eavesdropped as the doctor explained, "He has developed a partial blindness. Most likely it correlates to the horrid headaches. It is unclear if this is a temporary ailment. The fast development of it is quite strange. All in all, it could be a terrible migraine."

"Have you any treatments?" Lea asked as they exited the room. The doctor stated, "If he is still having trouble in a few days time, I can try to get a medicine together."

He then turned to Felix, "The best medicine right now is to please his ears with music. I know you will be quite good at that." He patted Felix on the shoulder.

After the doctor made his leave, Felix joined Ignaz once again in the music room. They kept the music soft and soothing as to not agitate Abraham. To their surprise, Abraham willed himself from his rest, to the music room. He took the utmost pleasure in hearing the two maestros.

~~~~

The next morning, the 18th of November, Ignaz stood in the main hall with his bags to leave. He had received his passport in the early hours. Felix told him, "Since this is to be a long parting, I very much promise to come to London again. My Vater would be willing to come along I'm sure."

"You are welcome to stay at Chester Place any day. Many thanks for letting me take your room in unexpected extendedness. I wish your family well." Ignaz picked up his bags and left to the carriage in haste. Felix returned back to the parlor where to his relief found Abraham reading. His sight still seemed a bother but he seemed in much calmness reading the last chapter of the book to finish it.

~~~~

Back in Leipzig at the Gewandhaus, things were in a turmoil as I continued organizing the orchestra in rehearsals. There were concerts to come, in which I had not known I'd be preparing. Felix's leave became quite longer than Hauser had mentioned.

Herr Schleinitz helped much as I worked in getting various symphonies and overtures prepared. There were notes of suggestions in the scores left by Felix. It helped, but certain things needed to be explained by Felix himself.

My honest wish was to play my violin and perform my intended duties. As concertmaster, it was common to conduct a few things, but not everything.

434

To my thanks, Schleinitz took to the music desk in rehearsals at times to let me play amongst the first violins so the other musicians could get used to my personal gestures.

A few more days bundled into another week of Felix's absence. Herr Schleinitz and Hauser were in a critical conversation concerning Herr Mendelssohn. I happened to walk in on it. Schleinitz assured Hauser, "Felix is a trustworthy man. There is obviously something going on. He wouldn't just abandon his position."

"It's been over an extra week with no word. True he has much vacation time, but without a word? I take that as carelessness. I say if one more week goes by, say bye to Felix as director." Hauser went away with a huff. Schleinitz fell into a fit of worry. He didn't want Felix to be fired from the job that suited him so well. I noticed that Schleinitz cared much about Felix so I tried to convince, "I am sure Felix will explain everything in the coming days. He is trustworthy; he will send a word."

Schleinitz nodded, but my words didn't soothe his worry. He in utter desperation questioned, "Where on earth is the man?"

~~~

[4]

As the simple casket lowered into the grounds of the Berlin cemetery, the scene brought a surreal sense. Lea and her children watched in silence.

Felix's mind was anything but silent. He didn't know whether he'd fall faint or vomit. His conscience kept him upright and his stomach settled by instructing: *Keep composure. Be a man. Take it. You must decide how to get on. Please your Vater.*

After the grave was covered, everything was said and done. Felix knew his old life had been severed. A new one was to begin. The carriage ride home gave way to his mind questioning the day. He became unsure what was real.

Upon arriving home, Felix felt a sureness that his father would be home to greet him or sitting in the parlor, book at hand. Yet upon entering the hollow estate, there was a cold reality. No Abraham greeted him in the main hall. When checking the parlor, his father was not reading his book there.

Fanny knew Felix to be in an utter state of realization. She stopped him in the corridor as he continued checking the house, "There's no point in trying to convince the day didn't happen."

Without any words, he fell in a hug and weeped into her shoulder. The fact of the matter hit him. He clung to Fanny tightly, ever so grateful to have his elder sister. She always watched over him, musically and mentally. He didn't know what he'd do without her.

~~~~

Three weeks later Felix's anguish really began to show. Like moving into a new house, life felt as if it had been there all along, until the obvious reminders were noticed.

As Felix played piano in the music room, the melodies were especially pretty and gentle. Yet it didn't feel the same as he was alone. His mother spent her time in the bedroom upstairs to mourn. Paul tended to business at the bank as Joseph needed all the help he could get.

436

He also worked to take charge of the estate. Fanny and Rebecka were in their own homes, living their own lives.

There was a loss of comfort knowing that Abraham wasn't in the parlor, enjoying the music or his book. The melodies seemed to be hanging in the air, no where to find enjoyment, except to calm Felix's sadness. He recollected the past few day's events:

Abraham had died on the 19th of November, in the morning half past 10. It happened so suddenly and in unexpectedness, but the manner was in his father's wishes if it ever came to be. His brother Joseph came as soon as hearing the news. He informed Felix and his siblings that their grandfather had died in the same manner and aged 59. The physicians could not name his malady.

After the fact, Felix still felt a determination to please his father. He wanted to be sure in the near future he was settled in a happy home and finished with the St. Paul oratorio that Abraham had wished to hear.

In the days to come, Lea took much comfort in her children and grandchildren. Felix stayed in Berlin for his mother. Yet, at the same time, the house was a torture of reminders. Each night, Felix retired to his bed only to stir awake at each hour, thinking he could not survive his loss. He cried as his chest physically ached with each heartbeat, but forced any whimper to be silent as to not disturb Lea or Paul.

Fanny visited the main house often for her mother, but mostly to comfort Felix. She knew he had clung to their father in recent years after much quarreling before. It would be one of the hardest realities for him to face.

At the writing desk in the music room, she found her brother sulking with his head resting on the desk. His oratorio manuscript underneath him, becoming soaked in tears.

"Felix?" Fanny tapped his shoulder. He sat up and stretched then looked at his sister. He wiped his eyes, dewed in liquid sadness. The sight of Fanny made him feel better. She pulled up a chair, "Working on the oratorio?"

"Trying to. I want it finished for the next Düsseldorf festival. What have you got?" Felix noticed in her hands she held music of her own.

"I finished a few songs. Wilhelm loved them and drew sketches to add ornament to them." Fanny handed him the music. Felix smiled at the pretty writing of Fanny and the intricate drawings penned by Wilhelm.

"They are lovely." Felix handed back the manuscripts. Fanny smiled, "Wilhelm is very encouraging. He would like his art sent to the print shop. It would make the music more appealing."

"You mean publish your music?" Felix knew where the conversation was headed. He set his pen down, crossing his arms. Fanny showed a glance of horror as Felix's demeanor had the resemblance of Abraham. She uncrossed his arms by holding his hands, "Felix, I know you disagree, but Wilhelm supports my idea. For now, I have a few other pieces I can publish under your name. At least grant me that."

"Alright..." Felix sighed, "Give them to me and I'll take them myself."

"Danke, my Bruder. In the future though, I shall find my way in publishing. Vater is not-"

"Don't you dare speak of Vater right now!" Felix blurted at Fanny. His tears reformed in his eyes. Fanny hugged him, "I am sorry. I shall not go further on this subject."

# Chapter XIX: Fallen

Mendelssohn, Paulus Overture [1]
Mendelssohn, On Wings of Song, orchestra arrangement [2]
Liszt, Lebestraum no. 3 [3]

## [1]

The new year of 1836 arrived and it was another day at the Gewandhaus. I did my best to keep rehearsals and concerts organized. Felix had not returned after two months of absence, but he sent a letter explaining everything about his father.

As I stood off to the side, listening to the orchestra to get an overview of progress, Herr Schleinitz raced to me with news, "Herr Mendelssohn is back! A carriage arrived less than an hour ago!"

"Wonderbar!" I made my exclamation as someone entered the auditorium. They looked tired and somber, taking slow flowing steps towards the stage. It was Felix. He brightened up upon noticing me, "Ferdinand," he quietly rushed to me so as to not disturb the orchestra. He grabbed a folio and handed it to me. I opened it to find a finished oratorio.

"Copies need to be made then it shall be ready to rehearse. It's the St. Paul oratorio." He explained. I nodded, "I can definitely help with the copies."

"Danke so much for filling in for me, I'm sorry I was gone in such an absence." His eyes showed slight tears. I assured, "You have nothing to be sorry about. My grievances to you."

Felix nodded then continued to the orchestra to tend to them. I grabbed my violin, finally able start my true position as concertmaster. The concert being prepared included the works of Mozart, Handel and Beethoven. Felix was particularly intrigued by the coronation anthem of Handel.

For Mozart's concerto in D minor, he sat at the keys as I conducted. It was my position to conduct the concertos.

With each week closer to the next concert, Felix had a determination to put all energy into his work. His oratorio had been copied and rehearsed, turning it into a grand piece of sound. The musicians were pleased with it. Since I took part in copying it, I admitted to Felix, "I noticed you took quite a bit of inspiration from Bach's music."

"You could tell?" Felix blushed some. I rolled my eyes in a tease, "You are obsessed."

In the evenings after work, Felix invited me to his apartment to practice some sonatas. We frequently played through Beethoven's Kreutzer Sonata as he adored the way I interpreted it. Sometimes his pupil Mr. Bennett joined at the keys as Felix took up the viola for various chamber works. The time spent entrusted a well rounded friendship.

~~~~

With the next public concert, the house was full and the music filled the auditorium to satisfactory. The crowd took full enjoyment in hearing music of old. At the last piece, the Mozart concerto, Felix sounded his best. In surprise, he played the cadenza in the first movement differently than in rehearsals. The rendition was the most divine. After the frivolous performance, he lifted his hands from the keys with spirit.

Afterwards, Felix roamed the halls backstage to cool down. Everyone else packed up to leave. One of the second violinists, an old fellow, went to Felix. His aged face brightened, "Felix, I have to congratulate you on that suburb cadenza in that first movement."

"Dankeschön." Felix chimed.

"Years ago I myself heard Mozart play that work in this very hall. Since then I have not heard any other play the cadenza as good, that is, until today." He smiled. Felix felt a wave of awe knowing the man had heard Mozart himself.

~~~~

In February of 1836, Felix turned seven and twenty. He had much happiness in Leipzig and never wanted to forgo his work there. Yet to much dismay, the committee of the Düsseldorf Festival sent a request that he conduct his new oratorio.

When reading the request, Felix felt torn. He thought Düsseldorf was behind him, but the directors, particularly Herr Immermann, reminded that he promised to conduct every now and again. Within the month, he set out from Leipzig on another leave of absence. He planned to not be gone too terribly long or sidetracked. Yet, it did not fathom in his mind that his heart had a mind of its own.

~~~~

"But who is to direct the choir there!?" Schadow exclaimed loudly at Felix. A note was in his hand. Felix assured him, "I am sure Herr Schelble will find someone, he has plenty of other options."

"But he asked for you because he trusts you. I strongly disapprove of the decline." Schadow scolded. Felix gave a sigh. Herr Schelble, a friend, was the director of the St. Cecilia choir in Frankfort on the Main. He sent a letter requesting Felix to fill in for him as he was struck with illness. Felix didn't want to as he wanted to get back to Leipzig.

The Düsseldorf festival was hosted the evening prior and he conducted his oratorio with tremendous success. His luggage was packed to make his leave, but this note hindered his route, "I can't be absent from Leipzig anymore, I have duties there." Felix grabbed his two bags and hatbox. Schadow asked in desperation, "Who is filling in for you right now?"

"The Konzertmeister, Ferdinand David."

"See, you have someone there fulfilling duties. I shall inform him of the situation. There is no director in Frankfort so you are going as I shall ensure it. Schelble is letting you stay at his large home. His maid and mother-in-law are there. Schelble and his wife are visiting their property in Swabia upon his doctor's request. Your friend Herr Hiller is here so I will send him with you to help...and to ensure that you go." Schadow stated. Felix gave a huff as he was given no choice.

~~~~

When the carriage arrived at Frankfort on the Main, Felix gave an unhappy sigh while staring out the coach's window. Hiller, who was sitting next to him assured, "Don't worry, this engagement will be good. This happens to be my home city. My Mutter still lives here. Besides, look at the large house of Schelble." He pointed to a mansion-like house coming into view.

A maid exited the house when the carriage pulled up. She greeted Felix with utmost enthusiasm, "It is so kind of you to come. A good room is prepared. Herr Schelble thanks you ever so."

Felix nodded and unloaded his luggage. Hiller stayed in the coach as he planned to stay with his mother. He told Felix, "I shall find you later this week with my Mutter. I want you to meet her."

"Alright." Felix waved as the carriage moved on. The maid then let him inside and showed him down a corridor of rooms. Each one had its own charm with fresh linen on the beds and fine decor. The maid told him, "You may choose any room you wish."

Felix noticed a room with a window facing the Main, giving a splendid view of boats and ships. Once unpacked and settled, he felt happier. The reception at the home was kind and they had an excellent piano.

Schelble's mother-in-law had taken charge of the home for the time being. She was a kind woman.

Felix became acquainted with the St. Cecilia choir the next day to start his duties. Each member of the chorus deemed to have good morale so Felix got along fine. The work would be well and manageable. He became thankful for the fill in as he realized it made his days calm and restful with plenty of music.

In the week, Hiller and his mother rang the bell to Schelble's home. The maid let them enter. Madame Hiller had much anticipation in meeting Felix as her son described him. She had a pan of homemade pound cake. The maid informed, "Felix is in the living room taking a nap."

"That's alright," Herr Hiller assured, "I know he won't mind being woken, he naps much." They entered the living room to find Felix on the sofa in a deep snooze. Hiller tapped him awake, "Felix, my Mutter is here."

"Oh!" Felix shook away his tiredness. He looked at the motherly aged woman who had a warm smile and bright eyes of amber. Her hair was a rich brown, similar to Hiller's. She dressed in modesty. Felix addressed her, "Pleased to meet you Madame."

"It's a pleasure. My son told me so much of you. I brought pound cake if we have tea." She set the pan at the coffee table. The maid headed to the kitchen, hearing Madame Hiller's comment.

Felix sat up from laying down to have a proper posture in front of the guests. Hiller and his mother took the chairs on the other side of the coffee table. As they spoke, Madame Hiller's attention veered mostly to Felix. She had become fascinated by him. Hiller noticed his mother asking Felix an awful lot of questions, "So you obviously enjoy a hearty meal by the foods you say are your favorites. Will you like the pound cake I made? There is butter I brought along."

"I'm no fan of butter, but I'll definitely eat cake." Felix chimed as the maid set down a tray of tea. Madame Hiller then assured as she unwrapped the cake, "I shall in future invite you over to dinner. I'll be sure lamb is roasted or fine pasta cooked."

With tea, pound cake and more talk, Madame Hiller absorbed as much information Felix had to give of his interests. A plan was forming in her mind. She didn't dare give a hint as to what she was up to. Herr Hiller knew his mother and could read her better than most. She was up to something.

After the teapot emptied and the cake ate up, Madame Hiller suggested, "I'm inclined to go for a walk with the both of you. We need some fresh air."

"Sure!" Both Felix and Hiller chimed at the same time. Everyone stood to grab their coats and cloaks. When exiting the main doors, Felix and Hiller were surprised to see a beautiful little carriage standing in the drive with a dolled up horse in flowers. Madame Hiller hopped in, "I secretly got a carriage for us instead. We can ride in style around the country."

"Nice." Felix stepped in along with Hiller. The three of them plus the coachman took an excursion through the countryside. Fine summer air filled their noses. The warmth of the sun forced them to set their coats aside. As they rode along, a quaint cottage came into view.

"That cottage looks quite beautiful." Felix stated. Madame Hiller explained, "That's where Madame Jeanrenaud is residing with her children. It is the house of her parents. She is a widow of a French clergyman, August Jeanrenaud who had been stationed in a church here in Frankfort. He died years ago in the prime of his life. Madame Jeanrenaud is now forty years young, healthy and radiant. Her children are in their late adolescence."

"That's quite a sad loss for them." Felix gazed at the home, feeling the hurt from his own loss. Madame Hiller suggested, "Later I can introduce you to them. They are a sweet family. You must meet them at least once."

"I'd be glad to." Felix kept his eyes at the cottage, admiring the beautiful flower garden and decorative ivy. Madame Hiller gave a spirited smile. The carriage continued on along the path lined with trees. The horse pulling seemed to be in a stubborn mood, halting without reason. It agitated the coachman. He lashed at the horse with a whip, "Go on you stupid animal!"

The horse bellowed and reared, shaking the carriage. Felix felt a sudden wave of nervousness and got out of the carriage. He felt bad for the horse and yelled at the coachman, "The horse is not a bother! Don't be agitating it or it will cause an accident!"

The horse continued being unsteady. Hiller and his mother got out as well. The coachman told them, "Get back in, it is fine."

"Nein. We are walking." Felix stormed off. Herr Hiller and Madame Hiller followed behind. They were close to town so it wasn't a taxing stroll. Felix's mood became irritable but Madame Hiller calmed him down, "Let us get back and have dinner together at my home. There is a piano."

"Alright." Felix took a deep breath from his frustration. The rest of the way to town was cheerful as they got their exercise. After passing through some streets, they came to a decent home on a corner. It was the Hillers' home.

Herr Hiller showed Felix around as Madame Hiller helped the maid in preparing dinner. It was a toasty home, conveying a comforting essence. The parlor contained the piano. Past that, was Hiller's room. He showed it to Felix as it was a nice place. It looked like a miniature home of its own with a nice leather sofa and coffee table next to the fireplace.

By dinner time, the table was set with a meal of wine, fish and cheese. When sitting down, Madame Hiller told Felix, "You said you like wine and cheese, so I decided to include such in dinner."

"Danke."

"In turn you must play piano."

"Of course." Felix gulped a fair amount of wine being sure to pair cheese with it. The fish had good flavor with various spices. In discussion, Felix laughed over the occurrence with the coachman, forgetting that he had been so irritable in the day.

After dinner, they took their wine to the parlor and Felix went to the keys. He played many soothing adagios from concertos. As he added his own touch to each piece, Madame Hiller whispered to her son, "He is a wonderful man, that Felix."

After a few more calm pieces, he went into some Bach inventions for something different. Yet the delight in those rendered Felix to become hot with excitement. Bach's music, plus wine, built up much energy in him. Herr Hiller stood and went to his friend who seemed about ready to jump from the piano bench and run around.

"Felix, I think you need to cool down, go sit on the sofa in my room." Hiller pulled him away from the piano. Felix jumped up and pranced to Hiller's room, flopping onto the leather couch. It cooled his inner energy. He fell asleep as the nearby fireplace crackled soothingly. Hiller of course let him spend the night.

~~~~

The next week, Felix continued his routine with the Frankfort choir. A majority of rehearsals were used to prepare music for the church as that was a standard engagement of the chorus. Felix of course had them practice cantatas and oratorios of Bach as well as his own music.

446

During a run through Felix's oratorio, he sat in a pew to hear how the music echoed in the decently large church. He wanted to be sure the sound bouncing off the walls didn't get too entangled. As he sat, enjoying the echo giving the right effect, someone unexpected sat beside him. It was Julius Reitz. They didn't greet as they both had their attention to the choir.

When the work finished, Felix stood and called to the singers, "Excellent work, be sure to sing the pianissimo softer, it was a bit overbearing, otherwise rehearsal is done for today." Felix then turned to Julius, "What is bringing you to Frankfort?"

"I needed a break from the Düsseldorf choir and decided to see how your project was faring. I see you are well."

"Ja, I'd say this engagement is better than I thought. I still hope to return to Leipzig soon."

"Schadow received a letter from Schelble and told me to inform you of it. He could be out for the winter as his doctor suggested he go to Hüfingen for fresh air. You may not have to be here that long but until we find someone to fill in long term…" Julius indicated that Felix would be stuck in Frankfort for a while. Felix didn't want to think about it and changed the subject, "Herr Hiller is here, we should visit him."

"How nice, I'd like to visit him." Julius joined Felix out of the church to Hiller's home. Upon knocking at his door, Hiller answered and looked in the utmost excitement. Without addressing Julius in welcome, he informed, "Rossini is here!"

"Rossini?" Julius questioned.

"*The* Rossini?" Felix echoed. Hiller nodded, his face blushing red. He gestured them to come in, but Julius sighed, "I don't feel proper in meeting the man." He turned back. Hiller gasped at Julius, "Ahhhhh! How can you decline!?"

Julius was already many paces down the street. Felix assured, "I'll come in. This is something I can't pass by."

Hiller guided him in and there he was, sitting in the main room. The composer Rossini, enjoying coffee. The aged man looked up as Hiller brought his friend, "Why hello there. You must be a close acquaintance of Herr Hiller."

"Ja." Felix could hardly believe he was talking to Rossini. Hiller further explained, "This is Herr Felix Mendelssohn, a well off composer in every aspect...except opera, if I dare say." Hiller teased. Felix didn't mind the comment as it was in part truth. Rossini on the other hand was a highly regarded composer of opera.

"I've heard your name, I know you are quite good," Rossini then gave a witty remark, "I'm sorry but I never learned your first name before. Felix...sounds like something I'd name a feline."

Hiller burst into laughter. Felix chuckled not letting the comment hurt him. Rossini continued with witty speech, keeping them both laughing. He then commented on a more serious note,"This country, Germany, is quite different in music and culture. Bach is quite a different way of music, but it's fascinating to learn new things. Of course I'm Italian by heart in music, but I am fine anywhere as long as I get the list of wines at the hotels."

"What of Beethoven? Have you an opinion?" Felix questioned. Rossini nodded, "He had excellent works. I think at times my operas distracted audiences from him."

Hiller then spoke up, "In my days as a pupil of Hummel, he took me to visit Beethoven. He was at his deathbed, which I shan't forget. I have the lock of hair Hummel took." Hiller went to a desk and grabbed a locket. He handed it to Rossini, explaining, "Hummel gave me the locket as a parting gift."

"Quite a bit of history with that." Rossini handed back the locket, "Fascinating. Now Felix, I am interested in hearing you play piano. Please, indulge me in some fine music."

Felix sat at the keys and played a caprice. He felt confident, but it faded as he thought he heard Rossini muttering, giving unflattering comments. The whispers of the old man crept in his mind, making him believe Rossini did not care for the music.

~~~~

The next day Felix and Hiller went to the baths on the main for a swim. Felix practiced a back stroke against the current. Hiller dived about, scavenging the riverbed. Felix paused his exercise and told Hiller as he came to the surface of the water, "If your Rossini goes on muttering such things as he did yesterday, I won't play him anything more."

"What did he mutter? I did not hear anything." Hiller was confused.

"But I did, when I was playing my F sharp minor Caprice, he muttered between his teeth 'Ca sent la Sonate de Scarlatti."

"Well, that's nothing so very dreadful"

"Ah—Ba!" Felix continued on swimming. Hiller shrugged, more interested in a coin he found from diving. He had to be careful as some glass bottles had been thrown in the main. The two soon left the river to head back to Hiller's home.

Rossini stayed in Frankfort a few days more to learn more about Ferdinand Hiller as that was his main reason for coming. Felix joined them after choir rehearsals and still played music for Rossini as the man sincerely wished it. Felix still felt he didn't altogether like his music.

After Rossini made his leave of Frankfort, Madame Hiller invited Felix to accompany her to meet the Jeanrenaurd family. She had been invited to tea so thought it the perfect way to introduce Felix. Felix had much excitement in seeing the pretty cottage again. Herr Hiller had other engagements, so it was only Madame Hiller and Felix in the chaise to the home.

When arriving, they entered the front door into a large open room where a fine wood staircase was contained. The cottage had two stories and appeared just as dazzling on the inside as it did outside. A woman walked in from another room. She had dark curled hair and wore a dark maroon dress. It was not black as her husband had died seventeen years ago, but still dark to show she was still a mourning window. This was Madame Elizabeth Jeanrenaud.

"Greetings." The widow's French tone was bubbly and her face bright contrary to her attire. Madame Hiller and Felix gave nods in response. As soon as Elizabeth laid eyes on Felix, she felt a sense of pure happiness. She fell into a gaze. Madame Hiller's smile gave a hint to Felix as to why she brought him here.

Elizabeth induced conversation, speaking with good German, "My dear one, I have been told much about you. Music is a favorite subject of mine. I especially love the organ works of Bach."

"They are quite good." Felix smiled as she had much charm. She then mentioned, "You must meet my children."

"Of course." Felix followed her to a sitting room. There sat three young adult children. Two girls and one boy.

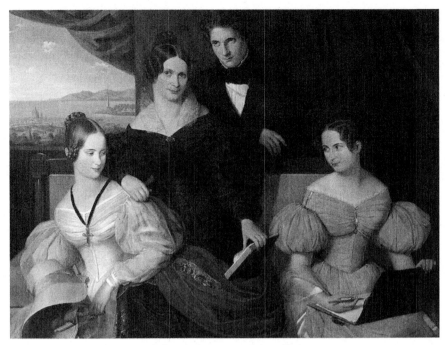

*(The Jeanrenaud Family)*

One of the girls was busy, braiding her hair. The boy was at the writing desk, penning a letter. Elizabeth gave their names, but Felix only caught one of them. The other girl sitting in her lonesome, working at cross-stitch.

## [2]

Felix heard the harps of love strumming when he gazed at the sight before him. Her shining dark copper hair was rich, her blue eyes shone like the morning dew, her face was the most beautiful thing he had ever settled his eyes upon. Her vibrant name echoed in his mind. Cécile.

It felt as if his heart had grown a pair of wings, to soar out of his chest in the essense of song. His lungs halted as the angel before him swept every ounce of breath away. The feeling of butterflies fluttered and tickled his stomach, enticing the violets of romance to giggle within him, forcing a blossoming smile, yet not in a nervous way. He couldn't believe it; he was in love.

His mind frolicked like a fawn in a pasture, until Madame Hiller tapped his shoulder, "Felix?"

"Ja?" Felix shook from his swooning doze. Elizabeth asked, "You are staying for dinner? Madame Hiller tells me you have a taste for roasted lamb."

"Ja." Felix nodded.

"We have time for tea before dinner, so let us sit down." Elizabeth sat on an empty sofa. The chair next to Cécile happened to be open. Felix thought she looked lonely, but before he had the chance, Madame Hiller took his arm, "Come Felix." She escorted him next to Elizabeth. In turn, Madame Hiller took the spot near Cécile.

"So, Felix," Elizabeth's tone gave much charm, "I am glad that you ended up in Frankfort. Are you here for some time?"

"It is in question. I do wish to be back in Leipzig as soon as I can."

"Leipzig sounds like a good city. Have you a nice home there?"

"Ja, I do enjoy it." Felix answered politely. She went on asking other questions, but it only made her hopes obvious. She wanted a relationship that would lead to marriage. Being a widow, she had no husband to help provide for her family. Felix had an occupation, was well off socially and had the means financially for a family.

As a maid brought tea, Felix veered much of his attention towards the brewed herbs. Madame Hiller spoke up, trying to keep Felix induced in conversation. She revealed his interests and dislikes. Felix felt a pang of self embarrassment, wishing them to find another subject to talk about.

Elizabeth was just another typical lady enthralled by him, mostly gazing at his coat as it gave him a refined figure. Cécile sat rather in boredom, but glanced whenever Felix smiled or laughed.

At the hour of dinner, Elizabeth escorted Felix to the dining room. He helped her get seated as it was a proper gesture of a polite man. She tapped on the chair next to her, ensuring he sat beside her. To his luck, Cécile happened upon the seat on the other side of him.

When Elizabeth paused in her speech, Felix turned to Cécile, "Wie geht's?"

Cécile stared at him in confusion. He added tenderly, "Sprichst du Deutsch?" Felix sensed that she didn't know what to say, so he shifted, "Parle Français?"

"Oui."

"How are you?" Felix asked in her language. She smiled, "Very well."

"Sorry for not conversing in French earlier, you must have been bored out of your mind."

"No, I assure I wasn't." She admitted in a blush. Felix then asked, "How old are you?"

"Nineteen. You?"

"Twenty seven." Felix was happy to say. Elizabeth noticed Felix speaking much with Cécile, so she intervened in German, "My dear Felix, how is it you like dinner? Does it look well?"

"Ja, it is tasty." Felix replied. He tried to speak more to Cécile but both Madame Hiller and Elizabeth did what they could to distract him. Dinner soon came to a close and Madame Hiller determined that it was time to leave.

Before exiting the cottage, Elizabeth questioned, "You do intend to return?"

"Of course." Felix assured. Both Madames gave way to excitement in their line of thought, but Felix had other intentions. He made sure to give Cécile a farewell wave.

On the carriage ride home, Madame Hiller asked Felix, "So how do you like Madame Jeanrenaurd?"

"She is charming."

"She very much appreciated your visit. I am ever so glad you are inclined to go back." Madame Hiller smiled. The carriage stopped at Schelble's home so Felix disembarked. Madame Hiller went on her way to her own home.

When returning to his rooms, Felix found some letters at the desk. One gave way to surprise. Schelble's doctor determined it best he recover at his home, so he'd be returning in the week. A few other letters were from Düsseldorf, begging him to conduct more concerts. There were arrangements made for someone else to fill in the Frankfort position; Ferdinand Ries, a composer and former pupil of Beethoven agreed to come.

Just as Felix had felt comfortable in Frankfurt, he had to move on. He had been instructed to leave straight away, so he packed up his belongings and loaded a carriage. Hiller decided to keep his mother company so Felix would be journeying alone. Before setting off, he penned a note to the Jeanrenaurd family of his situation. He planned to return after the engagements in Düsseldorf.

~~~~

On arriving at Schadow's home, Schadow was away on business so Felix had the whole place to himself. To ensure the house was fine, Schadow left notes of instruction. There were servants to help as well.

Felix spent his days in relative calmness with a few concerts here and there. The majority of his time was spent in leisure; going on walks, attending painting lessons, composing or riding his horse to the Rhine for baths. Swimming was a common activity as it was relaxing on hot days and a convenient option to keep clean. The other bathing option was to haul water to a tub and heat it manually, which was a painstaking process; unless you had servants.

Felix liked to exercise, so going to the Rhine was the perfect option. Yet, choosing to swim in an open body of water in partial wilderness had dangers. Sometimes the water looked more shallow than it was.

Felix parked his horse in the tall grass by the riverbank to let it graze. He then set his shoes and stockings aside along with his coat. He only wanted to soak his feet and wade some. When dipping his toes in the water, he noticed the river appear murky as if some fish had kicked up dirt in the riverbed. The water felt fine, so he stepped in and walked along the shallow bank.

The horse grazed in all peacefulness. It was the most content creature as Felix was the best horseman a horse could wish for. He had scattered apples about in the grass giving the horse an option of a treat while munching on grass.

Suddenly, a strange splash in the water caused the horse's ears to prick. It lifted its head from grazing. Felix, its precious owner, was nowhere in sight. The horse trotted up to the riverbank. The water was murky and the horse hadn't the best of eyesight. A few bubbles were reaching the surface in one spot.

In relying on its ears, it could hear a muffled scream. It stepped in the water to find that it was a deep section. The horse didn't lose its stance and didn't make any hesitation to bite onto the collar of Felix's shirt. It pulled him to the surface, dragging him a few paces from the riverbank.

The horse then nudged Felix as he laid motionless. He stirred some when his state of shock began to ease. In sitting up, he frantically hugged his horse at its nose, ever so thankful for a trusty steed. He winced in standing as his ankle ached. Felix knew he sprained it when toppling from a drop in the river's depth. It had some bruising.

After stretching, he managed to walk but limped. He put his stockings, shoes and coat on to help warm his chilled state then mounted his horse to ride home.

When he entered the stables, Felix disembarked the equine. As he walked it to the stall, the stableman noticed his limp, "Are you hurt?"

"I slipped at the Rhine." Felix gave him the horse's reins. The stableman suggested, "There is a doctor that lives across the street, I can call him over to your place of stay. Just to be sure you're alright."

"Danke." Felix sighed, tired of such mishaps. He hobbled back to Schadow's house. When he entered, he changed into dry lounging clothes and rested on the sofa. A slight knock tapped at the door and an old gentleman with a bag entered. He greeted Felix kindly, "How are you doing? I hear you sprained an ankle."

"Ja, the river was deeper than I thought." Felix showed him his ankle. It was now quite dark in bruising. The doctor went to him and looked at it. He moved it some, "It is quite fine, only the bruising is quite bad. I shall prescribe leeches. It will help with inflammation. I'll run home and get some."

Felix gave a sigh as the doctor headed out. Leeches weren't fun. With letters he distracted his thoughts. One from Hiller rendered quite ironic. He happened to have a worse accident from a bath. He stepped on a shard of glass hidden in the water. His foot was hurt terribly. He left the churning details in the letter.

456

The injury rendered Hiller ill and a doctor suggested he find fresh air in Homburg near a mineral spring. Madame Hiller accompanied her son. Felix penned a nice letter of comfort.

The old doctor soon came back with a porcelain jar. He set it on the coffee table then had Felix rest his leg on the table. Felix felt squeamish as the doctor grabbed a handful of the slimy, bloodthirsty creatures.

"Do I need that many?" Felix asked in hesitation, "Are you sure this will help? Isn't this rather an old practice?"

"You'll need quite a few as your ankle might swell. I was taught in my schooling that it's effective. It's either the leeches or I stick you myself." He set some leeches on the bruised ankle. It didn't feel like anything at first, but after a while they began to hurt. He tried to distract himself by writing letters and composing. The doctor passed his time by penning notes.

After an hour, Felix noticed his concentration became hazy. In fatigue he asked, "How long is this to go on?"

"A little bit longer." The doctor watched Felix fall in and out of wakefulness, noting the observation in a journal. Just before he fell faint, the doctor put the leeches back in the jar then bandaged the ankle well. He then ordered a maid to bring him a hearty dinner. Felix laid comfortably on the sofa, sleeping in the meantime. The doctor stayed to make sure he was alright.

The maid came back with a beef stew. Felix forced himself to sit up and eat in order to get strength back. The treatment for his ankle rendered more taxing than the injury itself.

~~~~

After a few days of healing and regaining strength, Felix had to decide whether to return to his duties at the Gewandhaus in Leipzig or not.

His heart was calling him to Frankfort on the Main as it panged for Cécile. Felix packed his bags in haste, answering his beating love.

When arriving at Frankfort, he was kindly welcomed at Schelble's home. Herr Schelble had much gratitude that Felix had filled in at the St. Cecilia choir earlier. Ferdinand Ries had taken the position now, so Felix had more time to concentrate on his own business.

The next day, Felix visited the lovely Jeanrenaud cottage. Elizabeth greeted Felix with the utmost pleasure, "Oh, my Felix. I'm ever so glad you're back." Her bubbly tone sounded warm. She guided Felix to the main room. To his hopes, beautiful Cécile sat in a chair, knitting. She looked ever so calm and carefree.

Elizabeth took a spot on the sofa, gesturing Felix to sit by her. He consented though he wished to be in the empty chair beside Cécile. His heart fluttered with longing as she glanced at him. Elizabeth induced conversation in German. Felix responded in much politeness, but when given the opportunity, he included Cécile in the conversation by switching to French. Elizabeth tried to keep the speech German. She commented to Felix when the language changed, "You have such a way with words in your Mutter tongue, bitte, spricht Deutsch."

"I feel that your daughter should be in conversation with us." Felix looked to Cécile who was concentrating on her yarn. Her hands were starting to get in a knot. Elizabeth consented, "Alright, French it is, but I will admit, your accent doesn't suit the language."

~~~

Over the next few weeks, Felix's visits to the Jeanrenaud home became more and more frequent. In much of the time he kept his reserve for Cécile, waiting for the right moments. He got to know her better by watching her demeanor. His quest of love began to hinder all else activity. He admitted in writing to his sister Rebecka:

*Frankfort, July 2nd, 1836*

*Dear Rebecka Dirichlet,*
*Such is my mood now the whole day; I can neither compose nor write letters, nor play the piano; the utmost I can do is sketch a little....*

*—Felix*

~~~

The Hillers made their return to Frankfort, so Felix spent much time at their home. He often rested on the couch in Ferdinand's room after dinner, thinking only of Cécile. Hiller noticed his friend's lovestruck state, "If you are so fallen for Elizabeth, you should ask her in marriage already."

"It is not Elizabeth that has captured my soul."

"It's not?" Hiller had confusion. Felix admitted, "Her daughter Cécile has so much beauty, I cannot think of anything but her grace, her eyes, her way of speech…"

"Be careful," Hiller shut the door to his room, "if my Mutter hears your words, both she and Elizabeth will fall in disappointment. Elizabeth wants you as her husband and my Mutter is trying to help, hence why she introduced you to the family."

"I knew that from day one. Though Elizabeth is kind, I cannot love her. If I became her husband, I'd be Cécile's step Vater. I find such a scenario too awkward. Besides, Cécile is closer in age to I." Felix pondered the situation.

"I shall help you in any way I can." Hiller assured. Felix smiled while in a dream, "Dankeschön my friend. Cécile has so much charm in my eyes, you have no clue how much this means to me. I plan to propose.

Here is the ring." Felix opened a jewelry case containing the most humble diamond ring. Hiller stated, "It's beautiful."

As the two continued speaking, Felix's love interests were seeping straight into the ears of Madame Hiller, who was eavesdropping behind the closed door. The information hindered her plans. She murmured to herself, "I shall get you Felix to wed Elizabeth. I shall."

~~~

In Felix's next visit to the Jeanrenaud cottage, he deemed himself ready. He was going to ask Cécile into a betrothal. He wore a most charming suit and made sure the ring was safe in his coat pocket. A carriage was ordered for a ride in the countryside. It would take them to a beautiful floral garden.

When he arrived at the home, a servant let him in. Elizabeth greeted him alone in the main hall. She smiled, "My dear Felix. You are dressed in such dashing attire. Bitte, I have freshly brewed tea in the parlor."

"Danke." Felix followed her. To his dismay, Cécile wasn't sitting in her chair. Elizabeth mentioned as they seated on the sofa, "I had my children go do more productive things than sit here. I felt we needed time to speak, just you and I."

"Oh…" Felix tried to think of a way to ask about Cécile. He sipped some tea as Elizabeth once again induced conversation. She was soon to notice Felix was enticed to ask something. He didn't seem to know how. She had high hopes, so implied,"Felix dear one? Have you something to ask me?"

"Ja, I've had something on my mind a while."

"You have?" She was quick to set her teacup down and hold Felix's hands. He hesitated as she would fall in disappointment. She sensed his shyness so assured, "My darling, you don't have to be shy. Ask away."

460

She gently caressed his chin. Felix knew he needed to speak up before she got too touchy, "Will you-"

"I do!" Elizabeth in an instant grabbed him at his waist and pulled him into a kiss. She completely interrupted his question. Madame Hiller walked in from eavesdropping nearby. She announced, "I shall start preparing wedding arrangements."

"Wait-" Felix tried to speak up. Elizabeth continued interrupting him. She asked while searching him, "Where is the ring?"

"Madame," Felix nudged her hands away, "You didn't hear my question. I asked, will you tell me where your eldest daughter Cécile is."

"You did?" She felt confused. Felix nodded. Madame Hiller questioned, "Why do you want to see Cécile? You've hardly spoken to her. You've been in more company with Elizabeth."

"I love Cécile with every pulse of my heart, breath of my lungs; she has captured my soul." Felix fell into a swoon. Elizabeth disrupted his moment, "But my daughter doesn't know German." She slowly held him at his sides again. Felix tried to scoot away, but the small sofa prevented it. Elizabeth sensed he was uncomfortable, but pulled him closer, assuring in all smoothness, "I would be good and loyal to you. If you would only consent in marriage."

Both Madames eyed Felix, giving the strongest pressure he had ever felt. Elizabeth kept her grasp at his waist, making the feeling all the more worse. To scold her boldness towards him, he decided to speak his mind, "Madame Jeanrenaud. You are good, kind and charming. Yet, your demeanor towards me after today has shown that we are not suited for each other."

"Bitte, I'm sorry if I offended you." She instantly let him go. He stood from his seat becoming stern, "I want to know where Cécile is. I've ordered a carriage for a ride in the country."

Elizabeth gave a somber glance, but led Felix to the dining room, where Cécile sat, painting. Felix stood beside her, watching the beautiful art form on the page. He had no idea she painted so skillfully. She glanced up at Felix, blushing as he admired the work. Elizabeth explained to her daughter, "Felix would like to take you on a carriage ride through the country."

"Oh. I'd be glad to." Cécile stood up, setting her crafts aside. Felix escorted her to the pretty gig sitting outside. He helped her step in then joined her in sitting. When the carriage set off, Felix felt much joy to have in depth conversation with Cécile. They had much in common in the likes of art and music. Cécile loved the compositions of Chopin, so she had enthralment to know Felix was friends with him.

Soon the carriage stopped outside a beautiful fenced garden. Felix hopped out and escorted Cécile along the fencing with the fall plants in bloom. At the main gate where they stopped, the iron design had elegance of its own. Felix faced Cécile declaring, "Today, I am going to ask you something. There were reasons for my frequent visits." He got on his knees while holding her hands, "You. You were my reason. I love you and if you consent, I would be the most pleased man in the world if you would accept my engagement."

"This is the most surprising thing I've ever encountered," she gazed at him. Felix gave way to worry, but she finished, "I love surprises." She kissed him as he stood back up. His face radiated with the most blissful smile. Felix's thoughts then blared at him, "Oh! I almost forgot!" He grabbed the jewelry case from his coat. Before even opening it, Cécile hugged him. Felix knew he caught the perfect girl. She loved him for who he was as it didn't take the sight of a diamond to convince her.

~~~~

Felix wasn't the only man falling in love. Back in Leipzig, I myself had found the love of my life. In my travels I had many patrons that contributed to my music career. Particularly the Liphart family in my time in Estonia. The Liphart daughter, Sophie, had captivated my heart.

After I found my steady career in Leipzig as concertmaster, we reunited. In due time I proposed and we wedded. Since Sophie and her family were of nobility, the marriage brought a decent fortune with it.

Felix soon returned to Leipzig to meet Sophie von David and celebrate his own betrothal among friends. The occasions gave way to a dinner party at the new year with gifts and songs. Felix's wedding was to be in May, but he had to endure a separation from Cécile in the meantime. He sat quietly looking rather dismal. Herr Schleinitz called to him, "Felix, you should compose something right now of your romance."

"Alright." Felix took a manuscript and pencil a lady handed to him. He penned under the shelter of a napkin before the pine-apples were finished. Others were eating sweet cakes. Felix came up with a four part choral and the guests sang it to perfection.

After a night of celebration, we continued our regular duties at the Gewandhaus. It was a busy season as there were many new and hopeful composers sending music.
With each symphony the orchestra ran, Felix was pleased with not one.

"Ferdinand," Felix addressed me as we sat in the seats of the auditorium, observing the music, "I thank you ever so much for filling in for me, but where did these symphonies come from?"

"There have been many aspiring composers sending in their work. The committee strongly suggested I work them out until you came back. They want new music. It's all a hash."

"We will work through a few of these, but Hiller recently composed an overture that I'd like rehearsed. It is ready to hand out." Felix grabbed a folio of parts. I gathered some and helped in handing them out. Felix then took his place at the conducting desk as I sat in my seat amongst the orchestra.

In running the piece, I gave many gestures to help the musicians get through it. Felix instructed after hearing it once, "Be sure to watch the tempo, we tend to be slow."

"Violins, be sure to follow my bowings," I added, "A down bow on the second cadence suits best."

"From the top." Felix held his baton up. The musicians followed and ran the piece a second time. It was deemed much better, so the rehearsal ended on a good note.

On returning home, Felix found quiet time to dig into letters. He received a response from Ignaz as Felix questioned if he knew of any new composers that were decent in sound. Moscheles mentioned Chopin but also the excellent technique of a pianist by the name of Thalberg. With these up and coming pianists, Ignaz stated concerning his own skill:

*I need to practice more to keep up with the times.*

In other business, another concern was Fanny. She had much insistence on publishing. Every now and again, she sent Felix a composition. To him, they seemed rather rushed. His opinion on her wish did not waver, yet their mother knew of Fanny's desire and wanted Felix to consent, so she wrote, praising her music. Felix wasn't a fool and knew the intent so replied:

*Dear Mutter,*

*You write to me about Fanny's new compositions, and say that I ought to persuade her to publish them. Your praise is, however, quite unnecessary to make me heartily rejoice in them, or think them charming and admirable; for I know by whom they are written. I hope, too, I need not say that if she does resolve to publish anything, I will do all in my power to obtain every facility for her, and to relieve her, so far as I can, from all trouble which can possibly be spared her. But to persuade her to publish anything I cannot, because this is contrary to my views and to my convictions.*

*We have often formerly discussed the subject, and I still remain exactly of the same opinion. I consider the publication of a work as a serious matter (at least it ought to be so), for I maintain that no one should publish, unless they are resolved to appear as an author for the rest of their life....and from my knowledge of Fanny I should say she has neither inclination nor vocation for authorship. She is too much all that a woman ought to be for this. She regulates her house, and neither thinks of the public nor of the musical world, nor even of music at all, until her first duties are fulfilled. Publishing would only disturb her in these, and I cannot say I approve of it...if she resolves to publish, either from her own impulse or to please Hensel, I am, as I said before, quite ready to assist her so far as I can; but to encourage her in what I do not consider right, is what I cannot do.*

*–Felix*

*~~~*

**The month of May couldn't have come soon enough. Felix went to the finest tailor in Leipzig to be fitted for his wedding attire. He wanted an elegant suit. The tailor crafted special fabrics together to give Felix the desired look. He sewed decorative pearly buttons on the waistcoat.**

The waistcoat itself was black with silver embroidery of an ivy leaf pattern. It looked refined over the white undershirt. The cravat was made with fine black silk. Black pants and shiny shoes completed the outfit.

Once obtaining the fine suit, Felix took a coach to Frankfort to be reunited with his bride to be. Yet, before the marked day, Madame Hiller and Elizabeth would not let Felix see Cécile as they wanted her appearance to be a surprise, so Felix stayed at Schelble's home.

On the 28th of May, the meant to be simple and seldom occasion occurred. Among the few observers were Cécile's family, Hiller and his mother. The wedding took place in the French church that Cécile's father had occupied. Their vows were held in Cécile's mother tongue. It was quite strange to hear someone so thoroughly German harangue in French. Felix's accent was quite noticeable. Cécile spoke in pure grace and beauty.

At the end of the ceremony, the new couple pressed lips in the most passionate kiss. With the moment lasting a while, Elizabeth cried into Madam Hiller's shoulder. Other ladies' eyes became wet with tears as well.

Afterwards, everyone proceeded out of the church to the Jeanrenaud home where they celebrated with cake and champagne. A small group of singers joined the party to share a wedding song Hiller had composed for the couple. Felix and Cécile sat together as they listened to the pleasing tune. The ladies of the choir looked to Felix with much remorse as they had admiration for him, but alas, he was now married. Their tones had much vibrato to impress him.

At the late hour, everyone grew tired. Felix and Cécile needed rest as a carriage was hired for the next morning to take them to their place of honeymoon. They headed for a guest room which had a double bed. Elizabeth rushed to them before they got up the stairs, "Oh no, no, no. Cécile, you are sleeping in your own room tonight. I do not want to be a grandmother yet."

"Oh Mother!" Cécile blushed in embarrassment. Felix chuckled and continued up the stairs. Cécile obeyed her mother for the time being, but the young couple had a whole honeymoon to spend together without interference.

~~~

In the forenoon of the next sunny day, Felix and Cécile arrived in the charming town of Freiburg-im-Breisgau. Clear streams ran through the streets and glorious hills, mountains, plains and valleys could be seen on the town's outskirts. Both took part in sketching and painting.

Felix felt that he needed to brush up on drawing. When watching Cécile sketch, he knew he could learn a lot from her. As he shaded a mountain side, Cécile noticed his pencil giving the wrong texture. She instructed, "Here, shade it this way."

Felix let her take the pencil and she lightly coloured in circles rather than straight lines. It made the mountain in more liking to the real thing. Felix couldn't help but kiss her in thanks. Together they composed a journal of their journey.

Felix worked on music as well. Cécile sat next to him on a hillside as she enjoyed watching the notes form on the page while basking in the warm sun. Felix penned some sacred music based on the 42nd Psalms as well as a second piano concerto. The surroundings of spring blossoms and green grasses made his ideas flourish.

After spending the daylight hours roaming hills, the evening hours were spent at a hotel, known to be highly maintained. Felix had sent a letter of notice ahead of time for a reservation. He didn't want the trip to be overly extravagant but made sure to find a reputable place of stay.

The lobby of the hotel had much elegance and the manager greeted them kindly. He led them upstairs to a master suite. When entering, Felix and Cécile gave gasps of awe.

The main room contained sitting space with a fireplace. A bouquet of red roses sat on the mantle. There was a dining table set in the corner, complete with candles and French champagne. A separate room contained the bedroom where a decent sized bed sat. Rose petals were dusted on top of the fine white bedding.

Once they unpacked, they settled in the sitting room next to the warming fireplace. It was then they realized they were completely alone. Felix in the moment began to think it surreal he had married. He recollected his conversation those years ago at the university with his teacher, Humboldt.

"Honey? Is something on your mind?" Cécile coined a sweet address. Felix was not used to being called such, but it felt flattering, "Much is on my mind I guess. It feels strange that we are really married. You are actually my wife." He caressed her at the shoulders. She gazed in return. Their glances soon led to noticing each other's features.

[3]

Ceicel's blue eyes sparkled in the light of the fireplace, mesmerizing Felix's whole soul. Her blushing cheeks had such colour of rose buds and her copper hair glistened from the firelight. Fine French perfume gave a pleasing scent. She wore a modest navy blue evening gown, detailed with dark red and orange blossoms. The dress gave a perfect silhouette of her pure stature as a beautiful woman. Her etiquette shone whilst holding a glass of champagne before dinner.

Ceicel was infatuated by the wisps of dark hair and deep black eyes that gave Felix a completion of a heartwarming human being. His sideburns were whisking some but still trimmed enough to look well maintained. His outfit was the same from the wedding. Cécile couldn't help but notice the silver leaf pattern on the black waistcoat which correlated with the vibrant white sleeves of the undershirt. She knew Felix had been to England, obtaining a sense of fashion there. Though he was born in Berlin, she knew she had found an Englishman at heart.

Their gazes fixed at each other's eyes. Felix couldn't help but caress Cécile's chin with ever such elegance. He leaned into a blissful kiss. Her face had a softness, making her all the more a sweetheart of a woman. He then caressed her at the shoulders, her graceful arms adding attractiveness. His wistful kisses moved to her elegant neck, making her heart glimmer inside.

Cécile was rather distracted as she gently held him at the waist, not being overbearing. Once he smiled, showing he was comfortable, she held him more. Felix's inner feelings fluttered as her hand brushed his waistcoat. Cécile gazed intently at his silhouette. He wasn't at all heavy weighted, but his body had substance with shapely hips, a slimmed waist and a torso nicely shaped at the tummy. It gave him a cute essence.

As the kissing and holding continued, the arrow of love struck them both, piercing their inner souls. Their two hearts had joined as a whole in all purity. Before things got 'too' saucy, there was a knock on the door. Both Felix and Cécile sat up from their love session. A servant came in, setting a fancy dinner of lamb chops with a splendid sauce of bourbon. On the side were persimmons and slices of drunken goat cheese. Fine wine accompanied the course.

After the servant left them to it, Felix and Cécile ate in complete pleasure without a care in the outside world. It was their time to fully indulge in nice things. Desert consisted of sharing slices of cheesecake drizzled in raspberry-chocolate sauce.

When the plates were emptied, they settled their stomachs with more wine. It made them both tired, but not too 'tired.' Ceicel eyed Felix as he gulped down the last bit of red wine. He set the finished glass aside, noticing his wife's gazes. She stood from her seat and gracefully headed to the bedroom, gesturing Felix to follow.

Whether it was the wine or the anticipation, he felt as if he were floating her way. He followed her with hearts surrounding his line of vision. When closing the bedroom door behind him, he knew the night would be complete with good passionate love.

# Chapter XX: The Victorian Era

Handel, Zadok the Priest [1]
Schubert, C Major Symphony 'The Great' [2]

June 1838

## [1]

The highly ornamented carriages gracefully circled the large roundabout. Guards marched on foot as others sat on the backs of horses, guiding the large coaches in an organized manner.

In one particular cab, a girl sat, wearing fine garments. She was nervous, anxious and in mourning all at once. The streets were filled with the citizens of England, trying to get a glimpse of the young girl hidden within the enclosed coach. Excitement filled every face and pair of eyes.

Meanwhile, in the Abbey of Westminster, the choir waited with their sheets of music in front of them. The papers were illuminated as each chorister's stand held a candle for light. Music was already echoing through the cathedral as the interlude of the orchestra gave the greatest sound of anticipation.

Outside, the carriages were arriving and a finely dressed parade formed. It was an occasion filled with the dukes and duchesses. The music of Handel could be heard escaping through the open door.

Soon, the biggest carriage arrived. The young girl inside was escorted out with the highest care. As soon as exiting the privacy of the coach and into the public eye, she kept her head raised in confidence. She joined in the center position in the lines of escorts.

As the choir almost could not bear the wait, the grand procession of guards entered in a slow manner. The voices then burst into the pinnacle of the piece as those seated in chairs stood in respect. Everyone was looking at the girl of 18, who was the center of attention as she proceeded in the company of guards, squires and priests.

The girl then sat at the throne with the proper garments of a coronation. After given the golden scepters, the main priest walked up to the throne and raised the royal crown over the woman's head. Everyone in the Abbey held their breath.

Once the crown was placed in elegance, the attendees filled the cathedral with rejoice. Their queen had been crowned. She sat at the throne in all maturity and confidence. Her leadership was now deemed an official engagement. Every duke and duchess admired the young woman's stance before her people as she kept her face serious in expression, refraining from smiling too much. She couldn't help it at least a little with all the joy filling the cathedral.

(Queen Victoria 1838)

The queen then stood in pride with her adorned gown and crown. The scene gleamed as the sun's light had appeared and shone through the windows. The attendees clapped in cheer once more then they all joined their voices together in unison to a chant and said:

'God save the Queen! Long live the Queen! God save the Queen!' 'May the Queen live forever!' 'Amen, amen, hallelujah, hallelujah, halle'

The choristers sang their ascending lines in cheer as the entire procession headed for the open world so the citizens of England could see their new ruler. It was the mark of a new era.

Queen Victoria was now crowned.

~~~

Felix set down the newspaper with the reports of the Queen's coronation. It was the headline of every paper in Europe. After setting it aside, he continued eating his eggs and sausages. The table was noisy as Cécile held their crying infant.

Felix leaned back into his chair, rubbing his eyes, feeling the heaviness under them. Their five month old child had been wailing for hours on end. Little Carl was in an ill state. Felix had held him through the night as Cécile needed sleep. She was under the weather as well with chills and a sniffle.

Felix wished for a few hours of rest, but he had work and a family to provide for. He had purchased a large apartment, settled on the second floor of a complex in Leipzig. The building was settled in Lurgenstein's Garten; the first home on the left. It had an open view over the gardens, fields and city. Felix's salary enabled him to purchase a nice home, modern to the new era.

On entering the flat, the first room was a hall containing a dining table and a few chairs. To the right was a large sitting room then bedrooms. To the left was the nursery and a fine drawing room. A kitchen area held a stove and a servant, Johann, had been hired to tend to the housework. Johann was more of a close family friend rather than one hired to work, which made the home all the happier.

*(The Mendelssohn home in Lurgenstein's Garten)*

As Cécile feared she was catching a fever, she headed for bed, making Felix take Carl for the day. Felix took little Carl with him to the parlor. He sat at the writing desk, caressing his child while penning notes on a manuscript. Carl woke, his beaming little eyes stared at his father. Felix paused his writing and smiled at his son's cute face. Carl had been born on the 7th of February, 1838.

The child's sickness had to have lifted as he smiled back. Yet, the smile soon turned sour. Carl cried...and cried...and cried. Felix tried to keep working while rocking Carl to sleep, but his ears were suffering in the process. He now knew how Fanny felt when she wanted to compose, but was occupied with a child. It didn't quite occur to him, even as the man of the house, he'd be quite occupied with his child. He didn't want to be the sort that handed the baby off to the servant.

Felix set his quill down and carried the crying child to the nursery that he and Cécile had put together. The room had a cozy fireplace with a rocking chair in front of it. Felix sat to see if that would put the baby to sleep.

Right away, Carl quieted. Felix hummed tunes that came to mind. The child was quite lucky to get such a good lullaby. He soon fell asleep.

Felix continued humming, being sure to hum choral melodies of Bach. With the warm room, the rocking of the chair; his own hums put himself to sleep.

Cécile, with a blanket draped over her shoulders, walked into the nursery to such a lovely sight. Her sleeping husband and baby. The low glowing fireplace illuminating their cozy state. She savored the moment, noting in her mind that she wanted more children.

~~~

The past months before settling his family in Leipzig gave much opportunity. Shortly after he and Cécile's honeymoon, Felix took a trip to London to premiere his second piano concerto. His Paulus oratorio was also performed, taking part in the Birmingham music festival. Beforehand it was supposed that the new queen was to watch, but it did not appear so at the event.

The journey rendered a typical trip to Britain with sea sickness, but this time also with a deep homesickness more than anything else. Cécile wasn't beside him and the newly married man longed ever so to be with her. He almost couldn't bear the three weeks away.

After England, Felix feared he'd be called away from Leipzig again as the St. Cecilia choir in Frankfort lost another director. Ferdinand Ries had unexpectedly died after a terrible illness with jaundice and fever. Schelble still wasn't fit to return. Thankfully Hiller filled in, but he was having his own sadness as his former teacher Hummel passed away in October of 1837.

In the early summer of 1838 Felix and Cécile paid a visit to Berlin to meet Felix's mother and siblings. The stay was well, but long. They went to various concerts together, including ones at the Sing-Akademie. Felix had much disappointment in the performances there.

The music had lost much of its lust since Zelter's death. It didn't feel the same. To Felix's dismal the choir sang some of his music. Many times Cécile had to hold her husband's arm as he wanted to get up and scold the performance. She kept whispering sweetly to him, "Dear husband, do be calm."

Felix made it through the performances and had a good couple of months with family. They seemed to like Cécile, but were a bit surprised that Felix fell in love at first sight after years of being rather uninterested in the idea of marriage.

Felix now was back and well established in Leipzig, conducting many concerts and reviving compositions of old. Each work was performed in historical order to help the audiences get a grasp of history. His use of the bâton deemed him one of the most prolific conductors. The regular work at the Gewandhaus and at home made life at the moment feel prosperous.

~~~

"Ferdinand…" Sophie, my wife sighed as she handed me my violin case. It was early morning and time to head to the Gewandhaus. She continued, "Must there be work this week? I feel it an unwise decision."

"It has already been decided that rehearsals must commence this week. Any musician available must be there as we can't afford to forego the soon coming concerts. I must have a living for you and our future child." I stated. My wife gave another quiet sigh. She had reason for much worry. The winter had arrived, which was nothing too alarming, but in the season, a terrible outbreak of the measles spread like wildfire throughout Leipzig and other cities of Germany.

I had my luck for the time being as I had not caught it. Other members of the orchestra had not been so lucky. Many were stuck at home with the illness, including Felix. Like every time he was away from the Gewandhaus, I was the one to take over.

I wished rehearsals to be postponed, but Herr Schleinitz and Hauser agreed as the Konzerthaus needed funds to stay sufficient, postponing concerts in the coming spring was out of the question.

Any able musicians were to show up for regular rehearsals, which was a small number. Herr Schumann still had his health and helped tend to business, but soon left for an excursion to Vienna shortly after the winter came. He was to not return until spring.

I exited my apartment complex, entering the streets, slippery with ice. Though the sun seeped between buildings in rising, the air was desperately cold. A storm in the night had formed trenches of thick snow, forcing me to walk. Carriages were getting stuck in the snow piles. Others were forced to walk as well. When passing someone on the pavement, everyone, including myself, held a handkerchief over our face so as to not contract the horrid measles.

My home wasn't far from Lurgenstein's Garden where Felix lived. As I passed by, I looked up at the second story of windows. The curtains were all shut, giving the level a darkened appearance. I hoped my friend and his family were alright.

~~~

In the Mendelssohn home, Johann the servant went to and fro everywhere in the apartment. Cleaning, cooking and caring for the family. Felix, Cécile and little Carl were all ill of measles. In the midst of the terrible sickness, Johann set up a bed in the nursery so Cécile could be with Carl. Felix took the main bedroom to stay separate.

Cécile wrote to her family back in Frankfort to occupy herself when not sleeping, informing them of the illness. She was determined that her child, husband and herself would pull through it. When the news reached her mother, in a day's time as it felt, Elizabeth arrived at the home in a burst of worry for her daughter and grandchild. She came without a notice, but Johann arranged an extra bed in the drawing room.

Soon after settling her luggage, Elizabeth walked towards the nursery. Before entering, she peeked into the main bedroom. Felix was out as a candle. She turned back for the time being and continued to the room where Cécile sat in the rocking chair, holding little Carl. Both looked quite pale and in bad health. Carl showed signs of the rash that measles caused.

"Mother! I'm so happy to see you." Cécile's ill expression healed at the comfort of seeing her mother.

"My poor Cécile and my poor Carl! I'm here to help with what I can," Elizabeth was careful not to get too close, "I shall help keep things clean and in order so Johann can have a rest."

"I love you so much." Cécile felt much happiness. The three of them heard Johann give a big sigh of relief as he overheard while bringing a tray of food. Elizabeth was quick to ask, "Has Felix eaten yet?"

"Nein, I have another tray ready, but he's been sleeping all day. He doesn't eat much when ill." Johann explained. Elizabeth assured, "I'll be sure he eats." She left the room for the kitchen. There she found a tray of lunch consisting of chicken noodle soup. It wasn't hot nor cold, but needed to be eaten. She took it to Felix's room, where he was in a hard sleep.

"Felix dear…" Elizabeth sweetly called in her usual bubbly tone. Felix was too deep in sleep to hear. One of his ears were temporarily deafened from the illness. She called again while setting the tray on the nightstand, "Felix, the soup will get cold, you must eat." She tapped on him, "You need to eat."

Felix laid motionless, too weak to will himself awake. Elizabeth sat at the edge of the bed, waiting for a response. He had the same ill, pale look as Cécile, but in contrast, his eyes had a foggy appearance as he opened them.

478

"You should sit up." Elizabeth grabbed a damp cloth to clean his eyes. It helped him wake but his vision rendered a blur. He knew as he had suffered measles before that it would take time for his ear and eyes to heal. It would be a challenge to continue work even weeks after the illness had lifted.

Felix finally sat up and took the tray of food. He hoped it would give him energy. As he ate, Elizabeth induced conversation. Her tones were like windfull flutes depicting blooming flowers while a desperate oboe lingered, rendering the conversation uncomfortable. Even though it was cheerful talk, Felix knew she still wished to have had Cécile's place as his wife. She didn't seem to try to keep away as she had with Cécile and Carl.

Felix viewed her as she was: a mother-in-law. In the moment Elizabeth was beginning to act more and more like one. Her speech began to tire him. She veered from innocent conversation to asking, "I wonder what caused my daughter and grandson to catch such illness. You must have gotten it from someone you work with."

"It's spreading all over the city. Cécile could have got it at the dress shop or something, I could have caught it at work or walking around, who knows. Don't imply that I'm to blame." He set the finished tray at the nightstand. Elizabeth sat closer, "If anything happens to my daughter or grandson, you are responsible."

"You shouldn't get this close to me or you'll catch sickness."

"I am not scared of sickness. I'm being careful." She made sure he was cozy. As she tucked his blanket, her charming voice fell into a whisper, "If you had married me and stayed in Frankfort, such a sickness wouldn't have beseeched you."

"This could have happened to anyone." Felix retorted, starting to perspire. Elizabeth constantly felt his forehead, checking his temperature.

It was more a bothering gesture than helpful. She wasn't a doctor. Carl could be heard crying in the other room. Felix's head and neck already ached, but the cries added to it, "Have Johann call for a physician. My wife, child and I need a professional."

"I'm capable of helping. Besides there's probably no doctors available. This disease is likely affecting every household." She used a dampened cloth to cool him down. He knew the next fortnight was going to be long. Especially with his mother-in-law staying.

~~~

With every passing day accumulating to two weeks, Felix's eyesight improved. His work of composing and editing had added up from his absence so he worked in bed. His ear still beseeched him, but he resorted to catching up on letters when he felt unable to concentrate on music. Ignaz wrote, informing that his whole family had been struck terribly ill as the measles had reached England. Felix worried about his family in Berlin. Lea informed that the only one to get ill was Fanny.

Felix wrote responses to the Moscheles family and his sister, hoping everyone would make a fast recovery. The same he wished for himself. His bedroom door seemed to be always on the move like a baker's door with Elizabeth coming hither and thither to check on him. Felix hid his manuscripts, letters and pens under the blanket each time she came, knowing she would take them away.

Recently, she had been reading books about home remedies. There were recipes that included all sorts of teas and calming herbs. She did research to find something for Felix's ear. There were many options and to Felix's utter dismay, she of course tried each one. None of them worked and moreover added to his annoyance. In the latest attempt, she cleaned his ear with a mix of olive oil. It felt rather gross and still rendered his ear useless. Felix snubbed at her, "Nothing is going to work! Leave me alone goddammit!"

"If you'd hold still! You're so irritable!" She huffed trying to dap more oil in his ear. Felix pulled the blanket over his head. Once she left, he grabbed a hidden pen and manuscript. Composing was his only comfort in the time being.

"You are not to be working when you are to be resting!" Elizabeth scolded. Felix looked up in not noticing her return, "I have to get this done eventually. I'm the one providing for my family." He continued editing the score. She forced the papers from him. His mind sunk into boredom as she took them out of the room.

In her next leave, Felix snuck a blank page of letter paper from the nightstand's drawer and wrote to Hiller of his ailments and anxiety:

*My dear friend,*

*...I have been keeping in my room a fortnight and you may imagine my agony, not being able to hear properly...it is the same illness that beseeched me four years prior and my hearing then was off for six weeks...I cannot quite help being anxious, as, till now, in spite of all remedies, there is no change, and often I do not even hear people speaking in the room.*

*Besides this there is another still greater anxiety, from which I hope every day to be released, and which does not leave me for a moment. My mother-in-law has been here a fortnight, you know for what reason. When you see your whole happiness, your whole existence, depended upon one inevitable moment, it gives you quite a peculiar sensation.*

*–F. M. B.*

~~~

The warm spring of 1839 helped cure the sickness of the winter. I felt much relief as things were soon back to normalcy. Felix made his return in due time as I had an engagement of my own. I had composed a violin concerto for myself and made arrangements to find my way around London to have it performed. Felix helped gladly by sending a letter to Mr. Moscheles to become acquainted with me. Mr. Bennett, Felix's pupil, had recently composed a piano concerto so decided to join me.

Before the carriage set off, Felix spoke at the window, giving goodbyes. He assured, "Mr. Moscheles is a good man, be sure to say hallo for me." Felix turned to Bennett, "Play well and have fun. Your concerto will impress. Ferdinand, you do the same. London will love your music."

"Felix," responded I, "Bitte, will you someday write a violin concerto? It is my wish as I really want one from you."

"We shall see. In due time." Felix waved as the carriage went on.

After Bennett and I left, Felix went home to take a walk in the garden. The floral bushes and greens were beginning to bud. As he strolled about, he saw his brother Paul walking along the fencing outside the garden. He had not informed of a visit.

"Paul!" Felix called. Paul looked towards the garden then rushed through the gate to Felix, "My Bruder, it's so good to see you up and in health. I can't imagine how terrible that illness must have struck. The disease had reached Berlin, Fanny was in a bad state for weeks."

"How is she? Is she alright?"

"Fine now. Playing her piano and organizing salons." Paul assured. Felix gave a sigh of relief, "Mutter is well also?"

"Never better." He chimed. They both nodded and were silent a minute.

482

Paul seemed ready to say something and finally build the courage to mention, "I don't know if you know, but your first piano concerto is to be played at a concert in Berlin."

"Oh, how nice."

"Fanny is making her public debut."

"Oh how nice- wait what!?" Felix gave way to shock. Paul nodded. Felix felt a mix of pride and confusion all at once. He didn't know whether to be happy or in irritation. His mouth made words for him, "Good for her. She must be so excited, I'm sure the concert will go over well."

"Ja, I'm happy for her. If Vater was here, he'd be going crazy." Paul chuckled. Felix felt a sting of sadness, but refused to show it. His thoughts pondered over the old memories of Fanny arguing with Abraham. Paul interrupted his thinking, "Let's go back inside. I've much to discuss as I came for good reason. You have a billiard table?"

"Ja, there's one in a game room on the main floor."

"Good, we can talk while getting a game going." They headed towards the complex.

As Felix set the billiard table, Paul threw a few darts. The room had many games such as chess, a table for cards and a few board games for the tenants to share. Once their game of billiards started, Paul seemed to speak business right away, "I came here to tell you of the ideas going around Berlin."

"Oh, do say." Felix struck the white ball, but made no score. Paul continued, "Crown Prince Frederick William IV is strongly suggesting that an academy of sorts is to be started in Berlin. He wants something for the instruction of music and other arts as well.

There are no specific plans yet, but he thought you may be interested. I've decided to do what I can to help. Herr Massow is the one trying to adhere to the King's wishes."

"That would be good for Berlin, but how involved does he want me? If he wants me to become an instructor, I'd have to leave Leipzig, my occupation and move my family to a new home."

"It's only something to think about right now. No official plans have been set. Prince Frederick really wants you back in Berlin as it would give the city something honorable." Paul made a score in the game. Felix shrugged, missing his strike again, "I'll think about it. When the plans become official, I'll give my answer. I have many projects around here I'm working on. I'm to host some organ concerts to raise money for the St. Thomas school. I want a monument for Bach to be put up as to make the school a historical site. It will help concerts there get more of an audience."

"That sounds like a good idea. Maybe you still could have your duties here and teach in Berlin. Frederick at least wants you to visit."

"That sounds flattering, but seems a hassle going back and forth. It would be more practical to have an academy here so I could stay with the Gewandhaus. Yet I do so much music I even at times get tired of it. Concerts, rehearsals, practice and I receive requests to teach but have no time because of my regular duties. A few pupils here and there are alright, but otherwise, I'm booked. I've been painting to get away from it all."

Paul nodded then suggested, "You should at least write Her Massow an answer in the least. It is the Crown Prince we speak of so you should strongly consider this idea."

"I will think about it." Felix assured.

~~~

The next week after Paul's visit brought a calm within the house. There happened to be no rehearsals or work at the Gewandhaus. Felix spent his time at home sketching new ideas at the writing desk in the parlor. Cécile sat on the sofa, with little one year old Carl on her lap.

The room was brightened with the mid-morning sun streaming in. Felix felt in all comfort as the cups of coffee were still fresh and steaming. Cécile poured a dab of fresh cream in her cup, "That cream Johann brought from the market is so rich. It makes a superb coffee."

"I shall have to try some." Felix dipped his pen in the inkwell, holding a thought. He penned the notes on his mind, then got up. As he went to grab the cream canister, he paused, looking at Cécile and Carl. Cécile asked, "Something on your mind?"

"Ja…" Felix sounded concerned. Cécile felt startled, but her husband continued, "My heart is just so full of joy at the sight of my beautiful wife and child." He grabbed the cream and sat back down. Cécile smiled, chuckling, then casually commented, "I hope your heart is not too full for us. You'll have to save room for one more."

Felix near choked on his coffee. He turned around towards Cécile, "You mean you're pregnant!?"

"I am sure!" Cécile nodded. Felix set his cup down and sat next to her on the sofa. They kissed in happiness. Little Carl laughed in a happy mood. It made a joyful sight.

~~~

Later in the evening after dinner, Felix took his scores and manuscripts with him to work while relaxing in bed. Cécile took Carl to the nursery then joined Felix by reading a book. As Felix composed, he grabbed a handkerchief sitting at the nightstand. His mouth itched for something to chew at. It was a habit by now.

He unconsciously chewed as his mind submerged in music. Cécile noticed him biting the cloth, "You'll chew a hole through that."

Felix shook from his thinking, noticing he was near eating the handkerchief. He threw the slobbery thing aside then continued writing, "I believe I know a possible idea for a future oratorio."

"That's nice." Cécile didn't take her eyes from her reading. Felix continued, "I've looked at various things to base it on. I think the account of Elijah would favor. It is a mere idea as I have much other work. Herr David lately has suggested a violin concerto. One in e minor runs in my head, the beginning of which gives me no peace. I hope to have it prepared next winter, but don't know where I want the music to go yet."

"I'm sure you'll figure it out honey." She didn't turn her head. Felix didn't turn from his score, assuming she cared. Suddenly the bell rang. Felix sat down his papers, "Who could be here at this hour?" He headed to the main door. Johann reached it first. When he opened it, Robert Schumann pressed in with overwhelming excitement, "My friend! You will not believe what I have come across! You are going to love this." He eagerly laid a score on the dining table. Felix examined the aged manuscripts. It was a symphony in C by Franz Schubert.

While studying the melodies, Felix deemed it a solid piece of music. Schumann explained, "I came back from Vienna not even an hour ago. Straight here I had to come. This is an important discovery. I don't think this poor score has been heard by an orchestra. I will help you in any way to get it performed. I'll get instrument copies made."

"This can be worked out. Now it is late, I imagine you need to get home and unpack yet." Felix yawned. Robert placed the score back in his satchel, "I am sorry in coming at this hour but I had to. After this is heard, I believe the music of Schubert will become a standard at every concert hall."

~~~

486

In the bustling city of London, I came with the most decent success. My concerto was played on the 18th of March and was received humbly. The concert gave way to invitations to musical gatherings as everyone wanted to hear the violin concerto of 'Ferdinand David'.

It pleased me very much. I stayed in the Moscheles' home at Chester Place. There, the days became some of the best. I had become a favorite acquaintance. Ignaz especially gained a deep friendship as my visit would be the start of a long one between us.

After Mr. Bennett's concert of his piano concerto, Ignaz threw a little after party at Chester Place. It was a simple, yet a capital gathering with champagne to go along with meat and cheese. Ignaz's family was in good cheer. Charlotte was on the couch, sitting with her daughter Emily, helping her knit. Emily became a good pianist and often played with her father. At times doing concerts with him. Little Felix Moscheles was in his fifth year, drawing on a page. The whole atmosphere of the house felt as a happy home should be.

Ignaz turned to me, "All that Felix mentioned in his letter of you is quite true. You are a capital violinist."

"Thank you. Before I came to England I suggested Felix write a violin concerto. Maybe soon there will be another for me to perform."

"That would be splendid," Ignaz nodded, "but don't get too anxious. I know Felix. Sometimes he can get things done in the snap of the fingers, other times I think he throws things aside. Keep on him and he'll get a great concerto ready."

"Don't worry, I shall. He has written to me something of interest. Schumann found a score of Schubert's in Vienna. A symphony. The Gewandhaus has been rehearsing it and it's premiere to the world is in a few days hence."

"Interesting. He should bring it to London sometime."

"I don't think we would have to wait long for that." I smiled. Little Felix Moscheles came up to me. The boy asked, "When is 'uncle' Felix to visit? I want help drawing."

"He'll come in due time dear one. He can't stay away from London long." I chuckled at the child's cute tone. He then ran off to go play and such. Ignaz continued the conversation, "What did you think of Mr. Bennett's piano concerto?"

"Suburb. He's a well rounded artist." I answered. Mr. Bennett stood a few paces away speaking to a group of musicians. He glanced my way with a smile, overhearing my comment. In reply he called to me, "The violin concerto of Ferdinand David has to be the best work for violin in our time!"

~~~~

March 22nd 1839

[2]

The sound of horse carriages rattled towards the Konzerthaus. A whispering crowd settled in the auditorium with only a few familiar with the composer Franz Schubert. Yet, they had not heard a symphony by him.

"Do you think they will like it?" Schumann questioned at the stage door. Felix gave assurance, "I am positive it will go wonderfully. It looks like the hour has struck."

"I'll be watching from the box." Schumann jogged off. Felix took his baton and stationed himself before the orchestra. The musicians lifted their instruments. Before counting in, Felix glanced at the box above the floor seating closest to the stage. Robert sat, tapping his fingers nervously on the balcony. The auditorium had its profound silence. Felix shut his eyes, taking in the moment.

A violist grumbled at him, wanting to get on with it. Felix opened his eyes and gave his gesture of counting. No one would be leaving the concert hall without knowing the name Franz Schubert.

~~~

The musicians all drank in cheer at the tavern after the well recepted concert. Schumann, Felix, Schleinitz and Hauser took a table to drink Bier and Prost the night away. Herr Hauser informed, "The audience is so impatient for another hearing of Schubert, I have made the arrangements for a second concert a week from today."

"It deserves all of the performances it can get!" Schumann cheered. Felix turned to him, "Since you adore it so much, why don't you conduct it?"

"Well...I actually won't make it to the next one as I already have much to do that week. I'm going to be visiting Herr Wieck's home to sort something out. I have affections for Clara and she for me. We want to marry." Schumann sipped some Bier.

"You two are perfect together." Felix stated, "I'm sure Freidrich sees that and will give his consent."

"That is the problem. I've asked. He threatened to shoot me."

"Herr Wieck?" Schleinitz questioned, "He is harsh at times as a teacher, but not as a man, he couldn't have meant it."

"Oh he did," Schumann had a surge of fear in his eyes, "I know him as a teacher and a man. He is not what you think. To you he may be dignified, but in reality he is crazy. I'm going there again to ask for the hand of Clara. If he threatens me again, I shall go to court!"

"If you'd like, I would be willing to help you talk to Friedrich." Felix suggested. Robert shook his head, "Danke Felix, but this is something I must do myself. Even if it takes years, I want to put all of my effort in. Plus I don't want you on Herr Wieck's bad side." With that, Robert got up and grabbed his coat to leave. Felix was tired after a few mugs of Bier so followed soon after.

~~~

In my return from London, I made it in time for the next performance of Schubert's symphony. It felt good to be back at the Gewandhaus doing my regular duties. Felix and I together kept the sound of the orchestra in good standing. In conducting great symphonies, Felix gave much artistic finishes with his expressive features. His behavior at the conducting desk wasn't all that noticeable with his movements short and decided. He began, turning his right side to the orchestra. A mere glance at the first fiddle, then a slight look the other way was sufficient.

In this case, the music of Schubert rang out. It was a full house as the attendees of the first performance told their friends of how good the work was. The moment of excitement didn't last long. Before finishing the first movement, a man's voice carried across the auditorium, "Fire! Fire!"

The shouts startled the entire crowd and everyone flooded out in fright. Felix and the orchestra stayed put on stage, looking about for flames. By the time the public fled, it was realized such an alarm was false. Felix set down his baton, "There goes that concert."

I gave way to a sigh of disappointment as the other musicians packed up. Felix noticed my state and came to me, "Ferdinand, are you alright?"

"It's so disheartening how fragile a good performance can be."

"Don't get too much in a fuss, there are plenty of other opportunities. This was just one of those concerts. I am positive the next will be amazing." He patted my shoulder.

490

Herr Schleinitz came up to us, "I must speak to you two. Tomorrow Herr Hauser is conducting a small concert, it would be nice to add this symphony at the end. It will be a full house."

"I'd be obliged to conduct it." Felix smiled, then turned to me, "When something doesn't go right, something better comes along." He then turned away, skipping out of the auditorium. I packed my violin and headed home myself.

Everything was made up for the next evening. After the originally planned program, the audience gave way to much surprise as Herr Hauser left the conducting desk and Felix took his place. Some attendees cheered out in excitement. I took my stance in my chair as Felix clicked his bâton against the desk. He glanced at me then counted. I gave my gesture with the bow of my instrument and the other musicians followed my lead.

Though there were no alarms or disruptions during the whole of the Schubert symphony, fire flared all around with the music itself igniting flames of sound.

~~~

In July of 1839, Felix and Cécile took a leisurely carriage ride through the woods. The sun was setting beautifully in the outskirts of Leipzig, giving a romantic sense. Crickets and toads chirped as a few lighting bugs began to appear in the twilight.

Cécile enjoyed the calm and needed all that she could get. Her belly was heavy with the child; due in only a few months. Felix expressed overjoy and could not wait to see if it were a boy or girl. As the carriage rode on, they discussed names.

"If it's a boy, I want him to be Felix jr.. If a girl, Marie." Cécile stated. Felix nodded then gave his input, "I think Paul would suit a boy. After his uncle would be nice. I do like Emily if a girl."

Cécile laughed, "I should get first say as I'm the one having the child."

"Maybe it will come to us when it's born." Felix gave her a kiss. Cécile kissed him back. The evening couldn't have been nicer. As the sun disappeared, lamps were lit among the trees. Felix pricked up his ears as a choral melody echoed through the woods. It was a cappella. One of his own pieces.

The carriage paused so Felix and Cécile could go see where the music came from. Though it was dark, the lamps guided them. Felix stepped a pace or so in front of Cécile to be sure she wouldn't trip on anything. They walked only a few paces and the music grew louder. Soon they entered a scene of gathered musicians and spectators. Most of them were friends. It was a Fête in the forest.

"Oh, dear Felix..." Herr Schleinitz came to Felix from among the gathered, "You arrived early. It was to be a surprise."

"I do apologize. I didn't know this was to be so. It all sounds and looks well." Felix glanced at the choir singing. It echoed against the trees. Spectators listened and joined in outdoor games. The lamps illuminated the lovely scene. Felix and Cécile found a picnic table where a group played cards. There was much fruit circulating the tables including strawberries, cherries and oranges. Drinks of wine, ice and raspberry syrup were passed around as well.

Cécile found much company. Madam Schleinitz, Constanze, sat across from her beside Herr Schleinitz. She smiled, "Cécile, you look so beautiful with child. How can your husband stand to leave for work each day?"

"It's hard for him." Cécile glanced at Felix. He was busy listening to the music. The small chorus singing gave Felix so much excitement that he often stood up at the end of a piece, danced about on one leg as he called to them, "Again, again, bitte, once more!"

Constanze then commented, "At the same time, I don't know how you handle his energy."

"Felix dear," Cécile felt a slight embarrassment and pulled him back to his seat, "be calm." She held his arm. Felix still watched the chorus. They sang 'The Lark's Song' three times with repeats. Felix didn't want the moment to end.

Later on, tables were moved aside to open a space for dancing. Most of the spectators skipped about. There were a few actors among them, acting out scenes as they danced. One nearby noticed Felix dancing with Cécile and joked a bit by imitating Felix. He had a quill and paper, pretending to compose while chewing away at a handkerchief. Felix chuckled at the sight. Cécile whispered, scolding Felix, "I wish you'd stop that handkerchief chewing, you're influencing others, it's gross."

Felix shrugged and they continued dancing away in the lovely night. Everything felt perfect.

~~~

Felix jumped awake from a knock at the door. He was laying on the sofa in the parlor. His body was tired from a concert the night before. It was the busy month of October. He forced himself to sit up and rubbed his face awake. The door was knocked again and the bell rang. Felix stood from the sofa to answer. The clock near the door read nine in the morning. He opened the door and in the most surprise he found Klingemann standing in the doorway.

"Karl! Do come in!" Felix let him in with the warmest smile. Karl shook his hand tightly, "I came straight from London. I thought it time I'd check out your home here."

After they greeted, they walked to the parlor. Cécile came from the nursery, holding their new child Marie. Born on the second of October. Little Carl crawled about behind her.

Klingemann couldn't believe his eyes at such a sweet family. He had not met Cécile nor the children. He gasped in awe, "Such a perfect family!"

"Dankeschön." Felix stood proud. He then gestured Klingemann to sit so they could catch up. It began well with tea and such, but Karl sighed to Felix, "I say I do have some sour news. Professor Rosen passed away."

"He did!? He was such a kind man." Felix gave a sigh, remembering Mr. Rosen in his trips to London. Klingemann suggested, "But let us talk of happier things, you've had too much loss to worry about in the past few years."

Felix nodded with slight sadness but found another subject, "My sister Fanny and her husband are planning a trip to Italy. I wrote to Fanny giving advice on everything she needs to check out there. It felt quite fun writing to her. I miss that trip. I miss London as well."

"Other than Mr. Rosen, London hasn't changed too much. Ignaz and Charlotte still reside at Chester Place with their children. Little Felix Moscheles seems to like drawing. Ignaz said he constantly catches him sneaking into the ink and trying to scribble on the floors."

"Maybe he is to be an artist someday." Felix laughed. Klingemann chuckled, "I don't know, but if that's the case, you may need to visit to teach him some things."

"Maybe." Felix smiled.

# Chapter XXI: Gutenberg

**Mendelssohn, Symphony no. 2 'Lobgesang' [1]**

**Year of 1840**

**[1]**

Felix watched intently as the blank stride of paper was compressed under the printing press, given a pattern of ink. It became one of his latest works he had deemed ready for publishing. The satisfaction of getting it hard copied made him ever so grateful for the discovery of the press.

The print master chose the next set of blocks. There were plenty of tiles to get what was needed as much music had been printed before. The publisher made sure the pressman understood where the notes should be if a block needed to be etched or carved.

As things came together, more beautiful sheets of music were produced. Upon holding a fresh crisp reproduction, Felix felt a spurt of excitement. His mind sprang out with music.

In a hurry, he raced home from the print shop. He sat at the writing desk with a pen and manuscript. A gleaming light from the orchestra came together in the form of chords as if the sun were rising in song. The melodies poured like fine Bier.

It so happened that the coming June was the 400th anniversary of Gutenberg's printing press. Felix determined it to be the perfect opportunity to write a work inspired by such. He started making outlines, taking seriously the details of his craft. If something could look nice, he took the time to make it that way. His good handwriting he learned from Eduard Reitz, made the music look all the more artistic.

Felix decided the work should be a symphony. A full one with choir. Since Beethoven's 9th symphony, which was the first to include the use of human voices, other composers began following that pattern. Berlioz was the first to coin the term Choral Symphony. Felix preferred his to be a Symphony Cantata in relation to Bach's chorale music. To fit the theme of a Cantata more so, he worked it out as a 'Lobgesang' or 'Hymn of Praise,' basing it on biblical text.

It became a large work consisting of thirteen movements. To the average person, the score appeared as a large jumble, but Felix had it carefully organized.

Felix's busy life by no means ceased in the midst of creating such a taxing project. There were still rehearsals to conduct, a house to take head of, a wife to tend to and children to feed.

*(Mendelssohn in 1840)*

The more Felix soaked himself into his regular duties, the more he craved to compose; all day every day. Some days he was bestowed with his wish, but most days he hardly managed penning a bar. It seemed the seconds, minutes and hours slipped away at each stroke of the pen.

When he did obtain a day to himself, hours were spent at the writing desk in the parlor. He feverishly penned as to not waste a moment. The nice fountain pen strode smoothly on each manuscript, better than any old quill.

At the noon hour, Cécile wandered up behind him, "Why don't you go eat lunch. I just got Marie to nap and I have letters I want to write. You have hoarded the desk all morning."

496

"Alright." Felix got up, taking his papers to the dining room. Johann had set a plate of cheese, bread and olive oil. Two year old Carl sat at the table, playing with his slices of cheese.

"Stop playing with your food. Eat." Felix scolded. Carl gave his father a silly smirk but obeyed. Felix ate while penning his score. Every now and again, a hum or phrase escaped his mouth in thought. Carl began to mimic, "Da-da-da-"

Felix couldn't help but smile as his son had been progressing in learning to speak. Every moment of his small voice gave Felix joy. Felix turned to Carl, "You know, that was quite a good idea." He wrote a little segment of the phrase that made sense musically. Carl giggled, now knowing he had influence. He tried to mimic more to be funny, but Felix concentrated on his own mind.

~~~

When June came, Felix's hard work paid off. He finished his symphony cantata. Despite anticipating future revising as everything else, he deemed it ready for the copyist. It helped hasten the process of preparing it for rehearsals.

When rehearsals did commence, the days became long. Oftentimes, Felix was hardly home; leaving in the early morning to the Gewandhaus only to return to his family at a late hour. His wife and children didn't like such stretches of time.

One evening, at the dark tenth hour, Felix sighed as he walked into the house. Cécile sat in the parlor, sewing by the warm fireplace. The children were put to bed already. After Johann took his coat, Felix flopped onto the sofa next to Cécile. She glanced at him, "How was work today honey?"

"Tiring. There are many upcoming concerts."

"I'm sure once these concerts come and go, you'll get a break."

"I hope so. Right now Liszt and Thalberg are in the city."

"I thought you weren't fond of Liszt." Cécile indicated confusion, not turning from her needlework. Felix shrugged, "I've become more acquainted. Socially he has changed for the better. At the piano, his independence of finger can scarcely be equaled. The other directors insisted he come. Yet, his concerts are at a high price which of course is making all of Leipzig grumble. Thalberg though, you would not believe. I find him the most superb pianist of our time. Later this week I am to host a soirée for Liszt at the Gewandhaus if you want to come. There will be wine, cakes and music."

"I'd like to." Cécile nodded, finishing up in darning a pair of stockings. Felix brushed off all his tiring thoughts, "Anyways, how were the children today?"

"Good. They went to bed on time...I almost forgot, you did receive a letter. It's from Herr Hiller." She handed him a folded note. Felix opened it and read in quietness. The crackling fireplace gave a sense of peacefulness. Yet, the calm was disrupted by a light whimper. Cécile looked up from her fabrics to see Felix's face pouring with tears.

"What does it say?"

"Herr Hiller lost his Mutter." Felix felt the loss of his father flood back into his mind. Cécile set her stocking down and hugged her husband. They both snuggled a while.

~~~~

The next week, the street surrounding the Mendelssohn apartment was filled with nothing but musical passages of Bach. Felix had been practicing various fugues and chorales for the past eight days. The efforts were for a concert at the St. Thomas school where Bach had once directed.

Felix wanted to raise money for a monument to be put up in memory of Bach as to make the place a destination. In turn it would help the chorus there flourish. The school happened to be near the Mendelssohn apartment.

*(St. Thomas Church, watercolour by Felix)*

After finishing up last minute practicing, Felix packed up his music to head out to the school. Cécile gave him a kiss before he left for work. Before exiting the house Felix paused, turning to Cécile, "I wanted to ask, do you think it's possible we could invite Herr Hiller to stay with us for a while? I want to help him find comfort from his loss."

"I don't see why not. I'll have Johann organize a bed in the drawing room as he did when my mother visited."

"Danke. I'll write to Hiller. Anyways, see you later." Felix gave a parting kiss then walked to the St. Thomas school in gratitude. To his hopes, the concert caused a good crowd to assemble, all eager to hear the organ works of Bach.

Felix took his spot at the grandest of all instruments, the organ. He set his music on the stand and began the recital without haste. The nine pieces he presented earned him 300 dollars. A decent amount for a decent memorial.

After the success, Felix returned home and went to the writing desk to organize letters. First he read the received mail. Each letter contained requests to judge various music competitions. The composer Spohr was hosting them in Vienna. Felix had much respect for Spohr, but could not accept to judge such things. He had done so in local events but after doing so, vowed to decline offers of competitions. He deemed them far too distracting and gave an unwell outlook in composing for a prize.

Felix set the business notes aside and grabbed a fresh leaf of paper. He wrote a heartfelt letter to Herr Hiller, giving grievances then inviting him to the home. While finishing it, Cécile came into the parlor with another letter. She set it beside Felix as he signed his current writing. He then folded the letter and handed it off for Johann to send.

After wiping away his mild tears, Felix opened the next note. It was another request, but not concerning music. He informed Cécile, "The artist Herr Rietschel would like me to his studio. He wants to make a cast of my hand."

"That would be nice. A cast of your lovely piano hands."

"I have time today, so I'll go." Felix cleaned up the desk. He took the note with Rietschel's address along with him when going out to find a cab. An open gig passed by so Felix boarded it for a ride to a quaint wooden home settled between two apartment complexes.

After knocking at the door, a man wearing a muddied apron answered. He seemed near Felix's age and had a complexion of intellectual standing. His brown hair had bits of marble dust drizzled about.

"Are you Herr Ernst Rietschel? The sculptor?" Felix questioned.

"Ja, ja. Excuse my messy state, do come in." Ernst gladly gestured him into his humble studio. It was a large open room containing workspace for sculpting and pottery. Living space with necessities such as a stove and bed were settled in one area. It was kept simple as the main means of living was art itself. Felix always adored these artists' way of life.

The workspace at the moment had a few marble busts in progress. Felix then noticed a bucket of plaster. Beside it sat a few casts of hands. Some were chipped, while others fine and polished. Ernst explained, "As you can see, I have been practicing hand casts. Ignore those chipped ones, those were first attempts. I thought you'd be an excellent subject as one of your piano hands would make a nice sculpture."

"It looks like fun." Felix had excitement to dunk his hands in plaster. Herr Rietschel mixed the liquid plaster and added water to keep it from hardening. He then had Felix dip his right hand into it. They waited until the plaster firmed up. Felix pulled his hand out then watched Ernst take a different mix of plaster and fill the mold.

When it became solid, he flipped the whole bucket to put the block of plaster on the table. He used a hammer and chisel to break it apart. Inside, the hand cast stayed in perfect contact. Felix looked at it with intrigue, "Surely I'll pay you for this."

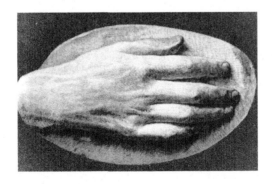

*(Cast of Mendelssohn's hand)*

"Nein, it was practice." Ernst cleaned up bits of plaster then handed the finished product to Felix.

"Dankeschön."

"I am primarily a sculptor of busts, so in future if you need one done, come to me." Ernst mentioned. Felix nodded then went on his way.

~~~~

The next week, I paid a visit to the Mendelssohn apartment. Felix had a stir of excitement as he showed me the hand cast. I found it quite interesting, but questioned, "Doesn't not Herr Rietschel reside In Dresden?"

"He is visiting. His studio is set up in a fine wood home."

"Intriguing. He is probably the best sculptor in Germany." I stated. Felix nodded then mentioned, "Herr Hiller is to be coming today. He will be staying a while to heal from the loss of his Mutter. We should go for a walk as we have time before he comes." He fetched his coat from the entryway. I grabbed mine and we headed out.

*(The Small Market, watercolour by Felix)*

It was a normal afternoon in Leipzig. People were at work, children were at play after their schooling and horses clopping to and fro. We strolled to the markets to skim the fresh produce. Many displays were full of color.

One young girl had a stand of imported fruits. Many of which appeared quite strange. One sort had the colors of pink with hints of green, looking like scales. Felix picked one up, "What are these?"

"That is dragon fruit. It's from a sort of cactus. They originated from Taiwan." The girl informed with bright excitement, "I will admit, dragon fruit is my favorite."

"Interesting." Felix debated buying one, yet after seeing the price, discarded the idea. We took home persimmons and an assortment of wines instead. On coming to the complex, a carriage was parked on the street side in front. Herr Hiller climbed out with a bag of luggage. Felix and I rushed to him, greeting him with friendly embraces.

"Please, do come in, a bed is prepared for you in the drawing room." Felix took his luggage in the house. Hiller followed him to get settled. Meanwhile, I set our market purchases on the dining table to share. I found a few wine glasses in the cabinet. Felix came back and grabbed a block of cheese from the kitchen storage. He sliced a few pieces of drunken goat cheese along with the persimmons.

By the time Hiller settled, we had our wine party set. Felix wasn't hasty to start gulping down the aged fermented grape juice. He always swallowed it with immense satisfaction. Hiller tasted each sort before choosing one to fill his glass. I picked a sweet red wine.

Cécile walked in with surprise, "Felix!"

"Ja honey?" Felix perceived her tone scornful. She came closer to the table, "Why didn't you tell me you were hosting a wine party? Can I join."

"Of course." Felix kindly stood and in a gentlemanly fashion helped her get seated. The rest of the evening was filled with talk, wine and cheese tasting.

~~~

The next morning, Felix, Cécile and the two children sat at the breakfast table. Hiller got around to waking and joined them. Johann set out a simple start to the day with coffee, bread and butter. The coffee was quite dark, so Hiller added much cream. The bread appeared light and fresh with the crust dusted in flour. Creamy, salted butter topped it all off.

After Hiller took his serving of food, he noticed Felix dunking his bread in coffee like a young schoolboy rather than eat it with butter. Hiller questioned, "Don't you like fresh butter?"

"I despise it. It tastes like salted lard."

"It does not. It's creamy." Hiller ate another bite of buttered bread. Felix rolled his eyes and ate his coffee dunked bread. Little Carl played with his bread, causing Felix to scold the boy. Cécile was busy holding Marie.

When breakfast ended, Felix and Hiller headed out to the markets. They had planned to compose music in the day and wanted snacks while doing so. As they skimmed the apples and oranges, the girl selling the imported fruit called to Felix, "Come here."

"Ja?" Felix went to her. She pointed to the dragon fruit, "I'll give you a deal on the dragon fruit, they need to go before they spoil."

"I'll buy two so my friend and I can both try it." Felix made his purchase. Hiller found a few plums then they left the market. In returning to the apartment, Felix put the fruit in a bowl and set it on the table. It looked quite pretty with the pink and green dragon fruit beside the purple plums.

Hiller grabbed a folio of his compositions in progress. Felix took his folder from a shelf. The two composers sat opposite of each other, writing in peacefulness, dipping pens in the same inkstand. Their silence only broke on rare intervals by a joke or other. They needed not the piano though the entire setting.

In a break, Hiller grabbed a dragon fruit to try. While breaking it open with a knife, Felix giggled in finishing up a piece.

"What did you write?" Hiller was curious.

"A piece inspired by yesterday's wine." Felix took the other dragon fruit for himself. Upon biting it, it's sweet taste was kiwi like. Hiller took Felix's paper to examine it. It was titled 'Liebe und Wein (Op. 50 no. 5).'

"I believe it would sound best by a group of drunken men, but not too drunk. Just enough to sing with jolly." Felix stated. Hiller chuckled then noticed Felix grab a large score. When seeing the title he recognized that it was the recent 'Lobgesang' Felix had completed. It was already in print. Hiller asked, "Why are you still penning on that? Is it not finished?"

"Revising," Felix corrected, "every brushstroke counts." He adjusted dynamic markings. Hiller then noticed drafts of the work laying nearby. The system Felix used in concern to writing the choruses puzzled him. He questioned in reproach, "Why are you using C clefs for all of the voices and why is the alto line in the soprano clef? It makes everything inconsistent."

"You are perfectly right, but it is not my fault. It was Zelter's way, and I accustomed myself to it from the very first," Felix admitted. Hiller turned back to his own work. He had a few pieces for piano that could be completed by supper.

When the hour of super did come, Johann set the table for a scrumptious meal of baked potatoes. He had excellent cooking skills causing everyone to make quick work of the food.

Afterwards, Felix and Hiller went to the parlor where the piano was situated. It happened to be acquired from the committee of the Gewandhaus, presented to Cécile after Felix settled in Leipzig with his new wife. It was an excellent instrument. Felix and Hiller used the remainder of the evening to test out their compositions.

~~~

The next day rendered similar to the last. Sharing ink at the dining table. Felix held a completed d minor trio with immense satisfaction. Hiller looked at it but his expression gave way to worry. In his opinion he found a small misgiving, "Those broken chords in the piano passages seem a bit old fashion, does it not? I think they shouldn't be broken and played normally. It should have richness of passage."

"Do you think that this would make the thing any better? The piece would be the same and so it may remain as it is." Felix crossed his arms like a child refusing to listen.

"But," Hiller answered, "You have often told me, and proved to me by your actions, that the smallest touch of the brush, which might conduce to the perfection of the whole, must not be despised. An unusual form of arpeggio may not improve the harmony, but neither does it spoil it-and it becomes more interesting to the player."

Felix replied with nothing and went to the piano to prove his point over Hiller and vise versa. They worked it over and over. In the end, Hiller was triumphant in changing Felix's view. In turn, Felix with his conscientiousness had to take the lengthy task of rewriting the whole pianoforte part. It pained him, but the piece would turn out better among musicians as it would allow them to show off their skills.

After much correcting, Felix suggested, "Why don't we do something else besides bicker over our ways. I say we should invite Herr David with us for a walk to the Rosenthal."

"Alright." Hiller complied, putting his music away. They both grabbed their coats and headed down the cold street.

There at my apartment, they invited me to join them. I had finished my practice and work, so took the stroll far out into the Rosenthal with them. Felix suggested, "We should stop at the café and play a game of billiards."

"I'm game." I answered. Hiller shrugged, "Sure." In truth he believed Felix's latest passion for billiards to be a very passing indulgence. Hiller had played much but admitted knowing nothing of the game. He couldn't judge if Felix was as clever at it as he was in everything else.

When entering the café and beginning a game, the visiting continued. Felix liked repeating or bringing up any funny expression, joke or piano passage he liked. While speaking about piano he stated, "We should have brought Herr Schumann along. He would have had much to say about the music we talk about. I think highly of his opinions."

"Robert is too busy in his life right now with work, newspapers and trying to approach Clara in marriage." I informed, "It could take years as I heard that Herr Weick is causing all sorts of scandal against Robert."

"Really, what sorts of things?" Felix questioned.

"All dreadful lies that Robert can not sustain a living. Herr Weick wants money from both Clara and Robert."

"I hope things work out for them soon." Felix hit a ball with the stick, missing the hole. He sighed in frustration. Billiards were not his forte in reality.

~~~

Hiller's stay at the Mendelssohn home soon added to a few days. He decided it was time to find his own lodgings so as to not burden the family. A nice hotel suited in which he could retreat and be alone.

The choice also alluded to the fact that being around Felix all so often made it bound to catch him in a fit of frustration or irritability. The happy, innocent, carefree man could turn into the most heated creature imaginable. Whether it were a bad day or a case of writer's block, Felix's energy could channel sourly in a flash.

Hiller happened at his home on one such occasion. Johann answered Hiller's knock and let him in. The poor servant seemed tired. Grunts of frustration could be heard coming from the parlor. Hiller headed there and found Felix sitting at the writing desk, scribbling on a manuscript. Other papers sat about crumpled up or torn.

Felix furiously scratched at the desk, not noticing Hiller watching. Hiller felt frightened at his friend's fury towards himself. He stood quietly, deciding not to consult him yet. Felix's anger soon cooled, but he became restless in a feverish way. He snapped at himself in almost a crying tone, "Why can't I just get it!? Why can't I just write it!? What is wrong with me!? I'm stupid! UHHHH!"

"What is the matter with you?" Hiller finally called.

"There I have been sitting for the last four hours trying to alter a few bars of a song and can't do it." Felix threw his pen. Hiller glanced towards one of the bedrooms where Cécile stood. She rolled her eyes, "It's that sort of day...where I'm caring for three children..."

Hiller turned back to Felix to see what he was grumbling over. It was a quartet for men's voices. He had twenty different versions, most of which would have satisfied anyone.

"What you could not do today in four hours, you will be able to do tomorrow in as many minutes." Hiller grabbed Felix's hand to stop him from scratching at the desk. Felix calmed down after the sensible suggestion. Hiller decided he wasn't going to visit long.

508

Before heading out the door, he told Johann, "Be sure Felix doesn't drink anything with caffeine. No coffee or black tea. Only herbal."

"I think that's for the best." Johann agreed. Hiller made his leave. As soon as he did, Felix called to Johann, "Johann! Fetch me a fine brew of coffee!"

"I'll get you something." Johann went to the cabinet and chose chamomile tea with honey to calm him, and the household.

~~~~

"Felix!" I called from the entryway of the Mendelssohn apartment during a busy afternoon, "The orchestra needs you to play Beethoven's fifth piano concerto for a concert, Clara is under the weather."

"Just a minute." Felix shuffled about in the parlor, fumbling drawers. I waited by the door, glancing at the clock. It was half past noon and I needed Felix to the Gewandhaus before one. I was to conduct as the concertos were my duty. All became quiet in the parlor. I called again, "We need to go now."

In getting no answer I walked into the house more. To my surprise I found Felix at the writing desk, sitting in his concert attire. He was in the middle of penning a piece for men's voices with much ease, his mood chipper in doing so. Felix then stood from his seat, ready to go. Cécile was dressed to attend as well, leaving the children with Johann.

Upon getting in a carriage to the Konzerthaus, a sore throat began to beseech Felix. By the time we reached our destination, he developed a cough. Cécile with her wifely worries asked, "Are you alright to play?"

"I'll make it through." Felix assured as the carriage halted. Cécile gave a sigh as her husband ran off to meet with the orchestra. Herr Hiller joined with Cécile as I hurried off to catch up with Felix. The concert hall was packed, but I heard a mix of murmurs. Some were disappointed that Clara wasn't playing, but others were excited that Felix was the fill in.

When it came time to start, Felix entered the stage. He put a handkerchief in his pocket as if he'd blown his nose. I could tell he had a head cold, yet the man pursued on by sitting at the keys. He sat patiently as I joined the orchestra at the conducting stand. With the gesture of the hand, the musicians burst forth the strong Eb major chord. Felix then strode the arpeggios in grace yet sniffing from a runny nose.

After the first movement, the real struggle came during the Adagio as a coughing fit commenced, nearly halting his playing. Some in the audience whispered in suspense, but Felix pulled through. As the concerto went on, the less spirited his playing became, but in an odd sense it sounded better than his at home practice. With a sense of relief he managed to finish the challenging third movement.

After the concert, Hiller escorted Cécile outside. As they waited for Felix near the front doors, some ladies nearby spoke of the performance. One sighed, "Oh that poor Felix, he appeared so tired. I heard Clara Wieck was ill. That's why she didn't play."

"I dare say," the other lady commented, "I wouldn't call Felix poor. I would rather say that poor Cécile, his wife."

"What do you mean?" Another asked. The lady explained, "Her husband is such a cruel, inhuman man. He is barbarous to her!"

Cécile and Hiller pricked their ears in confusion. The ladies were obviously envious, wishing they were Felix's wife. When they walked off, Cécile and Hiller burst into laughter. Felix soon caught up with them, "What has got you two in a laugh?"

"Oh nothing," Cécile caressed her husband's chin, "I have the happiest life with you."

Felix smiled and the three headed back to the apartment. Hiller decided to join in dinner as it was still early evening. Felix went straight to the sofa upon returning home. When he was out of sorts, sleep was his best resource. Hiller found it quite strange as he napped for hours, so deep in slumber.

When Johann deemed dinner ready, Felix woke with capital appetite. Everyone ate a nice beef stew together. Afterwards, Felix spent time visiting with Hiller. In speaking, when a conversation was quiet or calm, Felix had a tendency to jump into a comical subject or a serious one.

As he and Hiller lounged calmly, Felix asked in a slight burst, "Do you believe in the progress of humanity?"

"How, in what way do you mean?"

"I don't speak of machines, and railways, and all those things, but I ask if you think that mankind becomes better and more remarkable as time goes on?"

"I guess it doesn't cross my mind much..." Hiller felt indifferent. Felix gave way to a yawn. It was only a quarter of an hour of conversation and he said with the air of a spoiled child, "I am still quite tired." He laid back on the sofa, stretched out, mumbling slightly, "Rest is so delicious." Within a few minutes he gave way to soft snores.

Cécile walked in as Hiller stood from his chair. She glanced at Felix apologizing, "Sorry he's being a bad host. He can go on in that way for days but then is fresher than ever."

"Nature is his cure from his busy life." Hiller gazed at Felix, who was shifting about in his sleep.

"That may be, but I'm calling for a doctor tomorrow. I think he's unwell."
Cécile stated. Hiller then mentioned, "I thank you both for hosting me, but
tomorrow I am to start my journey to Italy. It will be early morning so
please give Felix my goodbyes."

"I will. Thanks for coming." Cécile smiled. With that, Hiller made his leave.
~~~

Felix awoke the next morning still on the sofa, groggy as ever. He snoozed,
but was unpleasantly bothered as someone lightly pressed on his throat. In
opening his eyes, he realized it was a doctor checking his vitals. Cécile
stood nearby waiting to hear the diagnosis. Felix felt he had a head cold but
nothing serious. He forced himself to sit up, "I assure I am fine, it's only
a chill."

The doctor nodded, but continued his work. Felix didn't enjoy the
unexpected check up and tried to hasten it by perking up as to seem
healthy, but inside he was tired to the bones. Cécile stepped up, "Is it
really only a chill? You've been sleeping hours upon hours since the
concert yesterday."

"I see." The doctor checked Felix's eyes. They were that of an exhausted
man. The doctor stated, "I believe you are overworking yourself with
conducting and piano. It wasn't the best idea to perform with a cold as it
may turn severe. I know that September and October are the start of the
busy season so I suggested you rest the weeks before then. Your body
needs it."

"I will res-." Felix fell asleep mid-sentence. The doctor turned to Cécile,
"Next time he wakes, try to get him to bed. It will be better for him." The
doctor left. Cécile noted everything to be sure her husband obeyed
the orders.

The whole of the August month consisted of rest and regaining health. It felt like fresh air, but doing completely nothing got boring. Felix thought the extra time to be suitable for composing, but Cécile set limits.

When September came, the concert proposals were back in motion and the next weeks were booked. Felix's symphony, 'Lobgesang' was in high demand, attracting the likes of the royal courts in Germany. The King of Saxony attended the second performance at the Gewandhaus.

At that concert, the chorus and orchestra sounded their best. Felix gestured the cadence at the end of the first half, deeming it perfect so far. Before the start of the second half, someone interrupted by tapping on his shoulder. Felix glanced to find Herr Schleinitz.

"It's the middle of a concert, what do you want?" Felix whispered in annoyance.

"The King wants you." Schleinitz pointed towards the audience. Felix turned around to see the King of Saxony nod at him. Since it was an order of royalty, Felix abandoned the conducting desk, leaving the perfect performance on hold to pass through the double row of ladies.

Once Felix reached the seats of the royal court, the King spoke in the most friendly manner, "Excuse my halting the concert, but I couldn't help but tell you how superb the music sounds."

"I am happy that your majesty is pleased." Felix gave a polite bow.

"Bitte now, carry on." The King gestured him to the stage. Felix obeyed and continued with the second half of the symphony. The orchestra and chorus echoed with a pleasant reverb through the large hall.

When the grand performance finished, the clapping lasted minutes upon minutes. Every musician bowed then dispersed. As Felix packed up his music, whispers behind him gasped, "The King is coming to him this time!"

Felix turned around and the King of Saxony was passing through the row of ladies, "My dear Mendelssohn! That was the most excellent concert I've ever attended!" His manner of speech had such animation, "That music resonated through my ears. Those voices, the orchestra, everything was so perfect! Bitte, you must come to Dresden."

"I am sorry, but I am due in England in a few weeks. If you come to Birmingham you would hear it again." Felix explained. The King sighed then patted Felix on the shoulder, "I shall be patient for your return."

~~~

On the 18th of September, Felix arrived in the city that was a second home to him, London. He was to be in Birmingham, but decided to make time to stay at Chester Place with the Moscheles family. Cécile stayed home in Leipzig with the children.

When Felix entered Chester Place, Ignaz greeted him, "Welcome! You've made it an hour before dinner. Klimgemann and Mr. Chorely have joined."

"Excellent." Felix had excitement as he saw little Felix Moscheles frolic about. When the boy noticed Felix senior, he paused. In a burst of unexpectedness, little Moscheles ran to Felix and tapped his hand, "Tag, you're it!"

"I'll get you." Felix immersed himself into the child's game. He chased and managed to tag him. The two ran about the house and it went on vice versa. At times, little Moscheles jumped with so much energy, it made the house near shake.

"Felix!" Charlotte scolded her child. Both Felix and little Felix looked at her. Charlotte looked towards little Felix, "Don't be jumping. Why don't you and Felix go do something more calm, like sketching."

514

"Yes mum." The young boy grabbed a sketchbook. Felix watched him doodle with much interest. Little Felix penciled a tree then tried to sketch an axe to chop it down. Yet he wasn't sure how to start it. He made a line but already felt dissatisfied. Felix senior instructed, "Here, let me help." He took the pencil, forming a line to make the drawing the desired object. Young Moscheles smiled and continued on.

Dinner soon commenced and everyone took their seating. Felix sat between Klingemann and Ignaz. Mr. Chorely sat across from them along with Charlotte and the children. It was a handsome meal of shepherds pie. As the group took their plates, Mr. Chorley asked Felix, "So that 'Hymn of Praise' is to be performed in Birmingham?"

"Ja, are you and Klingemann joining Ignaz and I?" Felix questioned as he put extra cheese on top of the minced meat. Klingemann confessed, "I believe the trip shall be only you and Ignaz. I am bombarded with work and Mr. Chorely is as well."

"I will be coming to Leipzig," Mr. Chorely added, "If Ignaz still has plans to go."

"Yes, I am stopping there on my way to Prague." Ignaz politely took a bite of vegetables. Felix brightened, "I had no clue you were coming, I do offer my home if you need a place to stay."

"I'll see, but a hotel will do me fine." Ignaz assured. The evening ended after finishing the hearty plates. Desert consisted of creamy English trifles.

~~~

On the 20th of September, Felix and Ignaz arrived at the Stork Hotel in Birmingham. It wasn't tall, but it had a quaint tavern feel. The rooms were clean and comfortable. Their stay in Birmingham was a busy one right from the start.

Before unpacking anything, Felix was requested to rehearsals for the concert that afternoon. Though the day was already booked, he found time to make sketches for Felix and Emily Moscheles.

*(Sketch of Birmingham)*

The concert hall was settled in an interesting neighborhood, full of commotion. The brick streets were bustling with nicely dressed people. Everything about Birmingham had a properness to it. The feel of it made time slip away. Felix felt as if one second he were penciling in a sketchbook then in rehearsals the next. The orchestra was organized and always ready. Soon he was conducting the 'Hymn of Praise' before a massive audience.

After finishing, the audience left, leaving the concert hall in an echo of silence. Felix stuck around the stage with a group of friends, including Ignaz.

A large organ had been built into the wall of the concert house, so Felix felt the need to check it out. For three quarters of an hour, he played as if he'd neither been hearing nor conducting, only as if the day had just begun.

Felix and Ignaz returned to the hotel and had supper in the tavern. There were foods in Birmingham that Felix had not tried before. Though he hated butter, his favorite dish became bread and butter pudding. The soft bread with freshly melted butter appealed to his taste. He obtained the recipe to take home.

Before leaving back to London, Felix roamed the street and happened upon a fabric shop selling sewing supplies. He remembered that Charlotte was struggling to get projects finished as her old pair of scissors had dulled, so Felix purchased a fine new pair.

Hours later in a carriage, Felix and Ignaz returned to Chester Place, but not to stay long. Ignaz packed for a trip through Germany to Prague. While he was busy, Felix presented Charlotte with the scissors. She had much happiness as her fabric work would be much easier. In turn she presented him a new cravat, another that he would have to figure out. Felix tried to tie it on the spot but couldn't get it to sit right on his shirt collar, "These new cravats are so hard to tie."

"Pin it up." Charlotte pronounced the magic words. All problems were solved. By the time the ordeal with the cravat ended, Ignaz was ready to go. Charlotte gave Felix an umbrella to barrow, figuring Ignaz could bring it back.

At the harbor, the luggage was piled together. Mr. Chorely was still on his way. Felix sketched the scene in the meantime. A sad grey chill filled the surroundings whenever leaving London.

*(Packing up. \*Notice the Stork Hotel in the background and a pair of scissors formed into a stork.)*

Chorley soon showed up and the three travelers carried their belongings on the ferry. Felix had much in his hands, but managed. When stepping on the dock to board, he dropped the umbrella. It fell in the water and the folded thing sank. Ignaz gave an irritated sigh as it was technically his. Felix had never made Mr. Moscheles upset so fell in utter silence. He settled his luggage, feeling a complete klutz. The stuffy air only lasted so long as the harsh waters towards Germany made Ignaz forget about the umbrella.

Before reaching Leipzig, the group made rest stops in Hamburg and Berlin. In Berlin, Felix paid a visit to his family. His mother and siblings were living well. Paul was now married and making a life at the bank house. Lea still had plenty of company at the estate with Fanny and Wilhelm living nearby. She was satisfied as long as her grandchildren visited.

Felix and Ignaz also paid a visit to the Konzerthaus in Berlin, where Felix sketched the layout of it. He couldn't help but doodle music as well.

*(Rough Seas and Konzerthaus Layout)*

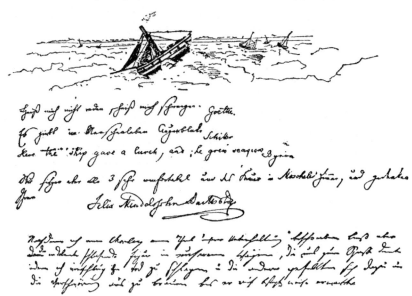

In finally coming to Leipzig, Chorely and Moscheles settled in a hotel. Felix went home, happy to be with his family. His children missed him ever so. Carl jumped at him until he picked him up. Cécile held little Marie. The child reached for her father, so Felix cuddled both Cécile and Marie. Carl budded in of course. The relief of being home cured every ounce stress.

In the evening, Felix invited Ignaz and Chorely to dinner. Johann began cooking a large chicken pot pie to share. It gave a pleasant smell through the home. The children impatiently waited for the food. Ignaz and Chorely looked about the home, impressed with the cozy atmosphere. Felix got them settled in the parlor with some light coffee then said, "Excuse me a moment, I'll be back." He ventured off to a room down the hall.

As Felix was gone, little Carl came into the parlor, intrigued by the guests. He listened to them speak while heading for the piano. Ignaz glanced at Carl with a smile. The boy asked, "Do you play like my papa?"

"I don't know." Ignaz set his cup down. He sat next to Carl, "Let's find out." Ignaz held his arms towards the keys. Instead of placing his fingers, he made his hands into a fist and began playing melodies as so. Carl giggled loudly while watching. Felix came back to the parlor, laughing at such a sight.

"Dinner is ready!" Johann called. Everyone went to the dining room and sat around the table. The large supper pie looked so appetizing. Felix told Johann, "It looks beautiful, good job."

"Danke. There is another pie as well. A desert one." He brought a pecan pie to the table, "It is for after the healthy stuff." He eyed the children and Felix. Johann joined the table and everyone began eating. Felix mentioned, "Tomorrow evening there is to be a musical party. Herr David has been organizing it as I've been gone. The orchestra, chorus and guests are to be there."

"Sounds like fun." Mr. Chorley sipped some wine. Johann then stood, "Oh, I almost forgot. I tried that recipe you gave me Felix." He left and came back with a plate of bread and butter pudding. Felix looked at it with excitement. Cécile had confusion, "I thought you hated butter."

"I do, but in this dish, it tastes good." Felix took a few scoops of the pudding.

~~~

That next evening, I watched in satisfaction as many guests poured into the Gewandhaus for the party I had organized. There were 300 invited plus the chorus of 140 voices and the orchestra. Everyone had excitement as the champagne passed around. A few musicians began to play tunes to entertain the oncoming guests.

I waited patiently for Felix as I had not seen him since he took his trip to Birmingham. Many guests stopped to speak with me, all asking, "Herr David, are you going to play tonight?"

"Ja, Ja, of course." I pandered in reply. A few minutes before the hour, Felix came walking with Ignaz, Cécile and another man through the doors. It made the crowd all the more eager, whispering, "Mendelssohn and Moscheles both have come!"

The group of four spotted me right away. When they reached me, Felix introduced the man I had not seen before, "Ferdinand, this is Mr. Chorely. Mr. Chorely, This is Herr David."

"How do you do?" Chorely shook my hand. I nodded, "Very well, Danke."

Our group then proceeded towards the stage. Guests now were scattered and in a chatter with their French bubbly and hors d'oeuvre. Felix jumped right into the party as he liked anything social. Cécile kept at his side as she noticed a gaggle of ladies encircling him.

While most ladies were kind towards them, a few whispered and gazed at Cécile, still wishing to be in her place. Though Cécile heard every remark, Felix was oblivious to it as his heart only looked to his precious gem of a wife.

Soon the chorus and orchestra beckoned me to the stage. Felix was distracted in an animated conversation, so I took the back of his coat collar and pulled him away from the circle of guests. Felix noticed the waiting musicians, so followed me on the stage.

After I sat in my chair with my violin, Felix stood with his hands raised to conduct. Every musician gave him a tilt of the head. His bâton wasn't in his hand. He noticed and pulled one from his sleeve. It made the orchestra chuckle. The party only got better with good music; some serious and other ones for fun. It made for a memorable night.

~~~

The time came all too soon for Ignaz and Mr. Chorley to make their leaves. For Mr. Chorely, he had to head back to England straight away. Ignaz was continuing his journey to Prague to visit his mother. Felix asked Ignaz sadly while helping him gather luggage, "When is your carriage coming?"

"Well this time I decided to try something new. I'm going to take the train to Prague."

"Oh, interesting." Felix felt curious as the rail system was becoming more and more popular. Over the last few years, train stations were being built in each city. There was one in Leipzig.

Felix took the carriage with Ignaz to the station to check it out. When they arrived, the train's whistle blew like a steam boat. Towards the front, rail men were preparing coal to burn. Ignaz stated, "Well, I guess I'll find out how fast this will get me to Prague."

As the whistle blew once more, Ignaz boarded. He waved as the train chugged out of the station. Felix waved back, finding such a machine interesting. He then returned home in a dull quietness.

After the leave of guests, the days at the house became calm with rest. It felt good to be back in a normal, healthy routine. Not too busy but not too lazy. Whenever Felix worked at the writing desk in the parlor, little Carl continuously went to the piano asking, "How does uncle Moscheles play?"

Felix set his pen down and sat by Carl. He tried to imitate Ignaz's funny way of playing with his fists. The melody he tried was in A flat, 6/8 time. It sounded quite miserable but entertained Carl. A knock at the door interrupted the bonding moment. Felix got up to answer, finding his brother Paul.

"Come in." Felix smiled at the unexpected visit. He guided him to the parlor. Johann gathered a tray of tea together. Paul seemed to be on important business as he had a folio of various papers. When Felix sat next to him with the hot herbal water, Paul began, "I have come with an important engagement. Remember when I mentioned that Frederick William the IV wanted to organize an academy of music in Berlin? Well, now that he has been crowned King, he has furthered the plans for a school of arts."

"Really? That would be good for Berlin. Of course there is the Sing-Akademie, but a school dedicated to the teaching of specific subjects would do the city well." Felix nodded with satisfaction. Paul explained further, "There are to be four classes. Painting, sculpture, architecture and music. A director will be appointed for each subject. The King has officially chosen you to direct the music department." Paul handed him a letter of approval.

"You mean he appointed me a position that I know not much of? Let alone fully agree?" Felix tilted his head.

"Well, the school is not formed yet, so there is nothing to worry about now, but it is the King that appointed you. Once again I strongly suggest you to comply. There will be plenty of concerts to conduct at the royal theater; sacred and secular, you'll make a good sum and be close to the family home. Mutter misses you."

"It sounds good, but what about my position here? I do not want to give it up. I am fortunate with my salary here in Leipzig."

"Well, Herr Massow, a correspondent of the King sent me this to give you," Paul handed Felix a letter of Frederick William himself discussing a sum of three thousand Thalers. Felix looked at it, still doubtful. Paul pushed, "It is the King of Prussia we are talking about."

"I do want to please his majesty, but for now I shall keep my reserve of the matter until the plans are more detailed. I promise to visit Berlin in the spring, but I tell you that I do not want to foolishly give up my station here at the Gewandhaus."

"There is still time to think." Paul stood up, "Like I said, the academy is still being planned out so you don't have to leave Leipzig for a while." He grabbed his coat to leave for his hotel. As soon as the door shut, Felix gave an anxious sigh, wondering what mess this would turn out to be.

~ ~ ~

Before the end of 1840, Felix hosted a dinner party at his home where friends came to sing and eat roast beef. The celebration was in part for his friends Robert and Clara, who were both now Schumann. They had been wedded for a few months. Felix had not the chance to do something for them, so decided this to be a perfect opportunity.

As dinner commenced, Robert sat between his bride and Felix. He grabbed a score from a folder and showed Felix, explaining, "This is my newest work. I'm having it copied. Is there any way to have it performed at the Gewandhaus?"

"Let me see." Felix examined it. It was titled 'Spring Symphony.' The music looked well; quite well in fact. Felix nodded, "There shall be a concert early in the new year."

"Dankeschön!" Robert cheered, becoming the happiest a man could be. He gave Clara a light kiss in his joy. Schleinitz who was sitting across from Felix asked, "Felix, so I hear you are to be in Berlin sometime in the spring?"

"It's only a short visit to see what the King has planned for the academy there. He appointed me director but I don't know what all of the details are. I don't want to abandon Leipzig." Felix noticed Cécile, who was beside him, become troubled in expression. He forgot to tell her the news.

After everyone left for the evening, Cécile stayed at the table with Felix. She spoke her mind, "Felix. I don't think you should go to Berlin. You were gone so much in England and I don't think I can handle moving the children to a new city."

"I know honey. I don't want to move either, that is why I'm only visiting, to try to organize someone else to be director. It is not for a few months yet. After I conduct Robert's symphony I will try to make my trip to Berlin as short as possible. I do want to visit my family. Paul told me that my Mutter is missing me terribly."

"Paul is trying to get you to stay in Berlin."

"He's just doing what the King wanted." Felix made an understanding tone. Cécile added, "There's something else. Another reason. We have a nice home here and it's been so good to the children..." She trailed off.

"And?" Felix wanted her to continue. Cécile blushed, "With our growing family it will only make it more of a challenge."

"You're pregnant again!" Felix jumped in excitement. Cécile hugged him tightly, "I feel that this place is the best for us."

"I know." Felix embraced with many kisses. Little Carl peeked from around the corner, "Ew!"

"Carl! It's bedtime." Felix went to the boy and picked him up. Little Marie had been put to bed before the dinner party. Carl fussed, "Nein bed! Nein bed! Chocolate!"

"It's too late for sweets. If you don't sleep, you'll have no energy for tomorrow." Felix tucked him in. He sat beside him, humming him to sleep. It put Carl in deep slumber right away.

After the children were settled for the night, Felix went back to the parlor where Cécile sat. The fireplace illuminated the room. He sat next to her to enjoy the peaceful night at home. Cécile turned to him and they both had a moment of cuddling. Felix assured, "I will not give up our life in Leipzig."

*Side note about the Gutenberg Cantata: Mendelssohn wrote a Cantata, aside from his second symphony, dedicated to Gutenberg. The original composition of it rather fell into obscurity. Later in the 1850s, after Mendelssohn's death, the melody was arranged into the Holiday Hymn of 'Hark the Herald Angels Sing'.

# Chapter XXII: The Academy of Berlin

Schumann, Spring Symphony movement I [1]
Handel, Arrival of The Queen of Sheba [2]

## [1]

Excitement filled the Gewandhaus while Felix was in a sweat at the conducting desk. The orchestra was presenting Robert Schumann's 'Spring Symphony'. Clara Schumann had begged her husband to compose a symphony, so Robert complied as he loved his wife ever so.

The date of the premiere couldn't have fit the music any better, happening in the spring on March 31st 1841. The music gave way to a floral essence of blossoms blooming in the awakening of warm weather. With Felix's help and the cooperative audience, the music went over well.

When the last chord echoed through the Gewandhaus, there was a moment of silence. It was not until Felix turned around that the crowd gave a handsome applause. Felix looked up at Robert who was sitting in one of the boxes along with Clara. Their faces gleamed with smiles. Felix bowed then gestured towards Robert, giving credit. The concert was one to remember.

In returning home, from the afternoon concert, Felix was welcomed by three year old Carl who dashed for a hug. Two year old Marie crawled about. Cécile then came, holding the newest family member, little Paul.

Felix gave Cécile a smooch then admired the baby, named after his brother. He deemed his growing family to be the best he could wish for, but in somberness Felix sighed, "I must go pack, Berlin awaits." He headed towards the bedroom. Cécile followed him, still holding the child, "Felix, must you listen to that Herr Massow? I know his letter had importance, but must you go?"

"Herr Massow is a correspondent of the King of Prussia. I can't ignore his requests. What he writes are the King's wishes. I'm evidently the director of this academy that doesn't exist yet, so I am to help it get organized." Felix continued packing for an early morning leave. Cécile said no more, only giving a sigh.

~~~

A long carriage ride later to Berlin, the coachman parked the horses at Leipziger Straße no. 3. The estate looked the same as always, settled in it's quiet neighborhood with its sense of home. Felix exited the coach and entered the estate to be greeted overwhelmingly by Lea, "Mein Sohn! You're getting too old! I can't believe you're my 32 year old child!"

"Love you Mutter." Felix embraced. His mother had aged, but in good sense. Though the outside of the home appeared the same, the inside felt hollow. Coming back wasn't the same after Abraham's death. Felix rather wished to be with his wife and children.

After settling in his old room, he came back downstairs. His brother Paul happened to be home and greeted Felix in the parlor with a sigh of relief, "I'm so glad you decided to come."

"I'm glad to be with family." Felix didn't sound enthralled. He then turned to see a dark haired man sitting in the chair closest to the fireplace. He appeared ambitious with his hands full of various formal papers.

"This is Herr Massow." Paul introduced. Felix didn't know the man's true personality, but the fact that he was sitting in his father's old chair didn't help with first impressions. In greeting, Massow stood and shook Felix's hand, "I'm eager to start our business right away. It is the King's wishes that these plans are fulfilled in capital timing."

"Alright, but may a tray of tea be set? I'm weary from the travel."

"Of course, I could use a cuppa myself." Massow replied. Paul sent a maid to do the task. Felix sat on a couch as Massow returned to the chair. Paul pulled up another chair beside the coffee table.

When tea was set, Massow initiated the meeting, "These here are the proposals that the King has organized thus far." He set the papers on the coffee table. There were many contracts, all of them concerning Felix. One contained the proposal of terms, deeming him future director and kapellmeister of the future academy. Another discussed the pre-salary of three thousand thalers and other money concerns. The last had the plan of action to form the academy, but it wasn't descriptive.

"If you sign the contract concerning your salary, the King will pay the said pre-amount straight away." Massow explained.

"Let me look at this more," Felix skimmed the contract. Towards the bottom, a term of agreement was printed small and fine. It stated that if he signed, he was to keep in Berlin for a year. With that, he was risking his job at the Gewandhaus and his family's welfare in Leipzig.

"I don't think I want to sign." Felix felt pressure as Massow handed him a pen. Paul gave input, "I know a year sounds like a lot, but it will go fast. Your family will be happy in Berlin. The city will have much to offer. Three thousand thalers will do you good."

"It's a proposal of the King." Herr Massow persuaded further. Felix took the pen in hesitation. He held it over the empty line. In the midst of the suspense, he set the pen down, "I can not agree to this contract, however, I do intend to help get this academy organized. It seems that the King doesn't know what is all needed, so I shall make a list."

"I have blank paper." Massow handed him a leaf. Felix spoke as he wrote the list, "This is for the music department as that is what my duty is to help put together. There must be a head teacher of composition, a head for solo singing, a head for choral singing and a head for pianoforte playing.

Also teachers for the history of art and music. These courses of study are to last three years and every winter a certain number of concerts are to take place. I want the instruction to be top notch and technical perfection in art."

Herr Massow watched Felix write the requirements and felt a bit overwhelmed. The King most likely had not thought of all the technicalities. After Felix finished the paper, Massow put it in his folio and went on his way.

The days passed after the conference and Felix found himself aimlessly lounging around. He thought his stay to be pointless, but Lea enjoyed every second of his company. Paul only visited when Massow returned with King's instruction. It was in the form of a letter.

As Felix read his majesty's writing, Massow summarized, "He is letting you off for the time being, so you may go back to Leipzig. He will request you back once things progress. He still wishes you to sign for the salary, so adjusted the terms. The year-long stay does not apply."

"Alright." Felix took a pen and signed the contract, earning him three thousand thalers. With that, Felix left Berlin, hoping he didn't make any foolish moves.

~~~

"You did what!?" Cécile had a fit of fury. Felix sat at the dining table, his hands rubbing his throbbing head. He had told Cécile that he signed the contract. She snapped, "You are tied up to the King's orders now that he has paid you. I bet in a few months time he will make you go back and stay, forcing us to move there!"

"I'm sorry honey. I was careful, but when the terms were eased it sounded good. I thought a few extra thalers would be nice."

"A few extra thalers? A few extra!? He paid you three thousand! A little too good to be true? With that amount he'll expect you to do whatever he wishes."

"He knows I have a family and life, I'm sure he'll be flexible."

"He is a King. He does whatever he wants."

"Personally, I don't think he will request me back for a while. He thought he had an academy going, but I made a list inquiring what he actually needed. I have my doubts on who, if anyone, will fill those positions." Felix distracted his thoughts by holding his child Paul, but gave a sigh as his wife headed for the bedroom in somberness. Felix handed little Paul to Johann as he needed to talk to Cécile.

When following her to the bedroom, she ignored him. Felix pursued to make amends, "Cécile, I am sure things will work out. I do want to stay here."

"Felix, stop, I am not in the mood." She put her hand in his face, "Talk to the hand."

"Cécile, bitte. We need to talk." Felix gave her puppy eyes. Cécile crossed her arms, but it didn't last long as her husband's expression warmed her heart. She sighed in despair, "Oh what am I to do with you?"

"Give an array of kisses." Felix showered her in short smooches. Cécile smiled as it made her feel loved. Her temper dispersed and their amends were made.

~~~~

It was not until after the spring and the majority of the summer, that the month of August brought the unwanted call back to Berlin. It was just as Cécile had predicted. Herr Massow sent notice that King Frederick William wanted to meet Felix face to face on the matter of the 'progressing' academy.

In packing, Felix laid out various outfits, toiletries and music. He made sure to pack extra necessities as he feared the King would make him stay in Berlin for a long stretch of time.

Before leaving, the family assembled in the dining room to give their farewells. Felix first turned to Johann, "Take good care of everyone."

"You have not a thing to worry about." Johann assured. Felix gave his wife and children parting hugs and kisses. Little Marie clung to her father's ankle as Carl wrapped his arms around his legs begging, "Papa! Stay!"

"My darlings." Felix bent down to them, "I have to be gone a while, but I shall be back in due time. I will write much and be back in the blink of an eye." He then stood up and looked to Cécile who was holding little Paul. She had tears, knowing he wouldn't be back so soon. Felix's eyes dewed, "This is the sourest apple a man can eat." With that, he turned for the door.

Carl frantically followed his father, but Johann picked the boy up, trying to comfort him. The child's desperate cries echoed through the apartment halls. Each step down the stairs felt like a knife to the heart for Felix. He had to fight the tugging strings of love that begged to calm his baby. Leaving by carriage only worsened the feeling as the clopping of the horses' hooves felt like pounds at his chest, longing to stay.

~~~

"Why would Felix come back? He is too busy adhering to the orders of the King of Prussia." A flautist stated. A hornist added, "I heard he was paid a great sum."

"Gentleman." I rummaged some chords on my violin. The chatter halted and the musicians looked towards me. I had taken up the task of watching over the Gewandhaus during Felix's absence. The musicians had their doubts, so I tried to calm their gossip, "I don't think we should be quick to make assumptions. Felix has not given me word of his resignation.

He is only in Berlin as he must obey the King. That doesn't mean he intended to be there in the first place."

The musicians shrugged in the moment and rehearsals carried on. Herr Schleinitz and Hauser both still had the expressions of worry, so after rehearsals I mentioned privately, "I received a letter from Felix. He believes nothing will become of anything in Berlin as no one can make up their minds. They are having the most difficult time in finding instructors; not only in the music department but also the other subjects."

"As long as you are willing to fill in for him, we have your word." Hauser stated. I nodded, hoping Felix would return as soon as possible. It felt a hopeless situation as it was the King of Prussia wavering the direction of Felix's job.

It didn't take long for the weeks to become months with the Gewandhaus still under my direction. The year of 1842 had arrived and Felix still remained in Berlin. It was a sad sight as Cécile brought little Carl to concerts to give the boy and herself closure from Felix's absence. Each time his music was to be performed, they came, sitting in the same front corner seats.

At one concert containing Felix's piano concerto, I entered the stage, headed for the conducting desk. Before starting the performance, I glanced at the corner seats. This time they were empty.

~~~

In Berlin, Felix lazed about the parlor of the estate. He kicked back on the sofa and stared at the ceiling, studying the intricate designs as he had nothing better to do. All was quiet and boring after having returned from the residence of King Frederick. He had called Felix to another drawn out meeting about the nonexistent academy of Berlin.

Felix at this point started to devise a plan to leave the city. He thought up excuses. The most convincing was to speak of his family, deeming it too hard to move his wife and children to a different city. He decided to use that excuse at the next meeting.

"Felix!" Lea burst into the room ever so happy, "My grandchildren are here! Oh I'm so happy to finally meet little Paul! Why didn't you tell me Cécile was coming with them?"

"What!?" Felix faced palmed as his whole plan was ruined. Little Carl sprinted into the parlor, "Papa!" He jumped onto Felix's lap. Felix hugged him tightly. Cécile came, holding Marie.

"Oh, I am just so excited." Lea couldn't contain her joy as she held baby Paul. She then suggested, "I should invite Fanny and Rebecka over with their children. I want all of my grandchildren."

Paul senior came downstairs, hearing the commotion. He went to see the baby Lea held, "So this is the one named after me."

"Ja, maybe he will grow to be a banker just as you." Felix replied. He then turned to Cécile, his tone a tinge moody, "So Johann let you come?"

"Oui. He will manage the house fine." She answered, sensing that he wasn't in complete acceptance. Paul discreetly left the parlor to go pen a letter to Herr Massow, now knowing it was practical for Felix's family to move to Berlin.

Felix caught him heading for the drawing room, so set Carl down. He caught up to his brother in the corridor, "Bitte, Paul, I know you are going to write to Herr Massow. The King need not know my family is here."

"Herr Massow and the King should know."

534

"Why is it any of their business?" Felix protested. Paul crossed his arms, "Look, I know you do not want to be here in Berlin but it is the wish of the King of Prussia. I think you should take such a task more seriously. It would keep your family in good standing."

"Paul." Felix scolded, "You are being a spitting image of our Vater right now. Stop it."

"Vater's ideals were sensible and you need to adhere to them."

"I did the best I could to please him and I proved that I can keep a family with music. We fought so long over name and occupation. I don't care about the station, I care for my happiness and I happened to find work that I love to support my family. Yet it could all go away because a majesty wants me here and I am to listen because he is of high station and will bring me a higher standing. In honesty, I'd rather reject the royal affair altogether!"

"Felix!" Paul hit him in the shoulder, "You shouldn't speak like that. If you are this upset over it, you should discuss this to his majesty himself."

"The next time he requests me, I shall say something."

~~~

June 1842

"Hmm. I see..." the man in formal attire sank deep in thought while sitting at his throne. Felix kneeled before him in a beg, fidgeting with his top hat in nervousness. He had confessed his feelings to his majesty, King Frederick, on the matter of living in Berlin. It was a blunt speech, but Felix kept his stance in all properness.

"My dear Mendelssohn," Frederick spoke lightly, "you know how this city needs something to better it. You grew up and belong here at heart. It would upset me if you refused to station yourself here. I mean hurt me deeply as a friend."

"Bitte. I have a happy occupation and home in Leipzig. It pleases me and supports my family. I need not anything more than that." Felix clasped his hands. Frederick gave a sigh, giving the direct statement, "I do not give my consent. I hate to give orders to a friend, but I can not let you go."

Felix near melted from the disheartening statement. He stood back up with a somber expression. Frederick felt bad as Felix strode towards the exit. Before he got out of sight, the King called, "Wait! Come back a second."

Felix returned and Frederick grabbed a letter. He explained, "I have a cousin who now resides in England with his wife. He is a composer himself in his spare time and he adores your music. I think it would be best if you gave this letter to him by hand...and you'll get a break from Berlin. I know you like London."

"Danke." Felix brightened up. He took the letter with care, "What is the name of your cousin?"

"Albert. Prince Albert, the husband of Queen Victoria." The King's information caused Felix to race out of the Palace in excitement. He felt as if a cloud had been lifted. Though this trip was to be temporary, he wanted any way to get out of Berlin. Yet, on his way back to the estate, he realized that his children would have to part with both parents. It was time Cécile had seen Felix's favorite destination and met Charlotte Moscheles. To compensate, Lea would be having the time of her life with the grandchildren.

When dashing through the front door of the home, he found Cécile in the parlor, knitting. Felix called from the doorway, "Pack your bags honey, let my Mutter watch the children, we are going to London!"

~~~

# [2]

On the morning of July 14th 1842, the high trotting horses of a grand coach entered the grand gates, unlocking the drive to Buckingham Palace. As they clopped closer, Felix could not believe his eyes at such a scene. The yard was picturesque, let alone the palace itself.

The coach parked on the fine graveled terrain. A servant dressed in fine attire opened the carriage door and gave Felix a hand upon stepping out. Once on Buckingham's grounds, he turned about in circles, distracted by it all. The servant steadied Felix by the arm to escort him up the main stairs.

When entering through a door, Felix turned, looking at all of the decor inside Buckingham. The servant kept guiding him until stopping at the Grand Gallery. There, in a comfortable chair towards the corner sat a gentleman. For being in a royal palace, his clothes appeared on the casual side, but still formal for any commoner. A tray of tea sat at the end table beside him. His dark brown bangs slightly fell out of place whilst reading a book. Upon hearing footsteps, he looked up.

"Your Majesty," the servant bowed lightly, "this is Herr Mendelssohn of Berlin. He has come to deliver a letter from King Frederick William the IV."

"Ah! You are Felix! I have always wanted to meet you!" The man had a thick German accent. Felix discerned this to be Albert, so he bowed in introduction, "I am happy to give you this." He handed Albert the letter. The servant rolled his eyes at hearing Felix's accent. A mutter left his mouth, "Great, another German."

Albert gestured the fickle servant to leave and invited Felix, "Bitte, sit and have tea. There's an extra cup."

"So your cousin tells me you compose?" Felix sat. Unlike every other time around royalty, he felt comfortable. Albert didn't seem the judging spirit.

He spoke earnest of heart, "Ja. When time allows and I have a lot for a husband. I do work, but it's such a different concept when your wife is the one running the country. I'm always there to assist, but it feels backwards at times as if I'm a house husband..." He seemed to be venting his thoughts. Felix listened and nodded as he cared about the man's feelings. Albert continued, "I have an organ and my wife also adores your music. You should come to dinner tomorrow evening, it would be a pleasure."

"Of course." Felix couldn't pass such an engagement. He had a few more sips of tea then headed back to Chester Place, where he and Cécile were staying.

The home was quite busy with Ignaz at the keys and little Felix nearby, playing with toy soldiers, giving them sound effects as he placed them about. Charlotte, Cécile and Emily joined in a circle of seats, knitting. Felix skipped in the midst of them, "I sent the letter to Albert and he invited me to dinner!"

"When?" Cécile asked.

"Tomorrow."

"Enjoy it. It sounds a bit too formal for us; Charlotte is taking Emily and I to the theater to watch some plays." Cécile helped Emily untangle a knot in her yarn. Felix joined Ignaz at the piano to partake in duets and improvisations.

Little Felix felt a comfort whenever his father and Felix were at the piano. He couldn't help but pause his games to watch their creative minds collaborate. Deep within he knew that he would forever remember the duo.
~~~

The next afternoon, Felix sat at the piano with an array of ideas. He had much on his mind concerning the evening that was to be spent with the British Monarchs.

The only way to make it come sooner was to occupy himself. Yet the composing occupied him a bit too much. Ignaz walked into the parlor, "Felix? Aren't you to be at the palace?"

"Oh Ja!" Felix jumped up from the instrument, noticing time had slipped away. Dinner at Buckingham had commenced at the hour. In a sprint, Felix got dressed into something formal. Ignaz stopped him before he left and straightened his cravat, "There, now you are presentable."

"Danke!" Felix raced out the door, hopping onto the nearest cab.

Meanwhile at the Palace, Albert and Victoria sat at the large table with their guests. They felt in a flutter. Felix's reserved seat remained empty. Albert hoped he had not offended Felix in any way. Victoria showed an air of disappointment. She had looked ever so forward to meeting Herr Mendelssohn. Dinner ended without sight of him.

The men stood as the ladies dispersed the table, including Victoria. When the men headed towards the smoking room, Albert left them in that event as usual. He preferred to be with his wife in the evenings rather than an after dinner smoke.

Victoria, Albert and a few other ladies scattered about the parlor, drinking champagne. After the hopes of Felix coming were lost, a servant escorted him into the parlor. Albert brightened up, greeting him straight away. Victoria stationed herself off to the side to study Felix before conversing with the man that composed the music she ever so loved.

In her first impressions, she guessed he was 35 or 36 in age. He had dark hair, lightly curled in wisps. The receding bangs gave him a fine intellectual forehead. She discerned him to be Jewish and his stature, short yet delicate, dressing in modest attire. She found herself captivated by his pleasing expression as he shook Albert's hand warmly.

Victoria approached Felix as he in turn gave a polite bow. He seemed rather lost in speech, not knowing whether he should speak first. Victoria had a welcoming tone, "It is nice that you were able to make it here. Please, take some champagne."

"Danke." Felix grabbed a glass. Victoria corrected him in a kind manner, "Do say thank you. Try to keep your speech English. After all this is England." She glanced at an older servant nearby. They had a grudge over the fact that most of the royal court were of German descent.

"Sorry, th-ank you." Felix tried his best to pronounce the TH. Victoria smiled in being pleased. Albert rolled his eyes discreetly then suggested, "Let us not waste time standing here, let us go to the music room."

"I will allow you to escort me." Victoria held her arm towards Felix. Felix gladly held it and followed Albert. They walked a few corridors down then came to a beautiful open room with a piano. It looked ever so beautiful. The organ sat in the room as well but that was too loud for the evening.

Victoria gestured Felix to sit at the piano. He eagerly seated himself and played right into his 'Lieder ohne Worte.' Victoria and Albert sat in chairs nearby, watching Felix play with such passion. Their ears were comforted at the pieces they formally played to each other.

"Can you give me a theme to improvise on?" Felix questioned after ending a cadence. Victoria suggested, "Rule Britannia."

"The Austrian anthem." Albert gave his input. Felix began immediately, trying each melody. To start, he added exquisite harmonies to the chosen pieces. The couple had never heard anything so beautiful. In a variant, both themes were blended together and changed over from one to the other. He put such feeling into each variation with rich powerful chords and modulations. At one moment, he played the Austrian anthem with his right hand and Rule Britannia with his left.

Between Victoria and Albert, they suggested more themes. Each improvisation filled them with the greatest admiration. By the time Felix raised his arms to finish for good, he could hardly keep his eyes open. Victoria stood and escorted him to a chair, "Oh you poor thing, you are exhausted. You should have said something when we kept making requests."

"No, I had a lot of fun." He felt better, resting his fingers and brain. Albert went to the keys and Victoria joined to play a set of 'Lieder ohne Worte.' Felix watched as they duetted to their hearts' content, making the music sing with true passion. Since they loved it so much, Felix grabbed an arrangement of his Scottish Symphony which he transformed into a piano duet. The symphony itself had become increasingly popular after a benefit concert back in June, earning £650 for the sufferers of the Hamburg fire.

Victoria and Albert lifted their hands in grace from the keys. Felix handed Victoria the music, "I'd like to give this to you."

"Ah! The Scottish symphony. This has to be one of your finest." She glanced it over.

"I am happy to dedicate it to you. Scotland is a wonder of a place." Felix recollected his trip to Scotland from thirteen years ago. Together the royal couple studied the arrangement until the evening's end.

~~~

The time was soon coming for Felix and Cécile to part from England. Cécile showed sadness as she had become best of friends with Charlotte and young Emily. Felix never liked to depart from the smokey nest. There were still a few days yet before the leave was to be, so Prince Albert sent for Felix again as they had not played the organ.

When Felix arrived, he found Albert alone in the music room, organizing various scores on a stand. The room felt fresh with air breezing in from an open window, letting the morning dew of the sun seep in. Albert told Felix with much excitement, "I have many pieces of Bach I think you will enjoy."

"Wunderbare!" Felix sat at the organ, ready to play. He got excited whenever coming across an organ. Albert chuckled as Felix corrected his language, "Wonderful!" He read the first piece setting at the instrument. It was a three part fugue. Albert listened in content as the music was played with ease. Felix then tried experimenting with a few pieces he had been composing.

While they were distracted, a gust of wind pressed in from the window, wobbling the music stand beside it. The manuscripts dispersed all over the floor. Victoria entered the room, dressed quite informally for a Queen, "Albert, remember we have to leave for Claremont in an hour's time," she then noticed the scattered mess, "Heavens, how untidy!" The Queen got down on her hands and knees, picking up the leaves of paper. Meanwhile, Felix turned to Albert, begging, "Please play me something before you go, so I can tell all of Germany of it."

*(Albert playing organ for Victoria and Felix)*

542

"Alright." Albert traded spots with him and played a chorale by heart with charm and accuracy. Victoria joined in listening with much pleasure after having picked up the mess.

Albert gestured Felix back to the instrument after a piece. Felix sat again and played a section of the St. Paul oratorio. To his joy, the royal couple began singing the chorus together. Albert managed the stops of the organ quite cleverly.

The young prince of Gotha then entered. Felix continued on as the fellow royals spoke together. Their speech had chipper tones. Victoria then turned to Felix as he finished a piece, "Have you any new songs? I am fond of singing the published ones."

"You ought to sing one to him." Albert inclined.

"I don't know..." Victoria became bashful, "Maybe we will try the 'Spring Song' in B flat. That is, if it's still here. All of my music is packed for Claremont."

"I will check," Albert rushed off. He was gone a fair amount then returned, "It's already packed."

"Couldn't it possibly be unpacked?" Felix ventured. Victoria gave a sigh, "We must send for Lady M." She rang one of the servant bells. The servants dispatched, but none came with any music. Victoria decided to go herself.

While she was away, Albert grabbed a small case sitting on a shelf nearby. He handed it to Felix, "She begs you will accept this gift as a memento."

"Dankeschön." Felix opened it to find it's contents to be a beautiful ring on which was engraved: V. R. 1842. He tried it on. As he admired the jewelry, the Queen came back. Felix put the ring in its case and pocketed it.

Victoria explained, "Lady M has gone and she's taken all my music with her, it's really most annoying."

"Could you pick another song that you know, so I can hear you?" Felix chimed. Victoria looked to her husband. It seemed that she was rather making excuses. Albert assured Felix, "She will sing you something by Gluck."

"But let us go to the piano in my room, that one would suit best." Victoria explained as the Princess of Gotha entered. All five in the group proceeded through various rooms and corridors to the Queen's boudoir. There a piano sat in grace. Beside it stood a very plump rocking horse and two large bird cages, one containing a parrot.

Felix found where the music was stacked, so flipped through it. He rummaged a while until he found his first set of songs. The duchess of Kent then joined the group, speaking among them.

"Can you sing one of these instead of Gluck?" Felix asked Victoria, interrupting their chatter.

"Yes, but first we must get rid of the parrot, or he will scream louder than I can sing." She explained. Albert rang the bell for the servant, but the Prince of Gotha spoke up, "I'll take it out."

"Please allow me!" Felix came forward as he wanted to get to the music. He lifted the big cage and carried it out. The servants coming up to answer the bell were astonished at the gesture. Felix returned and seated himself at the keys, "Now. What shall you sing?"

"I do like Schöner und schöner schmückt sich." Victoria set the music at the stand. Felix set his hands at the notes and began. When the voice part entered, the Queen sang charmingly. The whole piece went well with only a small mistake when she sang D when it was to be D sharp.

For an amateur Felix never heard the last sustained G sung more purely or naturally. Victoria smiled after finishing and stated,"That is one of my favorite pieces. You compose so well."

"Well..." Felix adjusted his cravat, "My sister Fanny actually wrote that one..."

"Oh really? You have a sister?"

"Ja...could we choose one of my pieces now?"

"We could try as long as you help me much." She inquired. Felix nodded and grabbed 'Lass dich nur nichts dauern.' It was played and sung faultlessly. Felix had much on his mind to say but it wasn't the moment to indulge in extravagant compliments, so he thanked her well. Victoria sighed, "Oh, if only I hadn't been so frightened! I generally have a pretty long breath...."

"You did excellent." Felix stated warmly. Albert then skimmed the music and chose 'Es ist ein Schnitter' to sing. His tone had a heartfelt fullness. When it finished, Felix improvised the chorale Albert had played earlier at the organ, mixing it with the melody of the song he just sung. Everyone listened with intrigue at the cleverly interwoven melodies.

Usually Felix felt that when he wanted to improvise well, it never turned out as he wished. It would have spoilt his morning, but this time all was pleasing. His fingers gently played to a closing chord, completing the sweet music.

"I hope you come back to England again soon and pay us another visit." Victoria smiled. Felix turned to her, assuring, "Don't worry, I shall come back."

It was then time for everyone to be on their way. Felix savored his walk to the main doors which didn't last long. Outside Buckingham, there were many beautiful carriages waiting for the Queen and her company. The palace's flags were lowered, indicating Her Majesty's leave.

Felix found a cab for commoners and took it to Klingemann's home. The afternoon brought rain so he rushed into the complex. He knocked at the door and Karl answered happily, "Cécile is here. She got caught in the rain too!"

"I have to talk!" Felix pressed in. Cécile sat in the small parlor with a tray of tea. Felix set his coat aside to join and warm himself. Karl grabbed coffee. As soon as he sat, Felix told them everything of the morning's events.

After hours of talking, the rain calmed and the sun came out, drying the dewed city. Felix stood and stretched, asking Klingemann, "Would you want to go on a stroll with me? I could use the exercise. Cécile, you may come too."

"I should be getting back to Chester Place. Charlotte and Emily are almost done sewing a few things." She put on her cloak. The three headed out, but Felix and Karl went their own way up a street. It led to an open field to stroll around. Felix sighed, "In a few days my wife and I are to be back in Berlin. The King is making everything a mess with the academy. I want to go back to Leipzig; anywhere but Berlin."

"You don't have to be in stress yet. Your brother Paul wrote to me. He and his wife are going to Switzerland and want you and Cécile along. King Frederick has given consent as there is no progress with the academy."

"Oh! This is pleasing, danke Karl!" Felix rushed off to Chester Place to inform Cécile that they would be leaving for Switzerland by morning.

~~~

In August of 1842, Felix, Paul and their spouses found themselves in the calming country of Switzerland, staying in Interlachen. The inn happened to be where Felix had previously been refused years prior on his pedestrian tour as the landlady thought him too shabby. She was now welcoming. It felt as if that tour happened yesteryear ago but it had been eleven years since his two year European excursion.

The scenes of the alps were even better with family. The trip wasn't terribly long but filled with hiking and beautiful landscapes. It rained at times but it didn't sour anything. Felix found one of his former guides though the country, Michael. He now had a good strong home with a wife and children. Felix and Paul stayed with them during a long hike. Michael enjoyed singing to his extremely pretty wife. Felix gave the children some trifles and toy soldiers he bought at Untersee when hiking out there.

After staying at Michael's residence, Paul and Felix hiked at Grimsel then headed back to the inn where their wife's were. They then moved on from there as Paul wanted to see Zurich. After that, Paul and his wife decided to head back to Berlin. Cécile asked Felix while packing as well, "Before you and I head back to Berlin, can we stop in Frankfort to visit my mother?"

"I don't know..." Felix hesitated. Cécile remarked, "It will keep you out of Berlin longer."

"Alright." Felix complied. Paul assured before disembarking, "I will inform Herr Massow. If the King requests you, I will write." With that, they went their separate ways.

~~~

After long weary travel, Felix and Cécile arrived in Frankfort on a cold downpour. The darkened evening gave a bitter chill. The couple huddled together in the carriage to keep warm. The coachman soon parked at the humble Jeanrenaud cottage. Candles were lit inside, indicating the residents were still awake.

When pounding at the door, Elizabeth happened to answer. She in a rush let the shivering couple inside. They both took off their drenched coats. Elizabeth scolded, "You shouldn't be traveling in such rain."

"That's why we came here." Felix stated. Elizabeth went to her daughter and admired her pretty girl, having not seen her in a long while. She then turned to Felix, looking at him intently, "The little of six years has definitely aged you." She gazed at his hair, which had receded some. Felix tried to brush the edge of his bangs, not in likes of her comment. He told her in return, "I see the years have shown on you."

"I'm aging well for my age." She smiled in sourness. Since it was late, Elizabeth showed the two to a guest room where they settled and decided to get much needed slumber. The light thunder helped drift them to sleep.

The next morning at breakfast, a large stack of hotcakes had been made to share. Fresh maple syrup accompanied. While eating, Elizabeth mentioned to Felix, "Your friend Ferdinand Hiller still resides in the city, with his new wife."

"I shall have to pay a visit. Did he find a girl in Italy?"

"I believe so. She sings like an angel." Elizabeth poured some syrup. Felix finished his food then went on his way to greet his friend that he had not seen in a while. He resided in the same home as before, acquiring it after his mother's death.

When knocking at the door, Hiller answered. He gave a hard shake of the hand in greeting, "It's so good of you to visit! Come bitte!" He let Felix in. When entering the sitting room, a pretty Italian lady sat at the writing desk. Hiller introduced, "Darling, this is my friend Felix that I've talked to you about."

"Oh, Ciao!" She turned around. Felix greeted back in her language, "Ciao!"

548

"You must sing for him." Ferdinand suggested, "He will adore your voice. I'll accompany at the keys." Hiller went to the piano. Frau Hiller stood and stationed herself beside the instrument. Together they bloomed into song. Felix sat, listening to the woman's soft tones. It was perfect. When the piece finished, Ferdinand told Felix, "There is a favor I'd like to ask."

"Ja?" Felix was in wonder. Hiller explained, "The painter Carl Müller is in town and he was going to come sketch my wife, but I'd also like him to sketch you."

"Oh I don't know..." Felix felt a pang of self consciousness. The comments Elizabeth spoke echoed in his mind. He gave Hiller his opinion, "Maybe another time."

"Bitte, I have not a sketch of you. If you're worried about your appearance, trust me, you look fine." Hiller tried to convince him. Felix shrugged, but all was interrupted when the bell rang. Ferdinand went to answer, "That's probably Herr Müller." He came back with a man holding a pencil and sketchbook. As the artist gathered his supplies, Frau Hiller spoke up to him, enticing, "Before you sketch me, my husband and I very much would like a sketch of our friend here."

"Bitte-" Felix sighed, covering his face. Hiller begged, "Come on Felix, it's only a sketch, you look fine."

"Okay. I'll let a drawing pass under one condition. Frau Hiller sings through the setting." Felix sat decently to look proper. Hiller went to the piano and Frau Hiller sang at once. Felix watched her, fazed by her lovely sound. Herr Müller began sketching Felix's expression. The music seemed to fill his heart with a calming joy. It took 16 songs of various lengths to complete the sitting.

*(Felix watching Frau Hiller sing)*

~~~

In October, Felix received a letter from Paul, calling him back to Berlin. Felix sighed upon reading the letter, but informed Cécile. Though they stayed in Frankfort for a month, it felt short lived.

Traveling in the mid autumn wasn't fun. The leaves were a pretty yellow, but the cold blasts forced them to make many stops to find a hot stove. They missed the warm cottage in Frankfort. To shelter for a night, they found a small ruddy inn.

Cécile huddled in the bed trying to keep warm. The room had a chilled dreariness to it with the woodwork looking bitter with frost. Felix sat at the writing desk, wearing his coat and wool gloves. He was reading a letter he received on the road.

It was from a man who enjoyed his 'Lieder ohne Worte' and had a question on Felix's thoughts, comparing words to music. Felix penned a reply, giving his feelings:

*Dear Marc-André Souchay*

*...There is so much talk about music, and yet so little really said...I believe words do not suffice for such a purpose, and if I found they did suffice, then I certainly would have nothing more to do with music. People often complain that music is ambiguous, that their ideas on the subject always seem so vague, whereas every one understands words; with me it is exactly the reverse; not merely with regard to entire sentences, but also as to individual words; these too seem to me so ambiguous, so vague, so unintelligible when compared with genuine music, which fills the soul with a thousand things better than words...because the words of one person assume a totally different meaning in the mind of another, because the music of the song alone can awaken the same ideas and the same feelings in one mind as another, a feeling which is not however, expressed by the same words...*

*Felix Mendelssohn Bartholdy*

After he finished penning the letter, Cécile begged, "It's so cold in here and getting late, please come to bed."

"I'll put more wood in the fireplace first." He wrapped his letter then grabbed a few logs by the hearth, setting them in the kindling fire. After the fire heated more, Felix laid in bed next to Cécile. She scooted over but the bed was not meant for two. They both were nearly falling off. Felix blew out the candle after they seemed somewhat settled.

After the room darkened, Felix huddled in the blanket, hoarding it. Cécile pulled it back, making her the one hoarding it.

Felix turned over trying to get comfortable, but it moved the blanket again. Cécile snapped, "Stop taking the blanket!"

"I hardly have any of it." Felix groaned. Cécile fluffed her pillow in annoyance. In Felix's tossing about, he accidentally kicked her. She in turn hit him on the shoulder.

"Ow!" Felix snapped. Cécile huddled closer to stop his irritation. Felix managed to get some shut eye while Cécile gave a breath of relief. She began to lightly dream of frolicking sweet smelling flower fields, picking lilies and roses. Yet, her fragrant dreams were distastefully disrupted when a bursting loud fart echoed in the room. She gave a small sigh, ignoring it...until the stench caused her to sit up, "Felix! Really!?" She looked at him. He was snoring, but a smirk formed on his face. Cécile rolled her eyes and went to sleep.

The next morning, Felix awoke with an aching back. He sat up to notice he was on the hardwood floor, having fallen out of bed. Cécile had the entire bed to herself. He gave a huff and stood back up. Cécile awoke soon after and asked, "Get enough sleep?"

"In truth, nein. At least today we will be back in Berlin. I'm only pleased to get there as to be in a good bed." Felix packed up their things. As soon as Cécile got out of bed and dressed, they left the cold inn.

~~~

Bach in Berlin, Felix stood before King Frederick. His majesty was at his throne in thought as usual, not speaking a word. Felix piped up, "So what progress has been made?"

"The academy positions still need to be filled."

"So nothing has changed?" Felix stared at him. The King huffed a sigh, giving a suspense that Felix could not stand.

Felix inquired, "Why can I not go somewhere that offers work? Leipzig is where I feel most at home. My family is happy there. I feel useless in Berlin."

"So your saying I'm not offering a sustainable job for you?" The King's tone was displeased. Felix was quick to deny, "Nein, I'm trying to think for my family's happiness."

"Well, before you speak to me anymore of wanting to leave, discuss the matter with your Bruder and Herr Massow. I will then call you back here." He gestured Felix to leave. His actions were rather careless. Felix left calmly, but inside, his blood boiled.

When Felix returned to the estate, Cécile saw him walk in with disparity. She asked, "How was it?"

"He wants me to talk to Paul and Herr Massow. They will only try to convince me to stay. The King didn't even want to hear my plan. No matter how angry it makes the man, we are leaving in eight days time." Felix hugged Cécile. Lea rushed into the entryway upon eavesdropping, "You had better not leave me so soon."

"Mutter, we must." Felix felt a terrible pain at seeing his mother in such distraught. She usually was calm and seldom, giving only glimpses of her inner feelings, but now her sorrow showed greatly. Felix felt as if his heart was being crushed within him as Lea embraced him with sobs. He hugged her then went to go find Paul. Fortunately, his brother was coming down the stairs upon hearing his mother's tears. He questioned, "What is the matter with Mutter?"

"I told her my family and I are leaving in eight days."

"Does the King approve?"

"He sent me off to talk to you and Massow. I've made up my mind, I'm not letting you try to sway my plan." Felix put his hands on his hips. Paul sighed, "Alright, I will inform Herr Massow."

~~~

The next day, Felix went back to the King's residence in the company with Herr Massow. Felix feared that he'd be facing the King's anger. Yet, to his surprise, they found him in good humor. He greeted Felix kindly, "How is my musician getting along today? In a better spirit than last time?"

"I have come to give my farewells." Felix stood sternly, "In a week hence I am returning to Leipzig with my family to continue my duties there. To fill the request here, I am sure there is another man perfect for it." He finished his simple speech.

The King sat in thought, then replied, "I know I can not compel you to remain, but it will give me heartfelt regret if you leave me. The plans I had for you are now frustrated, you leave a void that can't be filled. Yet if you name any capable person that can execute plans as you could, then send them to me and I will entrust them, but I believe you will be unable to name anyone I could approve of..." As the King continued into much detail, Felix felt he was being put on the spot. King Frederick topped his speech off with a cherry by guilting, "I also hear that your Mutter is so disappointed that you are going so soon. It must hurt so much to see her in such a state."

Felix subconsciously clutched his chest, feeling the ache in his heart. In truth, he did not care a thing about the King's opinion, but seeing his mother crying, he couldn't stand. It was the only kink in his plan. The King was doing anything to get to Felix.

"How about I return to Leipzig as I planned and when this academy is fully in progress, I mean in seriousness, then I will return." Felix gave a stern statement. King Frederick nodded, "I will approve your leave, but, you are not near out of duty to me. There are commissions that I require. A few plays that I enjoy need some incidental music.

I will write these requests so as you don't forget them. The ones I want done are Œdipus Coloneus and The Midsummer Night's Dream. You have an overture done for the Midsummer, but it needs music throughout it."

"I will stay in your service and fulfill these commissions." Felix bowed politely. Before leaving, Frederick added, "And one more thing. Since you are leaving, I hope you haven't used up the three thousand thalers that I paid you. I'll need half of it back since my original ideas have not been seen."

"I'll get it to you." Felix sighed within. They then separated after an hour and a quarter conversation. While heading out through the main halls, Herr Massow skipped in excitement, repeating happily to Felix, "Surely you can never now think of going away? With these new commissions."

"I've already made my decision. I can adhere to the King's proposals in Leipzig." Felix walked ahead of him. Massow stopped his jolly stature and followed in a huff.

At home Felix wrote the necessary letters to give up half of the salary given to him. Cécile had known the whole thing too good to be true all along. Felix was relieved that he had not spent the extra money.

When business was finished, Felix grabbed a few pages and wrote a long letter to Ignaz, describing everything that happened. His pen, he let run away with words. He needed someone to vent to, yet, he couldn't write too much as Cécile wanted the next page.

Little did Felix know, Ignaz had exciting plans on his own.

# Chapter XXIII: The Academy of Leipzig

Mendelssohn, Scherzo (II) from 'Midsummer Night's Dream' [1]
Mendelssohn, Wie der Hirsch Schreit, Psalm 42 [2]
Mendelssohn, Wedding March, orchestra version [3]


[1]


In London, at Chester Place, Ignaz paced about the dining room. Charlotte sat at the table, running her fingers through her hair. There was a moment of silence until Charlotte couldn't stand it any longer, "So you want our family to move to Leipzig?"

"Felix is to start an academy there and suggested that I be head. I know we thought about Berlin, but Felix informed me of the King's failure to make a school there. I'll have a better chance at getting work in Leipzig."

"Are you sure we can afford it? What of Chester Place? It's been such a good home." Charlotte sighed somberly. Ignaz gave a disheartened tone, "I will miss it dearly, but the London we know is changing. I'm struggling to keep up and I think Germany will give me more opportunity. I'll ask Felix about the living costs. As you know he's quite a good house agent."

"You're lucky you came across that boy those years ago." Charlotte stated. Ignaz chuckled, "That I am."

~~~


Back in Leipzig, Felix was penning a wistful scherzo of the flutes on a scratch piece of paper. The ideas flowed as he wasn't at the writing desk in the parlor. Instead, he had acquired his own workspace by moving the children to another room and transforming the nursery into an office. It became his sanctuary of comfort and privacy.

*(Felix's Study)*

The room contained a sturdy desk with shelving, making it perfect for storing scores in progress. The mantle of the desk and the wall above were decorated with watercolor landscapes as well as portraits of family. A nice one of Fanny was set out.

On the other wall, a large oak cabinet with paneled glass doors stood. Felix had favorable decor on top of it, including a bust of Johann Sebastian Bach. Opposite to the room's door, a window looked out into the sunset, over the meadows and fields. Near the window was a conducting desk and to complete the room, a quaint little clavier. Perfect for composition and practice. Felix enjoyed every bit of his man cave.

Felix continued penning outlines of music for the Shakespeare play. He wanted to keep his word on the King's commissions so he disciplined himself to be sure it was ready in due time. Yet, the days were hindered with distraction. His luggage from Berlin had not been received, so he was without his books and scores. He used scratch paper for the time being.

When bags began returning, he was too busy unpacking to chip away at composing. If he found time, he often sat, only to realize he had nothing but writer's block with the King's requests. In an attempt to get his brain going he managed to complete a sonata for piano and cello.

During his composition time, there was a light knock at the door and Cécile came, bringing in a few letters. She left them beside Felix as he was submerged in his work. While she left, she casually mentioned, "I'm pregnant again."

Felix set his pen down and looked to her, smiling. It made him chuckle inside over the fact that out of his siblings, he ended up with the most children.

Felix then grabbed the letters to read. One was from Ignaz and the other from Paul. He opened Ignaz's first. They had been writing back and forth concerning Ignaz's plan to move his family from England to Germany.

Felix had the utmost excitement that he considered Leipzig. It would be a dream come true for the two musicians to be united in the same city. Felix enticed Ignaz further as he planned to start an academy of art in Leipzig. A few event led Felix to arrange such an idea:

The King of Saxony had heard of the struggles in Berlin with King Frederick. When Felix made his leave of Berlin, it wasn't long before Felix received an offer from the King of Saxony. To be respectful, Felix made a trip to Dresden to thank the King verbally, but declined any positions. Before returning home, the King showed him something of interest. It was the will of an old man that passed containing twenty thalers to establish an Academy of Art in Leipzig. Felix accepted to see it done by the next winter, giving a full year. He felt that he would have a clean conscience knowing there was a successful academy in Leipzig.

Almost as soon as putting the plans under way, in which Felix made sure got organized accordingly, the King of Prussia heard of it. He wasn't fond of the idea, but instead of scolding Felix, he tried to make the plans in Berlin sound more hopeful. Felix received notice after notice of King Frederick entitling him honors such as general music director and sofourth. Felix wasn't fond of each polished title as he didn't know how to live up to the old ones.

After taking care of business with Ignaz's letters, he turned to the carefully folded note from his brother Paul. Felix felt nervous opening it as there was a high chance he was begging him back to Berlin. After pausing a second, Felix gave a sigh and just opened it.

[2]

In the parlor, Cécile was sipping hot cocoa while watching little Carl play with toys. He looked so cute with the set up of small wood animals, using his imagination. As the boy continued to play, Cécile suddenly heard a deep somber whimpering. She set her cup of cocoa down to go check it out. It was coming from Felix's office. She cracked open the door, "Honey?"

At the desk, Felix sat, staring in fear at the open letter before him. Tears were seeping from his eyes like never ending rivers. The most melancholy sounds were being produced by his voice.

"Felix honey?" Cécile went to him, "What is the matter?"

"My- mmu..." Felix couldn't bring himself to form words. Cécile glanced at Paul's note dated the 12th of December 1842. The message was simple. Lea had died.

"Come to bed for now." Cécile nudged him to get up. Felix stayed seated, grabbing blank paper. He began penning to Paul. Cécile took the pen from him, "You do not need to write right now. Come to bed."

Felix stood, sniffling much. His state caused him to be in a fog, so Cécile escorted him to bed. As soon as his head hit the pillow, he slept his sorrows away. Cécile felt the need to make him as cozy as possible, so she added extra pillows and blankets, making him snug. She then grabbed lavender oil and put some on his nose in hopes it would keep him calm. It was uncertain if he would wake in an emotional or irritable state so she did all she could to avoid the latter.

After he looked to the standards a spa would deem relaxed, Cécile made sure the room was dark and quiet. His mourning session would last a few days so she decided to sleep elsewhere.

~~~

The whole of the next fortnight consisted of deciding what was to be done with the old beloved Berlin estate of Leipziger Straße No. 3. Paul owned it, but had no use for the main house as he resided in the Bankhaus. Fanny and Wilhelm still lived in the guest house. Rebecka and her husband resided elsewhere.

560

In letters, Paul began offering the estate to Felix and his family as he didn't want to see the grand home Abraham had purchased go to waste. Felix felt that it needed to be decided further with his other siblings. He didn't want to move his family and get entangled in Berlin. In the moment it was all too much as Felix couldn't gather every thought. The point of his family's union was now gone. He and his siblings were children no longer. The next visit with them would be enough of a trial.

In the means of music, Felix couldn't fathom a note. He rather used his time to be thankful for his wife and children. They regularly bonded together with activities. The children of course loved it as their father took the utmost pleasure in teaching them how to sketch windmills. Eventually Felix's old love of music returned. He began writing again, but felt most comfortable if his children were playing nearby.

Concerning people outside the home, Felix felt horrid around them. Herr Schleinitz paid a visit, assuring him not to rush back to work. To start into a routine, Felix took up transcribing, instrumentation and other half mechanical tasks at home. The automatic work helped occupy his emotional void.

~~~

It was hardly a week later at the Gewandhaus that I felt a melancholy air pass through the musicians as our beloved director returned. We expected Felix to be in utter quietness, but rather he came in his usual way; ready to take care of business. Herr Schleinitz had warned him that the first day back would be the hardest, but there was a fact to the matter: sooner or later the terrible day would have to come and go.

The chorus had joined the orchestra for the day. Felix directed with much grace, letting the music calm his aching heart. After running a few pieces, an alto came forward to sing 'Wie der Hirsch schreit'. It was then Felix's inner feelings showed, becoming overcome. He tried to hold in his state with an occasional sigh, but everyone knew it to be the cry of longing.

With each bar, the harder it was for Felix to keep composure. He seemed to be stressing himself as to not let a whimper leave his mouth. I knew that he needed to be excused, so I gestured the orchestra to a halt. When I looked back to the conducting desk, Felix was already exiting the nearest door. I set my violin down to go check on him.

In the hall, I found him sitting on the ground, against the wall. His eyes were dewed from giving free vent to tears. As soon as noticing me his state of emotion reverted from the deep mourn. He forced a smile, "Herr David. Sorry, I am out of sorts."

"Nein, it is fine, I came to check on you."

"Danke. I think the worst of it is finished." He wiped a tear. I patted his shoulder. He then mentioned, "I mean to have you and Schumann over to my place to discuss academy plans. Tomorrow I need a day alone, but the next I'm free."

"That works for me," I assured. His face began to show signs of holding tears, so I told him, "It is alright to cry. It's not healthy to hold in hard emotions." I gave a friendly embrace as tears poured from his eyes in the middle of my comfort. His cries spilled all over my shoulder. Once he calmed, we returned to rehearsals.

~ ~ ~

"Alright, it is January and the new year of 1843," Felix stated happily, "The plans for the academy are making rapid progress."

"I shall accept to be one of the first teachers." I nodded. Herr Schumann added, "I'll take care of the announcements in the papers." He penned notes. The three of us were at the dining table in Felix's home, discussing the Leipzig academy.

"Excellent," Felix wrote on a few note cards, "For starts, I shall give public presentations at the Gewandhaus to show what will be taught.

When things get going, I'd like to make it a requirement of each member of the orchestra to contribute in some way to the school. Most will teach their specific instrument."

"Sounds fair." I agreed. Felix finished his note cards, "I have my first presentation ready, so I am going to head to the Konzerthaus."

"I'll go with." I grabbed my coat to follow. Schumann trailed behind but went separate ways to the printing shop to take care of the advertising.

At the Gewandhaus, I joined the crowd gathered in the small hall, who wanted a taste of what teachings the upcoming school had to offer. Many young listeners were in hopes to be future students. Felix came before the interested spectators with his presentation, "Now, today I shall be speaking publicly about what will be taught concerning music theory classes. To give an example, I shall explain 6-4 chords."

Felix walked up to a blackboard with staff lines set up behind him. He explained firstly, "To make this easier, I will write the example, using the key of C major. No sharps or flats. The chord I will write will be a G major chord in the key of C, so a major dominant chord." He drew the notes G, H * and D on the bass clef in their proper spaces. To show that it was the major dominant chord, he put a capital roman numeral V under it.

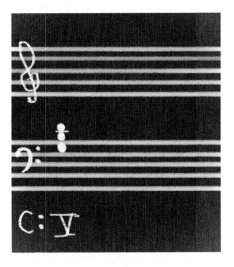

(G Major Triad)

*In German lettering of music, the Bb is B and the B is H

"So a G major chord is the dominant because the note G is a fifth from C; five spaces above C." Felix tried to be thorough in teaching, knowing some knew nothing of music, "Now, this chord is stacked as a triad, in root position, meaning the lowest note in this case is G." He glanced at his audience to be sure they followed. Most everyone nodded.

"The next chord I will write is also a G major chord" He wrote on the board. This time next to the roman numeral, he placed a 6-3.

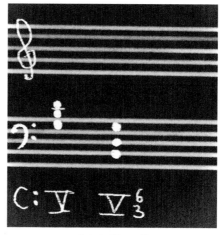

*(6-3 Chord)*

"As you can see, I wrote using the same notes, but placed them in different positions. This is still a G major chord because when organized into a stacked triad G is the lowest. This new way I wrote it, H is the lowest. This is what is called inverting chords. The numbers beside the V symbol indicate that it's the first inversion. H is the lowest, so six intervals above that is G and three gives D. When reorganized into a triad, it shows that it's originally a G major chord. This now brings me to discuss 6-4 chords." Felix chalked a third chord on the staff, writing next to the roman numeral a 6-4.

564

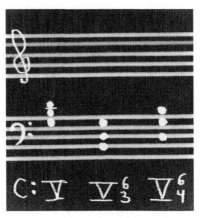

*(6-4 Chord)*

"Just like the other two chords, this is a G major chord, but this time in second inversion. The lowest note in this case is D. The numbers meaning that six intervals above D gives H and four above gives G. Reorganized, it makes a G major triad. To find out how to tell what sort of chord you are looking at, you must know the key of the music. That is the starting point to tell if the chord is tonic, supertonic, mediant, subdominant, dominant, submediant, or a leading tone/subtonic. To tell if it's inverted, it can be stacked into triads to show the original chord. The chords I described more commonly look like this:"

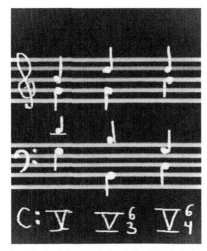

*(G Major Chords in root, 1st and 2nd inversion)*

565

"Inverting chords gives more options and variety for choral and counterpoint rules. The numbers are known as figured bass, in which can help a musician, particularly keyboardists, to fill in the chords freely with the indications given. In the time of J S Bach, it was common for a harpsichordist to accompany the orchestra, using figured bass to create an accompaniment." Felix closed his lecture. A few aspiring students asked him an array of questions afterwards.

After tending to questions, the members of the orchestra gathered in the auditorium for regular rehearsals. There were many preparations within the Gewandhaus concerning concerts. Felix happened upon a new symphony written by a man from Denmark. His name was, A. W. Gade; only 26 years of age and a professor of music in Copenhagen. Though Felix had a hard time searching for new favorable works, he concluded one thing was for sure: those Scandinavians knew how to make music.

After rehearsing Gade's symphony, Felix went to a writing desk and penned a letter, inviting Gade to come to Leipzig in the near future. After giving the note to a postman, Felix headed back home before the noon hour. When opening the apartment door, he found his family seated at the dining table as Johann served lunch. Upon seeing Felix, young Carl left his seat and ran to his father, "Papa, Papa, piano! Piano!"

"After lunch." Felix guided him back to the table. Carl had lately been eager to learn piano as Ignaz had sent a present of music, 'The Harmonized scales.' It was a set of 59 pieces for a juvenile performer and teacher. As the student played the scales in various tempos and rhythms, the teacher gave a full accompaniment.

Carl was proud of his gift, but in reality Felix got the most enjoyment out of it. Usually he took time after breakfast to teach Carl his notes. They worked on other things as well besides music, such as writing letters. Carl had crooked handwriting, but he was still quite young. Felix loved every moment of helping him.

After lunch had commenced, Carl rushed to the keys. Felix followed close behind and tested Carl on notes, "Where is C?"

"C!" Carl pressed the correct note.

"H?"

"H!"

"B?" Felix knew he struggled more with the black keys. Carl froze, "Um..." He scanned the keyboard then slowly thumbed a B. Felix smiled, "Correct. You are doing quite splendidly today."

Before they got to 'The Harmonized Scales' a knock at the door disrupted them. Cécile answered and came to the parlor, escorting Herr Schumann. Robert smiled immensely at seeing little Carl beside Felix. Felix was about to stand, but Robert begged, "Oh please, stay seated. Let me hear you two at least a little, this is far too adorable not to watch."

"Papa, this one." Carl pointed to the F major scale. Felix placed his hands and Carl began playing his scale exercise. The accompaniment was clever but simple for Carl to follow. Robert couldn't help but smile.

Once a few scales were played, Carl went away to go find toys to play with instead. Music was tiring after a while. Felix stood and gestured Robert to sit on the sofa. Schumann sat and explained, "I know you've been searching for new composers and works to perform; in my outings of critiquing, I've happened upon a young man that may be worth your while. He has interest in sending a symphony. His name is Richard Wagner. He also showed interest in the future Academy."

"Ah. I would be glad to meet him. I happen to be free later tonight after I get the children to bed. I do warn, it may be chaotic when you come." Felix chuckled as little Carl came back, giving his father a mischievous glance. He ran to Felix's lap, attacking him with hugs.

Robert laughed, then said, "This evening will work, Wagner is rather in a trance to meet you." He stood. Felix tried to get up, but Carl was wrestling. He hit Felix in the face roughly. Felix in an instant became stern, "Carl! You do not hit, now stop this and go to your room!"

"Sorry Papa." Carl went off in tears. Robert commented of the somber child, "Poor little thing."

"He's cute on the outside. Don't let him deceive you." Felix warned. Robert chuckled, then made his leave.

~~~~

Later that evening, after dinner finished, the house was in turmoil as the children complained of not wanting to go to bed. Young Paul cried, Marie huffed and Carl snapped at his father, "I am not going to bed."

"You are going now. No buts!" Felix pointed down the hall. In the midst of the chaos, there was a knock on the door. Felix went to answer and let Herr Schumann and Wagner in.

"Please excuse me for a moment." Felix apologized, turning back to his children. Cécile carried wailing Paul to the bedroom. The two eldest took more convincing. Felix warned Marie, "If you don't go to bed, you get no desert tomorrow."

Instantly she ran to her bed. Carl crossed his arms, "That doesn't fool me anymore."

"Carl! Go to bed." Felix nudged him. Carl nudged back but sprinted as he knew he wasn't to do such a thing. Felix chased and picked up the angsty child. He then took him to the bedroom. Cécile took care of the rest of the matter so Felix could tend to the guests.

When he returned, Robert gave a warm smile. Herr Wagner rather appeared in disgust. Felix assumed it to be the young man's nature, so held out his hand, "It's a pleasure to greet you here...Richard."

"A pleasure?" He lightly shook Felix's hand in reluctance. It struck Felix odd that Wagner had such a strange demeanor towards him, discreetly wiping their handshake off on his coat.

As an awkward silence came, Felix took note of a score in Richard's hands, "What is it you have? It appears to be a symphony. Let's take it to my office."

Robert and Richard followed Felix down the hallway. Once they got to the office, Felix sat at his desk, Robert pulled up a chair and Richard took a seat at the small clavier. Felix then skimmed Richard's symphony. It seemed to have captivating qualities, but at the same time appeared a typical composition of romanticism. Felix nodded, keeping an enthused expression, hiding his opinion. To avoid any questions he suggested, "Why don't I get us coffee." He got up. Schumann mentioned, "Excuse me a moment but I must use the restroom before we get to business."

"I'll show you where it is." Felix went out the door with Robert, leaving Richard alone. In his moment by himself, Wagner stood and ventured to Felix's desk. An intriguing piece in progress sat. Richard read it, letting it play in his head.

[3]

The beginning had a fanfare of excitement. The trumpets sounded like gold pillars, leading the whole orchestra to a royal chord. It was like a bride and groom exiting the aisle in grace after reciting their vows of marriage.

Though the music had a whimsical essence of purity, Richard had his own opinions of Felix. Musically speaking, there were points Wagner did not care for.

He intended to give Felix a piece of his mind if he agreed to perform his symphony. Felix conducted at faster tempos and Wagner wasn't going to have it for his music. Yet, it wasn't only the music he felt in a trifle about. There was something else that he could not get past. It concerned Felix himself. To Herr Wagner, the only thing that came to his mind was Felix's heritage and family background.

"Oh, I see you intently looking at my march I'm working on." Felix came back in with a tray of coffee. He set it on a nearby end table. Richard jumped, excusing, "I was only glancing."

"What do you think of it? It's a commission for King Frederick."

"It looks...alright." Wagner reluctantly took a cup of coffee as Felix handed it to him. He quickly moved away as Felix went to sit at the desk. It boggled Felix as this young man seemed so skittish around him. He asked Richard, "Is something the matter?"

"Nein." He set the coffee aside. Felix knew there was something as Herr Wagner began glaring, giving a rather threatening look. Turning to his desk, Felix felt a sense of tension in waiting for Robert. As he penned some music, Richard came, looking over his shoulder. Felix ignored him and continued writing. All was fine until a snotty remark came from Wagner's mouth, "You're just writing this for the King's money."

~~~

Schumann came into the corridor, heading back to Felix's office. The sound of arguing made him rush. Cécile peeked from the children's room in wonder, but turned back not wanting to wake the children.

When entering the office, Robert found Richard and Felix snapping at each other. Felix hissed, "Your music is exaggerated!"

"You conduct Beethoven's music far too fast!" Richard spewed his opinions, "Your music also portrays nothing but childish themes of fairy tales; the notes prancing about like a weak innocent fawn, like yourself! If I wrote a wedding piece, it would be the utmost standard work for a bride and groom to walk the aisle to!"

Felix threw down his pen, about to stand, but Robert scolded the both of them, "Order! Order! This is to be a gentlemanly meeting. Let us have coffee." He took a cup. Felix obeyed. Wagner still refused. Robert sighed, but enticed, "Why don't you play a bit of the Klavier, so Felix can hear you."

"Fine." Richard turned to the keys and began a work of his. Felix listened, knowing the man had talent, but the attitude soured his liking. He knew truly why Wagner hated him. There would be no convincing, deeming them enemies for life...and thereafter.

~~~

That same evening, I was headed to Felix's home with my violin at hand. We were going to discuss the violin concerto I requested. Felix wanted to try out some sections to see what needed editing. He had been working at the concerto off and on throughout the past few years. I hoped that it would have come together sooner, but the commissions of King Frederick hindered his time.

When I came to the apartment, I knocked lightly. Schumann happened to answer. He and Herr Wagner were getting their coats to leave. I had not become acquainted with Wagner so I set my violin case down, took my gloves off to give a shake of the hand. The stern face glared at me in utter disgust. He commented to Felix, "Be sure to keep my symphony in mind." Richard then budded past me out the door. Schumann sighed to us, "Sorry for this hassle." He followed Wagner.

"What was that all about?" I felt quite confused. Felix assured, "Don't feel bad, he is just that way towards people like you and I. Let's move on to something better. I'll get the concerto score."

I followed Felix to his office. There he set his violin concerto score in progress at the conducting desk. I opened my violin case and tuned the fine instrument. Felix grabbed another score that was a mess on his desk and shoved it in the cabinet. He stated, "That Wagner left his symphony with me. I think I'll tell him I misplaced it or something. Anyways, let's look at the concerto." Felix gestured me to start at the beginning.

I played the opening to the first interlude after the ascending octaves. The sound pleased Felix. He then went to business, "So the phrase starting at measure 76, when the violin enters again, I wondered if that would be better at an octave higher. Right now I have it starting at H5 going up to G and so on. It seems to me that it would sing more at a higher range, but you try it."

"Alright." I held the violin to my chin and played the phrase up the octave then in the written form. After switching back and forth, I stated, "It is true that it sings in the higher voicing, but there is a warmth that erupts from the original version."

"I felt a good sense in the lower version so we shall keep it that way. Now, I do have a cadenza in the first movement, but contrary to what you know and you may not agree, but I don't want the cadenza improvised. I want it as written."

"Are you sure?" I enticed, "Are you truly sure you don't want me to add my own touches in the moment?"

"I do want your input. In fact, if you wish, write in what you think needs to be added. Though I do like your improvising, I don't want this done in the spur of a moment. Bitte, don't deceive me in the performance." He flipped to the written solo.

572

"I'll try not to." I looked at it and sight read through it. Some challenging sections caused me to review what he wrote. I added things so it made more sense from the perspective of a violinist. Felix seemed pleased, but the second time I ran it, I veered slightly into my own world.

"I think I can manage the written version. I'm happy as long as there are no notes held dreadfully long. I swear if you do, I shall add a trill." I spoke in all seriousness.

"Of course. I know you." Felix chuckled then explained, "The next thing I must mention is that each movement should be continued into the next. No pauses between."

"There is no break in the work?"

"Nein, I am tired of the audience clapping between every moment, so I shall train them not to." Felix stated. I shrugged a little at these ideas, but continued on. In the last movement of the work, Felix mentioned, "I mean for the last movement to complement the skill of your right hand, so please, have fun with it."

"I shall." I bowed a few phrases of it.

After working on things here and there, Felix moved to discussing the future Academy of Leipzig. He informed, "34 pupils have already sent their names to be students. So far the teachers are to be you, Robert and Clara Schumann, Herr Hauptmann, Herr Pohlenz, Herr Becker and I. I'm in search of a singing master as I do not want the teaching of singing to be done away with. I ever so want Ignaz Moscheles to be head of the school. Did I tell you that he has plans to move here?"

"Nein, but that would be great."

"I would be more tedious in getting things together but there is so much music I'm revising and then there is the 100th anniversary of the foundation of Leipzig subscription concerts. We are to have a super for the orchestra." Felix gave a tired sigh. I assured, "Things will progress with time."

~~~

A week or so later, Felix paced about the parlor, anxious as ever. It was nearing the midnight hour and Cécile was yelling from the bedroom, having a child. A doctor was with her, tending to the occasion. All Felix could do was wait. He felt nervous as he did each time. Johann made sure the other children stayed in their room.

After the passing of another hour, a baby's cries echoed. The doctor came to the parlor informing, "Congratulations. You have another son." He guided Felix to where Cécile laid in bed, holding the baby, freshly wrapped in a blanket. Felix sat at the bedside to get a closer look at the child. Cécile stated, "This one should be Felix Jr., he looks like a Felix to me."

"I like that name." Felix kissed her.

Besides gaining a new member of the family, other things were being accomplished. In concern of the St. Thomas school, Felix raised money by giving more organ concerts. His hard work paid off as the Bach monument was placed near the school. Felix couldn't help but feel proud as the elegant statue sparkled in the sunlight. It was obvious who his favorite composer was. Felix was also on the lookout for old pieces to revive. He hoped to find a copy of Mozart's 'Die Zauberflöte' in the original German.

By mid-February, the Academy of Leipzig progressed enough to commence. The classes came together through experience and trial, teaching ten sinecures; the rest wanting instruction were to pay 75 thalers a year. Felix spent much of his time at the academy to teach classes. He planned to do so for a short while, at least until the school increased and generalized.

The school made a fair start with new pupils joining daily, causing lessons to increase, in turn making the need for more staff. There was no trouble in finding teachers as there were plenty of musicians from the orchestra. Five directors had been chosen who were inclined in the system of organizing a Konservatorium, but none of them were musical, hence the reason Felix wanted Ignaz to be head of the Academy.

The project did not go by without any troubles. Two maladies were afflicting things. The directors wanted to enlarge and expand even more by building houses and hire rooms. Felix felt they were wishing to jump ahead. He believed the two large rooms, giving simultaneous lectures were sufficient.

The other malady had to do with the students. All of the pupils wanted to compose and theorize, while Felix believed the principal thing that ought to be taught is sound practical work - sound playing, keeping in time, sound knowledge of sound music; to teach them what is good music first so then they can make well rounded music. Out of that, all other knowledge would grow of itself. Felix wished art to be far from a mere handicraft.

As Herr Schumann gave a lecture on music interpretation in one room, Felix held a theory class in the other. He was working with a group of students who were young in the ways of music. They had finished a lesson in intervals. While the class worked on homework, a group of students giggled together.

"What's so funny?" Felix asked in a curious tone as he glanced up from his desk in the midst of work. One student murmured, "Major fifth."

"Ok don't be swearing now." Felix scolded. Another student asked, "What was that one song by Chopin you played the other day?"

"Piece." Felix corrected, "Music without words is a piece."

"Explain your 'Songs without Words.'" Another student looked up from their paperwork. Felix face palmed. He concentrated on a letter he was penning to Ignaz, calculating a dry estimate of income and cost of living to move to Leipzig. Felix concluded that the total pay request for students would be 200 thalers per annum. An amount decently equal to the cost of living. Yet, English men, who lived rather better, required 250 to 300 thalers. Felix did some maths and the equivalence. In English money it was around 50 to 60 pounds.

There was much satisfaction in his work day at the academy, writing to Ignaz while the students worked obediently in the background. Yet, such moments couldn't last a mere minute. Felix grabbed a letter stashed in his folder. It was from Berlin. He didn't feel like thinking about that city, but he couldn't ignore the royal letter forever.

The first glance at it agitated him. Herr Massow had poured the King's begs into words for Felix to return to Berlin. There was to be a conference held, giving Felix a new title of high standing. The inquiry embarrassed him as he didn't want to be like some composers who had more decorations than good compositions.

King Frederick overestimated him as he began spewing commissions on top of the ones in progress. The long chorale of Felix's, 'Herr Gott. Dich loben wir' was to be arranged for chorus and orchestra. In the coming weeks, Felix worked his tail off to complete it. It became the most tiring thing he had ever attempted. Things were still not organized in Berlin academy wise. He wrote to his brother Paul, wanting to write directly to the King, breaking off every affair with Berlin, but did not feel justified to do so. Though he wanted to be in Leipzig by inclination, he felt drawn to Berlin by the promises he made to the King.

In the entire affair, Felix felt so angry and bewildered by the King's demands. Herr Tieck, another correspondent of the King frequently wrote as he was in charge of making sure Felix was fulfilling the commissions. The pressure made Felix feel physically ill over matters.

To top it off, the King decided to come to Leipzig for a concert at the year's end. Felix knew he would have to adhere to the King face to face.

With that to come, he and his family would have no choice but to lose their home in Leipzig. Felix didn't agree with it nor thought it fair, but concluded that he would have to make the heart aching decision of choosing someone to take over as director of the Gewandhaus.

# Chapter XXIV: Incidental Music

Mendelssohn, Lied mit Chor from 'Midsummer Night's Dream' [1]
Jethro Tull, Locomotive Breath [2]
Mendelssohn, Dance of the Clowns from Midsummer [3]
Mendelssohn, 'Through the House' (Finale with narrative) Midsummer [4]
Spring song [5]

## [1]

Felix stood in his office, penning a score at the conducting desk. He glanced outside the window where the chilled snow glowed in the twilight. With ideas forming, his pen flowed with ease on each leaf of manuscript paper. The writer's block had lifted and his imagination flourished on the incidental music for 'A Midsummer Night's Dream.'

Out of King Frederick's commissions, the Shakespeare play yielded the most progress, due in part that the overture was completed years prior. The new parts were coming together beautifully. Felix found the project quite unique and intriguing.

There had to be a balance between music and story, so he made sure to be especially specific when it came to the dynamics. If the music deemed too quiet, it was mere background to fill the void of the speaking voice. Too loud and the story would be drowned out. It was more about letting the music submerge the listener into the land of pixies and sprites.

At the same time, it therefore made spoken poetry an instrument of its own, working in harmony with the orchestra. Sometimes the music paused depending on context, so Felix practiced through the play at the Klavier to line things up. It was to be in the original English as well as translated to German, so it took time in that aspect.

On the first notice of the finished product, his Majesty wanted the 'Midsummer Night's Dream' presented at the new palace in Berlin. The engagement would be the intended means of moving Felix and his family out of Leipzig.

Though Felix knew he had no choice, Cécile downright disagreed with the whole matter. She spoke with her arms crossed, "We can not leave our home behind. There must be a way to convince his Majesty."

"Darling. I've done all I can. It is a bit hard to convince royalty without being offensive. I am to find someone to fill the position at the Gewandhaus." Felix felt a pain in his heart in hearing his own words.

"How can you think of giving up the position that you love so much? We are so happy here. The children are well here. Is there any way out of this?"

"I don't see a way out. This is the instruction of the King." Felix sighed hopelessly. Cécile pleaded, "At least give the job to Herr David."

"I will ask him." Felix assured.
~~~

"I don't know..." I sighed, leaning back into my chair. Felix became exasperated as he sat in my parlor, after asking me to take his position. He begged, "You are the one I most trust. I intend to be back. As soon as I fulfill my promises to the King, I'll be back and that concerto will be ready for a premiere by then, and-"

"Felix, bitte." I silenced his ramblings. He hushed and I continued with my honesty, "I do not think I am suited for your job. I am comfortable as Konzertmeister and I wish not to compromise my position."

Felix gave another somber sigh, not knowing what to do. He set his coffee down and stood up to leave. I felt a pang of guilt so suggested, "Why don't you contact Herr Hiller on the subject?"

579

"I could try, but he and his wife reside quite comfortably in Frankfort." Felix grabbed his coat and left it at that. I continued sipping my coffee, pondering the whole situation. My wife Sophie joined me for quality time.

Meanwhile, in haste Felix went home to write a letter. When entering his office, little Carl was at his desk, messing with the inkwell; splotching the pen over a thankfully blank manuscript.

"Carl! What are you doing here?"

"Papa! Mama said I could write music!" Carl dotted random notes on a staff, his arms covered in sticky black ink. He dipped the pen back in the inkwell, but bumped it with his hand, tipping it off the desk. The little boy groaned as the staining liquid flowed onto the carpet. He turned to his father's tapping foot. Felix had his hands on his hips. A long silence commenced.

"Papa...I'm sorry." Little Carl set the pen down. Felix sternly pointed towards the door. Carl stood and obeyed, but before he left, Felix grabbed his arm, halting him. He held his hand up to give discipline. Carl in an instant clenched his eyes shut, knowing what was to come. Felix halted a minute as he felt a reminisce of his own father within him. He had not been to such a point with his child.

"Carl." Felix calmed his tone and loosened his stance. Carl looked up to Felix in fright and whispered, "Ja Papa?"

"Go to your room for the rest of the day. You shall not have dessert after supper." He firmly stated. Carl didn't moan or groan. He quietly listened and went to his room on his own. Johann came by the office and noticed the mess on the floor, "Oh dear, I'll go to the market to get something to clean that."

"Danke." Felix nodded, while grabbing a rag to sop up some of the ink. He then sat at his desk with fresh letter paper. The manuscript Carl scribbled, Felix set aside to save it. He still thought the attempt was cute. To continue with business, Felix began writing to Hiller, requesting he take the position as director of the Gewandhaus. It was a hard task to shape words for the request. Each line of the pen felt like a blade to his heart. He did not want to give up directing at the Gewandhaus but forced his hand to write otherwise to Hiller. Little did he know, the new year 1843 was to compromise their life long friendship.

~~~

At the St. Thomas church weeks later, I joined Felix to attend a performance of the oratorio Samson. We stood in the lobby while the crowd around us streamed into the main hall. Felix had his arms crossed in nervousness. I glanced at the clock and mentioned in our waiting, "This should be a nice concert to attend before you leave Leipzig."

"I guess..." Felix had pangs of sadness in his voice. He suddenly fell into a doze. I looked up to where his gaze settled to see Herr Hiller coming our way. He had agreed to come take Felix's position at the Gewandhaus. This concert was a little something for us to spend time together before Felix was to make his leave. Without a word we carried on into the church hall and found seating in a center pew.

Felix sat between Hiller and I. He turned to me in small talk, but kept silent otherwise. Hiller minded his own business, waiting for the concert to commence. I couldn't help but notice the slight gêne developed between them. Felix had a pang at seeing the man who was to fill the position he so loved and gave up so willingly. Hiller sensed the change in his once close friend, who now had a melancholy towards him. Their feelings lasted throughout the whole evening of the oratorio.

The next day, I headed to the hotel where Hiller took a temporary stay. With me was a young eleven year old violinist named Joseph Joachim.

He was an excellent musician and already had high skill at the violin. He looked up to the musicians of the Gewandhaus such as I, but mostly to Felix. In the moment I was taking the young child to meet Herr Hiller, but a worry came when I found Felix and Hiller speaking with coffee in the hotel lobby.

I feared Felix's mood to be soured, but in joining them, the uncomfortable sensation between the two disappeared. Another guest seemed to distract from the matter. Sitting across the way on a couch was the young Danish composer Niles Gade. He greeted Joachim and I in all kindness. Young Joachim of course greeted Felix in his usual excitement. Felix had the boy sit beside him and they spoke of all sorts of things. Joachim couldn't have felt happier, but did not have a guess that Felix would be going away. Any sadness was hidden with talk and smiles.

"We should go out somewhere today. This is a lively group." Hiller looked at his surrounding friends. I suggested, "Why don't we go to the theater this evening? There are a few stage plays going on."

"After that we could supper together in my rooms." Hiller added. Everyone stood to go on the outing. Joachim stuck to Felix as if he were his papa. Through the whole time of attending a few plays, the mood of our group was well. A vast difference from the bitter air the evening prior.

When we returned to Hiller's hotel room for supper, everyone gathered at the small table. The food was simple, consisting of bread, an assortment of cheeses and wine. Hiller spoke after gulping down a serving of wine, "I am happy to say that my wife will be joining me in a few days, after I purchase a new place here in Leipzig."

"Is she happy to come?" I asked. Hiller nodded, "She can't wait."

Felix was too busy taking to Joachim to pay attention to the conversation. Rather he was purposely ignoring such talk until Niles asked Felix, "Isn't it nice that Frau Hiller will be in the city?"

"I'm exceedingly happy for Herr Hiller." Felix turned from Joachim in high spirits. I sensed Felix's real mood through his positivity. Hiller did as well, knowing he was truly anxious over the matter.

Later in the week, Hiller made his first meet with the Gewandhaus orchestra. I took my seat with Joachim close by as my shadow. He wanted to be a concertmaster in his future. Soon after the rest of the musicians seated, Felix stood before the orchestra somberly, announcing, "My dear friends, as you may have heard, I must leave Leipzig for a long while. In that time, you shall have a new director." He gestured Hiller to the conducting desk. A few members of the orchestra gasped, including young Joachim beside me. The talk of our circle of friends didn't give hint to him of Felix's leave. His heart broke to pieces in seconds.

"This is Ferdinand Hiller, a very good composer and he will be a suitable director." Felix introduced. He then went to the piano as Hiller flipped through the scores. I announced to the orchestra, "We shall rehearse Felix's g minor concerto. He will perform that for his last concert here. Though it is my duty to conduct the concertos, I am allowing Hiller to conduct to give him a welcome." I looked to Felix with a nod. Hiller held up his hands and counted in.

~~~~

After rehearsals, Felix returned home tired and worn. He couldn't wait to get into lounging attire and go to bed. Cécile questioned him as he walked by the dinner table, "Are you going to bed before supper?"

"I'm quite exhausted." Felix headed to the bedroom. Cécile followed, grabbing a note, "This letter came today from Herr Bendemann, the artist. He is having a gathering tonight at his house. Clara Schumann and you are to play music. You must eat before you go."

"At least let me nap." Felix flopped in bed, instantly falling into slumber.

Cécile let him sleep the fifteen minutes before Johann finished setting the table. Felix got up feeling somewhat refreshed. When eating, he made capital work of his meal then headed out on the next engagement.

Bendemann's home bustled with guests. The artist welcomed Felix, guiding him to the piano. Clara stood nearby, holding a glass of wine as if she were taking a break. Felix sat at the keys and began Beethoven's Appassionata. The guests gathered around to catch the sweet tones.

At the end of the Andante, he let the final chord of the diminished seventh ring on for a long time as if he wanted to impress it forcibly on all present. He turned to Clara, "You must play the Finale."

"Nein! Felix, seriously! You finish it." She near choked on her sip of wine. Everyone waited with the diminished seventh over their heads, anticipating the finale. The unresolved discord moved Clara to the piano. The end of the sonata was worthy of the beginning. Felix had much enjoyment with his circle of friends, Yet, life in Leipzig was soon coming to a halt.

~~~

On the first of October, Felix's farewell concert was held at the Gewandhaus. People packed the auditorium. I took my seat with the other musicians close to follow. Felix sat in all grace at the piano while Hiller entered to take his spot at the conducting desk in all professionalism. There was no hesitation for the music to start. As soon as every musician has their instrument set, Hiller counted in.

It was a wonder watching Felix put so much heart into his playing in the moment. He glanced at Hiller every so often, but kept his mind towards the voice of his instrument. I rather noticed Felix's eyes gleam with regret. He didn't want to leave the Gewandhaus so savored every note he touched. Hiller stood proud and conducted as if he could not wait for Felix to be out of the picture.

After the concerto's end, the audience applauded with a roar. Felix stood and bowed. When the rest of the musicians bowed, Felix glanced back at me. I saw a tear exit his eye before he walked off. He left the stage without any handshakes as he was too saddened to give farewells.

Felix headed for the exit as he didn't want to be in Hiller's way when the dispersing crowd gave their congratulations to the new director. In the lobby, young Joachim came across Felix and tugged at the back of his coat, stopping his fast leave. Felix turned to the boy who was in tears, asking, "You aren't really leaving Leipzig are you?"

"I'm sorry but I must. I hope to come back, but that I can not tell. Stick to Herr David. You will learn a lot from him." Felix gave Joachim an embrace then headed for home. It was going to be a long night as his family was to pack for the early morning train. He thought he would have had more time, but between letters from Paul and Herr Massow in concern to the King's demands, Felix smelled a rat and decided to set off on the first train to Berlin the next day.

Cécile had a head start in gathering their belongings. Johann helped the children pack. Felix walked into the house to his children in a state of confusion. Little Carl cried while Marie had excitement in thinking they were going on a road trip. Young Paul and Felix Jr. were indifferent. They were too young to understand what was happening. Carl's upset emotions worried Felix so he sat down with the child, "What is the matter?"

"I don't want to be away from you." He sniffled. Felix explained, "We are leaving together. I'm not leaving you."

"That's not what mama says. She says you are going to Berlin and we are visiting grandma Lizzy." He poured his tears onto Felix's lap. Felix gently moved him aside to stand and went to the bedroom where Cécile was packing.

"Explain why Carl thinks I'm leaving you and the children."

"I'm not going to live in Berlin. The King is going to waste your time again. When there is nothing left to do in Berlin, I expect you to come to Frankfort." She kept packing. Felix ran his fingers through his hair. She then explained, "Our train leaves in the afternoon, so I expect that you'll be gone by the time I wake."

"Ja, but I'm sure the King wants us to have a life in Berlin eventually."

"He wants you to make a life there, he doesn't truly care about your family." Cécile finished a suitcase then flopped into bed, adding, "Johann is coming with the children and I." She shut her eyes to sleep. Felix sighed, packing a suitcase then leaving the rest for the morning. He tucked the children in their beds then headed back to the bedroom to get a good night's rest himself.

~ ~ ~

## [2]

Before the dawn or rattling of carriages, Felix rose out of bed. After a morning wash and fresh outfit, he fully woke himself by fetching a spot of coffee. He gathered the last of his luggage while Cécile peacefully kept in her dreams. Before Felix left the bedroom, he kissed his wife tenderly. She stirred awake and kissed back, quite intensely, but huddled back to sleep.

Felix then went to the childrens' room and gave them kisses. Marie, Paul and Felix Jr. kept out like blown candles. Little Carl managed to stir awake. He clung to his Papa, hugging his neck. Felix kissed him then gently pried his hands away. Carl cried hopelessly while watching his father go. Johann met Felix in the dining area, giving a farewell. This was yet another hard leave to Berlin.

Felix headed out into the dark morning and found a carriage to take him to the train station. The locomotive was rolling in at the hour.

586

Felix went to the ticket booth to purchase his pass to Berlin. A few others were in line for the early train. The whistle blew indicating the time to board. The scent of steam filled the air, burning Felix's nose. A mix of oil and grease were added to the stench.

As Felix headed towards a boxcar, he felt nervous with the modern means of travel. The train jerked as the breaks were soon to be let up. It whistled once more. Felix put all second thoughts behind and stepped on.

The locomotive chugged away. The wheels screeched much when turning. Once moving straightforward it sped up to get to Berlin in capital timing. Instead of days in a carriage, the trip would be hours.

The dark morning soon transformed into a light afternoon of grey clouds, bright with a mist. He glanced out the window every now and again, watching the fields pass by quickly in view.

As the train continued to chug, the pistons scraped against the tracks. Felix wasn't sure if he favored going by carriage in the context of the moment. Each passing minute was taking him closer to the city he desired not to see. He couldn't change his mind now. There was no stopping the train. Life didn't slow down.

Felix happened upon a newspaper to read. It had many articles to keep him occupied. The long paragraphs finally gave his eyes a dreariness with the passing hours. Slowly he dropped it onto his lap to drift into a dream. It seemed to start pleasant; like floating on air with the train's whistle puffing clouds of smoke.

He soon began to recollect over everything and everyone. Hiller's happiness of going to Leipzig was a sting to Felix's emotions. It gave him worry as he hoped to get his position back once he returned. Being separated from Cécile and the children gave another angst of anxiety. He pictured little Carl's desperate face each time his Papa left him. Cécile's bewitching blue eyes full of tears gave another torment.

On the other hand, the worst wrench in his mind were the demands of King Frederick. The King's orders began blaring in his head along with the screeching train whistle, giving him a migraine. He wanted the train to turn around, but it couldn't slow down. The engine chugged faster and faster.

Felix's dream veered into a surreal fear of the boxcar swaying on an unstable bridge. In reality, Felix leaned against the window, but in his wakeful mind, the cold glass felt like a gust of wind. The dream went back into the floating feeling, but it didn't last as it turned into a falling dream. Just before his brain anticipated the ground, he jumped awake in a fright to the whistle's scream, declaring it had arrived at its destination. He grabbed his bags and rushed out into Berlin.

His first stop was the Bankhaus, where he found Paul. Their uncle Joseph still resided there as well. It felt nice to be around family, but bitter at the same time as Lea was now gone. Felix and Paul went to the living room for some coffee and to catch up. They first discussed the main house of Leipziger Straße No. 3.

"I have found a family interested in the estate." Paul informed, "Before I close the sale on it, I'd like to make sure you were alright with it."

"I am alright with it. There are many precious memories there, but I don't see my family and I owning it. It is better for it to have a new family to enjoy it. Who is the family?"

"Boeckh. I believe they will take care of it." Paul assured. Felix then confessed to Paul, "I was wondering, I wish not to be intrusive, but I need a place to stay. If it's not too much for you, otherwise I could ask Fanny and Wilhelm."

"Why don't I organize something for you. I know Fanny and Wilhelm are quite busy these days and this house has much commotion with business. I'll get you a room at the best hotel in Berlin." Paul handed him money.

"Danke." Felix accepted, but rather felt that Paul didn't want to deal with him. His brother slyly added, "Be sure to be on the lookout for apartments. I hear there are many decent ones for a family of six."

"Don't count on it." Felix replied ryely. He made his leave of the Bankhaus to go find the hotel. It was settled in a well to do neighborhood with nice accommodations.

After getting a room and relaxing, Felix deemed the hotel to be his favorite. Though it was clean and modest, it still felt nothing like being with family. Felix laid in bed and longed for his parents, as well as heartfelt quality time with his siblings.

~~~~

Eight days after settling, a letter from King Frederick came, summoning him to the palace. Felix hoped it was for a real conversation, not a mere dinner request.

When he came to the palace, Felix's hopes crumbled as the servant escorted him towards the dining hall. There, at the foot of the long table sat his Majesty and Herr Massow. King Frederick had a lavish dinner plate before him while Massow had a pile of papers. On the other side of the King, across from Massow, was another lavish plate of cheese and sausage accompanied by wine.

"Felix, come sit, I do hope you are hungry. I know you like wine, so I paired the finest cheeses and meats with it." Frederick pointed to the seat. Felix walked the way and sat down. Rather than eat, he watched Massow scribble signatures on various documents. The King ate grapes and fine bread. He looked to Felix, "Go on, eat. We have much to discuss, I can't have you talking on an empty stomach."

Felix grazed at the different cheeses, trying each kind. Herr Massow began business, "These are the new documents concerning concerts and pay that his Majesty would like you to sign." He handed Felix a pen.

Felix looked at each one with caution and didn't sign anything he deemed impractical. The King explained his main request, "I want the 'Midsummer Night's Dream' premiered at the new palace. I have an orchestra and choir at my disposal. They will grant you 11 rehearsals beforehand. The performance is to be the 14th of October."

"Sounds sufficient enough." Felix finished his wine. By the time his plate had been emptied, the meeting ended. Felix then ventured off to meet with the orchestra.

The musicians and actors rehearsed in the auditorium of the new palace to get a sense of the acoustics. They adapted quickly to Felix's conducting. Each performer was top notch and chosen well. It surprised Felix that something concerning music had progressed in Berlin. At the same time not a word of the academy was said. Felix knew nothing was moving forward in that aspect. The extravagant orchestra and professional stage actors were to entice Felix to stay. It was tempting as he felt his music flowing together.

~~~

## [3]

On a train to Berlin, Hiller, Gade, Joachim and I were on our way to surprise Felix by coming to the premier of 'The Midsummer Night's Dream.' We laughed and had a party in the boxcar, excited to see how Felix was holding up. We knew he wasn't fond of the city so we thought our visit would cheer him.

When arriving at the new grandiose palace, everyone in attendance wore their best. We had appropriate attire, even young Joachim. His fine little suit made him feel proper.

I couldn't help but chuckle as he stood with confidence in posture. He had the most anticipation to see Felix once again. I hoped to find Felix beforehand, but the crowded audience flowed towards the auditorium, forcing our group to follow.

We seated in a balcony of the pearly hall containing a stage. King Frederick could be seen on the ground floor along with the rest of the court. He sat in all properness, speaking to a correspondence beside him.

When the modern furnishing of gas lighting dimmed, the stage was illuminated. I noticed the King's expression brighten as he watched Felix enter the orchestra pit. Everything in the moment was as the King wanted. A shiny new palace and good music to attract the likes of the court.

When everything was set, Felix counted into the overture. Everyone recognized the flutes' windfull chords and captivating tones. It gave them the anticipation to hear the whole play.

The fresh music after the overture gave the utmost enchanting incidental accompaniment to Shakespeare's lines. The actors performed capitally, though, the lovely and popular actress Charlotte von Hagen would have been more in her sphere in a drawing room or ballet than as the elfin Ariel.

Everything regarding performance was to Felix's wishes. The comic scenes were amusing and the whimsical parts most poetic. The entr'actes were played without any pause whatsoever. It was indispensable for proper effect.

A long pause was introduced in the middle of the performance to offer refreshments to the people belonging to the court. It caused a half hour to be taken up with loud talking and moving about while others were quiet. That whole scenario portrayed disrespect to art in Felix's ideals. Nevertheless, the play carried on after the court got their break.

I couldn't help but find intriguing aspects with each piece. The overture was recapped and recycled throughout various passages; from the flute's wind to the donkey's calls. The ending gave the utmost satisfaction. Along with the flutes, the narration went as so:

[4]

Through the house give glimmering light,
By the dead and drowsy fire:
Every elf and fairy sprite
Hop as light as bird from brier;
And this ditty, after me,
Sing, and dance it trippingly.
First, rehearse your song by rote
To each word a warbling note:
Hand in hand, with fairy grace,
Will we sing, and bless this place

Above all, even the great Shakespeare verses, the incidental music alone would be enough to stamp Mendelssohn as one of the cleverest of tone-masters. Though his late father would be rolling in his grave, Felix's muse flourished in the world of sprites. The phrases of violins tickled the nerves in tone. It affected Felix, giving him spurts of energy as he conducted.

The voices of the chorus beautifully resonated as if transforming the scene of the stage into a real land of fairies. Shakespeare's plays were solid on their own, but without such music, the listeners would have been captivated in a much different sense.

Among the ladies in song, a soprano stood out in a solo. Her voice floated over all other melodies with her graceful lines of:

'First, rehearse your song by rote,
To each word a warbling note:
Hand in hand, with fairy grace,
Will we sing, and bless this place'

I turned to Joachim who appeared ever so transfixed. The eyes of his boyish face showed the glimmer of what he saw in the music.
Each note contributed to a scene of purple blossoms beside a sparkling blue lake in the glow of the moon.

For myself, I had the most intrigue for the violin phrases that came fourth, giving the sparkle to the sprites. Hiller and Gade were watching Felix's conducting for the majority of the performance. They were fascinated by the musical context and what the instruments mimicked. Whether it was a twinkle of a pixie, an elf or elfin or the call of a burrow; it all had a part in the composition.

I glanced down towards the front row seats on the ground floor. The royal court watched in their usual manner. The ladies waving their fans, moving about with a feather or so in their hair. The gentleman sat, appearing bored as ever, whether they truly were or not.

King Frederick watched in happiness, but often whispered his options to the royal beside him. It couldn't be heard from afar, but Felix, being only a few feet in front of him became annoyed with the stirs of rich people.

Once the interlude of the chorus faded down, the actor at the head of the stage stepped forward, ready to speak his next lines. The flutes entered again:

Now, until the break of day,
Through this house each fairy stray,
To the best bride-bed will we,
Which by us shall blessed be;
And the issue there create
Ever shall be fortunate.
So shall all the couples three
Ever true and loving be;
And the blots of Nature's hand
Shall not in their issue stand.
Never Mole, harelip, nor scar,
Nor mark prodigious, such as are
Despised in nativity,
Shall upon their children be.
With this field-dew consecrate,
Every fairy take his gait;
And each several chamber bless,
Through this Palace, with sweet piece;
And the owner of it blest
Ever shall in safety rest.
Trip away; make no stay;
Meet me all by break of day.

The music fell into another interlude once more in which was slow and sweet. It felt all too soon for the play to come to a close, but everything had to come to such a point eventually. The next great lines ended the music for the night:

If we shadows have offended,
Think but this, and all is mended,
That you have but slumber'd here
While these visions did appear.
And this weak and idle theme,
No more yielding but a dream,
Gentles, do not reprehend:

594

if you pardon, We will mend:
And, as I am an honest Puck,
If we have unearned luck
Now 'scape the serpent's tongue,
We will make amends ere long;

Else the Puck a liar call;
So, good night unto you all.
Give me your hands, if we be friends,
And Robin shall restore amends.

After the clapping of the court and commoners, Felix turned and bowed. Every other performer followed. Frederick William walked the few feet to the orchestra pit, telling Felix in excitement, "My dear Felix, with this work, we must soon have the next plays performed. Your music is the best Berlin has to offer."

"I'll see what can be done." Felix had an air of annoyance. It was obvious, especially around other members of the court, that the King treated him as his pet. Felix didn't want to stay in the city based on the fact he was a favorite of the King.

A duchess came up and assured Felix, "I can't wait to come back and hear more." She curtsied then left with her duke. Her comment made Frederick all the more eager. Felix braced himself as Fredrick gripped him at the shoulders, livingly stating, "You shall have to get the next one done right away."

"As I said, I will see what I can do." Felix bowed slightly. Frederick smiled once more then trotted away with his party. Felix gave a sigh standing alone in the pit. He then looked up at the thinning audience. Out of them, he spotted his group of friends, so sprinted off to catch up in the lobby.

"Herr David!" Felix spotted me first. Young Joachim jumped with excitement and hugged Felix. Niles, Hiller and I gathered around. After greetings, Hiller suggested, "Let's go out to dinner."

"Where to?" Niles asked.

"We can go to Postam and have dinner at the Einsiedler." Felix pointed out. Everyone agreed and took a carriage there.

At the restaurant, our table was lively with food and drink. We spoke much about the concert. Felix for the most part seemed satisfied and pleased, yet mentioned, "I was quite enraged by that break for the court. It was a waste of a half hour. I felt it was a disregard of artist consideration."

"But it still went fine." I stated. Felix shrugged in irritation. Joachim assured Felix, "That music was the best, it outweighs any antics of those needy nobles."

"Danke." Felix quietly answered. Hiller finished his plate last then stated, "I guess we had better be heading back to Leipzig, there's much work to do."

"You have that right." I commented, then turning to Felix. The expression on his face became somber, especially towards Hiller. Hiller had the air of knowing the soured relation between them. Things might have smoothed over had not Felix been called to Berlin.

After a quick shake of the hand, Hiller headed out. Gade gladly offered a healthy shake. Joachim sighed much, not wanting to leave Felix behind. Lastly I gave my goodbye. Felix had a few tears and told me plainly, "I am going to do all I can to be anywhere but here."

"You will be back at the Gewandhaus soon. We still have a violin concerto to premiere." I grabbed my bag then joined my group. Felix stayed at the table, lonely and sad.

~~~~

After the success of the 'Midsummer Night's Dream,' King Frederick was overly anxious to have the next commissions finished. To make things harder, he added new ones into the list. In the course of a fortnight Frederick wanted presented at the palace: Athalia, Antigone, Eumenides and Medea.

Felix frantically wrote music for Athalia, having it done in a few days as Frederick wanted that one immediately. Yet, typically of the King, the concert never happened that soon. In reality, the other plays would not get finished as promised. There wasn't enough time nor motivation. To lighten his load, Felix refused the commission for 'Eumenides'. He knew it would upset the King ever so, but he didn't know what else to do.

Herr Massow returned the book for Felix then wrote up a report on him for refusing. When presenting the news, Frederick sulked in irritation, "Does Felix know that he has hurt my feelings?"

"He believes that this alone can't be put to music, but the whole trilogy would require much more time." Massow explained.

"That would be all the better, but it could not prevent Mendelssohn composing for the 'Eumenides', which in itself, may be regarded as a splendid whole." Frederick sounded in deeper remorse. Massow didn't know what to say, but jumped as his Majesty abruptly hissed, "This affair is not over, I refuse to drop it. He shall compose for me as he is my subject. I shall be sure he continues to be a loyal subject!"

"Why don't you give the work to another artist? At least for this one, I think Felix may need a break from your commissions." Massow loosely suggested, "I know you want Felix to do it, but if you want it done, there are many eager artists who would take a commission from the King."

"I'll think it over..." Frederick gestured Massow to leave. Outside the room, Herr Tieck was in the corridor, catching bits of the drama. As soon as Massow came out and shut the door behind him, Tieck asked, "Is the King's precious musician being disobedient?"

"He is starting to refuse work." Massow sighed, "It will only pain the King more once I get around to telling him that he also refused to compose songs for 'Wie es euch gefällt.'"

"I am going to confront Felix. It is not like him to refuse so much." Tieck hurried out of the palace. Massow followed, "I shall come as well." They both headed for the hotel.

When they found Felix's room, they knocked. Felix answered and let them in, not speaking a word. He sat at the dining table where music in progress sat. Massow asked without intent, "Have you been working the hours away?"

"Ja." Felix rested his head on his arm as he fumbled with his pen. Tieck then spoke up with worry, "Why are you choosing to displease the King? Why are you refusing commissions?"

"I need time to elapse between the 'Midsummer,' he has commissioned a lot." Felix huffed. Massow suggested, "At least write for the 'Eumenides'. The King is deeply saddened with you. You have time, so your excuse is insufficient. You can not annoy the King too horribly as he loves you far too much. Yet, I don't want trouble to arise."

"The 'Eumenides' is too difficult and impractical to organize for chorus and orchestra; for me at least. I can make an attempt to solve this problem by suggesting someone else to do it." He spoke his truth. Massow ran his fingers through his hair, "The King wishes to stay in good standing with you."

"Well then I should go speak with him to get things straight. I'd rather be honest on my feelings of everything going on in Berlin. All of these grandiose academy plans- none of which are coming together." Felix stood and put on his coat. Herr Massow and Tieck followed him.

At the palace, the King was surprised to see Felix pay a visit. When he walked in, Frederick cheered, "My Felix, what brings you? Have you finished anything? Herr Massow tells me you have refused a commission. It does pain me to hear that."

"It is true." Felix stood in all politeness, "I find your demands too hard."

"What an absurd thing to hear from the mouth of a musician." The King stood in disappointment. He walked up to Felix to face him. Felix felt a heart stopping tension but managed to speak kindly, "I have other priorities, if you want me to speak in truth. My family is staying in Frankfort and I wish to be with them. I am not apt on staying here. I have a name that could replace me. You would find sufficient means of what you want done, music wise and academy wise."

"Bitte, my dear one, whenever you are here you always speak of leaving as if you're trying to escape a danger. I assure you, I am no threat to you, you are too precocious of a subject to harm. No other could replace your capabilities. I find it hard to believe you found a man to replace yourself."

"I have, his name is Herr Naumann, a perfectly fine musician." Felix bowed politely. Frederick smiled at his gentlemanly demeanor, but tried to be more convincing, "Your Bruder Paul won't be happy with what you are doing to my requests. This Herr Naumann is not you, therefore can not compose like you. I wanted the trilogy of 'Agamemnon, Choëphoræ and Eumenides' done, but you are refusing to do one."

"Leave my Bruder out of this. He does not have any rule over my choices. I can not promise three plays if I deem one impossible. I speak in truth and honesty again, I have been in turmoil trying to figure out your confusing demands."

"You confuse me!" The King's tone became rough. He grabbed Felix by the jaw, "You are an excellent composer that I deem good enough to fulfill my wishes. Yet you say you can't! I mean to be your friend, but now I don't know. Your speech is quite absurd as if you do not care that you are speaking to his Majesty!"

"Maybe if you were more reasonable then I'd get more done!" Felix's mouth began spewing his thoughts. Frederick told him in bluntness, "If you keep going with this attitude, I will have to impose my authority as King." He gave a grizzly glare. Felix calmed down a few notches then spoke softly, "How about I get the rest of 'Antigone' done while I am in Frankfort. I'll send it as soon as it's finished. Herr Naumann can do the rest of your commissions."

"Fine. Maybe it's best that you go." The King roughly let him off.

Right away Felix went back to his hotel, packed and took the next coach to Frankfort. He didn't visit his siblings before his leaving as he didn't want to hear their disapproval of the matter.

As the coach neared Naumburg, the decent July weather calmed Felix's mood so he penned letters giving his siblings farewells. For Paul, he worked on a painting he titled 'The Jungfrau.' It had been in progress since their trip to Switzerland yesteryear ago. He hadn't had time to finish it. The memory of the place was still fresh in his mind, but it didn't always come out on the canvas. He had to wash out the forest a second time as he wanted to get it right.

When the carriage rode closer to Frankfort, Cécile sent notice, informing that the family was settled in a home in Soden, near Frankfort.

600

Felix felt much relief to find a quaint wood house on the outskirts of town, giving it country air.

Right when stepping out of the carriage with his luggage, his children screamed, "Papa!" Little Carl and Marie sprinted out the front door. Young Paul clumsily followed behind. Cécile came, holding Felix Jr..

After being tackled with hugs by his children, Felix entered the house. Johann took his coat and luggage, assuring, "I have a plate of food for you. Your family ate already, but I made sure there was some left."

"Danke." Felix was ever so thankful to have a trustworthy servant. His famished state caused him to wolf down the full serving of beef and potatoes. After that, he went to bed for a hard rest.

With the rubbish of Berlin behind him, Felix had the most peace at the home in Soden. Each day he rose out of bed at six after having nine and a half hours of sleep. Early strawberries were available for breakfast to accompany coffee. The morning hours were most enjoyable when sitting by the open window, watching the children play in the garden with dear Johann.

During the crisp afternoons, Felix found apple trees and huge oaks to lay under. Sometimes a man from a nearby farm drove his swine herd, disturbing his relaxation. As he napped after getting a fill of rich pears and apples, one of the pigs ventured away from the herd. It decided to graze beside Felix. It snorted into his ear while hoarking on grass. Felix sat up and called to the farmer, "Bitte! Go elsewhere with your animals!"

The man listened, gathering his hogs away, causing the stray one to follow. Felix sassily turned over in the grass to get cozy, continuing his rest, that is, until little Carl rushed to his father, "Papa! Please play!" He ran around the yard with Marie. Felix stood and stretched, then joined in their game of tag. Cécile stood nearby with a canvas, painting.

Felix couldn't cease to rejoice at the sight of his healthy family. Cécile especially looked well, tanned by the sun without the least trace of former indisposition. He paused in playing and went to her. The canvas had a beautiful scenic landscape of the blue hills with the winding Main and Rhine. Felix admired his wife and her talents. He then gazed towards the children, who were in health with a tan from their days in the garden.

Each day continued with lunch at two O'clock to finish with dinner at eight, leading to bedtime at ten. In the entirety of the season, Felix never felt so much as himself.

*(Mendelssohn family at Soden, sketch by Felix 1844)*

Every Saturday the family went to town for the markets. The confectioner sold thread and shirt buttons in which Felix needed to mend a few of his linens. Cécile enjoyed browsing the fabrics for future dresses and clothes for the children.

Outside the thread shop, little Paul ran towards a group of women who were selling cherries. The four year old always made a bargain on the fruit.

The women selling them thought he was the cutest child and couldn't help but give him a few. Meanwhile, Felix enjoyed a stand where 'punch' was sold and drank.

After the market, it was time to go back home. The children continued their play outside while Felix and Cécile had sweet strawberries at the dining table. Cécile took up the newspaper to read. Felix gazed out the window, feeling a sense of peace while watching the children frolic the green grass. He turned back to Cécile and mentioned, "I wrote to my sister Fanny. I invited her to come here for a fortnight. She should be here tomorrow."

"Oh nice." Cécile smiled, sipping water. It was fresh from the Asmannshäuser spring. She stood, "I'll be sure there is a bed for her." She left to make arrangements.

The next day, Fanny arrived in the early afternoon. She came in time for lunch. Felix was in the utmost joy at her presence. Almost right away they began discussing composition together. Fanny shared her work and Wilhelm's sketches. Felix looked at them with awe, "Wilhelm must be so proud to have such a talented wife and you proud of him. I mean to ask, when you return home, can you send me that organ piece I composed for your wedding? A publisher wants me to put together a collection of organ music."

"Of course, but you left Berlin in such haste. Paul is in a rut about your leaving. Why don't you come back to get your music?"

"I have made my decision to stay out of Berlin long term. Besides, soon I must go to Zweibrücken for a festival. After that I am making my next trip to Britain. London of course. I've also been invited to Dublin to be presented with a doctorate at the university there."

"Oh, so now my Bruder is to be doctor Mendelssohn." She gave a joking tone. Felix chuckled, then begged, "When you return home, please have Sebastian write. I'd love a letter from him."

"Of course." Fanny nodded.

~~~~

In April of 1844, Felix set off on his next trip to England. Cécile and the children stayed in Soden as it seemed too much of a hassle. The ordeal of him going to Britain reached the ears of Berlin society. They thought it 'very wrong' that Felix decided to go there instead of composing for King Frederick. Felix didn't care about such drama and felt his happy self when visiting the Moscheles family at Chester Place, arriving on the 8th of May.

Right away, Felix was received enthusiastically in London society with conducting and composing. Among concerts, he took part in a performance with Ignaz and Thalberg in Bach's triple concerto. Also, young Joseph Joachim who was now thirteen years of age and an astounding violinist, made his way to London for a public debut. He featured in Beethoven's violin concerto with Felix conducting.

Away from concerts, Felix spent his time at Chester Place with young Felix Moscheles who was becoming quite the artist. Together they practiced sketching. In other aspects, Felix senior enjoyed testing the boy on his Greek and Latin studies. Young Moscheles had a sharp mind, even when quizzed on the spot.

On one occasion, while young Moscheles recited his language studies, Felix doodled on sketch paper. He began incorporating music into it, thinking it a good present for Ignaz. Klingemann visited later in the day and came up with lines of poetry. Emily Moscheles wrote down his lines with her nice handwriting.

*(Sketch for Ignaz)*

When the late evening came, Felix presented the sketch to Ignaz, who found the page most amusing. Ignaz then tried to herd young Moscheles to bed, but the boy groaned as Felix sat at the piano, "I don't want to go to bed. I want to hear Felix."

"Alright, you can stay up, but only for a little bit." Ignaz allowed. Young Moscheles cheered and flopped on the sofa. Ignaz sat by Felix at the keys and together they improvised various tunes. Young Moscheles savored every note, but it didn't last long. After one piece, Ignaz made the child retire for the night.

Felix and Ignaz then continued on with a few tunes. After running through a piece of Handel, Ignaz informed Felix, "The Handel Society wants you to make a new addition of Handel's Messiah. A concert has been announced on the first of June."

Felix nodded then stated, "In the addition, I want the music true to the score. If anything is added, it must be clear who intended what. I should have the thing prepared in due time." Felix continued at the keys with a soft melody. It gave a soothing end to the night.

~~~~

## [5]

On the 30th of May, Felix found himself taking a carriage to Buckingham Palace. Victoria and Albert invited him as soon as they heard that he was in London. Felix found them both in the drawing room, organizing music of Albert's. Each work pleased Felix, making him give way to comments, "These are excellent. I must hear you play them."

"Let us move to the music room." Victoria grabbed a few sheets. Albert took the rest and Felix followed them to the music room. There they played all of the beautiful pieces. Felix watched with content as the royal couple had such talent that wove together perfectly. Albert then told Felix, "Your turn."

"Alright." Felix went to the keys. He played a few sections of the 'Midsummer Night's Dream' then two songs without words. After that, Victoria joined with her voice in her favorite works, most of which happened to be Fanny's.

Before it was Felix's time to go, he grabbed a book of music from his folder, "I've arranged seven of my 'Songs without Words' as a duet for you to play together."

"Thank you dear Mendelssohn," Victoria chimed, "but before we part, you and I must play one together."

"Of course." Felix gestured her to sit at the keys beside him. Victoria chose 'Spring Song.' They played it beautifully. Albert daydreamed while watching his wife's pretty hands press the keys in grace.

When it finished, Felix then mentioned, "I have a concert coming on the 10th of June if you'd like to join. The orchestra is performing the incidental music to 'A Midsummer Night's Dream."

"We shall." Albert became excited. Victoria questioned, "The play will be in the original English I imagine?"

"Of course." Felix nodded, "Now I bid you both farewell." He departed the palace in happiness.

~~~

Days later at the said concert, Felix conducted in a theater containing a packed audience. The music echoed well and made the sound all the more magical and majestic. Victoria and Albert took up seats in the center front row as any royals would. They were only ten steps away from the pit where Felix counted the orchestra.

Victoria enjoyed watching the play while Albert, being a musician, rather found most of his attention towards Felix. He was intriguing to watch with his conducting gestures. His bâton and outfit made him appear most professional.

After the closing of the performance, the crowd gave way to yells, "Encore! Encore!" The demands were relentless. Felix turned and noticed Victoria and Albert shouting along, so faced back to the orchestra and had the musicians replay a few of the most popular sections. The Wedding March seemed to receive the best applause. Victoria was especially intrigued by it. She determined that when her children married in the future, the march would be an excellent choice of post vow music.

~~~~

A month later, after much fun and success, Felix gathered his luggage to depart from England. Little Felix Moscheles helped him, but in sadness. Felix senior felt so disheartened as silent tears dripped from little Moscheles' cute face.

"We will see each other again. You still have much to learn with drawing." Felix senior assured. The boy felt much better after being spoken to. Ignaz came and made sure nothing was left behind. He then informed Felix, "We shall not be parted too terribly long. Emily and I will be in Frankfurt in the autumn as I have a concert."

"Really!" Felix jumped in excitement. He then picked up his bags, now able to leave in satisfaction. The long trip back to Soden felt normal. A needed happiness and comfort was granted when he reunited with his family.

~~~

When autumn came, Ignaz and Emily kept their word. They arrived in Frankfurt in September. Felix joined them at the Konzerthaus, crammed full of people excited to hear the music of Moscheles. While Ignaz and Emily were elsewhere warming up, Felix stood by a friend named Rosenhain. They watched as more and more people flooded into the auditorium. Felix felt worried and told Rosenhain, "What will Frankfurters say when they find no seats? Let us try to hire some chairs. Come along!"

Rosenhain followed Felix as he went in search of more chairs. It was no easy task. The Konzerthaus had no extra. They resorted to taking a carriage out to various hotels, but each was crowded, having none to spare. The last place they checked was a small inn in which to their luck had four dozen chairs. Felix informed the landlord, "These must be sent to the Konzerthaus immediately."

"But who is to pay?" Inquired the landlord.

"A great artist, Moscheles, who is giving a concert. It is alright; your money is safe." Felix grabbed a few chairs. The landlord called to him, "Stop a minute! These great artists often give concerts, pocket the money, and then disappear. I must have something down."

Felix gave a sigh, setting down the chairs. Both he and Rosenhain emptied their pockets, which amounted to a little cash. The landlord took it and thankfully said, "On your way."

"Vielen Danke!" Felix and Rosenhain took what they could carry in their arms. They then stuffed the chairs outside of the carriage's cab to hurry back to the Konzerthaus.

With the extra chairs, everyone was able to find a seat, making the concert goers comfortable and pleased with the music. Ignaz played at his best and his daughter Emily joined him in a duet at the keys. It made for great success.

On the way home, Emily sat next to Felix in the carriage cab as he drew a sketch of the evening's go-abouts, doodling the chairs stuffed in the cab. Emily noticed he quit the sketch with the horse unfinished. She pointed it out, "You must draw in the horse."

"I can't draw that by heart." Felix admitted, penning a few words and lines of music for Ignaz to read and remember.

*(Searching for seating)*

The carriage rode to the hotel where Ignaz took stay. There, the musicians from the concert greeted them in the lobby with a 'punch' party set up. A piano was situated there as well. Both Ignaz and Felix were enticed to play spirited music. Most of the drinks happened to be passed to Felix. He played much Beethoven at the keys, each work sounding more drunk than the last. Through the hours, he had guzzled down 212 glasses of 'punch' fortissimo! The night ended with wonderful moonlight and singing in the street.

By morning Felix had a headache.
~~~~

"Nein!" Felix gave a dry reply. His throat stung in sourness. It was the season of spring and he had planned to make a trip to Leipzig to conduct his e minor violin concerto in its premiere. Just before making arrangements to leave from Frankfort, Felix caught illness.

"I am sorry, but you can not travel. I fear fever is soon to set in," the doctor sighed, "you have caught a strain of the measles."

"But this was the last day I could leave to make it in time! That concerto took me six years and it's too late to postpone the concert. I feel fine right now, I can conduct." Felix sat up. The doctor made him lay back, "Nein, you are not leaving the bedroom. You will spread sickness and a rash is already developing on your neck." He pointed out a redness on his throat.

"Who is to conduct then!?" Felix scoffed. Cécile overheard and came into the room, asking, "Does not Herr David usually conduct the concertos?"

"But this is a violin concerto. He plays violin." Felix stated in the obvious. He then huffed, "Get me some letter paper, I must write to Ferdinand."

Cécile grabbed a pen and paper. Felix viciously took it and wrote, explaining his situation. In his overwhelmed state, he gave way to a horrendous coughing fit.

~~~

I sighed upon receiving Felix's letter. It had arrived the night of the concert. Sofie, my wife, knew I was not happy. After I took in the information, I told her, "I must go find a fill in to conduct tonight. Hiller is away and I'm playing violin. It may be a challenge." I grabbed my coat and rushed out to the Konzerthaus.

Musicians were here and there, preparing for the evening. I found no one I was looking for, so headed back outside. When exiting the main door, I coincidentally bumped into Niles Gade in all my worry. He stopped and asked, "Everything alright?"

"Nein! Bitte! Can you conduct the concert tonight? Felix is ill."

"Of course." Niles smiled.

# Chapter XXV: The Violin Concerto

Mendelssohn, Violin concerto in e minor movement 1 [1]
(Violin concerto movement 2) [2]
(Violin concerto movement 3) [3]

*The whole concerto should be continuous in correlation with the book, but markers are given to indicate where each movement is to start. The 1844 version of the piece is preferred.

March 13th 1845

[1]

In the crowded Gewandhaus, Niles Gade counted the orchestra in. My violin entered soon after, singing the flowing motif that had been fermenting in Felix's mind six years prior; now being poured out as if it were fine wine. Sweet and extravagant to the taste, but a mature drink only enjoyed at the most special occasions. The audience listened as if they were tasting every tone. Each instrument had its own distinct hint of flavour.

I used my efforts appropriately to be sure every ear captured my instrument. The entirety of the work revolved around the auditorium with capital acoustics. The orchestra's accompaniment complemented the violin with skill.

As my bowings galloped the sound upward, the orchestra followed, leading to the climax of the phrase where the orchestra blared out.

I ran my fingers to play the strong acceding octaves. The orchestra gave another blaring flare. I bowed a second run of broken octaves that led the work into an interlude.

Though I stood, keeping my stance, I glanced at the people seated towards the front. They were in a state of bliss, surrounded by the mystique of the piece that had come together through careful craftsmanship. Each musician had pleasure in taking part in the concerto. The interlude gave them a chance to exercise their skill as a whole.

I held my violin to my chin again, ready for my next entry so as to not be late. This work in its premier was deemed not to be forlorn in the generations to come.

~~~~

Back in the home in Soden, Felix was stuck in bed, feeling like death. His ill state wasn't the main factor, but it was because he longed so terribly to be conducting the premier of his violin concerto. He had worked so hard to get it to that point and he couldn't fathom the fact that he missed it.

To top it off, the doctor now declared him too unwell to leave bed. He didn't believe the man's words, until fever finally began consuming him. It sent a weakness over his body, making it not matter whether he wanted to leave bed or not. He felt as if a weight were on his chest and the contents of his stomach felt a muddle, ready to spill out his mouth. Drips of sweet drizzled off his forehead.

Johann helped in any way he could by fetching tea and herbs. The doctor feared the fever to be dangerous, so mixed various medicines that he determined were far more effective than mere plants. It was in question whether the tinctures truly worked or not. Most doctors, especially older ones, mixed things through trial and error, causing repercussions. To Felix's thanks, none of the sour medications hurt him, but they rather made him drowsy on top of the ill fatigue.

After taking a dose of a tincture the doctor found effective, Felix sank into bed. The sweating slowed and a real restful slumber commenced. Johann gave sighs of relief, "Thank goodness something worked."

"Ja, hopefully he sleeps the rest of the night. It will give a good chance for the fever to lift." The doctor penned down his medicinal recipe.

Meanwhile, dreams were flourishing in Felix's mind. He felt a warming happiness, riding his old horse through a blossoming flower field, surrounded by a mystical forest. The horse pranced about the open land before stopping to graze. Felix dismantled the equine to smell the pink wild roses. He then fell back into a bed of soft lush grass as the twilight enticed fireflies to hover about.

Felix lived up the moment in which sprung a lullaby of melody into his head. He hummed it unconsciously outside of the dream world, only to realize it was a segment of his precious violin concerto.

The doctor adjusted his spectacles whilst listening to Felix chirp and whistle various melodies. There was too much talent in the hums to deem it mad behavior. The doctor rather enjoyed the singing and listened with pleasure. He asked Johann, "Does he hum often?"

"Ja, when composing of course, but it is especially tuneful when he is lullabying the children to sleep." Johann smiled at Felix's peaceful state.

Yet, in a sudden flash, Felix woke in utter restlessness, trying to get up. The worry over his concerto became stronger than the medication. The doctor instantly stood from his seat and tried to calm him, "You can not leave bed, you are in a feverish state."

"But the concert!" Felix became delirious, "I need to be there!" He stirred in a sweat. Johann grabbed a handkerchief and wiped the pouring sweat from Felix's face. The doctor explained while holding him down, "The fever is worsening and causing a panic."

"I will fetch water." Johann left the room.

"I don't want water, I need to be at the Konzerthaus!" Felix's tone had desperation. He then turned to the doctor in fury, "This is your fault! I could have left!"

"You are being completely unreasonable." The doctor grabbed his arms as Felix tried to shove him away.

"Let go of me!" Felix began to scream. The poor fellow shivered as if he were cold to the bones. On the other hand, his forehead was burning.

When Johann returned with a pail of water, he set it on the floor. He then dampened a rag and placed it on Felix's head to cool him down. The doctor told the servant, "Stay beside him while I get him medicine."

"Of course." Johann attempted to calm Felix by giving him water. He drank much as his dry mouth begged for hydration. It also seemed to lift his delirious state. The doctor came back after mixing a tincture together. Felix sighed upon seeing the vial of syrup, "Is that going to make me groggy as everything else you've given me?"

"This will make you sleep fully, I am sure of it." He gave Felix a harty spoonful. The horrid taste of the thick, sticky syrup took much effort to manage down his throat.

After a few minutes, Felix blinked heavily, becoming too exhausted to move. The slumber that came over him appeared deep. The doctor gave a sigh of relief, "That at least calmed his nerves." He grabbed a stethoscope to check Felix's pulse. When listening to him, his breathing was slow, but the beats of his heart were ramping. Something more than the fever was firing his nerves.

Felix inside was fully awake with the anxiety of the concert lingering within him. His main asset of worry was of the cadenza in the first movement. He hoped it would go as written with no impromptu moves.

~~~~

The concert at the Gewandhaus continued with the orchestra slowing towards the cadenza. In reality, it was my decision whether to improvise or not. Felix was not present to say otherwise and audiences loved my personal input in compositions. A daring choice it was, with only mere moments to decide.

When the flayal of my bowings drove the music on, I braced myself as the accompaniment came to an utter echo of silence.

Without any hesitation I gracefully embarked on the arpeggios and broken chords. My fingers followed what dear Felix had written. Each note he had penned was worth the while for this performance. He had specifically made it to correlate with the skill of my bowing hand.

Everyone's attention pertained to nothing but my old violin. The dimmed lights of the auditorium still glowed a twinkle, looking like stars from the stage. It was an unforgettable, magical sense.

The air of the stage felt like a vent of space; cool in temperature with a sense of nothingness while all else sat in silence to watch me caress my instrument. My hard sweat spewed in the midst of the workout of playing a perfect rendition.

The deed had been done. I played to Felix's wishes.

After the rest of the piece, the premier was received with immense success. I gave my bow then shook Gade's hand, only to find myself skipping out of the Konzerthaus in pure joy.

At my home, I straight away changed from my concert attire to something travel worthy and packed a bag or so. Sophie came into the bedroom as I finished gathering my things. She asked, "How was the concert?"

"It went just as imagined. I'm taking a trip to Frankfort as I must visit Felix. It will give him closure if I tell him how well it went."

"Travel safe." Sophie pecked my forehead in wifely tenderness. I gave my goodbyes to my children then set off by coach in the darkened night.

The carriage trudged for a day and a half before reaching the quiet wood home in Soden near Frankfort. It was the late-afternoon and Felix's children were running about in the garden. When they saw me, they rushed my way.

"Hallo Herr David!" Young Carl exclaimed. The others jumped happily. I greeted, then continued to the house. Cécile greeted me warmly, but her eyes were full of trouble. She explained, "Felix has had a terrible case of the measles. The doctor said his fever should lift, but it seems to only stay steady."

"May I see him?" I asked.

"It is best you speak to him as he is overwhelmed about the concert." She guided me to the bedroom. I entered to see a doctor sitting in a corner chair, giving a sigh of relief. I turned to see Felix in bed, snoring softly, dreaming and humming. I instantly caught that it was the melody of his concerto. The doctor explained, keeping his voice low, "He had been humming that melody all evening. I wish I had my own lullabies to myself."

"He's probably having nightmares over the concerto, wondering if I played it right." I chuckled.

As soon as sensing my presence, Felix shot up in his usual way of excitement. The doctor face palmed as Felix spoke frantically, "Ferdinand, did the concert go well? Did you play the cadenza as I intended? Did the audience like it? Who conducted? I wished ever so to be–"

"Felix," I gave a stern tone of voice, "I will tell you everything once you calm down."

"Alright." He patted the edge of the bed, wanting me to sit by him. I went ahead and sat, but still distanced enough to not catch any illness.

"So, how did it go." Felix changed his manners all together to be calm and polite. I smiled, "It was the best concerto I have ever played."

"Really!?" The excitement flared again. The doctor scolded, "Be calm or I'll give you another dose of medicine before you finish the conversation."

"Sorry." Felix glared at the physician in annoyance. He turned to me commenting, "All he does is stuff me full of tinctures."

That's it," the doctor stated, "I'm sick of the attitude. I'm going to try something new. Something that will work in the snap of the fingers. My colleague from Dublin came up with the solution last year."

"Do I want to know?" Felix gave a puff of exasperation. I watched the doctor stuff the medicine into something that didn't look all together appealing. A syringe. Felix's eyes widened in nervousness. The doctor took a tight hold of Felix's arm, rolling up his sleeve. The ruddy, speckled rash from the illness appeared quite terrible. Felix questioned as the doctor seemed to rather fumble with the dreadful thing, "Do you even know what you're doing?"

"I watched my colleague use these." He didn't hesitate to stick his arm. Felix jumped and spewed his opinion, "Your colleague's invention sucks."

"Shut up, you'll be asleep in the next minute." The doctor pushed on the plunger to force the medicine in. Felix fell in a state of drowsiness before the full dose of the tincture was injected. He fought hard to keep awake.

I knew it was my company he wanted, so wrapped up our conversation by assuring, "You will be there for the next performance of the concerto. I promise you. You have my word."

"If this illness would not consume me-" Felix flopped back onto his pillow in a cold sweat.

~~~

## [2]

A week or so later Cécile sat on the sofa in the parlor to catch up on knitting. Felix strode in wearing his lounging robe and slippers. He had a steeping cup of lemon ginger tea. Cécile gave a smile of thankfulness when he sat beside her. He looked tired from indisposition, but he had healed from the fever.

"Is the lemon tea helping with the cough? Johann said it was the best remedy." Cécile scooted closer to her husband.

"Ja, it's helping. It's better than all of those disgusting syrups and dreadful shots the doctor gave me." Felix then sipped the hot liquid in silence. The fireplace crackled, warming the room. Cécile could sense his thoughts, "Is something on your mind?"

"I've been thinking about our home here lately. Although I do miss Leipzig, we are so peaceful in the Frankfort countryside. If the future allows, we should build ourselves a home to our liking. It could be anything we want, a cottage or a wooden house. We would always have a garden with fresh strawberries and sparkling water from the finest spring-"

"Felix darling." Cécile interrupted, "We are happy visiting here, but Leipzig is where we prosper. In all honesty, do you want to live this close to my mother?"

"Good point, never mind." Felix left the sofa and turned to the writing desk to catch up on letters. He penned things here and there but nothing exciting.

"Felix darling?" Cécile crept up behind him, holding him at the shoulders. Felix grabbed her hand, soaking up the affection, "Ja honey?"

"Are you by chance going to write to Chopin anytime soon?"

"I haven't a reason, why?"

"Well, you know how I adore his music. I wondered if he could send something for you to play me. I'd be pleased to hear something new from him."

"I can ask. I hear that he spends most of his time writing these days. He doesn't perform publicly as he used to."

"Merci." Cécile kissed her husband on the neck. Felix grabbed a blank page and began his wife's request:

*My dear Chopin,*

*This letter comes to you to ask a favour. Would you, out of friendship, write a few bars of music, sign your name at the bottom to show you wrote them for my wife, Cécile, and send them to me? Whenever I wish to give my wife a great pleasure I have to play to her, and her favorite works are those you have written.*

*Your friend,*

*Felix*

~~~~

A week or so later, the post brought a few letters. The first one contained the most exciting news as Johann dished out supper.

Klingemann was engaged and soon to be married. The circumstances had been a long time pet wish to Felix. Upon reading the news, he got up from his dining chair and danced about the room for a full five minutes. Cécile raised a brow, "Are you out of your senses?"

"Nein, I've waited so long for this moment! Klingemann is getting married!" He continued his happy dance. The children loved their father's energy and the three eldest joined by dancing around him. Cécile casually asked as Felix was overcrowded by his children, "When should we plan our next child?"

"Next child? I think we have our hands plenty full right now." He sat back at the table to eat the stew before it chilled. The children followed. Cécile gave a sigh, then pestered him by muttering, "Bach had twenty children."

"That seems a bit excessive." Felix gave an eye roll. Little Carl spoke up, "Can we get another sister so Marie has a friend."

"Maybe one more." Felix gave in. Cécile in an instant stood from the table in delight. She handed Felix Jr. to Johann then went to her husband, giving him a kiss on the cheek, "I shall get the bed ready for tonight."

"Wait—" Felix was rather not expecting that. Cécile hurried off. Felix shrugged and continued eating. He opened the other received letter containing music. It was from Chopin:

*Dear Felix,*

*Just try hard to imagine, my dear friend, that I am writing by return of post... If please present it from me to Mrs Mendelssohn.*

*Frederick Chopin*

Felix hid the enclosed music when Cécile returned. She grabbed her satchel, "I'm going to town to get more fabric. Marie needs a new dress."

"Take your time honey." Felix inquired as she left. He finished up his dinner then went to the piano to try the new piece. It was a short Mazurka in Ab major with Chopin's signature at the bottom. Cécile obviously wanted a night of *quality time*, so he made preparations by practicing the work beautifully before her return.

When the latter part of the evening came, the children were ordered to bed. Johann took care of any complaints as Felix had business to tend to. He returned to the piano, waiting for his wife.

A half hour later, Cécile came home with her needed fabrics. The minute she entered, her heart swooned as the piano echoed a new piece of music. She knew it to be Chopin's composition by the flow of it. In haste she put her purchases away then spruced up her hair before entering the living room. There, she found Felix sitting with a posture of romance at the keys. The fireplace illuminated the room.

Cécile sat next to him, watching his hands delicately press each note with purpose. When the piece finished, Cécile kissed her husband. She stated between pressing lips, "Where are the children?"

"Put to bed." Felix assured.

"Excellent." Cécile maneuvered her hands to his hips. He in turn held her gracious shoulders to shower her neck with passionate kisses. Each press of his sweet lips felt as a brushing of rose petals.

When their session became too in-depth for the piano bench, they moved to the sofa. There, Felix romantically moved aside the shoulder sleeves of Cécile's dress to get a bare hold on the woman's radiant arms. Her light skin felt of fine silk, smooth to the touch. He breathed in her floral perfume, letting the fresh scent fill his nose.

With his gesture, Cécile moved her hold to Felix's waist. She then unbuttoned his waistcoat and undershirt. Felix's heart pounded once her vibrant hands grasped his torso, causing him to lay back as if falling into a bed of spring flowers.

In his state of being paralyzed from love, Cécile leaned over him to give her touches. She ran her hands along the slight curve of his waist. Felix's stature was petite for a man, but his figure had a luscious shape. From regular exercise, his tummy was fit, but after being full of dinner and wine, it was lush and soft like a bundle of violets. Completing his body's essence of cuteness was the little belly button, ever so rounded and delicate. Felix gave way to giggles and chirps of melody as he felt Cécile's soft touches slowly seep into it like a hummingbird gently tasting a succulent blossom.

In an attempt to keep a romantic stature, Felix caressed Cécile's beautiful hips. The dress she wore articulated her small curvy body, with a silhouette of utmost elegance to Felix's liking. He moved his hands to her neck and chin, admiring her gorgeous face. Her blue eyes pierced his soul.

Cécile smiled at the various tunes the spark of her hand caused Felix to bellow and whinny. Yet, after a few more moments of savoring his music, she sat up. Felix begged her, "Bitte, ich brauche mehr Küsse." He tugged at her dress to entice her back.

"Alright." Cécile leaned over him, unable to help herself. She kissed his neck and moved each pressing smooch towards his ear to whisper, "It's time for bed."

"Must we leave our moment here?" Felix breathed onto her shoulder.

"Come to bed." Her tone had indication. He fluttered, feeling her touches once more frolic about his belly. She was then quick to pull him from the sofa as if stealing him away. He followed beside her to the bedroom where the session continued its course.

~~~~

## [3]

After the full seasons of spring and summer, the latter part of 1845 brought the busy season of October at the Gewandhaus. Each week contained a plethora of concerts. The successful days were full of energy while other moments begged for rest.

One concert took the utmost work to prepare: Felix's violin concerto. It had not seen the stage since its premiere. The composer inquired that he conducted the second showing, but it took time to schedule the concert as other engagements constantly booked out the Konzerthaus. In thankfulness a perfect day happened to be free in October and all of Leipzig packed the Gewandhaus.

The beat of the timpani bellowed. Flares of the trumpets took part in a ravishing fanfare. My violin chirped in joy. Felix found himself at the conducting desk with utmost excitement in finally getting to see his concerto performed. He had waited ever so patiently to have the concert organized. I of course felt inclined to take up as the soloist.

Though Felix's conducting was commonly subtle, he was moving about with much excitement at the joyful last movement of the work. He was in pure happiness at the moment in time, music wise and life wise.

The stretch of the year caused many great things to commence. Felix moved his family back to Leipzig, where they found a modest apartment on KönigStraße. Niles Gade's abide happened to be only a few paces away, making Felix feel even closer to his friends.

(Mendelssohn Haus, KönigStraße)

Along with moving, Felix returned to the duties at Gewandhaus. Hiller wanted to move on, so allowed Felix to reacquire the position as director.

In regards to family life, Cécile was heavy in pregnancy, due in only a few months' time. She felt most comfortable in the lavish parlor of the new apartment. Felix meanwhile worked away in his office, composing music and writing letters.

He had received exciting news from Ignaz, who was making official arrangements to move his family to Leipzig, where he would devote his time as a head of the Konservatorium.

Felix straight away wrote about the differences between London and Leipzig, giving a rough outcome on expenses. Before giving a solid cost amount, Felix set his pen down. He left his office to find Cécile, "Are you by chance organizing the account books today?"

"Yes. In fact I shall do that now." She set her knitting aside and grabbed the books. Felix followed her to the dining table.

Together they sorted out their costs per annum. He studied the bills carefully to get the real sum of a cheerful home. A lot went into the costs, but each factor had importance.

After consulting Cécile, Felix returned to the writing desk and penned:

The price of a flat consisting of seven or eight rooms, with kitchen and appurtenances varies from 300 to 350 thalers. Servants would cost 110 thalers per annum, depending on what is required. Male servants are not as common as they cost 3 to 12 thalers a month. A good cook gets 40 thalers a year. A housemaid 32 thalers. If you add a lady's maid, to sew and make dresses, you would reach the mentioned figure. Adding a man servant would increase cost, but most don't need one. Wood is an important expense for the kitchen stove and heating costs 150 to 200 thalers for a family of five with servants. Rates and taxes were next to nothing. 8 to 10 thalers a year covered it all.

To help you get a better idea of cost, a thaler is equal to three shillings or 75 cents. In other words, your family would live comfortably with 1,800 to 2,000 thalers.

Yours,

Felix

~~~~

By December, Cécile had her fifth child, Elizabeth. Felix complied with his wife's wishes of naming the baby after the newborn's grandmother. He rather used the nickname of Lili.

With a growing family, Felix found his hands full, trying to give attention to each child. Adding to the mayhem, concerts at the Gewandhaus only became busier. The next performance involved a growing name in the singing world.

A Swedish woman by the name of Jenny Lind was sweeping concert halls with her soprano voice. In haste the board of directors at the Gewandhaus invited her to perform.

On the day of her coming, word spread like wildfire through Leipzig. Rehearsals took up the hours prior to the evening's concert. While Jenny was being introduced to the musicians by her manager, all of the men swooned over the young maiden's beauty. All but I. I thought her to be pretty of course, but I had a wife. There was nothing to be overdrawn to. Felix had a warm smile towards the girl; in much manner as I. Yet, that changed when she began to sing.

As soon as Felix heard the sheer power of her sparkling voice, it caused his heart to feel as if it were growing wings. The pulses of love hurt as it was treacherous. He had felt the same way when first laying eyes upon Cécile. The aches of a torn heart hindered his conducting and the musicians slowly began to fall out of time.

I looked up from my music to find Felix in a daze of infatuation. Jenny kept singing, but struggled as the orchestra became a muddle. I seemed to be the only conscious man in the moment so took charge, "Männer! Männer!" Everyone halted and turned to me. I continued, "Shouldn't we be playing in time for Miss Lind?"

"Ah Ja, of course." Felix shook himself awake, "From the top."

The rest of rehearsals went to satisfaction. Jenny smiled at me, feeling more confident. I blushed inside a tad, but still wasn't fazed. Felix's desire of the soprano only grew with each note her angel of a voice.

After rehearsing the hours away, the Konzerthaus hosted a packed audience. It was an obedient crowd that wanted to savor every note of Jenny Lind. Felix conducted as if he were floating on clouds.

He watched only her, causing me to articulate my gestures more so to help guide the other musicians. His forming affections for the soprano really began to irritate me.

After the performance, Lind managed to make her exit after much applause and roar. It took a great deal of time for the crowd to silence. Felix was soon to follow behind her, but I packed my violin in haste and halted him, "Herr Schleinitz is having a gathering at his home, his wife is making cake."

"I'll join, but I must go speak with miss Lind." He wandered off. I followed him down a corridor to the dressing room that Jenny took up. He knocked and Lind allowed him to enter. Meanwhile, I waited outside. Patiently.

Inside the dressing room, Felix sat at a chair, visiting with Jenny as she did her hair at the vanity. He was in a trance with his heart skipping, but couldn't be overly anxious towards her. She seemed to enjoy Felix's company but not in the same air.

"I had much enjoyment here." Jenny commented, "I shall have to return."

"Please do, this had to be the best concert I've ever conducted." Felix chimed with a smile. Jenny saw his expression through the mirror. She sensed his feelings in the moment, so finished up her hair and turned to him. Felix felt butterflies attack him as her eyes gazed at him.

"Felix." Her tone had a serious nature. Felix shook from his daydream and noticed her posture was not of love. She continued speaking, "I know why you wanted to come and speak with me. It is the case with every gentleman. You will help me with my career so I intend to keep our relationship on the basis of that." She stood. Felix stood as well, now in a disheartened state.

Jenny sighed at seeing him so sad, but there was a fact to the matter. She grabbed her cloak to leave. Before putting it on, Felix offered, "Please, let me help you with that. I can at least be a well mannered gentleman."

"Alright." She handed him her cloak. Felix made the moment slow by taking his time to place it on her. Jenny felt a small spark in her heart as his hand brushed her shoulder. She turned around to face him, causing Felix to hold her at the arms. His feeling of love went all over as she gave an unexpected kiss to the side of his neck. She whispered in his ear, "Write to me." With that she left for the evening.

When Lind exited the dressing room, I bowed politely. Felix followed behind her, putting on his top hat, ready to leave. He appeared to be the utmost chipper. I interrogated as we went down the corridor, "What took you so long? I thought you were only giving a few praises."

"I did." Felix skipped in his step. I eyed him in suspicion. He gave a confused expression as I took him at the shoulders and stopped him in the hall. I spoke seriously, "Felix. I know there was something more."

"What do you mean?" Felix kept an innocent tone as he tried to keep his neck covered by his cravat. I sighed and moved the cravat to see a kiss mark on his neck. Felix gulped as I warned in an all scolding nature, "Felix. I do not know your intent with Jenny, but I sure hope that you remember that Cécile and your children love you. You should never risk losing that."

"I'm sorry, I don't know what came over me." Felix apologized. We continued out of the Konzerthaus and found a carriage to Schleinitz's home.

The whole time at the little get together, Felix appeared out of place. He spoke none while sitting in the parlor and didn't seem to care about Frau Constanze Schleinitz's homemade cake. I thought his demeanor to be rude, so handed him a slice of cake, "Felix, Frau Schleinitz would be happy if you ate some of her cake."

"I'm not hungry." Felix stated as if I had disrupted something. I knew he was thinking about Jenny, so forced him to take the cake while whispering, "Get your act together and stop thinking about Miss Lind."

"Fine." Felix glared at me. It wasn't like him to give such expressions. I turned from him and continued enjoying the gathering. Felix ate the cake, but as soon as the late hour struck, he left in eagerness.

Upon entering his apartment, Felix went straight to his office, feeling the need to conceal himself. He sat at his desk, contemplating love altogether. Picking up a fresh leaf of paper, Felix wrote as to get rid of his deceitful feelings. He filled the page with lines of his underlying love wishes. After signing it, he addressed the note to Jenny Lind.

# Chapter XXVI: The Oratorio

Fanny Hensel Mendelssohn, Das Jahr, April [1]
Fanny Hensel Mendelssohn, Hiob Cantata [2]
Felix Mendelssohn, Elijah Overture and Help Lord [3]
Chopin, Funeral March [4]
Fanny Hensel Mendelssohn, Lobgesang, Kantate für Soli [5]

## [1]

The new year of 1846 gave to a fresh start. Felix was working on his next coming project. The Elijah oratorio. Progress on the composition had accelerated since coming up with the outline. Yet, to satisfy Felix's standards, it would take a lot more editing. His picky nature in revising made the whole affair no easy task.

On the other side of things, Fanny flourished in completing music, sending them Felix's way to inspect. Felix adored her way of expression, but felt grateful that she stayed compliant to his ideals on the basis of publishing.

After admiring his sister's music, he turned back to his own. The early spring morning brought muse and motivation. He completed a large section of his score before the noon hour, so decided to cool down from such thinking by taking a coffee break.

When entering the parlor, he found Cécile darning a pair of stockings. Felix sat by her, noticing she appeared especially beautiful that morning. His wandering eyes made her look up from sewing, "Yes honey?"

"I want your portrait painted. You look so beautiful. I shall hire an artist today." Felix went to pen a commission. Cécile stopped him to make a deal, "Darling. If I am to get my portrait painted, you must also. An updated one would suit me."

"Alright." Felix sighed, "Only because you are so ravishing." He headed to his office and wrote a request to a well respected artist by the name of Eduard Magnus.

Hours later, the painter made time for Felix and Cécile to his studio. They wore fine attire for formal portraits. Magnus welcomed them to his workspace with utmost excitement to paint the Mendelssohn couple. He first gestured Cécile to a chair set in front of a canvas, "Come sit here."

Cécile sat and Magnus asked, "What shall we add for an even more dashing portrait?"

"How about this elegant rose." Felix picked up the flower from a plethora of props. He handed it to Cécile and it added grace. She already appeared quite fancy with her red fur scarf draped around her arms. It matched the sparkling ruby ring placed on her finger.

Magnus began his craft after she posed in all beauty. Felix watched as the outlines formed his wife's figure. He couldn't help but blush as it transformed into the most gracious portrait. Each stroke of color made it all the more real.

The painting took a long setting to finish, but it was worth the wait. Felix admired it to the full. Cécile became curious about it as her husband stood with his mouth dropped in awe. She came to the canvas to see it herself. The turnout rendered her very pleased.

"Now it's your turn." Cécile pointed Felix to the chair. Before sitting down, he adjusted his coat and cravat. His hair he tried to fluff. While doing so, Felix questioned his wife,"Honey, do I look alright?"

"You look fine darling. Don't fuss so much about your appearance." She smiled as she found him to be handsome. Felix had many self conscious thoughts as he wasn't the young man he had been in his twenties. He was still young, being thirty seven, but time would only rush forward.

632

When he sat and posed with a subtle smile, Magnus began outlining Felix's face. Cécile gleaned constantly while comparing her husband to the portrait in progress. Hours later, Magnus signed the finished product, "Done."

*(Cécile and Felix Mendelssohn)*

Felix stood to check it out. Upon seeing his face staring back at him on the canvas, he gave a sigh of unsureness. He looked at both paintings sitting together. Magnus in a fright asked, "What's wrong?"

"Nothing, each is painted to perfection." Felix glanced at a mirror, comparing his reflection. Cécile asked, "What is the matter?"

"It's just that you look so good with beautiful youthfulness. Why am I aging so prematurely!?" Felix fluffed his hair some. Cécile chuckled, but assured her husband, "You aren't as bad as you think. Some hair is receding, but nothing to beat yourself over. Plus, you wanted to grow out your sideburns. You can't expect to look ten years younger with them."

"I love you." Felix gave her a kiss. Cécile knew how to speak to her husband.

Though Cécile's wifely words made him feel better, the next few weeks contributed to his self consciousness. His lifestyle consisted of frequent stress, work and fatigue; all in which affected his health.

Relentlessly, he put immense effort into providing for his family of five children. He conducted concerts multiple times a week or performed on the piano. When he wasn't at the Gewandhaus, he spent his time feverishly working on the Elijah oratorio. To top it off, there was soon to be a music festival in Birmingham, meaning another trip to England.

Felix hoped to finish the oratorio beforehand, but the processes of editing and revising hindered his wishes. Cécile caught onto his constant hardship on himself, so gave him reminders to calm down. Felix complied and decided not to rush the composition for the sake of his own health.

To keep from tiring out on the oratorio altogether, he made decisions on other aspects such as the printing and publishing. He thought it would be a decent idea to have the orchestra parts printed in Germany, but the vocal parts in England. The language he primarily chose to use was English. He had translations in German but intended many performances in England.

In regards to the price of the work, he reviewed his past compositions for ideas. He had made £25 for the Hymn of Praise, £30 for Antigone, £12 for a piano and violin duo, £24 for Walpurgisnacht, £47 for the incidental music for 'A Midsummer Night's Dream,' (not including the overture), £4 for 'Hear my Prayer O Lord,' £10 for the violin concerto, £25 for a book of six 'Lieder ohne Worte,' £10 for a trio in d minor, £20 for a trio in c minor and £20 for six songs.

Felix set aside his financial decisions, still indecisive. He moved on to a pile of letters from the postman. Most came from his siblings.

Before reading those, one from Jenny Lind was slipped in the pile. He opened it quietly after being sure his office door was shut.

It was a response to his love letters over the past couple months since their first meeting. Jenny's replies began to dishearten him. He requested that she sing at the Birmingham festival for he had written a high F-sharp in the oratorio, specifically pertaining to her voice.

Concerning the festival, she was booked, being in high demand otherwise. Relationship wise, her writing gave the hint that his expressions of love were too much. He needed to keep his feelings towards his wife and children.

Felix felt a stab to his heart, so penned another longing love letter. He rather put pressure on her by writing outlandish things, saying he would die without her. She was to be making her London debut in the next year so Felix planned to attend.

After dealing with Jenny's letter, Felix turned to his siblings' notes. They were from Paul and Fanny. He read Paul's first, learning exciting news that he and his wife had a child. The boy was named Ernst Mendelssohn. Felix smiled upon reading his brother's descriptions of the child. Each addition felt so welcoming after losing so much.

With Fanny's letter, each line caused Felix's warm heart to grow cold. His dear sister had made an agreement with a couple of publishers who wanted the music of Fanny Hensel put in the market. With Wilhelm on her side, she agreed to accomplish what she had wanted all her life.

[2]

In a deep rage within, Felix clutched the letter, crinkling it. When the sister he looked ever so up to made her public debut, he had second thoughts, but this was a line crossed in his ideals.

The reminiscences of Abraham's standards had taken over Felix's once indifferent encouragement as a young child.

(Fanny Hensel [Mendelssohn])

It wasn't so much on the basis of her being a woman as Abraham's reasoning alluded to. Clara Schumann was a decent example of a lady making her way in the world. Felix's basis concerned that Fanny began pursuing her wishes after Abraham's death. It stung his inner heart that she veered so far from their father's standards. Felix wrote back to her for the time being, hiding his true feelings:

*Dear sister,*

*I send you my professional blessing on becoming a member of the craft...may you have much happiness in giving pleasure to others; may you taste only the sweets and none of the bitterness of authorship; may the public pelt you with roses, and never with sand.*

*Your Bruder,*

*Felix*

Felix set the pen down, folded the note and handed it to Johann for sending. Within the next few weeks, the Elijah oratorio would be ready for the Birmingham festival, so Felix made plans to pass through Berlin to give Fanny a piece of his true mind.

~~~

636

"Bruder! Do not question my choices. I am my own woman and have a husband as my head. He is tolerant of my decision." Fanny scolded Felix, who was standing in the entryway of the Hensel home. He had not yet settled in a guest room and had already blown into a spiel at his sister. Fanny continued, "If I had known you were visiting to tell me your opinions, in which I know every one, I would not have agreed to let you stay."

"What else did you expect dear sister? I don't understand how you could deceive our late Vater!" Felix became red. Fanny bellowed back in a boil, "I sometimes don't know if I am talking to my dear Bruder Felix or arguing with my Vater!"

"I am not Abraham!" Felix crossed his arms. Wilhelm walked in at the commotion with young Sebastian trailing behind. Felix quieted upon noticing his brother-in-law's stern stance while putting a comforting arm around his wife.

Sebastian looked to his Uncle in fear, never seeing him act as so. Felix felt the embarrassment and didn't say another word. Fanny then took his luggage, "I'll show you to the guest room."

Felix followed behind her to a comfortable room upstairs. Her air in demeanor was stern when leaving him to settle. Felix relaxed in his lonesome until his nerves were calm. He then headed back downstairs where in the corridor, he heard Fanny and Wilhelm in the parlor. Their conversation caused him to eavesdrop.

"I think it would be better if he stayed with Paul, he seemed to know how to handle him when he is in such a state." Wilhelm stated. Fanny shook her head, "I know him better than Paul in honesty. He is fine here. Felix just needs to come to terms then he will return to his cheerful mood. Paul tends to send him to a hotel even though he has room-" She paused her speech as Felix quietly entered.

The three of them seated around the coffee table. A servant brought tea at the hour. Felix sipped his cup, remaining quiet. Wilhelm and Fanny continued visiting, but on a different subject. It was innocent talk of art as Wilhelm had many commissions to paint portraits. Felix joined the conversation by speaking of his watercolours, but Fanny purposely mentioned to Wilhelm, "I did choose which drawings I want for my music. They will look well in print."

"Good." Wilhelm smiled, gazing at Fanny with infatuation. They both jumped from their subtle moment by a slam of a teacup. Felix leaned back in his seat, arms crossed. Fanny glared at him, "I know you do not agree with my publishing, but it is happening. You can not convince me otherwise."

"I can't believe you would be so bold!" Felix shot up from his seat, becoming fearfully overcome with his dark side. Only on a few occasions in younger years had Fanny seen her brother in such a state. Their father's stern voice had been the one to check the torrent of words.

Fanny didn't know what to say as Felix scolded at her loudly, "You should be concentrating on your family! You are the woman of a household! Do you think you could handle the constant demand of a music career!?"

"Bitte Bruder! Enough!" Fanny's eyes dewed with tears. Felix continued on in a raging hiss. His voice gave way as if he were on the brink of passing out in his rage.

Wilhelm did not tolerate the behavior any longer when his wife began to cry. He went to Felix and smacked him in the face until he shut up. It took a few hard slaps, but Felix seemed to come back to his senses. His face stung from the hits but it needed to be done. Wilhelm then escorted him to the guest room. Fanny noticed as her brother left, he rubbed his head as if it ached from all of his distressing emotions.

~~~~

Days later after leaving Berlin and taking a steamer across the sickening channel to England, Felix arrived in Birmingham. Straight away he became soaked into a full routine of conducting rehearsals. On top of it, his emotions did not cease to disturb him.

One morning, his stresses caught up and he slept in an hour late. His throbbing head enticed him to dream more, but when daylight shone in his room, Felix rushed out of bed to get dressed.

Each morning a maid brought coffee and a cup sat at the table. Felix took a swig, but grimaced. It had run cold. To get his caffeine for the day, he went out to a street vendor. Many people happened to be circling about to get their morning brew, so Felix waited, tapping his foot in annoyance.

After purchasing a steaming cup, he wandered about to find a carriage. None of course were available. By the time one parked, Felix was running extremely late. He boarded it by any means to carry on his way to the concert hall.

[3]

When arriving, the musicians were set to rehearse. They didn't appear in the most chipper of mood. Felix quietly took his place. When picking up his bâton, he heard a member of the chorus scorn in a whisper, "A late man is a lazy man."

"Alright, let's start at the beginning." Felix ignored the remark, raising his arms to count. Before any music, a trombonist sneered, "A waste of a morning. I still believe he shouldn't be conducting nor composing sacred works as so."

"Halt, halt, halt." Felix set down his bâton, "Are we here to criticize me? I ran late. It has nothing to do with my composing nor other old worn out squabbles."

639

"I thought you took being on time an important virtue!" A bassoonist hissed. Felix glared at the man, "Sometimes even the most pious of people are late." He picked up his bâton, "Eins, zwei, drei!" He counted. None were ready. A flautist in the front blabbered, "We speak English here."

"I'm about done with all your saucy remarks!" Felix set down the bâton once more. The festival directors encouraged Felix to keep going by sending out the troublemakers. It left Felix worried about the performance. He didn't like unnecessary things as so.

~~~

In the packed concert hall, the first full performance of Elijah went exceedingly well to Felix's surprise. The overture was grooving with the trumpets and hits of the drum. Overall, there were no mistakes in the first part. The second half had a few, but nothing trifling. The memorable concert came and went with the audience adoring the passion in the mega production. Felix determined that the next performance would be even better as it was to be presented to the London public.

On the 18th of August, Felix arrived at his smoky nest. Rehearsals for the oratorio commenced in small groups at the Moscheles' home of Chester Place. Ignaz was enthralled when supervising each segment and couldn't wait to attend the big London performance.

Young Felix Moscheles was fascinated by the music coming together, but sometimes the composer's loud singing in the guest room next door disrupted young Moscheles' Greek and Latin studies.

The boy gave a huff as Ignaz happened to enter the room. He asked his son, "What is the matter?"

"Why does Uncle Felix edit so much? I thought it was done. Why is he still singing?"

"Well." Ignaz sat on the bed next to young Moscheles, "Felix is especially picky. Since I've known him, he has told me, 'Always room for improvement.' It's like you with your drawing." Ignaz then left so his son could continue studying. Young Moscheles shrugged.

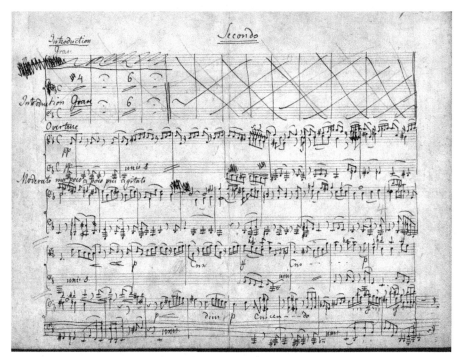

*(A page of a piano arrangement of Elijah)*

On the 28th of August, the concert hall crowded up with people, including Ignaz among them. Anticipation circulated when the musicians were set. Felix stood proud when counting them into the grandiose overture.

Each moment built on top of the last until reaching the climax where the entry of the chorus burst into a plea of help. Their desperate d minor tone had a similar air to that of Mozart's infamous requiem.

Ignaz watched Felix submerge himself in directing such a massive plethora of musicians. It made him look all the more tired and worn at heart from years of endlessly working and traveling. Composing such a large work in the midst of it all only put weights on the burden of exhaustion.

The performance had a long way to go as this was no unfinished one hour requiem. This was an intense two hour production, finished by the composer himself.

Felix perused on, mouthing lyrics as to get the singers to remember the correct intention. Every voice, tone and rosin of the bows filled the concert hall with purpose, reaching every ear.

When the grand performance did finish, no one left the concert hall without a positive remark. Ignaz especially adored the work. He found Felix backstage and exclaimed, "Felix! That was brilliant!"

"Thank you." Felix blushed with satisfaction, the sweat still heating his face. Ignaz handed him a handkerchief. While drying his forehead, a man who had been sitting behind the choir came up to Felix in overwhelming excitement. He effusively embraced the composer whilst exclaiming with a thick French accent, "That music was the best I've ever heard! Merci for such a grandiose sound!'

"You're welcome." Felix smiled warmly. The Frenchman then out of the blue tried to give a kiss. Felix leaned his head back to avoid him. Ignaz intervened and pried the man away, "Bugger off." He nudged the Frenchman until he went on his way.

"Thank you." Felix chuckled at the humorous occurrence. He then sighed to Ignaz, "I'm leaving London tonight. We probably won't see each other for a while."

"Well, you have a lot of packing to do. We can still chat, as I must begin the process of packing my family and I's things."

642

"You're moving to Leipzig!" Felix cheered, having forgotten Ignaz's plans. They continued on in complete ecstasy to Chester Place.

~~~~

Back at the Gewandhaus, I burst with joy to see Felix return to Leipzig. Yet, it was double the excitement when Ignaz walked in with him. He remembered me well from my stay at Chester Place and had great happiness in meeting me again. I asked him, "How long are you in the city?"

"My family and I have moved here. Thanks to Felix, he arranged a temporary place for us. I shall soon purchase a permanent home and work at the Konservatorium." He smiled nonstop. Felix spazzed out from heart bursting happiness. All of his dreams of living in the same city as Ignaz had come true. He cheered with a leap, "Ignaz is really here!"

"It's a good thing he is. He can help me deal with your endless energy." I joked as Ignaz calmed his jumping and turning about. Once he let up, I explained, "The orchestra has been rehearsing Mozart's G minor symphony. I hope you're up for it."

"Of course." Felix chimed, "We should be sure the last movement is more moderate. I want things expressed clearly." He headed towards the auditorium. I followed and took my regular seat among the musicians with my violin. Ignaz observed from the stage side while Felix counted in from the conducting desk. It made for a perfect day at work.

~~~

Later that week, it was a great feeling when working at the academy with Ignaz there. He taught piano lessons in one room while I took the other for a lecture on interpreting music when conducting. The full class of students gained knowledge of the many fundamentals.

Felix on the other hand wasn't at the academy very often. He wanted the ones designated to teach to take over. Every now and again he came for specific lectures as it was a requirement that every member of the Gewandhaus have a part in contributing to the Konservatorium. He didn't want to forego his own rules.

As I dozed at my desk after teaching, my class silently penciled in their homework. The piano from Ignaz's instruction resonated through the walls. His student played fluidly, halting only at times. In the moment, my mind trailed. I happened to wonder what Felix was doing; whether it were free time painting or if he was in his office, writing some great composition or just regular old work.

~~~

"I swear! You need to control your children!" Elizabeth Jeanrenaud snapped at Felix who was chasing little Felix Jr.. The boy was in the midst of running away from nap time.

Meanwhile, mischievous Carl was in the kitchen, lifting little Paul to dig into the biscuit jar. Marie stood nearby, arms crossed, "Papa is going to yell at you both."

"Papa need not know." Carl took a handful of sweets from Paul. Marie ran off to taddle. She found her mother in the parlor, but Cécile was occupied with baby Lili, who cried for no such reason. Felix Jr. sprinted through with tears as well. He found the pile of Marie's toys so kicked them in the pathway of the corridor. It was a set of small wood animals. Felix Senior hurried in, but stepped on the wood while wearing stockings but no shoes. He yelled out of the painful annoyance, "Dammit! Marie, pick up your things!"

"You broke my favorite toy horse!" Marie burst into a tantrum of tears. Carl sprinted into the room, a mouth full of biscuits, "Vater swore!"

"Papa needs to wash his mouth out with soap!" Little Paul copied his older brother. Cécile gave a sigh as baby Lili cried louder. She took the child to a more quiet room.

"This is the most outrageous household on earth! My daughter is doing her best while you are swearing and letting your children do whatever!" Madame Elizabeth overcrowded her son-in-law with a scold.

"I am sorry that my hands are full." Felix rubbed his foot. He put the broken toy aside to fix later. Marie picked up the rest of the mess. Things seemed to calm down after getting the parlor cleaned up. Felix found Felix Jr. hiding under the coffee table, so made him come out and go to bed for a while.

Carl and Paul snuck back to the kitchen, but Johann stood before them, arms crossed. The open biscuit jar and their messy mouths said it all. Felix soon came and noticed the situation. He didn't speak, but guided the two boys straight to their beds.

Lastly, Felix went to Cécile, who still held crying Lili. Felix took the child and she instantly calmed. Lili had wanted her papa all along. Cécile rolled her eyes being a tad jealous. Felix eventually took little Lili to her crib then returned to the parlor to flop on the sofa with a sigh of relief. The only disruption became Elizabeth's ongoing nags, but luckily she left for Frankfort in the afternoon.

Later that evening, Felix invited Ignaz to a rehearsal of Elijah at his home with a few singers. There was to be a concert, but sections of the choir needed extra time. I was invited as well and came in before any chorus members showed up. On entering the parlor, Felix sighed to Ignaz, "I don't know when I'll ever get this oratorio officially published. It's had plenty of performances, but I revise it nonstop. It's a horrid disease."

"I'm sure you'll decide what you want soon enough." Ignaz assured. Felix then changed the subject, "How is your new settlement in Gerhard's Garden?"

"Quite well. It has much history as it marks where the battle of Leipzig contested. I do say, it makes for a humble abode."

"That's good." Felix nodded as the bell rang. He got up to answer, letting in various members of the choir. Gradually his apartment filled up with singers. A few directors stopped by when rehearsals commenced. Ignaz and I stood off to the side, watching Felix instruct the chorus. At times we gave our input, but Felix knew for the most part what he wanted from their voices.

"Out with the vowels! Who made the hea-vans and the wa-ters." Felix exaggerated the pronunciation. He flipped pages in the score, "No. 5: 'Rather err on the side of vigor than on the side of drowsiness. No 8: from the very beginning the music must sound fresh, not only towards the end. No 20: I want to hear tone, what one might call music."

The singers heeded his council and sang their second rounds carefully. Once they did everything to his standard, Felix let them off for the night. Ignaz and I were exhausted ourselves so returned to our homes for much needed slumber.

Felix on the other hand went to his office to continue work. He had tiredness but an array of music, other than the oratorio, sat at his desk. Over the past months, the King of Prussia still tormented Felix with requests by way of post. To please his Majesty, Felix happened to finish a whole Liturgy, but it had yet to be copied and organized.

While putting the manuscripts in order, Johann strode in with a cup of tea. Strong chamomile by the scent. Felix set the cuppa at his desk, taking in the warm vapors of heated herbs.

646

Johann admitted of the tea, "Cécile wants you to bed, so I put something in to make you sleepy. It is quite strong, so I would drink it and be going. You've had a long day."

"I could use good rest, but I must finish this." Felix stated, not turning from his livelihood. Johann pushed the cup towards him, "Cécile wants you to bed now."

"Alright." Felix sighed, sipping down the tea. It tasted of lavender and chamomile with a tinge of mint. He set the cup down then continued working. Johann cleared his throat, "Aren't you going to bed?"

"The tea takes time to give effect I imagine." Felix excused with a smirk. Johann chuckled, "Sometimes you're more stubborn than your children when it comes to bedtime. Don't fall asleep on the desk." The servant took the cup and saucer. While holding the delicate china, his hands gave way to shaking uncommonly. Felix asked in worry, "Johann, are you alright?"

"Ja, I am a little out of sorts tonight." He turned for the door. Before exiting, he unexpectedly stumbled in a fall, dropping the teacup. Felix shot up from his seat, "Johann!"

"What happened?" Cécile rushed in at hearing the fall. She wore her night cap and gown. Felix ordered, "Help me get him to his room."

"Of course." Cécile took hold of Johann's arm while Felix had the other. Together they pulled their friend to his feet. Johann managed to stand, but needed all of the help he could get. His arms and legs felt as if they were weights. Felix noticed his face had a puffiness to it.

"I don't know what has come over me." Johann's face beamed with sweat. He walked steadily to his cozy room. It was the best place for him at the moment.

Once Johann got settled in his bed, Felix told Cécile, "I will go get a doctor." He put on his coat to go out, but a wave of drowsiness came over him. It was the sleepy tea. Cécile noticed him fight tiredness so offered, "Felix, let me go fetch the doctor. The tea I told Johann to give you will have you asleep in the streets."

"Bitte, Hurry." Felix pleaded while heading to the parlor. Cécile in a flash got dressed and grabbed her cloak. Before leaving the home, Felix was already snoring on the sofa. It made Cécile hurry all the more to the nearest home of a doctor. One resided only a few blocks away.

At the door, she rang the bell. It took many rings, but a maid finally answered, "Ja, Madame?"

"Please, I need to speak with the doctor. It is urgent." Cécile begged. The maid sighed, "It is late, can't you wait until morning?"

"Please, the servant of my house has fallen desperately ill, he needs help now." Cécile tried to convince. The maid went to shut the door on her, but in thankfulness, the doctor came down the stairs, "What is going on at this hour?"

"Please, my family's dear friend is severely ill." Cécile explained. The doctor nodded as the look in her eyes caused him to take action, "Head home and I will be there shortly. You are Frau Mendelssohn are you not? I know where your home is, so I'll come after I get dressed."

"Thank you so very much." Cécile ran back to her apartment. When she entered the parlor, Felix was in a deep slumber. She tapped him until he awoke, "A doctor is coming soon."

"Excellent. I don't know what Johann mixed in that tea, but it blew me out as a candle." He shook off his remaining tiredness.

The doctor then knocked at the door and Cécile let him enter. Felix greeted with relief. The middle aged man introduced himself, "My name is Walther. I hear your servant is ill?"

"Ja, our precious friend. This way." Felix guided Walther to Johann's room. After entering, Felix turned back to the parlor to let the physician do his work. He waited patiently with Cécile, the both of them full of worry for their dear Johann. It took many uneasy ticks of the clock before Walther returned with news.

"Your servant is ill with dropsy."

"Will he recover?" Felix questioned. Walther sighed, "With time. He will be in bed a long while. I will be sure to visit often." He made a quiet leave, leaving a somber air behind. Felix sensed things weren't as easy as the man made it sound. There was now a completely unexpected anxiety for the family. A bombardment of housework.

"How are we to take care of everything?" Cécile questioned, "You know I am busy all day with the children and you must work. Now we don't have a servant to help with the daily tasks, on the contrary, Johann will need consistent care."

"We will work out something." Felix assured, running his fingers through his hair, "We can not send off our dear friend because he is ill. That would be horrid. He is far more to us than any old servant. He is our friend."

"I could get my mother to come back." Cécile suggested. Felix shook in disagreement, "Nein. If she mixes in this, I assure you, I will die of anxiety. Let us leave all until morning. It is late and we need sleep. Besides, a little work around the house shan't stress me."

## [5]

Two months passed. Johann still remained in bed, growing daily worse.

Felix took up the work of a servant on top of his regular duties. The experience gave a whole new meaning to their precious Johann's chores. Their maids came and went to help, but they had tasks of their own that took up enough time. No one could truly replace Johann.

Cécile chose to tend to the children and the kitchen as any woman would. Her cooking skills were sufficient and she made wise decisions when going to the markets for healthy food. The older children enjoyed helping her, especially when biscuits and cakes were being baked.

Felix cleaned and supplied the utilities such as firewood, candles and of course kept an eye on Johann. Watching the servant suffer through the days was only icing on the cake. Walther came by to help, but he could only do so much. Felix often left the door to Johann's room open when playing piano so the poor man could find some enjoyment.

A fortnight into Johann's illness, there had been improvements, so Felix persisted in doing the work of the servant that he so highly valued. The chores made him value the man all the more.

After a long day of composing, chores and super, Felix flopped onto the sofa, with a sigh. Cécile took the seat next to him in the same manner. Each day left the couple beat to the bones. The children were off playing with toys and whatnot.

"Felix?" Cécile lifted her head from a micro nap.

"Ja honey?"

"Did you remember to take care of the chamber pots today?"

650

"Oh Nein…" Felix rubbed his face in annoyance. The maids had left for the day, so Felix was stuck in dealing with the matter. He got up to get the nose burning, disgusting chore over with. After which, he made sure to wash himself extremely well.

To get the lingering smell off his mind, he tended to the kitchen dishes. He filled the sink with soapy water until many bubbles appeared. Little Carl couldn't resist but to join in the case. He 'helped' by playing with the fluffy suds. The father and son laughed together in tossing bubbles.

Such positivity didn't last. Cécile entered the room, teared at the eyes. Felix washed the soap off his hands, "What is it?"

"I think we had better get Walther. Johann is not moving or breathing." Cécile sounded quite mortified. Felix dropped the plate he was drying, breaking it. He sprinted off into the servant's bedroom to find Johann in the deep sleep of death.

While staring at him, Felix felt an emotional pain in his gut. It wasn't with a sense of fear, but with a push to do what was needed. He turned out of the room. Carl came up behind him asking, "Vater, why did you drop the dish?"

"Go back to the parlor with your Mutter. Don't come anywhere near this room." Felix shut the door. Carl opened his mouth to testify, but Felix snapped, "Listen to me now!" He pointed down the hall. Carl sprinted off. Felix grabbed his coat and went out into the cold rain.

When desperately ringing at Walther's door, the doctor answered straight away. He gestured to Felix, "Bitte, step inside, you'll catch a chill."

"You must come back to my home." Felix tried holding his sniffles. The rain covered up his tears. The doctor understood and hurried out.

~~~~

The coming days were nothing but a gloom. Johann's death put Felix in a grave mood, lasting a long time. It was due to watching his friend suffer so much, becoming worse and worse, having a moment of hope, then followed by his sudden death. The funeral didn't help. Johann's mother and sister arrived the day after he was buried. It distressed Felix all the more seeing their faces as they couldn't be sent for in time.

There was a great deal to do with Johann's belongings. He had trunks of items and clothes. Felix spent the remaining days of the year organizing with the servant's mother and sister. Together they happened upon a letter containing Johann's last will. It was utmost heartfelt and touching.

~~~~

At the start of the new year of 1847, things seemed to brighten. Felix stumbled upon a score of Bach's b minor mass, which cheered him a bit from the dreary months before.

With the third of February arriving, Felix turned eight and thirty years of age. On that day, the Moscheles family invited the Mendelssohn family to their home. Charlotte was in the mood to bake, so she took advantage of Felix's addition in age. She organized the whole day with treats, cake and little plays for the children to act out.

Cécile and Charlotte watched their cute children act while they sipped tea. Felix seated in a rocking chair, enjoying the entertainment. In one scene, Charlotte had made Ignaz dress as a cook. He burst into the room with an apron and frying pan, making Felix burst into laughter.

Little Felix Moscheles followed close behind to act out conducting in all cuteness while his father played the piano. Felix senior rocked the chair to and fro, along with the beat of the music as a natural response. The gathering had turned out the most memorable.

~~~

Weeks later after getting back into a routine of work and composing, a letter from Fanny came in the post. Her name was signed, but Felix opened it to find a sketch and note by Sebastian. His nephew had taken up art, like his father Wilhelm. Felix adored the drawing and the boy's handwriting so wrote back a loving letter:

*Leipzig February 22nd, 1847*

*Dear Sebastian,*

*I thank you very much for the drawing, which as your own composition, pleases me extremely, especially the technical part, in which you have made great progress. If, however, you intend to adopt painting as a profession, you cannot too soon accustom yourself to study the meaning of a work of art with more earnestness and zeal than its mere form...study very thoroughly how the outer form and the inward formation of a tree, or a mountain, or a house always must look, and how it can be made to look, if it is to be beautiful, and then produce it with sepia or oils, or on a smoked plate; it will always be of use, if only as a testimony of your love of substance. You will not take amiss this little sermon from such a screech-owl as I often am, and above all, do not forget the substance, - as for the form (my lecture), the devil may fly away with it, it is of very little value.*

Fanny had enclosed music along with her son's letter, seeking advice on a scherzo. Felix knew it was most likely a piece she wanted to publish. He gave his honest opinion to Sebastian as he would, critiquing any of his sister's music:

*Tell your mother that I quite agree with her about the scherzo. Perhaps she may one day compose a scherzo serioso; there may be such a thing,*

*Your Uncle,*

*Felix M. B.*

~~~

The months drove by and the April of 1847 naturally brought Felix back to London. His oratorio of Elijah had become in high demand for concert goers. Starting on the 23rd, performances commenced at Exeter Hall. The building's grand acoustics brought satisfaction to the ears.

For the second performance, Queen Victoria and Prince Albert attended. They hadn't the opportunity to hear the fairly new composition. Felix made sure the musicians sounded capital for his royal friends. Albert was especially impressed with the work. He penned a handwritten inscription on the program paper of his pleasing opinions.

When May arrived, Felix was still in London, so Victoria invited him to Buckingham Palace, insisting on a quick visit. Felix complied and came for an hour to play new works at the keys. One of which was an idea for an opera. He stated after running a segment, "I intend to use the story of Lorelei for the opera. Another oratorio often hovers in the form of melody in my head, but I still don't know if either of these projects are worth the while."

"Please," Albert assured, "These new outlines are extravagant, don't let them go."

"Thanks, but I still am not all that confident in them yet." Felix pressed the keys to a melody. Victoria spoke up, "If you happen to get your opera going, you should strongly consider the soprano Jenny Lind. She has been the talk of Europe. I shall be at her debut here in London."

"What is the performance?" Felix knew Jenny was to be making her debut but didn't know the details. Victoria smiled, "It is an Italian version of Meyerbeer's opera 'Robert le diable.' She is to sing the part of Alice."

"Oh, I shall have to attend." Felix nodded. Though he did not care for Meyerbeer, he could sit through any opera to hear Jenny. It would also be the perfect opportunity to discuss 'Lorelei' and other subjects.

To finish up music with the royal couple, Victoria chose three songs to sing. Her voice soothed all stresses. Once finished, Felix removed his hands from the instrument. Victoria testified kindly, "Since I sang, you must improvise on themes of my choosing."

"Alright." Felix obeyed. The Queen then named various melodies from operas and royal music. Felix played each one in a very pretty way, branching them off into their own little worlds of added harmonies, varying in rhythm in carrying on. After finishing, Felix could hardly lift his arms. Victoria's smile made her cheeks a rosy pink, "You have given me so much pleasure, now what can I do to give you pleasure?"

"I'd love to see your children play in the nursery. I miss my children as they are miles away at home. I'd love to sit and talk commonly." Felix felt the need to touch base with home life. Victoria nodded and she escorted Felix that way. Albert had other business so left them.

In the nursery, a nanny was watching over five children, ranging from ages one to seven. Victoria and Felix entered and took seating beside them. Felix smiled at the children, who were busy at play. It made him think of his own family. Victoria casually asked, "How many kids do you have?"

"Five as well. Three boys and two girls. All living together in a decent apartment."

"Sometimes I wonder what it's like living in a normal home. Having a palace doesn't mean a peaceful life when you are expected to run a country." The Queen sighed. Felix explained, "My home is peaceful, but the children have their days and there's much work to tend to in providing for them."

"I guess there are good sides and bad sides to either lifestyle." Victoria watched as her eldest daughter gleamed a smile at the guest. Felix's visit lasted a while longer, but his tiredness forced him to head back to his place of stay, where he rested up for the next phase of events in London.

~~~~

On the fourth of May, Felix, accompanied by his friend and critic of music Mr. Chorley, went to the opera featuring Jenny Lind. The concert hall became crowded with every seat filled. Felix and Chorley took up seating in a box off to the side, yet close to the stage.

Victoria and Albert could be seen in the front row on the ground level. Felix waved and the royal couple returned the gesture in all properness. Chorley chimed, "Aren't you ever so special. You get a wave from them."

"I only know them, no big deal." Felix teased his friend. The musicians then settled with their music and instruments. Everyone quieted when the conductor entered the pit and counted them in. Chorley had pen and paper to write up what he observed in the music and the audience's reaction to give a proper report in critiquing.

After the intense overture, the curtains opened and the acting commenced. Felix rather dozed off, but his attention refocused when Lind's tender voice brightened the entire house. Chorley looked to Felix, who had a smile of bliss on his face in taking full indulgence in Lind's talents. When turning in a glance to Chorley, it appeared as if a load of anxiety had been released from his mind. On paper, Chorley noted his observations in Felix's noticeable demeanor.

Concerning Jenny, she sang with the voice of an angel of dignified beauty. Her light hair and graceful stance captivated the stage. Felix watched her in utter awe. When the opera reached its end, a standing ovation occurred in the entirety of the house.

Felix left the box in a hurry to meet Jenny backstage. Yet, there in the corridor surrounding her dressing room, was a mob of men. They were cheering and begging to meet Lind. A few guards stood towards the front to keep anyone from getting in the room.

Felix slid his way through the crowd with ease, but once the men noticed him, one called out, "That is Mendelssohn; he would surely be able to meet Jenny before any of us."

"Wait-" Felix yelped as the ones surrounding him clutched onto his coat. They managed to lift him and the whole group crowd surfed him to the back of the line. Felix puffed in annoyance after being dropped on the ground. He stood again and attempted to squeeze his way through, but only to be shoved back. A voice behind him huffed, "Don't even bother. It's impossible now to meet Jenny."

Felix turned around to see a young man sitting against the wall in a drear. He had a thick Danish accent. Felix joined next to him and sighed, "If only she knew I was here, I'd meet her again."

"It is the same with me." The man rested his chin on his palm. Felix questioned, "Is not your name Hans?"

"That it is. Hans Christian Andersen." He held out his hand, "I'm visiting London, having much hope to meet Lind again. We are friends you see."

"You know, I did write music based on 'The Fair Melusine.'" Felix shook his hand happily. Hans gave a surprised expression, "Really? The music must have turned out well...at least I hope."

"I loved it, the musicians did not." Felix chuckled a tad. Hans nodded, but they were interrupted when one of the guards came up to them. He asked Felix, "Are you Herr Mendelssohn? Jenny would like to speak with you."

"Ja, I will come, but only if my new friend Hans can tag along."

"Of course." The man led them around to the crowded doorway. Felix and Hans entered in haste. Jenny was sitting at the vanity, doing her hair. She turned upon hearing people come in. Hans smiled non stop and enthused, "Jenny! I have come all the way from Denmark to meet you again, my friend!"

"Oh, how pleasant." Jenny did not seem all that happy with him. Felix felt somewhat out of place as Hans obviously had affections for her. Jenny made quick work of his conversation giving indications of annoyance. Hans got the point and made his exit.

"Madame Lind." Felix smiled as they were now alone, "I wanted to mention that I have a new idea for an opera that I want you to take part in. It is titled 'Lorelei.'"

"How nice." Jenny's tone trailed off as Felix walked close to her. He caressed her at the shoulders,"You should come back to Leipzig so we can work on the opera together."

"I don't know...I am quite booked now across Europe."

"You could make time between tours to visit." Felix leaned his face towards hers. Jenny avoided the kiss, "Felix, I do not want your letters anymore. I do care about you, but I can not ruin you in reputation."

"We could still be together." Felix sneaked a peck to her lips. Jenny smacked him hard in the face, "I'm sorry. Leave now."

"But-"

"Out!" She pointed at the door. Felix obeyed, feeling a complete stupidity within himself. He realized his affections for Jenny were nothing but a passing thing. It could not compare to the love of his wife and children. He didn't know what came over him.

~~~

On the 5th of May, Felix joined Prince Albert for an organized concert of ancient music at the Hanover square rooms. Felix performed a prelude and fugue by Bach on an instrument the papers described, 'One of the worst in the metropolis.' Any badness in sound was blamed on the old instrument itself.

Afterwards, Felix spoke to Albert one last time before his leaving of London. It was good company, but strange in feeling. A sudden tiredness came over him; so strong that even Albert noticed. The Prince commented in concern to the composer's state, "Be sure to get good rest. Travel will add to your taxing fatigue."

"I will. Before I make my leave, I'll sleep in my room a day or so. Please, give this to Victoria," Felix grabbed a gift, "It's for yourself as well."

Albert inspected the manuscript handed to him. It was a piano arrangement of 'Songs Without Words,' op 85 no. 6 as a duet. With immense thanks, Albert stated, "My wife and I will have utmost joy in playing these."

"See you in the future." Felix left, finding a carriage to his place of stay. One parked nearby so Felix boarded it.

## [6]

While the horse pulled the vehicle down the street, Felix watched the bustle of London around him. From his first visit to the smoky nest, things had changed in concern to social and mechanical progress. It made him sigh thinking upon how fast the years had gone by with his memories of England.

The carriage soon parked beside the humble hotel. Felix disembarked and trudged inside with exhaustion. As soon as arriving at his rooms, Felix dropped his bag, flopped into bed and slept, slept, slept.

~~~

On the 8th of May, Felix made the hard journey back to Germany. Cécile informed that she and the children were once again visiting the countryside home in Frankfort. It gave Felix a sense of comfort that he would enjoy the beautiful garden and relaxation.

Yet, before making it to Frankfort, the fun wasn't over as he made a stop in Leipzig at the Gewandhaus. There was a concert to conduct. Though he admitted being quite tired, the concert went pleasing. He didn't want to waste time afterwards so found a coach headed for Frankfort. It traveled through the night and the whole of the next day.

The coachman woke Felix when the carriage arrived in the city. Still yet, Felix had to find a way to the countryside. He stepped out into a bright afternoon, ever so weary. A horse clopped by, pulling a gig, so Felix jumped on. He paid the boy driving to take him to said address.

After going down a long dirt path and arriving at the wood home, Felix felt the needed relief. He struggled to keep awake while dragging his feet to the front door. Eventually he made it inside to feel the comfort of a crackling fireplace. His children excitedly greeted him, causing him to wake up more. Each child begged to be kissed and cuddled.

As Felix held Marie, Cécile walked in to see the cutest sight of the two giving eskimo kisses. Their cute noses budded a while before Felix set the girl down to give Cécile a most welcoming smooch. He asked her, "Has anything happened since I've been gone?"

"Not much. A letter from your brother is sitting in the bedroom, otherwise that is it." Cécile informed. Felix nodded and headed that way. A fresh letter lay peacefully on the nightstand. He picked it up and unfolded it:

*My most dear Brother*

*By the time this reaches you, the worst has come and gone in hours passed. There is not a single way to go about this letter in light terms for your sake for I know that no matter what, it will hurt in the most unimaginable way. Hours ago, passed and gone, during one of her musical matinées, our dear sister, Fanny, succumbed from a sudden collapse. She is no longer with us, Fanny is dead-'*

Before Felix read anymore, he looked up at the ceiling. Gobs of thick tears filled his eyes. He dropped the letter, unable to look at it. It did not exist in his mind; until with each glance, the horrid writing only became more real. His tired state caused him to stumble back. In a sudden flare of high emotion, he in a rage, began throwing things about in the bedroom.

A wood chair was toppled with a loud crash against a shelf. Books and papers fell, making a mess. In pure despair Felix grabbed a handful of manuscripts and tore at them. The beautiful notes being shriveled to nothing. His world had been ruined. The reason for breath, writing and hearing of melody were now pointless. The pain of the news felt as if a knife had severed everything within him, but left him alive to be in torturous agony.

In a dizzy spell Felix turned about, trying to regain balance. The twirl of the moment caused his senses to numb. With a sudden jolt, he fell forward, grunting after his head hit against the bedpost. He landed on the wood flooring with the terrible letter beside him. The writing echoed in his mind as his vision faded into darkness.

# Chapter XXVII: Fanny's Requiem

Mendelssohn, String Quartet no. 6 in f minor [1]
Mendelssohn, Nachtlied op 71, 6 [2]
Beethoven, Funeral March from Symphony no. 3 (movement 2) [3]

## [1]

Felix, to his own surprise, woke to someone poking at his face. A little voice bellowed, "Papa?" It was young Marie. He opened his eyes slightly. Her innocent mind believed him to be playing, so she tugged at his coat. Felix turned onto his side, but in complete disorientation. His head sharply ached. Yelps escaped his mouth, causing Cécile to burst in the room. She carried young Marie out then frantically went to her husband.

"What did you do!? You've bruised your head!" She examined the injury.

"Auch!" Felix winced as Cécile touched where the bedpost hit him. She sighed, "I'm going to have to call for a doctor."

"Nein, I don't need a doctor. I'm sick of such hassles." Felix forced himself to sit up. He then remembered the horrid letter on the floor. The sight of it caused him to weep. Cécile did not understand his reasons for such emotions. His sudden screeching cries of utter despair frightened her.

"What ever is the matter?" She brushed the sides of his hair in an attempt to calm him. His glossed eyes looked at her, giving no effort to answer, only spilling with tears. Cécile noticed the opened letter from Paul beside him. She grabbed it carefully upon noticing Felix whimper at it.

Once skimming it, everything in an instant was realized. The news caused her to tear up as well. Cécile set the note aside and tightly hugged her husband. Felix cried the hardest he had ever known into her shoulder. He struggled to breath between each trying weep.

After the lengthy moment of emotions, Cécile encouraged Felix to get up. He stood, but walked in a somber stride of foot to bed. He huddled under the covers, burying his head between the pillow and blanket. Cécile let him be and took the children to bed. They sensed the emotional output and naturally questioned, 'Why is Papa so sad? 'What happened?'

Cécile settled them in their room and explained aunt Fanny's death. The children understood the situation after dealing with Johann's death. They went to sleep in silence. Cécile headed to go sleep herself after giving the exhaustively hurtful news. When crawling into bed, she had to move Felix more towards his side. Being practically dead asleep, he didn't wake in the slightest. Her sleep didn't fare as deep, having too much worry on her mind.

~~~

The days to come did not pull Felix out of mourning by any means. Sympathy letters constantly came, only making him fill with anxiety. He couldn't fathom a note to compose without the dear sister he looked up to personally and musically. When he tried to conjure a melody, it all seemed so empty and desolate.

Hours he sat at the writing desk with a manuscript; blank. The children frequently came to him at their mother's request to cuddle. It was then he felt happiness. Though they were young, each child had much to say. Felix could look and listen to them for hours.

~~~

A week or so later, Cécile received a letter from Paul. He and Wilhelm were planning a trip to Switzerland to find fresh air and wanted Felix's family to join. Cécile thought it would help heal her husband's damaged heart, so went to him to suggest the trip.

In opening the bedroom door, it was completely darkened. Felix sat in a chair, facing the window.

He aimlessly gazed at the curtains covering the outside view. Cécile face palmed, knowing it was all he had been doing for hours. She went up beside him, "Why don't you open the curtains, it will brighten the room. It is a beautiful spring day."

"I like it dark in here. It suits my soul." Felix answered back, rather in irritability. Cécile continued with Paul's idea, "Your brother and Wilhelm are going to Switzerland. They want us to join."

"I don't want to go. I'm much too tired."

"Felix. You need a calming trip. What better than the beautiful alps? We must take our canvases to paint."

"I don't think I'm energized enough." Felix looked up at Cécile. She had a moment of not recognizing her husband who normally had a spirit of adventure. Even through previous losses, this channel of behavior was nothing compared to what he was resorting to.

In giving him a hug, Cécile's comfort seemed to release his bright personality. He professed his love, "You are my darling."

"You are mine as well." Cécile pecked a kiss. The moment lasted until she let go. Felix's eyes glossed in saddens with sniffles to accompany. Cécile stated, "I'm going to make the arrangements for us to go to Switzerland. The children ought to love it."

~~~

That summer, Felix, Cécile and the children were crowded in a carriage, leisurely riding the country towards Switzerland. The weather was bright and warm. Cécile smiled, gazing at the fine scenic grasslands. She had her paints and canvas at hand, catching what the land had to offer. Marie, Elizabeth and Paul huddled beside their mother to watch her art.

Felix on the other hand sat with blank sketch paper. He watched the hills roll by, but found no muse. In honesty, he didn't want to be further from the comforts of home.

"Papa." Carl tapped his father's hand, "Draw something."

"Bitte. Bitte." Felix Jr. begged along. Their father began sketching a grassy field with a mountain coming into view. It was the first of many tall earthy structures that formed the Alps. The children gasped in awe, not having seen such a scene.

The carriage trekked many more miles before reaching the city of Interlachen. There, they met up with Paul and Wilhelm. Felix's emotions crushed him when exchanging embraces, but he bottled everything up as Paul was not the sensitive sort. Wilhelm had a sad air, but overall healed with the fresh Swiss weather.

"How good it is to see you Bruder." Paul held Felix at the arms after hugging. Wilhelm sensed Felix to be out of sorts, so handed him Swiss cheese and chocolate. The taste lifted the festering depression.

"Come, you must see the lovely inn." Paul gestured to Felix's family to follow a pretty path through the tall green grass. Wild flowers gave their aroma while the blue sky correlated with the colours of the scene. Birds chirped their soothing melodies whilst flying above.

The group hiked to a large wooden inn, settled at the edge of the city. It contained a tavern where hearty meals were cooked. Every person within the building was decent in manner. Felix and his family settled their luggage in an upstairs room. The atmosphere was humble and homely as ever.

After unpacking, the family then rejoined Paul and Wilhelm outside. There were many walnut trees giving comfortable shade from the beaming sun.

Felix sat under one with his watercolour supplies. To hide his underlying feelings, he decided to paint his sorrows away.

*(Interlachen, watercolour by Mendelssohn)*

Wilhelm came to see what Felix found of interest. The forming picture was a scene of Interlachen. Wilhelm admired it, but noticed something in complete absence from his brother-in-law.

"Have you not any music with you? I didn't see you bring any at all."

"I don't see the point of scribbling dots on a staff anymore." Felix made a petty brushstroke of the lake. Wilhelm looked at him in suspicion, "Do you mean that you are giving up music?"

"I need to carry on with better things."

"Is this about Fanny?" Wilhelm sat next to Felix. Felix kept his eyes to his art, not answering. Wilhelm encouraged, "Bitte, talk to me."

"I don't think I can ever fathom another note without Fanny. I have no one to look up to for a musical opinion anymore. No one can replace her critique." Felix's tears fell like the water he was painting. Wilhelm gave advice, "You shouldn't give up music. Fanny would want you to keep composing. When you write, you can always think of her because memories, happy ones, will breathe into the sound."

"I do have a piece in the works at the moment." Felix admitted, "It is a string quartet. Fanny is much on my mind when I'm penning it. I shall dedicate it to her." Felix continued painting, his eyes brightened with relief. Wilhelm nodded and left him alone with his art.

Though at times Felix became cheerful, his mood only inclined to return to the utter mourn. He didn't know how he was going to endure the time in Switzerland. Paul so strongly surmounted such feelings to utmost extent, which Felix concluded had to be hard on him.

Felix shrunk from the idea of suppressing emotions, but did his best for the sake of his younger brother. To let his thoughts pour, he reverted to writing. His pen flowed with one of the lines stating:

*God will make it right one day. This suits the beginning and end of all chapters.*

~~~

The stay in Switzerland hastened by and the group began their journeys home. On boarding a steamer out of Thun, Felix didn't want to be in extended separation from his siblings, so mentioned to Paul, "May I come to Berlin in September and stay?"

"That would be pleasant." Paul smiled. With that, the steamer docked and the families went their separate ways.

Felix and his family decided to return to the apartment in Leipzig. Cécile thought the busy city would occupy Felix from sulking.

The taxing ride home in a cramped carriage caused the children to become intensely restless. The relief of catching the distant sight of Leipzig was much needed.

When returning to the apartment, everything felt new and refreshing. Felix found muse to compose again, working hard at the string quartet for Fanny. The first movement had been penned in the uproar of his stress so thus conveyed it. The other movements implied the fond memories with his sister. He used the music to cope through his feelings.

On a positive note concerning something other than his sister, Felix earned 250 Guineas for the Elijah oratorio. It had been bought for publishing and Felix felt a much needed sense of accomplishment. He made his family content by giving them nice things with the extra money.

Though the tears seem to lessen, they were replaced by a different trifle. Uncommon headaches became frequent, giving stress to Felix's eyes. At times, he was forced to retire to bed. The state of his health gave him the reminisces of his father's malady. He hoped it to be a passing migraine, but the ache lingered as if waiting to turn ugly with a wrong move of the head.

~~~

"How long has he been in bed?"

"It's been two days!" Cécile exclaimed, "It is not normal."

Felix stirred awake to find Cécile speaking with Dr. Walther, so piped up, "I'm only trying to sleep off a migraine. It is nothing to worry about. The trip to Switzerland tired me. I am fine I assure."

"Well, let me know if anything is of concern. I'll leave you with a tincture for the headache." Walther handed him a glass bottle.

Felix took it, set it on the nightstand then huddled back to sleep. Cécile couldn't do anything but give a desperate sigh. As Dr. Walther headed out, Cécile stopped him in the parlor, "Please, I really think something is wrong."

"I understand Madame. I am only a few blocks away if you need me." The humble man assured kindly. Cécile then went off to tend to the children.

Hours later, Felix came out of the bedroom and sat in the parlor. Cécile gave way to surprise but relief. She sat next to her husband, "I hope that slumber got rid of the headache. Did you drink a dose of that tincture?"

"A bit of it. It seemed to help." Felix gazed at the crackling fireplace. Cécile gave him a kiss then stood, "I think pasta with pesto sounds good for super."

"Sounds good honey." Felix smiled, but in reality didn't feel all that hungry. He got off the sofa and went to his office, preferring to put his creeping somberness into his string quartet.

~~~

The days dragged with Felix's welfare plummeting. He wasn't healing from the true ache in his heart. For hours he began to sit in his office with his composition, only to often halt the work's progress to caress a portrait of his beloved sister. It became a distraction on its own.

The lack of motivation soon affected other leisurely activities and health. He found no worth in reading or sketching. The joy of food; a pointless endeavor.

Cécile didn't know what else to do when his fragile state became apparent. She tried to entice him to eat by having his favorite foods prepared. Felix sat at the table to talk with his family, only to leave after a bite or so. The children, primarily young Carl, even knew his behavior to be unnatural.

One day while Felix napped on the parlor sofa, Cécile gave way to a sigh. Without anymore doubting, she penned a note. Despite knowing that Felix would object, she summoned Dr. Walther to the home.

When the doctor arrived, Cécile welcomed him in and explained her concern, "Felix isn't eating and I fear his health is deteriorating."

"Where is he?" Walther questioned. Cécile pointed towards the parlor. The doctor glanced in at Felix who was snoring his sorrow away. Walther then turned back to the dining room, "Well Madame," He took a seat at the table. Cécile did the same and listened closely to the doctor's explanation.

"It sounds to me that his mourning is afflicting his mental state. He needs to come to terms. My suggestion is that he visit his sister's grave and stay in his home city with his other siblings a while. It may be the cure for this terrible case of nostalgia."

"Are you sure that is the best option? I know my husband and seeing her grave could really hurt him."

"I think it to be the only humane option," Walther then declared without hesitation, "Otherwise this sort of illness will be treated with leeches, bloodletting, purging the stomach; anything to get rid of it."

"Oh dear." Cécile changed color at hearing the list.

"I am not mental!" Felix unexpectedly snarled, coming in with his arms crossed. He didn't accept such talk that left his wife unsettled, "It is rather unnecessary of you to be in my house, speaking such absurd things."

"Please, I am only here to help. Your wife is worried about you." Walther stood and went to Felix, observing his behavior. Felix's agitation only grew, "Get out of my house and leave me be." His energy channeled into an overwhelmed state. Cécile sensed it straight away and rushed to caress her husband, "Do be calm."

670

"I fear all of those trips to Switzerland have finally caught up!" Walther became stern of voice, "The clanking cowbells have damaged your brain cells causing this nostalgia."

"That's not true!" Felix tried to get after him, but Cécile clung to his sleeves, preventing any fighting. The doctor concluded while grabbing his bag, "If you do not come to terms, the second option of treatment shall be what I enforce. I advise you to take my first suggestion seriously." He left, shutting the door behind him with the air of a thunderstorm commencing.

~~~

A week later, with the high influence of Cécile, Felix found himself taking a train back to Berlin. The technology of the locomotive had become more efficient and faster; too rapid for his liking. It made Felix miss the calmness of the older days.

As he sat in his lonesome, gazing out the window, a middle aged lady took the seat across from him. Her curiosity made her gaze upon the younger man in wonder. He wore all black, from the top hat in his hands to his shoes. The only color that the outfit yielded was a near closed, red rose on his lap.

"Excuse me Junge Herr," the lady questioned, "Are you by chance a widower?"

"Nein." Felix looked up in confusion. The woman gave a puff of disappointment, then remarked in utter rudeness, "You're too thin anyways." She changed seats, not understanding his distress. Felix felt a sense of unnecessary hurt at the comment.

When reaching Berlin, Felix took a carriage straight to the cemetery. The gated garden of death had an unflattering gothic essence with the bundles of flowers before each rotting stone.

He walked a little dirt path trailing through the grass of a special shade of green until he came to the dreadful sight.

There, a fresh lap of stone stood out of the ground. Felix set his beautiful rose down beside it, only to fall to his knees with a puff of pure weeping despair whilst reading the engraved name:

### Fanny Hensel-Mendelssohn Bartholdy
### 1805-1847

Felix whimpered in woe and sorrow, wishing ever so to be sitting under the piano in the old Berlin home, taking in every note of those Bach preludes, played ever so perfectly by his sister. Her life had given him the meaning of music, but now the wick of the candle was used up.
There was no meaning.

Felix picked himself back up. He dizzily stumbled in standing being faint in the head. A hand fell on his shoulder to steady him, "What are you doing here?"

"Wilhelm?" Felix turned around to hug him tightly in cries. Wilhelm embraced back in confusion, "Is it wise for you to come here? Your wife wrote to me about your state. I think this is too much."

"It was the doctor's suggestion to cure my severe 'homesickness.'" Felix tiredly explained. Wilhelm knew this to be far more taxing than helping. He suggested, "Why don't you come stay with me, I know it may be hard but at least it is close to the main house of the estate."

"I feel exhausted." Felix's eyes blinked in sleepiness. Wilhelm confessed his worry, "Are you sure that doctor really has your welfare in mind?"

"I'm sure he does. Besides, Cecile encouraged it as well." He glanced back at the grave with gobs of tears. There was something more. Wilhelm gently took Felix at his shoulders, "What are you not telling me?"

Felix stayed quiet a moment, trying to hold everything in. He wished he were as strong as his brother Paul, but the stress in his chest caused him to burst into tears, "The doctor wants me to come to terms or the alternative option of treating my state involves nothing but horror!"

"If he even tries anything, I shall be sure to find out." Wilhelm gave a tight protective hug, "That is the last thing you need plaguing your mind."

"Danke." Felix had his head buried in Wilhelm's shoulder, sopping it with tears. He didn't have a parent or older sister to cry to anymore. Wilhelm let him vent his feelings, knowing they had been bottled too long. They then proceeded to the Hensel home.

When arriving, young Sebastian had a happinesses in seeing his uncle. Felix watched the adolescent work at landscape drawings. Wilhelm gave a proud smile, "Taking after me."

"These are so well, I'm impressed." Felix commented. Sebastian gave a nod, "Dankeschön."

Felix then wandered the house to burn his remaining emotions off. It seemed well at first, but he came to Fanny's music sanctuary. The large room that used to hold such beautiful creativity, now sat in the dark light of desolation.

*(Fanny's Music Room)*

Felix felt his sorrow coming back. Before tears came, Wilhelm guided Felix from the room, "I know what will lift your spirits. I'm going to make a portrait of you. I need an updated one, so since you're here..."

"Are you sure you want one? In my current state?"

"You look fine, any mild flaws can be fixed by a stroke of paint. You know my use of shadow. Just change that black undershirt to a white one. Your outfit needs variation."

"Alright." Felix left to change.

When coming back, Wilhelm had a canvas set up in the drawing room. Felix sat in the chair against the wall, posing in properness with a hint of a smile.

674

"Perfect." Wilhelm began the outlines. Sitting in one position for hours was usually a taxing affair, but with Wilhelm and Sebastian to keep him company, Felix had a fulfilling comfort. The missing link in which gnawed at him wasn't gone, but rather felt elsewhere in the house.

In the time of getting painted, Wilhelm had to calm Felix from moving as there was much laughter in their visiting. The occurrences made the duration of the setting last longer, but every added minute was one more of healing joy.

"There." Wilhelm set his brush down. Felix jumped up from his seat to have a look. He smiled as it was definitely in the style of Wilhelm Hensel. The shadowing, lighting, colour scheme and smoothness of brush portrayed the expression.

*(Felix Mendelssohn 1847)*

~~~~

After a wholesome stay in Berlin, Felix returned home in a new light. He carried on with composing, drawing, reading and taking care of himself. Cécile could not believe it, but her husband had pulled himself out of the dark hole of despair. The doctor's suggestion had worked.

Felix even began returning to his duties at the Gewandhaus and Konservatorium. It happened to be the raging month of October, so he kept fully occupied. Almost too much so. The effects of overworking began to yield effects of their own.

On one free day, Ignaz paid a visit to the Mendelssohns' home. He had not seen Felix in some time as their busy lives intertwined less and less since their families' get together.

Upon entering the home he found Felix at work in his office. A deep sense of separation beseeched Ignaz. His dear young friend had changed in that span of wavering time. He watched Felix write away at his desk, his already small stature appeared more so drained from stress. His face showed a tinge of unnatural paleness.

"Felix?" Ignaz hardly formed his name. Felix looked up to see his old friend. In his eyes, Ignaz aged due to the normal cycle of life. It was evident that they both gave expressions of surprise towards one another. A silence commenced between them, but Ignaz broke it, "I feel it has been so long since our last meet."

"We must go to the piano." Felix stood from his desk, "I have completed a new work. It's a string quartet." He took the score along with him to the piano in the parlor. Ignaz joined beside him to begin their session firstly with Bach.

Felix, in his usual way, had excitement when playing duets of his favorite composer. It made Ignaz feel relieved in sensing the bright spirit of his friend. Yet, it didn't last when Felix showed him the string quartet.

Right at the intense beginning, Ignaz listened closely. The harsh power of expression was not the Felix he knew. It was so very rare to hear his desperation and rage. The other movements calmed, but had somber tones of depression. Ignaz groaned within, knowing that Felix was shaken to his heart's core at his sister's loss.

~~~~

On the 8th of October, the day proved to be a busy one. The students of the Konservatorium were taking their examinations for reception. I gathered my bag for the full day of work ahead. Before hurrying out the door, Sofie stopped me, "Ferdinand! Don't forget your lunch."

"Danke honey!" I grabbed the small bag she had especially made for me. My children were still sleeping as it was the early hour. The course of the years gave me a decent family.

When arriving at the academy, I was quite happy to see Felix heading in beside Mr. Moscheles. I had not seen the two side by side in months past, so it gave a nice air of friendship. The state of Felix's busy life was no surprise to me as it was to Ignaz. I saw Felix near everyday with the regular work at the Gewandhaus.

"Herr David," Felix called as I caught up, "I have organized some things to test the students on if you don't mind."

"Sure, the more they can do, the better." I joked. We headed for the main classroom. There, the hopeful students sat at their desks, paper and pencils at hand. Felix smiled while making a comment, "Quiet as mice."

I gathered my stack of theory tests to hand out. Meanwhile, Felix did his own thing at the blackboard, writing examples of thorough bass (figured bass). He explained before the exam started, "Along with your tests, on separate paper, I want you to work through these examples I have written."

While the room sat in silence with nothing but moving pencils, Felix used the time to sketch landscapes on paper. Ignaz watched it all form on the page, thinking them to be the most lovely. I on the other hand took the exam papers one by one as each student finished.

After the last was turned in, Felix invited Ignaz and I out for a walk in Rosenthal. I declined, "I have to get these papers corrected. You and Ignaz should spend time together."

"Alright, but later tonight you must join us at my home. Julius Reitz is in town as well." Felix informed.

"I shall have time then." I adjusted my reading spectacles and continued correcting papers. Felix and Ignaz trotted out with happiness. I had much pleasure in seeing Felix content after such a dreary phase.

Once every theory test was checked and nicely stacked, I put my things away then grabbed my bag. It was the late afternoon, so I stopped at my home for a snooze then headed to Felix's apartment.

When coming to the door of the Mendelssohns' home, it sounded full of excitement with the children at play and the adults lively in conversation. Cécile answered the door in the midst of laughter. She guided me to the parlor where Felix, Ignaz and Julius Reitz were in animated conversation. A bottle of fine wine was passed about to fill their small elegant glasses.

I looked to Felix's children who were in their own happy chatter. Carl, the eldest, was nine years of age. Ignaz had brought along his son, young Felix.

The boy was now in his adolescence, being fourteen. Though there were gaps in age, all of the children got along.

"Ferdinand," Felix Senior looked to me, "we were discussing a question that you may be able to help us untangle."

"What is it?" I inquired.

"Who is better? Bach or Beethoven? I do advise that you pick the first." Felix implied. Julius gave his opinion, "Beethoven helped further the feeling of music. Though I do have immense respect for Bach, I think Beethoven did something quite extraordinary. Take the ninth symphony for example."

"I'm quite indecisive. I like them both all too much." Ignaz put his arms up in a shrug. I gave my answer, "I believe that no matter who you compare, Bach should be regarded as the best. Music would be a lot different without him. Yet, it is a pleasure to play Beethoven's symphonies with an orchestra."

"I accept that answer." Felix nodded, sipping his glass of white wine. He then looked to young Felix Moscheles who had his books of Greek and Latin studies at hand. Felix Senior quizzed him in the spur of the moment, "What is the aoristus primus of τύπτω, Felix?"

"Um..." young Moscheles was startled at the sudden question, "To strike?"

"Good!" Felix chimed then stood, "Super is ready. It's lamb chops and potatoes." He headed to the dining room. The children eagerly followed the adults.

The large meal consisted more of lamb and potatoes. There was an assortment of fruit, cheese and a freshly toasted pecan pie to finish it off. Dinner lasted many hours into the night.

~~~~

The following day, the ninth of October, began as any other. Felix rose out of bed at five, had coffee then started composing. Much came into progress such as his 'Lorelei' opera. He still edited the Elijah oratorio and the Italian symphony, which had been recovered from its close call.

Concerning the popular Elijah oratorio, a proposal by letter had been made to have it performed in Vienna. Felix had not seen that city of music in a great while, so had anticipation to go.

Later that afternoon, Felix wrapped up his desk work to head out to the home of Herr and Frau Frege. Madame Livia Frege was a well standing soprano who worked with Felix on various occasions. Their home was settled in a quaint complex, one of the nicest in Leipzig.

Herr Frege answered Felix's knocks, "Livia is in the music room."

"Excellent." Felix heard the woman's powerful voice carry in practice. When he entered the music room, Livia turned with a smile, "Ah, Felix, there you are."

"Hallo Frau Frege." Felix gave a polite nod of the head. He then sat at the piano with music, handing her copies. Herr Frege asked, "May I offer you anything? Coffee? Tea?"

"A spot of tea would suit me." Felix answered.

"Excellent, I have some Lapsang Souchong brewing." Herr Frege went off. Livia and Felix began their rehearsal with various songs, each one fitting her voice perfectly. Felix woke more when Herr Frege returned with the tea. It made for an even more productive session.

"What should we do for the last piece?" Felix thumbed his music. A slight headache came over him in the moment, but nothing alarming. He thought it to be the dose of the strong smokey tea.

680

"What about this Nachtlied? It looks nice."

"That is a good choice." Felix took up the music.

## [2]

When they began, the music had an ambience with his gentle playing and her soft, glowing voice. The savory bliss lasted, but only so long. When Livia reached a stronger section, the piano halted with a clunking chord. Turning towards the instrument, Livia saw Felix hunched over the keys, gripping his head. Flashes of pain forced him to give way to sudden screams.

"Felix? What is wrong?" She rushed to him. The screeches caused Herr Frege to sprint in. He instantly sat Felix up. Livia gave way to a panic as Felix's eyes were rolling in a faint. His expression conveyed nothing but a torturous ailment.

"Go fetch a doctor now!" Herr Frege ordered his wife. Livia ran off straight away. Herr Frege continued to keep Felix upright, but knew he needed to be put to bed. In carefulness, he slid his arm under Felix's legs and used the other to get a hold on him. Frege managed to pick him up and take him to a guest bed.

Felix hyperventilated as Herr Frege tried to settle his head on the pillow. Every position caused distress. The violent headaches felt like claps of thunder directly hitting him, causing a plethora of screaming and wailing. It soon led Felix into the deep depths of unconsciousness.

~~~~

"Honey." A gentle voice echoed. Felix stirred at the sound of Cécile beside him. He looked about, adjusting his vision. Cécile's voice echoed again, "Honey, can you hear me?"

Felix shut his eyes again to let his eyes rest a moment longer. His headaches had dispersed, giving a thankful relief. Once his sight sorted, he opened his eyes to see that he was in his own bed in his own home.

"How did I get back here?"

"Herr Frege and Dr. Walther brought you. You were at the Feges' home for a day or so but Walther determined it safe to get you back in your own bed."

"What happened to me?" Felix sat up, feeling weak. Cécile sighed, "Walther thinks it could be the stress of overworking. In honesty, he doesn't know. He said he would consult other doctors for advice. I noted the illness that took your father, grandfather, mother and sister. Hopefully this will get sorted before it gets any worse."

"That sounds hopeful in itself..." Felix shuttered, knowing so much of his family had succumbed to such symptoms. Cécile headed for the door, "I shall get you some tea. That should calm your nerves and mine. Walther instructed that you stay as calm as possible."

"Danke..." Felix could tell she was holding in every cent of worry for his sake. He laid back in bed to ponder over things. Cécile came back with fresh chamomile tea. Felix sipped from the elegant cup and saucer with much satisfaction. It was what he needed. Cécile then grabbed a glass bottle of medicine, "Walther prescribed this and instructed that it be taken twice a day."

"Does it taste as bitter as everything else he leaves for me?"

"He did warn that this one doesn't have a pleasant taste." She poured a fair amount on a spoon. The dark liquid's texture flowed like thick molasses. He hesitated when she held to his mouth. It smelled like tar. Cécile didn't waste time and made him take it.

He swallowed with much distaste, "After I recover, in which I expect not to take longer than a fortnight, I intend to visit Paul in Berlin. Also towards the end of the month is that festival in Vienna–"

"Felix." Cécile halted his speech, "Walther does not think you will recover in that amount of time. This will take longer than you intend."

"We shall see about it." Felix didn't believe her words. In his mind, this ailment was but a small misfortune that he could pull himself out of. He drank the rest of his tea to get rid of the medicine's taste, then laid back in bed to heal himself with dreams.

~~~

The days rolled by with nothing but rest. Felix regained enough strength to go about the house and sit in the parlor if he wished. He went to his office on occasion, but Cécile limited his time writing. Many letters had accumulated over the week as friends and family heard of the sudden attack of illness. Paul was left especially worried as it sounded all too familiar in concerns to the family. Felix tried to reassure his younger brother by penning:

*Leipzig, October, 25th 1847*

*Dearest Brother,*

*I thank you a thousand times for your letter today, and for the hint you give about coming here, which I seize with the utmost eagerness of heart. I really did not know till today what you say about my plans. God be praised, I am now daily getting better, and my strength returning more and more; but to travel this day week to Vienna (and that is the latest period which will admit my arriving in time for rehearsal of their Musical Festival) is an idea which cannot possibly be thought of.*

There is no doubt, however, that my improvement in health is day by day greater and more sure, so I have written to ask if I may delay coming for a week; but, as I said, I place little faith in the practicality of the whole thing, and it seems I must remain here. In no case can I attempt to travel before eight days from this time....

After, however, these interrupted performances, which must now be carried through, that I positively undertake no new ones, are quite settled. If it were not necessary to keep one's promise! But this must be done, and now the only question is whether I shall see you again on Saturday? Say Yes to this; I believe you would do me more good than all of my bitter medicine. Write me a couple of lines soon again, and be sure you agree to come. My love to you all! And continue your love for your:

Felix Mendelssohn Bartholdy

~~~

## [3]

I stood at the chalkboard on the subtle Wednesday mid-morning on the third of November, teaching a group of students. They listened with every bit of attention. The subject was one of most importance concerning composition. Sonata form.

"Alright, so as we discussed in regards to fugal form, sonata form begins with an exposition. Instead of subjects and counter subjects, this form utilizes themes and transitions. In the exposition of sonata form we have our first theme in the tonic key then a transition in which may be tonic to dominant, or tonic to relative major concerning minor keys. Someone tell me what is next." I scanned for a student to answer, "Ja, Baumfelder?"

"Theme zwei. The key can be dominant or relative major concerning minor keys."

"Excellent. Also, a third theme is optional and a codetta. Their keys are in the same manner as the second theme. Now, what comes next?" I skimmed the students again. No hands were raised, so I explained, "We now move on to the development. This is where a number of creative things may occur. There is no standard design or key pattern; a variety may be used and more themes may be added.

The third section, the recapitulation, makes the piece return to the first group of themes to recap the work. A transition will connect the second theme and so on. After that, a coda in the tonic key is likely to end the work." I glanced back at my students who were penciling notes in a moment of being enlightened by knowledge.

After the lecture and giving the pupils their assignment, I sat at my desk to catch up on grading quizzes. Everything had a calm air. Ignaz was elsewhere for the day, so no piano echoed through the wall.

In the silence of work, the classroom's door opened and closed. I looked up to see Niles Gade. His shoes, tapping against the flooring with each step towards my desk. He fidgeted with his hat nervously in his hands.

Never shall I forget Gade's coming to me at the Konservatorium.

Niles came close, keeping his words calm and quiet, "I have come to inform. Dear Felix has been struck with another attack of illness. This time it's a matter of life and death."

"Nein." My voice cracked as I stood. The students looked up, sensing something urgent. I ran ahead of Gade out of the Academy to the Mendelssohns' apartment, hitching a ride on a moving trolly carriage.

When arriving, the first sight I found were the ones gathered in the parlor: Ignaz, Charlotte, Herr Schleinitz and Constanze Schleinitz. They gazed up as I entered.

I in honesty did not know what to expect, yet their faces said it all and I was met with the tidings that there was no hope. The reality caused me to leave the parlor to the dining room, where for a quarter of an hour, my tears gave way.

Ignaz came and sat at the table with me. He tried to comfort, "Felix is ever so a person of energy. Let us hope it will be enough to pull him through." He patted my shoulder. His expression showed rather the opposite. He had seen Felix. I knew the reality inside.

Once I regained composure and felt calm enough, I slowly made my way to the death chamber. Outside the bedroom, Herr and Frau Frege, along with young Felix Moscheles sat anxiously. I paused as a doctor quietly stepped out of the room. His name was Dr. Hammer. He informed, "Felix appears to be resting well now. If there are no fresh attacks on the nerves or lungs, the apparent calm may lead to a happy turn."

When the doctor turned back into the room, I followed behind. There were three doctors watching in turn at Felix's bedside. At the moment, it was Herr Hammer. The other two were Dr. Clarus and Walther.

Cécile sat in the room of course, knitting to keep her mind straight. She consistently glanced at her husband as if waiting for him to wake in a normal state, but alas, Felix laid on the bed, unconscious.

The doctors were doing what they could to figure out the malady that caused such strokes and thunderclap headaches. All that could be discerned was his family's trait of succumbing to the ailment. It happened to hit Felix earlier than the others.

At the strike of the second hour, the peacefulness ceased as another attack of the illness set in. Felix stirred in a sudden flurry, giving way to terrible shrieks at his aching head. Hammer summoned the other doctors to the room. Dr. Walther took charge of the whole ordeal. He tried to make Felix more comfortable by shifting him in bed.

It caused the shrieks to turn into screeches, which unfortunately persisted for hours until 10 o'clock at night.

After using up his voice, Felix resorted to humming as if music were passing through his train of mind. The sweet melody calmed everyone's worry. Yet, the peace was soon interrupted as the humming exhausted Felix, making his head sharply ache. He gave way to screams, each one chilling as the hour passed.

By 11 o'clock, his cries ceased and he laid quiet, only breathing heavily. Since things winded down, everyone visiting decided to retire for the night. There was still a spark of hope for the next day.

~~~

Before the light of the dawn broke on the fourth of November, a few regathered at the Mendelssohn home, including myself. Concerning Felix, his pain appeared to have abated, but I looked at him, only to notice that his face was that of a dying man.

Young Felix Moscheles came into the room to inquire, but the sight only gave the early adolescent disheartening news. It was clear the end was approaching. He turned back from the room to vent his tears elsewhere. I went to follow, but stopped in the anteroom of the death chamber to find Ignaz sitting, journal at hand. Tears gushed down his face as the pen calmly wrote his meditations. He couldn't stand to see that young boy he met those years ago die still young yet.

I moved to the parlor where Herr Schleinitz was on the sofa, slumped in a sleep. His wife Constanze silently knitted beside him to occupy herself. The passing hours brought nothing new. Everyone's emotions were on their toes, but things kept steady for the time being.

When evening rolled around, past the hour of dinner, more acquaintances arrived. Joachim, now sixteen years of age, came as soon as hearing the news. To him it was the worst tragedy.

He had looked up to Felix in many ways over the course of a few short years. Following Joachim was my wife Sophie and her friend Hedwig Salomon.

No one dared speak as we all sat, paralyzed in thought. On occasion, Felix's children shouted as any young kids, but the essence of suspense caused them to look around in fright as if they had done something bad. Cécile often hushed them.

Meanwhile, I penned a letter to the other directors of the Gewandhaus, calling off a concert that had been planned within the week. As I finished it up, Gade broke the silence, "We can take turns resting at my place. It is only a few paces down the street."

"I think that's a good idea." Herr Schleinitz yawned. Joachim gave his answer, "I want to stay wherever Herr David is."

"I shall go to Gade's." I finished up the letter, my eyes feeling heavy. It didn't fathom in my mind how exhausted I was. Gade turned to Hedwig, "Would you like a place to rest?"

"Nein, I'm alright. I'm going to head to my hotel." She declined. My wife had brought extra pillows along, so gave them to those who needed them. She and Constanze decided to stay with Cécile. Ignaz remained in the anteroom while Felix Moscheles had disappeared.

When leaving for Gade's home, Hedwig left at the same time. She rather followed our group down the pavement as if she couldn't help but be in the company of friends. Gade noticed and offered, "Would you like to stay at my house?"

"Nein, I am heading for my hotel." She declined in hesitation. Gade stopped, falling away from the group, "Are you sure? It is quite alright."

"Ja, I am sure, my hotel is not far." Hedwig thought it too bold to be walking with men, so turned at the street corner. Joachim called to Gade, "Are we walking too fast?"

"No," Niles caught back up. He led the group into his home, which was nearby. It was a warm and humble place, perfect for a rest. Everyone took a spot to get cozy and acquire much needed shuteye. Herr Schleinitz passed out on the couch straight away, Joachim took a spot on another sofa, Gade went to his bedroom while I found a nice cushioned chair.

It took an effort to relax, but eventually I shut my eyes, only to open them again to a frantic knock at the front door. Niles rushed to answer, finding Dr. Clarus calling. He had nothing but concern on his face as he spoke.

"Gentlemen, it would be wise to return to Felix's home. His breathing has begun to slow. It shan't be much longer." Clarus turned back. I got up and woke Herr Schleinitz, who upon hearing the situation, gushed tears in silence. Our group's settling at Gade's home had not lasted a mere hour. No one spoke nor complained on the short walk back to the Mendelssohn apartment.

When entering, the scene was that of a tragedy. Paul had arrived and he was transfixed with grief. Rebecka had not come and Dr. Clarus was urgently writing notes. Paul begged him, "Oh please let her come!"

"I'm doing all I can. Time is not on our side at the moment." Clarus folded his current letter. Paul knew deep inside she would not make it as Felix's breaths were far too slow and labored, but there was always that remaining ounce of hope.

When the ninth hour came around, Cécile stood in the corridor, instructing the children to go to bed. Little Lili and Felix Jr. went with ease, sensing that it was best they slept. Paul and Marie had some fuss, but their mother's daring expression made them question nothing.

Young Carl couldn't be convinced. Being the eldest, he knew something bad was going to happen. He asked in bewilderment, "Why can't I see papa?"

"He is far too ill." Cécile held back tears. Carl sensed the seriousness and glanced at his parents' bedroom, the door partly open. He caught a glimpse of his father in bed, paled in the face while struggling with each heaving breath.

"Please Carl, to bed." Cécile begged, nudging her son. Carl nodded, knowing the fact of the matter. He listened to his mother and turned for bed. Cécile then returned to her husband, keeping strong in her struggle.

It was then everyone gathered in the bedroom to be beside Felix. The reality of the moment caused all chests to ache. Paul still wished for his dear sister Rebecka to have come, but it was an impossible endeavor now. Even if she had arrived at the outskirts of the city, she would be too late. The ordeal caused his usually strong and upheld sense of emotions to break. Tears melted off his face like oozing lava. He went to Felix and whispered everything he wanted to tell him in his ear. Felix appeared to feel the warmth of his brother's sweet words.

When the struggle for life became feebler and fainter, Cécile couldn't hold anything in anymore. She kneeled at Felix's pillow with floods of tears, holding tightly his still graceful piano hands. Contrary to the rest of Felix's state, they still appeared ready to play any concerto or sonata on the spot.

Paul, Schleinitz, Ignaz, young Felix Moscheles and I then stood in deep silent prayer. With the breathing seeping away, young Moscheles looked up at Felix. In his mind, the scene gave the reminiscing sound of a passage from the funeral march in Beethoven's third symphony, where the hero lies, breathing his last; the sands of life gradually running out.

The doctors stood off to the side, counting each dry breath. They took notes as if to make some sort of conclusion or discovery.

Felix's air soon turned calm and peaceful, his diaphragm moving ever so slightly. It then gave a pause.

At 24 passed 9, the air he held escaped his mouth. He breathed his last.

With her hot tears, Cécile was persuaded to leave by Dr. Clarus, escorting her out. Young Felix Moscheles did not know what to make of the scene. The man he was named after was now gone. To give his personal farewell, the adolescent pressed a kiss on Felix's forehead before it grew cold in the damp dew of death.

*(Mendelssohn on his deathbed)*

# Epilogue

Mendelssohn, Nocturne from a 'Midsummer Night's Dream' [1]

## [1]

The next morning, everyone who had known and loved Mendelssohn wanted to pay their respects at the deathbed. The house, stairwell and entrance of the complex became crowded with people ranging from members of the orchestra, friends, family to concert attendees. Outside in the courtyard, couples strolled by to mourn the loss of such a staple in musical society, who was far too young to have his melodies silenced.

It was now many hours after the occurrence. The respected ones arrived for the corpse, which by now was quite pale and riggored. The sight was to everyone's dismay as it was transported by casket to a carriage-hearse.

While most followed alongside the carriage down the street, I stayed behind at the apartment. I happened upon young Moscheles standing in the doorway of Mendelsson's office. The adolescent sketched it, being sure to add the details in decor. The sheets of music were left, stacked in an organized fashion, just as orderly Felix liked it. My heart hurt too much, so moved on from the lonely office to join the procession outside.

FUNERAL OF MENDELSSOHN, AT LEIPZIG.

*(Mendelssohn's office after the composer's death, by Felix Moscheles)*

On the 8th of November, a beautiful and dignified funeral was held. A choir of five hundred sang, accompanied by organ and trombones. The music echoed through the main hall of the Paulinerkirche. Felix's casket sat a few paces before the musicians.

With the lid open, he was laying peacefully in a bed of mourning flowers as if the music were soothing his deep breathless sleep.

After the funeral service, the casket remained in the church until 10 o'clock at night. A small group including myself, stood around when the lid was slid over. My heart lurched, watching Felix, still so young, become inclosed.

With that, Ignaz, Robert Schumann and Niles picked up the casket and proceeded outside to a carriage headed for the train station. Felix was to be laid to rest in Berlin.

I walked home after all was done. My breath felt like ice while looking up at the sky, illuminating a night blue by the glow of stars. Each one twinkled and glimmered. It was a sight to find enjoyment in, but in my cold heart, all I felt was the train chugging away.

~~~

That next week, a concert in memory of Mendelssohn commenced. I was too heartbroken to take my spot among the violins, so watched from the audience. The whole concert was but a tragic torture. Lingering across the entire Gewandhaus was the feeling of something missing.

The musicians' faces expressed sorrow, having followed their beloved director's corpse out of the church only days prior. It seemed impossible to have music again feel the same. The tones of the instruments themselves seemed to have a weep of their own. Each horn held their notes as If trying to hold on a moment longer. The strings' emotions came from within their wooden frames. To keep beauty, the woodwinds flourished and embellished like the beautiful blossoms placed before a grave.

694

I listened, but my mind felt rather blank with the wavering flutes pulling at my heartstrings, still in disbelief that Felix was no more. His music remained alive as ever, making it hard to fathom the circumstance.

Herr Hiller, now director of the Düsseldorf orchestra, sat beside me. He could hardly listen to the tones of the young man he once knew, creative in every aspect of art. Tears left Hiller's eyes through the whole thing, wishing at heart that he could have made better amends with Felix.

~~~

Never again shall I feel that same November chill when taking a stroll through the wooded outskirts of Leipzig. The bitter trees were dewed with frost and the coloured leaves were crisp under my feet.

I looked out to find the sun setting a bright gold, sparking over a babbling brook. In the clearance of foliage were fields, bare from harvest in which gave an air of desolation. Not another soul wandered about, which I rather preferred in my moment of being. A large rock laid amongst the frosty grass, so I sat upon it. My thoughts soaked in the lonely air, recollecting everything up to this point. It was bound to come.

Felix, with his limited time alive, by no means wasted a minute. The adventures, discoveries, music; each one being but a moment in history. Whether his music lived on or not, it was in the least that his efforts pursued in the years to come.

Had he not pursued the performance at the Sing-Akademie of Bach's oratorio leaves in question if some of the greatest music considered should be as lost as it was before. Thanks to Felix's envision for discovery, the public welcomed the revival of old compositions and the music became as we know it today.

Felix in the end, wished his own compositions to live on, using his strength to give even his smallest songs the perfection in which always hovered before him, but were it conceivable that all his works perished, the remembrance of his poetic nature would alone suffice to afford the German public that such a being was born and bloomed there.

Though I have told you this story of Felix, the true factor of influence upon him was his dear sister Fanny. Her death ultimately caused his own demise. The malady that affected their family factored into his death, but in truth, it was the heartbreak of losing his reason for hearing melody that finished him. Fanny was the source that ignited Felix's desire to make beautiful music. She was the reason he took such care in revising his compositions, so that each work became the best it could be.

Now, as the sky is growing dark, I must be getting home; so in conclusion to this biography of Felix Mendelssohn, I leave you with a quote of his concerning the music composed over the course of his short life:

*'Ever since I began to compose, I have remained true to my starting principal: not to write a page because no matter what public, or what pretty girl wanted it to be thus or thus; but to write solely as I myself thought best, and as it gave me pleasure.'*

*—Felix Mendelssohn Bartholdy*

# Credits and Things

Mendelssohn Scottish Symphony fourth movement [1]

## [1]

If all of [Felix's] intimate friends had been writers, each would have had something extraordinary and something different to record; each would have whole volumes to write about him. — Robert Schumann

## About the Author

Abigail Smith is a classical guitarist, composer and music novelist from Belmond Iowa. She likes music history along with a spot of tea.

# Picture Credits

Cover: Felix Mendelssohn: Moritz Oppenheim, 1864;
Wikimedia Commons; Jüdische Museum der Stadt Frankfurt am Main

Mendelssohn's signature; Wikimedia Commons; Felix Mendelssohn

Tea and Guitars logo: Abigail Smith 2019

The Hamburg Home: Artist unknown; Gutenberg Project;
Certain Masterworks

Abraham Mendelssohn Bartholdy: Wilhelm Hensel 1829;
Staatliche Museen zu Berlin

Lea Mendelssohn Bartholdy: Wilhelm Hensel 1823; Wikimedia Commons

Jakob Salomon Bartholdy: Julius Schnorr von Carolsfeld 1823; Wikimedia

Carl Friedrich Zelter: Carl Begas 1827; Wikimedia Commons
Sing Akademie zu Berlin

Carl Maria von Weber: Caroline Bardua 1821; Wikimedia Commons
Staatliche Museen zu Berlin

Felix playing piano to Goethe: artist unknown; Wikimedia Commons

Young Felix Mendelssohn: Wilhelm Hensel; 1822 Wikimedia Commons
Staatliche Museen zu Berlin

Young Fanny Mendelssohn: Wilhelm Hensel 1822
Staatliche Museen zu Berlin

Ignaz Moscheles: Ludwig Albert von Montmorillon 1820; Wikimedia
Bibliothèque nationale de France

Sing Akademie zu Berlin: Eduard Gaertner 1843; Wikimedia Commons

The Bank Haus: Abigail Smith 2020

Rebecka Mendelssohn: Wilhelm Hensel 1823; Wikimedia Commons
Staatliche Museen zu Berlin

Leipziger Straße No 3, Berlin: Artist rendition (Demolished in the 1930s); Abigail
Smith 2020

Adolf Bernhard Marx; Wilhelm Hensel
Staatliche Museen zu Berlin

Beethoven's Funeral: Franz Xaver Stöber 1827; Wikimedia Commons

Hegel's lectures in Berlin: Franz Kugler 1828; Wikimedia Commons

Fanny Mendelssohn: Wilhelm Hensel 1829; Wikimedia Commons
Yale University Music Library

Wilhelm Hensel by Wilhelm Hensel 1829; Wikimedia Commons

Karl Klingemann: August Grahl 1850ish; Wikimedia Commons

Journal des Dames et des Modes 1829, Costumes Parisiens: Wikimedia

Watercolour of Durham 1829: Felix Mendelssohn;
Courtesy of Staatsbibliothek Berlin

Chapel Ruins at HolyRoodhouse: Louis Daugerre 1824; Wikimedia Commons
Walker Art Gallery

Felix Mendelssohn: James Warren Childe 1829; Wikimedia Commons

Karl Klingemann 'The Fair Maid of Perth': Felix Mendelssohn 1829;
Bodleian Library, Oxford University

Dunollie Castle: Felix Mendelssohn 1829;
Bodleian Library, Oxford University

Fingal's Cave Music sketch; 1829 Mendelssohn: Wikimedia Commons
Fingal's Cave: Abigail Smith 2020

The steamers and boats: Mendelssohn 1829; Wikimedia Commons

Loch Lomond: Felix Mendelssohn 1829;
Beinecke Library, Yale University

Coed Du Hall, colorized from a photo from 1900

Learning to drive a Dennett: Henry Thomas Alken 1824;
courtesy of Louis Allen

Goethe and Mendelssohn: Moritz Daniel Oppenheim 1864; Wikimedia
Jüdische Museum der Stadt Frankfurt am Main

Felix Mendelssohn: Horace Vernet 1831; Wikimedia Commons

Hector Berlioz: Emile Signol 1832; Wikimedia Commons

Watercolour of Florence: Mendelssohn 1831; Wikimedia Commons

Friedrich Kalkbrenner: Auguste Bry; Wikimedia Commons

Lieder ohne Worte manuscript: Mendelssohn 1832; Gutenberg project,
letters to Moscheles

Fredrick Chopin: Eliza Radziwllowna 1826; Wikimedia Commons

Felix Mendelssohn: Eduard Bendemann 1833; Wikimedia Commons

Paul Mendelssohn: Wilhelm Hensel
Staatliche Museen zu Berlin

Felix Moscheles in Crib: Felix Mendelssohn 1833; Gutenberg Project

Chester Place: Felix Mendelssohn 1833; Gutenberg Project

Bei der Wiege manuscript: Mendelssohn and Klingemann; Gutenberg Project

Friedrich Schadow: Carl Christian Vogel von Vogelstein 1821; Wikimedia
Staatliche Kunstsammlungen Dresden

Felix Mendelssohn: Shadow 1834; Wikimedia Commons
Staatliche Museen zu Berlin

Felix Mendelssohn: From a drawing by Mücke 1835;
Gutenberg Project Colorized

The Gewandhaus interior: Artist unknown 1800s Colorized
Original sketch; Library of Congress

The Gewandhaus with music of Cherubini: Felix Mendelssohn 1836; Wikimedia
Library of Congress

Ferdinand David: Johann Georg Weinhold; Wikimedia Commons

Lea and her children in mourning: Abigail Smith 2021

The Jeanrenaud Family: Bernhard Schlösser 1835
The Frankfurt Museen

Queen Victoria: George Hayter 1838; Wikimedia Commons
Royal Collection

Lurgenstein's Garten: Artist Unknown, postcard circa 1900; Wikimedia

Mendelssohn: Johann Heinrich Schrumm 1840;
Image courtesy of Sotheby's London

St. Thomas Church: Mendelssohn 1838; Wikimedia Commons

Cast of Mendelssohn's hand: Artist unknown; Letters of Mendelssohn;
Gutenberg Project

Der klyne Groenmarkt: Mendelssohn 1836; Wikimedia Commons

Birmingham: Mendelssohn 1840; Letters of Mendelssohn; Gutenberg Project

Leaving London: 1840; Letters of Mendelssohn; Gutenberg Project

Rough Seas: Mendelssohn 1840; Letters of Mendelssohn; Gutenberg Project

Berlin Konzerthaus layout: Mendelssohn; Letters of Mendelssohn;
Gutenberg Project

Albert playing organ for Victoria and Felix: G. Durand 1842; Wikimedia

Mendelssohn: Carl Muller 1842;

Letters of Ferdinand Hiller 1874

Felix's Study: Photograph: Zarafa 2006;
Wikimedia Commons, Public Domain

Chalk board: Abigail Smith 2020; Felix mentioned he gave
presentations on 6-4 chords

Mendelsshon family at Soden: Mendelssohn 1844; Gutenberg Project;
Certain Masterworks

Sketch for Ignaz: Mendelssohn, Klingemann, Emily Moscheles;
Gutenberg Project, letters

Searching for seating sketch: Mendelssohn 1844; Gutenberg Project,
Letters of Mendelssohn

Mendelssohn Haus on KonigStraße; Albert Henry Payne 1850: Wikimedia
Commons, Stadtgeschichtliches Museum Leipzig

Cecile and Felix Mendelssohn: Eduard Magnus 1846; Wikimedia Commons
Staatsbibliothek Berlin

Fanny Hensel [Mendelssohn]: Moritz Daniel Oppenheim 1842; Wikimedia

Page of piano arrangement of Elijah Overture: Mendelssohn 1846; Wikimedia Commons Library of Congress

Watercolour of Interlachen: Mendelssohn 1847; Wikimedia Commons

Fanny's Music Room: Julius Eduard Wilhelm Helfft 1849; Wikimedia Smithsonian Design Museum

Mendelssohn: Wilhelm Hensel 1847; Wikimedia Commons Stadtmuseum Düsseldorf

Mendelssohn on his deathbed: Eduard Bendemann Gutenberg Project, Letters of Mendelssohn

Mendelssohn's funeral Cortège JosephJoachim.com Robert W. Eshbach

Mendelssohn's office: Felix Moscheles 1847; Gutenberg project letters of Mendelssohn, Sketch from a watercolor, sketch colorized

Photo of Abigail Smith

# Other various sources

Recollections of Eduard Devrient
Diary entries of Queen Victoria
Letters of Anne Taylor
Letters of Karl Klingemann
Letters of Ferdinand David
Letters of Joseph Joachim
Letters of Abraham Mendelssohn
Letters of Lea Mendelssohn
Various facts from Robert Schumann

**A narrated audio version of the book can be found at the Tea and Guitars Youtube Channel**

Printed in Great Britain
by Amazon